Applied Psychology

BPS Textbooks in Psychology

BPS Blackwell presents a comprehensive and authoritative series covering everything a student needs in order to complete an undergraduate degree in psychology. Refreshingly written to consider more than North American research, this series is the first to give a truly international perspective. Written by the very best names in the field, the series offers an extensive range of titles from introductory level through to final year optional modules, and every text fully complies with the BPS syllabus in the topic. No other series bears the BPS seal of approval!

Each book is supported by a companion website, featuring additional resource materials for both instructors and students, designed to encourage critical thinking, and providing for all your course lecturing and testing needs.

For other titles in this series, please go to **www.bpsblackwell.co.uk.**

Applied Psychology

EDITED BY

GRAHAM DAVEY

This edition first published 2011 by the British Psychological Society and Blackwell Publishing Ltd.

Reprinted February 2013 ; March 2014 ; November 2014 ; December 2015

BPS Blackwell is an imprint of Blackwell Publishing, which was acquired by John Wiley & Sons Ltd in February 2007.

Registered office
John Wiley & Sons Ltd, The Atrium, Southern Gate, Chichester, West Sussex, PO19 8SQ, United Kingdom.

For details of our global editorial offices, for customer services and for information about how to apply for permission to reuse the copyright material in this book please see our website at www.wiley.com.

Library of Congress Cataloging-in-Publication Data

Davey, Graham.
    Applied psychology / Graham Davey.
      p.   cm. — (BPS textbooks in psychology)
    Includes bibliographical references and index.
    ISBN 978-1-4443-3121-9 (pbk.)
      1. Psychology, Applied.   I. Title.
  BF636.D38 2011
  158—dc22

                                                       2010053068

A catalogue record for this book is available from the British Library.

Set in 11/12.5pt Dante MT by MPS Limited, a Macmillan Company, Chennai, India
Printed and bound in Italy by Printer Trento Srl, Trento

The British Psychological Society's free Research Digest e-mail service rounds up the latest research and relates it to your syllabus in a user-friendly way. To subscribe go to www.researchdigest.org.uk or send a blank e-mail to subscribe-rd@lists.bps.org.uk

Commissioning Editor: Andrew McAleer
Assistant Editor: Georgia King
Marketing Managers: Fran Hunt and Jo Underwood
Project Editors: Nicole Burnett and Juliet Booker

Brief Contents

Contents

CHAPTER 9 Stress, Coping and Health **171**

Fiona Jones, Daryl O'Connor, Charles Abraham & Mark Conner

CHAPTER 19 Educational Psychology: Research on Cognitive and Biological Factors 385

Andy Tolmie

Contributors

Charles Abraham, University of Exeter, UK

Robin Banerjee, University of Sussex, UK

Adrian Banks, University of Surrey, UK

Jim Boyle, University of Strathclyde, UK

Mark Conner, University of Leeds, UK

Graham Davey, University of Sussex, UK

Tracey Devonport, University of Wolverhampton, UK

Michelle Davies, University of Central Lancashire, UK

Charlie Frowd, University of Central Lancashire, UK

Neil Gredecki, University of Central Lancashire, UK

Carol Ireland, Mersey Care NHS Trust, UK

Jane Ireland, University of Central Lancashire, UK

Fergal Jones, Canterbury Christ Church University, UK

Fiona Jones, University of Hertfordshire, UK

Andy Lane, University of Wolverhampton, UK

Almuth McDowall, University of Surrey, UK

Lynne Millward, University of Surrey, UK

Daryl O'Connor, University of Leeds, UK

Karen Rodham, University of Bath, UK

Andrew Tolmie, Institute of Education, UK

Polly Turner, Ashworth Hospital, Lancashire, UK

Preface

Of those UK psychology graduates who take employment immediately after graduation, around 15–20% enter professional and applied occupations (HESA: Standard Occupational Classification [SOC] of UK Psychology graduates). However, for many more, the reason for choosing an undergraduate degree in psychology is their interest in applied psychology and a desire to use psychological knowledge to help solve personal and social problems. This student interest in applied psychology has led to some significant changes in the way we teach undergraduate psychology over the past 10 years or so. Instead of being restricted to final-year options and electives, applied psychology courses are frequently offered alongside core courses at Level 2 and – more radically – as an integrated part of foundation teaching at Level 1. Indeed, to cater for this desire for knowledge of applied psychology, most psychology departments now have faculty dedicated to this teaching at both undergraduate and postgraduate level.

This textbook has been designed to satisfy these changing needs for applied psychology teaching at all undergraduate levels. It provides detailed coverage of the academic and professional aspects of six main fields of applied psychology. These are clinical psychology, health psychology, forensic psychology, educational psychology, occupational psychology and sports and exercise psychology. Each applied section consists of five chapters, with the first chapter providing an introduction to that applied area and the last chapter focusing on professional and training issues. The remainder cover core knowledge of the applied area and discuss the research base that has contributed to the development of that applied field. The text is written to be accessible to Level 1 Introductory Psychology students, and also to provide the core knowledge and professional information that students at Levels 2 and 3 would require.

The text is supplemented by a range of features designed to facilitate effective teaching and learning. They include:

- *Focus Points:* These provide more in-depth discussion of particular topics that are conceptually important, controversial or simply of contemporary interest. These are often linked to everyday examples – such as high-profile news items – that allow the reader to consider the issues in a contemporary, everyday context.

- *Activity Boxes:* These offer the reader an opportunity to engage in active learning about a topic by completing a task or activity. Examples of such activities include simple experiments designed to demonstrate a particular phenomenon, opportunities for further reading and research, or topics and questions suitable for small-group discussion. The instructor or teacher may want to make use of these activities when structuring their class teaching.

- *Research Methods:* These boxes contain detailed descriptions of methods used in applied psychology research, and describe the pros and cons of individual methods and their potential uses.

- *Case Histories:* Most chapters contain case histories providing individual examples of how applied psychologists provide help, advice, support and services for people across a range of settings and contexts.

- *Theory to Application Boxes:* These boxes are designed to facilitate understanding of the link between applications, research and theory, and describe how applications emerge from core psychological theory or how the need to deal with practical problems in applied psychology has given rise to developments in psychological theory.

- *Self-Test and Essay Questions:* At the end of each chapter the reader will encounter self-test and essay questions. These are designed to test the reader's absorption of basic factual and conceptual knowledge. Instructors and teachers can also use these questions as a basis for discussing key material in class or in small-group discussions.

- *Texts for Further Reading and Relevant Journal Articles:* All chapters have an extensive bibliography of further reading for the interested reader or the advanced-level student who needs further detail on specific topics. These are organised into texts for further reading and relevant journal articles. The journal articles provided cover reviews of specific topics, seminal discussion of critical conceptual and theoretical issues, studies describing important research in an area, or discussions and descriptions relevant to applied practice. Nowadays, students in higher education have regular free electronic access to many journal articles via their HE institution, and this was one of the main reasons for including a full and extensive list of journal articles for students to pursue – hopefully at minimal cost to themselves.

- *Glossary:* There is a full and comprehensive glossary of concepts and terms at the end of the book, which readers can refer to for quick and ready definitions of key terms. At the beginning of each chapter there is also a list of key terms used in the chapter. When each term first appears in the text, it is highlighted in bold and is either described or defined at that point. Highlighting these terms makes them easy to locate, and the list of key terms can serve as a revision checklist.

- *Website:* An associated website (www.wiley.com/college/davey) provides additional information covering teaching and learning resources, links to relevant applied psychology sites and additional information on all areas of applied psychology, including new, emerging and developing areas of application.

Finally, a book of this diverse nature would not have been possible without the dedication, knowledge and skills of all those applied psychologists who have contributed so diligently to this final product. Many have had to write and think in ways that they may well have not been familiar with before and they have all risen to those challenges – it has been a privilege to work with all of them.

Graham Davey
Brighton, March 2011

1 Introduction

GRAHAM DAVEY

LEARNING OUTCOMES

WHEN YOU HAVE COMPLETED THIS CHAPTER, YOU SHOULD BE ABLE TO:

1. Describe the main areas of applied psychology, including some newly developing and emerging areas.
2. Describe and critically evaluate the standards of conduct, performance, ethics and proficiency required of practitioner psychologists.

KEY WORDS

Clinical Psychology • Community Psychology • Consumer Psychology • Counselling Psychology • Educational Psychology • Environmental Psychology • Evidence-Based Practice • Forensic Psychology • Generic Standards • Health Professions Council (HPC) • Health Psychology • National Institute for Health & Clinical Excellence (NICE) • Neuropsychology • Occupational Psychology • Profession-Specific Standards • Protected Titles • Sport & Exercise Psychology • Standards of Proficiency

CHAPTER OUTLINE

ROUTE MAP OF THE CHAPTER

This is an introductory chapter that will describe in basic terms what applied psychology is, its integral relationship with research and how the different applied psychology professions are regulated. The chapter will continue by discussing standards of conduct, performance, ethics and proficiency for practitioner psychologists, and will describe some of the knowledge, understanding and skills required by individual practitioner psychologist professions. At the end of the chapter we also describe some newly emerging areas of applied psychology that are not covered in detail in this volume.

1.1   WHAT IS APPLIED PSYCHOLOGY?

It is not easy to come up with a simple definition of applied psychology that covers all of the circumstances in which psychological knowledge is applied and also encompasses the professional nature of much applied psychology. However, just as psychology is the scientific study of human behaviour, applied psychology is *the professional application of psychological knowledge to the solution of problems associated with human behaviour*. These problems may be at the level of the individual, in the case of clinical psychology and the treatment of individual mental health problems; at the level of an organisation, such as occupational psychology and its role in making organisations better places in which to work; or at the level of society in general, such as health psychology and its role in changing the health behaviours of the nation. While most applied psychology involves the application of existing psychological knowledge to practical problems (and you will find many examples of this in our 'Theory to Application Boxes' throughout the text), many of these problems are so politically and socially urgent that the practitioners dealing with these issues have to develop theory and practice almost on the hoof. You will find many examples in this text where the urgency of providing services and solutions has actually led to the development of psychological theory rather than vice versa.

The main areas of applied psychology can be defined by a number of features:

- The nature of the problems that require a solution.
- The target populations who normally serve as clients.
- The competencies required to develop and evaluate solutions to problems.
- The unique combinations of these factors.

For example, while Clinical Psychology addresses mainly mental health problems, deals with clients and patients who exhibit these problems, and consists of practitioners with specialised knowledge of interventions for these problems, the profession of clinical psychology is defined by all three of the above characteristics. Similarly, Sports & Exercise Psychology has evolved as a profession that addresses issues to do with sport and physical performance, deals with sportsmen, sportswomen and associated professionals, and requires knowledge of factors that can facilitate and enhance sporting performance. These unique combinations of problems, client groups and competencies have given rise to a number of influential applied psychology professions, and some examples of the types of problems faced by different groups of applied psychologists are provided in Activity Box 1.1. You might like to read through these examples to get a flavour of the main types of problems faced by different applied psychology professionals.

In the United Kingdom, the main fields of applied psychology are reflected in the different professional Divisions currently represented within the British Psychological Society (BPS). Figure 1.1 provides a list of the major Divisions currently represented in the BPS and shows how membership of these Divisions has changed since the year 2000. You can see from this figure that the main areas of applied psychology are **clinical**, **occupational**, **educational**, **forensic**, **health**, **sport & exercise**, **counselling**, **neuropsychology**, and teaching

---

clinical psychology the branch of psychology responsible for understanding and treating mental health problems.

occupational psychology the professional application of psychological knowledge to organisations to make them better places in which to work.

educational psychology psychology as applied to educational practice and related research.

forensic psychology the application of psychological knowledge within the criminal justice system.

health psychology the professional application of psychological knowledge to the solution of problems associated with human health behaviour.

sport & exercise psychology a profession dealing with sport and physical performance requiring knowledge of factors that can facilitate and enhance sporting performance.

counselling psychology the application of psychological knowledge generally to therapeutic practice.

neuropsychology the study of the structure and function of the brain related to psychological processes and behaviours.

Applied psychology is the application of psychological knowledge to the solution of problems associated with human behaviour. Below are six case histories, each outlining a specific behaviour-related problem, which will give you a flavour of the types of issues facing applied psychologists. Can you identify which type of applied psychologist would be most likely to be involved in seeking solutions for each of these problems? Choose from Clinical Psychologist, Health Psychologist, Forensic Psychologist, Educational Psychologist, Occupational Psychologist and Sports & Exercise Psychologist.

1. Sandy is a female middle-distance runner who competes at a national level. She had complained of lack of confidence in her abilities. She recognised that she was less confident and was unable to control her nerves in competitions in which she faced strong opposition. This caused her to tighten up during the race, particularly in her shoulders, affecting her running style. (From Lane, 2008)

2. Despite receiving a good deal of information about condoms and their role in preventing unwanted pregnancies, only about 1 in 3 teenagers in the classes receiving this information reported actually using condoms. Why do most of them fail to use condoms? Is the information given to them in a form they can understand? What will motivate them to use condoms?

3. Michael is a 13-year-old student in a secondary school whose parents wanted to know whether he might be better placed in a small unit for young people with dyslexia/specific literacy difficulties. He had been experiencing difficulties with reading and spelling throughout his school career, and on transfer to secondary school had struggled with homework, despite the best efforts of a skilled special needs support department. In conversation, it was apparent that he was an articulate and thoughtful young person and tests showed that his level of verbal comprehension lay within a high average range for his age. (From Frederickson *et al.*, 2008)

4. Jim had recently been made redundant from a skilled manufacturing job, was experiencing difficulties in his marriage and had started to drink to excess. Jim was expressing serious suicidal intent and had taken three life-threatening overdoses in the previous six months. He was spending money he could not afford on Internet gambling sites and was becoming increasingly hostile and aggressive to his wife, who he considered did not offer him the affection and attention he needed. (From Alwin, 2008)

5. Matt works in a company that sells phone and Internet services. His company takes communication very seriously and whenever there is an issue, a memo is sent out to keep everyone on top of things. The problem is that Matt feels overwhelmed by the amount of communication. He receives over a dozen e-mail memos every day and cannot remember everything that is sent to him in these memos. Matt is a very organised person, but simply doesn't know how to stay on top of things. (From Rothman & Cooper, 2008)

6. Consider two child sex offenders. The first is a 35-year-old married man who has been found guilty of molesting his daughter for the past 11 years while she was aged 4-14. The second is a single, 23-year-old man who had 'consensual' sexual intercourse with a 14-year-old boy four hours after meeting him in a local park. Neither man has any prior criminal history for sexual or nonsexual offences. Neither has a history of substance abuse. Neither man has ever been treated for a mental health problem. What risk does each of these two men pose for committing further sexual offences? (From Canter, 2008)

& researching. Over the past decade the most influential Divisions have been the Division of Clinical Psychology (DCP) and the Division of Occupational Psychology (DOP). Both have exhibited an increase in membership since 2000, with the DCP almost doubling its membership since that time. All other Divisions have shown a modest increase in membership over the past decade or so, indicating an increasing demand for applied psychologists of all types.

To become a member of a professional Division of the BPS, you must have an accredited undergraduate degree in psychology that makes you eligible for the Society's Graduate Basis for Chartered Membership (GBC) and the appropriate approved and accredited postgraduate training qualification for that applied profession that bestows on you the necessary competencies and skills required to practise professionally (see Section 1.3.3). Details of the required training routes and the qualifications

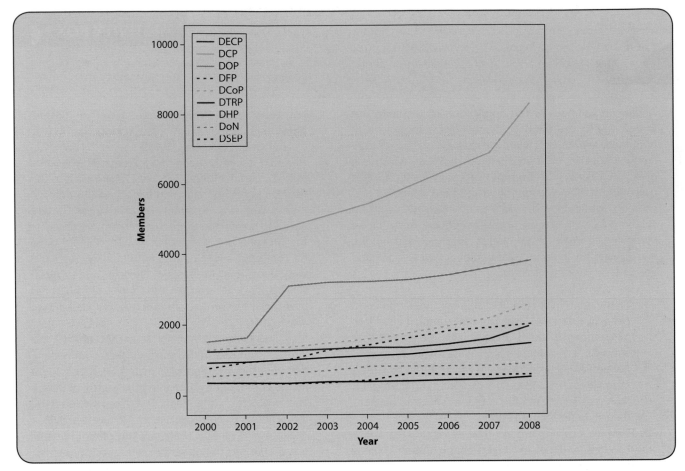

FIGURE 1.1 *Membership of the main practitioner Divisions of the British Psychological Society (BPS) between 2000 and 2008.*

Key: DECP = Division of Educational & Child Psychology; DCP = Division of Clinical Psychology; DOP = Division of Occupational Psychology; DFP = Division of Forensic Psychology; DCoP = Division of Counselling Psychology; DTRP = Division of Teachers & Researchers in Psychology; DHP = Division of Health Psychology; DoN = Division of Neuropsychology; DSEP = Scottish Division of Educational Psychology

needed to become a professional applied psychologist are also described in more detail in the final chapter of each applied section in this text.

1.2   RESEARCH AND APPLIED PSYCHOLOGY

Research is an integral part of applied psychology. It supplies most of the evidence-based theory that applied psychologists regularly adopt when looking for solutions to the problems they are required to address. Furthermore, in most fields of applied psychology, practitioners are trained as scientist- or researcher-practitioners. That is, research skills are a critical element of the approved training they receive before becoming eligible to practise

as applied psychologists. This does not mean that applied psychologists themselves regularly carry out research – in reality, the workload involved as a practising applied psychologist rarely gives time for the luxury of undertaking pure (or even applied) research. However, practitioners' research training provides them with the skills necessary for what is known as **evidence-based practice**. That is, these skills allow the applied psychologist to make objective assessments of the problems that need to be solved; to make decisions about what might be the most effective intervention in a situation based on existing theory and evidence; and to use objective and measurable methods to assess the success of an intervention (Harper, Mulvey & Robinson, 2003). This not only differentiates the applied psychologist from bogus practitioners and charlatans, but also makes them accountable

evidence-based practice practice whose efficacy has been proven through research using the scientific method.

for their actions and decisions against clear, objective, evidence-based criteria. For instance, a health or occupational psychologist who has been asked to develop a programme to improve either the physical or occupational health of a group of people will have to convince other professionals of the viability of their programme and that it is likely to be successful. To do this, they would use the common yardstick of research-based evidence to make their case.

In some areas of practice such as health and clinical psychology, there are already government agencies set up to assess the viability of interventions for a range of physical and mental health problems. In the United Kingdom, one such agency that attempts to assess and recommend effective interventions is the **National Institute for Health & Clinical Excellence** (known as NICE, www.nice.org.uk). It does this primarily by recommending treatments whose efficacy has been labelled as *evidence-based*; that is, whose efficacy has been proven through scientific research. As we shall see later, practitioner psychologists must adhere to proper standards of conduct, performance and ethics, and this means that their practice must be *transparent* (e.g. it must be clear why a particular intervention has been chosen, and why it might be successful) and their actions and decisions *accountable* (e.g. the intervention will produce results that are effective, worthwhile and financially acceptable). A knowledge of research skills supplemented by appropriate theory will allow a practitioner to provide objective evidence that an intervention is likely to be effective and will produce the outcomes that are predicted.

The relationship between research and practice is illustrated regularly throughout this book and is highlighted specifically in our 'Theory to Practice' feature boxes.

National Institute for Health & Clinical Excellence (NICE) an independent UK organisation responsible for providing national guidance on promoting good health and preventing and treating ill health.

1.3   REGULATION AND STANDARDS OF CONDUCT

1.3.1   The Health Professions Council (HPC)

Because practitioner psychologists all provide services, and in many cases do so to vulnerable groups of people (e.g. individuals with mental health problems), their practice needs to be properly regulated to protect the public from malpractice and exploitation from untrained individuals. Since 1 July 2009 practitioner psychologists in the UK have been regulated by an agency known as the **Health Professions Council (HPC)** (www.hpc-uk.org),

TABLE 1.1 *HPC Protected Titles.*

The Health Professions Council has designated these titles as 'protected titles'. That is, a practitioner is not allowed to advertise themselves as any of these types of applied psychologist unless they have met the training and performance criteria that allow them to be registered with the HPC.

Practitioner psychologist	• Practitioner psychologist • Registered psychologist • Clinical psychologist • Counselling psychologist • Educational psychologist • Forensic psychologist • Health psychologist • Occupational psychologist • Sport and exercise psychologist

and its role is to protect the public by ensuring that applied psychologists meet specified standards of training, professional skills, behaviour and health.

The HPC maintains a register of practitioner psychologists who meet these required standards, and it has also specified a set of **protected titles** that practitioners can use only if they are registered with the HPC. These protected titles are listed in Table 1.1, and the HPC has the authority to take out criminal prosecutions against anyone who uses these restricted titles when they are not properly trained or registered to do so. In addition, the HPC can take action against any practitioner psychologist who does not meet their standards of conduct, performance and ethics (see below), action that might include recommendations for further training and supervision, preventing a practitioner from practising for a specific period of time, or striking that person off the register for life.

Health Professions Council (HPC) the regulator of Practitioner Psychologists in the UK. The HPC aims primarily to protect the public and maintains a register of health professionals (e.g. Practitioner Psychologists) who meet set standards for their training, professional skills, behaviour and health.

protected titles a specified set of titles that practitioners can use only if they are registered with the HPC.

1.3.2   Standards of Conduct, Performance and Ethics

All practitioner psychologists are expected to keep to a general set of standards of conduct, performance and ethics that would be applicable to any practitioner working in the health professions generally. Adherence to these standards implies that the practitioner is 'fit to practice'; that is, has the skills, knowledge, character and health to practise their profession safely and effectively. A full set of these

TABLE 1.2 *Standards of Conduct, Performance and Ethics.*

Below is a list of the basic standards of conduct, performance and ethics required by the HPC of health professionals.

Your duties as a registrant
The standards of conduct, performance and ethics you must keep to

1 You must act in the best interests of service users.
2 You must respect the confidentiality of service users.
3 You must keep high standards of personal conduct.
4 You must provide (to us and any other relevant regulators) any important information about your conduct and competence.
5 You must keep your professional knowledge and skills up to date.
6 You must act within the limits of your knowledge, skills and experience and, if necessary, refer the matter to another practitioner.
7 You must communicate properly and effectively with service users and other practitioners.
8 You must effectively supervise tasks that you have asked other people to carry out.
9 You must get informed consent to give treatment (except in an emergency).
10 You must keep accurate records.
11 You must deal fairly and safely with the risks of infection.
12 You must limit your work or stop practising if your performance or judgement is affected by your health.
13 You must behave with honesty and integrity and make sure that your behaviour does not damage the public's confidence in you or your profession.
14 You must make sure that any advertising you do is accurate.
   This document sets out the standards of conduct, performance and ethics we expect from the health professionals we register. The standards also apply to people who are applying to become registered.

---

standards as defined by the HPC is set out in Table 1.2. In essence they attempt to ensure that practitioners:

- Respect the confidentiality, consent and interests of their clients/service users.

- Ensure that their skills are up to date and that they do not attempt to offer services that are outside the scope of their knowledge.

- Do not offer services if their physical or mental health will affect their practice.

- Behave honestly and responsibly in the way they advertise and conduct their practice.

The HPC considers complaints about registered practitioners from members of the public, employers, professionals and the police, among others, and will take action against individual practitioners if this code of conduct, performance and ethics has been breached.

1.3.3 Standards of Proficiency

More specifically, the HPC sets out **standards of proficiency** for practitioner psychologists. These represent a minimum set of standards necessary for the safe and effective practice of the profession of applied psychology, and applied psychologists must meet these minimum standards before they can be registered. In effect, these proficiency standards define the legitimate scope of an applied psychologist's practice based on the knowledge, skills and experience they possess. These standards are divided into **generic standards**, which apply to all practitioner psychologists (e.g. a practitioner must understand the need to respect the rights, dignity, values and autonomy of service users) and **profession-specific standards**, which are specific to individual applied psychology professions (e.g. a practitioner must be able to conduct assessments that are appropriate to the client groups relevant to their profession). In effect, these standards define the skills required for the application of practice and the knowledge, understanding and skills required to execute their practice. In addition, these standards of proficiency also define the training curriculum for applied psychologists, and in effect all training courses for practitioner psychologists must ensure that their students meet the minimum levels of knowledge and skills set out in

standards of proficiency in applied psychology, a minimum set of standards, necessary for the safe and effective practice of the profession, which applied psychologists must meet before they can be registered.

generic standards standards of conduct, performance and ethics applicable to any practitioner working in the health professions generally.

profession-specific standards HPC standards of proficiency representing minimum standards necessary for safe and effective practice by registered psychologists working in their individual applied psychology professions.

these proficiency standards in order to be registered with the HPC and to practise.

Table 1.3 replicates that section of the HPC's standards of proficiency for practitioner psychologists that defines the knowledge, understanding and skills required by individual practitioner psychologist professions. In addition, a list of approved courses for practitioner psychologists can be found on the HPC website at http://www.hpc-uk.org/aboutregistration/educationandtraining/approvedcourses_pp/.

TABLE 1.3 *Generic and Profession-Specific Knowledge, Understanding and Skills.*

The table provides information on the generic knowledge, understanding and skills required by practitioner psychologists (printed in black) and the profession-specific knowledge, understanding and skills (printed in blue). These skills provide the basis for the curriculums of applied psychology training courses, and can be found at http://www.hpc-uk.org/assets/documents/10002963SOP_Practitioner_psychologists.pdf.

Knowledge, understanding and skills

3a Knowledge, understanding and skills
Registrant practitioner psychologists must:

3a.1 know and understand the key concepts of the bodies of knowledge which are relevant to their profession-specific practice
- understand the structure and function of the human body, relevant to their practice, together with knowledge of health, disease, disorder and dysfunction
- be aware of the principles and applications of scientific enquiry, including the evaluation of treatment efficacy and the research process
- recognise the role of other professions in health and social care
- understand the theoretical basis of, and the variety of approaches to, assessment and intervention
- understand the impact of differences such as gender, sexuality, ethnicity, culture, religion and age on psychological wellbeing or behaviour

Clinical psychologists only
- understand the role of the clinical psychologist across a range of settings and services
- understand theories and evidence concerning psychological development and psychological difficulties across the lifespan and their assessment and remediation
- understand more than one evidence-based model of formal psychological therapy
- understand psychological models related to how biological, sociological and circumstantial or life-event-related factors impinge on psychological processes to affect psychological wellbeing
- understand psychological models related to a range of presentations including:
  - clients with presentations from acute to enduring and mild to severe;
  - problems with biological or neuropsychological causation; and
  - problems with mainly psychosocial factors including problems of coping, adaptation and resilience to adverse circumstances and life events, including bereavement and other chronic physical and mental health conditions
- understand psychological models related to clients:
  - from a range of social and cultural backgrounds;
  - of all ages;
  - across a range of intellectual functioning;
  - with significant levels of challenging behaviour;
  - with developmental learning disabilities and cognitive impairment;
  - with communication difficulties;
  - with substance misuse problems; and
  - with physical health problems
- understand psychological models related to working:
  - with individual clients, couples, families, carers, groups and at the organisational and community level; and
  - in a variety of settings including in-patient or other residential facilities with high-dependency needs, secondary health care, and community or primary care
- understand change processes in service-delivery systems
- understand social approaches such as those informed by community, critical and social constructivist perspectives
- understand leadership theories and models, and their application to service-delivery and clinical practice
- understand the impact of psychopharmacological and other clinical interventions on psychological work with clients

Counselling psychologists only
- understand the philosophical bases which underpin those psychological theories which are relevant to counselling psychology
- understand the philosophy, theory and practice of more than one model of psychological therapy

(Continued)

TABLE 1.3 (*Continued*)

Knowledge, understanding and skills

- understand the therapeutic relationship and alliance as conceptualised by each model
- understand the spiritual and cultural traditions relevant to counselling psychology
- understand the primary philosophical paradigms that inform psychological theory with particular regard to their relevance to, and impact upon, the understanding of the subjectivity and inter-subjectivity of experience throughout human development
- understand theories of human cognitive, emotional, behavioural, social and physiological functioning relevant to counselling psychology
- understand different theories of lifespan development
- understand social and cultural contexts and the nature of relationships throughout the lifespan
- understand theories of psychopathology and of change
- understand the impact of psychopharmacology and other interventions on psychological work with clients

Educational psychologists only
- understand the role of the educational psychologist across a range of settings and services
- understand psychological theories of, and research evidence in, child and adolescent development relevant to educational psychology
- understand the structures and systems of a wide range of settings in which education and care are delivered for children and adolescents
- understand psychological models related to the influence of school ethos and culture, educational curricula, communication systems, management and leadership styles on the cognitive, behavioural, emotional and social development of children and adolescents
- understand psychological models of the factors that lead to underachievement, disaffection and social exclusion amongst vulnerable groups
- understand theories and evidence underlying psychological intervention with children and adolescents, their parents or carers, and education and other professionals
- understand psychological models related to the influence on development of children and adolescents from:
    - family structures and processes;
    - cultural and community contexts; and
    - organisations and systems
- understand the theoretical basis of, and the variety of approaches to, consultation and assessment in educational psychology

Forensic psychologists only
- understand the application of psychology in the legal system
- understand the application and integration of a range of theoretical perspectives on socially and individually damaging behaviours, including psychological, social and biological perspectives
- understand theory and its application to the provision of psychological therapies that focus on offenders and victims of offences
- understand effective assessment approaches with individuals presenting with individual and/or socially damaging behaviour
- understand the application of consultation models to service-delivery and practice, including the role of leadership and group processes
- understand the development of criminal and antisocial behaviour
- understand the psychological interventions related to different client groups including victims of offences, offenders, litigants, appellants and individuals seeking arbitration and mediation

Health psychologists only
- understand context and perspectives in health psychology
- understand the epidemiology of health and illness
- understand:
    - biological mechanisms of health and diseases;
    - health-related cognitions and behaviour;
    - stress, health and illness;
    - chronic illness and disability;
    - individual differences in health and illness;
    - lifespan, gender and cross-cultural perspectives; and
    - long-term conditions and disability
- understand applications of health psychology and professional issues
- understand healthcare in professional settings

Occupational psychologists only
- understand the following in occupational psychology:

- human-machine interaction;
- design of environments and work;
- personnel selection and assessment;
- performance appraisal and career development;
- counselling and personal development;
- training;
- employee relations and motivation; and
- organisational development and change

Sport and exercise psychologists only
- understand motor skills, practice skills, cognition, learning and perception, and their impact on performance
- understand psychological skills such as:
  - arousal and anxiety;
  - confidence; and
  - coping and techniques such as relaxation, goal-setting, biofeedback, imagery, stress and inoculation
- understand exercise and physical activity including:
  - determinants, e.g. motives, barriers and adherence; and
  - outcomes in relation to mood, self-esteem and cognition;
- understand individual differences including:
  - personality;
  - motivation;
  - gender;
  - special groups; and
  - talent identification
- understand social processes within sport and exercise psychology including:
  - interpersonal and communication skills;
  - team cohesion;
  - group identity;
  - trust;
  - cooperation and competition; and
  - leadership
- understand the impact of lifespan issues
- understand the problems of dependence and injury

3a.2   know how professional principles are expressed and translated into action through a number of different approaches to practice, and how to select or modify approaches to meet the needs of an individual, groups or communities

3a.3   understand the need to establish and maintain a safe practice environment
- be aware of applicable health and safety legislation, and any relevant safety policies and procedures in force in the workplace, such as incident reporting, and be able to act in accordance with these
- be able to work safely, including being able to select appropriate hazard control and risk management, reduction or elimination techniques in a safe manner in accordance with health and safety legislation
- be able to select appropriate protective equipment and use it correctly
- be able to establish safe environments for practice, which minimise risks to service users, those treating them and others, including the use of hazard control and particularly infection control

Sport and exercise psychologists only
- be aware of the possible physical risks associated with certain sport and exercise contents

1.4   EMERGING AREAS OF APPLIED PSYCHOLOGY

In this book we deal with six of the main areas of applied psychology: namely Clinical Psychology, Health Psychology, Forensic Psychology, Educational Psychology, Occupational Psychology and Sports & Exercise Psychology. There are others that are of arguably equal importance in both a theoretical and an applied sense, but that we are unable to cover in required detail in a single text of this size. However, we have provided an introduction to these other and emerging applied areas of psychology in the book's associated website (www.wiley.com/college/davey), and hope that these will give the reader a flavour of how applied psychology is developing.

One important emerging and influential area of applied psychology is *Counselling Psychology*. This is a practitioner area that attempts to facilitate personal and interpersonal functioning across the lifespan, and to help a range of clients improve their wellbeing, resolve personal crises, alleviate distress and generally lead more fulfilling personal, social and occupational lives. Counselling psychologists will have received initial training as a psychologist, usually through taking a conventional undergraduate degree in psychology and acquiring skills at a postgraduate level that allow them to apply their psychological knowledge generally to therapeutic practice. Figure 1.1 shows that Counselling Psychology in the United Kingdom is a growing and influential profession, and in 2008 the BPS Division of Counselling Psychology was the third largest of the Society's practitioner Divisions.

Counselling psychologists work with clients with a variety of problems (for example the effects of childhood sexual abuse, relationship breakdown, domestic violence, major trauma) and/or symptoms of psychological disorder (such as anxiety, depression, eating disorders, post-traumatic stress disorder and psychosis). They offer an active, collaborative relationship that can both facilitate the exploration of underlying issues and empower people to confront change. Counselling psychologists' work provides services in a range of areas: NHS services (including primary care, Community Mental Health Teams, tertiary settings for psychiatric in-patients, specialist services for older adults, those with eating disorders, personality disorders or learning difficulties, and in general health-care settings where psychological services are offered), prison and probationary services, social services, voluntary organisations, occupational health departments, student counselling services and in independent/private practice. Further information on Counselling Psychology can be found on the book's associated website at www.wiley.com/college/davey.

Three other important emerging areas of applied psychology are Environmental Psychology, Consumer Psychology and Community Psychology. In its broadest sense, **environmental psychology** is the 'study of the interrelationships between the physical environment and human behaviour' (Burroughs, 1989) and will apply knowledge from important core areas of psychology – such as social psychology – to dealing with problems associated with the interaction between people and their environment. This covers how the environment can affect people and their behaviour (such as the effect of urbanisation on individual and group behaviour) and how people's behaviour can affect the

> **environmental psychology** the study of the interrelationships between the physical environment and human behaviour.

environment (such as the role that individual behaviour might play in global warming). As yet there is no distinct practitioner category known as environmental psychology, and most environmental psychologists tend to be academic psychologists or researchers who have an interest in tackling important environmental issues. Some do undertake consultancy work, and this may include advising on issues such as the effect of a particular building design on individual and group behaviour within an organisation (e.g. Parker *et al.*, 2004), or how crowds might behave in restricted environments such as carnivals or football stadiums (e.g. Batty, Desyllas & Duzbury, 2003).

Consumer psychology is the study of human responses to product- and service-related information and experiences. It draws heavily from the core areas of social psychology and cognitive psychology in order to help understand the beliefs, judgements, emotions, purchase decisions and consumption practices that are associated with consumer behaviour (Jansson-Boyd, 2010). Consumer psychologists may be involved in the study of the impact of advertising or product packaging on a consumer's purchasing decisions; others may be interested in how marriage, parenthood and other important life stages affect consumer behaviour. Like environmental psychologists, most consumer psychologists are academics or researchers who have an interest in understanding consumer behaviour. As such their primary activity is research, but their work is often of interest to advertising agencies and individual companies wanting to understand their product market and make their products more attractive.

> **consumer psychology** the study of human responses to product and service-related information and experiences.

Finally, **community psychology** is another rapidly developing area of applied psychology that deals with the relationships between the individual and the community and the wider society in which they live (Rudkin, 2003). To this extent, it is an area whose main practical aim is to enhance the quality of life through research and intervention strategies and programmes. It is an area that involves a range of health- and social-related professions, and involves understanding the relationships between social systems, wellbeing and physical and mental health generally. Community psychologists may find themselves dealing with individuals, groups of individuals, organisations and whole communities, and their interventions will aim to be as much preventative as ameliorative (such as developing programmes to help prevent drug abuse and dependency in deprived communities).

> **community psychology** the branch of psychology dealing with relationships between the individual and community and their wider society.

While these examples represent the most newly developing areas of applied psychology, there will certainly be many more emerging areas over the next 10–20 years. There is now a wealth of core psychological knowledge waiting to be applied in practical settings and to problems that are socially and politically urgent, so a burgeoning of applications is assured. In addition, most important research funders – such as the UK Research Councils – now require researchers to articulate and understand the applied impact of their research when making their funding applications. This will only mean more research that directly addresses applied issues or can be readily utilised to deal with personal and social problems.

SELF-TEST QUESTIONS

- What is the definition of applied psychology?
- What are the main areas of applied psychology as represented by Divisions of the British Psychological Society (BPS)?
- What is evidence-based practice and why is it an integral part of applied psychology?
- What is the Health Professions Council (HPC)?
- What are standards of conduct, performance and ethics?
- What is the difference between generic and profession-specific standards of proficiency?
- Can you name three emerging areas of applied psychology and describe their main characteristics?

ESSAY QUESTIONS

- What is applied psychology and what is its relationship to core psychological knowledge and research?
- Describe how practitioner psychologists are regulated and compare and contrast the standards of proficiency required for different types of practitioner psychologists.

TEXTS FOR FURTHER READING

Bayne, R. & Horton, I. (eds) (2003) *Applied Psychology*, London: Sage.
Coolican, H. (2007) *Applied Psychology*, 2nd edn, London: Hodder HE.

RELEVANT WEB LINKS

Health Professions Council (HPC), www.hpc-uk.org
National Institute for Health & Clinical Excellence (NICE), www.nice.org.uk

REFERENCES

Alwin, N. (2008) Working with people with a diagnosis of personality disorder, in G.C.L. Davey (ed.) *Clinical Psychology*, London: Hodder HE.

Batty, M., Desyllas, J. & Duxbury, E. (2003) Safety in numbers? Modelling crowds and designing control for the Notting Hill Carnival, *Urban Studies*, 40: 1573–90.

Burroughs, W.J. (1989) Applied environmental psychology, in W.L. Gregory & W.J. Burroughs (eds) *Introduction to Applied Psychology*, London: Scott Foresman & Co.

Canter, D. (2008) *Criminal Psychology*, London: Hodder HE.

Frederickson, N., Miller, A. & Cline, T. (2008) *Educational Psychology*, London: Hodder HE.

Harper, D., Mulvey, R. & Robinson, M. (2003) Beyond evidence-based practice: Rethinking the relationship between research, theory and practice, in R. Bayne & I. Horton (eds) *Applied Psychology*, London: Sage.

Jansson-Boyd, C.V. (2010) *Consumer Psychology*, Milton Keynes: Open University Press.

Lane, A. (2008) *Sport & Exercise Psychology*, London: Hodder HE.

Parker, C., Barnes, S., McKee, K. *et al.* (2004) Quality of life and building design in residential and nursing homes for older people, *Ageing & Society*, 24: 941–62.

Rothman, I. & Cooper, C. (2008) *Organizational & Work Psychology*, London: Hodder HE.

Rudkin, J.K. (2003) *Community Psychology: Guiding Principles and Orienting Concepts*, Upper Saddle River, NJ: Prentice Hall.

ANSWERS

Answers to Activity Box 1.1:

1. Sports & Exercise Psychologist
2. Health Psychologist
3. Educational Psychologist
4. Clinical Psychologist
5. Occupational Psychologist
6. Forensic Psychologist

Part I
Clinical Psychology

2 Clinical Psychology and Mental Health Problems

GRAHAM DAVEY

KEY WORDS

Abnormal Psychology ● American Psychiatric Association (APA) ● Behaviour Modification ● Behaviour Therapy ● Behavioural Model ● Classical Conditioning ● Client-Centred Therapy ● Cognitive Behaviour Therapy (CBT) ● Cognitive Model ● Comorbidity ● Demonology ● Diagnostic & Statistical Manual (DSM) ● DSM-IV-TR ● DSM-IV-TR Axes of Disorder ● Ego ● Ego Defence Mechanisms ● Empathy ● Humanist-Existentialist Approach ● Hybrid Disorders ● Id ● International List of Causes of Death (ICD) ● Learning Theory ● Mad Pride ● Maladaptive Behaviour ● Medical Model ● Multidisciplinary Teams (MDTs) ● Operant Conditioning ● Pathology Model ● Psychiatry ● Psychoanalysis ● Seizisman ● Service User Groups ● Somatogenic Hypothesis ● Statistical Norm ● Stigma ● Superego ● Syndrome ● Unconditional Positive Regard

CHAPTER OUTLINE

ROUTE MAP OF THE CHAPTER

This chapter begins the clinical psychology section by discussing the difficulties associated with identifying, defining and explaining mental health problems. The chapter begins by defining who clinical psychologists are and then discusses conceptual issues in the definition of mental health problems – especially issues that relate to the stigma and exclusion often associated with these problems. The chapter then progresses to discuss some fundamental approaches to explaining mental health problems, and finishes by describing current frameworks for classification.

I was a 22-year-old trainee working for a publishing company in London, and I was obsessed with food. I made a pact with myself to limit myself to less than 700 calories a day. This worked well for a while, but then I started binge eating, and my fear of gaining weight led me to make myself sick. Sometimes up to 5 or 6 times a day. This left me totally drained – both emotionally and physically, and my relationship with my partner began to go downhill rapidly. I really hated myself, and I felt fat and disgusting most days. If only I felt thinner I would feel better about myself. My GP eventually referred me to a clinical psychologist, who helped me to understand how my thinking was just plain wrong. He explained to me how I evaluated my self-worth purely on the basis of my weight and body shape. My thinking was also 'black and white' – I believed that foods were either 'good' or if not, they were 'bad'. During therapy I learned to identify and challenge my irrational thoughts about food and eating, this helped me to begin to eat relatively normally again, and I began to feel less anxious and worthless.

Elly's Story (from Davey, 2008)

2.1 HOW DOES CLINICAL PSYCHOLOGY AFFECT YOU?

Just like Elly, we all experience challenges and distress that will have a psychological impact on us. These include stress at work, an inability to cope with life's problems, feelings of worthlessness, having to deal with uncertainty, and experiencing losses and bereavements. Sometimes these experiences result in prolonged periods of distress and impairment in social, occupational and family functioning. Even if you haven't experienced this kind of distress yourself, it is quite probable that you have a family member or close friend who has.

Clinical psychologists are closely involved in helping people to recover from these kinds of problems. They attempt to help people understand the causes of their difficulties, provide interventions that can help to alleviate specific symptoms associated with their difficulties, and provide support and guidance through the period to recovery.

You are only likely to meet directly with a clinical psychologist if your symptoms are severe or enduring, but clinical psychology informs mental health services in many other ways. It provides a research basis through which new psychological interventions are developed and evaluated (Barker, Pistrang & Elliott, 2002), and it has developed principles of psychological treatment that are used by a range of mental health professionals, including psychiatrists, psychotherapists, counsellors, mental health and community psychiatric nurses, social workers and community support workers. Clinical psychology is also a theoretical and political driving force behind attempts in many countries to increase access to psychological therapies for those who need them (Clark *et al.*, 2009).

Clinical psychology should not be confused with **psychiatry**. The latter tends to have similar goals to clinical psychology, but focuses more on medication-based solutions to mental health problems. In contrast, clinical psychologists try to help people by facilitating their understanding of their thoughts and actions. You may already have heard of treatment approaches such as **cognitive behaviour therapy** or **CBT** (e.g. Kinsella & Garland, 2008). Clinical psychologists work closely with other professionals, such as doctors, social workers, probation officers and so on, and may specialise in helping specific groups of people such as children, adults, offenders, people with neurological disorders or people with learning disabilities (Jones, 2008).

So, although you may go through your life without ever meeting a clinical psychologist personally, the

psychiatry a scientific method of identifying the biological causes of mental health problems and treating them with medication or surgery.

cognitive behaviour therapy (CBT) an umbrella term for many different therapies that share the common aim of changing both cognitions and behaviour.

impact of clinical psychology on our evolving mental health services is significant.

2.2 WHO ARE CLINICAL PSYCHOLOGISTS?

Clinical psychologists are normally psychology graduates who have completed up to three years of intensive postgraduate training to learn the skills required for clinical practice. More detailed information about this training and the required skills is provided in Chapter 6. The training that these psychology graduates have received permits them to use the statutorily regulated title of 'chartered clinical psychologist'. In contrast, *psychiatrists* are medically trained doctors who have undertaken further training to specialise in mental health problems.

> **multidisciplinary teams (MDTs)** teams of workers from a range of disciplines specialising in different aspects of health and social care so that clients may receive holistic care.

Mental health provision is characterised by professionals working in **multidisciplinary teams (MDTs)** to provide a range of skills from different aspects of health and social care that will provide the basis for recovery and support. An MDT will discuss the best approach to dealing with individual patient cases – especially those that are complex and challenging. Table 2.1 provides descriptions of the members of a typical multidisciplinary team providing community mental health services (Jones, 2008). Within this team, the clinical psychologist's role will be to offer a perspective on each case based on their own professional skills. This may involve providing assessments either for diagnosis or for evaluation of a patient's needs, providing insights into the aetiology or causes of a patient's problems, or suggesting and conducting suitable therapeutic or rehabilitation interventions.

While clinical psychologists receive extensive training across a range of mental health problems using a variety of different theoretical approaches, most eventually specialise in working with one, or sometimes two, client groups, often within a preferred psychological approach (e.g. cognitive, behavioural, systemic, psychodynamic or humanistic; see Chapter 3). As an example of this, Focus Point 2.1 describes the work of a clinical psychologist who specialises in working with psychosis and within a preferred cognitive/behavioural approach.

Within the UK National Health Service (NHS), services are currently organised by client group. These include (i) children with mental health problems and physical health problems; (ii) working-age adults with mental health and physical health problems; (iii) older adults with mental and physical health problems; (iv) children

TABLE 2.1 *Multidisciplinary Teams.*

Clinical psychologists frequently work as members of multidisciplinary teams (MDTs). Part of the rationale for MDTs is that they can provide clients with more holistic care, since they include workers from a range of disciplines that specialise in different aspects of health and social care. Team members can include the following:

Team manager – usually a social worker or nurse by background, who is responsible for organising and managing the team.

Psychiatrists – medical doctors specialising in mental health, whose role includes making diagnoses, prescribing medication and being involved in assessments under the Mental Health Act, which can result in clients being involuntarily detained in hospital for assessment or treatment.

Psychotherapists, counsellors, clinical psychologists and **counselling psychologists** – professionals who can offer psychological assessments and interventions (some of the distinctions between these groups are discussed later).

Mental health nurses – nurses specialising in mental health, whose role includes monitoring clients' mental health, administrating medication and providing other support.

Social workers – professionals whose main focus is clients' social care needs (e.g. housing). Approved social workers are also involved in Mental Health Act assessments.

Occupational therapists – clinicians who specialise in assessing and training (or re-training) occupational and daily living skills.

Community support workers – individuals who do not normally have professional clinical qualifications, but can have considerable experience working with clients and may have in-service training and/or an NVQ.

Secretarial staff – responsible for administering the team (e.g. organising appointments and typing letters).

Source: After Jones (2008).

FOCUS POINT 2.1   A WEEK IN THE LIFE OF A CLINICAL PSYCHOLOGIST

WORKING WITH PSYCHOSIS: A CLINICAL PSYCHOLOGIST'S EXPERIENCE

I have worked with people with psychosis for the last five years. Most of the work that I have done has involved either cognitive behavioural therapy (CBT) or family intervention (FI) and has been provided through the NHS. When I started this work I was anxious about trying out these therapies with people with psychosis. I had experience of CBT working well in trauma, anxiety and depression but was unsure how the therapy would translate into psychosis.

A typical week would include a whole variety of very different tasks. The main focus of the work is the therapy itself but there is a lot that goes on alongside that. Usually I attend the Community Mental Health Team meeting where clinical cases are discussed and the team decides on who in the team is best for an individual to see. The team is made up of nurses, social workers, occupational therapists, psychiatrists and psychologists and each professional group takes a slightly different perspective on the case in hand.

In addition there are assessments to conduct. I will usually see three or four people a week for an initial assessment and then write up this information and take it back to the team meeting for allocation. Some more time is spent writing letters to clients or to GPs and also in speaking on the telephone to those people.

The bread and butter of the job is the clinical work itself. Psychosis is often confusing and terrifying for those who experience it. This may seem like a self-evident and simplistic statement. However, keeping a focus on the distress that people experience helps me a great deal in my work. It is easy to be blinded by the delusions and hallucinations and to fail to consider the confusion, distress and fear that so often goes with them. So, as a start point when working in psychosis I tend to try to consider what people

with psychosis have in common with other people rather than what sets them apart. In this way I can draw on my experiences of working in anxiety, depression and trauma when I meet, and try to help, someone with psychosis.

In my experience cognitive behavioural therapy can help someone make sense of psychotic experiences by helping them make links between emotional states, thoughts, beliefs, traumatic life events and psychotic symptoms. Helping people to make sense of psychotic and emotional experiences by discussing psychological formulations can help them make connections between seemingly unconnected events or beliefs and disabling and distressing psychotic symptoms. In order to succeed in this work it is first essential to engage well with a client. Engagement in CBT for psychosis is a big challenge to therapists. For some people having the time and space to talk through their experiences in detail is very liberating and although it is hard work (for all parties) can be very rewarding too.

Family interventions (FI) make up another large part of my clinical work. They have been designed to minimise the negative impact of a client's symptoms on carers and to reduce the risk of client relapse. Central importance is given to the task of defusing the large range of difficult emotions that psychosis can often engender in families, for example anger and fear. The intervention is based upon a positive view of individuals with psychosis and their caregivers; the strengths of the family unit are explicitly recognised and family members are mobilised as supportive therapeutic allies. I conduct the FI work with my colleague (who is also a clinical psychologist) and usually we try to see families in their own homes.

There is still a lot to learn about how psychology can help people with psychosis and that is what makes this area of work so challenging and rewarding. (From Davey, 2008)

with a learning disability; (v) adults with a learning disability; and (vi) people with brain injuries or neurological deficits. Depending on the locality and the nature of the mental health problems found there, individual NHS Mental Health Trusts may structure their service provision to reflect the needs of the area they serve.

For example, Figure 2.1 shows how services provided by the SussexPartnership Mental Health Foundation Trust are structured and managed around themes that reflect the underlying needs of the local community and the Trust's response to those needs. These include

a team dealing with Access (ensuring that those who require mental health services are able to access those services), Working Age clients (covering a range of psychological and mental health problems), Older People (who often have mental health problems combined with physical health problems), Child & Adolescent Services (including the involvement of educational and social services), Substance Misuse Services, Learning Disability and Secure & Forensic (for individuals who represent a danger to themselves or others or whose behaviour represents a criminal offence). Clinical psychologists will be

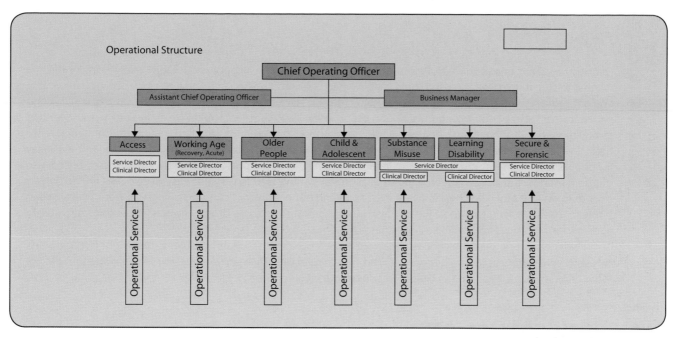

FIGURE 2.1 *SussexPartnership Mental Health Foundation Trust.* © Sussex Partnership NHS Foundation Trust 2009.

This figure shows how services provided by the SussexPartnership Mental Health Foundation Trust are structured and managed around themes that reflect the underlying mental health needs of the local community.

involved in each of these teams and play an active role in delivering mental health services for the community.

2.3 THE DOMAIN OF CLINICAL PSYCHOLOGY

So far we have briefly described who clinical psychologists are and a little about what they do. However, to understand the nature of clinical psychology requires a much broader understanding of:

- How we identify and define mental health problems.
- The theoretical frameworks within which we try to explain the causes of mental health problems.
- How we have attempted to classify and diagnose mental health problems.

Deciding what are proper and appropriate examples of mental health problems is not easy, and mental health issues are still very much associated with **stigma** and prejudice (Crisp *et al.*, 2000; see Section 2.4.2). Just because someone's behaviour deviates from accepted norms or patterns does

stigma a sense of shame felt by those as a result of having mental health problems.

not mean that they are suffering from a mental health problem, and just because we might use the term 'crazy' to describe someone's behaviour does not mean that it is the product of disordered thinking or some underlying psychological problem. Unlike medicine, we cannot attempt to define mental health problems on the basis that some 'normal' functioning (psychological, neurological or biological) has gone wrong. This is because (i) we are still some way from understanding the various causes that contribute to many mental health problems; and (ii) many forms of behaviour that require treatment by clinical psychologists are merely extreme forms of what we would call 'normal' or 'adaptive' behaviour.

For example, we all worry and we all get depressed at times, but these activities would often be considered normal and would not adversely affect our daily living. However, some people's experiences of worrying and depression are so severe that it causes them personal distress and prevents them from living a normal active and productive life (see Case History 2.1). In clinical psychology we have to make some decisions about when these 'normal' activities begin to represent mental health problems that require the services of mental health professionals, and this is a particularly tricky matter. We will address these issues in the following sections, beginning with how we should define what is and what is not a mental health problem.

ERICA'S STORY

I started using cocaine at thirteen. Before, I was using marijuana and alcohol and it didn't really work for me, so I wanted to step it up a level. I started using heroin when I was fifteen. I began using it to come down from cocaine and get some sleep. But I started liking the heroin high and started using it straight. Every day, after a while. Along with cocaine, I also began taking prescription drugs when I was thirteen. They were so easy to get. I never had to buy them or get them from a doctor. I would just get them from friends who had gone through their parent's medicine cabinet. I also thought that prescription drugs were 'safer' than other drugs. I figured that it was okay for people to take them, and if they were legal, I was fine. Like I said, prescription drugs were incredibly easy to get from friends, and it always seemed to be a last-minute thing. Heroin was also easy to get – all I had to do was go into town and buy it. My heroin use started spiralling out of control. I stopped going to school. I was leaving home for days at a time. My whole life revolved around getting and using drugs – I woke up shaking with anxiety almost every morning and I felt like I was going crazy. (Adapted from Davey, 2008)

To what extent do you think Erica's behaviour represents a mental health problem? You might like to discuss this with your fellow students before you read this chapter and then again after you have finished reading it. What differences has reading the chapter made to your views and why?

2.4 CONCEPTUAL AND CLASSIFICATION ISSUES IN CLINICAL PSYCHOLOGY

2.4.1 Defining Mental Health Problems

There are at least two reasons why defining mental health problems is a tricky business. First, unlike medicine, clinical psychology is still a relatively young science and we have some way to go yet before we will understand the causes of even the most common mental health problems. Because of this, we cannot simply base our definition of what is a mental health problem on causal factors – because we don't fully understand what these are. Secondly, many phenomena thought to represent mental health problems (e.g. anxiety, depression) range from being perfectly acceptable and even adaptive (e.g. anxiety at an impending exam, depression following the death of a loved one) to being distressing and disruptive (e.g. uncontrollable worrying, suicidal ideation), so where do we draw the line between what is acceptable and tolerable, and what is unacceptable and pathological? Let us look at some common examples of the way in which we might define whether a behaviour represents a mental health problem.

2.4.1.1 Deviation from the statistical norm

We can use statistical definitions to decide whether an activity or a psychological attribute deviates substantially from the **statistical norm**, and in some areas of clinical psychology this is used as a means of defining the criteria for a mental health problem. For example, in the area of learning or intellectual disability, if an IQ score is significantly below the norm of 100 this is currently used as one criterion for diagnosing a learning or intellectual disability. Figure 2.2 shows the distribution of IQ scores in a standard population, and this indicates that the percentage of individuals with IQ scores below 70 would be relatively small (i.e. around 2.5–3% of the population). However, there are at least two important problems with using deviations from statistical norms as indications of mental health problems. First, in the intellectual disability case, an IQ of less than 70 may be statistically rare, but rather than simply forcing the individual into a diagnostic category, a better approach would be to evaluate the specific needs of individuals with learning disabilities in a way that allows us to suggest strategies, services and supports that will optimise individual functioning. Rather than an approach based solely on categorising intellectual and adaptive impairments, the American Association on Intellectual & Developmental Disabilities (AAIDD) has recently promoted a more individualised assessment of a person's skills and needs. This approach emphasises that individuals have both strengths and limitations, and that an individual's limitations need to be described in a way that enables suitable support to be developed.

Secondly, as we can see from Figure 2.2, substantial deviation from the norm does not necessarily imply mental health problems, because individuals with exceptionally high IQs are also statistically rare, yet we would not necessarily be willing to consider this group of individuals as candidates for psychological intervention – would we?

statistical norm a statistical unit that is representative of the range of scores on a particular variable.

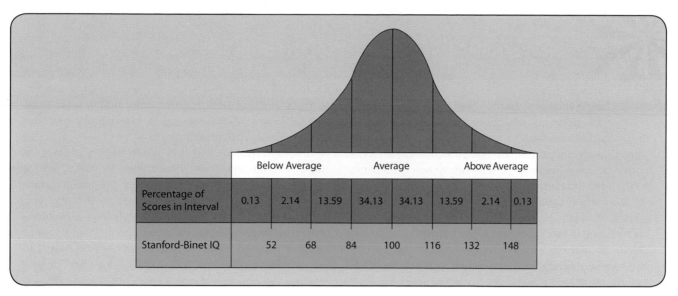

Below Average			Average		Above Average		
Percentage of Scores in Interval	0.13	2.14	13.59	34.13	34.13	13.59	2.14	0.13
Stanford-Binet IQ		52	68	84	100	116	132	148

FIGURE 2.2 *IQ scores.*

This figure represents a normal distribution curve for IQ scores. From this distribution it can be seen that 68% of people score between 84 and 116 points, while only 2.27% of people have an IQ score below 68 points. This graph suggests that around 2–3% of the population will have IQs lower than the 70 points that is the diagnostic criterion for mental retardation. However, the problem with basing a definition of psychopathology on scores that deviate substantially from the norm is that high IQ is also very rare. Only 2.27% of the population have an IQ score greater than 132 points.

Source: After Davey (2008).

PHOTO 2.1 *Substantial deviation from the norm does not necessarily imply mental health problems because individuals with exceptionally high IQs are also statistically rare. Yet we would not necessarily be willing to consider this group of individuals as candidates for psychological intervention – would we?*

2.4.1.2 Deviation from social norms

There is often a tendency within individual cultures and societies for the members of that culture or society to label a behaviour or activity as indicative of a mental health problem if it is far removed from what we consider to be the social norms for that culture. We assume (perhaps quite wrongly) that socially normal and acceptable behaviours have evolved to represent adaptive ways of behaving, and that anyone who deviates from these norms must have a mental health problem. However, it is almost impossible to use deviation from social norms as a way of defining such a problem.

First, different cultures often differ significantly in what they consider to be socially normal and acceptable. For example, in the Soviet Union during the 1970s and 1980s, political dissidents who were active against the communist regime were regularly diagnosed with schizophrenia and incarcerated in psychiatric hospitals. Among many in the Soviet Union at the time, this represented a genuine belief that anti-Soviet activity was indeed a manifestation of mental health problems – for example, anyone who wanted to protest against the perfect social system must be suffering from mental health problems (Goldacre, 2002)! Soviet psychiatrists even added to the official symptoms of schizophrenia by including categories such as 'reformist delusions' and 'litigation mania' to denote so-called mental illnesses, characterised

FOCUS POINT 2.2   MENTAL HEALTH PROBLEMS AND CULTURE

Mental health problems can manifest themselves in different forms in different cultures, and this can lead to some disorders that are culture-specific (i.e. have a set of symptoms that are found only in that particular culture). One such example is *Seizisman,* a state of psychological paralysis found in the Haitian community (Nicolas *et al.,* 2006).

The name literally means 'seized-up-ness' and refers to a state of paralysis usually brought on by rage, anger or sadness, and in rare cases happiness. Events that can cause Seizisman include a traumatic event (such as receiving bad news), a family crisis and verbal insults from others. Individuals affected by the syndrome become completely dysfunctional, disorganised and confused, and unresponsive to their surroundings (Laguerre, 1981). The following quote illustrates how viewing traumatic events while

working within a Haitian community that is attuned to the symptoms of this syndrome can actually give rise to these culture-bound symptoms.

'I remember over and over, when I was a UN Human Rights Monitor and I was down there in Port-au-Prince viewing cadaver after cadaver left by the Haitian army, people would say, "Now go home and lie down or you will have Seizisman". And I never really had a problem, you know? I never threw up or fainted no matter what I saw, but I started to feel "stressed", which is an American illness defined in an American way. After viewing one particularly vile massacre scene, I went home and followed the cultural model I had been shown. I lay down, curled up, and went incommunicado. "Ah-hah! Seizisman!" said the people of my household.' (Nicola *et al.,* 2006, p. 705)

by so-called dysfunctional beliefs that anti-Soviet actions were rational (Davey, 2008). However, since the collapse of the Soviet system, few would suspect that these kinds of beliefs and activities are representative of mental health problems.

Second, it is difficult to use cultural norms to define mental health problems because cultural factors seem significantly to affect how mental health problems manifest themselves. For example, culture can produce 'culture-bound' symptoms of psychopathology that seem confined to specific societies and can influence how stress, anxiety and depression manifest themselves. An example of a 'culture-bound' effect is described in Focus Point 2.2. Known as **Seizisman**, this is a state of psychological paralysis caused by stress and found almost exclusively in the Haitian community (Nicolas *et al.,* 2006).

Seizisman a state of psychological paralysis found in the Haitian community.

2.4.1.3   *Maladaptive behaviour*

One popular or lay view of mental health problems is that the thoughts and behaviours of people with mental health problems are in some way maladaptive. That is, the problem renders the individual incapable of adapting to what most of us would consider normal daily living. So such problems would normally affect whether a person could undertake and hold down a job, could cope with the demands of being a parent, develop loving relationships or function socially. In its extreme form, **maladaptive behaviour** might involve behaving in a way

maladaptive behaviour behaviour which inhibits a person's ability to adjust to a particular situation.

that is a threat to the health and wellbeing of the individual and others.

It is certainly the case that current diagnostic criteria for mental health problems, such as **DSM-IV-TR** (see Section 2.4.4.1),

DSM-IV-TR the most recent version of the *Diagnostic and Statistical Manual.*

do use deficits in social, occupational and educational functioning as one criterion for defining many mental health problems, but it is by no means the only criterion. The difficulty in defining mental health problems solely in terms of maladaptive behaviour is also apparent when we discuss forms of behaviour that we might call maladaptive, but would not necessarily want to label as problematic. For example, it can be argued that many activities that we might view as manifestations of psychological problems – such as worry or phobias – might not be representative of maladaptive behaviour but instead serve a protective or adaptive function. For example, many people view worrying as a positive activity that helps them think through problems and deal with daily issues (Davey, 1994). Similarly, a case can be made for suggesting that specific phobias such as height, water, snake and spider phobias are genuinely adaptive responses that protect us from exposure to potentially life-threatening situations (e.g. Seligman, 1971).

2.4.1.4   *Distress and impairment*

Later in this chapter we will look at some of the ways in which psychologists and psychiatrists have attempted to classify mental health problems. In order for symptoms to be diagnosed as a psychological disorder, one of the most common requirements is that they must cause 'clinically significant distress or impairment in social, academic, or occupational functioning' (DSM-IV-TR). It is clearly the case that many individuals with severe mental health problems do suffer considerable personal distress – often to the point of wanting to take their own lives.

Defining mental health problems in terms of the degree of distress and impairment expressed by the sufferer is useful in a number of ways. First, it allows people to judge their own 'normality' rather than subjecting them to judgements about their 'normality' made by others in society, such as psychologists or psychiatrists. Many people who are diagnosed with mental health problems originally present themselves for treatment because of the distress and impairment caused by their symptoms. Second, defining mental health problems in terms of the degree of distress and impairment experienced can be independent of the type of lifestyle chosen by the individual. This means that we do not judge whether someone has a psychological problem purely on the basis of whether they are perceived as productively contributing to society or not, but on the basis of how they are able to cope with the daily events that occur in their lives.

As attractive as this definition for defining mental health problems seems, it does have a number of difficulties, however. First, this approach does not provide any standards by which we should judge behaviour itself. For example, an adolescent regular drug user may admit that her substance dependency is beginning to cause her some distress, but should we consider that a teenager's drug addiction is in need of treatment only if she expresses unhappiness about her situation? Second, some forms of behaviour that are currently classified as mental health problems include so-called disorders in which diagnosis does not require the sufferer necessarily to report any personal distress or impairment. A good example of this is that group of disorders known as *personality disorders* (Alwin, 2008). For example, individuals diagnosed with borderline personality disorder or antisocial personality disorder (see Chapter 3) frequently exhibit behaviour that is impulsive, emotional, threatening and harmful to themselves and others. Yet they are rarely willing to admit that their behaviour is unusual or problematic.

2.4.1.5   Summary

None of these individual ways of defining mental health problems is ideal. They may fail to include examples of behaviour that we intuitively believe are representative of mental health problems (the distress and impairment approach); they may include examples that we intuitively feel are *not* examples of mental health problems (e.g. the statistical approach, the deviation from social norms approach); or they may represent forms of categorisation that would lead us simply to impose stigmatising labels on people rather than considering their individual

needs (e.g. the statistical approach). In practice, attempts to define and classify mental health problems use an amalgamation of all these approaches. An emphasis is placed on the degree of distress and impairment experienced by the individual and to a lesser degree the extent to which their behaviour may cause harm to themselves or to others.

2.4.2   Stigma and Mental Health Problems

The issue of defining mental health problems not only revolves around what criteria we use to define them but also the need to use terminology and criteria that minimise the stigma and exclusion that are often felt by people with mental health problems. For example, studies have suggested that stigmatising attitudes towards people with mental health problems are widespread and commonly held (Byrne, 1997; Crisp *et al.*, 2000; Heginbotham, 1998). In a survey of over 1700 adults in the UK, Crisp *et al.* (2000) found the following:

- The most commonly held belief was that people with mental health problems were dangerous – especially those with schizophrenia, alcoholism and drug dependence.
- People believed that some mental health problems such as eating disorders and substance abuse were self-inflicted.
- Respondents believed that people with mental health problems were generally hard to talk to.

People tended to hold these negative beliefs regardless of their age, the knowledge they had of mental health problems and whether they knew someone who had a mental health problem.

What generates these negative attitudes towards individuals with mental health problems? Some sectors of the popular media bear some responsibility for this and Focus Point 2.3 describes a recent example.

Furthermore, a term regularly used to describe people with mental health problems is 'abnormal'. For example, there are still numerous psycho-pathology courses and textbooks that use **abnormal psychology** in their title. Merely doing so implies that people suffering from mental health problems are in some way 'abnormal', either in the statistical or the functional sense – neither of which is necessarily true, because many forms of mental health problem (i) are common rather than

> **abnormal psychology** an alternative definition of psychopathology albeit with negative connotations in regard to being 'not normal'.

FOCUS POINT 2.3 MEDIA ATTITUDES TO MENTAL HEALTH PROBLEMS

The popular press can often present mental health problems in a way that propagates the stigmas attached to them. In September 2003, the ex-heavyweight champion boxer Frank Bruno was treated for depression at a psychiatric hospital, and the mental health charity Sane (www.sane.org.uk) subsequently criticised unsympathetic coverage of his illness in the media.

The BBC News website reported that an early edition of the *Sun* newspaper had the front page headline 'Bonkers Bruno

Source: Press Association.

Locked Up', which was later changed to 'Sad Bruno in Mental Home':

'Sane chief executive Marjorie Wallace said:"It is both an insult to Mr Bruno and damaging to many thousands of people who endure mental illness to label him as 'bonkers' or 'a nutter' and having to be 'put in a mental home'." (http://news.bbc.co.uk/1/hi/uk/3130376.stm)

(From Davey, 2008)

---

unusual (e.g. depression, worrying); and (ii) do not imply that any biological or psychological system is malfunctioning. However, the term 'abnormal' also has more important ramifications, because it implies that those people suffering mental health problems are in some way 'not normal' or are inferior members of society. In this sense, the 'abnormal' label may affect our willingness to include such individuals fully in everyday activities and may lead us to treat such individuals with suspicion rather than respect.

Individuals with mental health problems have become increasingly vocal about how mental health problems are labelled and perceived by others, and examples of groups set us to communicate these views include **service user groups** (groups of individuals who are end users of the mental health services provided by, for example, government agencies such as the NHS; Tait & Lester, 2005) and organisations such as **Mad Pride** (www.ctono.freeserve.co.uk), an organisation dedicated to changing the way in which society views people with mental health problems (Seaton, 2000). Activity Box 2.1 provides a brief quiz to test your own awareness and knowledge of mental health facts.

So, when considering how to define mental health problems, we must consider not only whether a definition is useful in the scientific and professional sense, but also whether it provides a definition that will minimise the stigma experienced by sufferers and facilitate the support they need to function as members of an inclusive society.

service user groups groups of individuals who are end users of mental health services provided, e.g., by the NHS.

Mad Pride a UK organisation dedicated to changing the way society views people with mental health problems.

2.4.3 Explaining Mental Health Problems

While defining what is and is not a mental health problem is challenging in itself, the issue of how we go about explaining mental health problems is equally taxing. Views about what causes mental health problems have changed significantly over the course of history, and it is instructive to understand how we have conceptualised this over time. For example, mental health problems are often accompanied by what appear to be changes in the individual's personality, and these changes in personality or behaviour are some of the first symptoms that are noticed. Historically, people tended to describe those exhibiting symptoms of psychopathology as being 'possessed' in some way, and many ancient civilisations, such as those in Egypt, China, Babylon and Greece, believed that such people were possessed by bad spirits (this is known as **demonology**). Sadly, it was assumed that the only way to exorcise these bad spirits was with elaborate, ritualised ceremonies that frequently involved direct physical attacks on the sufferer's body in an attempt to force out the demons (e.g. through torture, flogging or starvation). Not surprisingly, such actions usually had the effect of increasing the victim's distress and suffering.

demonology the belief that those exhibiting symptoms of psychopathology are possessed by bad spirits.

As cultures develop, so too do the types of causes to which they attribute behaviour. In particular, as we began to understand some of the biological causes of physical disease and illness, our conception of 'madness' moved very slowly towards treating it as a disease (hence the term 'mental illness'). This became known as the

A MENTAL HEALTH AWARENESS QUIZ   ACTIVITY BOX 2.1

See how many of the following questions you can answer correctly to test your own awareness of mental health issues.

1. Are mental health problems inherited?
2. Violence towards others is a symptom of which mental illness?
3. 35–50 year olds show the highest incidence of suicide – True or False?
4. People who talk about suicide are not likely to go on to do it – True or False?
5. Men are more likely than women to attempt suicide – True or False?
6. What proportion of people are known to experience mental health problems? Is it (a) 1 in 8, (b) 1 in 4 or (c) 1 in 6?
7. What percentage of GP consultations are for mental health problems? Is it (a) 30%, (b) 50% or (c) 25%?
8. Drugs such as cannabis and ecstasy can increase the risk of panic attacks, anxiety disorders and psychotic episodes – True or False?

9. At what age are mental health problems most likely to occur?
10. In a MIND survey of people who currently have or have previously experienced a mental health problem:
    (a) What percentage of these people said that they had been abused or harassed in public?
    (b) What percentage of these people claim to have been harassed, intimidated or teased at work because of a psychiatric history?
11. Mental Health Media (a campaigning organisation) has identified three major stereotypes of how people with a mental illness are portrayed by the media. One of these is sad and pitiable. What are the other two?

Source: Adapted from Student Psychological Health Project, Educational Development & Support Centre, University of Leicester and 'Looniversity Challenge', a mental health awareness quiz provided by mental health awareness group 'Fifteen Training & Development', Brighton, UK. First published in Davey (2008).

---

somatogenic hypothesis the theory that causes or explanations of psychological problems can be found in physical or biological impairments.

medical model an explanation of psychopathology in terms of underlying biological or medical causes.

somatogenic hypothesis or the **medical model**, which advocated that the causes or explanations of psychological problems could be found in physical or biological impairments (Small, 2006). There are many explanations of mental health problems that allude to biological causes, and these attempt to explain symptoms in terms of such factors as brain abnormalities (e.g. in dementia, autism), biochemical imbalances (especially imbalances of brain neurotransmitters) (e.g. major depression, bipolar disorder, schizophrenia) or genetic factors (e.g. learning disabilities, autism, schizophrenia), to name just a few (see Chapters 3–5).

However, while such biological factors may play a role in the aetiology of some mental health problems, biological explanations are not the only way in which psychopathology can be explained and biological dysfunction is by no means a factor underlying all mental health issues. As we shall see later, it is often a person's experiences that are dysfunctional, not their biological substrates. In contrast to the medical model, both psychodynamic and contemporary cognitive accounts of psychopathology (see below) argue that many psychological problems are the result of the individual acquiring dysfunctional

ways of thinking and acting, and acquiring these characteristics through normal, functional learning processes. In this sense, it is not the individual or any part of their biology that is dysfunctional, it is the *experiences* they have had that are dysfunctional and have caused them to think and act in the way they do.

2.4.3.1 Psychological models

Moving away from the medical model of psychopathology, some approaches to understanding and explaining mental health problems still see these as symptoms produced by an underlying cause (what is known as the **pathology model**), but a cause that is psychological rather than biological or medical. These approaches often view the cause as a perfectly normal and adaptive reaction to difficult or stressful life conditions (such as the psychoanalytic view that mental health problems are a consequence of perfectly normal psychodynamic processes that are attempting to deal with conflict). As such, psychological models of psychopathology tend to view mental health symptoms as normal reactions mediated by intact psychological or cognitive mechanisms, and not as the result of processes that are 'broken' or malfunctioning.

pathology model a view of psychopathology which sees symptoms as produced by underlying causes.

2.4.3.2 The psychoanalytic or psychodynamic model

This approach was first formulated and pioneered by the Viennese neurologist Sigmund Freud (1856–1939). As a result of his experiences treating individuals with hysteria and other psychological problems, he developed his influential theory of **psychoanalysis**. This was an attempt to explain both normal and abnormal psychological functioning in terms of how various psychological mechanisms help to defend against anxiety and depression by repressing memories and thoughts that may cause conflict and stress. Freud argued that three psychological forces shape an individual's personality and may also generate psychopathology. These are the id (instinctual needs), the ego (rational thinking) and the superego (moral standards).

psychoanalysis a term for the theory developed by Freud to explain normal and abnormal psychological functioning and for the psychotherapy derived from that theory.

The concept of the **id** was used to describe innate instinctual needs – especially sexual needs. As we grow up, Freud argued that it becomes apparent to us that the environment itself will not satisfy all our instinctual needs, and so we need to develop a separate part of our psychology known as the **ego**. This is a rational part of the psyche that

id in psychoanalysis, the concept used to describe innate instinctual needs – especially sexual needs.

attempts to control the impulses of the id, and **ego defence mechanisms** develop by which the ego attempts to control unacceptable id impulses and reduce the anxiety that id impulses may arouse. The **superego** develops out of both the id and the ego, and represents our attempt to integrate 'values' that we learn from our parents or society.

According to Freud, the id, ego and superego are often in conflict, and psychological health is maintained only when they are in balance. If these three factors are in conflict, our behaviour may begin to exhibit signs of psychopathology. Individuals attempt to control conflict between these factors and also reduce stress and conflict from external events by developing defence mechanisms. Table 2.2 describes some of these defence mechanisms together with some examples of how they are presumed to prevent the experience of stress and anxiety.

Conflict between the id, ego and superego together with Freud's theory of stages of development (see website)

ego in psychoanalysis, a rational part of the psyche that attempts to control the impulses of the id.

ego defence mechanisms means by which the ego attempts to control unacceptable id impulses and reduce the anxiety these may arouse.

superego in psychoanalysis, a development from both the id and ego which represents our attempts to integrate 'values' that we learn from our parents or society.

TABLE 2.2 *Defence Mechanisms in Psychoanalytic Theory.*

Each of the Freudian defence mechanisms described below functions to reduce the amount of stress or conflict that might be caused by specific experiences.

Denial – The individual denies that the source of the anxiety exists (e.g. I didn't fail my exam, it must be a mistake).

Repression – Suppressing bad memories or even current thoughts that cause anxiety (e.g. repressing thoughts about liking someone because you are frightened that you may be rejected if you approach them).

Regression – Moving back to an earlier developmental stage (e.g. when highly stressed you abandon normal coping strategies and return to an early developmental stage, for example by smoking if you are fixated at the oral stage).

Reaction formation – Doing or thinking the opposite to how you feel (e.g. someone who is angry with their boss may go out of their way to be kind and courteous to that person).

Projection – Ascribing unwanted impulses to someone else (e.g. the unfaithful husband who is extremely jealous of his wife might always suspect that she is being unfaithful).

Rationalisation – Finding a rational explanation for something you've done wrong (e.g. you didn't fail the exam because you didn't study hard enough but because the questions were unfair).

Displacement – Moving an impulse from one object (target) to another (e.g. if you've been told off by your boss at work, you go home and shout at your partner or kick the dog).

Sublimation – Transforming impulses into something constructive (e.g. redecorating the bedroom when you're feeling angry about something).

formed the major components of psychoanalytic theory. There is no doubt that the psychoanalytic model has been extremely influential, both in its attempts to provide explanations for psychopathology and in the treatments it has helped to develop, and as many as 20% of modern practising clinical psychologists identify themselves at least in part with a psychoanalytic or psychodynamic approach to psychopathology (Prokaska & Norcross, 2003). However, psychoanalytic theory does have some shortcomings, and it is arguably no longer the explanation or treatment of choice for most clinical psychologists, nor is it a paradigm in which modern-day evidence-based researchers attempt to understand psychopathology. This is largely because the central concepts in psychoanalytic theory are hard to define and measure objectively, and it is therefore difficult to conduct objective research on them to see if they are actually related to symptoms of psychopathology in the way that Freud and his associates describe (Erdelyi, 1992).

2.4.3.3   The behavioural model

Most psychological models have in common the view that psychopathology is caused by how we assimilate our experiences and how this is reflected in thinking and behaviour. The **behavioural model** adopts the broad view that many examples of psychopathology reflect our learned reactions to life experiences (Kazdin & Herson, 1980). That is, psychopathology can be explained as learned reactions to environmental experiences, and this approach was promoted primarily by the behaviourist school of psychology (Eysenck, 1959).

behavioural model an influential psychological model of psychopathology based on explaining behaviour.

During the 1950s and 1960s, many clinical psychologists became disillusioned by psychoanalytic approaches to psychopathology and sought an approach that was more scientific and objective. They turned to that area of psychology known as **learning theory** (see website) and argued that just as adaptive behaviour can be acquired through learning, so can many forms of dysfunctional behaviour (Davey, 1981). The two important principles of learning on which this approach was based are classical conditioning and operant conditioning. **Classical conditioning** represents the learning of an association between two stimuli, the first of which (the conditioned stimulus, CS) predicts the occurrence of the second (the unconditioned stimulus, UCS). The prototypical example of this form of learning is Pavlov's experiment in which a

learning theory the body of knowledge encompassing principles of classical and operant conditioning applied to explain and treat psychopathology.

classical conditioning the learning of an association between two stimuli, the first of which (the conditioned stimulus) predicts the occurrence of the second (the unconditioned stimulus).

hungry dog learns to salivate to a bell (the CS) that predicts subsequent delivery of food (the UCS) (see website; Davey, 1989). In contrast, **operant conditioning** represents the learning of a specific behaviour or response because that behaviour has certain rewarding or reinforcing consequences. A prototypical example of operant conditioning is a hungry rat learning to press a lever to obtain food in an experimental chamber called a Skinner Box (see website; Davey, 1989).

operant conditioning the learning of a specific behaviour or response because that behaviour has certain consequences.

These two forms of learning have been used to explain a number of examples of mental health problems. For example, classical conditioning has been used to explain the acquisition of emotional disorders, including many of those with anxiety-based symptoms. Some forms of specific phobias appear to be acquired when the sufferer experiences the phobic stimulus (the CS) in association with a traumatic event (the UCS) (e.g. dog phobia, accident phobia and dental phobia – Davey, 1989; Doogan & Thomas, 1992; Kuch, 1997). In contrast, operant conditioning has been used extensively to explain why a range of psychopathology-relevant behaviours may have been acquired and maintained. Focus Point 2.4 provides an example of how bizarre behaviours in schizophrenia may be acquired (Ayllon, Haughton & Hughes, 1965).

Other applications of operant conditioning to explaining mental health problems include how the stress-reducing or stimulant effects of nicotine, alcohol and many illegal drugs may lead to substance dependency (e.g. Schachter, 1982) and how the disruptive, self-harming or challenging behaviour exhibited by individuals with intellectual or developmental disabilities may be maintained by attention from family and carers (Mazaleski et al., 1993).

The behavioural approach led to the development of important behavioural treatment methods, including **behaviour therapy** and **behaviour modification**. For example, if psychopathology is learned through normal learning processes, then it should be possible to use those same learning processes to help the individual 'unlearn' any maladaptive behaviours or emotions (Kazdin & Hersen, 1980; see Chapter 3 and website).

behaviour therapy a form of treatment that aims to change behaviour using principles based on conditioning theory.

behaviour modification an approach to psychopathology based on the principles of operant conditioning (also known as behaviour analysis).

As influential as the behavioural approach has been over the years, it also has some limitations. For example, many psychopathologies are characterised by a range of cognitive factors such as information processing biases, belief schemas and dysfunctional ways of thinking, and learning theory jargon is probably not the best framework with which to describe these phenomena accurately

FOCUS POINT 2.4 CAN PERFECTLY NORMAL PROCESSES CAUSE BIZARRE BEHAVIOUR?

A revealing study by Ayllon, Haughton and Hughes in 1965 provides insight into some of the processes that might generate the kinds of bizarre and apparently irrational behaviour that characterise some mental health problems.

They used operant reinforcement methods to reward a female patient diagnosed with schizophrenia for carrying a broom.

Whenever she was observed holding the broom a nurse would approach her, offer her a cigarette, or give her a token which could be exchanged for a cigarette. After a period of this reinforcement, the patient was carrying the broom around for most of the day, and even taking it to bed with her when she slept.

At this point, the researchers called in two psychiatrists (who were unaware of the reinforcement schedule) to give their opinions on the nature of the behaviour. One of them gave the following reply:

'Her constant and compulsive pacing, holding a broom in the manner she does, could be seen as a ritualistic procedure, a magical action... Her broom would be then: (1) a child that gives her love and she gives him in return her devotion, (2) a phallic symbol, (3) the scepter of an omnipotent queen... this is a magical procedure in which the patient carries out her wishes, expressed in a way that is far beyond our solid, rational and conventional way of thinking and acting.' (Ayllon *et al.*, 1965, p. 3)

Source: Shutterstock.

First, this psychodynamic explanation given by one of the psychiatrists is a good example of how easy it is to over-speculate about the causes and meaning of a behaviour when the real causes are unknown.

Second, it shows how behaviour that is viewed as representative of psychopathology can be acquired through a perfectly normal learning mechanism (in this case operant reinforcement). (Adapted from Davey, 2008)

---

and inclusively. The cognitive approaches that we will describe next are probably more suited to describing and explaining these aspects of psychopathology.

2.4.3.4 *The cognitive model*

cognitive model an influential psychological model of psychopathology.

Perhaps the most widely adopted current psychological model of mental health problems is the **cognitive model**; one in four of all present-day clinical psychologists would describe their approach as cognitive (Prokaska & Norcross, 2003). Primarily, this approach considers psychopathology to be the result of individuals acquiring irrational beliefs, developing dysfunctional ways of thinking and processing information in biased ways. It was an approach first pioneered by Albert Ellis (1962) and Aaron Beck (1967).

Ellis argued that emotional distress (such as anxiety or depression) is caused primarily because people develop a set of irrational beliefs by which they need to judge their behaviour. Some people become anxious, for example, because they make unrealistic demands on themselves.

The anxious individual may have developed unrealistic beliefs such as 'I must be loved by everyone', and the depressed individual may believe 'I am incapable of doing anything worthwhile'. Judging their behaviour against such 'dysfunctional' beliefs causes distress. At around the same time, Aaron Beck developed a highly successful cognitive therapy for depression based on the view that depressed individuals have developed unrealistic distortions in the way they perceive themselves, the world and their future; this is described further in Chapter 5.

The view that dysfunctional ways of thinking generate and maintain mental health problems has been applied across a broad range of psychological problems, including both anxiety disorders and mood disorders, and has also been applied to the explanation of specific symptoms, such as paranoid thinking in schizophrenia (Morrison, 2001), anti social and impulsive behaviour in personality disorders (Young, Klosko & Weishaar, 2003), dysfunctional sexual behaviour in sex offenders and paedophiles (Ward *et al.*, 1997) and illness reporting in hypochondriasis and somatoform disorders (Warwick, 1995), to name but a few.

The cognitive approach has also been highly successful in generating an influential approach to treatment. If dysfunctional thoughts and beliefs maintain the symptoms of psychopathology, then these dysfunctional thoughts and beliefs can be identified, challenged and replaced by more functional cognitions. This has given rise to the broad-ranging therapeutic approach known as *cognitive behaviour therapy (CBT)*.

2.4.3.5 The humanist-existentialist approach

Some approaches to psychopathology believe that insights into emotional and behavioural problems cannot be achieved unless the individual is able to gain insight into their life from a broad range of perspectives. People not only acquire psychological conflicts and experience emotional distress, they also have the ability to acquire self-awareness, develop important values and a sense of meaning in life, and pursue freedom of choice. If these latter abilities are positively developed and encouraged, then conflict, emotional distress and mental health problems can often be resolved. This is the general approach adopted by humanistic and existential models of psychopathology, whose aim is to resolve psychological problems through insight, personal development and self-actualisation (Rogers, 2003).

An influential example of the **humanist-existentialist approach** is **client-centred therapy**, developed by Carl Rogers (1951, 1987). This approach stresses the goodness of human nature and assumes that if individuals are unrestricted by fears and conflicts, they will develop into well-adjusted, happy individuals. The client-centred therapist will try to create a supportive climate in which the client is helped to acquire positive self-worth. The therapist will use **empathy** to help understand the client's feelings and **unconditional positive regard**, by which the therapist expresses willingness to accept the client totally for who he or she is.

This type of approach tries to eradicate psychopathology by moving the individual from one phenomenological perspective (e.g. one that contains fears and conflicts) to another (e.g. one that enables the client to view him- or herself as a worthy, respected and achieving individual). However, humanistic and existentialist approaches are difficult to evaluate. Exponents of existential therapies tend to argue that experimental methodologies are inappropriate for estimating the effectiveness of such therapies,

humanist-existentialist approach an approach that aims to resolve psychological problems through insight, personal development and self-actualisation.

client-centred therapy an approach to psychopathology assuming that if individuals are unrestricted by fears and conflicts, they will develop into well-adjusted, happy individuals.

empathy an ability to understand and experience a client's own feelings and personal meanings and convey this understanding to the client.

unconditional positive regard valuing clients for who they are without judging them.

because such methods either dehumanise the individuals involved or are incapable of measuring the kinds of existential benefits that such approaches claim to bestow (May & Yalom, 1995; Walsh & McElwain, 2002). Nevertheless, such approaches to treatment are still accepted as having some value and are used at least in part by clinical psychologists, counselling psychologists and psychotherapists.

2.4.4 Classifying Mental Health Problems

The first extensive system for classifying mental health problems was developed by the World Health Organisation (WHO), which added psychological disorders to the **International List of Causes of Death (ICD)** in 1939. Despite this development, the mental disorders section in the ICD was not widely accepted, and in 1952 the **American Psychiatric Association (APA)** published its first **Diagnostic and Statistical Manual (DSM)**. In 1980, the APA produced a substantially revised and expanded DSM-III, which has come to be accepted as the most influential diagnostic system. The most recent version that is used is DSM-IV-TR (TR means 'text revision'), published in 2000. APA 'task forces' are already working on the next revision, DSM-V, which is due to be published in 2013. The ICD system is currently in its tenth edition (ICD-10), and most revisions of the DSM have been coordinated with the ICD to ensure some consistency of diagnosis across systems (see Cooper [1994] for a guide to the ICD-10 classification system).

International List of Causes of Death (ICD) the international standard diagnostic classification developed by the World Health Organisation.

American Psychiatric Association (APA) a scientific and professional organisation that represents psychiatry in the United States.

Diagnostic & Statistical Manual (DSM) an APA handbook for mental health professionals listing different categories of mental disorders and criteria for diagnosing them.

2.4.4.1 DSM-IV-TR

2.4.4.1.1 Defining and diagnosing mental health problems

Before attempting to classify mental health problems, it was necessary for the DSM to define what it considers to be a mental health problem. As we have already seen in section 2.4.1, this is not a simple matter. However, the DSM does attempt to put the emphasis on distress and disability as important defining characteristics.

DSM-IV-TR is a diagnostic manual that provides the following information:

- *Essential features* of the disorder (those that 'define' the disorder).
- *Associated features* (i.e. those that are usually, but not always, present).

- *Diagnostic criteria* (a list of symptoms that must be present for the patient to be given this diagnostic label).
- Information on *differential diagnosis* (i.e. information on how to differentiate this disorder from other, similar disorders).

Finally, an important feature of the DSM is that it avoids any suggestion about the cause of a disorder unless the cause has been definitely established. This means that diagnosis is made almost entirely on the basis of observable behavioural symptoms rather than any supposition about the underlying cause of the symptoms.

2.4.4.1.2   The dimensions of classification

DSM-IV-TR axes of disorder the five dimensions (axes) of classification in DSM-IV-TR.

DSM-IV-TR encourages clinicians to rate individuals on five separate dimensions, or axes (**DSM-IV-TR axes of disorder**), and these are listed in Table 2.3. Axes I and II cover the classification of mental health problems, with Axis I comprising the majority of common diagnostic categories such as anxiety disorders, depression, schizophrenia and so on. Axis II consists of personality disorders and intellectual disabilities, and covers psychopathologies that may be more chronic and long term. These disorders are separated onto two different axes to encourage clinicians to explore the possibility that some shorter-term disorders (e.g. a diagnosed anxiety disorder) may also be concurrent with a longer-term disorder (such as a personality disorder). Axes III, IV and V are

included so that the clinician can acquire a fuller appreciation of an individual's life situation. In particular, Axis IV allows the clinical psychologist to note any psychosocial, environmental, financial or family factors that might be influencing mental health problems.

2.4.4.2   Why do we need a classification system?

Categorisation and classification form an important first stage in the pursuit of knowledge about causes and aetiology. It would be difficult to discuss what causes mental health problems if there were not some form of classification that enabled us to understand how different causes relate to different symptoms. Secondly, classification is necessary if we are to organise services and support for sufferers effectively. For example, the needs of individuals with intellectual disabilities, major depression, an anxiety-based disorder or substance dependency are all very different, and demand different approaches and different means of support and intervention. Finally, whether we like it or not, modern-day society requires that we assess and classify people for a number of reasons, and this is also the case with mental health problems. For example, we might want to know whether a person is psychologically fit to stand trial for a criminal offence, whether a child has disabilities that will require special educational needs, or whether financial compensation or damages should be awarded to an individual because of psychological symptoms caused by the actions of others. Having said this, there are still many clinical psychologists who would argue that the diagnostic and

TABLE 2.3 *The Five Dimensions of Classification in DSM-IV-TR.*

DSM-IV-TR AXIS	Description	Examples
AXIS I	Clinical symptoms that cause significant impairment and disorders are grouped into different categories	Clinical Disorders (e.g. anxiety disorders, mood disorders, schizophrenia and other psychotic disorders etc.); other conditions that may be a focus of clinical attention
AXIS II	Long-term problems that may significantly affect how a person relates to the world	Personality Disorders (e.g. antisocial personality disorder, schizotypical personality disorder etc.) Mental Retardation
AXIS III	Physical or medical conditions that significantly worsen Axis I or Axis II disorders	General Medical Conditions (e.g. infectious & parasitic diseases, diseases of the circulatory system, injury & poisoning etc.)
AXIS IV	Any social or environmental problems that may impact on Axis I or Axis II disorders	Psychosocial & Environmental problems (e.g. unemployment, relocation, divorce or death of a loved one)
AXIS V	A rating of the individual's overall level of functioning	Global Assessment of Functioning

classification systems led by DSM have little utility when it comes to helping individual clients understand their own unique mental health problems, and merely help to stigmatise clients with a label that they will often find difficult to shake off (Boyle, 2007; May, 2007).

2.4.4.3 Problems with classification

While DSM-IV-TR provides an objective and reliable set of criteria by which mental health problems can be diagnosed, it is in many senses imperfect.

First, we have already mentioned that it does not classify psychopathology according to its causes, but does so merely on the basis of symptoms. This can be problematic in a number of different ways. For example, psychopathologies that look the same on the surface may have different causes, and as a consequence require different forms of treatment. Also, diagnosis on the basis of symptoms gives the illusion of explanation, when it is nothing more than a re-description of the symptoms (Carson, 1996). So, to say that 'she hears voices because she has schizophrenia' sounds like an explanation, but within DSM, schizophrenia is merely a collective term for the defining symptoms.

Second, simply using DSM criteria to label people with a disorder can be stigmatising and harmful. We have already noted that individuals with a mental health problem tend to be viewed and treated differently within society (Crisp et al., 2000). In addition, diagnostic labels actually encourage individuals to adopt a 'sick' role and can result in them adopting a long-term role as an individual with what they perceive as a debilitating psychopathology (Scheff, 1975).

Third, DSM diagnostic classification tends to define disorders as *discrete entities* (i.e. after being assessed, you will either be diagnosed with a disorder or you will not). However, much recent evidence has begun to suggest that mental health problems may be *dimensional* rather than discrete (Krueger & Piasecki, 2002). That is, symptoms diagnosed as a disorder may just be more extreme versions of everyday behaviour. For example, at times we all worry about our own life problems, some more than others. In extreme cases this activity can become so regular and persistent that it will interfere with our daily living and may meet DSM-IV-TR criteria for diagnosis as a disorder (e.g. generalised anxiety disorder, GAD; see Chapter 3). In such circumstances, the cut-off point for defining an activity such as worrying as a disorder becomes relatively arbitrary.

Fourth, DSM conceptualises mental health problems as a collection of hundreds of distinct categories of disorders, but in practice an individual client will often be diagnosed with two or more distinct disorders (e.g. an anxiety disorder such as obsessive-compulsive disorder and major depression). This is known as **comorbidity**, and what is interesting is that comorbidity is so common that it is the norm rather than the exception. For example, surveys suggest that up to 79% of individuals diagnosed with a disorder at some point during their lifetime will have a history of more than one disorder (Kessler *et al.*, 1994). This suggests that most disorders as defined by DSM may indeed not be independent, discrete disorders, but may represent symptoms of either **hybrid disorders** (a disorder that contains elements of a number of different disorders) or a more broad-ranging **syndrome** or *disorder spectrum* that represents a higher-order categorical class of symptoms (Krueger, Watson & Barlow, 2005; Widiger & Samuel, 2005).

> **comorbidity** the co-occurrence of two or more distinct disorders.

> **hybrid disorders** an illness containing elements of a number of different disorders.

> **syndrome** a distinct set of symptoms.

2.4.4.4 Summary

While DSM-IV-TR is not ideal, it is the most comprehensive classification system we have available, and while we have listed a number of criticisms of DSM it does have some advantages. We must also remember that DSM is an evolving classification system that takes into account criticisms of previous versions and develops to incorporate recent research. Thus, when DSM-V is published in 2013, it is likely to have attempted to address some of the problems with diagnosis that we have listed above.

2.5 CONCLUSIONS

This chapter has discussed some of the basic features of clinical psychology, clinical psychologists and how they work (see Chapter 6 for fuller coverage). We then discussed some of the conceptual issues that are central to defining what clinical psychology is, and these included (i) how we define mental health problems; (ii) how we try to explain the causes of mental health problems; and (iii) how we have developed ways of classifying mental health problems. There are no obvious and simple answers to any of these issues, but this chapter has attempted to guide you through the various different options and to present a balanced view on the pros and cons of defining, explaining and classifying mental health problems. An introductory chapter of this kind also has to cover some of the implications that these conceptual issues have for the social conception of mental health problems. Defining, explaining and classifying mental problems is as much about minimising the stigma associated with psychopathology as reaching an acceptable scientific conclusion to these debates.

SELF-TEST QUESTIONS

- What are the pros and cons of the medical model of mental health problems?
- Can you describe the basic concepts underlying psychoanalytic and psychodynamic approaches to mental health problems?
- What are the learning principles on which the behavioural approach to mental health problems is based?
- Who were the main founders of the cognitive approach to mental health problems, and what were their main contributions?
- How do humanistic-existential approaches to mental health problems differ from most of the others?
- What are the problems with using the normal curve to define mental health problems?
- How do cultural factors make it difficult to define mental health problems in terms of deviations from social norms?
- What are the pros and cons of using maladaptive behaviour or distress and impairment as means of defining mental health problems?
- What is the DSM classification system primarily designed to do?
- What are the five axes or dimensions of classification in DSM?
- DSM is not an ideal classification system. Can you describe some of the problems associated with this method of classification?

ESSAY QUESTIONS

- Is the presence of personal distress and impairment necessary for identifying symptoms as examples of mental health problems?
- What are the problems for the practising clinician of using a diagnostic system that does not classify mental health problems according to their causes?
- Are mental health problems simply a more extreme form of normal behaviour?
- What are the important similarities and differences in the ways in which different psychological models conceive of mental health problems?

TEXTS FOR FURTHER READING

American Psychiatric Association (2000) *Diagnostic and Statistical Manual of Mental Disorders*, 4th edn, Text Revision, Arlington, VA: American Psychiatric Press.

British Psychological Society (2000) *Recent Advances in Understanding Mental Illness and Psychotic Experiences*, Leicester: British Psychological Society.

Cooper, J.E. (1994) *Pocket Guide to ICD-10 Classification of Mental and Behavioural Disorders*, Oxford: Churchill Livingstone.

Davey, G.C.L. (2008) *Psychopathology: Research, Assessment & Treatment in Clinical Psychology*, Chichester: BPS Wiley-Blackwell.

Helzer, J.E. & Hudziak, J.J. (2002) *Defining Psychopathology in the 21st Century: DSM-V and Beyond*, Arlington, VA: American Psychiatric Press.

Maj, M., Gaebel, W., Lopez-Ibor, J. & Sartorius, N. (eds) (2002) *Psychiatric Diagnosis and Classification*, Chichester: John Wiley & Sons Ltd.

RELEVANT JOURNAL ARTICLES

Crisp, A.H., Gelder, M.G., Rix, S., Meltzer, H.I. & Rowlands, O.J. (2000) Stigmatization of people with mental illnesses, *British Journal of Psychiatry*, 177: 4–7.

Krueger, R.F. & Piasecki, T.M. (2002) Toward a dimensional and psychometrically-informed approach to conceptualising psychopathology, *Behaviour Research & Therapy*, 40: 485–99.

McNally, R.J. (2001) On Wakefield's harmful dysfunction analysis of mental disorder, *Behaviour Research & Therapy*, 39: 309–14.

Nicolas, G., DeSilva, A.M., Grey, K.S. & Gonzalez-Eastep, D. (2006) Using a multicultural lens to understand illness among Haitians living in America, *Professional Psychology: Research & Practice*, 37: 702–7.

Wakefield, J.C. (1997) Diagnosing DSM-IV – Part I: DSM-IV and the concept of disorder, *Behaviour Research & Therapy*, 35: 633–49.

REFERENCES

Alwin, N. (2008) Working with people with a diagnosis of personality disorder, in G.C.L. Davey (ed.) *Clinical Psychology*, London: Hodder HE.

Ayllon, T., Haughton, E. & Hughes, H.B. (1965) Interpretation of symptoms – fact or fiction, *Behaviour Research and Therapy* 3(1): 1–7.

Barker, C., Pistrang, N. & Elliott, R. (2002) *Research Methods in Clinical Psychology*, 2nd edn, New York: John Wiley & Sons, Inc.

Beck, A.T. (1967) *Depression: Clinical, Experimental and Theoretical Aspects*, New York: Harper & Row.

Boyle, M. (2007) The problem with diagnosis, *The Psychologist* 20: 290–92.

Byrne, P. (1997) Psychiatric stigma: Past, passing and to come, *Journal of the Royal Society of Medicine*, 90: 618–21.

Carson, R.C. (1996) Aristotle, Galileo, and the DSM taxonomy: The case of schizophrenia, *Journal of Consulting & Clinical Psychology*, 64: 1133–9.

Clark, D.M., Fonagy, P., Turpin, G. *et al.* (2009) Speaking up for IAPT, *The Psychologist*, 22: 466–7.

Cooper, J.E. (1994) *Pocket Guide to ICD-10 Classification of Mental and Behavioural Disorders*, Oxford: Churchill Livingstone.

Crisp, A.H., Gelder, M.G., Rix, S., Meltzer, H.I. & Rowlands, O.J. (2000) Stigmatization of people with mental illnesses, *British Journal of Psychiatry*, 177: 4–7.

Davey, G.C.L. (1989) Dental phobias and anxieties: Evidence for conditioning processes in the acquisition and modulation of a learned fear, *Behaviour Research & Therapy*, 27: 51–8.

Davey, G.C.L. (1981) *Animal Learning and Conditioning*, Basingstoke: Macmillan.

Davey, G.C.L. (1989) *Ecological Learning Theory*, London: Routledge.

Davey, G.C.L. (1994) Pathological worrying as exacerbated problem-solving, in G.C.L. Davey & F. Tallis (eds) *Worrying: Perspectives on Theory, Assessment and Treatment*, Chichester: John Wiley & Sons Ltd.

Davey, G.C.L. (2008) *Psychopathology: Research, Assessment & Treatment in Clinical Psychology*, Chichester: BPS Wiley-Blackwell.

Doogan, S. & Thomas, G.V. (1992) Origins of fear of dogs in adults and children: The role of conditioning processes and prior familiarity with dogs, *Behaviour Research & Therapy*, 30: 387–94.

Ellis, A. (1962) *Reason and Emotion in Psychotherapy*, New York: Lyle Stuart.

Erdelyi, M.H. (1992) Psychodynamics and the unconscious, *American Psychologist* 47: 784–7.

Eysenck, H.J. (1959) Learning theory and behaviour therapy, *Journal of Mental Science* 105: 61–75.

Goldacre, B. (2002) When hospital is a prison, *The Guardian*, July 16.

Heginbotham, C. (1998) UK mental health policy can alter the stigma of mental illness, *Lancet* 352: 1052–3.

Jones, F. (2008) What is clinical psychology? Training and practice, in G.C.L. Davey (ed.) *Clinical Psychology*, Oxford: Hodder HE.

Kazdin, A.E. & Hersen, M. (1980) The current status of behaviour therapy, *Behaviour Modification* 4: 283–302.

Kessler, R.C., McGonagle, K.A., Zhao, S. *et al.* (1994) Lifetime and 12-month prevalence of DSM-III psychiatric disorders in the United States: Results from the National Comorbidity Study, *Archives of General Psychiatry* 51: 8–19.

Kinsella, P. & Garland, A. (2008) Cognitive Behavioural Therapy for Mental Health Workers: A Beginner's Guide, London: Routledge.

Krueger, R.F. & Piasecki, T.M. (2002) Toward a dimensional and psychometrically-informed approach to conceptualising psychopathology, *Behaviour Research & Therapy* 40: 485–99.

Krueger, R.F., Watson, D. & Barlow, D.H. (2005) Introduction to the special section: Towards a dimensionally based taxonomy of psychopathology, *Journal of Abnormal Psychology* 114: 491–3.

Kuch, K. (1997) Accident phobia, in G.C.L. Davey (ed.) *Phobias: A Handbook of Theory, Research and Treatment*, Chichester: John Wiley & Sons Ltd.

Laguerre M.S. (1981) Haitian Americans, in A. Harwood (ed.) *Ethnicity and Medical Care*, Cambridge, MA: Harvard University Press.

May, R. & Yalom, I. (1995) Existential psychotherapy, in R.J. Corsini & D. Wedding (eds) *Current Psychotherapies*, 5th edn, Itasca, IL: Peacock.

May, R. (2007) Working outside the diagnostic frame, *The Psychologist* 20: 300–301.

Mazaleski, J.L., Iwata, B.A., Vollmer, T.R., Zarcone, J.R. & Smith, R.G. (1993) Analysis of the reinforcement and extinction components in DRO contingencies with self-injury, *Journal of Applied Behavior Analysis* 26: 143–56.

Morrison, A.P. (2001) The interpretation of intrusions in psychosis: An integrative cognitive approach to hallucinations and delusions, *Behavioural & Cognitive Psychotherapy* 29: 257–76.

Nicolas, G., DeSilva, A.M., Grey, K.S. & Gonzalez-Eastep, D. (2006) Using a multicultural lens to understand illness among Haitians living in America, *Professional Psychology: Research & Practice* 37: 702–7.

Prokaska, J.O. & Norcross, J.C. (2003) *Systems of Psychotherapy: A Transitional Analysis*, 5th edn, Pacific Grove, CA: Brookes/Cole.

Rogers, C.R. (1951) *Client-Centered Therapy*, Boston: Houghton Mifflin.

Rogers, C.R. (1987) Rogers, Kohut, and Erickson: A personal perspective on some similarities and differences, in J.K. Zeig (ed.) *The Evolution of Psychotherapy*, New York: Brunner/Mazel.

Rogers, C.R. (2003) *Client-Centered Therapy: Its Current Practice, Implications and Theory*, New York: Constable & Robinson.

Schachter, S. (1982) Recidivism and self-cure of smoking and obesity, *American Psychologist* 37: 436–44.

Scheff, T.J. (1975) *Labelling Madness*, Englewood Cliffs, NJ: Prentice-Hall.

Seaton, M. (2000) Talking sense, *London Evening Standard Magazine*, 17 March.

Seligman, M.E.P. (1971) Phobias and preparedness, *Behavior Therapy* 2: 307–20.

Small, M.F. (2006) *The Culture of our Discontent: Beyond the Medical Model of Mental Illness*, Washington, DC: Joseph Henry Press.

Tait, L. & Lester, H. (2005) Encouraging user involvement in mental health services, *Advances in Psychiatric Treatment* 11: 168–75.

Walsh, R.A. & McElwain, B. (2002) Existential psychotherapies, in D.J. Cain & J. Seeman (eds) *Humanistic Psychotherapies: Handbook of Research and Practice*, Washington, DC: APA.

Ward, T., Hudson, S.M., Johnston, L. & Marshall, L. (1997) Cognitive distortions in sex offenders: An integrative review, *Clinical Psychology Review* 17: 479–507.

Warwick, H.M.C. (1995) Assessment of hypochondriasis, *Behaviour Research & Therapy* 33: 845–53.

Widiger, T.A. & Samuel, D.B. (2005) Diagnostic categories or dimensions? A question for the Diagnostic and Statistical manual of mental Disorders – Fifth Edition, *Journal of Abnormal Psychology* 114: 494–504.

Young, J.E., Klosko, J. & Weishaar, M.E. (2003) *Schema Therapy: A Practitioner's Guide*, New York: Guilford.

ANSWERS

Answers to Activity Box 2.1:

1. They can be, but not always.
2. None. Violence towards others is not on any diagnostic criterion. For every person killed by someone with a mental illness there are roughly 70 deaths on the road and 10 alcohol-related deaths. We are far more likely to be assaulted by someone we know, in our own home, than by a random stranger with a mental illness. People with mental health problems are more likely to be victims than perpetrators of violence. Interestingly, approximately 70% of media coverage links mental distress to violence.
3. Highest risk group is 18–25 year olds.
4. False – most people who commit suicide usually tell someone of their intentions within the previous two months.
5. False.
6. (c) 1 in 4. However, this is only the number of people whom we know about, who have sought help. The associated stigma means that many will be too embarrassed to seek help.
7. 25% (source: National Service Framework for Mental Health, Department of Health).
8. True.
9. 16–25 years and over 65 years.
10. (a) 47%.
    (b) 38%.
11. (a) Comical and (b) violent to themselves and others. These stereotypes are found in fictional accounts and 'factual' reporting. This means that the key messages from the media are that if someone has a mental illness we should:
    - Feel sorry for them.
    - Be afraid of them.
    - Laugh at them.
    50% of people surveyed by Mind said that media coverage had a negative effect on their mental health. Effects included feeling more anxious or depressed and experiencing hostility from neighbours. A third of respondents said that family or friends reacted to them differently because of recent media coverage.

3 Common Mental Health Problems and Their Treatment

GRAHAM DAVEY

LEARNING OUTCOMES

WHEN YOU HAVE COMPLETED THIS CHAPTER, YOU SHOULD BE ABLE TO:

1. Describe the main characteristics of a range of mental health problems encountered by clinical psychologists.
2. Describe, compare and contrast the main theoretical approaches that clinical psychologists adopt when treating mental health problems.

KEY WORDS

Anorexia Nervosa (AN) • Antisocial Personality Disorder • Anxiety Disorders • Attention Deficit Hyperactivity Disorder (ADHD) • Autistic Spectrum Disorder (ASD) • Aversion Therapy • Axis I Disorders • Axis II Disorders • Beck's Cognitive Therapy • Behaviour Analysis • Binge-Eating Disorder • Bipolar Mood Disorder • Body Dysmorphic Disorder • Borderline Personality Disorder • Bulimia Nervosa (BN) • Case Formulation • Catastrophising • Client-Centred Therapy • Cognitive Therapy • Compulsions • Computerised CBT • Conduct Disorder • Conversion Disorder • Counterconditioning • Depersonalisation Disorder • Depression • Dissociative Amnesia • Dissociative Experiences • Dissociative Fugue • Dissociative Identity Disorder (DID) • Dream Analysis • Eating Disorders • Existential Therapies • Exposure Therapies • Externalising Disorders • Family Therapy • Flooding • Free Association • Functional Analysis • Gender Dysphoria • Gender Identity Disorder (GID) • Generalised Anxiety Disorder (GAD) • Gestalt Therapy • Hallucinogenic Drugs • Humanistic Therapies • Hypochondriasis • Intellectual Disabilities • Internalising Disorders • Interpretation • Learning Disability • Mania • Mental Retardation • Narrative Therapy • Obsessions • Obsessive-Compulsive Disorder (OCD) • Panic Disorder • Paraphilias • Personality Disorders • Pervasive Developmental Disorders (PDD) • Phobic Beliefs • Post-Traumatic Stress Disorder (PTSD) • Primal Therapy • Psychoanalysis • Psychotic Experiences • Schizophrenia • Sedatives • Sexual Dysfunctions • Somatisation Disorder • Somatoform Disorders • Specific Phobias • Stimulants • Substance Abuse • Substance Dependency • Systematic Desensitisation • Transference • Transpersonal Therapy • Unipolar Depression

CHAPTER OUTLINE

ROUTE MAP OF THE CHAPTER

This chapter is divided into two halves. The first half discusses the important categories of mental health problems as defined by DSM-IV-TR, and provides an insight into basic symptoms and diagnostic criteria. The second half discusses the main approaches to treating mental health problems and describes some of the various types of treatment methods used by clinical psychologists.

Below is a GP's referral letter to the clinical psychologist, Dr Potter. The letter provides basic information on the client and the reason for the referral.

Dear Dr Potter

Re: Mrs Joanna Hewittson, DOB 13/09/1979
    25 Canterbury Close, Gloucester

I believe this pleasant but anxious lady would benefit from a course of psychological therapy. She told me that she has been unable to leave home unaccompanied and has become increasingly housebound. She gets into a panic if she goes out on her own. She recalled a particularly bad panic attack a month ago when she collapsed in the local supermarket and was taken by ambulance to A & E. She had an ECG which was totally normal and was discharged. From what I gather the hospital was not very sympathetic and she feels very ashamed about the whole incident.

Joanna lives with her husband, Mark, and two children (Lianne, 7 and Jamie, 5). Mark works as an IT consultant and Joanna has not worked since having the children. A year ago the family moved down from Richmond, Yorkshire where she was born and brought up. Joanne is very close to her mother and it was a wrench to leave her friends and family including her two older brothers and sister, and this has led to Joanna reporting that she regularly feels depressed and worthless. They moved here to be closer to Mark's family. Joanne told me she doesn't get on with her mother-in-law whom she described as 'a bit of a snob.'

There is no significant family history of mental illness. However, Joanne told me her mother is a worrier and her sister went through a difficult time in her teenage years. I would be grateful if you would send her an appointment. (Adapted from Marzillier & Marzillier, 2008)

This referral letter is typical of many that clinical psychologists receive requesting help and advice. In this case, Joanna first took her problems to her GP, who then sought specialist advice and treatment for her from a clinical psychologist. This referral letter conveys a number of things. First, it hints at the nature of some of the symptoms that are causing Joanna distress, including anxiety, depression and panic attacks. Second, it also hints at some of Joanna's recent life experiences that may have contributed to these symptoms, including moving away from close family, a sense of isolation and difficult relationships with her in-laws. Third, it demonstrates how many factors may interact in a complex way to generate a set of problems and symptoms that an individual experiences, and this implies that each client will have a unique set of problems that need to be analysed and addressed. Clinical psychologists normally try to understand a client's problems through a process known as **case formulation** (Johnstone & Dallos, 2006; Tarrier, 2006). This is a key skill of the clinical psychologist and attempts to provide a theoretical rationale for how the person's problems have developed and how they might best be treated. This process will be discussed more fully in Chapter 6.

However, despite the uniqueness of each person's mental health problems, there are still some basic symptoms and processes that are common across many sufferers. Joanna's referral letter mentions symptoms of anxiety, depression and experiencing distressing panic attacks. These are symptoms that are common across many people with mental health problems, and can form the basis of how we categorise a person's problems and how we consider treating them.

case formulation a clinical psychologist's attempts to provide a theoretical rationale for how an individual's problems have developed and how they might best be treated.

The remainder of this chapter provides a description of the most common mental health problems encountered by clinical psychologists, providing examples of how they are categorised and how they can be treated. We will discuss the causes of mental health problems more fully in Chapters 4 and 5.

3.1 CATEGORIES OF COMMON MENTAL HEALTH PROBLEMS

Axis I disorders commonly diagnosed disorders such as anxiety disorder, depression and schizophrenia.

psychotic experiences experiences characterised by disturbances in thought and language, sensory perception, emotion regulation, and behaviour. Sufferers may experience hallucinations and develop thought irregularities leading to false beliefs or delusions about themselves and the world.

eating disorders serious disruptions of the eating habits or the appetite.

dissociative experiences a disorder in which the mind separates or compartmentalises certain mental contents from normal consciousness.

In Chapter 2, we discussed the diagnostic structure of DSM and how this is organised into a series of axes reflecting the nature of the psychological problem and whether it is likely to be an enduring problem or not. The following sections describe some of the most common **Axis I disorders** – including anxiety disorders, depression and mood disorders, schizophrenia and **psychotic experiences**, substance abuse and dependency, **eating disorders**, sexual and gender identity problems, somatoform disorders, **dissociative experiences** and disorders usually first diagnosed in infancy (e.g. autistic spectrum disorder). This is followed by a description of the main **Axis II disorders**, including personality disorders and intellectual disabilities.

3.1.1 Axis I Disorders – Clinical Symptoms that Cause Significant Impairment

Axis I disorders represent mental health problems that are diagnosed if they cause 'clinically significant distress or impairment in social, occupational, or other important areas of functioning'. However, when reading this section you should be clear about the following:

- Each mental health problem defined in Axis I does not have to be a discrete entity with absolute boundaries.
- Symptoms can be mild, moderate or severe.

- A person may often exhibit symptoms of more than one Axis I problem (known as comorbidity).
- Axis I problems may well be comorbid with Axis II problems.

3.1.1.1 Anxiety-based problems

Anxiety can often become so intense or attached to inappropriate events or situations that it becomes maladaptive and problematic for the individual (Lepine, 2002). This is when an anxiety disorder may develop. An **anxiety disorder** is an excessive or aroused state characterised by feelings of apprehension, uncertainty and fear. In a sufferer of an anxiety disorder the anxiety response:

- May be out of proportion to the threat posed by the situation or event (e.g. in **specific phobias**).
- May be a state that the individual continually finds themselves in and may not be easily attributable to any specific threat (e.g. in generalised anxiety disorder, or some forms of **panic disorder**).
- May persist chronically and be so disabling that it causes constant emotional distress to the individual, who is unable to plan and conduct their normal day-to-day living. This can result in an inability to hold down a regular job, maintain long-term relationships with friends, partners and family etc.

Anxiety-based problems are relatively common, and around 30–40% of individuals in Western societies will develop a problem that is anxiety-related at some point in their lives (Shepherd *et al.*, 1996). The five most common anxiety-based disorders are (i) specific phobias, (ii) panic disorder, (iii) **generalised anxiety disorder (GAD)**, (iv) **obsessive-compulsive disorder (OCD)** and (v) **post-traumatic stress disorder (PTSD)**, and the main characteristics of each of these are described in Table 3.1.

anxiety disorder excessive or aroused state characterised by feelings of apprehension, uncertainty and fear.

specific phobias excessive, unreasonable, persistent fears triggered by a specific object or situation.

panic disorder an anxiety disorder characterised by repeated panic or anxiety attacks.

generalised anxiety disorder (GAD) a pervasive condition in which the sufferer experiences continual apprehension and anxiety about future events which leads to chronic and pathological worrying about those events.

obsessive-compulsive disorder (OCD) an anxiety disorder characterised by uncontrollable obsessive thoughts and compulsive, ritualised behaviours.

post-traumatic stress disorder (PTSD) a set of persistent anxiety-based symptoms that occur after experiencing or witnessing an extremely fear-evoking traumatic event.

TABLE 3.1 *Anxiety-Based Disorders.*

Disorder & Lifetime Prevalence Rates	Definition	Key Features	Main Forms of Treatment
SPECIFIC PHOBIA (7.2%–11.3%)	Excessive, unreasonable, persistent fear triggered by a specific object or situation	Clinical phobias are usually restricted to a small group of objects and situations (e.g. animals, heights, water, blood and injury etc.) Twice as many females as males develop specific phobias Phobics acquire a set of threat-relevant beliefs that maintain their phobia	Exposure therapy Systematic desensitisation Flooding One-session rapid treatments
PANIC DISORDER (1.5%–3.5%)	The experience of repeated and uncontrollable panic attacks	Onset is common in adolescence or early adulthood, and normally following a period of stress Frequency of panic attacks can vary between one attack per week to frequent daily attacks Associated with fear of serious underlying medical condition or that the individual is losing control or 'going crazy'	Tricyclic antidepressants and Benzodiazepines Exposure-based treatments CBT
GENERAL ANXIETY DISORDER (GAD) (5%)	The experience of continual apprehension and anxiety about future events, leading to chronic and pathological worry	Pathological worry is the cardinal diagnostic feature of GAD GAD is twice as common in women as in men 12% of those who attend anxiety clinics will present with GAD Highly comorbid with a range of other anxiety disorders and major depression	Anxiolytics such as Benzodiazepines Stimulus control treatment CBT (including self-monitoring, relaxation training and cognitive restructuring)
OBSESSIVE-COMPULSIVE DISORDER (OCD) (2.5%)	Recurrent obsessions or compulsions that are severe enough to be time-consuming or cause distress	OCD onset is gradual and begins to manifest in early adolescence or adulthood – normally following a stressful life event Affects women more frequently than men The main compulsions are checking and washing behaviours – although these rarely occur together in the same individual Sometimes comorbid with other disorders such as major depression and eating disorders	Exposure & ritual prevention treatments (EPR) CBT Drug treatment (SSRIs) Cingulatomy
POST-TRAUMATIC STRESS DISORDER (PTSD) (3%–8%)	A set of persistent, anxiety-related symptoms that occur after experiencing or witnessing an extremely traumatic event	Following a severe traumatic event, women are significantly more likely to develop PTSD than men Experiences that are likely to cause PTSD include physical assault and rape, torture, prisoner of war and combat experiences, natural disasters such as floods and earthquakes, and motor vehicle accidents Main symptoms include increased arousal, avoidance and numbing of emotions, and re-experiencing of the traumatic event	Psychological debriefing Exposure therapy Eye-movement desensitisation and reprocessing (EMDR) Cognitive restructuring

3.1.1.1.1 Specific phobias

A specific phobia is defined as an excessive, unreasonable, persistent fear triggered by a specific object or situation. The phobic trigger normally elicits extreme fear and often panic, which usually means that the phobic individual develops avoidance strategies designed to minimise the possibility of contact with that phobic trigger. Phobics are normally aware that their fear to the phobic situation or event is excessive or unreasonable (in comparison either with the actual threat it represents or with the less fearful responses of other people), but they do acquire a strong set of **phobic beliefs** that appear to control their fear (i.e. irrational beliefs that the phobic object or situation is certain to cause harm; Thorpe & Salkovskis, 1997). Many psychological treatments for specific phobias are designed to challenge these dysfunctional phobic beliefs and replace them with more functional beliefs that foster an approach to and contact with the phobic stimulus.

Specific phobias are extraordinarily common, with surveys suggesting that a clear majority of the general population (60.2%) experience 'unreasonable fears' (Chapman, 1997) – although these fears are rarely severe enough to result in impairment or distress. Common phobias tend to focus on a relatively small group of objects and situations, and the main ones are animal phobias (including fear of snakes, spiders, rats, mice, creepy-crawlies such as cockroaches or invertebrates such as maggots and slugs), social phobia, dental phobia, water phobia, height phobia, claustrophobia, and a cluster of blood, injury and inoculation fears known as BII (Davey, 1997).

> **phobic beliefs** beliefs about phobic stimuli that maintain the phobic's fear and avoidance of that stimulus or situation.

PHOTO 3.1 *Most specific phobias tend to focus around a relatively small group of objects and situations, including animals such as snakes and spiders, and situations such as heights and enclosed spaces (claustrophobia).*
Source: Shutterstock.

3.1.1.1.2 Panic disorder Panic disorder is characterised by repeated panic or anxiety attacks. These attacks are associated with a variety of physical symptoms, including heart palpitations, perspiring, dizziness, hyperventilating, nausea and trembling (see Chapter 5). In addition, the individual may experience real feelings of terror or severe apprehension and depersonalisation (a feeling of not being connected to your own body or in real contact with what is happening around you).

Most people will experience at least one panic attack in their lifetime, but panic disorder is diagnosed when recurrent, unexpected panic attacks keep occurring, and are followed by at least one month of persistent concerns about having a further attack. The frequency of panic attacks in panic disorder can vary considerably between individuals, from one attack per week to frequent daily attacks. Panic disorder is associated with a number of fears and apprehensions that the sufferer develops. These include fears that the attacks indicate an underlying serious medical condition (e.g. cardiac disease, seizure disorder), even though repeated medical tests indicate no life-threatening illness. Others feel that they are losing control or simply 'going crazy'.

3.1.1.1.3 Generalised anxiety disorder (GAD)
GAD is a pervasive condition in which the sufferer experiences continual apprehension and anxiety about future events, which leads to chronic and pathological worrying about those events (Heimberg, Turk & Mennin, 2004). However, worrying for the individual with GAD has a number of features that make it disabling and a source of extreme emotional discomfort. For example, for the individual suffering GAD:

- Worrying is a chronic and pathological activity that is not only directed at major life issues (e.g. health, finances, relationships, work-related matters), but also to many minor day-to-day issues and hassles that others would not perceive as threatening (Craske *et al.*, 1989; Tallis, Davey & Capuzzo, 1994).

- Worrying is perceived as uncontrollable – the individual with GAD feels that they cannot control either the onset or the termination of a bout of worrying.

- Worrying is closely associated with the

catastrophising an example of magnification, in which the individual takes a single fact to its extreme.

catastrophising of worries – that is, worry bouts persist for longer in GAD, they are associated with increasing levels of anxiety and distress as the bout continues, and worrying seems to make the problem *worse* rather than better. While pathological and chronic worrying is the cardinal diagnostic feature of GAD, it may also be accompanied by physical symptoms such as fatigue, trembling, muscle tension, headache and nausea.

3.1.1.1.4 Obsessive-compulsive disorder (OCD)
OCD has two important and sometimes independent characteristics. **Obsessions** are intrusive and recurring thoughts that the individual finds disturbing and uncontrollable. These obsessive thoughts frequently take the form of causing some harm or distress to oneself or to some important other person (such as a partner or offspring). Common obsessions take the form of fear of contamination (i.e. contaminating oneself or important others), fear of directly or indirectly causing physical harm to others, and fears of expressing some immoral, sexual or aggressive impulse (Lee & Kwon, 2003). Obsessive thoughts can also take the form of pathological doubting and indecision, and this may lead to sufferers developing repetitive behaviour patterns such as compulsive checking or washing.

obsessions intrusive and recurring thoughts that an individual finds disturbing and uncontrollable.

Compulsions represent repetitive or ritualised behaviour patterns that the individual feels driven to perform in order to prevent some negative outcome happening. This can take the form of ritualised and persistent checking

compulsions repetitive or ritualised behaviour patterns that an individual feels driven to perform in order to prevent some negative outcome happening.

of doors and windows (to ensure that the house is safe) or ritualised washing activities designed to prevent infection and contamination. While the main compulsions are usually related to checking or washing, OCD can also manifest itself less regularly as compulsive hoarding (Steketee, Frost & Kyrios, 2003), superstitious ritualised movements or the systematic arranging of objects (Radomsky & Rachman, 2004).

3.1.1.1.5 Post-traumatic stress disorder (PTSD)
PTSD is a set of persistent symptoms that occur after experiencing or witnessing an extremely fear-evoking traumatic event. Such events include combat during a war, rape or other types of physical assault, child abuse, car or airplane crashes, or natural or human-caused disasters. The symptoms of PTSD are also somewhat different to those experienced in other anxiety disorders, and can be grouped into three main categories:

- *Increased arousal*, which includes an exaggerated startle response (Shalev *et al.*, 2000), difficulty sleeping, hypervigilance and difficulty concentrating.

- *Avoidance and numbing of emotions*, when the individual will attempt to avoid all situations or events that might trigger memories of the traumatic event, and there is a sense of detachment and a lack of feelings of positive emotion.

- *Re-experiencing*, when the individual regularly recalls very vivid flashbacks of events experienced during the trauma, and these images often occur in recurrent nightmares.

Associated problems and symptoms include depression, guilt, shame, anger, marital problems, physical illness, sexual dysfunction, substance abuse, suicidal thoughts and stress-related violence (Hobfoll *et al.*, 1991, 2001; Zatzick *et al.*, 1997).

3.1.1.2 Depression and mood disorders

depression a mood disorder involving emotional, motivational, behavioural, physical and cognitive symptoms.

mania an emotion characterised by boundless, frenzied energy and feelings of euphoria.

bipolar mood disorder a psychological disorder characterised by periods of mania that alternate with periods of depression.

Depression is the prominent emotion in mood disorders, but it can often be associated with its opposite – namely mania. **Mania** is an emotion characterised by boundless, frenzied energy and feelings of euphoria, and individuals who have a **bipolar mood disorder** frequently oscillate between deep depression and frenetic mania.

Depression involves emotional, motivational, behavioural, physical and cognitive symptoms. The *emotional* experiences of depressed individuals are usually restricted to negative ones and these are often described as 'sad, hopeless, miserable, dejected, and discouraged'. Depressed individuals exhibit a range of *motivational* deficits, including a loss of interest in normal daily activities or hobbies, and a lack of initiative and spontaneity. This lack of initiative may manifest itself initially in social withdrawal (depressed individuals regularly report wanting to stay where they are and to be left alone); appetite and sexual desire can also be significantly reduced. Depressed individuals often become physically inactive, stay in bed for long periods, and reports of decreased energy, tiredness and fatigue are common. Arguably the most disabling symptoms of depression are its *cognitive* features. In particular, depressed individuals tend to have developed extremely negative views of themselves, the world around them and their own future (Beck, 1987; Gable & Shean, 2000), and this generates *pessimistic* thinking where sufferers believe that nothing can improve their lot. This in turn leads to a lack of initiative, with individuals reporting impaired ability to think, concentrate or make decisions. This inability to affect the future also generates other problematic beliefs, such as a sense of worthlessness, shame and guilt. Because of this, many depressed individuals develop the dysfunctional belief that others would be better off if they were dead, and this can often lead to transient but recurrent suicidal thoughts.

There are two main types of clinical depression. The most common is major or **unipolar depression**, and the second is bipolar disorder. Table 3.2 summarises the main features of these two types of mood disorder.

3.1.1.3 Schizophrenia and psychotic experiences

unipolar depression a psychological disorder characterised by relatively extended periods of clinical depression that cause significant distress to the individual and impairment in functioning.

Psychotic symptoms can be crippling and are characterised by disturbances in thought and language, sensory perception, emotion regulation and behaviour. Sufferers may experience sensory hallucinations and also develop thought irregularities that may lead to pervasive false beliefs or delusions about themselves and the world around them. Individuals with psychotic symptoms often withdraw from normal social interaction because of these disturbances of perception and thought, and this can result in poor educational performance, increasing unproductivity, difficulties in interpersonal relationships, neglect of day-to-day activities and a preoccupation with a personal world to the exclusion of others. These symptoms can leave an individual feeling frightened and confused, and the presence of a number of these characteristic symptoms may lead to a diagnosis of **schizophrenia**. Importantly, no single symptom is indicative of a diagnosis of schizophrenia, and the diagnosis involves the identification of a variable set of symptoms indicative of impaired occupational and social functioning (see Table 3.3).

schizophrenia the main diagnostic category for psychotic symptoms.

3.1.1.4 Substance abuse and dependency

Traditionally, pathology associated with substance and drug use falls into two categories: substance abuse and substance dependence (Davey, 2008). **Substance abuse** can be considered as a pattern of drug or substance use that occurs despite knowledge of the negative effects of the drug, but where use has not progressed to full-blown dependence. Characteristics of substance abuse are:

substance abuse a pattern of drug or substance use that occurs despite knowledge of the negative effects of the drug, but where use has not progressed to full-blown dependency.

- Failure to meet many normal daily obligations because of the drug (e.g. repeated absences from work).
- Using the substance in ways that may be physically hazardous (e.g. drinking and driving).
- Legal problems resulting from behaviour caused directly or indirectly by the drug (e.g. being arrested for being drunk and disorderly).
- Continuing to use the drug even though it causes a range of personal and social problems and difficulties (e.g. quarrels with spouse or physical or verbal fights).

TABLE 3.2 *Depression and Mood Disorders.*

Disorder & Lifetime Prevalence Rates	Definition	Key Features	Main Forms of Treatment
MAJOR DEPRESSION (5.2%–17.1%)	Feelings of sadness, hopelessness, being miserable and dejected Motivational deficits, including loss of interest in normal daily activities Behavioural symptoms such as physical inactivity, decreased energy Physical symptoms such as insomnia or hypersomnia Cognitive features such as pessimistic thinking, negative beliefs about the world and hopelessness	Most prevalent of the main psychological disorders Commonly comorbid with other Axis I and Axis II disorders Twice as common in women than in men Associated with imbalances in brain neurotransmitters such as serotonin and norepinephrine Associated with negative biases in ways of thinking and processing information	Medication (such as trycyclic drugs, MAOIs and SSRIs) Electroconvulsive therapy (ECT) Psychoanalysis Social skills training Behavioural activation therapy Cognitive therapy Mindfulness-based cognitive therapy (MBCT)
BIPOLAR DISORDER (0.4%–1.6%)	Periods of mania that alternate with periods of depression	Periods of extreme mania alternate with periods of major depression In Bipolar II disorder, depression alternates with mild manic episodes (hypomania) 10–25% of first-degree relatives of sufferers have also reported significant symptoms of mood disorder	Medication (lithium carbonate) Electroconvulsive therapy (ECT) Cognitive therapy in conjunction with appropriate medication

Definitions of dependence and abuse differ primarily in terms of severity, with substance dependence being more severe than substance abuse – particularly in terms of tolerance and withdrawal effects and in the degree of disruption to daily living caused by the substance. **Substance dependence** can be loosely defined as the continued use of the substance *despite* its problematic consequences, and key features of abuse and dependency are listed in Table 3.4.

A particularly important aspect of substance use disorders is that they are highly comorbid with a range of other Axis I and Axis II disorders, and there is an especially strong association of lifetime mood and anxiety disorders with substance use disorders (Merikangas *et al.*, 1998). Examples of substances that are commonly involved in substance abuse and dependency are **stimulants** (e.g.

cocaine, amphetamines and caffeine), **sedatives** (e.g. barbiturates, alcohol and opiates, such as heroin) and **hallucinogenic drugs** (e.g. LSD and other hallucinogenics, cannabis and MDMA, better known as Ecstasy).

3.1.1.5 Eating disorders

There are three main eating disorders: anorexia nervosa, bulimia nervosa and binge-eating disorder. The main symptoms of **anorexia nervosa** are self-starvation and a refusal to maintain a minimally normal body weight. It is a disorder that afflicts mainly adolescent women, and tends to have an onset in early to middle teens following either a period of life stress or an intense period of dieting. High rates of comorbidity exist between anorexia and other Axis I and Axis II disorders such as major depression (Halmi *et al.*, 1991) and OCD (Hudson *et al.*, 1983; Wonderlich *et al.*, 1990).

Like anorexia nervosa, **bulimia nervosa** is also a disorder characterised by a fear of weight gain and a distorted perception of body shape. The main feature

substance dependence a maladaptive pattern of substance use, leading to clinically significant impairment or distress.

stimulants substances that increase central nervous system activity and increase blood pressure and heart rate.

sedatives central nervous system depressants which slow the activity of the body, reduce its responsiveness and reduce pain, tension and anxiety.

hallucinogenic drugs psychoactive drugs which affect the user's perceptions, either sharpening the individual's sensory abilities or creating sensory illusions or hallucinations.

anorexia nervosa (AN) an eating disorder featuring a refusal to maintain a minimal body weight, a pathological fear of gaining weight and a distorted body image.

bulimia nervosa (BN) an eating disorder featuring recurrent episodes of binge eating followed by periods of purging or fasting.

TABLE 3.3 *Schizophrenia and Psychotic Experiences.*

Lifetime Prevalence Rates	Definition	Sub-Types of Schizophrenia	Key Features	Main Forms of Treatment
0.5–2% **24 million sufferers worldwide** **No difference in prevalence rates between men and women**	Cognitive and emotional dysfunctions include dysfunctions of perception, inferential thinking, language and communication, behavioural monitoring, affect, fluency, productivity of thought and speech, and attention Main clinical symptoms include delusions, hallucinations, disorganised speech (incoherence), disorganised or catatonic behaviour, flat affect, poverty of speech and apathy	**PARANOID SCHIZOPHRENIA** Delusions or auditory hallucinations associated with persecution or grandeur **DISORGANISED SCHIZOPHRENIA** Disorganised speech, behaviour and flat affect **CATATONIC SCHIZOPHRENIA** Disturbances of motor behaviour (immobility), mutism etc. **RESIDUAL TYPE** Lack of prominent positive symptoms, but evidence of flat affect and other negative symptoms	A heterogeneous disorder in which no single symptom is a defining feature Consists of positive symptoms (distortions of normal functioning, e.g. hallucinations) and negative symptoms (diminution or loss of normal functions, e.g. flat affect and apathy) Develops through three well-defined stages: (1) prodromal stage, (2) active stage, and (3) residual stage Caused by a combination of a genetically inherited predisposition and environmental stress (a diathesis-stress perspective) Positive symptoms associated with excess activity of neurotransmitters such as dopamine Antipsychotic drugs can successfully suppress positive symptoms Most sufferers will require lifetime care and supervision, ranging from continuous medication and psychological and family-based treatments to longer-term community care and management	Hospitalisation and custodial care Electroconvulsive therapy (ECT) and psychosurgery Antipsychotic drugs Social skills training Cognitive behaviour therapy (CBT) Family interventions and family therapy Community care

of bulimia is recurrent episodes of binge eating (often eating more than a normal person's full daily intake of food in one episode) followed by periods of purging or fasting. In the *purging sub-type*, the individual regularly engages in self-induced vomiting or the misuse of laxatives, diuretics or enemas; vomiting is the most common form of purging and occurs in 80–90% of those who present for treatment. In the *nonpurging sub-type*, the individual will attempt to compensate for binging by indulging in excessive fasting or exercise. Most bulimia sufferers are not usually overweight compared to the norm for their height (Gordon, 2001), nor do they usually become underweight as a result of their bulimia.

binge-eating disorder an eating disorder characterised by recurrent episodes of binge eating.

Binge-eating disorder is characterised by recurrent episodes of binge eating, but without the associated purging or fasting associated with bulimia. As a result, those suffering from binge-eating disorder tend to be overweight, usually have a long history of failed attempts to diet and lose weight, and feel a lack of control over their eating behaviours that causes them significant distress. The main characteristics of these eating disorders are listed in Table 3.5.

3.1.1.6 Sexual and gender identity disorders

Disorders of sexuality and sexual functioning fit into three broad categories:

- **Sexual dysfunctions** – which represent problems with the normal sexual response cycle (e.g. lack of sexual desire or pain during intercourse).

- **Paraphilias** – which represent sexual urges or fantasies involving unusual sources of gratification (e.g. nonhuman objects or non-consenting individuals).

- **Gender identity disorders** – where the individual is dissatisfied with their own biological sex and has a strong desire to be a member of the opposite sex.

sexual dysfunctions disturbances in the processes that characterise the sexual response cycle or pain associated with intercourse.

paraphilias problematic, high-frequency sexual behaviours or unusual sexual urges and activities that are often directed at inappropriate targets.

gender identity disorder (GID) a sexual disorder where an individual is dissatisfied with his or her biological sex and has a strong desire to be a member of the opposite sex.

TABLE 3.4 *Substance Abuse and Dependency.*

Disorder and Lifetime Prevalence Rates	Definition	Key Features	Main Forms of Treatment (Both Abuse & Dependency)
SUBSTANCE ABUSE Lifetime prevalence rate: no systematic data	A pattern of drug or substance use that occurs despite knowledge of the negative effects of the drug, but has not progressed to full-blown dependence	Failure to meet many normal daily obligations because of the drug Using the substance in ways that may be physically hazardous Legal problems resulting from behaviour caused directly or indirectly by the drug Continuing to use the drug even though it causes personal and social problems	Self-help groups Drug-prevention schemes Residential rehabilitation Aversion therapy Behavioural self-control training (BSCT) Controlled drinking Cognitive behaviour therapy (CBT) Family & couple therapy Detoxification Drug maintenance therapy
SUBSTANCE DEPENDENCY Lifetime prevalence rate 5.1%	A cluster of cognitive, behavioural and physiological symptoms indicating that the individual continues use of the substance despite significant substance-related problems	Characterised by drug tolerance effects (need for increased amounts to achieve the same effects) Withdrawal symptoms indicate that the body requires the drug in order to maintain physical stability Lack of the drug causes a range of negative and aversive physical effects Preoccupation with attempts to obtain the drug Frequent unsuccessful attempts to cut down or quit the drug Frequent unintentional over-use Abandoning or neglecting important life activities because of the drug (e.g. neglecting family, work, education) Highly comorbid with other psychiatric disorders	

3.1.1.6.1 Sexual dysfunctions In general terms, a sexual dysfunction is characterised by 'a disturbance in the processes that characterize the sexual response cycle or by pain associated with sexual intercourse' (DSM-IV-TR, p. 535). Sexual dysfunction disorders have been categorised around the four stages of the sexual cycle, namely disorders of desire, disorders of arousal, disorders of orgasm and disorders of resolution. These are described in more detail in Table 3.6.

Diagnosing a sexual dysfunction is not as simple as referring to a list of criteria or symptoms, because the clinical psychologist has to make judgements about what is dysfunctional in the light of the client's sexual experience, age, religious views, cultural norms, ethnicity and upbringing. The clinician also has to decide whether the sexual problems that are referred are caused primarily by physical or medical conditions, and, if so, whether the client might be better referred for medical treatment, perhaps by a pain specialist or a gynaecologist. Finally, it is important to remember that many people may not be particularly satisfied with their own sexual performance or that of their partner, but manage to live their daily lives quite happily. A sexual dysfunction is diagnosed only when the condition is persistent, causes the client considerable distress, and causes significant interpersonal difficulty.

3.1.1.6.2 Paraphilias When high rates of sexual behaviour are channelled into unusual or very specific sexual activities, these are known collectively as *paraphilias*. DSM-IV-TR defines paraphilias as recurrent, intense, sexually arousing fantasies, sexual urges or behaviours generally involving (i) nonhuman objects (e.g. fetishes), (ii) the suffering or humiliation of oneself or one's partner (e.g. sexual masochism or sexual sadism), or (iii) children or other nonconsenting persons (e.g. paedophilia). From these categorisations it is clear that some paraphilias are *victimless* (e.g. fetishes and transvestic fetishism), while others will be defined in law as *sexual offences* (e.g. exhibitionism, voyeurism, paedophilia). Some require these activities to cause personal distress in the perpetrator to be diagnosed (e.g. fetishism), while others do not (e.g. paedophilia).

TABLE 3.5 *Eating Disorders.*

Disorder and Lifetime Prevalence Rates	Definition	Key Features	Main Forms of Treatment
ANOREXIA NERVOSA (0.5%)	Self-starvation and a refusal to maintain a minimally normal body weight	Afflicts mainly adolescent women with onset in early to middle teens Characterised by a pathological fear of weight gain and distortions of body image Highly comorbid with major depression and OCD Mortality rates are still unacceptably high (5–8%)	Antidepressant drug treatment (e.g. SSRIs) Interpersonal psychotherapy Family therapy
BULIMIA NERVOSA (1%–3%)	Recurrent episodes of binge eating followed by periods of purging or fasting	Recurrent episodes of binge eating followed by periods of purging or fasting Typical onset in late adolescence or early adulthood 90% of sufferers are female Characterised by a loss of control over eating patterns Associated with guilt, shame and high levels of self-disgust, low self-esteem and feelings of inadequacy A disorder closely linked to Western cultural ideals of body weight and eating behaviour Often comorbid with major depression and borderline personality disorder (BPD)	Antidepressant drug treatment (e.g. SSRIs) CBT
BINGE-EATING DISORDER (BED) (1%–3%)	Recurrent episodes of binge eating without associated purging or fasting	Characterised by recurrent episodes of binge eating Sufferers usually overweight or obese Associated with high levels of depression, impaired work and social functioning. Low self-esteem and dissatisfaction with body shape Incidence in women is 1.5 times higher than in men	Antidepressant drug treatment (e.g. SSRIs) CBT

3.1.1.6.3 Gender identity disorder (GID)

Some individuals develop a sense of **gender dysphoria** (unhappiness with their own gender) and feel that they have a sense of gender that is opposite to the biological sex with which they were born. In such circumstances, the individual may see themselves biologically developing as a man or a woman (e.g. growing a beard or developing breasts), but cannot shake off the belief that underneath the physical appearance they are of the opposite gender. This may lead them to cross-dress in clothes of the opposite sex or even seek surgery or take hormones to develop physical features indicative of the opposite sex. When this kind of gender dysphoria becomes problematic and causes significant personal distress and social and occupational impairment, it may be diagnosed as *gender identity disorder (GID)*.

> **gender dysphoria** a gender identity disorder in which an individual has a sense of gender that is opposite to his or her biological sex.

3.1.1.7 Somatoform disorders

Somatoform disorders are defined by the presence of physical symptoms suggestive of a medical or neurological condition, but full medical examination and tests provide no diagnosable evidence for an underlying medical condition. In order to be defined as a mental health problem, the symptoms must cause significant distress or impairment in social, occupational or other areas of functioning. Many individuals with somatoform disorders believe that their problems are genuinely medical and are often disbelieving when told there is no diagnosable evidence for a medical problem; those with symptoms that mimic neurological disorders genuinely believe that they have a disability. Common somatoform disorders include

> **somatoform disorders** the experiencing of physical symptoms suggestive of a medical or neurological condition for which there is no diagnosable evidence.

TABLE 3.6 *Sexual and Gender Identity Disorders.*

Disorder and Lifetime Prevalence Rates	Definition	Key Features	Main Forms of Treatment
SEXUAL DYSFUNCTIONS No prevalence rates available; see Table 9.14 for an estimated list of prevalence rates for specific sexual dysfunctions	A disturbance in the processes that characterise the sexual response cycle or by pain associated with sexual intercourse	Specific sexual dysfunction disorders include: *Disorders of desire:* Hypoactive sexual desire disorder Sexual aversion disorder *Disorders of sexual arousal:* Female sexual arousal disorder Male erectile disorder *Disorders of orgasm:* Female orgasmic disorder Male orgasmic disorder Premature ejaculation *Sexual pain disorders:* Dyspareunia Vaginismus	Direct treatments: • 'Stop-start' technique • 'Squeeze' technique • Tease technique • Directed masturbation training Couples therapy Sexual skills and communication training Self-instructional training Biological treatments: • Drug treatments • Hormone treatments • Mechanical devices
PARAPHILIAS Lifetime prevalence rates: no prevalence rates available	Recurrent, intense sexually arousing fantasies, sexual urges or behaviours generally involving (1) nonhuman objects (e.g. fetishes), (2) the suffering or humiliation of oneself or one's partner (e.g. sexual masochism or sexual sadism), or (3) children or other nonconsenting persons (e.g. paedophilia)	Specific paraphilias include: Fetishism Transvestic fetishism Sexual masochism and sexual sadism Exhibitionism Voyeurism Frotteurism Paedophilia The vast majority of the DSM-IV-TR diagnosable paraphilias are mainly male activities Some paraphilias are victimless (e.g. fetishes and transvestic fetishism) while others are defined in law as sexual offences (e.g. exhibitionism, voyeurism, frotteurism, paedophilia)	Behavioural techniques: • Aversion therapy • Covert conditioning • Masturbatory satiation • Orgasmic reorientation CBT Relapse-prevention training Hormonal and drug treatments
GENDER IDENTITY DISORDER (GID) Lifetime prevalence rates: estimated 0.003% in males and 0.001% in females	A sense of gender dysphoria in which the individual has a gender identity that is opposite to their biological sex	Also diagnosed in children Most individuals with GID want to change their biological sex and not their gender identity	Gender-reassignment surgery Psychological treatments designed to change gender identity beliefs

conversion disorder the presence of symptoms or deficits affecting voluntary motor or sensory function.

somatisation disorder a pattern of recurring, multiple, clinically significant somatic symptoms that require medical treatment and cause significant impairment in functioning.

body dysmorphic disorder a preoccupation with assumed defects in physical appearance.

hypochondriasis unfounded preoccupation with fears of having or contracting a serious disease or illness based on misinterpreting bodily symptoms.

dissociative amnesia an inability to recall important personal information that is usually of a stressful or traumatic nature.

dissociative fugue the instance of an individual suddenly and unexpectedly travelling away from home or work and being unable to recall some or all of his or her past history.

dissociative identity disorder (DID) a dissociative disorder characterised by the individual displaying two or more distinct identities or personality states that take turns to control behaviour.

depersonalisation disorder a disorder characterised by feelings of detachment or estrangement from the self.

(i) **conversion disorder**, (ii) **somatisation disorder**, (iii) **body dysmorphic disorder**, (iv) **hypochondriasis** and (v) pain disorder. The features of each of these somatoform disorders are described in Table 3.7.

3.1.1.8 Dissociative disorders

Dissociative disorders are characterised by significant changes in an individual's sense of identity, memory, perception or consciousness, and these changes can either be gradual or sudden, and transient or chronic. Symptoms of these disorders include an inability to recall important personal or life events (e.g. **dissociative amnesia**, **dissociative fugue**), a temporary loss or disruption of identity (e.g. **dissociative identity disorder**) or significant feelings of depersonalisation in which the person feels that something about themselves has been altered (**depersonalisation disorder**). Very often, these experiences will coincide with periods of stress or trauma, and it is common for individuals who have experienced severe trauma – such as combat troops or survivors of natural disasters – to experience these kinds of dissociative symptoms (Kozaric-Kovacic & Borovecki, 2005).

However, for some individuals these symptoms either become so severe that they significantly disrupt their day-to-day living, or become chronic conditions rather than temporary responses to stress, and cause significant distress to the individual. In such circumstances, they may become diagnosable as a dissociative disorder. Such disorders are commonly associated with severe psychological stress such as childhood abuse (Tyler, Cauce & Whitbeck, 2004) or life-threatening trauma, and are often associated with post-traumatic stress disorder (see Section 3.1.1.5 and e.g. Kozaric-Kovacic & Borovecki, 2005). The four main types of dissociative disorder are

PHOTO 3.2 *Cases of dissociative disorder increase significantly after war or natural disasters when individuals – such as these refugees fleeing from the genocide in Rwanda in 2000 – often experience life-threatening trauma well beyond that experienced during normal daily living.*
Source: Shutterstock.

(i) dissociative amnesia, (ii) dissociative fugue, (iii) dissociative identity disorder and (iv) depersonalisation disorder, and more features of these individual disorders are provided in Table 3.8.

3.1.1.9 Disorders first diagnosed during childhood

Clinical psychologists have tended to organise childhood psychological problems into two broad domains based on the general behavioural characteristics of the child. The first domain covers **externalising disorders**, which are based on outward-directed behaviour problems such as aggressiveness, hyperactivity, noncompliance or impulsiveness. The second domain covers **internalising disorders**, which are characterised by more inward-looking and withdrawn behaviours, and may represent the experience of depression, anxiety and active attempts to withdraw socially. The former are now more commonly known as disruptive

externalising disorders outward-directed behaviour problems such as aggressiveness, hyperactivity, non-compliance or impulsiveness.

internalising disorders inward-looking and withdrawn behaviours, which in children may represent the experience of depression, anxiety and active attempts to socially withdraw.

TABLE 3.7 *Somatoform Disorders.*

Disorder & Prevalence Rates	Definition	Key Features	Main Forms of Treatment for all Somatoform Disorders
CONVERSION DISORDER Lifetime prevalence rate <1%	The presence of symptoms or deficits affecting voluntary motor or sensory function	Common symptoms are paralysis, impaired balance, localised motor function weakness Neurological examination fails to reveal any underlying medical cause Usually develops in adolescence or early adulthood Symptoms may differ across cultures	Psychodynamic therapy Behaviour therapy • Changing reinforcement contingencies • Behavioural stress management • Exposure and response prevention CBT Drug treatments
SOMATISATION DISORDER Lifetime prevalence rates: 0.2–2% in women; <0.2% in men	Recurring multiple, clinically significant somatic symptoms that require medical treatment	Anxiety and depression are caused by the symptoms themselves Often comorbid with other Axis I disorders	
BODY DYSMORPHIC DISORDER Community prevalence rate 7%	Preoccupation with assumed defects in physical appearance	Complaints include flaws in facial features, hair thinning, acne, wrinkles, scars, vascular markings, facial hair, and body shape generally Associated with compulsive checking of physical features and avoidance of social situations Many seek cosmetic surgery in order to correct 'deficits' Often associated with depression and suicidal ideation	
HYPOCHONDRIASIS Community prevalence rate 1–5%	Unfounded preoccupation with fears of having or contracting a serious disease or illness based on misinterpreting bodily symptoms	Preoccupation with bodily functions (e.g. heart rate, coughs and ambiguous bodily sensations) Associated with intrusive thoughts about death and illness Sufferers readily seek medical opinion and medical knowledge but are unwilling to deny they have a illness	
PAIN DISORDER 12-month prevalence rate 8.1%	A preoccupation with, and fear of, pain itself	Pain is viewed as disabling, often nonlocalisable and described in negative emotional terms rather than sensory terms (e.g. 'pain is frightening' rather than 'pain is like a stabbing sensation') Associated with anxiety and depression	

conduct disorder a pattern of childhood behaviour exhibited by a child including fighting, lying and running away from home.

behaviour disorders, and include DSM-IV-TR diagnosable disorders such as **conduct disorder** and **attention deficit hyperactivity disorder** (ADHD) (see Table 3.9). As research on internalising disorders has progressed over recent years, this has enabled clinicians to develop a clearer understanding of childhood anxiety and depression, how these disorders are manifested and how they can be treated. Indeed, many of the specific anxiety disorders described in Section 3.1.1 have now been identified in children and adolescents, including OCD (Geller *et al.*, 2001),

attention deficit hyperactivity disorder (ADHD) a persistent pattern of inattention and/or hyperactivity-impulsivity that is at a significantly higher rate than would be expected for a child at their developmental stage.

TABLE 3.8 *Dissociative Disorders.*

Disorder & Prevalence Rates	Definition	Key Features	Main Forms of Treatment for all Dissociative Disorders
DISSOCIATIVE AMNESIA Prevalence rate in a community sample: 1.8%	An inability to recall important personal information that is usually of a stressful or traumatic nature	Amnesia may extend to a person's own behaviour (e.g. after having committed a violent act) There are five different types of memory disturbance in dissociative amnesia: localised, selective, generalised, continuous and systematised	Psychodynamic therapy Hypnotherapy Drug treatments
DISSOCIATIVE FUGUE Prevalence rate in the general population: 0.2%	The individual suddenly and unexpectedly travels away from home or work and is unable to recall some or all of their past history	Sufferers often do not have obvious signs of psychopathology In most cases, symptoms are relatively transient (i.e. <24 hours) Disorder becomes more common after traumatic events such as war and natural disasters	
DISSOCIATIVE IDENTITY DISORDER (DID) Prevalence rate in a community sample: 1.5%	The individual displays two or more distinct identities or personality states that take turns to control behaviour	Associated with an inability to recall autobiographical information DID sufferers have an average of around 13 different identities Alter identities usually take on a range of contrasting personalities Usually associated with severe childhood sexual or physical abuse Reported cases of DID have risen dramatically since 1980	
DEPERSONALISATION DISORDER 12-month prevalence rate: 0.8%	Feelings of detachment or estrangement from the self (such as living in a dream or standing outside themselves, watching themselves)	Sufferers often think they are 'going crazy' Many sufferers also report having *déjà vu* experiences Depersonalisation experiences can also occur when the individual is in a transitional physiological state	

GAD (Tracey *et al.*, 1997) and PTSD (De Bellis & Van Dillen, 2005).

In addition, some childhood mental health problems are characterised by serious abnormalities in the developmental process, and those that fall under the heading of **pervasive developmental disorders (PDD)** are usually associated with impairment in several areas of development. The most commonly diagnosed PDDs are autistic disorder (autism), Rett's disorder, childhood disintegrative disorder and Asperger's syndrome.

Autistic spectrum disorder (ASD) is an umbrella term that refers to all disorders that display autistic-style symptoms across a wide range of severity and disability. There is now general agreement

pervasive developmental disorders (PDD) a group of disorders characterised by serious abnormalities in the developmental process, usually associated with impairment in several areas of development.

autistic spectrum disorder (ASD) an umbrella term referring to all disorders that display autistic-style symptoms across a wide range of severity and disability.

that the autistic spectrum disorder consists of significant and observable impairments in three areas: (i) reciprocal social interactions, (ii) communication and (iii) imagination and flexibility of thought. These three areas are known as the *triad of impairments* (Brown, 2008). Case History 3.1 describes some of the behavioural traits of a child who was later diagnosed with autistic spectrum disorder. Table 3.9 describes some of the main features of these childhood psychological problems.

3.1.2 Axis II Disorders – Enduring Underlying Personality Conditions

Axis II describes long-term problems characterised by either personality problems or intellectual impairment, and these types of problems inevitably cause the

Axis II disorders chronic, long-term psychopathologies and disorders such as personality disorder.

AUTISTIC SPECTRUM DISORDER

After Adam's first birthday party his mother began to pay attention to some characteristics of her son's personality that didn't seem to match those of the other children. Unlike other toddlers, Adam was not babbling or forming any word sounds, while others his age were saying 'mama' and 'cake'. Adam made no attempt to label people or objects, but would just pronounce a few noises which he would utter randomly through the day.

At the birthday party and in other situations, Adam seemed uninterested in playing with other children or even being around them socially. He seemed to enjoy everyone singing 'Happy Birthday' to him, but made no attempt to blow the candles out on the cake – even after others modelled the behaviour for him.

His parents also noted that Adam had very few interests. He would seek out two or three Disney toys and their corresponding videotapes and that was it. All other games, activities and toy characters were rejected. If pushed to play with something new, he would sometimes throw intense, unconsolable tantrums. Even the toys he did enjoy were typically not played with in an appropriate manner. Often he would line them up in a row, in the same order, and would not allow them to be removed until he decided he was finished with them. If someone else tried to rearrange the toys he would have a tantrum.

As the months went by and he remained unable to express his wants and needs, Adam's tantrums became more frequent. If his mother did not understand his noises and gestures, he would become angry at not getting what he wanted. He would begin to hit his ears with his hands and cry for longer and longer periods of time. (Adapted from Gorenstein & Comer, 2004)

CLINICAL COMMENTARY

From a very early age, Adam exhibited symptoms of the triad of impairments typical of autistic spectrum disorder. He shows (1) no sign of engaging in or enjoying reciprocal social interactions (e.g. the lack of interest in socialising with others at his birthday party), (2) a significant delay in the development of spoken speech (illustrated by his failure to form word sounds, label objects, or express his wants and needs), and (3) a lack of imagination and flexibility of thought (as demonstrated by his inability to use toys in imaginative play and his inflexibly stereotyped behaviour towards these toys). (From Davey, 2008)

---

individual difficulties in relating to and adapting to the world. The two main Axis II categories are (i) personality disorders and (ii) intellectual disabilities (sometimes referred to as learning disabilities).

3.1.2.1 Personality disorders

personality disorders a group of disorders marked by persistent, inflexible, maladaptive patterns of thought and behaviour that develop in adolescence or early adulthood.

Personality disorders consist of a loosely bound cluster of subtypes that have the following common features:

- They are characterised by an enduring pattern of behaviour that deviates markedly from expectations within that culture.

- They are associated with unusual ways of interpreting events, unpredictable mood swings or impulsive behaviour.

- They result in impairments in social and occupational functioning.

- They represent stable patterns of behaving that can be traced back to adolescence or early childhood.

Two of the best known of these disorders are **borderline personality disorder (BDP)**, characterised by major and regular shifts in mood, impulsivity, temper tantrums and an unstable self-image; and **antisocial personality disorder (APD)**, characterised by a chronic indifference to the feelings and rights of others, lack of remorse, impulsivity and pursuit of the individual's own goals at any cost. Personality disorders are categorised as Axis II disorders because they represent long-standing, pervasive and inflexible patterns of behaviour. Individuals diagnosed with a personality disorder will frequently deny they have a problem, will often be unable to comprehend that their behaviour is contrary to conventional and acceptable ways of behaving, and will not associate their psychological difficulties with their own inflexible ways of thinking and behaving. As a consequence, such disorders are very difficult to

borderline personality disorder a personality disorder, featuring inability in personal relationships, a lack of well-defined and stable self-image, mood changes and impulsive behaviour.

antisocial personality disorder a personality disorder, the main features of which are an enduring disregard for, and violation of, the rights of others.

TABLE 3.9 *Childhood Mental Health Problems.*

Disorder Category	Disorder Sub-Types & Prevalence Rates	Key Features	Main Forms of Treatment for Childhood Mental Health Problems
DISRUPTIVE BEHAVIOUR DISORDERS	**ATTENTION DEFICIT HYPERACTIVITY DISORDER (ADHD)** **(3–7% of school-aged children)**	Lack of attention in academic, occupational or social situations Hyperactivity manifested as fidgetiness or excessive running or climbing when inappropriate Impulsivity manifested as impatience or difficulty delaying responses	Drug treatments • SSRIs for depression • Ritalin and other stimulants for ADHD Behaviour therapy • Bell-and-battery technique for enuresis • Systematic desensitisation • Reinforcement techniques • Behaviour management techniques Family interventions • Systemic family therapy • Parent training programmes • Functional family therapy (FFT)
	CONDUCT DISORDER **(Lifetime prevalence rate of 9.5%)** **OPPOSITIONAL DEFIANT DISORDER (ODD)**	Tendency to violent or aggressive behaviour Deliberate cruelty to people or animals Wanton vandalism or damage to property Lying, stealing, cheating and criminal theft Violation of the rights of others Associated with early onset of sexual behaviour, drinking, smoking, substance abuse and general risk-taking behaviour	CBT for both childhood anxiety and depression Play therapy
CHILDHOOD ANXIETY & DEPRESSION	**CHILDHOOD ANXIETY** • **Separation anxiety (2–5% of children & adolescents)** • **Obsessive-compulsive disorder (OCD) (prevalence unknown)** • **Generalised anxiety disorder (GAD) (<1% of 5–10 year olds)** • **Specific phobias (7% of 8–9 year olds)** **CHILDHOOD & ADOLESCENT DEPRESSION** **(2–5% of young children; 4–8% of adolescents, but with up to 25–28% lifetime prevalence rate for adolescents)**	Developing exaggerated fears that parents will die or become ill Associated with somatic complaints Intrusive, repetitive thoughts, obsessions and compulsions Regularly comborbid with tic disorders or Tourette's syndrome Associated with increased levels of pathological worrying Important childhood phobias include social phobia and animal phobias In younger children manifests as clingy behaviour, school refusal, somatic complaints and exaggerated fears In adolescence associated with sulkiness, withdrawal from family activities, loss of energy and feelings of guilt and worthlessness	

(Continued)

TABLE 3.9 (Continued)

Disorder Category	Disorder Sub-Types & Prevalence Rates	Key Features	Main Forms of Treatment for Childhood Mental Health Problems
PERVASIVE DEVELOPMENTAL DISORDERS (PDD)	**AUTISTIC SPECTRUM DISORDER (Umbrella Term)** **Autistic disorder (prevalence rate 0.05–0.13%)** **Rett's disorder (prevalence rate 0.005–0.01%)** **Childhood disintegrative disorder (prevalence rate 0.002%)** **Asperger's syndrome (prevalence rate 0.03%)**	Diagnostic criteria known as the 'triad of impairments' Children fail to develop a 'theory of mind' that allows them to understand the emotions and intentions of others 80% of those diagnosed with autistic disorder will have an IQ score <70	

treat because they represent ingrained ways of thinking and acting.

DSM-IV-TR lists 10 diagnostically independent personality disorders, organised into three primary clusters: (i) odd/eccentric personality disorders, (ii) dramatic/emotional personality disorders and (iii) anxious/fearful personality disorders. These, together with their main features, are listed in Table 3.10.

3.1.2.2 Intellectual disabilities

Intellectual disabilities are defined primarily by three criteria. They are characterised by:

- Significantly below-average intellectual functioning – usually based on a suitable measure of IQ.

- Impairments in adaptive functioning generally (e.g. an inability to master social or educational skills that would be expected for the individual's chronological age).

- These deficits being manifest before the age of 18 years and not being the result of any injury or illness that occurred later in life.

mental retardation a DSM-IV-TR-defined disorder in which an individual has significantly below-average intellectual functioning characterised by an IQ of 70 or below.

intellectual disabilities one of the two main Axis II categories, sometimes referred to as learning disabilities.

DSM-IV-TR still refers to the major form of intellectual disability as **mental retardation**, although this term is now considered too stigmatising, and does not convey the fact that individuals with intellectual disabilities can often learn a range of skills and abilities given appropriate education and opportunity. The term **intellectual disability** is becoming increasingly used in Europe and the United States to describe disorders of intellectual functioning, and in the United Kingdom the terms **learning disability** and *children with special educational needs* are frequently used to cover both disorders of intellectual ability and more specific learning disabilities.

learning disability an umbrella term to cover specific learning disabilities, intellectual disabilities and pervasive developmental disorders.

In DSM-IV-TR, intellectual disabilities are represented by the Axis II disorder Mental Retardation. The essential diagnostic feature of this disorder is significantly below-average intellectual functioning as measured by an IQ score of less than 70 (two standard deviations below the norm). The second main criterion is evidence of significant impairments or deficits in adaptive functioning, as evidenced by impaired skills in the following areas: communication, self-care, home living, social/interpersonal skills, use of community resources, self-direction, functional academic skills, work, leisure, health and safety. Finally, the onset of these impairments must have occurred prior to age 18 years.

The major causes of intellectual disability are biological in nature, and over 1000 forms of impairment based on genetic, chromosomal or metabolic abnormalities have been identified (Dykens & Hodapp, 2001). However, many researchers believe that an individual's resultant intellectual disability is also influenced considerably by environmental factors. For example, mild or moderate intellectual disability tends to occur more frequently in lower socioeconomic groups, indicating that poverty and associated deprivation may retard intellectual development (Borkowoski *et al.*, 1992; Brooks-Gunn & Chase-Lansdale, 1995). The characteristics of intellectual disabilities are summarised in Table 3.11.

TABLE 3.10 *Personality Disorders.*

Disorder & Prevalence Rate in General Population	Definition	Key Features	Main Forms of Treatment
CLUSTER A *(Odd/ eccentric disorders)*			
Paranoid personality disorder (2.5%–4.4%)	An enduring pattern of distrust and suspiciousness of others	External attributional style that blames others Higher prevalence rate in females than males	Medication (e.g. antipsychotic drugs) Psychodynamic therapies
Schizoid personality disorder (1.7%–3.1%)	'Loners' who have very few close relationships and fail to express a normal range of emotions	May be linked to autism in childhood	Medication (e.g. antipsychotic drugs) Psychodynamic therapies
Schizotypal personality disorder (0.6%–3%)	'Eccentric' behaviour marked by odd patterns of thinking and communication	Females tend to show positive symptoms while males show negative symptoms Highly comorbid with other PDs (particularly paranoid and avoidant) Has genetic and behavioural links to schizophrenia Exhibits attentional and memory deficits similar to those in schizophrenia Shows abnormalities in frontal and temporal lobes and enlarged ventricles similar to those found in schizophrenia	Medication (e.g. antipsychotic drugs)
CLUSTER B *(Dramatic/ emotional disorders)*			
Antisocial personality disorder (APD) (0.7%–3.6%)	A pervasive pattern of disregard for and violation of the rights of others. Impulsive, irresponsible and dishonest behaviour	Between 50% and 70% of males in prisons meet APD diagnostic criteria The best predictor of APD is a diagnosis of childhood conduct disorder There is a high incidence of APD in the parents of individuals with APD There is a higher concordance rate for APD in MZ than DZ twins, suggesting a genetic component Individuals with APD show low anxiety levels, failure to learn from negative consequences and neurological impairments indicative of impulsivity	Medication (e.g. atypical antipsychotic drugs) CBT Schema therapy Psychodynamic therapies Reasoning & rehabilitation treatment (R&R)

(Continued)

TABLE 3.10 (Continued)

Disorder & Prevalence Rate in General Population	Definition	Key Features	Main Forms of Treatment
Borderline personality disorder (BPD) (0.7%–2%)	A pervasive pattern of instability of interpersonal relationships, self-image and affect, and marked impulsivity	Associated with depression, deliberate self-harm, suicidal ideation and impulsive behaviour such as drug abuse, physical violence and promiscuity Highly comorbid with Axis I mood disorders and anxiety disorders 75% of those diagnosed are female Between 60% and 90% of individuals diagnosed report childhood neglect and physical, sexual and verbal abuse Around 44% of individuals with BPD are also diagnosed with bipolar disorder BPD is also highly comorbid with major depression, panic disorder, social phobia, substance abuse disorder, eating disorders and PTSD	Medication (e.g. antidepressants) Object-relations psychotherapy Dialectical behaviour therapy Psychodynamic therapies CBT Schema therapy
Narcissistic personality disorder (0.8%–1%)	A pervasive pattern of grandiosity, need for admiration and lack of empathy	May be a sub-type of APD	Psychodynamic therapies CBT
Histrionic personality disorder (1.8%–3%)	A pervasive pattern of excessive emotionality and attention seeking. Behaviour is often dramatic	Equally prevalent in males and females	Psychodynamic therapies CBT
CLUSTER C (Anxious/fearful disorders)			
Avoidant personality disorder (1%–5%)	A pervasive pattern of social inhibition, feelings of inadequacy and hypersensitivity to negative evaluation	Highly comorbid with social phobia and may be part of a broader social anxiety spectrum Having a family member diagnosed with either social phobia or avoidant PD increases the risk for both disorders two- to threefold Associated with avoidance behaviour generally Higher prevalence rate in females than males	Psychodynamic therapies CBT
Dependent personality disorder (0.4%–1.5%)	Pervasive and excessive need to be taken care of. Submissive and clinging behaviour and great difficulty making everyday decisions	Characteristics fall into categories of (1) abandonment fears, and (2) feelings of dependency and incompetence Higher prevalence rate in females than males Regularly comorbid with mood disorders, social phobia, obsessive-compulsive disorder and panic disorder	Object-relations psychotherapy CBT
Obsessive-compulsive personality disorder (OCPD) (1%–7.7%)	Exceptional perfectionist tendencies including preoccupation with orderliness and control at the expense of flexibility, efficiency and productivity	Only 22% of individuals with OCD are also diagnosed with OCPD	CBT

TABLE 3.11 *Intellectual Disabilities.*

Disability Category	Disability Sub-Types & Prevalence Rates	Key Features	Main Forms of Intervention & Care
INTELLECTUAL DISABILITIES	Prevalence rate of diagnosis of mental retardation (IQ <70) around 1%	Traditional criteria for intellectual disabilities based on an individual's limitations and impairments (e.g. low IQ) Contemporary approaches prefer to evaluate each individual's needs and then suggest strategies for support that will optimise functioning	Prevention strategies (e.g. genetic screening) Behavioural training procedures (e.g. use of applied behaviour analysis) Inclusion strategies (including accessibility strategies, sheltered workshops and supported employment settings)

3.1.3   Summary

This section has provided a descriptive overview of the main categories of mental health problem that are referred to clinical psychologists for assessment and treatment. However, each individual case is usually much more varied and complex than can be conveyed in a basic description of each disorder, and clinicians must use their skills, training and expertise to interpret symptoms, assess how an individual's problems may have developed as a result of their experiences and lifestyle, and determine how best to help them recover from their problems.

3.2   TREATING MENTAL HEALTH PROBLEMS

The distress and disruption that symptoms of mental health problems cause will often lead an individual to seek professional help and support for their problems. The first port of call is usually the individual's doctor or GP, and the GP may be able to offer sufficient help to deal with acute problems such as those involving depression, stress and anxiety. In most cases this support will be in the form of suitable medication, but it may also take the form of access to stress-management courses, short-term counselling or psychotherapy, access to self-help information or even **computerised CBT** (e.g. Van Boeijen *et al.*, 2005). In other cases, it may be necessary for the individual to be referred for more specific and specialised treatment, often involving a clinical psychologist as part of a multidisciplinary team.

computerised CBT an alternative to therapist-delivered cognitive behaviour therapy whereby an individual interacts with sophisticated software delivered via a variety of media.

The treatment that is provided for a mental health problem will depend on at least two factors: (i) the theoretical orientation and training of the therapist, and (ii) the nature of the problem. First, a therapist will tend to adopt those treatment practices that they have most experience with and were originally trained to use, and this will often involve therapies with a specific theoretical approach (e.g. a psychodynamic approach, a client-centred approach, a cognitive approach or a behavioural approach; see Chapter 6). Secondly, treatments may be chosen largely on the basis that they are effective at treating a certain type of mental health problem. In the UK, the National Institute for Health & Clinical Excellence (NICE) recommends treatments for specific mental health problems on the basis that their effectiveness is evidence based and empirically supported by scientifically rigorous research (www.nice.org.uk).

3.2.1   Theoretical Approaches to Treatment

Traditionally, popular therapies have been developed around a relatively small number of important theoretical approaches, and this section continues with a summary of how these theoretical approaches are adapted to treat mental health problems.

3.2.1.1   Psychodynamic approaches

The aim of most psychodynamic therapies is to reveal unconscious conflicts that may be causing symptoms of psychopathology. Most psychodynamic approaches assume that unconscious conflicts develop early in life, and part of the therapy is designed to identify life events that may have caused these unconscious conflicts. Once these important developmental life events and unconscious conflicts have been identified, the therapist will help the client to acknowledge the existence of these conflicts, bring them into conscious awareness and work with the client to develop strategies for change. One important form of psychodynamic therapy is **psychoanalysis**, and this is a type of therapy based on the theoretical works of Sigmund Freud. The aim of psychoanalysis is to bring any unconscious conflicts into awareness, to help the individual understand the source of these conflicts (perhaps by identifying past experiences or discussing the nature of important relationships) and to help the individual towards a sense of control over behaviour, feelings and attitudes. There are a number of basic techniques used by psychoanalysts to achieve these goals:

> **psychoanalysis** a term for the theory developed by Freud to explain normal and abnormal psychological functioning and for the psychotherapy derived from that theory.

- **Free association** – the client is encouraged to verbalise all thoughts, feelings and images that come to mind, and this process functions to bring into awareness any unconscious conflicts or associations between thoughts and feelings.

> **free association** a technique used in psychoanalysis where the client is encouraged to verbalise all thoughts, feelings and images that come to mind.

- **Transference** – the analyst is used as a target for emotional responses, and the client behaves or feels towards the analyst as they would have behaved towards an important person in their lives. This allows the client to achieve understanding of their feelings by acting out any feelings or neuroses that they have towards that person.

> **transference** a technique used in psychoanalysis where the analyst is used as a target for emotional responses.

- **Dream analysis** – Freud believed that unconscious conflicts often revealed themselves in symbolic forms in dreams, and this made the analysis of dream content an important means of accessing unconscious beliefs and conflicts.

> **dream analysis** the analysis of dream content as a means of accessing unconscious beliefs and conflicts.

- **Interpretation** – the skilled psychoanalyst has to interpret information from all of the above sources and help the client to identify important

> **interpretation** in psychoanalysis, helping the client to identify important underlying conflicts.

underlying conflicts and to develop ways of dealing with these conflicts.

Psychoanalysis represents a quest for self-knowledge, where an individual's problems are viewed in the context of the whole person and, in particular, any conflicts they may have repressed. It can be an effective treatment for many people with moderate to severe anxiety or depression-based problems – especially when other, more conventional therapies have failed.

3.2.1.2 Behaviour therapy

In the 1940s and 1950s there was a growing dissatisfaction with the medical or disease model of psychopathology, and also with the unscientific approaches to psychopathology being generated by many psychodynamic theories. These dissatisfactions led psychologists to turn towards learning theory (see this book's website, www.wiley.com/college/davey) and this gave rise to the development of what came to be known as behaviour therapies. Two distinctive strands of behaviour therapy developed from these assumptions. The first was a set of therapies based on the principles of classical conditioning (see website), and the second based on principles of operant conditioning (see website). While the former group of therapies continues to be known as behaviour therapy, the latter group has also come to be known as behaviour modification or **behaviour analysis**. The term behaviour therapy is often used even more eclectically nowadays to refer to any treatment that attempts to change behaviour directly (rather than, say, cognitions), whether the underlying principles are based on conditioning or not.

> **behaviour analysis** an approach to psychopathology based on the principles of operant conditioning (also known as behaviour modification).

3.2.1.2.1 Therapies based on classical conditioning principles
The most famous Behaviour Therapy techniques to apply classical conditioning principles are **flooding**, **counterconditioning** and **systematic desensitisation**. These have collectively come to be known as **exposure therapies** (Richard &

> **flooding** a form of desensitisation for the treatment of phobias and related disorders in which the patient is repeatedly exposed to highly distressing stimuli.

> **counterconditioning** a behaviour therapy using conditioning techniques to establish a response that is antagonistic to the psychopathology.

> **systematic desensitisation** an exposure therapy based on the need to expose clients to the events and situations that evoke their distress and anxiety in a graduated and progressive way.

> **exposure therapies** treatments in which sufferers are helped by the therapist to confront and experience events and stimuli relevant to their trauma and their symptoms.

FOCUS POINT 3.1   EXPOSURE THERAPIES

It was Wolpe (1958) who first argued that many forms of emotional disorder could be treated using the classical conditioning principle of *extinction*. The assumption was that if emotional problems such as anxiety disorders were learned through classical conditioning, they could be 'unlearned' by disrupting the association between the anxiety-provoking cues or situations and the threat or traumatic outcomes with which they have become associated. In practice, this means ensuring that the anxiety-provoking stimulus, event or situation is experienced in the absence of accompanying trauma so that the former no longer comes to evoke the latter. These techniques are collectively known as *exposure therapies* (Richard & Lauterbach, 2007) because they are all based on the need to expose the client to the events and situations that evoke their distress and anxiety – so that they can learn that they are no longer threatening (see Davey, 1998). Wolpe (1958) also introduced the principle of *reciprocal inhibition*, in which an emotional response is eliminated not just by extinguishing the relationship between the emotion-inducing cue and the threatening consequence, but also by attaching a response to the emotion-inducing cue that is incompatible with anxiety (e.g. relaxation).

FLOODING

Flooding is an extinction-based therapy procedure involving therapist-directed prolonged exposure to the anxiety-eliciting stimulus or situation. Flooding can be conducted *in vivo* or *in vitro*, the latter by asking the client to imagine extended contact with their phobic stimulus. It is not necessary for high levels of fear to be elicited during the flooding experience, and mere exposure appears to be the sufficient condition. Studies have demonstrated that flooding is significantly more effective than placebo treatments, indicating that its success is not simply the result of client expectations (Gelder *et al.*, 1973).

COUNTERCONDITIONING

Counterconditioning is also a procedure based on Pavlovian extinction principles, but as well as extinguishing the emotional conditioned response (CR) it develops an acceptable alternative CR (such as relaxation). A more structured variation of the counterconditioning procedure is known as systematic desensitisation by reciprocal inhibition (Wolpe, 1958).

SYSTEMATIC DESENSITISATION

With this technique, the therapist constructs a ranked list of events or stimuli to which the client reacts with increasing fear or anxiety (the fear hierarchy). The client is then trained to relax while at the same time being exposed to the stimulus condition at the bottom of the fear hierarchy. When the client feels quite relaxed in this situation, they then progress on to the next most fear-inducing event on the hierarchy. This technique involves extinction of the anxiety response through graduated exposure to the anxiety-eliciting stimuli, and counterconditioning of a response incompatible with anxiety (relaxation) to these stimuli (the principle of reciprocal inhibition). It is one of the most durable and successful of all the behaviour therapy procedures.

Lauterbach, 2007) because they are all based on the need to expose the client to the events and situations that evoke their distress and anxiety (see Davey, 1998). Focus Point 3.1 provides a description of some of the main exposure therapies, and Activity Box 3.1 provides you with some guidance on how to construct a fear hierarchy for one of your own fears or phobias in a way similar to that used in systematic desensitisation.

aversion therapy a treatment based on classical conditioning which attempts to condition an aversion to a stimulus or event to which the individual is inappropriately attracted.

Aversion therapy is another treatment based on classical conditioning, but in these procedures a stimulus (e.g. alcohol) is paired with aversive outcomes (e.g. sickness-inducing drugs) in order to condition an aversive reaction to that stimulus (e.g. Lemere & Voegtlin, 1950; Voegtlin & Lemere, 1942). However, while aversion therapy for some problems (such as alcoholism) has been shown to have some therapeutic gains when used in conjunction with broader community support programmes (Azrin, 1976), addictive responses are often very resistant to this form of treatment, and there is very little evidence that aversion therapy alone has anything other than short-lived effects (e.g. Wilson, 1978).

3.2.1.2.2 Therapies based on operant conditioning principles

Operant conditioning principles have mainly been used in therapy in three specific ways:

- To try to understand what rewarding or reinforcing factors might be maintaining an

CREATING A FEAR HIERARCHY FOR A SPECIFIC PHOBIA – FLYING PHOBIA

ACTIVITY BOX 3.1

The following provides a step-by-step example of how to create your own fear hierarchy.

Overview

The fear hierarchy will contain situations or scenes involving some aspect of taking an airplane flight. These situations will most likely be situations you have actually experienced, but they can also be situations that you fear experiencing even though they have never actually happened to you. For example, you may want to include the item 'The airplane has to turn around and return to the airport in an emergency' even though this has never actually happened to you. The important point is that items included in an anxiety hierarchy describe situations which produce varying levels of anxiety, some more worrisome than others – this is what hierarchy means, and the details of this will be presented below.

You should describe the items on your anxiety hierarchy in sufficient detail to enable you to vividly imagine each one. It might be sufficient to say, 'Standing in line at the ticket counter,' but saying, 'Standing in a long line at the crowded ticket counter, with nothing to do but wait to get my luggage checked,' might be more graphic. Remember that items are most effective if they can help you experience the event in your imagination, not just describe it.

Creating Your Anxiety Hierarchy

You should attempt to create about 16 or 17 situations at the beginning. Most people tend to discard some items in the sorting process, so you can expect to end up with about 10 to 15 items in your final hierarchy. To aid in sorting the items, write each one on a separate index card.

As was mentioned earlier, the situations or scenes in your hierarchy should represent a fairly well-spaced progression of anxiety. The best way to achieve this goal is to first grade the anxiety of each item by assigning it a number on a scale from 0 to 100, where 100 is the highest level of anxiety imaginable and 0 is no anxiety (complete relaxation). Write this number on the back of the index card for the item being graded. At this point, you need not worry about how well-spaced the items are; just give each item the first number grade that 'pops into your head'.

When each item has an anxiety grade, your next step will be to sort the cards into 5 piles. Each pile will represent a different category of anxiety, as follows:

Pile	Anxiety Grade
Low Anxiety	1–19
Medium Low Anxiety	20–39
Medium Anxiety	40–59
Medium High Anxiety	60–79
High Anxiety	80–100

The goal here is to end up with at least two items in each pile. If this does not happen, you will have to go back and re-evaluate some items or create some new items. When you have finished, combine all the cards into one pile that is ordered from lowest to highest anxiety. This is your personal Fear of Flying anxiety hierarchy. Set the cards aside for one day.

It helps to check the accuracy of your ordering by shuffling the cards the next day or so. Without looking at the grades on the back of the cards, re-order them. Then check the grades to see if your second ordering is the same as the first. If not, make some adjustments. You don't have to waste a lot of time with this; just try to get an order that feels right and that represents a fairly smooth progression from low to high anxiety.

Sample Fear of Flying Anxiety Hierarchy

The following is a sample hierarchy to help you develop your own hierarchy. Your items should, of course, be more fully detailed. Also note that any item's *relative anxiety level* does not necessarily relate to its *temporal sequence*.

- Packing luggage
- Making reservations
- Driving to the airport
- Realising you have to make a flight
- Checking in
- Boarding the plane
- Waiting for boarding
- Taxiing
- In-flight service
- Moving around the cabin
- Climbing to cruising altitude
- Descending
- Waiting for departure
- Taking off
- Landing
- Turbulence

Source: http://www.guidetopsychology.com/sysden.htm.

inappropriate or maladaptive behaviour – this is known as functional analysis (e.g. trying to understand what factors might be maintaining challenging or aggressive behaviours in individuals with intellectual disabilities).

- To use reinforcers and rewards to try to establish new or appropriate behaviours (e.g. to establish self-help or social behaviours in individuals who have become withdrawn because of their mental health problems).

- To use negative or punishing consequences to try to suppress or eliminate problematic behaviours in need of urgent attention (e.g. to eliminate or suppress self-injurious behaviours in individuals with intellectual disabilities or severe autistic symptoms).

functional analysis the use of operant conditioning principles to try to understand what rewarding or reinforcing factors might be maintaining behaviour.

A **functional analysis** is where the therapist attempts to identify consistencies between problematic behaviours and their consequences – especially to try to discover whether there might be a consistent event or consequence that appears to be maintaining the behaviour by rewarding it. For example, self-injurious or challenging behaviours may be maintained by a range of reinforcing consequences, such as the attention the behaviour may attract or the sensory stimulation it provides. Identifying the nature of the consequence allows the therapist to disrupt the reinforcement contingency and, if necessary, reduce the frequency of that behaviour through extinction (Malaleski *et al.*, 1993; Wacker *et al.*, 1990). Functional analysis has been adopted across a range of clinical settings, including controlling aggressive or challenging behaviour (O'Reilly, 1995) and tantrums (Darby *et al.*, 1992).

3.2.1.3 Cognitive therapies

In the past 25 years, one of the most impressive developments in our understanding of psychopathology has been our evolving insight into the cognitive factors that play important roles in causing and maintaining psychopathology. For example, some mental health problems are caused by dysfunctional 'ways of thinking' – either about the self or the world (e.g. in major depression) and many anxiety disorders are characterised by a bias towards processing threatening or anxiety-relevant information (e.g. generalised anxiety disorder, see p. 40) or interpreting ambiguous information negatively (e.g. panic disorder, see p. 40). In both cases these biases act to develop and maintain anxiety. If such cognitive factors are maintaining symptoms, then developing treatments that try to address and change these dysfunctional cognitive features is important.

One early form of **cognitive therapy** based on these assumptions is known as **Beck's cognitive therapy**. Beck argued that depression results when the individual develops a set of cognitive schemas (or beliefs) that bias them towards negative interpretations of the self, the world and the future. Any therapy for depression must therefore address these schemas, deconstruct them and replace them with more rational schemas that do not always lead to negative interpretations. Beck's cognitive therapy does this by engaging the depressed individual in an objective assessment of their beliefs, and requires them to provide evidence for their biased views of the world. This enables the individual to perceive their existing schemas as biased, irrational and overgeneralised.

Out of these early pioneering attempts at cognitive therapy developed what is now known as cognitive behaviour therapy (CBT), which is an intervention for changing both thoughts and behaviour, and represents an umbrella term for many different therapies that share the common aim of changing both cognitions and behaviour (see Focus Point 3.2). A CBT intervention usually possesses most of the following characteristics:

cognitive therapy a form of psychotherapy based on the belief that psychological problems are the products of faulty ways of thinking about the world.

Beck's cognitive therapy a form of therapy that considers depression is maintained by 'negative schema' leading depressed individuals to hold negative views about themselves, their future and the world.

- The client is encouraged to keep a diary noting the occurrence of significant events and associated feelings, moods and thoughts in order to demonstrate how events, moods and thoughts might be interlinked.

- With the help of the therapist, the client is urged to identify and challenge irrational, dysfunctional or biased thoughts or assumptions.

- Clients are given homework in the form of 'behavioural experiments' to test whether their thoughts and assumptions are accurate and rational.

- Clients are trained in new ways of thinking, behaving and reacting in situations that may evoke their psychopathology.

CBT is generally perceived as an evidence-based and cost-effective form of treatment that can be successfully applied to a very broad range of psychopathologies (Butler *et al.*, 2006).

FOCUS POINT 3.2   COGNITIVE BEHAVIOUR THERAPY (CBT) FOR PANIC DISORDER

The following transcript gives an example of how a cognitive therapist (T) would try to challenge the catastrophic beliefs of a panic disorder sufferer (P) who believes that signs of an impending panic attack are signals for an imminent heart attack.

P: When I'm panicking, it's terrible I can feel my heart pounding; it's so bad I think it could burst through my chest.

T: What thoughts go through your mind when your heart is pounding like that?

P: Well I'll tell you what I think; it's so bad that I think I'm going to have a heart attack. It can't be good for your heart beating like that.

T: So you're concerned that anxiety can damage your heart or cause a heart attack.

P: Yes, it must do you some damage. You hear of people dropping down dead from heart attacks caused by stress.

T: Do you think more people have stress in their lives than die of heart attacks?

P: Yes, I suppose so.

T: How can that be if stress causes heart attacks?

P: Well, I suppose it doesn't always cause problems. Maybe it does only in some people.

T: Yes, that's right; stress can cause some problems in some people. It tends to be people who have something wrong with their hearts in the first place. But stress is not necessarily the same as sudden anxiety or panic. When you panic your body releases adrenalin which causes the heart to speed up and your body to

Source: Shutterstock.

work faster. It's a way of preparing you to deal better with danger. If adrenalin damaged the heart or body, how would people have evolved from dangerous primitive times? Wouldn't we all have been wiped out?

P: Yes, I suppose so.

T: So maybe panic itself doesn't cause heart attacks, there has to be something physically wrong for that to happen. When people have had heart attacks they are often given an injection of adrenalin directly into the heart in order to help start it again. Do you think they would do that if it damaged the heart even more?

P: No I'm sure they wouldn't.

T: So, how much do you now believe that anxiety and panic will damage your heart?

Source: Wells, A. (1997) *Cognitive Therapy of Anxiety Disorders*, Chichester: John Wiley & Sons Ltd, pp 123–4.

3.2.1.4   *Humanistic therapies*

humanistic therapies psychotherapies that attempt to consider the 'whole' person and not just the symptoms of psychopatholgy.

Gestalt therapy a humanistic therapy that takes into account all aspects of a person's life and experience to bring about a sense of the whole person, characterised by a sense of self-awareness and integration.

Throughout the twentieth century, many psychotherapists felt that psychological therapy was becoming too focused on psychological and behavioural mechanisms, or on psychological structures (such as personality), and was losing sight of both the feelings of the individual and the individual themselves. As a consequence, a number of what are called **humanistic therapies** developed, including **Gestalt therapy** (Perls, 1969), **existential therapies** (Cooper, 2003), **primal therapy** (Janov, 1973), **narrative therapy** (Freedman & Combs, 1996), **transpersonal**

therapy (Wellings, Wilde & McCormick, 2000) and, arguably the most successful, **client-centred therapy** (Rogers, 1961) (see website). These therapies had a number of factors in common:

- They espoused the need for the therapist to develop a more personal relationship with the client in order to help the client reach a state of realisation that they can help themselves.

- They were *holistic therapies*, in that they emphasised the need to consider the

existential therapies humanistic therapies orientating themselves around a shared concern relating to human lived experience, its 'givens' and meanings.

primal therapy a form of psychotherapy created by Arthur Janov based on the theory that a client's buried birth or childhood distress can resurface as neurosis, the treatment of which occurs through the client's 'return' to the 'primal scene' to re-experience and resolve the old trauma.

narrative therapy variously a term referring specifically to the ideas and practices of Michael White and David Epston, as well as the general term for psychotherapy that used stories and 'storying' to make meaning.

transpersonal therapy any form of therapy which places emphasis on spirituality, human potential or heightened consciousness.

client-centred therapy an approach to psychopathology assuming that if individuals are unrestricted by fears and conflicts, they will develop into well-adjusted, happy individuals.

'whole' person, and not just those 'bits' of the person that manifest problems.

- Therapy should be seen as a way of enabling the individual to make their own decisions and to solve their own problems rather than imposing structured treatments or ways of thinking on the individual.

- Humanistic therapies espouse the need for the therapist–client relationship to be a genuine reciprocal and empathetic one, rather than the limited, skilled professional–referred client relationship that exists in many forms of psychological therapy.

- Increasing emotional awareness is a critical factor in alleviating psychological distress, and is necessary before the client can begin to resolve life problems.

In much the same way as psychoanalysis has evolved, humanistic therapies developed not just as therapeutic procedures, but also as a process for fostering personal self-growth. The general approach places relatively little emphasis on how the person's problems were acquired, but attempts to eliminate symptoms by moving the client from one phenomenological state (e.g. a state of anxiety, depression etc.) to another (e.g. one that enables clients to view themselves as worthy and respected individuals).

3.2.1.5   Family and systemic therapies

family therapy a form of intervention involving family members designed to treat mental health problems arising from the relationship dynamics within the family.

Family therapy is a form of intervention that is becoming increasingly helpful as a means of dealing with mental health problems that may result from the relationship dynamics within the family (Dallos & Draper, 2005). Family therapy has a number of purposes:

- It helps to improve communications between members of the family – especially where communication between individuals might be the cause of mental health problems in one or more family members.

- It can resolve specific conflicts – for example between adolescents and their parents.

- It may apply *systems theory* (attempting to understand the family as a social system) (see website) to treatment by trying to understand the complex relationships and alliances that exist between family members, and then attempting to remould these relationships into those expected in a well-functioning family (the latter may usually involve ensuring that the primary relationship in the family – between the two parents – is strong and functional; Minuchin, 1985).

In family therapy, the therapist or family therapy team meets with those members of the family willing to participate in discussion about a topic or problem raised by one or more members of the family. In the case of an adolescent eating disorder, the parents may have raised the issue of how their child's eating disorder affects family functioning, and this may be explored with the family over a series of meetings (Dallos & Draper, 2005). Family therapists are usually quite eclectic in the range of approaches they may bring to family therapy, and these may include cognitive-behavioural methods, psychodynamic approaches and systemic analyses, depending on the nature of the problem and its underlying causes. In many cases, family therapists may focus on how patterns of interaction within the family maintain the problem (e.g. an eating disorder) rather than trying to identify the cause (the latter may be seen as trying to allocate blame for the problem within the family). Over a period of between 5 and 20 sessions, the family therapist will attempt to identify family interaction patterns that the family may not be aware of, and suggest to family members different ways of responding to one another.

3.2.2   Summary

Each of the treatment approaches we have discussed in this section can be used to treat a range of different mental health problems, and we have provided a few examples to show how these treatments work in practice. However, clinical psychologists may well be skilled in using more than one of these approaches and, indeed, a combination of approaches may be used to address specific mental health problems (e.g. the use of both CBT and behaviour therapy techniques to treat anxiety problems). While the traditional mode of treatment delivery is in one-to-one, face-to-face meetings or sessions between a therapist and a client, the pressing need to treat ever-increasing numbers of individuals referred with symptoms of mental health problems means that over-stretched clinical psychologists and service providers often look to find more cost-effective and efficient ways to deliver treatment interventions. Focus Point 3.3 provides some examples of the modes of treatment delivery that have been developed to supplement the traditional one-to-one therapist–client model.

FOCUS POINT 3.3   MODES OF TREATMENT DELIVERY

With political and social pressures mounting to increase access to psychological therapies, over-stretched clinicians and service providers often look to find more cost-effective and efficient ways to deliver treatment interventions. Some of these are described below.

GROUP THERAPY

Therapy can also be undertaken in a group and not just on a one-to-one therapist–client basis. Group therapy can be useful:

- When a group of individuals share similar problems or mental health problems (e.g. self-help groups).
- When there is a need to treat an individual in the presence of others who might have a role in influencing the mental health problems (e.g. family therapy).

Group therapies can have a number of advantages, especially when individuals:

- May need to work out their problems in the presence of others (e.g. in the case of emotional problems relating to relationships, feelings of isolation, loneliness and rejection).
- May need comfort and support from others.
- May acquire therapeutic benefit from observing and watching others.

There are now many different types of group therapy (Block & Crouch, 1987), including *experiential groups* and *encounter groups* (which encourage therapy and self-growth through disclosure and interaction) and *self-help groups* (which bring together people who share a common problem, in an attempt to share information and help and support each other – e.g. Alcoholics Anonymous, www.alcoholics-anonymous.org.uk).

E-THERAPY

The rapid growth of the Internet over the past 10–15 years has meant that people now have almost immediate access to information about mental health problems; e-mail provides another potential form of communication between therapists and clients. As a result, more and more therapists and practitioners are using e-mail as an integral part of the treatment they provide (Hsiung, 2002).

THERAPY BY TELEPHONE

Most clients telephone their therapists, if only to schedule an appointment, but the telephone can also provide a means of facilitating and conducting treatment (e.g. Ludman *et al.*, 2007) and studies have found that therapy by telephone is both effective and acceptable (Leach & Christensen, 2006). Telephone therapy may prove to be an effective form of intervention when clients live in remote or inaccessible areas, and it is a mode of delivery that can save time and reduce travel costs.

COMPUTERISED CBT (CCBT)

Because a treatment such as CBT has a highly organised structure, it lends itself well to delivery by other modes and as a package that might be used independently by the client. In recent years, computerised CBT (CCBT) has been developed as an alternative to therapist-delivered CBT, and consists of highly developed software packages that can be delivered via an interactive computer interface on a personal computer, over the Internet or via the telephone using interactive voice response (IVR) systems. The UK Department of Health has recently recommended the use of two CCBT packages:

- *Beating the Blues*® as an option for delivering computer-based CBT in the management of mild and moderate depression.
- *Fear Fighter*™ as an option for delivering computer-based CBT in the management of panic and phobia (Department of Health, 2007).

Beating the Blues consists of a 15-min introductory video and eight 1-hour interactive sessions, including homework to be completed between sessions. The programme helps the client identify thinking errors, challenge negative thoughts and identify core negative beliefs, and provides help and advice on more adaptive thinking styles (www.ultrasis.com). *Fear Fighter* is a CBT-based package for phobic, panic and anxiety disorders and is divided into nine steps, with support available from trained helpers via telephone calls or e-mails throughout treatment. The package helps clients identify specific problems, develop realistic treatment goals, and monitor achievement through self-exposure (www.fearfighter.com).

Studies comparing CCBT with other forms of support and intervention are still in their infancy, but Kaltenthaler *et al.* (2004) found that five studies showed CCBT to have equivalent outcomes to therapist-led CBT, and four studies found CCBT to be more effective than the usual GP treatment.

3.3   CONCLUSIONS

This chapter has discussed some of the main categories of mental health problem that are encountered by clinical psychologists. We then moved on to describe some of the important theoretical approaches to treatment that are adopted to tackle these problems. However, it must be stressed that everyone who presents with a mental health problem is different. Their symptoms differ in complexity and severity and their history of experiences will often be unique. This means that the clients seen by clinical psychologists will not always fit easily and simply into individual diagnostic categories, nor will they all respond to the same forms of treatment. This is a major challenge to the skills and expertise of the clinical psychologist, and these practical issues are discussed more fully in Chapter 6.

SELF-TEST QUESTIONS

- What are the most common phobias?
- Can you describe the main symptoms of a panic attack and the diagnostic criteria for panic disorder?
- What is the cardinal diagnostic feature of GAD?
- Can you describe what *obsessions* and *compulsions* are and provide some examples of each?
- Can you describe the main symptoms of PTSD and how they may differ from the symptoms found in other anxiety disorders?
- What are the two main mood disorders?
- What are the important characteristics of psychosis?
- What is the difference between substance abuse and substance dependency?
- What are the three main eating disorders defined by DSM-IV-TR?
- What are the three main groups of sexual and gender identity disorders?
- What are the four main categories of somatoform disorders?
- What are the main features of dissociative disorders?
- What is the difference between externalising and internalising childhood mental health problems?
- What are the three clusters of personality disorders listed in DSM-IV-TR, what are the disorders listed in each cluster, and what are their main defining features?
- Can you describe both the traditional and more recent alternative approaches to defining intellectual disability?
- Can you describe some of the basic techniques used by psychoanalysts?
- Can you describe the behaviour therapy techniques that are based on classical conditioning?
- Can you describe an example of cognitive therapy?
- What is family therapy and how is it conducted?

ESSAY QUESTIONS

- Describe how clinical psychologists categorise mental health problems. What are the important characteristics of the main categories?
- Compare and contrast the main principles in any two of the following psychotherapies: psychoanalysis, behaviour therapy, cognitive therapy or humanistic therapy.

TEXTS FOR FURTHER READING

Dallos, R. & Draper, R. (2005) *An Introduction to Family Therapy: Systemic theory and practice*, Milton Keynes: Open University Press.

Davey, G.C.L. (2008a) *Psychopathology*, Chichester: BPS Wiley-Blackwell.

Davey, G.C.L. (2008b) *Clinical Psychology*, Oxford: Hodder Arnold.

Dobson, K.S. (2002) *Handbook of Cognitive-Behavioural Therapies*, New York: Guilford Press.

Richard, D.C.S. & Lauterbach, D.L. (2007) *Handbook of Exposure Therapies*, New York: Elsevier.

Rogers, C.R. (2003) *Client Centred Therapy: Its Current Practice, Implications and Theory*, London: Constable & Robinson.

REFERENCES

Azrin, N.H. (1976) Improvements in the community-reinforcement approach to alcoholism, *Behaviour Research & Therapy* 14: 339–48.

Beck, A.T. (1987) Cognitive models of depression, *Journal of Cognitive Psychotherapy* 1: 5–37.

Block, S. & Crouch, E. (1987) *Therapeutic Factors in Group Psychotherapy*, New York: Oxford University Press.

Borkowski, J.G., Whitman, T.L., Passino, A.W. *et al.* (1992) Unraveling the new morbidity – adolescent parenting and developmental delays, *International Review of Research in Mental Retardation* 18: 159–96.

Brooks-Gunn, J. & Chase-Lansdale, P.L. (1995) Adolescent parenthood, in M.H. Bornstein (ed.) *Handbook of Parenting, Vol. 3: Status and Social Conditions of Parenting*, Mahwah, NJ: Erlbaum.

Brown, A. (2008) Autistic spectrum disorder, in G.C.L. Davey (ed.) *Clinical Psychology*, Oxford: Hodder HE.

Butler, A.C., Chapman, J.E., Forman, E.M. & Beck, A.T. (2006) The empirical status of cognitive-behavioral therapy: A review of meta-analyses, *Clinical Psychology Review* 26: 17–31.

Chapman, T.F. (1997) The epidemiology of fears and phobias, in G.C.L. Davey (ed.) *Phobias: A Handbook of Theory, Research and Treatment*, Chichester: John Wiley & Sons Ltd.

Cooper, M. (2003) *Existential Therapies*, Beverly Hills, CA: Sage.

Craske, M.G., Rapee, R.M., Jackel, L. & Barlow, D.H. (1989) Qualitative dimensions of worry in DSM-III-R generalized anxiety disorder subjects and nonanxious controls, *Behaviour Research and Therapy* 27(4): 397–402.

Dallos, R. & Draper, R. (2005) *An Introduction to Family Therapy: Systemic Theory and Practice*, Milton Keynes: Open University Press.

Darby, K.M., Wacker, D., Sasso, G. *et al.* (1992) Brief functional assessment techniques to evaluate aberrant behavior in an outpatient setting: A summary of 79 cases, *Journal of Applied Behavior Analysis* 25: 713–21.

Davey, G.C.L. (1997) A conditioning model of phobias, in G.C.L. Davey (ed.) *Phobias: A Handbook of Theory, Research and Assessment*, Chichester: John Wiley & Sons Ltd.

Davey, G.C.L. (1998) Learning theory, in C.E. Walker (ed.) *Comprehensive Clinical Psychology: Foundations of Clinical Psychology, Vol. 1*, New York: Elsevier.

Davey, G.C.L. (2008) *Psychopathology: Research, Assessment and Treatment in Clinical Psychology*, Chichester: BPS Wiley-Blackwell.

De Bellis, M.D. & Van Dillen, T. (2005) Childhood post-traumatic stress disorder: An overview, *Child & Adolescent Psychiatric Clinics of North America* 14: 745.

Department of Health (2007) *Improving Access to Psychological Therapies (IAPT) Programme*, London: Department of Health.

Dykens, E.M. & Hodapp, R.M. (2001) Research in mental retardation: Toward an etiologic approach, *Journal of Child Psychology & Psychiatry and Allied Disciplines* 42(1): 49–71.

Freedman, J. & Combs, G. (1996) *Narrative Therapy: The Social Construction of Preferred Realities*, New York: WW Norton & Co.

Gable, S.L. & Shean, G.D. (2000) Perceived social competence and depression, *Journal of Social & Personal Relationships* 17(1): 139–50.

Gelder, M., Bancroft, J.H.J., Gath, D. *et al.* (1973) Specific and non-specific factors in behaviour therapy, *British Journal of Psychiatry* 123: 445–62.

Geller, D., Biederman, J., Faraone, S. *et al.* (2001) Developmental aspects of obsessive-compulsive disorder: Findings in children, adolescents, and adults, *Journal of Nervous & Mental Diseases* 189: 471–7.

Gordon, A. (2001) Eating disorders: 2. Bulimia nervosa, *Hospital Practice* 36(3): 71–2.

Gorenstein, E.E. & Comer, R.J. (2004) *Case Studies in Abnormal Psychology*, 4th edn, New York: Worth.

Halmi, K.A., Eckert, E., Marchi, P. *et al.* (1991) Comorbidity of psychiatric diagnoses in anorexia-nervosa, *Archives of General Psychiatry* 48(8): 712–18.

Heimberg, R., Turk, C. & Mennin, D.S. (2004) *Generalized Anxiety Disorder: Advances in Research and Practice*, New York: Guilford Press.

Hobfoll, S.E., Spielberger, C.D., Breznitz, S. *et al.* (1991) War-related stress – addressing the stress of war and other traumatic events, *American Psychologist* 46(8): 848–55.

Hudson, J.I., Pope, H.G., Jonas, J.M. & Yurgeluntodd, D. (1983) Phenomenologic relationship of eating disorders to major affective-disorder, *Psychiatry Research* 9(4): 345–54.

Hsiung, R.C. (2002) (ed.) *E-therapy*, New York: WW Norton & Co.

Jacobsen, L.K., Southwick, S.M. & Kosten, T.R. (2001) Substance use disorders in patients with posttraumatic stress disorder: A review of the literature, *American Journal of Psychiatry* 158(8): 1184–90.

Janov, A. (1973) *Primal Scream: Primal Therapy – The Cure for Neurosis*, New York: Abacus.

Johnstone, L. & Dallos, R. (eds) (2006) *Formulation in Psychology and Psychotherapy: Making Sense of People's Problems*, London: Routledge.

Kaltenhaler, E., Parry, G. & Beverly, C. (2004) Computerized cognitive behaviour therapy: A systematic review, *Behavioural & Cognitive Psychotherapy* 32: 31–55.

Kozaric-Kovacic, D. & Borovecki, A. (2005) Prevalence of psychotic comorbidity in combat-related post-traumatic stress disorder, *Military Medicine* 170(3): 223–6.

Leach, L.S. & Christensen, H. (2006) A systematic review of telephone-based interventions for mental disorders, *Journal of Telemedicine & Telecare* 12: 122–9.

Lee, H.J. & Kwon, S.M. (2003) Two different types of obsessions: Autogenous obsessions and reactive obsessions, *Behaviour Research & Therapy* 41: 11–29.

Lemere, F. & Voegtlin, W.L. (1950) An evaluation of aversive treatment of alcoholism, *Quarterly Journal of the Study of Alcoholism* 11: 199–204.

Lepine, J.P. (2002) The epidemiology of anxiety disorders: Prevalence and societal costs, *Journal of Clinical Psychiatry* 63: 4–8.

Ludman, E.J., Simon, G.E., Tutty, S. & Von Korff, M. (2007) A randomised trial of telephone psychotherapy and pharmacotherapy for depression: Continuation and durability of effects, *Journal of Consulting & Clinical Psychology* 75: 257–66.

Mazaleski, J.L., Iwata, B.A., Vollmer, T.R., Zarcone, J.R. & Smith, R.G. (1993) Analysis of the reinforcement and extinction components in DRO contingencies with self-injury, *Journal of Applied Behavior Analysis* 26: 143–56.

Marzillier, J. & Marzillier, S. (2008) General principles of clinical practice: Assessment, formulation, intervention and evaluation, In G.C.L. Davey (ed.) *Clinical Psychology*, Oxford: Hodder HE.

Merikangas, K.R., Mehta, R.L., Molnar, B.E. *et al.* (1998) Comorbidity of substance use disorders with mood and anxiety disorders: Results of the International Consortium in Psychiatric Epidemiology, *Addictive Behaviors* 23(6): 893–907.

Minuchin, S. (1985) Families and individual development: Provocations from the filed of family therapy, *Child Development* 56: 289–302.

O'Reilly, M.F. (1995) Functional analysis and treatment of escape-maintained aggression correlated with sleep deprivation, *Journal of Applied Behavior Analysis* 28: 225–6.

Perls, F.S. (1969) *Gestalt Therapy Verbatim*, Moab, UT: Real People Press.

Radomsky, A.S. & Rachman, S. (2004) Symmetry, ordering and arranging compulsive behaviour, *Behaviour Research & Therapy* 42(8): 893–913.

Richard, D.C.S. & Lauterbach, D.L. (2007) *Handbook of Exposure Therapies*, New York: Academic Press.

Rogers, C.R. (1961) *On becoming a person: A therapist's view of psychotherapy*, Boston, MA: Houghton-Mifflin.

Rogers, C.R. (2003) *Client Centred Therapy: Its Current Practice, Implications and Theory*, London: Constable & Robinson.

Shalev, A.Y., Peri, T., Brandes, D. *et al.* (2000) Auditory startle response in trauma survivors with posttraumatic stress disorder: A prospective study, *American Journal of Psychiatry* 157(2): 255–61.

Shepherd, M., Cooper, B., Brown, A. & Kalton, C.W. (1996) *Psychiatric Illness in General Practice*, London: Oxford University Press.

Steketee, G., Frost, R.O. & Kyrios, M. (2003) Cognitive aspects of compulsive hoarding, *Cognitive Therapy & Research* 27(4): 463–79.

Tallis, S., Davey, G.C.L. & Capuzzo, N. (1994) The phenomenology of non-pathological worry: A preliminary investigation, in G. Davey & F. Tallis (eds) *Worrying: Perspectives on Theory Assessment and Research*, Chichester: John Wiley & Sons Ltd.

Tarrier, N. (2006) An introduction to case formulation and its challenges, in N. Tarrier (ed.) *Case Formulation in Cognitive Behaviour Therapy*, Hove: Routledge.

Thorpe, S.J. & Salkovskis, P.M. (1997) The effect of one-session treatment for spider phobia on attentional bias and beliefs, *British Journal of Clinical Psychology* 36: 225–41.

Tracey, S.A., Chorpita, B.F., Douban, J. & Barlow, D.H. (1997) Empirical evaluation of DSM-IV generalized anxiety disorder criteria in children and adolescents, *Journal of Clinical Child Psychology* 26: 404–14.

Tyler, K.A., Cauce, A.M. & Whitbeck, L. (2004) Family risk factors and prevalence of dissociative symptoms among homeless and runaway youth, *Child Abuse & Neglect* 28(3): 355–66.

Van Boeijen, C.A., van Oppen, P., van Balkom, A.J.L.M. *et al.* (2005) Treatment of anxiety disorders in primary care practice: A randomised controlled trial, *British Journal of General Practice* 55: 763–9.

Voegtlin, W.L. & Lemere, F. (1942) The treatment of alcohol addiction: A review of the literature, *Quarterly Journal of the Study of Alcohol* 2: 717–803.

Wacker, D.P., Steege, M.W., Northrup, J. *et al.* (1990) A component analysis of functional communication training across three topographies of severe behavior problems, *Journal of Applied Behavior Analysis* 23: 417–29.

Wellings, N., Wilde McCormick, E. (eds) (2000) *Transpersonal Psychotherapy*, Beverly Hills, CA: Sage.

Wilson, G.T. (1978) Aversion therapy for alcoholism: issues, ethics, and evidence, in G.A. Marlatt & P.E. Nathan (eds) *Behavioral Assessment and Treatment of Alcoholism*, New Brunswick, NJ: Center for Alcohol Studies.

Wolpe, J. (1958) *Psychotherapy by Reciprocal Inhibition*, Stanford, CA: Stanford University Press.

Wonderlich, S.A., Swift, W.J., Slotnick, H.B. & Goodman, S. (1993) DSM-III-R personality-disorders in eating-disorder subtypes, *International Journal of Eating Disorders* 9(6): 607–16.

Zatzick, D.F., Marmar, C.R., Weiss, D.S. *et al.* (1997) Posttraumatic stress disorder and functioning and quality of life outcomes in a nationally representative sample of male Vietnam veterans, *American Journal of Psychiatry* 154(12): 1690–95.

4 The Causes of Mental Health Problems: Schizophrenia and Autistic Spectrum Disorder

GRAHAM DAVEY

LEARNING OUTCOMES

WHEN YOU HAVE COMPLETED THIS CHAPTER, YOU SHOULD BE ABLE TO:

1. Describe, evaluate and compare the main biological, psychological and developmental/social theories of the causes of schizophrenia.

2. Compare and contrast theories of the aetiology of autistic spectrum disorder.

3. Describe and evaluate how theories couched in biological, cognitive and developmental/social theories attempt to understand mental health problems at different levels of explanation.

KEY WORDS

Abnormal Attributional Processes • Adoption Studies • Aetiology • Amphetamine Psychosis • Asperger's Syndrome • Communication Deviance • Concordance Studies • Diathesis-Stress Perspective • Dopamine • Dopamine Hypothesis • Downward Drift • Empathising-Systematising Theory • Executive Functioning • Expressed Emotion • Orienting Response • Phenothiazines • Sally-Anne False Belief Task • Social Labelling • Social-Selection Theory • Sociogenic Hypothesis • Theory of Mind • Twin Studies

FOCUS POINT 4.1 THE GENETICS OF INHERITING MENTAL HEALTH PROBLEMS

Huntington's disease is a degenerative neurological condition that can often give rise to dementia, and it is caused by a dominant mutation in a gene on the fourth chromosome. Each person has two copies of this gene (each one called an allele), one inherited from each parent. In the case of Huntington's disease an individual only needs one copy of the mutant allele to develop the disease. Parents randomly give one of their two alleles to their offspring, so a child of a parent who has Huntington's disease has a 50% chance of inheriting the mutant version of the gene from their parent. A grandchild of a person with Huntington's disease has a 25% chance of inheriting the mutant gene and so developing the disease.

The gene for Huntington's disease is dominant, and so the disease can be inherited only if one parent has the mutant gene. In this case, inheriting the mutant gene is the primary factor in the affected individual developing the disease. In other mental health problems where genetic factors have been established as important (e.g. schizophrenia), inheritance is only one of a number of factors that has been found to contribute to the development of symptoms, and this has led researchers to advocate a diathesis-stress model in which inherited factors provide a vulnerability to develop symptoms, but these symptoms do not appear unless the individual encounters stressful life experiences.

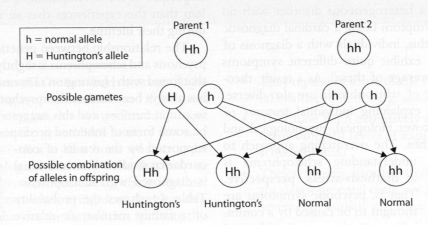

TABLE 4.1 *Concordance Rates for Individuals with a Diagnosis of Schizophrenia.*

Relation to proband	% diagnosed with schizophrenia
Spouse	1.00
Grandchildren	2.84
Nieces/nephews	2.65
Children	9.35
Silblings	7.30
Dizygotic (fraternal) twins	12.08
Monozygotic (identical) twins	44.30

Source: After Gottesman, McGuffin & Farmer, 1987.

in communication between family members), which may give rise to the development of psychosis. In order to examine the genetic basis more carefully, many researchers have undertaken **twin studies**, in which they have compared the probability with which monozygotic (MZ) and dizygotic (DZ) twins both develop symptoms indicative of schizophrenia. MZ twins share 100% of their genetic material, whereas DZ twins share only 50% of their genes, so a genetic explanation of psychotic symptoms would predict that there would be greater concordance in the diagnosis of schizophrenia in MZ than in DZ twins. This can clearly be seen in Table 4.1, where the concordance rate for MZ twins is 44%, but falls to only 12% in DZ twins. As convincing as these data may seem, there are still problems in interpreting twin studies. For example:

> **twin studies** studies in which researchers compare the probability with which monozygotic and dizygotic twins both develop symptoms indicative of a psychopathology in order to assess genetic contributions to the psychopathology.

- MZ twins will always be the same sex, whereas DZ twins may not be.
- MZ twins are usually physically identical, unlike DZ twins, and this may lead to family and friends treating MZ twins more similarly than they would DZ twins (i.e. MZ twins could experience more similar environmental factors than DZ twins).
- MZ twins are likely to have shared the same placenta prior to birth, whereas DZ twins do not, and this would mean that any inter-uterine abnormalities would be more likely to affect both MZ twins through the shared placenta (Davis & Phelps, 1995; Davey, 2008).

However, many of these difficulties of interpretation can be overcome by studying the *offspring* of MZ and DZ twins rather than the twins themselves (Gottesman & Bertelsen, 1989). If one MZ twin develops psychotic symptoms and the other does not, any genetic element in psychosis should still show up in the children of *either* of the two MZ twins. That is, the children of the MZ twins should still exhibit similar rates of risk for schizophrenia (because they have inherited the same predisposition), even though one of their parents developed schizophrenia and the other did not. This is exactly what Gottesman and Bertelsen (1989) found: 16.8% of the offspring of the MZ twins who were diagnosed with schizophrenia were likely to develop psychotic symptoms themselves, and 17.4% of the offspring of the MZ twins who were *not* diagnosed with schizophrenia were also likely to develop psychotic symptoms. This suggests that a genetic risk factor has been passed on to the offspring, even though one set of parents did not develop schizophrenia themselves.

Another way of tackling the problems of identifying the influence of genetic inheritance and environmental experience is to look at the incidence of schizophrenia in children who are biologically similar but have been reared apart (**adoption studies**). If there is an important genetic element to psychosis, then we would expect the children of a mother diagnosed with schizophrenia to have similar probabilities of developing schizophrenia regardless of whether they have been reared with their mother or not. A seminal study by Heston (1966) compared 47 adopted children who were reared apart from their schizophrenic biological mothers with 50 control adopted children whose mothers were not diagnosed with schizophrenia. He found symptoms of psychosis in 16.6% of the adopted children of the schizophrenic mothers, and no symptoms in the adopted children of mothers without schizophrenia. Studies of adopted children conducted in Denmark have shown similar results. Kety (1988) and Kety *et al.* (1994) found that adopted children who develop psychotic symptoms are significantly more likely to have had biological relatives with a diagnosis of schizophrenia (21.4%) than adoptive relatives with a diagnosis of schizophrenia (5.4%).

> **adoption studies** research conducted on children who are biologically similar but have been reared apart.

These types of study provide strong evidence for a genetic component to schizophrenia and psychosis. However, some more recent adoption studies suggest that genetic liability still interacts with environmental factors to predict the development of psychotic symptoms. Wahlberg *et al.* (2004) found that in adopted children, inherited genetic factors were an important predictor of a diagnosis of schizophrenia, but only in combination with certain environmental factors found in the adopted home environment. In this particular study, an adopted child was more likely to be diagnosed with schizophrenia if they had a biologically inherited predisposition *and* they were also brought up in an adopted home environment where there were dysfunctional communication patterns. While genetic inheritance is an important predictor of psychotic symptoms, this is further evidence that genetic factors interact with environmental factors in a way predicted by diathesis-stress models.

If, as seems likely, there is a genetic component to psychosis, how is it transmitted between related individuals, and how does this inherited component influence the development of psychotic symptoms? Using techniques such as *genetic linkage analyses* (see Research Methods Box 4.1), genes associated with the development of psychotic symptoms have been identified primarily on chromosomes 8 and 22 (Kendler *et al.*, 2000) and also on chromosomes 2, 3, 5, 6, 11, 13 and 20 (Badner &

Genetic Linkage Analysis

In recent years, much effort has been directed at attempting to identify the specific genes through which the risk for psychosis may be transmitted (Harrison & Owen, 2003), the chromosomes on which these genes are located (Kendler *et al.*, 2000), and how these genes and their possible defects may give rise to psychotic symptoms (Andreason, 2001). These endeavours have primarily involved *genetic linkage analyses*, in which blood samples are collected in order to study the inheritance patterns within families that have members diagnosed with schizophrenia. Linkage analyses work by comparing the inheritance of characteristics for which gene location is well known (e.g. eye colour) with the inheritance of psychotic symptoms. If the inheritance of, for example, eye colour follows the same pattern within the family as psychotic symptoms, then it can reasonably be concluded that the gene controlling psychotic symptoms is probably found on the same chromosome as the gene controlling eye colour, and is probably genetically linked to that 'marker' characteristic in some way.

Gershon, 2002; Levinson *et al.*, 2002). These findings make it clear that if there is a genetic predisposition to psychotic symptoms, it is not transmitted solely through a single gene. This may be because psychosis represents a number of rather different psychopathologies, each of which contributes to the heterogeneity of schizophrenia as a diagnostic category (Joober *et al.*, 2002). Even if there is an important inherited component to psychosis, as the data suggest, then what is it that is transmitted genetically that gives rise to psychotic symptoms? We do not yet know enough about the specific genes implicated in psychosis, but if the involvement of individual genes were confirmed, this may well help us to identify dysfunctions in specific biochemical pathways and molecular mechanisms that are implicated by these genes.

4.1.1.2 Brain neurotransmitters

Brain neurotransmitters are the chemicals that help neurones to communicate with each other and thus are essential components of the mechanisms that regulate efficient and effective brain functioning. During synaptic transmission, neurones release a neurotransmitter that crosses the synapse and interacts with receptors on neighbouring neurones, and most neurotransmitters relay, amplify and modify signals between neurones. There are many different types of neurotransmitter and they can be grouped according to either their chemical structure or their function. One important neurotransmitter that has been implicated in the development of mental health problems is dopamine. **Dopamine** has many functions in the brain, including important roles in regulating voluntary movement, motivation and reward, and is critically involved in mood, attention and learning.

dopamine a compound that exists in the body as a neurotransmitter and as a precursor of other substances including adrenalin.

Because cognition and behaviour are very much dependent on the efficient working of brain neurotransmitters such as dopamine, it is not surprising that many researchers have suspected that the thought disorders, hallucinations and behaviour problems characteristic of the diagnosis of schizophrenia may be caused by malfunctions in these brain neurotransmitters. A theory of schizophrenia that has been most prominent over the past 50 years is known as the **dopamine hypothesis**, and this account argues that the symptoms of schizophrenia are importantly related to excess activity of the neurotransmitter dopamine. There are a number of factors that have led to the implication of excess dopamine activity.

dopamine hypothesis a theory which argues that the symptoms of schizophrenia are related to excess activity of the neurotransmitter dopamine.

First, the discovery of antipsychotic drugs that helped to alleviate the symptoms of psychosis (such as the **phenothiazines**) led to the discovery that such drugs acted by blocking the brain's dopamine receptor sites and so reduced dopamine activity (Schneider & Deldin, 2001).

phenothiazines a group of antipsychotic drugs that help to alleviate the symptoms of psychosis by reducing dopamine activity.

Second, during the 1970s it was noticed that there was a strong link between excessive use of amphetamines and a syndrome known as **amphetamine psychosis**. When taken in high doses for long periods, amphetamines produce behavioural symptoms in humans and animals that closely resemble symptoms of psychosis. These include paranoia and repetitive, stereotyped behaviour patterns (Angrist, Lee & Gershon, 1974). Subsequently we have learned that amphetamines produce these disturbed behaviour patterns by increasing brain dopamine activity, and giving amphetamines to those diagnosed with schizophrenia actually increases the severity of their symptoms (Faustman, 1995).

amphetamine psychosis a syndrome in which high doses of amphetamines taken for a long time produce behavioural symptoms that closely resemble symptoms of psychosis.

Third, brain imaging studies have indicated that individuals diagnosed with schizophrenia show excessive levels of dopamine released from areas of the brain such as the basal ganglia – especially when biochemical precursors to dopamine, such as dopa, are administered to the individual (Carlsson, 2001; Goldsmith, Shapiro & Joyce, 1997).

Finally, post-mortem studies have found increased levels of dopamine and significantly more dopamine receptors in the brains of deceased schizophrenia sufferers – especially in the limbic area of the brain (Kapur & Seeman, 2001).

So, how might excess dopamine activity be involved in the production of psychotic symptoms? It might be that dopamine receptors in those diagnosed with schizophrenia are too sensitive, and messages being transmitted by this system are sent too often and too easily. This could give rise to the disorganised thinking and communication styles typical of psychosis, which is consistent with the fact that dopamine neurons are known to play a critical role in controlling and guiding attention (Cohen *et al.*, 1988). In addition, a number of brain imaging studies have confirmed that individuals diagnosed with schizophrenia have more dopamine receptors in the brain, and that these are often more sensitive than those receptors found in nonsufferers (Goldsmith, Shapiro & Joyce, 1997).

4.1.1.3   Summary

Over many years now, research into the biological factors underlying schizophrenia has focused on genetic determination and the role of abnormalities in brain neurotransmitters, and we have a significant understanding of these factors. Parallel research on cognitive factors has enriched this understanding, and we look at this in the next section.

4.1.2   Cognitive Factors

There is no doubt that cognitive processes (and their dysfunction) can be identified in the aetiology of many psychotic symptoms. Cognitive theories are involved in explaining these symptoms in a number of important ways:

- They can be used to describe the cognitive and behavioural deficits that may be caused by possible underlying biological dysfunctions (e.g. excessive dopamine activity may give rise to attentional deficits that can be described in terms of dysfunctions of normal cognitive processes).

- Some basic cognitive processes may be directly involved in shaping some of the deluded thinking and bizarre behaviour typical of psychosis (e.g. a tendency to attribute negative events to external sources may give rise to paranoid beliefs).

4.1.2.2   Attentional processes

One of the most obvious characteristics of psychosis is the individual's seeming inability on some occasions to make simple associations between relevant events (e.g. sticking to the theme of a conversation), but on other occasions making associations that are irrelevant (e.g. being unable to prevent themselves from 'clanging' or emitting words that rhyme). These opposing tendencies seem to reflect deficits in attentional processes, where the individual seems unable to focus attention on relevant aspects of the environment (under-attention) or pays too much attention to irrelevant aspects of the environment (over-attention).

One characteristic of normal attentional processes is the **orienting response**, which is a physiological reaction consisting of changes in skin conductance, brain activity, heart rate and blood pressure. These responses occur naturally when the individual is presented with a novel or prominent stimulus, and they indicate that the stimulus is being attended to and processed. However, around 50% of individuals diagnosed with schizophrenia show abnormalities in their orienting reactions, suggesting that they are not attending to or processing important environmental stimuli (Olbrich *et al.*, 2001). Studies have shown that individuals with a diagnosis of schizophrenia are highly distractable, and perform poorly at cognitive tasks when they are also presented with irrelevant, distracting stimuli or information (Wielgus & Harvey, 1988). This inability to screen out irrelevant stimuli or to ignore distractions correlates highly with many of the positive symptoms of schizophrenia (e.g. disturbances of thought and language; Cornblatt *et al.*, 1985) and may well be a contributing factor to the disordered thought and communication exhibited by individuals diagnosed with schizophrenia.

> **orienting response** a physiological reaction consisting of changes in skin conductance, brain activity, heart rate and blood pressure.

4.1.2.2   Attribution and information processing biases

Of specific interest to cognitive theorists are the delusional beliefs that are regularly developed during psychotic episodes, and over 50% of individuals diagnosed with schizophrenia are diagnosed with paranoid schizophrenia (Guggenheim & Babigian, 1974). This raises the issue of why so many sufferers should develop these particular kinds of delusions. Some researchers have pointed out that paranoid delusions may be the result of **abnormal attributional processes**, which suggests that they have a bias towards attributing negative life events to external causes (Bentall, 1994; Bentall &

> **abnormal attributional processes** biases or faults in the normal attribution process which may lead to errors in the interpretation of one's own and others' behaviour.

Kinderman, 1998, 1999; Bentall *et al.*, 2001). For example, Kaney and Bentall (1989) found that patients with paranoid delusions made excessively stable and global attributions to negative events (just like depressed individuals), but also attributed positive events to internal causes and negative events to external causes. A subsequent study by Bentall, Kaney and Dewey (1991) found that this tendency of individuals with paranoid delusions to attribute negative events to external causes was only evidenced when there was a perceived threat to the self – they did not necessarily attribute negative events to external sources when describing the experiences of others. The preceding studies all suggest that individuals exhibiting paranoid delusions have developed a bias towards attributing negative events to external causes. At the very least, this attributional bias will almost certainly act to maintain paranoid beliefs, and maintain their delusions that someone or something external is threatening them.

In addition, Freeman (2007) has argued that people vulnerable to paranoid thinking try to make sense of unusual internal experiences by using those feelings as a source of evidence that there is a threat, and they then incorporate other evidence around them to substantiate that belief (e.g. interpreting the facial expressions of strangers in the street as additional evidence that they are threatened). But why do some people develop these suspicious interpretations? Freeman argues that they often occur in the context of emotional distress, are frequently preceded by stressful events (e.g. difficult interpersonal relationships, bullying, isolation) and happen against a background of previous experiences that have led the person to have beliefs about the self as vulnerable, others as potentially dangerous and the world as bad. Other factors may also be involved in setting the conditions for an interpretational bias that will generate paranoid beliefs.

Freeman *et al.* (2002) have argued that four factors are important in contributing to the development of cognitive biases involved in persecutory ideation:

- Anomalous experiences (such as hallucinations) that do not appear to have a simple and obvious explanation (and are therefore open to biased interpretations).

- Anxiety, depression and worry, which would normally cause a bias towards negative thinking and threatening interpretations of events.

- Reasoning biases on the part of the individual that lead them to seek confirmatory evidence for their persecutory interpretations rather than question them.

- Social factors, such as isolation and trauma, which add to feelings of threat, anxiety and suspicion.

PHOTO 4.1 *Suspicious Minds.*

People vulnerable to paranoid thinking try to make sense of unusual internal experiences by using those feelings as a source of evidence that there is a threat, and they then incorporate other evidence around them to substantiate that belief (e.g. interpreting the facial expressions of strangers in the street as additional evidence that they are threatened). Freeman (2007) argues that these paranoid interpretations often occur in the context of emotional distress, are often preceded by stressful events (e.g. difficult interpersonal relationships, bullying, isolation) and happen against a background of previous experiences that have led the person to have beliefs about the self as vulnerable, others as potentially dangerous and the world as bad. In addition, living in difficult urban areas is likely to increase the accessibility of such negative views about others.
Source: Shutterstock.

This view is supported by evidence suggesting that individuals with persecutory delusions have high levels of negative mood, such as depression (Freeman, Garety & Kuipers, 2001) and rarely consider alternative (nondelusional) explanations of their experiences (Freeman *et al.*, 2004). Interestingly, this cognitive model of persecutory delusions can also be applied to understanding why psychoactive drug use (such as cannabis) can increase the risk of developing schizophrenic symptoms, discussed more fully in Focus Point 4.2.

FOCUS POINT 4.2   CANNABIS USE AND PSYCHOTIC SYMPTOMS

Brian, my brother, started smoking at a very young age, in his teens. He was a daily smoker and he used to smoke the equivalent of a pack of cigarettes a day. I had a phone call once from the police in High Wycombe saying they had found him. He was talking like a Rastafarian and he believed he was John the Baptist. I had to get him sectioned which absolutely broke the family up. My father and mother had very old-fashioned ideas about mental illness – you didn't speak about it – and they practically disowned him. He came to live with me. He would be awake all night and sleep all day. One doctor asked me if he was smoking cannabis and I said he was – she believed that was what triggered his downfall. They put him on medication because they believed he was schizophrenic – he was hearing voices, saw messages in the paper and was having delusions of grandeur. I believe the last time anyone saw him was around High Wycombe in 1996 and he was basically living the life of a down-and-out. I believe his problems were brought on by the smoking. He had to live 28 days off it while in hospital and he improved. He seemed in better shape to me.

Source: Shutterstock.

This BBC news interview describes how one woman believed that smoking cannabis had caused her brother to develop psychotic symptoms. There has long been a view that regular psychotropic drug use may be related to the development of psychotic symptoms, and in recent years this has focused on the relationship between cannabis use and subsequent diagnosis of schizophrenia (Arsencault *et al.*, 2004). Concern about the possible relationship between cannabis use and schizophrenia has been fuelled by a dramatic increase in cannabis use by adolescents and young adults over the past two decades (Smart & Ogbourne, 2000) and the possible impact this might have on mental health if there is a causal link between cannabis use and psychotic symptoms.

Cross-sectional studies have shown that individuals diagnosed with schizophrenia use cannabis significantly more often than other individuals in the general population (Degenhardt & Hall, 2001). Some have argued that this relationship between cannabis use and schizophrenia reflects a form of 'self-medication', in which individuals may start using cannabis because of a predisposition for schizophrenia (Khantzian, 1985). However, others have argued for a direct causal link between cannabis use and schizophrenia, and case history studies frequently describe psychotic episodes being preceded by the heavy use of cannabis (Wylie, Scott & Burnett, 1995).

Prospective studies that have monitored cannabis use and psychotic symptoms in individuals over a lengthy period appear to indicate that there is indeed a causal link between cannabis and the development of psychotic

symptoms. First, Andreasson *et al.* (1987) found a dose–response relationship between cannabis use at 18 years and later increased risk of psychotic symptoms. Subsequent prospective studies have found that 18 year olds meeting the criteria for cannabis dependence had rates of subsequent psychotic symptoms that were twice the rate of young people not meeting these criteria (Fergusson, Horwood & Swain-Campbell, 2003). Also, this relationship could not be explained by high cannabis use being associated with any pre-existing psychiatric symptoms (Fergusson, Horwood & Ridder, 2005). Statistical modelling of these longitudinal data show that the direction of causality is from cannabis use to psychotic symptoms and not vice versa (Fergusson, Horwood & Ridder, 2005). In addition, further studies have demonstrated that cannabis use increases the risk of psychotic symptoms, but has a greater impact on those who already have a vulnerability to schizophrenia (Verdoux *et al.*, 2003; Henquet *et al.*, 2005).

So if there is a causal link between cannabis use and schizophrenia, what is the mechanism that mediates this link? First, there may be a neurological explanation. Recent research suggests that cannabis has an important effect on brain chemistry, and the compound tetrahydrocannabinol (THC) that is found in cannabis can release the neurotransmitter dopamine (Tanda, Pontieri & Di Chiara, 1997). Excess dopamine activity has been identified in the aetiology of schizophrenia, and heavy cannabis use may therefore raise brain dopamine activity to levels triggering psychotic episodes. Alternatively, Freeman *et al.* (2002) have argued that anomalous experiences (that do not have a simple and obvious explanation) are one of the fundamental factors contributing to the development of delusional thinking, and psychoactive street drugs such as cannabis are likely to increase the frequency of such anomalous experiences. If the individual is in an anxious state and already feeling isolated, these anomalous experiences are likely to be interpreted threateningly and give rise to the persecutory and paranoid ideation often found in schizophrenia. (From Davey, 2008)

4.1.2.3   Summary

What is interesting about these cognitive explanations of paranoia and paranoid schizophrenia is that they allude to ways of thinking that are a common feature of most of our thinking. That is, they result from biases in the way we interpret information, attribute causes to events, and collect evidence to confirm or disconfirm our beliefs. They are rarely the result of chaotic or random thought processes. Understanding the development of paranoid thinking in this systematic way enables us to develop interventions that will help to correct such biased thinking and alleviate the distress associated with severe paranoia (Freeman *et al.*, 2006).

4.1.3   Developmental/Social Factors

In addition to the biological and cognitive features that may give rise to symptoms of schizophrenia, developmental/social perspectives attempt to supplement the diathesis-stress view of schizophrenia by identifying social, cultural or familial factors that generate stressors that could precipitate psychotic symptoms.

4.1.3.1   Social factors

The highest rates of diagnosis of schizophrenia are usually found in poorer inner-city areas and in those of low socioeconomic status, and this has given rise to two rather different sociocultural accounts of schizophrenia. The first is known as the **sociogenic hypothesis**. This claims that individuals in low socioeconomic classes experience significantly more life stressors than individuals in higher socioeconomic classes, and these stressors are associated with unemployment, poor educational levels, crime and poverty generally. Having to endure these stressors may trigger psychotic symptoms in vulnerable people. A study conducted in Denmark indicated that factors associated with low socioeconomic status may be risk factors for psychosis, and these include unemployment, low educational attainment, lower wealth status, low income, parental unemployment and lower parental income (Byrne *et al.*, 2004). Studies conducted on immigrants have also indicated that such groups have a higher incidence of the diagnosis of schizophrenia, and this has been attributed to the stress caused by many of the initial consequences of immigration, such as language difficulties, unemployment, poor housing and low socioeconomic status (Hjern, Wicks & Dalman, 2004).

An alternative explanation for the fact that individuals diagnosed with schizophrenia appear to have low socioeconomic status is that the intellectual, behavioural and motivational problems afflicting individuals with psychotic symptoms mean that they will suffer a **downward drift** into unemployment, poverty and the lower socioeconomic classes *as a result of their disorder*. This is known as the **social-selection theory** and claims that individuals displaying psychotic symptoms will drift into lifestyles where there is less social pressure to achieve, no need to hold down a regular job, and they can cope with their difficulties on a simple day-to-day basis. This hypothesis is supported by the fact that many individuals diagnosed with schizophrenia may have parents with high socioeconomic status, even though they themselves are living in poverty-ridden areas of towns and cities (Turner & Wagonfeld, 1967).

One final sociocultural view of schizophrenia is known as **social labelling**, in which it is argued that the development and maintenance of psychotic symptoms are influenced by the diagnosis itself (Modrow, 1992). In particular, if someone is diagnosed as 'schizophrenic' then it is quite possible (i) that others will begin to behave differently towards them and define any deviant behaviour as a symptom of schizophrenia; and (ii) that the person who is diagnosed may themselves assume a 'role' as someone who has a disorder and play that role to the detriment of other – perhaps more adaptive – roles. At the very least this is likely to generate a self-fulfilling prophecy, in which a diagnosis leads to the individual, their family and friends behaving in ways that are likely to maintain pathological symptoms.

4.1.3.2   Familial factors

There is a general belief across most theoretical perspectives on schizophrenia that the characteristics of the family are in some way important in making an individual vulnerable to acquiring psychotic symptoms, and research has implicated the importance of patterns of interactions and communications within the family.

Recent research has identified a construct called **communication deviance (CD)** in families, which is related to the development of psychotic symptoms. CD is a general term used to describe communications that would be difficult for an ordinary listener to follow and that

---

sociogenic hypothesis the theory that individuals in low socioeconomic classes experience significantly more life stressors than individuals in higher socioeconomic classes.

downward drift a phenomenon in which individuals exhibiting psychotic symptoms fall to the bottom of the social ladder or even become homeless due to impairment.

social-selection theory the theory that individuals displaying psychotic symptoms will move into the lower socioeconomic classes as a result of their disorder.

social labelling the theory that the development and maintenance of psychotic symptoms are influenced by the diagnosis itself.

communication deviance a general term used to describe communication that is difficult for ordinary listeners to follow and leaves them puzzled and unable to share a focus of attention with the speaker.

leave them puzzled and unable to share a focus of attention with the speaker. Such communications would include:

- Abandoned or abruptly ceased remarks or sentences.
- Inconsistent references to events or situations.
- Using words or phrases oddly or wrongly.
- Employment of peculiar logic.

Studies have demonstrated that CD is a stable characteristic of families with offspring who develop psychotic symptoms (Wahlberg *et al.*, 2001). When children with a biological predisposition to schizophrenia have been adopted and brought up in homes with adopted parents who do not have a biological predisposition for schizophrenia, CD has been found to be an independent predictor of the adopted child developing psychotic symptoms (Wahlberg *et al.*, 2004). This suggests that CD is a risk factor for a diagnosis of schizophrenia that is independent of any biological or inherited predisposition, and that CD is not simply the product of a shared genetic defect between parents and offspring.

Another construct that has been closely linked to the appearance and reappearance of psychotic symptoms is known as **expressed emotion** (EE). The importance of the family environment in contributing to psychotic symptoms was first recognised when it was found that individuals who left hospital following treatment for psychosis were more likely to relapse if they returned to live with parents or spouses than if they went to live in lodgings or with siblings (Brown, Carstairs & Topping, 1958). From this it was discovered that many of the discharged patients were returning to environments where communications were often hostile and critical. This led to the development of the construct of EE, which refers to high levels of criticism, hostility and emotional involvement between key members of a family, and some examples of high EE are shown in Activity Box 4.1.

Since its development, EE has been shown to be a robust predictor of relapse (Kavanagh, 1992) and, in particular, relapse involving positive psychotic symptoms. Families high in EE tend to be intolerant of the patient's problems and have inflexible strategies for dealing with their difficulties and symptoms. High EE families also have an attributional style that tends to blame the sufferer themselves for their condition and the consequences of their symptoms (Barrowclough, Johnston & Tarrier, 1994; Weisman *et al.*, 2000). It is not clear how high EE

> **expressed emotion** a qualitative measure of the 'amount' of emotion displayed, typically in the family setting.

ACTIVITY BOX 4.1

Families with high levels of expressed emotion (EE) exhibit (i) high levels of criticism, (ii) hostility towards the individual diagnosed with schizophrenia, (iii) intolerance of the sufferer's problems, (iv) inflexible strategies for dealing with the symptoms of schizophrenia, (v) blaming the sufferer themselves for their symptoms and behaviour, and (vi) a tendency to attribute the sufferer's behaviour to global, stable causes, making it difficult to conceive of change and improvement.

Can you identify these characteristics in the fragments of conversation below? These are statements made by members of families with high EE talking about the individual who has been diagnosed with schizophrenia.

> Four days ago he told my wife that he was going to kill the police … now whether that's just bravado, that's just childish, the sort of thing a child would do.

> He has this thing that he is the most important person and they'd have to wait for him, so he'd have to miss appointments.

> He knows I don't like swearing, so he would continue to swear … I think he did it just to be difficult.

> When he came back with his funny ideas about blacks' persecution and natural health I just thought it was typical Nicholas picking things up en route, he's not too strong a character and tends to absorb other people's views.

> The other day she threatened to top herself. Now that is not her, that is not an expression that she would use. It's completely out of character with her … It's a bit of emotional blackmail; she wants me to take her home.

> She's a bit on the lazy side, and she's not very logical. If you are cleaning a place out, she'll help, but she won't finish things.

> He was smoking very heavily, which he hadn't been doing before … he really wasn't the smoking type, you know, he got with some friends who smoked and he kept on smoking.

(From Davey, 2008)

within a family might influence a tendency to relapse – if indeed there is a causal relationship between high EE in a family and sufferer relapse. However, some studies have suggested that interventions to moderate the high EE levels in a family may actually have a beneficial effect on relapse, suggesting a possible causal link between high EE and relapse (Hogarty *et al.*, 1986; Tarrier *et al.*, 1988).

4.1.4   Summary of Research on Schizophrenia

The over-arching explanation of schizophrenia is one of *diathesis stress*. That is, individuals who develop psychotic symptoms have an inherited vulnerability to develop these symptoms (diathesis) which are likely to be triggered by experiencing environmental stressors. We have discussed a mixture of biological, psychological (cognitive) and sociocultural theories of psychosis, and these rather different types of explanation are by no means mutually exclusive. They all aim to explain different features of schizophrenia, often at different levels of description.

4.2   AUTISTIC SPECTRUM DISORDER

Autistic Spectrum Disorder (ASD) is characterised by impairment in several areas of development. Early symptoms are that the child seems withdrawn, has failed to develop normal means of communication, appears uninterested in his or her surroundings and has difficulty learning new skills. There is general agreement that autistic spectrum disorder consists of significant and observable deficits in what is know as a triad of impairments. These are (i) reciprocal social interactions, (ii) communication and (iii) imagination and flexibility of thought.

Case History 3.1 in Chapter 3 describes the behaviour of Adam, a young child exhibiting symptoms of autistic spectrum disorder. Consistent with the triad of impairments typical of autistic spectrum disorder, Adam shows:

- No sign of engaging in or enjoying reciprocal social interactions (e.g. the lack of interest in socialising with others at his birthday party).

- A significant delay in the development of spoken speech (illustrated by his failure to form word sounds, label objects or express his wants and needs).

- A lack of imagination and flexibility of thought (as demonstrated by his inability to use toys in imaginative play and his inflexibly stereotyped behaviour towards these toys).

Clinical psychologists can take a pivotal role in coordinating services and interventions for autistic spectrum disorder, which will involve providing families with support and information about the disorder and will often involve partnership working between health, education, social-care and voluntary-sector organisations through the local Children & Adolescent Mental Health Services (CAMHS) (Brown, 2008).

The causes of autistic spectrum disorder are beginning to be unravelled and it is becoming clear that there is a significant genetic element. However, in individual cases there is also likely to be a contribution from environmental factors, such as peri-natal risk factors (e.g. maternal infections during pregnancy). The various combinations of genetics and environmental risk factors may be the reason why autistic syndrome disorders vary so much in their symptomatology and their severity. As we shall see below, it is now accepted that autistic syndrome disorder is caused primarily by aberrant brain development, which gives rise to the range of impairments in cognitive abilities and social understanding exhibited by sufferers.

4.2.1   Biological Factors

4.2.1.1   Genetic factors

There has been evidence available for some time that the social and language deficits and psychological problems reminiscent of autistic spectrum disorder often have a family history (Folstein & Rutter, 1988; Piven & Palmer, 1999). In particular, there is evidence for a strong familial aggregation of autistic symptoms, as demonstrated in studies of sibling re-occurrence risk (i.e. studies investigating the probability of developing autism given that an individual's sibling is autistic). These studies have estimated that the rate of autism in the sibling of someone with autism ranges between 2% and 14% (Bailey, Phillips & Rutter, 1996; Jorde *et al.*, 1990), which is significantly higher than the 0.05–0.2% prevalence rate found in the general population. Autistic spectrum disorder also appears to cooccur with several known genetic disorders such as phenylketonuria, fragile X syndrome and tuberous sclerosis (Reiss & Freund, 1990; Smalley, 1998), implying a genetic link in its aetiology. There are also familial links between autistic spectrum disorder and other psychological problems. For instance, affective disorders are almost three times more common in the parents of autism sufferers than in the parents of children suffering from tuberous sclerosis or epilepsy. While we might expect that having a child with a disability might precipitate such psychological problems, a majority of parents of autistic children developed their affective disorder before the birth of the child (Bailey, Phillips & Rutter, 1996).

Numerous twin studies have confirmed this genetic component to the disorder. In studies comparing concordance rates in MZ and DZ twins, Folstein and Rutter (1977) found concordance in 4 out of 11 MZ twins, but none in DZ twins. Subsequent twin studies have found concordance rates of between 60% and 91% for MZ twins and between 0% and 9% for DZ twins (Bailey *et al.*, 1995; Rutter *et al.*, 1990; Steffenberg *et al.*, 1989). In addition, more recent twin studies have also demonstrated that each of the symptom components of autistic disorder – social impairments, communication impairments and restricted repetitive behaviours – all individually show high levels of heritability (Ronald *et al.*, 2006).

Despite confirmation from a variety of sources that autistic spectrum disorder has a significant genetic component, it has so far not been possible to identify clearly the genes responsible for transmitting the disorder. This suggests that a single gene is not responsible for the expression of autism, that as many as 15 different genes may be involved (Santangelo & Tsatsanis, 2005) and that, even when there is strong evidence to suggest the involvement of a single gene, the significance of the gene in terms of brain development has been difficult to determine (Muhle, Trentacoste & Rapin, 2004). This suggests that autistic spectrum disorder is a complex condition that may involve a range of different genetic influences affecting symptom expression and severity.

4.2.1.2 Peri-natal factors

Peri-natal factors may play a significant role in determining intellectual impairment and the same may be true in the case of autistic spectrum disorder. A range of birth complications and pre-natal factors have been identified as risk factors in the development of autistic spectrum disorder, including maternal infections, such as maternal rubella during pregnancy (Chess, Fernandez & Korn, 1978), intra-uterine exposure to drugs such as thalidomide and valproate (Stromland *et al.*, 1994; Williams *et al.*, 2001), maternal bleeding after the first trimester of pregnancy (Tsai, 1987) and depressed maternal immune functioning during pregnancy (Tsai & Ghaziuddin, 1997). However, many of these risk factors have been identified only in individual case reports, and they probably account for a very small percentage of cases of autistic spectrum disorder (Fombonne, 1999; Muhle, Trentacoste & Rapin, 2004). For example, studies suggest that congenital rubella infection has been found to be present in less than 0.75% of autistic populations – largely because of the near eradication of the disease in western countries (Fombonne, 1999).

Some studies also claim to have linked autism to postnatal events such as a link between autistic spectrum disorder, inflammatory bowel disease and administration of the measles, mumps and rubella (MMR) vaccine (Wakefield *et al.*, 1998). This claim caused some controversy in the UK at the time, because it led to many parents refusing to have their children immunised with the vaccine and so put them at significant risk of these infections. However, subsequent studies have failed to corroborate an association between administration of MMR and autism (e.g. Madsen *et al.*, 2002). In addition, recent studies have also failed to find any association between infectious diseases in the first two years of life and autism. Rosen, Yoshida and Croen (2007) found that children with subsequent diagnoses of autism had no more overall infections in the first two years of life than children without autism.

In conclusion, while a very small minority of cases of autism may be linked to peri-natal factors such as those outlined above, congenital and peri-natal factors are probably not the primary causes of the disorder.

4.2.1.3 Brain functioning deficits

There is now a good deal of converging evidence from autopsy studies, fMRI studies and studies measuring EEG (electroencephalogram) and ERP (event-related potentials) that autism is associated with aberrant brain development. Autopsy studies of individuals diagnosed with autistic spectrum disorder have revealed abnormalities in a number of brain areas, including the limbic system and the cerebellum. For example, neurons in the limbic system are smaller and more dense than normal, and the dendrites that transmit messages from one neurone to another are shorter and less well developed (Bauman & Kemper, 1994). Abnormalities in the cerebellum appear to correspond to deficits in motor skills such as impaired balance, manual dexterity and grip, often found in individuals with autistic spectrum disorder (Gowen & Miall, 2005). Finally, autopsy studies have also shown overly large brain size and enlarged ventricles in the brain (Bailey *et al.*, 1998), and many of these abnormalities are typical of pre-natal stages of brain development.

Anatomical and functional imaging studies have supplemented the evidence from autopsy studies and given us an insight into how brain abnormalities in autism progress during different developmental stages. They have confirmed that individuals with autism have abnormalities in a number of brain regions, including the frontal lobes, limbic system, cerebellum and basal ganglia (Sokol & Edwards-Brown, 2004), and they also confirm that autistic individuals have larger brain size and significantly poorer neural connectivity than nonsufferers (McAlonan *et al.*, 2005).

Taken together, these sources of evidence indicate that individuals with autistic spectrum disorder exhibit abnormalities in a number of different brain areas. These brain areas exhibit both anatomical (i.e. structural) abnormalities and functional abnormalities (i.e. they do not appear to be able to fulfil the cognitive functions they do in normally developed individuals). These abnormalities appear to be determined by a period of abnormal brain overgrowth in the first two years of life (hence studies showing that autistic individuals develop oversize brains), followed by abnormally slow or arrested growth, and this deviant brain growth occurs at a time during development when the formation of brain circuitry is at its most vulnerable (Couchesne, 2004).

4.2.2   Cognitive Factors

Depending on the severity of their symptoms, individuals with autistic spectrum disorder clearly have problems attending to and understanding the world around them. Most notably, they have difficulty with normal social functioning. In severe cases they may be withdrawn and unresponsive, while less severe cases may exhibit difficulty in reciprocal social interaction, including deficits in communication and in understanding the intentions and emotions of others.

Some theorists have argued that these deficits in social skills are a result of deficits in cognitive functioning (Rutter *et al.*, 1994). First, individuals with autistic spectrum disorder appear to exhibit deficits in **executive functioning**, and this means that they have poor problem-solving ability, difficulty in planning actions and controlling impulses and attention, and in inhibiting inappropriate behaviour, and these deficits all have an impact on the ability to act appropriately in social situations. Second, some theorists have argued that individuals with autistic spectrum disorder lack a '**theory of mind**' (**TOM**). That is, they fail to comprehend normal mental states, and so are unable to understand or predict the intentions of others. Finally, the **empathising-systematising theory** has been developed to help explain some of the nonsocial features of autism such as the narrow interests, need for sameness and attention to detail displayed in the behaviour of individuals with autistic spectrum disorder.

executive functioning processes that are involved in planning and attentional control.

theory of mind the ability to understand one's own and other people's mental states.

empathising-systematising theory particularly relevant to autism spectrum disorder, this theory seeks to classify people on the basis of their skills in two factors – empathising and systemising.

4.2.2.1   Deficits in executive functioning

Individuals with autistic spectrum disorder generally perform poorly on tests of executive functioning, suggesting that they may have difficulty effectively problem solving, planning, initiating, organising, monitoring and inhibiting complex behaviours (Ozonoff & McEvoy,

1994; Shu *et al.*, 2001). Consistent evidence for executive functioning deficits has been found in adults, adolescents and older children with autism (McEvoy, Rogers & Pennington, 1993). However, determining the significance of poor performance on tests of executive functioning is difficult, because executive functioning tasks require the integration of a range of more basic cognitive abilities, such as shifting attention, memory, sequencing events and inhibiting responses.

Nevertheless, even when the basic cognitive processes required for successful executive functioning are analysed separately, individuals with autistic spectrum disorder exhibit deficits in a number of these skills, including categorisation and concept formation (Minshew, Meyer & Goldstein, 2002), shifting attention (Akshoomoff, Courchesne & Townsend, 1997; Belmonte, 2000), planning and abstract problem solving (Hill & Bird, 2006) and short-term and long-term memory (Bachevalier, 1994; Klinger & Dawson, 1996). However, evidence suggests that they fail to exhibit deficits in cognitive inhibition (inhibiting inappropriate responses; Kleinhans, Akshoomoff & Delis, 2005; Ozonoff & Strayer, 1997) or in tests of semantic fluency (Boucher, 1988; Manjiviona & Prior, 1999). Thus, depending on the degree of severity of the disorder, individuals with autistic spectrum disorder may only be deficient in some of the basic cognitive skills required to complete executive function tasks successfully, and not in others.

4.2.2.2   Theory-of-mind deficits

One influential account of autistic spectrum disorder claims that the fundamental problem for individuals with autism is that they fail to develop a 'theory of mind' (Baron-Cohen, 2001; Baron-Cohen, Leslie & Frith, 1985). That is, individuals with autism fail to develop an awareness that the behaviour of other people is based on mental states that include beliefs and intentions about what they should do and, as a result, individuals with autism fail to understand the intentions of others. There are a number of ways to test whether a child has developed a 'theory of mind'. One traditional method is known as the **Sally-Anne false belief task** (Baron-Cohen, Leslie & Frith, 1985), described more fully in Research Methods Box 4.2.

Sally-Anne false belief task a method used to test whether a child has developed a 'theory of mind'.

Even adults with high functioning autism (such as **Asperger's syndrome**) also exhibit theory-of-mind deficits on some measures. For example, many of the traditional tests of theory of mind are rather static and somewhat removed from the dynamic situations that an individual with autism will experience in real life. To make such tests more

Asperger's syndrome severe and sustained impairment in social interaction and the development of restricted, repetitive patterns of behaviour, interests and activities.

RESEARCH METHODS BOX 4.2

The Sally-Anne False Belief Task

How can we measure whether someone can understand the intentions of others? Baron-Cohen, Leslie and Frith (1985) designed an imaginative procedure that has been used many times to assess theory of mind abilities in a range of clinical populations. This is known as the *Sally-Anne False Beliefs Task*. In this procedure two dolls are used to act out the story shown above, and at the end children are asked 'Where will Sally look for her marble?' Children who have developed a theory of mind will say that when Sally comes back from her walk she will look in the basket for her marble because they will understand that she has not seen Anne move it. Children who are unable to understand that others have different beliefs from themselves will say that Sally will look in the box because that is where they themselves know it is.

Baron-Cohen, Leslie and Frith (1985) conducted this test with three groups of children, all with a mental age of over 3 years. One group was diagnosed with autistic disorder, one with Down syndrome, and the third group consisted of normally developing children. Most of the children with autism answered incorrectly (saying Sally would look in the box) while most of the children in the other two groups gave the right answer (saying Sally would look in the basket). The inclusion in the study of a group of children with Down syndrome showed that the failure on this task of children with autism could not be attributed to their learning difficulties more generally. In addition all children correctly answered two control questions 'Where is the marble really?' and 'Where was the marble in the beginning?' demonstrating understanding of the change in the physical location of the marble during the story. (From Frith, 2003)

This is Sally. This is Anne.
Sally has a basket. Anne has a box.

Sally has a marble. She puts the marble into her basket.

Sally goes out for a walk.

Anne takes the marble out of the basket and puts it into the box.

Now Sally comes back. She wants to play with her marble.

Where will Sally look for her marble?

akin to everyday experiences, Heavey *et al.* (2000) devised the Awkward Moments Test, in which participants view a series of television commercials and then are asked questions about the events in each. Individuals with Asperger's syndrome were significantly less able to answer questions about the mental state of the characters in the commercials than an age- and gender-matched control group without autism. However, the two groups did not differ on scores on questions related to recall of events within the television clips (a memory test), suggesting that the poorer scores on mental state questions by Asperger's syndrome participants were not simply due to a memory deficit. Because of these difficulties in understanding the mental states of others, individuals with autistic spectrum disorder will undoubtedly have difficulty indulging in symbolic play with others, actively participating in human interactions and forming lasting relationships.

4.2.2.3 The empathising-systematising theory

More recently, some researchers have argued that theory-of-mind deficits may help to explain many of the social and communication difficulties experienced by individuals with autistic spectrum disorder, but such deficits do not easily explain the nonsocial features of behaviour, such as narrow interests, need for sameness and attention to detail. Baron-Cohen (2002, 2009) has argued that theory-of-mind deficits only address the difficulties that people with autism experience and do not address their areas of strength. He suggests that individuals with autistic spectrum disorder may even have superior skills in *systematising* – that is, analysing or constructing systems to understand the world – and they do this by noting regularities, structures and rules within systems. This leads such individuals to focus on fully understanding individual systems, such as collectible systems (e.g. distinguishing between types of stones), mechanical systems (e.g. a video-recorder), numerical systems (e.g. a train timetable), abstract systems (e.g. the syntax of a language) and motoric systems (e.g. bouncing on a trampoline) (Baron-Cohen, 2009). This is a helpful way of explaining the narrow interests, repetitive behaviour and resistance to change/need for sameness found in autistic spectrum disorder. It is this desire to systematise that differentiates autism from other psychopathologies that also exhibit theory-of-mind deficits (e.g. schizophrenia, borderline personality disorder, conduct disorder) (Corcoran & Frith, 1997; Dodge, 1993; Fonagy, 1989). The empathising-systematising theory also helps to explain the inability to 'generalise' in autistic spectrum disorders (Wing, 1997). Baron-Cohen (2009) provides the following example:

> The typical clinical example is a teacher who teaches a child with autism to perform a task in one setting (e.g. taking

PHOTO 4.2 *Constructing Systems to Understand the World.*

Individuals with autistic spectrum disorder or Asperger's syndrome may have superior skills in systematising – that is, analysing or constructing systems to understand the world – and they do this by noting regularities, structures and rules within systems. This leads such individuals to develop relatively narrow interests and focus on fully understanding individual systems, such as collecting train numbers.

a shower at home) but has to reteach it in a new setting (e.g. taking a shower at school). Consider though that if the child is treating the situation as a system, the unique features of each (e.g. how the shower at home differs to the shower at school in the detail of their temperature control functions or the angle and height of the shower-head) may be more salient than their shared features (e.g. that both require getting in, turning the shower on, turning it off, and getting out). (Baron-Cohen, 2009, pp. 72–3)

4.2.3 Summary of Research on Autistic Spectrum Disorder

This section on research into the aetiology of autistic spectrum disorder has revealed a range of factors that can influence the development of autistic symptoms. On the biological side these include a genetic or inherited component, some potential peri-natal factors and brain-functioning abnormalities, which may give rise to the characteristic social, cognitive and behavioural deficits found in autism. In addition, psychological factors include executive functioning and theory-of-mind deficits, which help to explain the social and communication deficits found in autism, and the empathising-systematising theory, which points to a desire to systematise the world that helps to explain the narrow interests, repetitive behaviour and resistance to change/need for sameness found in autistic spectrum disorder.

SELF-TEST QUESTIONS

- What is the diathesis-stress perspective that is used to explain the aetiology of psychotic symptoms?
- Concordance studies, twin studies and adoption studies are used to determine the extent of genetic factors in psychosis. Can you give examples of these types of method?
- What are genetic linkage analyses and how are they used to identify the specific genes through which the risk for psychosis may be transmitted?
- What is the dopamine hypothesis and how did the role of dopamine in psychosis come to be discovered?
- A number of cognitive biases have been implicated in the development of some psychotic symptoms. What are these biases and how might they contribute to factors such as delusional thinking?
- What are (i) expressed emotion and (ii) communication deviance, and what is the evidence that they constitute a risk factor for the development of psychotic symptoms?
- What is the evidence for autistic spectrum disorder being an inherited disorder?
- What peri-natal factors might contribute to autistic symptoms?
- What kinds of study have contributed to our understanding of brain abnormalities in autistic spectrum disorder?
- What cognitive deficits have individuals with autistic spectrum disorder been shown to have?

ESSAY QUESTIONS

- How can delusions and hallucinations be understood psychologically?
- What is the diathesis-stress perspective that is used to explain the aetiology of psychotic symptoms?
- What is the dopamine hypothesis and how did the role of dopamine in psychosis come to be discovered?
- Describe the triad of impairments typical of Autistic Spectrum Disorder and how the impairments may present and affect a person's life throughout the life span.
- Describe and evaluate the evidence for autistic spectrum disorder being an inherited disorder.

TEXTS FOR FURTHER READING

Bentall, R.P. (2003) *Madness Explained: Psychosis and Human Nature*, London: Allen Lane.

Bentall, R.P. (ed.) (2004) *Models of Madness: Psychological, Social and Biological Approaches to Schizophrenia*, Hove: Brunner-Routledge.

Green, M.F. (2001) *Schizophrenia Revealed: From Neurons to Social Interactions*, New York: W.W. Norton.

Hirsch, S.R. & Weinberger, D.R. (2003) *Schizophrenia*, Oxford: Blackwell Science.

Volkmar, F.R., Paul, R., Klin, A. & Chen, D.J. (eds) (2005) *Handbook of Autism and Pervasive Developmental Disorders: Diagnosis, Development, Neurobiology, and Behavior: 1,* Chichester: John Wiley & Sons Ltd.

Volkmar, F.R., Paul, R., Klin, A. & Chen, D.J. (eds) (2005) *Handbook of Autism and Pervasive Developmental Disorders: Assessment, Interventions, and Policy: 2,* Chichester: John Wiley & Sons Ltd.

Wing, L. (2003) *The Autistic Spectrum: A Guide for Parents and Professionals*, London: Constable and Robinson.

RELEVANT JOURNAL ARTICLES

Baron-Cohen, S. (2009) Autism: The empathizing-systematizing theory, *The Year in Cognitive Neuroscience* 1156: 68–80.

Bentall, R.P., Corcoran, R., Howard, R., Blackwood, N. & Kinderman, P. (2001) Persecutory delusions: A review and theoretical integration, *Clinical Psychology Review* 21: 1143–92.

Fergusson, D.M., Horwood, L.J. & Ridder, E.M. (2005) Tests of a causal linkage between cannabis use and psychotic symptoms, *Addiction* 100: 354–66.

Freeman, D. (2007) Suspicious minds: The psychology of persecutory delusions, *Clinical Psychology Review* 27: 425–57.

Harrison, P.J. & Owen, M.J. (2003) Genes for schizophrenia? Recent findings and their pathophysiological implications, *The Lancet* 361: 417–19.

Wahlberg, K.-E., Wynne, L.C., Keskitalo, P. *et al.* (2001) Long-term stability of communication deviance, *Journal of Abnormal Psychology* 110: 443–8.

Wearden, A.J., Tarrier, N. & Barrowclough, C. (2000) A review of expressed emotion research in health care, *Clinical Psychology Review* 20: 633–66.

REFERENCES

Akshoomoff, N.A., Courchesne, E. & Townsend, J. (1997) Attention coordination and anticipatory control, *International Review of Neurobiology* 41: 575–98.

Andreason, N.C. (2001) *Brave New Brain: Conquering Mental Illness in the Era of the Genome*, New York: Oxford University Press.

Andreasson, S., Allebeck, P., Engstrom, A. & Ryberg, U. (1987) Cannabis and schizophrenia: A longitudinal study of Swedish conscripts, *The Lancet* ii: 1483–6.

Angrist, B., Lee, H.K. & Gershons, S. (1974) Antagonism of amphetamine induced symptomatology by a neuroleptic, *American Journal of Psychiatry* 131(7): 817–19.

Arseneault, L., Cannon, M., Witton, J. & Murray, R.M. (2004) Causal association between cannabis and psychosis: Examination of the evidence, *British Journal of Psychiatry* 184: 110–17.

Bachevalier, J. (1994) Medial temporal lobe structures and autism: A review of clinical and experimental findings, *Neuropsychologia* 32(6): 627–48.

Badner, J.A. & Gershon, E.S. (2002) Meta-analysis of whole-genome linkage scans of bipolar disorder and schizophrenia, *Molecular Psychiatry* 7(4): 405–11.

Bailey, A., Lecouteur, A., Gottesman, I. *et al.* (1995) Autism as a strongly genetic disorder – evidence from a British twin study, *Psychological Medicines* 25(1): 63–77.

Bailey, A., Luthert, P., Dean, A. *et al.* (1998) A clinicopathological study of autism, *Brain* 121: 889–905.

Bailey, A., Phillips, W. & Rutter, M. (1996) Autism: Towards an integration of clinical, genetic, neuropsychological, and neurobiological perspectives, *Journal of Child Psychology and Psychiatry and Allied Disciplines* 37(1): 89–126.

Baron-Cohen, S. (2001) Theory of mind and autism: A review, in L.M. Gliddon (ed.) *International Review of Research in Mental Retardation*, Vol. 23, San Diego, CA: Academic.

Baron-Cohen, S. (2002) The extreme male brain theory of autism, *Trends in Cognitive Science* 6: 248–54.

Baron-Cohen, S. (2009) Autism: The empathizing-systematizing theory, *The Year in Cognitive Neuroscience* 1156: 68–80.

Baron-Cohen, S., Leslie, A. & Frith, U. (1985) Does the autistic child have a theory of mind? *Cognition* 21: 37–46.

Barrowclough, C., Johnston, M. & Tarrier, N. (1994) Attributions, expressed emotions, and patients' relapse – an attributional model of relatives' response to schizophrenic illness, *Behavior Therapy* 25(1): 67–88.

Bauman, M.L. & Kemper, T.L. (1994) Neuroanatomic observations of the brain in autism, in L. Bauman & T.L. Kemper (eds) *The Neurobiology of Autism*, Baltimore, MD: John Hopkins University Press.

Belmonte, M. (2000) Abnormal attention in autism shown by steady-state visual evoked potentials, *Autism* 4: 269–85.

Bentall, R.P. (1994) Cognitive biases and abnormal beliefs: Towards a model of persecutory delusions, in A.S. David & J. Cutting (eds) *The Neuropsychology of Schizophrenia*, London: Lawrence Erlbaum.

Bentall, R.P. & Kinderman, P. (1998) Psychological processes and delusional beliefs: Implications for the treatment of paranoid states, in S. Lewis, N. Tarrier & T. Wykes (eds) *Outcome and Innovation in Psychological Treatment of Schizophrenia*, Chichester: John Wiley & Sons Ltd.

Bentall, R.P. & Kinderman, P. (1999) Self-regulation, affect and psychosis: Social cognition in paranoia and mania, in T. Dalgleish & M. Power (eds) *Handbook of Cognition and Emotion*, London: John Wiley & Sons Ltd.

Bentall, R.P., Kaney, S. & Dewey, M.E. (1991) Paranoia and social reasoning – an attribution theory analysis, *British Journal of Clinical Psychology* 30: 13–23.

Bentall, R.P., Corcoran, R., Howard, R., Blackwood, N. & Kinderman, P. (2001) Persecutory delusions: A review and theoretical integration, *Clinical Psychology Review* 21: 1143–92.

Boucher, J. (1988) Word fluency in high-functioning autistic children, *Journal of Autism & Developmental Disorders* 18: 637–45.

Brown, A. (2008) Autistic spectrum disorders, in G.C.L. Davey (ed.) *Clinical Psychology*, Oxford: Hodder HE.

Brown, G.W., Carstairs, G.M. & Topping, G. (1958) Post-hospital adjustment of chronic mental patients, *The Lancet* 2(Sept. 27): 685–9.

Byrne, M., Agerbo, E., Eaton, W.W. & Mortensen, P.B. (2004) Parental socio-economic status and risk of first admission with schizophrenia – a Danish national register based study, *Social Psychiatry and Psychiatric Epidemiology* 39(2): 87–96.

Cardno, A.G., Marshall, E.J., Coid, B. *et al.* (1999) Heritability estimates for psychotic disorders – The Maudsley twin psychosis series, *Archives of General Psychiatry* 56(2): 162–8.

Carlsson, A. (2001) A half-century of neurotransmitter research: Impact on neurology and psychiatry (Nobel lecture), *Chembiochem* 2(7–8): 484.

Chess, S., Fernandez, P. & Korn, S. (1978) Behavioral consequences of congenital rubella, *Journal of Pediatrics* 93: 699–703.

Cohen, R.M., Semple, W.E., Gross, M. *et al.* (1988) The effect of neuroleptics on dysfunction in a prefrontal substrate of sustained attention in schizophrenia, *Life Sciences* 43(14): 1141–50.

Collins, F.S. & McKusick, V.A. (2001) Implications of the human genome project for medical science, *Journal of the American Medical Association* 285: 540–44.

Corcoran, R. & Frith, C. (1997) Conversational conduct and the symptoms of schizophrenia, *Cognitive Neuropsychiatry* 1: 305–18.

Cornblatt, B.A., Lenzenweger, M.F., Dworkin, R.H. & Kimling, L.E. (1985) Positive and negative schizophrenic symptoms, attention, and information-processing, *Schizophrenia Bulletin* 11(3): 397–408.

Courchesne, E. (2004) Abnormal brain development in autism spectrum disorder, *Biological Psychiatry* 55: 47S–163.Davey, G.C.L. (2008) *Clinical Psychology*, Oxford: Hodder Arnold.

Davis, J.O. & Phelps, J.A. (1995) Twins with schizophrenia – genes or germs, *Schizophrenia Bulletin* 21(1): 13–18.

Degenhardt, L. & Hall, W. (2001) The association between psychosis and problematic drug use among Australian adults: Findings from the National Survey of Mental Health & Well-Being, *Psychological Medicine* 31: 659–68.

Dodge, K.A. (1993) Social-cognitive mechanisms in the development of conduct disorder and depression, *Annual Review of Psychology* 44: 559–84.

Faustman, W.O. (1995) What causes schizophrenia?, in S. Vinogradov (ed.) *Treating Schizophrenia*, San Francisco: Jossey-Bass.

Fergusson, D.M., Horwood, L.J. & Ridder, E.M. (2005) Tests of causal linkages between cannabis use and psychotic symptoms, *Addiction* 100(3): 354–66.

Fergusson, D.M., Horwood, L.J. & Swain-Campbell, N.R. (2003) Cannabis dependence and psychotic symptoms in young people, *Psychological Medicine* 33(1): 15–21.

Folstein, S. & Rutter, M. (1977) Infantile-autism – genetic study of 21 twin pairs, *Journal of Child Psychology and Psychiatry and Allied Disciplines* 18(4): 297–321.

Folstein, S.E. & Rutter M.L. (1988) Autism – familial aggregation and genetic-implications, *Journal of Autism and Developmental Disorders* 18(1): 3–30.

Fombonne, E. (1999) Are measles infections or measles immunizations linked to autism?, *Journal of Autism and Developmental Disorders* 29(4): 349–50.

Fonagy, P. (1989) On tolerating mental states: Theory of mind in borderline personality, *Bulletin of Anna Freud Centre* 12: 91–115.

Freeman, D. (2007) Suspicious minds: The psychology of persecutory delusions, *Clinical Psychology Review* 27: 425–57.

Freeman, D., Garety, P.A., Fowler, D. *et al.* (2004) Why do people with delusions fail to choose more realistic explanations for their experiences? An empirical investigation, *Journal of Consulting and Clinical Psychology* 72(4): 671–80.

Freeman, D., Garety, P.A. & Kuipers, E. (2001) Persecutory delusions: Developing the understanding of belief maintenance and emotional distress, *Psychological Medicine* 31(7): 1293–306.

Freeman, D., Garety, P.A., Kuipers, E., Fowler, D. & Bebbington, P.E. (2002) A cognitive model of persecutory delusions, *British Journal of Clinical Psychology* 41: 331–47.

Freeman, D., Garety, P.A., Kuipers, E. *et al.* (2006) Delusions and decision-making style: Use of the Need for Closure Scale, *Behaviour Research & Therapy* 44: 1147–58.

Frith, C.D. (2003) *Autism: Explaining the Enigma*, 2nd edn, Oxford: Blackwell.

Goldsmith, S.K., Shapiro, R.M. & Joyce, J.N. (1997) Disrupted pattern of D-2 dopamine receptors in the temporal lobe in schizophrenia – a postmortem study, *Archives of General Psychiatry* 54(7): 649–58.

Gorenstein, E.E. & Comer, R.J. (2004) *Case Studies in Abnormal Psychology*, 4th edn, New York: Worth.

Gottesman, I.I. & Bertelsen, A. (1989) Confirming unexpressed genotypes for schizophrenia – risks in the offspring of Fischers Danish identical and fraternal discordant twins, *Archives of General Psychiatry* 46(10): 867–72.

Gottesman, I.I., McGuffin, P. & Farmer, A.E. (1987) Clinical genetics as clues to the real genetics of schizophrenia (a decade of modest gains while playing for time), *Schizophrenia Bulletin* 13(1): 23–47.

Gowen, E. & Miall, R.C. (2005) Behavioural aspects of cerebellar function in adults with Asperger syndrome, *Cerebellum* 4(4): 279–89.

Guggenheim, F.G. & Babigian, H.M. (1974) Catatonic schizophrenia - epidemiology and clinical course – 7-year register study of 798 cases, *Journal of Nervous and Mental Disease* 158(4): 291–305.

Harrison, P.J. & Owen, M.J. (2003) Genes for schizophrenia? Recent findings and their pathophysiological implications, *The Lancet* 361: 417–19.

Heavey, L., Phillips, W., Baron-Cohen, S. & Rutter, M. (2000) The Awkward Moments Test: A naturalistic measure of social understanding in autism, *Journal of Autism and Developmental Disorders* 30(3): 225–36.

Henquet, C., Krabbendam, L., Spauwen, J. *et al.* (2005) Prospective cohort study of cannabis use, predisposition for psychosis, and psychotic symptoms in young people, *British Medical Journal* 330(7481): 11–14.

Heston, L.L. (1966) Psychiatric disorders in foster home reared children of schizophrenic mothers, *British Journal of Psychiatry* 112(489): 819.

Hill, E.L. & Bird, C.A. (2006) Executive processes in Asperger syndrome: Patterns of performance in a multiple case series, *Neuropsychologia* 44(14): 2822–35.

Hjern, A., Wicks, S. & Dalman, C. (2004) Social adversity contributes to high morbidity in psychoses in immigrants – a national cohort study in two generations of Swedish residents, *Psychological Medicine* 34(6): 1025–33.

Hogarty, G.E., Anderson, C.M., Reiss, D.J. *et al.* (1986) Family psychoeducation, social skills training, and maintenance chemotherapy in the aftercare treatment of schizophrenia, 1. One-year effects of a controlled-study on relapse and expressed emotion, *Archives of General Psychiatry* 43(7): 633–42.

Joober, R., Boksa, P., Benkelfat, C. & Rouleau, G. (2002) Genetics of schizophrenia: From animal models to clinical studies, *Journal of Psychiatry & Neuroscience* 27(5): 336–47.

Jorde, L.B., Masonbrothers, A., Waldmann, R. *et al.* (1990) The UCLA University-of-Utah Epidemiologic Survey of Autism – genealogical analysis of familial aggregation, *American Journal of Medical Genetics* 36(1): 85–8.

Kaney, S. & Bentall, R.P. (1989) Persecutory delusions and attributional style, *British Journal of Medical Psychology* 62: 191–8.

Kapur, S. & Seeman, P. (2001) Does fast dissociation from the dopamine d2 receptor explain the action of atypical antipsychotics? A new hypothesis, *American Journal of Psychiatry* 158: 360–69.

Kavanagh, D.J. (1992) Recent developments in expressed emotion and schizophrenia, *British Journal of Psychiatry* 160: 601–20.

Kendler, K.S., Myers, J.M., O'Neill, F.A. *et al.* (2000) Clinical features of schizophrenia and linkage to chromosomes 5q, 6p, 8p, and 10p in the Irish study of high-density schizophrenia families, *American Journal of Psychiatry* 157(3): 402–8.

Kety, S.S. (1988) Schizophrenic illness in the families of schizophrenic adoptees – findings from the Danish National Sample, *Schizophrenia Bulletin* 14(2): 217–22.

Kety, S.S., Wender, P.H., Jacobsen, B. *et al.* (1994) Mental-illness in the biological and adoptive relatives of schizophrenic adoptees – replication of the Copenhagen Study in the rest of Denmark, *Archives of General Psychiatry* 51(6): 442–55.

Khantzian, E.J. (1985) The self-medication hypothesis of addictive disorders – focus on heroin and cocaine dependence, *American Journal of Psychiatry* 142(11): 1259–64.

Kleinhans, N., Akshoomoff, N. & Delis, D.C. (2005) Executive functions in autism and Asperger's disorder: Flexibility, fluency, and inhibition, *Developmental Neuropsychology* 27(3): 379–401.

Klinger, L.G. & Dawson, G. (1996) Autistic disorder, in E.J. Marsh & R.A. Barkley (eds) *Child Psychopathology*, New York: Guilford Press.

Levinson, D.F., Lewis, C.M. & Wise, L.H. (2002) Meta-analysis of genome scans for schizophrenia, *American Journal of Medical Genetics* 114(7): SL2.

Madsen, K.M., Hviid, A., Vestergaard, M. *et al.* (2002) A population-based study of measles, mumps and rubella vaccination and autism, *New England Journal of Medicine* 347: 1477–82.

Manjiviona, J. & Prior, M. (1999) Neuropsychological profiles of children with Asperger's syndrome and autism, *Autism* 3: 327–56.

McAlonan, G.M., Cheung, V., Cheung, C. *et al.* (2005) Mapping the brain in autism. A voxel-based MRI study of volumetric differences and intercorrelations in autism, *Brain* 128: 268–76.

McEvoy, R.E., Rogers, S.J. & Pennington, B.F. (1993) Executive function and social communication deficits in young autistic-children, *Journal of Child Psychology and Psychiatry and Allied Disciplines* 34(4): 563–78.

Minshew, N.J., Meyer, J. & Goldstein, G. (2002) Abstract reasoning in autism: A dissociation between concept formation and concept identification, *Neuropsychology* 16(3): 327–34.

Modrow, J. (1992) *How to Become a Schizophrenic: The Case against Biological Psychiatry*, Everett, WA: Apollyon Press.

Muhle, R., Trentacoste, S.V. & Rapin, I. (2004) The genetics of autism, *Pediatrics* 113(5): E472–E486.

Olbrich, R., Kirsch, P., Pfeiffer, H. & Mussgay, L. (2001) Patterns of recovery of autonomic dysfunctions and neurocognitive deficits in schizophrenics after acute psychotic episodes, *Journal of Abnormal Psychology* 110(1): 142–50.

Ozonoff, S. & McEvoy, R.E. (1994) A longitudinal-study of executive function and theory of mind development in autism, *Development and Psychopathology* 6(3): 415–31.

Ozonoff, S. & Strayer, D.L. (1997) Inhibitory function in nonretarded children with autism, *Journal of Autism and Developmental Disorders* 27(1): 59–77.

Piven, J. & Palmer, P. (1999) Psychiatric disorder and the broad autism phenotype: Evidence from a family study of multiple-incidence autism families, *American Journal of Psychiatry* 156(4): 557–63.

Reiss, A.L. & Freund, L. (1990) Fragile X syndrome, DSM-III-R, and autism, *Journal of the American Academy of Child and Adolescent Psychiatry* 29(6): 885–91.

Ronald, A., Happe, F., Price, T.S., Baron-Cohen, S. & Plomin, R. (2006) Phenotypic and genetic overlap between autistic traits at the extremes of the general population, *Journal of the American Academy of Child and Adolescent Psychiatry* 45(10): 1206–14.

Rosen, N.J., Yoshida, C.K. & Croen, L.A. (2007) Infection in the first 2 years of life and autism, *Pediatrics* 119: E61–U18.

Rutter, M., Bailey, A., Bolton, P. & Lecouteur, A. (1994) Autism and known medical conditions – myth and substance, *Journal of Child Psychology and Psychiatry and Allied Disciplines* 35(2): 311–22.

Rutter, M., Macdonald, H., Lecouteur, A. *et al.* (1990) Genetic-factors in child psychiatric-disorders, 2. Empirical-findings, *Journal of Child Psychology and Psychiatry and Allied Disciplines* 31(1): 39–83.

Santangelo, S.L. & Tsatsanis, K. (2005) What is known about autism – genes, brain and behaviour, *American Journal of Pharmacogenomics* 5: 71–92.

Schneider, F. & Deldin, P.J. (2001) Genetics and schizophrenia, in P.B. Sutker & H.E. Adams (eds) *Comprehensive Handbook of Psychopathology*, 3rd edn, New York: Kluwer Academic/Plenum.

Shu, B.C., Lung, F.W., Tien, A.Y. & Chen, B.C. (2001) Executive function deficits in non-retarded autistic children, *Autism* 5(2): 165–74.

Smalley, S.L. (1998) Autism and tuberous sclerosis, *Journal of Autism and Developmental Disorders* 28(5): 407–14.

Smart, R. & Ogbourne, A. (2000) Drug use and drinking among students in 36 countries, *Addicitve Behavior* 25: 455–60.

Sokol, D.K. & Edwards-Brown, M. (2004) Neuroimaging in autistic spectrum disorder (ASD), *Journal of Neuroimaging* 14(1): 8–15.

Steffenburg, S., Gillberg, C., Hellgren, L. *et al.* (1989) A twin study of autism in Denmark, Finland, Iceland, Norway and Sweden, *Journal of Child Psychology and Psychiatry and Allied Disciplines* 30(3): 405–16.

Stromland, K., Nordin, V., Miller, M., Akerstrom, B. & Gillberg, C. (1994) Autism in thalidomide embryopathy – a population study, *Developmental Medicine and Child Neurology* 36(4): 351–6.

Tanda, G., Pontieri, F.E. & DiChiara, G. (1997) Cannabinoid and heroin activation of mesolimbic dopamine transmission by a common mu 1 opioid receptor mechanism, *Science* 276(5321): 2048–50.

Tarrier, N., Barrowclough, C., Vaughn, C. *et al.* (1988) The community management of schizophrenia – a controlled trial of a behavioral intervention with families to reduce relapse, *British Journal of Psychiatry* 153: 532 42.

Tsai, L.Y. (1987) Pre-, peri- and neonatal factors in autism, in D.E. Berkell (ed.) *Autism: Identification, Education and Treatment*, Hillsdale, NJ: Erlbaum.

Tsai, L.Y. & Ghaziuddin, M. (1997) Autistic disorder, in J.M. Weerner (ed.) *Textbook of Child and Adolescent Psychiatry*, Washington, DC: American Psychiatric Association.

Turner, R.J. & Wagonfeld, M.O. (1967) Occupational mobility and schizophrenia, *American Sociological Review* 32: 104–13.

Verdoux, H., Gindre, C., Sorbara, F., Tournier, M. & Swendsen, J.D. (2003) Effects of cannabis and psychosis vulnerability in daily life: An experience sampling test study, *Psychological Medicine* 33(1): 23–32.

Wahlberg, K.E., Wynne, L.C., Hakko, H. *et al.* (2004) Interaction of genetic risk and adoptive parent communication deviance: Longitudinal prediction of adoptee psychiatric disorders, *Psychological Medicine* 34(8): 1531–41.

Wahlberg, K.E., Wynne, L.C., Keskitalo, P. *et al.* (2001) Long-term stability of communication deviance, *Journal of Abnormal Psychology* 110: 443–8.

Wakefield, A.J., Murch, S.H., Anthony, A. *et al.* (1998) Ileo-colonic lymphonodular hyperplasia, non-specific colitis and autistic spectrum disorder in children: A new syndrome?, *Gastroenterology* 114(4): A430–G1753.

Weisman, A.G., Nuechterlein, K.H., Goldstein, M.J. & Snyder, K.S. (2000) Controllability perceptions and reactions to symptoms of schizophrenia: A within-family comparison of relatives with high and low expressed emotion, *Journal of Abnormal Psychology* 109(1): 167–71.

Wielgus, M.S. & Harvey, P.D. (1988) Dichotic listening and recall in schizophrenia and mania, *Schizophrenia Bulletin* 14: 689–700.

Williams, G., King, J., Cunningham, M. *et al.* (2001) Fetal valproate syndrome and autism: Additional evidence of an association, *Developmental Medicine and Child Neurology* 43(3): 202–6.

Wing, L. (1997) *The Autistic Spectrum*, Oxford: Blackwell.

Wylie, A.S., Scott, R.T.A. & Burnett, S.J. (1995) Psychosis due to skunk, *British Medical Journal* 311(6997): 125.

5 The Causes of Mental Health Problems: Anxiety and Mood Disorders

GRAHAM DAVEY

LEARNING OUTCOMES

WHEN YOU HAVE COMPLETED THIS CHAPTER, YOU SHOULD BE ABLE TO:

1. Describe, evaluate and compare the main biological and psychological models of anxiety symptoms such as panic attacks, chronic worrying, and pervasive intrusive thoughts.

2. Compare and contrast biological and cognitive theories of the causes of depression.

3. Describe and evaluate how theories couched in biological and cognitive terms attempt to understand mental health problems at different levels of explanation.

KEY WORDS

Anxiety Disorders • Anxiety Sensitivity • Attribution Theories of Depression • Battered Woman Syndrome • Biological Challenge Tests • Catastrophic Misinterpretation of Bodily Sensations • Hopelessness • Hyperventilation • Increased Access to Psychological Therapies (IAPT) • Inflated Responsibility • Information Processing Biases • Intolerance of Uncertainty • Intrusive Thoughts • Learned Helplessness • Monoamine Oxidase (MAO) Inhibitors • Negative Schema • Negative Triad • Norepinephrine • Panic Attack • Perfectionism • Pessimistic Thinking • Selective Serotonin Reuptake Inhibitors (SSRIs) • Serotonin • Suffocation Alarm Theories • Thought Suppression • Thought–Action Fusion • Tricyclic Drugs • Worry

CHAPTER OUTLINE

6 Clinical Psychology: Training and Development

FERGAL JONES

LEARNING OUTCOMES

WHEN YOU HAVE COMPLETED THIS CHAPTER, YOU SHOULD BE ABLE TO:

1. Describe some of the key stages and choices in the training and career development of clinical psychologists.

2. Provide an overview of the main competencies needed by clinical psychologists, and how these are developed in training.

3. Have some sense of how these competencies relate to clinical practice.

KEY WORDS

Assessment • British Psychological Society (BPS) • Cognitive-Behavioural • Competencies • Consultant Clinical Psychologist • Continuing Professional Development (CPD) • Evaluation • Formulation • Graduate Basis for Chartered Membership (GBC) • Intervention • Psychodynamic • Reflective Practitioner • Research • Scientist-Practitioner • Social Constructionist • Systemic

CHAPTER OUTLINE

TABLE 6.2 *Frequently Asked Questions about a Career in Clinical Psychology.*

What income can I expect while I am training?	Usually starting from £25 472 (for 2010)
What salary can I expect when I am fully trained?	Usually starting from £30 460 within the NHS (for 2010)
What job opportunities are there?	The majority of clinical psychologists are employed within the NHS. Some may work in academia or privately.
What unique skills will I learn?	A wide range of skills, e.g. skills in assessment, formulation, intervention and evaluation, and research skills.
What qualifications and experience should I have prior to training?	A good undergraduate degree that confers graduate basis for chartered membership (GBC) with the BPS, and clinical or clinically related experience. Some applicants will have relevant higher degrees and/or further research experience.
What further training and development can I do once I have qualified?	Once qualified it is expected that clinical psychologists will receive ongoing supervision from a more experienced colleague and undertake continuing professional development (CPD). Sometimes the latter involves reading papers or attending short workshops. Some clinical psychologists choose to do more substantial further training, e.g. a degree or diploma in a specific form of psychological therapy. Further training may have to be self-funded in part or in full.
What particular qualities will employers look for?	This is likely to vary between employers. However, NHS Trusts now typically expect clinical psychologists to provide more than direct clinical work with clients. For example, they will typically expect clinical psychologists to provide training and consultation to other staff members, and to be involved in supporting audits and service evaluation.
What career progression opportunities are there?	As clinical psychologists become more experienced they are expected to become involved in supervising more junior colleagues. Some go on to become consultant clinical psychologists, whose jobs will include a significant management component.
Will my training make me an attractive proposition for other careers? If so, which careers?	Perhaps, but given that the training is quite specific, it would probably only be worth doing this training if you planned to work as a clinical psychologist either clinically and/or in academia.
What are the hours of work?	Within the NHS clinical psychologists are typically paid to work a 37.5-hour working week, excluding breaks, if they work full time. Some clinical psychologists may work longer hours than this, without additional pay, given the busy nature of their jobs. Part-time posts are also available.
What are the working conditions like?	Before applying to clinical psychology training it is worth gaining some experience working within a clinical setting in the NHS, to see if this is an environment that suits you.
Will I have a job for life?	In the past this has tended to be the case. The future is likely to depend on economic conditions.
Where can I go for further information?	www.leeds.ac.uk/chpccp and www.bps.org.uk

and be able to provide evidence of their academic, clinical and research abilities and potential. The training itself usually comprises a three-year doctorate combined with a salaried post in the NHS. Key competencies developed during training include the ability to conduct, evaluate and apply research, the ability to assess, formulate, intervene and evaluate interventions, the ability to support other staff, and the capacity to reflect. These competencies are further developed following qualification through continuing professional development and by receiving supervision.

During their training, clinical psychologists work with a range of different client groups using a range of different approaches. Once qualified, they tend to specialise in working with one or two of these client groups, and may decide to do further training in a specific therapeutic approach. As clinical psychologists become more senior, the amount of direct client contact they have tends to reduce and their supervisory and management responsibilities tend to increase.

SELF-TEST QUESTIONS

- What are the key stages involved in clinical work?
- What is a formulation and why is it important?
- What are the differences between the scientist-practitioner model and the reflective-practitioner model?
- What are the main competencies that a clinical psychologist will develop during training?

TEXTS FOR FURTHER READING

Dallos, R. & Draper, R. (2005) *An Introduction to Family Therapy: Systemic Theory and Practice,* Buckingham: Open University Press.
Hall, J. & Llewelyn, S. (2006) *What Is Clinical Psychology?* Oxford: Oxford University Press.
Knight, A. (2002) *How to Become a Clinical Psychologist: Getting a Foot in the Door,* Hove: Brunner-Routledge.
Lemma-Wright, A. (1995) *Invitation to Psychodynamic Psychology,* London: Whurr.
Lindsay, S. & Powell, G.E. (2007) *The Handbook of Clinical Adult Psychology,* Oxford: Routledge.

RELEVANT WEB LINKS

American Psychological Association, www.apa.org
British Psychological Society, www.bps.org.uk
Clearing House for Postgraduate Courses in Clinical Psychology, www.leeds.ac.uk/chpccp
European Federation of Professional Psychologists' Associations, www.cop.es/efppa
Psyclick, a website for people who want to become clinical psychologists, http://psyclick.org.uk

REFERENCES

Barlow, D.H., Hayes, S.C. & Nelson, R.O. (1984) *The Scientist Practitioner: Research and Accountability in Clinical and Educational Settings.* New York: Pergamon Press.
Beck, J.S. (1995) *Cognitive Therapy: Basics and Beyond,* New York: Guilford Press.

Dallos, R. & Draper, R. (2005) *An Introduction to Family Therapy: Systemic Theory and Practice,* Buckingham: Open University Press.

Hall, J. & Llewelyn, S. (2006) *What Is Clinical Psychology?* Oxford: Oxford University Press.

Huey, D.A. & Britton, P.G. (2002) A portrait of clinical psychology, *Journal of Interprofessional Care* 16: 69–78.

Kuyken, W., Watkins, E.R. & Beck, A.T. (2005) Cognitive-behaviour therapy for mood disorders, in G. Gabbard, J. Beck & J. Holmes (eds) *Concise Oxford Textbook of Psychotherapy,* Oxford: Oxford University Press.

Lemma-Wright, A. (1995) *Invitation to Psychodynamic Psychology,* London: Whurr.

Lindsay, S. & Powell, G.E. (2007) *The Handbook of Clinical Adult Psychology,* Oxford: Routledge.

Nightingale, D.J. & Cromby, J. (1999) *Social Constructionist Psychology: A Critical Analysis of Theory and Practice,* Buckingham: Open University Press.

Schön, D.A. (1983) *The Reflective Practitioner: How Professionals Think in Action,* New York: Basic Books.

Part II
Health Psychology

7 What Is Health Psychology?

CHARLES ABRAHAM, MARK CONNER, FIONA JONES & DARYL O'CONNOR

LEARNING OUTCOMES

WHEN YOU HAVE COMPLETED THIS CHAPTER, YOU SHOULD BE ABLE TO:

1. Define and describe the discipline and profession of health psychology.

2. Explain what is meant by the biopsychosocial model of health and illness.

3. Identify the psychological sub-disciplines that contribute to health psychology research and practice.

4. Explain why theory building is important in science and how theoretical development provides the foundation for intervention design.

5. Explain how induction can be used to develop theories.

6. Explain why a randomised control trial provides a good test of an intervention.

7. Explain why in developed countries, distribution of wealth within a country is a better predictor of the nation's health than total national wealth.

8. Describe how socioeconomic status, stress and health are related.

9. List a series of behaviour patterns that predict good health and longevity.

10. Describe the information–motivation–behavioural skills model.

11. Discuss why health-related information may not affect motivation and behaviour.

12. Describe the social ecological model of change.

13. Describe the key stages that are needed to plan a successful behaviour change intervention according to the intervention mapping model.

14. Define primary, secondary and tertiary prevention.

15. List four things that a doctor could do in any consultation to maximise patient satisfaction and adherence.

KEY WORDS

Adherence • Behavioural Determinants • Biopsychosocial Model • Community-level Intervention • Deduction • Differential Exposure Hypothesis • Differential Vulnerability Hypothesis • Elicitation Research • Epidemiological Transition • Health Inequalities • Induction • Information–Motivation–Behavioural Skills Model • Intervention Mapping • Job Insecurity • Meta-analytic Study • Motor Skills • Needs Assessment • Predictive Validity • Primary Prevention • Randomised Control Trial • Secondary Prevention • Self-efficacy • Self-regulatory Skills • Setting Change Objectives • Social Ecological Model of Change • Social Skills • Socioeconomic Hierarchies • Socioeconomic Status • Tertiary Prevention

CHAPTER OUTLINE

7.1 AN ACADEMIC DISCIPLINE AND A PROFESSION

Can the stress of taking examinations compromise students' health? It can. Understanding the link between psychological process and health is the domain of health psychology. Health psychology lies within an academic discipline focused on a series of research questions concerning health and wellbeing. It is also a profession comprising trained practitioners who have a set of competencies enabling them to initiate change at individual and social levels. In this chapter we will outline the nature of the discipline and illustrate some of the work in which professional health psychologists may be involved.

Psychology is the scientific study of perception, memory, cognition (e.g. attitudes and beliefs) emotion, personality, behaviour and interpersonal relationships. All these areas of study are relevant to health psychology because all are important to our health and to our responses to illness. The World Health Organisation defines health as:

a state of complete physical, mental and social well-being and not merely the absence of disease or infirmity. (WHO, 1948, p. 100)

Health psychologists seek to identify and understand the determinants of 'physical, mental and social well-being', focusing on physical health rather than mental illness. Matarazzo (1980, p. 118) provides the following definition of health psychology:

Health psychology is an aggregate of the educational, scientific and professional contributions of the discipline of psychology to the promotion and maintenance of health, the prevention and treatment of illness, the identification of etiologic and diagnostic correlates of health, illness and related dysfunction and the improvement of the health care system and health policy formation.

This much-cited definition highlights:

- The key aims of health psychology; that is, to promote health and prevent illness.

- The scientific focus of research into the causes and processes underpinning health and illness (this is what Matarazzo means by 'etiologic and diagnostic correlates').

- Key priorities of professional practice in health psychology, for example improving health care by focusing on the behaviour of health-care professionals and how health care is delivered.

When thinking about these definitions consider Activity Box 7.1.

To summarise:

- Health psychology is an academic discipline focused on research questions. It is also a profession comprising trained practitioners who initiate change at individual and social levels.

- Health psychology aims to promote health and prevent illness, as well as research causes and processes underpinning health and illness.

- Professional health psychologists work towards improving health care and the delivery of health care.

7.2 A BIOPSYCHOSOCIAL MODEL OF HEALTH

Health psychologists investigate processes linking individual perceptions and beliefs to biological processes and behaviours. For example, how a person perceives their work demands and copes with these demands will determine their stress levels (see Chapter 9). This, in turn, may affect the biological functioning of their cardiovascular and immune systems (see Chapter 8). Health psychologists also study social processes including the effect of social and economic position in society on our wellbeing as well as face-to-face interactions with others (e.g. work colleagues), because these structures and social processes shape perceptions, beliefs and behaviour. In addition, health psychologists investigate social processes involved in health-care delivery. For example, the way in which

biopsychosocial model an integrated model of health psychology drawing on many other disciplines, including biology, medicine, social psychology, developmental psychology and economics in order to provide a comprehensive picture of the causes and processes underpinning health and illness.

health-care professionals talk to their patients may influence whether or not they take their recommended medication. This in turn affects biological processes that determine the optimal functioning of the body. Health psychologists integrate research from across these areas to build a **biopsychosocial model** of health (Schwartz, 1980); see Figure 7.1.

When research enables us to develop good models or theories that describe underlying causal processes, this establishes the evidence we need to design interventions that will change these processes. If we know how a system works we can plan interventions to change its operation. For example, if we have a good model of who is likely to suffer most stress and how such stress is generated (see Chapter 9), we can think about helping people to reduce stress. Professional health psychologists use research findings and models to assess individuals and to design and evaluate interventions that can change

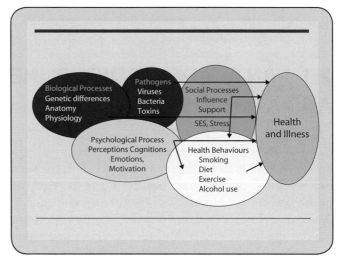

FIGURE 7.1 *A biopsychosocial model of health and illness.*

perceptions, beliefs, behaviours and social relationships. These in turn can affect health-related behaviour, quality of life, health and disease. Health interventions operate at different levels, ranging from those focusing on the individual to those designed to change society.

7.2.1 Integrating Models and Findings across Academic Disciplines

Health psychologists need to draw on cognitive, social, developmental and organisational psychology as well as economics, sociology, neuroscience, biology and medicine. The stress–health relationship, considered in detail in Chapters 8 and 9, provides an excellent illustration of the need for a biopsychosocial model of health. Stress results from our perception of the demands made on us by the environment and our beliefs in our own capacity to deal with those demands. If our perception of our own resources is increased by social or financial support, this is likely also to reduce stress and its negative effects

(Peirce *et al.*, 1996). If the perceived demands exceed our perceived resources, this may have immediate effects on our autonomic nervous and endocrine systems, which in turn may lead to deterioration in cardiovascular and immune functioning, increasing the likelihood of stroke, heart attack, infection and cancer (see Chapter 9 and Abraham *et al.* [2008] for further details).

Chapter 10 will discuss how social and developmental psychology has influenced work in health psychology. For example, personality traits can affect wellness and longevity directly though biological processes or through health behaviours like exercise and healthy eating. At the same time, developmental approaches have influenced understanding of how personality traits develop, for instance as a result of family relationships. Social psychology has also enabled us to examine processes of persuasion and cognitions (e.g. beliefs and attitudes) that shape health behaviours.

To summarise:

- Health psychology draws on many other disciplines, including biology, medicine, neuroscience, sociology, social psychology, organisational psychology, developmental psychology and economics, in order to provide a comprehensive picture of the causes and processes underpinning health and illness.
- This integrated model is referred to as a *biopsychosocial* model of health.

7.3 CONSTRUCTING AND TESTING PSYCHOLOGICAL THEORY

Like all psychologists, health psychologists seek to *describe, explain, predict* and *change* the processes, systems and outcomes that they study. Try to think of different aspects of life that will determine a person's health – see Activity Box 7.2.

The construction of theories allows scientists to share evidence-based descriptions of systems that can then be used to predict what might happen if some element or process in that system changed. For example, a description of personality differences (see Chapter 10) can be used to predict differences in how people will process information and how they will behave. If this is supported by evidence, it might imply that health-care professionals should use different communication and persuasion materials for people who have different personalities (Williams-Piehota *et al.*, 2005). So building a good descriptive theory can not only help us understand psychological processes, but also, potentially, improve the effectiveness of service delivery.

7.3.1 Observation and Induction

Theory development often begins with the observation of associations. For example, in the 1950s two cardiologists noticed that many patients with heart disease spoke quickly and were more agitated than others (Friedman & Rosenman, 1974). These *associations* between a set of behaviours and disease prevalence led to proposals regarding individual differences underlying differences in the propensity to cardiovascular disease and shaped initial thinking about the 'Type A' behaviour pattern (see Chapter 10 for details). Developing a theory in this way, based on repeated observation of the same association, is called **induction**. This process can generate important insights, but identification of associations (or correlations) does not, in itself, *explain* those

> **induction** observation of repeated associations which is often the first step in theory building.

associations. For example, Russell (1912) considered the case of an inductivist turkey that was always fed at 9 a.m. Many observations in different weathers and seasons confirmed this association between time and feeding. Nonetheless, the rule or theory that 'I am always fed at 9 in the morning' was not sustained over time, because on Christmas Eve morning the turkey was not fed!

WHAT ASPECTS OF LIFE ARE IMPORTANT TO HEALTH?

ACTIVITY BOX 7.2

Thinking about your society generally, who is healthy and who is not? What differences between people predict better or poorer health? Think about things people do that improve or damage their health. What about the family they were born into or where they live? Make a list of particular factors that you think may shape a person's health.

7.3.2 Theory Testing the Development of Measures

To *explain* observed associations, psychological theory must transcend the identification of correlations and articulate causal processes and mechanisms. The development of theory following from initial ideas about Type A behaviour pattern and cardiovascular disease provides a useful example (again see Chapter 10). In this case the explanation involved psychological responses to threat perception, the experience of stress and the impact of stress on the cardiovascular system (see Chapter 8). Type A people were thought to continually perceive themselves to be short of time to meet their goals and to perceive other people as threats to their wellbeing. The resultant stress was thought to create above-average wear and tear on the cardiovascular system and so create a risk factor for heart disease. This illustrates how observed associations can lead to the development of theoretical explanations. However, the same association may be explained in different ways.

Theories can also operate at different levels. For example, the psychological processes involved in threat perception and the experience of stress are different in kind from the physiological processes involved in the narrowing of peripheral blood vessels, increased heart rate and the release of cortisol. Yet both types of theories are necessary to provide an explanation of why and how stress-related perception can make heart disease more likely (see Chapter 8).

Theory identifies characteristics that can be measured and measures enable us to distinguish between types of people in terms of psychological and physiological processes. Consequently, new theoretical explanations can generate new measures. For example, different measures of Type A behaviour pattern were developed. Using the structured interview (SI; Rosenman *et al.*, 1975), the interviewer elicited impatience and hostility and monitored the interviewee's nonverbal behaviour (including their expressions, speed and style of communication, body posture and agitation). This allowed scoring on exhibited Type A behaviour. By contrast, the Jenkins Activity Survey (e.g. Jenkins, Zyzanski & Rosenman, 1971) is a self-report measure assessing Type A behaviour on the basis of respondents' reports.

predictive validity the extent to which a test or measure can predict a specified outcome.

The **predictive validity** of these measures has been tested by examining how effectively they predict heart disease. For example, Matthews (1988), in a **meta-analytic study** (which combines evidence from many other studies), found that the SI significantly predicted heart disease

meta-analytic study a study which combines evidence from many other studies and generates an average effect size across studies.

across studies while the Jenkins Activity Survey did not (see Chapter 10 for further details). This difference in findings indicated that being categorised as Type A did not always mean that one was more likely to develop a heart attack, suggesting that the theory needed modification. Subsequent work indicated that it was not Type A behaviour but a particular component of this personality type, namely the tendency towards interpersonal hostility, that makes heart disease more likely (Miller *et al.*, 1996, Ch. 4). Hostility was better measured by the SI, which is why it proved to be a better predictor of later heart disease.

Scientists' ability to measure processes described by theory depends on the development of measures and equipment. For example, the development of functional magnetic resonance imaging has allowed neuroscientists to address new questions about brain function. Similarly, the development of new questionnaires or interview techniques can also help psychologists gather new evidence and, as a result, better define the processes described in psychological theory – as happened with the focus on hostility rather than Type A behaviour generally.

7.3.3 Deduction, Theory Building and Evaluation of Interventions

Once scientists have found evidence supporting theories based on observed association (using induction), deductive reasoning becomes possible. **Deduction** involves drawing conclusions from premises that are assumed to be true. For example, if we accept the following premises – (i) those who score highly on the Jenkins Activity Survey exhibit more Type A behaviour; (ii) those who exhibit more Type A behaviour are more likely to suffer from cardiovascular disease; and (iii) Jim scored highly on the Jenkins Activity Survey – then we can deduce that Jim is more likely to suffer from heart disease than other people. Such reasoning provides the foundation for testing theories. Once we can deduce that outcomes should follow from our theory, we can test whether what we observed supports our theory. So if Jim, and people like him, suffer from heart disease, the theory may provide a good description of reality. If, however, this proposition is not supported by the evidence – as proved to be the case with the Jenkins Activity Survey measure – there may be something wrong with the theory or the measure. In this particular case, the theory had to be modified because the findings did not support it. This has happened many times in the development of psychological theories.

A theory that is supported by evidence may provide the foundation for designing an intervention to change the systems that the theory describes. If that intervention

deduction the process of drawing conclusions from premises assumed to be true.

is found to be effective through research, this adds to the evidence that the theory provides a good description – and is useful. For example, Davidson *et al.* (2007) found that an intervention designed to reduce hostility did, in fact, result in less hostility (both using self-report and observational measures) and, in addition, six months later those who had received the intervention spent fewer days in hospital compared to a control group who had not received the intervention (see Theory to Application Box 10.1 for details). In this case a theory-based intervention was found to enhance health and reduce health-care costs. Experimental work like this provides important evaluations of the effectiveness of interventions, so helping health psychologists decide what does and does not work (Michie & Abraham, 1994).

randomised control trial an experiment in which people are randomly allocated to an intervention group or a control group for comparison purposes.

A **randomised control trial** is an experiment in which people are randomly allocated to an intervention group or a control group (Sibbald & Roland, 1998). This allows a comparison between what happens in the intervention group and what would have happened if the intervention had not been used (i.e. in the control group). The randomisation attempts to control for individual characteristics that might affect the results. For example, if there were more people who had high hostility in the control group than the intervention group, this could lead to misleading results – for example, the intervention might look less effective than it really was. Randomisation makes it likely that such individual factors are evenly distributed between intervention and control groups and so rules out the possibility that such differences can explain the findings of the study.

Summarising this section, we have noted how early theory development can explain the observation of associations between events. This is called induction. The implications of theories can then be tested using available or new measures using deductive reasoning. If the implications are supported by evidence, the theory provides a useful predictive model of the events in question. This can then provide the basis for developing theory-based interventions, which, in turn, can be tested using experimental methods such as randomised control trials.

To summarise further:

- Health psychologists seek to *describe, explain, predict* and *change* the processes, systems and outcomes that they study. Theories can be used to predict what might happen if some element or process in that system changed.

- Repeated observation of associations is often the first step in theory building. This is known as induction. To *explain* observed associations, theory must go beyond noting that two elements are linked and describe causal processes and mechanisms. Theory and technological advances generate new measures that, in turn, can be used to test theory.

- Once we have a theory that describes how a system works and is supported by evidence, we can design interventions to change that system – e.g. to prevent heart attacks. Interventions can be tested using experiments such as randomised control trials.

7.4 THE SOCIAL AND SOCIETAL CONTEXT OF STRESS AND HEALTH

Clean water, good food, clean, damp-free housing and low-density living in which people can sleep well are all prerequisites of good health. Poverty deprives people of these basic needs and so is associated with poorer health. In many developing countries, the most effective way to improve health is to increase national wealth so that people can afford to live healthy lives. However, wealth and poverty are also important to health in developed countries. In one UK city, for example, two babies born within 10 miles of one another on the same day but from families with contrasting economic fortunes have quite different life expectancies. The baby from the more privileged background can be expected to live up to 28 years longer (Commission on Social Determinants of Health, 2008). Thus **health inequalities** are an important focus for health psychologists.

health inequalities differences between the health and life expectancy of individuals affected by social and economic factors, amongst others.

7.4.1 Wealth Distribution, Socioeconomic Hierarchies and Health

If we increased the wealth of the UK, would the population have better health? Surprisingly, the answer to this question appears to be 'no' – or not substantially. Why? In developed countries, increases in national wealth such as gross national product and average income are weakly associated with life expectancy. Above a certain threshold, increases in national wealth do not translate into increases in longevity. Wilkinson (1996, p. 29) calls this the '**epidemiological transition**'. The link between wealth and health remains strong *within* developed countries, but

epidemiological transition a wealth threshold which, when crossed by a country, means that increased national wealth has little effect on the overall health of the population.

changes in national wealth do not translate into enhanced population health.

The explanation lies in the distribution of wealth within countries. In the United Kingdom, for example, the richest 1% of the population owns about one-fifth of national wealth and the richest 5% owns two-fifths. By contrast, the poorest 50% (half the population) own only 7% of the national wealth. The impact of national wealth can only affect overall population health if that wealth is shared by the poorest. This is why Wilkinson (1996) found only a small correlation between gross domestic product and national life expectancy among (developed) Organisation for Economic Co-operation and Development countries ($r = 0.30$), but a large correlation between income distribution and national life expectancy in economically developed countries ($r = 0.86$).

Wilkinson considered England and Japan to illustrate this relationship. In 1970 the populations of England and Japan had very similar life expectancies. The two countries also had very similar income distributions; that is, a similar proportion of wealth was owned by the poorest 50%. However, between 1970 and the 1990s Japan's income distribution equalised, so that the poorest came to own more of the national wealth and incomes clustered around the average income (or mean). At the same time, the distribution of incomes in the United Kingdom became more widely distributed, with increasing differences between the richest and poorest. Statistically, we would say that the standard deviation of wealth ownership decreased in Japan but increased in the UK. In this period, Japan's life expectancy increased dramatically, while the UK moved down the international longevity league tables. Thus, in affluent countries, health is much more strongly predicted by individuals' position within **socioeconomic hierarchies** than the wealth of their nation.

socioeconomic hierarchies different levels of financial status in society.

7.4.2 Health Risks and the Benefits of Health Behaviour Change

Health behaviour change (for example giving up smoking, which is strongly linked to lower life expectancy) may be more beneficial for the better off. A wealthy person enjoying good food and accommodation, having a low work-strain job (see Chapter 9) with high job security and perhaps employing others to help with everyday tasks (including child care), has few influences that predict poor health. By contrast, a poor person with fewer resources, coping with high daily demands, has many risk factors, perhaps including high work stress and job insecurity. **Job insecurity**, for example, strongly adds to work

job insecurity lack of security concerning one's job which adds to work stress and impacts on one's health.

stress (Strazdins *et al.*, 2004) and job insecurity is an everyday stressor for many people in developed countries. Consequently, the wealthy smoker who gives up is likely to have a greater impact on their future health than a poorer person, because the poorer person retains more health risk factors in their everyday life. Consequently, when someone from a poor background says 'If the cigarettes don't get me something else will', they are, sadly, reflecting the reality revealed by research into health risk factors. This is one reason why it is more difficult for health professionals to change the health behaviours of poorer people.

This creates a problem for health promoters (including health psychology practitioners) who aim to improve the health of those with the worst health and lowest life expectancies, thereby reducing health inequalities. Adopting health-promoting behaviour patterns predicts better health and longevity. Therefore, the promotion of such behaviours (e.g. high levels of physical activity and appropriate calorie intake) is a public health priority. Unfortunately, however, changes in such health-related behaviours may be more difficult among groups with the greatest health risk because:

- A lower, daily quality of life may reduce motivation to live longer.
- Health-damaging behaviours (such as smoking and drinking alcohol) may be seen as important ways of coping with everyday stressors.
- These changes may have less impact on their future health because structural aspects of society (including wealth distribution) expose them to a greater range of health risks.

7.4.3 Socioeconomic Hierarchies, Stress and Health

Socioeconomic status (SES) can be measured in terms of individual wealth or income. The impact of SES on health is not explained by differences between health behaviours of wealthy and poorer members of societies. For example, cardiovascular disease (creating a risk of stroke or heart attack) is associated with SES and this relationship is not eliminated after other risk factors such as smoking are taken into account. Socioeconomic hierarchies have an independent impact on health (Adler *et al.*, 1994; Carroll, Bennett & Davey-Smith, 1993). An alternative theory focuses on the relationship between SES and stress. The **differential exposure hypothesis**

socioeconomic status a summary measure of a person's economic and social position (compared to others) based on income, education and/or occupation.

differential exposure hypothesis a theory that proposes that the higher prevalence of health problems in low socioeconomic status groups is associated with a greater exposure to psychological stressors.

differential vulnerability hypothesis a theory that suggests that low socio economic status individuals are less well equipped to cope with stressors because they have fewer material and social resources.

proposes that the higher prevalence of health problems in low-SES groups is associated with a greater exposure to psychological stressors. In addition, the **differential vulnerability hypothesis** suggests that low-SES individuals are less well equipped to cope with stressors because they have fewer material and social resources (e.g. they have less money to buy healthy foods, fewer effective coping strategies and limited social support networks). So some members of society are chronically exposed to greater stress than others and are simultaneously less able to cope with such stress, so that stress has a major impact on their physical health.

The relationship between social hierarchy, stress and physical health has also been observed in animal studies. For example, Sapolsky's (1993) work shows that baboons who have lower positions in dominance hierarchies show higher levels of stress-related hormones, indicating more frequent stress responses that could be detrimental to immune functioning. These lower-dominance animals also have higher resting blood pressure and their blood pressure returns more slowly to resting levels following stressful encounters, creating a risk for cardiovascular health (see Chapter 8). So the biological processes that explain, in part, the impact of socioeconomic factors on health appear to be part of our evolutionary history.

Summarising this section, we have noted how wealth and resources affect health and that the health of developed nations depends on the distribution of wealth within countries. We have seen how one's position in the socioeconomic hierarchy can have an important impact on health and longevity. This can be partially explained by greater everyday exposure to demands combined with fewer resources to cope among those lower in the socioeconomic hierarchy.

To summarise further:

- Clean water, good food, clean, damp-free housing and low-density living in which people can sleep well are prerequisites of good health. Yet in developed countries, increases in national wealth are only weakly associated with life expectancy. In these countries, health is much more strongly predicted by individuals' position within socioeconomic hierarchies than the wealth of their nation.

- This relationship between socioeconomic status and health is likely to be due in part to the greater exposure to stress of poorer people and their simultaneous lack of resources to cope with these demands.

7.5 HEALTH-RELATED BEHAVIOUR PATTERNS AND HEALTH PROMOTION

SES and one's genetic make-up are important determinants of our health, but research demonstrates that individual behaviour patterns are also crucial to health, illness and longevity. Behaviour change is, therefore, a key focus for health psychologists. It can have large effects on individual and public health and can be undertaken by individuals themselves.

Attempts to improve public health by promoting individual behaviour change have a long history, but have become more important as evidence of the importance of behaviour patterns to health has been consolidated. For example, nearly 2000 years ago the Greek leader Diogenesin commissioned a wall etched with messages taken from the teachings of the philosopher Epicurus. The wall included 25 000 words written over 260 square metres and emphasised the importance of quality of life, self-reflection and self-regulation. As far as we know no randomised control trial was undertaken to test the effect of the wall on the city's citizens! Nonetheless, this ambitious public health intervention can be seen as a direct precursor to the leaflets and websites commissioned by modern health services.

7.5.1 Behaviour Patterns and Health

Research consistently shows that lifestyle factors predict how long we live.

Consider the two studies highlighted in Table 7.1. The Alameda County study researched nearly 7000 people over 10 years in the United States (Belloc &

TABLE 7.1 *Behaviour Patterns that Predict Longevity.*

Alameda County study Belloc & Breslow, 1972, USA	Norfolk Prospective Population study Khaw et al., 2008, UK
Adequate regular sleep	
Regularly eating breakfast	
Not snacking between meals	
Not smoking	Not smoking
Maintaining appropriate body weight	
Being physically active	Being physically active
No excessive alcohol consumption	No excessive alcohol consumption
	Healthy eating habits

PHOTO 7.1 *Behaviour Patterns Predict Health And Longevity.*
Source: Shutterstock.

Breslow, 1972). The Norfolk Prospective Population study followed 20000 people in the United Kingdom (Khaw *et al.*, 2008). Both studies emphasise that smoking, physical activity, alcohol consumption and eating a healthy diet are associated with mortality. The Alameda study also suggests that other behaviour patterns may contribute to a longer life. Further research shows that the leading causes of death in the United States are tobacco use (18%), poor diet and physical inactivity (17%) and alcohol consumption (3.5%), accounting collectively for almost 40% of all premature deaths (Mokdad *et al.*, 2004; Photo 7.1).

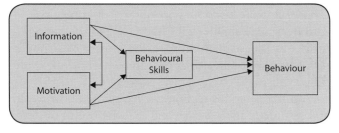

FIGURE 7.2 *The information–motivation–behavioural skills model.*
Source: Fisher & Fisher (1992).

7.5.2 Identifying Individual-level Change Targets

> **behavioural determinants** underlying causes of behaviour including beliefs, attitudes and intentions.

> **information–motivation–behavioural skills model** provides a useful guide to identifying key behavioural determinants.

If we want to help people change health-related behaviours, we first need to know what psychological processes or **behavioural determinants** are responsible for their current behaviour and, consequently, what changes in behavioural determinants are most likely to trigger behaviour change. The **information–motivation–behavioural skills model** (IMB; Fisher & Fisher, 1992; see Figure 7.2 and Focus Point 7.1) provides a useful guide to identifying critical behavioural determinants.

Imagine that our target group are sexually active young people who are not adequately protecting themselves against pregnancy and sexually transmitted infections. Do they have enough information? If no, then what information do they need? If yes, then are they motivated to use condoms and other contraceptives? If no, what elements of motivation are they lacking? If yes, do they lack skills to translate their motivation into action? The IMB approach recommends that researchers answer these questions before deciding what change techniques should be included in a behaviour-change intervention. This initial research is called **elicitation research** because it seeks to elicit or diagnose the deficits or problems that explain why people are not taking actions that are in

> **elicitation research** seeks to elicit or diagnose the deficits or problems which explain why people are not taking actions that are in their own interests.

FOCUS POINT 7.1   INFORMATION–MOTIVATION–BEHAVIOURAL SKILLS MODEL (IMB)

The information–motivation–behavioural skills model has been used to develop a number of interventions that have been found to be effective in changing health-related behaviour patterns. Some of these are listed and described on the Center for Health, Intervention and Prevention website at the University of Connecticut (www.chip.uconn.edu).

For example, Fisher *et al*. (1996) developed an intervention to reduce the risk of human immunodeficiency virus (HIV) infection among US college/university students. The intervention promoted better *information* using a slide show and a large-group discussion, which focused on how HIV could be transmitted from one person to another and how this could be effectively prevented. For example, this session included discussion of the risks involved in

different sexual behaviours, the effectiveness of condoms, where to buy condoms and how to decide about safer sex. In addition, the intervention attempted to bolster *motivation* in small-group discussions led by another (previously trained) student, followed by large-group discussions led by a professional health educator. These sessions targeted personal susceptibility to HIV and attitudes and subjective norms relating to condom use (see Chapter 4). The intervention also used role-play sessions led by trained students to allow students involved in the intervention to practise the *social skills* required to negotiate condom use effectively. Finally, *self-efficacy* and *manual skills* relevant to condom use were enhanced using a video in which students modelled correct handling and use.

WHAT INFORMATION DO PATIENTS WANT?   ACTIVITY BOX 7.3

Write down 5–10 types of information that someone who was ill might want. How would a patient acquire this information? Now think about what might go wrong if the patient did not have the information they wanted. For

example, how might they act so as to impair their health? See Coulter, Entwistle & Gilbert (1999) for research into what patients say they want to know and how this corresponds to the information that is provided, e.g. with medication.

their own interests. When we have identified missing behavioural determinants through elicitation research, intervention planning can begin.

There are many reasons why people may not have the right information. The information they want may not be available at all, so they are unaware of a potential health threat. Alternatively, information may not be easily available when they need to make decisions about action. For example, do young people know where to get contraceptives (e.g. condoms) in the evening and do they know how to use them correctly? Available information may not be in a form that people can understand. Communications from health services sometimes use technical terms and unfamiliar vocabulary. For example, in a survey of leaflets provided by palliative care units (Payne *et al*., 2000) two-thirds had poor readability scores and so would only be understood by 40% of the population.

In addition, information presented by disliked sources or sources thought to be poorly informed or untrustworthy are unlikely to be believed and so will not shape beliefs, attitudes and behaviour. We will consider aspects of persuasion in Chapter 10 and an introduction to the presentation of information is provided by Abraham *et al*. (2008). For now, however, think about the question posed in Activity Box 7.3.

Once good information is available in an easily understood form from reliable sources, health promoters can focus on motivation. In Chapter 10, we will consider models that identify elements of motivation that may be missing in relation to any particular behaviour for any particular group. Specifically, we will discuss the theory of planned behaviour and the 'major theorists' model (see Figures 10.3 and 10.4). For example, young people may wrongly believe that sexual partners would not approve of condom use. Identification of missing elements of motivation (e.g. others' approval) enables intervention designers to choose messages and change techniques that precisely target these missing elements, thereby bolstering motivation and promoting behaviour change.

If motivation is established, interventions may seek to develop missing behavioural skills. Abraham *et al.* (2008) distinguish between three classes of prerequisite skills. First are **self-regulatory skills**, which are needed to control action planning and performance of action sequences. For example, Schinke and Gordon (1992) describe an intervention that aimed to develop self-monitoring and planning skills that could be used to control and avoid interaction leading to unprotected sex. The acronym SODAS, standing for Stop, Options, Decide, Act and Self-praise, was used in this intervention. By remembering these stages young people were learning to regulate their own action so as to avoid unprotected sex. It was designed to help young people reduce risk behaviour.

self-regulatory skills skills used to control everyday action including, e.g., goal setting, planning and self-monitoring.

motor skills those involved in bodily movement and functioning.

Second, **motor skills** may be required. For example, can young people easily take a condom out of its packet and roll it onto an erect penis without damaging the condom or putting it on the wrong way? In one of our studies we offered training in condom-handling skills and gave young people who demonstrated good skills a condom proficiency certificate. This increased their confidence and skills relevant to condom use.

social skills the ability to interact successfully with other people.

Third, **social skills** may be required. For example, heterosexual young women in particular must negotiate condom use with their sexual partners. Being effective at such negotion may require assertiveness and practice. Role-play sessions are often used in interventions to develop such skills.

self-efficacy the belief that one can perform an action or series of actions successfully.

Skill development enhances **self-efficacy**, which is the belief that one can perform an action or series of actions successfully. As we shall see in Chapter 10, self-efficacy is important to motivation and to the successful performance of action. Consequently, interventions regularly aim to increase people's self-efficacy to adopt and maintain health-related behaviours. A number of successful behaviour-change interventions have been based on the IMB and some of these have been evaluated using long-term follow-up (e.g. after 12 months in the case of Fisher *et al.*, 2002).

7.5.3 A Multilevel Framework for Promoting Health Behaviour Change

Changing health behaviours often depends on changes at different levels. For example, changing availability of condoms and changing social norms in relation to condom use may require changes at school level (e.g. Fisher *et al.*, 2002). Similarly, promoting greater physical activity may be achieved through worksite interventions (see Abraham & Graham-Rowe [2009] for a review). Sometimes national legislation may be required. For example, changing the price of alcohol may be critical to changing alcohol consumption (WHO, 2009). However, differential alcohol prices between neighbouring countries encourage people to bring (and smuggle) alcohol across borders, so international action may be required to change some health behaviours. Health psychologists may be involved in interventions at individual, family, community, organisation, national and international levels. This view of behaviour change targets is embodied in the **social ecological model of change** (Kok *et al.*, 2008), which is illustrated in Figure 7.3.

The North Karelia Project, which began in Finland in 1972, provides a good illustration of a **community-level intervention**. The project targeted smoking, diet and blood pressure and used leaflets, radio and television slots.

social ecological model of change a model emphasising the different levels at which intervention may be required to successfully change behaviour.

community-level intervention a health initiative using media and resources at the level of the community, such as local radio and voluntary organisations.

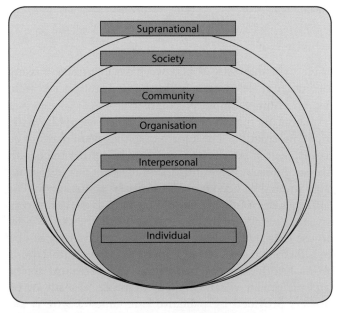

FIGURE 7.3 *Levels of behaviour-change intervention.*
Source: Kok et al. (2008).

TABLE 7.2 *Characteristics Associated with Effectiveness in Interventions Targeting Community Change.*

- Targeting behaviour patterns with immediate health consequences, such as alcohol misuse or sexual risk taking
- Targeting young people to prevent uptake of health-risk behaviours
- Combining institutional policy change with theory-based behaviour-change interventions
- Involving communities themselves in intervention design

Source: Hingson & Howland, 2002.

In addition, voluntary-sector organisations, schools and health and social services were involved. This comprehensive intervention was found to be effective in reducing smoking and cholesterol levels (e.g. Vartiainen *et al.*, 1998).

In a review of evaluations of such comprehensive community interventions (including the North Karelia Project), Hingson and Howland (2002) identified four factors that were associated with greater intervention effectiveness. These are shown in Table 7.2.

The National Institute for Health and Clinical Excellence (NICE), which advises on best practice and cost effectiveness in the UK National Health Service, published guidance on how to promote health behaviour change in 2007. A useful introduction is provided by Abraham *et al.* (2009) and an eight-page summary can be downloaded (see www.nice.org.uk/Guidance/PHG/Published for various public health guidance provided by NICE). The NICE guidance on behaviour change underlines the importance of assessing and intervening to change the social context in which health-related behaviour develops and is sustained. This may involve health promoters in attempting to remove social and financial barriers as well as policy development focusing on ways to alleviate local poverty, limited employment and educational opportunities. Thus as well as developing individual-level interventions, health psychologists must also be able to lobby for policy changes to promote health effectively (Schaalma *et al.*, 2004).

7.5.4 Planning Health Behaviour Change Interventions

intervention mapping a step-by-step method for planning, developing and evaluating behaviour change interventions.

Developing effective interventions to change health behaviour can be complex. The '**intervention mapping**' model (Bartholomew *et al.*, 2006) provides a useful guide to planning.

- The first step is a **needs assessment**, which involves clarifying *if* and *how* the target group needs to change and precisely specifying the target behaviour. As we have noted, this involves elicitation research and identification of informational, motivational and skills deficits.

  needs assessment initial research to ascertain what, if anything, needs to change to enhance the health and wellbeing of a group.

- The second stage is **setting change objectives**, which involves identifying behavioural determinants and change mechanisms (e.g. changing subjective norms – see Chapter 4).

  setting change objectives identifying behavioural determinants and change mechanisms.

- The third stage involves a theoretical design linking behavioural determinants and change mechanisms to a set of change techniques (see below).

- The fourth stage is the translation of this theoretical design into a practical plan. This will involve reviewing and creating materials and methods (e.g. leaflets, lesson plans and websites).

- Once materials are selected and manuals have been written to describe how the intervention is to be delivered, the fifth stage, implementation, begins. This involves identifying those who will deliver the intervention (e.g. teachers in schools or worksite managers) and negotiating its use with them.

- The sixth and last stage is evaluation. This involves conducting research to discover whether the intervention is effective, for example a randomised control trial.

As the intervention mapping approach suggests, planning includes selecting appropriate change targets, adopting the appropriate theoretical models that explain change mechanisms and applying the most relevant change techniques. The importance of these elements was endorsed by a review of reviews examining the effectiveness of school-based health-promotion interventions targeting sexual, substance abuse and nutrition behaviours. Peters *et al.* (2009) found strong evidence that effective school-based interventions across all three domains shared the five characteristics listed in Table 7.3.

The components that intervention designers use can be selected from lists of available behaviour-change techniques on the basis of the behavioural determinants identified through elicitation research into the target group and the target behaviour. A list of behaviour-change techniques that have been reliably identified across a range of behaviour-change interventions is provided by Abraham and Michie (2008).

TABLE 7.3 *Characteristics Associated with Effectiveness in School-Based Interventions.*

- Use of theory in the intervention design
- Targeting social influences, especially social norms
- Targeting cognitive and behavioural skills
- Providing training for those delivering the intervention
- Including multiple components

Source: Peters *et al.,* 2009.

Does planning matter to effectiveness? Mullen, Green and Persinger (1985) examined 70 studies evaluating interventions designed to improve patient education. These studies were selected because they were methodologically sound and assessed the effectiveness of the intervention in terms of increased knowledge and **adherence** to medical advice (that is, following recommendations made by healthcare professionals). The researchers developed six criteria identifying aspects of good intervention planning and found that the best predictor of intervention effectiveness was the planning quality score derived from these six criteria. Thus good planning is critical to intervention effectiveness.

adherence following advice provided by health care professionals.

In this section we have seen how important behaviour patterns are to health and longevity and considered a series of models that can be used to develop and test interventions designed to change health-related behaviours. The information–motivation–behavioural skills model identifies key prerequisites to establishing health behaviours. By checking whether people have good information, that the elements of motivation are in place and assessing relevant skills, we can design more effective behaviour-change interventions. Interventions may also target organisations, such as schools and communities, and research helps us understand what intervention characteristics and which change techniques are associated with effective intervention. The intervention mapping model emphasises that good planning is a prerequisite to intervention effectiveness.

To summarise:

- Differences in behaviour do not explain the link between socioeconomic status and health. Nonetheless, those who sleep well, exercise, eat a good diet (including eating fruit and vegetables) and avoid smoking and excessive alcohol consumption are healthier and live longer.
- In order to develop interventions that will change health-related behaviour, we should first check which determinants (or antecedents) of behaviour are present in a population. The

information–motivation–behavioural skills model provides a useful guide to critical behavioural determinants.

- Information needs to be carefully prepared and presented if it is to influence motivation and behaviour. Self-regulatory skills, motor skills and social skills may be required to translate motivation into action.
- Health psychologists may be involved in individual, family, community, organisation, national and international interventions to change health-related behaviour patterns. Such interventions need to be carefully planned. The intervention mapping model highlights six key stages from needs assessment through to evaluation.

7.6 ENHANCING HEALTH CARE THROUGH BEHAVIOUR CHANGE

The focus by Mullen *et al.* (1985) on adherence reminds us that behaviour change is not only relevant to the prevention of illness, often referred to as **primary prevention**. It is also important to improving the effectiveness of treatment and health-care services. The extent to which patients follow health-care professionals' advice (that is, adherence) can be critical to their health. Interventions designed to change patients' behaviour are often referred to as **secondary prevention**. The behaviour of health-care professionals affects public health through their ability to persuade patients to adhere and through good practice, including, for example, limiting the spread of disease through infection-control behaviours.

primary prevention interventions to prevent illness.

secondary prevention interventions designed to change patients' responses to their illness and so prevent long-term damage.

As people live longer in affluent countries they are also more likely to develop long-term physical illnesses such as hypertension, asthma, diabetes, coronary heart disease, heart failure and chronic pain. For many of these conditions there is no cure, so providing good professional care and supporting high-quality self-management become the goals for health services. Interventions designed to promote coping with illness or minimise the effects of established illness, rather than prevent illness, are often referred to as **tertiary prevention**. Seeking

tertiary prevention interventions designed to promote coping with illness or minimise the effects of established illness, rather than prevent illness.

and maintaining good social support (see Chapter 8) and maintaining high self-efficacy (see Chapter 10) in relation to managing illness are very important to patients with long-term illnesses.

7.6.1 Improving Adherence

While some elements of health care, such as surgery, require little active involvement from patients, most health care depends on patients changing their behaviour. A doctor may make an accurate diagnosis of a health problem and prescribe effective medication to a patient. However, the effectiveness of this work in terms of health improvement depends on the patient collecting the medication and then taking it as directed. So the doctor's effectiveness depends on how successful they have been at changing the patient's behaviour. As we have noted, following advice provided by health-care professionals is called adherence. When patients, like Julie in Case History 7.1, do not adhere to such advice, their health may suffer. In Julie's case her asthma may be poorly controlled, so making serious attacks more likely.

Surprisingly, across a range of recommended health- and illness-related behaviours, between 15% and 93% of patients do not follow health-care professionals' advice (see Abraham et al. [2008] and Myers & Midence [1998] for more details). Even when the consequences may be fatal, some patients may not adhere to prescribed medication. For example, in a prospective study of heart, liver and kidney transplant patients, Rovelli et al. (1989) found that 15% were nonadherent. Nonadherence led to organ rejection or death in 30% of these cases, compared to only 1% among adherent patients.

Why are patients nonadherent? There may be a variety of reasons. Some patients intend to follow advice but forget or find it difficult to do so, resulting in partial adherence. Others may suspend medication to test their health or (like Julie) to avoid real or imagined side effects. Some patients fear medication dependency, while others may disagree with the doctor's diagnosis or the prescribed treatment and deliberately take more or less than was advised (Donovan & Blake, 1992). Knowing why patients do not adhere is important to designing interventions or changing health professionals' practice to promote better adherence. Improving adherence is important, both because health-care effectiveness depends on adherence and because nonadherence is expensive, since it leads to further demands on health-care systems, including additional hospital admissions.

How the patient feels about the person giving health-care advice is likely to shape how that patient thinks about the recommended action. If a patient feels that her doctor is not interested in her problem or has not understood it, this may undermine confidence in the doctor's advice. Consequently, patient satisfaction is significantly correlated with adherence. For example, in a well-known study of paediatric consultations, Korsch et al. (1968) found that mothers who were very satisfied with their doctor's warmth, concern and communication were three times more likely to adhere than dissatisfied mothers.

Given the importance of patient satisfaction to adherence, it is interesting to discover that doctors' own satisfaction with their work is a predictor of patients' adherence. In a two-year prospective study, DiMatteo et al. (1993) found that doctors' satisfaction with their work was a significant predictor of patients' future adherence. This study also showed that doctors' self-reported

CASE HISTORY 7.1

Julie is a teenager who has been diagnosed with asthma. Her doctor explained that she should be using a preventative steroid inhaler every day to control her symptoms and prevent her from having asthma attacks. During the consultation at which the doctor prescribed the inhaler, the doctor asked Julie if she understood and Julie said she did. But did Julie have enough information to fully understand and take appropriate action? (See Activity Box 7.3.)

Initially, Julie started taking the preventative steroid inhaler as advised. Then she watched a television programme about the side effects of steroids on body builders and began to worry about the potential long-term effects of using the steroid inhaler. She continued to worry about these side effects and stopped using the inhaler.

In fact, Julie did not need to worry because the steroid dose she was taking was very low and the threat of asthma attacks is more serious than any – very unlikely – side effects. What could Julie's doctor have done to make it more likely that she would keep taking her preventative steroid inhaler?

willingness to answer all their patients' questions, regardless of the time involved, was positively associated with adherence. Doctors who are happier in their work may be more willing to answer questions and may engender greater satisfaction in their patients, so enhancing patient satisfaction and adherence.

We will consider the importance of social support to coping with stress in Chapter 9, but social support is also important to adherence. In a review summarising 122 studies reporting associations between social support and adherence, DiMatteo (2004) found that adherence (compared to nonadherence) was 3.6 times more likely among those receiving practical support than among those who did not have such support. Similarly, the risk of nonadherence was 1.35 times higher if patients were not receiving emotional support than if they had such support. A lack of social support may also increase the impact of daily demands and life events, which may, in turn, allow less priority for self-care goals, including adherence.

So can health psychologists, and health-care professionals generally, improve adherence? Yes, at least to some extent. Haynes *et al.* (2005) examined the outcomes of randomised control trials that measured adherence to medication and included a clinical or health outcome; that is, studies that measured adherence and whether people in the intervention condition showed greater health benefit. For short-term prescriptions they found that 44% of interventions had an effect on both adherence and at least one clinical outcome. For longer-term treatments, 45% led to improvements in adherence, but only 31% led to improvement in a clinical outcome. The research also identified behaviour-change approaches and techniques that were used in successful interventions. For short-term drug treatments, they found that counselling, written information and a personal phone call could boost adherence. However, for long-term treatments, no particular technique and only some complex interventions led to improvements in health outcomes. Those that were successful in improving adherence to longer-term care included combinations of more convenient care, providing information, counselling, reminders, self-monitoring, reinforcement, family therapy, psychological therapy, crisis intervention, telephone follow-up and additional supervision. Thus it is challenging to improve adherence to long-term medication to the extent that such improvements have an impact on clinical outcomes. Nonetheless, this research provides a good basis for improving adherence to short-term care in practice and for designing and evaluating further interventions targeting longer-term adherence.

7.6.2 *Improving Health-Care Professionals' Consultations*

Meetings with health-care professionals are crucial to patients' understanding of their health and health problems. We have seen too that such consultations shape patients' adherence. Consequently, the way in which health-care professionals manage consultations with patients determines their own professional effectiveness. For example, the doctors whose patients were satisfied with their doctor's warmth, concern and communication in Korsch *et al.*'s study (see above) were more effective in shaping mothers' behaviour and, thereby, enhancing their children's health. So psychological study of consultations may provide advice to health-care professionals on how to maximise the impact of their consultations.

Many models of successful doctor–patient consultations have been developed, including the Calgary-Cambridge model (Silverman, Kurtz & Draper, 2005). These models identify key stages or tasks (Pendleton *et al.*, 1984) that allow doctors (and other health-care professionals) to manage their consultations in a manner that will maximise patient care, satisfaction and adherence. They can be used to develop training methods that will help health-care professionals optimise their interactions with patients; see Focus Point 7.2 for details.

Such models have emphasised the importance of shaping the consultation to the patient's needs. Evidence suggests that patients are less likely to be satisfied and so less adherent if consultations do not focus on their needs. For example, in a study which involved observing more than 800 consultations with family doctors (or general practitioners), Little *et al.* (2001) found that patient satisfaction was related to doctors building a relationship or partnership during consultations and taking a positive approach. Moreover, patients reported fewer symptoms one month after the consultation when doctors had adopted a positive approach. Helping patients adopt a positive approach to their illness and to develop self-efficacy may be especially important to those with long-term illnesses. For example, Moskowitz, Epel and Acree (2008) found that feeling positive and 'enjoying life' was associated with longevity among people with diabetes and those older than 65.

Summarising this section, we have seen that understanding why patients do or do not follow advice given by health-care professionals can help us change the behaviour of health-care professionals and, thereby, help them become more effective at changing patients' behaviour. In particular, we have seen that the way in which consultations are managed can have an important effect on whether or not patients adhere.

FOCUS POINT 7.2   UNDERSTANDING AND EFFECTIVELY MANAGING CONSULTATIONS BETWEEN HEALTH-CARE PROFESSIONALS AND THEIR PATIENTS

Source: Shutterstock.

Think about the last consultation you had with a doctor. Did this consultation shape your behaviour? For example, did you take any recommended medication as advised or did you change any other health-related behaviours? Try to remember what was said in the consultation.

Now have a look at the two lists below. The Calgary-Cambridge model of doctor–patient consultations (Silverman, Kurtz & Draper, 2005) identifies six stages. These are very briefly summarised below. In addition, Pendleton *et al.* (1984) identified seven tasks that need to be achieved to maximise the effectiveness of a doctor–patient consultation. These are also summarised below. We can see that these two models overlap, but may also complement one another.

Finally, returning to your own consultation, think about how it compared to the two lists below. Did your doctor complete these tasks? Do you think this affected the extent to which the consultation shaped your behaviour?

THE CALGARY-CAMBRIDGE MODEL OF DOCTOR–PATIENT CONSULTATIONS

1. *Initiating the consultation*, including greetings and introductions and identifying the reason(s) for the consultation.

2. *Gathering information*, including understanding the patient's beliefs and concerns.
3. *Building a relationship,* including showing interest and communicating appreciation of the patient's concerns.
4. *Providing structure*, including summarising what has been said.
5. *Explanation and planning*, including providing information in a manner that is easily understood and remembered and developing a shared plan for treatment and care.
6. *Ending* the consultation.

SEVEN TASKS IDENTIFIED BY PENDLETON *et al.* (1984)

1. Define the reason for the consultation, including the nature and history of the problem, its effects and the patient's concerns and expectations.
2. Consider other problems, including risk factors that exacerbate the problem.
3. Choose an appropriate action for each problem in negotiation with the patient.
4. Achieve a shared understanding of the problem(s).
5. Involve the patient in the management of problems and encourage acceptance of responsibility by the patient.
6. Use time and resources appropriately.
7. Establish and maintain a relationship with the patient.

Together these two models highlight the important features of effective doctor–patient consultations. Understanding the important phases and tasks involved in effective consulting means that doctors and other health-care professionals can be trained to develop effective consultation skills. Applying these skills will allow them to maximise the impact of their care and the adherence of their patients.

To summarise further:

- As well as promoting health-enhancing behaviours (primary prevention), health psychologists also work on changing patients' responses to their illness (secondary prevention). Following health-care professionals' advice (or adherence) provides a good illustration. Understanding the reasons for nonadherence can help us develop

effective interventions to increase adherence.

- Patient satisfaction with consultations predicts adherence. Therefore if health-care professionals, including doctors, can improve their patients' satisfaction, they may be able to increase adherence. A number of models describe how doctors can maximise the impact of their consultations on patient satisfaction and adherence.

7.7 CONCLUSION

Health psychologists may be researchers who develop and test biopsychosocial theories that explain the mechanism underpinning health and illness. The mechanisms underpinning health and illness span many disciplines, so health psychology draws on a range of related research literatures. Health psychologists may also be practitioners who develop theory-based interventions to change health-related behaviour patterns. Many health psychologists are simultaneously researchers and practitioners. Interventions may be aimed at changing mechanisms and systems at different levels from the individual to the international. They may also be aimed at preventing ill health or at maximising the self-care of patients who are already ill. Interventions may target patients directly (for example aiming to reduce hostility or increase adherence) or they may focus on the behaviour of health-care professionals who themselves can shape patient behaviour. In each case, the aim is to enhance health and the effectiveness of such interventions must be tested.

SELF-TEST QUESTIONS

- What is health psychology?
- Explain induction and deductive reasoning.
- Is the health of a nation predicted by the overall wealth of that nation?
- Why is socioeconomic status linked to health?
- Describe the information–motivation–behavioural skills model.
- Describe the social ecological model of change.
- What is the difference between primary and secondary prevention?
- List four things that a doctor could do during a consultation to maximise adherence.

ESSAY QUESTIONS

- Providing information is not enough to change behaviour. Discuss in relation to theory and research findings.
- One's parents' wealth is a key determinant of one's health. Explain why, considering poorer developing and richer developed countries.
- Why is theory important to the development of behaviour change interventions?
- Why do patients not always follow the advice of their doctors and what can we do to increase adherence?
- How can the effectiveness of doctor–patient consultations be maximised? Discuss with reference to relevant research.

TEXTS FOR FURTHER READING

Abraham, C., Conner, M., Jones, F. & O'Connor, D. (2008) *Health Psychology: Topics in Applied Psychology*, London: Hodder Arnold.
Sarafino, E.P. (2006) *Health Psychology: Biopsychosocial Interactions*, 5th edn, New York: John Wiley & Sons, Inc.
Sutton, S., Baum, A. & Johnston, M. (2004) *The SAGE Handbook of Health Psychology*, London: Sage.

RELEVANT JOURNAL ARTICLES

Adler, N. & Matthews, K. (1994) Health Psychology: Why do some people get sick and some stay well, *Annual Review of Psychology*, 45: 229–59.

Friedman, R., Sobel, D., Myers, P., Caudill, M. & Benson, H. (1995) Behavioral medicine, clinical health psychology and cost offset, *Health Psychology* 14: 509–18.

Kaplan, R.M. (1990) Behavior as the central outcome in health care, *American Psychologist* 45: 1211–20.

Kok, H., Schaalma, H., Ruiter, R.A.C. & van Empelen, P. (2004) Intervention mapping: A protocol for applying health psychology theory to prevention programmes, *Journal of Health Psychology* 9: 85–98.

Lemieux, A.F., Fisher, J.D. & Pratto, F. (2008) A music-based HIV prevention intervention for urban adolescents, *Health Psychology* 27: 349–57.

Luszczynska, A., Sobczyk, A. & Abraham, C. (2007) Planning to lose weight: RCT of an implementation intention prompt to enhance weight reduction among overweight and obese women, *Health Psychology* 26: 507–12.

Matarazzo, J.D. (1980) Behavioral health and behavioural medicine: Frontiers for a new health psychology, *American Psychologist* 35: 805–17.

Schwartz, G.E. (1980) Testing the biopsychosocial model: The ultimate challenge facing behavioral medicine? *Journal of Consulting and Clinical Psychology* 50: 1040–53.

RELEVANT WEB LINKS

Center for Health, Intervention and Prevention, University of Connecticut, www.chip.uconn.edu

National Institute for Health and Clinical Excellence, a page showing published public health guidance, www.nice.org.uk/Guidance/PHG/Published

UK Department of Health, www.nhs.uk/Pages/HomePage.aspx

Wikipedia entry, http://en.wikipedia.org/wiki/Health_psychology

REFERENCES

Abraham, C. & Graham-Rowe, E. (2009) Are worksite interventions effective in increasing physical activity? A systematic review and meta-analysis, *Health Psychology Review* 3: 108–44.

Abraham, C. & Michie, S. (2008) A taxonomy of behavior change techniques used in interventions, *Health Psychology* 27: 379–87.

Abraham, C., Conner, M., Jones, F. & O'Connor, D. (2008) *Health Psychology: Topics in Applied Psychology*, London: Hodder Education.

Abraham, C., Kelly, M.P., West, R. & Michie, S. (2009) The UK National Institute for Health and Clinical Excellence (NICE) Public Health Guidance on Behaviour Change: A brief introduction, *Psychology Health and Medicine* 14: 1–8.

Adler, N.E., Boyce, T., Chesney, M.A. *et al.* (1994) Socio-economic status and health: The challenge of the gradient, *American Psychologist* 49: 15–24.

Bartholomew, L.K., Parcel, G.S., Kok, G. & Gottlieb, N.H. (2006) *Planning Health Promotion Programs: An Intervention Mapping Approach*, San Francisco: Jossey-Bass.

Belloc, N.B. & Breslow, L. (1972) Relationship of physical health status and health practices, *Preventive Medicine* 1: 409–21.

Carroll, D., Bennett, P. & Davey Smith, G. (1993) Socio-economic health inequalities: Their origins and implications, *Psychology and Health* 8: 295–316.

Commission on Social Determinants of Health (2008) *Closing the Gap in a Generation: Health Equity through Action on the Social Determinants of Health. Final Report of the Commission on Social Determinants of Health.* Geneva: World Health Organization, http://whqlibdoc.who.int/publications/2008/9789241563703_eng.pdf.

Coulter, A., Entwistle, V. & Gilbert, D. (1999) Sharing decisions with patients: Is the information good enough? *British Medical Journal* 318: 318–22.

Davidson, K.W., Gidron, Y., Mostofsky, E. & Trudeau, K.J. (2007) Hospitalization cost offset of a hostility intervention for coronary heart disease patients, *Journal of Consulting and Clinical Psychology* 75: 657–62.

DiMatteo, M.R. (2004) Social support and patient adherence to medical treatment: A meta-analysis, *Health Psychology* 23: 207–18.

DiMatteo, M.R., Sherbourne, C.D., Hays, R.D. *et al.* (1993) Physicians' characteristics influence patients' adherence to medical treatment: Results from the medical outcomes study, *Health Psychology* 12: 93–102.

Donovan, J.L. & Blake, D.R. (1992) Patient non-compliance: Deviance or reasoned decision-making, *Social Science and Medicine* 34: 507–13.

Fisher, J.D. & Fisher, W.A. (1992) Changing AIDS-risk behavior, *Psychological Bulletin* 111: 455–71.

Fisher, J.D., Fisher, W.A., Bryan, A.D. & Misovich, S.J. (2002) Information-motivation-behavioral skills model-based HIV risk behavior change intervention for inner-city high school youth, *Health Psychology* 21: 177–86.

Fisher, J.D., Fisher, W.A., Misovich, S.J., Kimble, D.L. & Malloy, T.E. (1996) Changing AIDS risk behavior: Effects of an intervention emphasizing AIDS risk reduction information, motivation, and behavioral skills in a college student population, *Health Psychology* 15: 114–23.

Friedman, M. & Rosenman, R.H. (1974) *Type A and Your Heart*, New York: Knopf.

Haynes, R.B., Yao, X., Degani, A., Kripalani, S., Garg, A. & McDonald, H.P. (2005) Interventions for enhancing medication adherence, *Cochrane Database of Systematic Reviews* 2005, Issue 4. Art. No.: CD000011. DOI: 10.1002/14651858.CD000011.pub2.

Hingson, R.W. & Howland, J. (2002) Comprehensive community interventions to promote health: Implications for college-age drinking problems, *Journal of Alcohol Studies* 14: 226–40.

Jenkins, C.D., Zyzanski, S.J. & Rosenmann, R.H. (1971) Progress toward validation of a computer-scored test for the type A coronary-prone behavior pattern, *Psychosomatic Medicine* 33: 193–202.

Khaw, K.T., Wareham, N., Bingham, S., Welch, A., Luben. R. & Day, N. (2008) Combined impact of health behaviours and mortality in men and women: The EPIC-Norfolk prospective population study, *PLOS Medicine* 5, open access doi:10.1371, http://medicine.plosjournals.org/perlserv/?request=get-document&doi=10.1371/journal.pmed.0050012.

Kok, G., Gottlieb, N.H., Commers, M. & Smerecnik, C. (2008) The ecological approach in health promotion programs: A decade later, *American Journal of Health Promotion* 23: 437–42.

Korsch, B.M., Gozzi, E.K. & Francis, V. (1968) Gaps in doctor–patient communication: 1. Doctor–patient interaction and patient satisfaction, *Pediatrics* 42: 855–71.

Little, P., Everitt, H., Williamson, I. *et al.* (2001) Observational study of effect of patient centredness and positive approach on outcomes of general practice consultations, *British Medical Journal* 323: 908–11.

Matarazzo, J.D. (1980) Behavioral health and behavioural medicine: Frontiers for a new health psychology, *American Psychologist* 35: 805–17.

Matthews, K. (1988) Coronary heart disease and type A behavior: Update on and alternative to the Booth-Kewley and Friedman (1987) quantitative review, *Psychological Bulletin* 104: 373–80.

Michie, S. & Abraham, C. (2004) Interventions to change health behaviours: Evidence-based or evidence inspired? *Psychology and Health* 19: 29–49.

Miller, T.Q., Smith, T.W., Turner, C.W., Guijarro, M.L. & Hallet, A.J. (1996) A meta-analytic reveiw of research on hostility and physical health, *Psychological Bulletin* 119: 322–48.

Mokdad, A.H., Marks, J.S., Stroup, D.F. & Gerberding, J.L. (2004) Actual causes of death in the United States, 2000, *Journal of the American Medical Association* 291: 1238–45.

Moskowitz, J.T. Epel, E.S. & Acree, M. (2008) Positive affect uniquely predicts lower risk of mortality in people with diabetes, *Health Psychology* 27(Suppl.): S73–S82.

Mullen, P.D., Green, L.W. & Persinger, G. (1985) Clinical trials of patient education for chronic conditions: A comprehensive meta analysis, *Preventive Medicine* 14: 75–81.

Myers, L.B. & Midence, K. (1998) Concepts and issues in adherence. In L.B. Myers & K. Midence (eds), *Adherence to Treatment in Medical Conditions* (pp. 1–24). Amsterdam: Harwood Academic Publishers.

Payne, S., Large, S., Jarrett, N. & Turner, P. (2000) Written information given to patients and families by palliative care units: A national survey, *The Lancet* 355: 1792.

Peirce, R.S., Frone, M.R., Russell, M. & Cooper, M.L. (1996) Financial stress, social support and alcohol involvement: A longitudinal test of the buffering hypothesis in a general population survey, *Health Psychology* 15: 38–47.

Pendleton, D., Schofield, T., Tate, P. & Havelock, P. (1984) *The Consultation: An Approach to Learning and Teaching*, Oxford: Oxford University Press.

Peters, L.H.W., Kok, G., Ten Dam, G.T.M., Buijs, G.J. & Paulussen, T.G.W.M. (2009) Effective elements of school health promotion across behavioral domains: A systematic review of reviews, *BMC Public Health* 9: 182, doi:10.1186/1471-2458-9-182.

Rosenman, R.H, Brand, R.J., Jenkins, C.D., Friedman, M., Straus, R. & Wurm, M. (1975) Coronary heart disease in the Western Collaborative Group Study. Final follow-up experience of 8 1/2 years, *Journal of the American Medical Association* 233: 872–7.

Rovelli, M., Palmeri, D., Vossler, E., Bartus, S., Hull, D. and Shweizer, R. (1989) Compliance in organ transplant recipients, *Transplantation Proceedings* 21: 833–44.

Russell, B. (1912) *Problems of Philosophy*, Oxford: Oxford University Press.

Sapolsky, R.M. (1993) Endocrinology alfresco: Psychoendocrine studies of wild baboons, *Recent Progress in Hormone Research* 48: 437–68.

Schaalma, H.P., Abraham, C., Gillmore, M.R. & Kok, G. (2004) Sex education as health promotion: What does it take? *Archives of Sexual Behaviour* 33: 259–69.

Schinke, S.P. & Gordon, A.N. (1992) Innovative approaches to interpersonal skills training for minority adolescents, in R.J. DiClemente (ed.) *Adolescents and AIDS; A Generation in Jeopardy*, Newbury Park, CA: Sage.

Schwartz, G.E. (1980) Testing the biopsychosocial model: The ultimate challenge facing behavioral medicine? *Journal of Consulting and Clinical Psychology* 50: 1040–53.

Sibbald, B. & Roland, M. (1998) Understanding controlled trials: Why are randomised controlled trials important? *British Medical Journal,* 316: 201.

Silverman, J., Kurtz, S. & Draper, J. (2005) *Skills for Communicating with Patients*, 2nd edn, Oxford: Radcliffe Medical Press.

Strazdins L., D'Souza, R.M., Lim, L.L., Broom, D.H. & Rodgers, B. (2004) Job strain, job insecurity, and health: Rethinking the relationship, *Journal of Occupational Health Psychology* 9: 296–305.

Vartiainen, E., Paavola, M., McAlister, A. & Puska, P. (1998) Fifteen-year follow-up of smoking prevention effects in the North Karelia Youth Project, *American Journal of Public Health* 88: 81–5.

Wilkinson, R.G. (1996) *Unhealthy Societies: The Afflictions of Inequality*, London: Routledge.

Williams-Piehota, P., Pizarro, J., Schneider, T.R., Mowad, L. & Salovey, P. (2005) Matching health messages to monitor-blunter coping styles to motivate screening mammography, *Health Psychology* 24: 58–67.

World Health Organization (1948) Preamble to the Constitution of the World Health Organization as adopted by the International Health Conference, New York, 19–22 June, 1946; signed on 22 July 1946 by the representatives of 61 States (*Official Records of the World Health Organization* 2: 100) and entered into force on 7 April 1948.

World Health Organization (2009) Preamble to the Constitution of the World Health Organization as adopted by the International Health Conference, New York, 19–22 June, 1946; signed on 22 July 1946 by the representatives of 61 States (*Official Records of the World Health Organization,* 2: 100) and entered into force on 7 April 1948.

8 A Biopsychosocial Approach to Health Psychology

Daryl O'Connor, Fiona Jones, Mark Conner & Charles Abraham

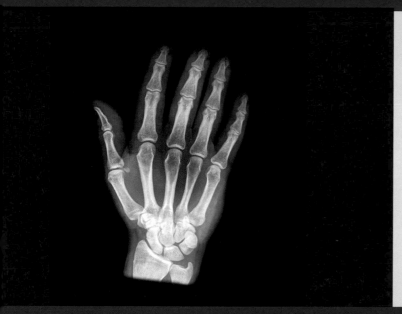

LEARNING OUTCOMES

WHEN YOU HAVE COMPLETED THIS CHAPTER, YOU SHOULD BE ABLE TO:

1. Describe the basic features of the central nervous system.
2. Explain how the body responds to psychological stress.
3. Understand the role of psychological factors in the experience of pain.
4. Discuss how psychoneuroimmunology (PNI) plays a role in illness processes such as developing the common cold and in wound healing.

KEY WORDS

Adrenal Glands ● Antibody-Mediated Immunity ● Atherosclerosis ● Autonomic Nervous System ● Behavioural Pathways ● Biofeedback ● Brain ● Cardiovascular System ● Cell-Mediated Immunity ● Central Nervous System ● Cerebrum ● Cognitive Techniques ● Common Cold ● Cortisol ● Cytokines ● Diencephalon ● Endocrine System ● Forebrain ● Gate-Control Theory ● Hindbrain ● Hypothalamic-Pituitary-Adrenal (HPA) Axis Response System ● Hypothalamus ● Immune System ● Limbic System ● Midbrain ● Myocardial Infarction ● Nerves ● Nervous System ● Operant Techniques ● Pain Management ● Parasympathetic Division ● Peripheral Nervous System ● Pituitary Gland ● Progressive Muscle Relaxation ● Psychobiological Pathways ● Psychoneuroimmunology ● Respiratory Infectious Illness ● Somatic Nervous System ● Spinal Cord ● Stress Response ● Sympathetic Adrenal Medullary (SAM) System ● Sympathetic Division ● Telencephalon ● Thalamus ● Wound Healing

CHAPTER OUTLINE

ROUTE MAP OF THE CHAPTER

In this chapter we will consider the main biological pathways through which psychological factors influence physical health and illness. The body's physical systems, including the central nervous system, the endocrine system, the cardiovascular system and the immune system, will be introduced. Next, we consider how these basic biological processes may be affected by factors such as psychological stress. In particular, we will outline how activation of the hypothalamic-pituitary-adrenal (HPA) axis and the sympathetic adrenal medullary (SAM) system are linked to increased risk of heart disease. Then we will provide an overview of the gate-control theory of pain, the role of psychological factors in the experience of pain and pain management. Finally, we will introduce research into psychoneuroimmunology and discuss how psychological factors can affect the immune system, focusing on susceptibility to upper respiratory illness and the speed of wound healing.

8.1   INTRODUCTION

The biopsychosocial model (see also Chapter 7) proposes that health and illness are influenced by psychological factors (e.g. personality, cognition, emotion) and social factors (e.g. social class, ethnicity, people in your social world) as well as biological factors (e.g. viruses, bacteria). Within this context, there is increasing evidence that psychological factors such as stress (see Chapter 9) affect health directly by causing changes in blood pressure and hormones for example. Psychological factors can also influence health indirectly by changing health behaviours (e.g. exercise, diet, smoking). This is known as the **behavioural pathway**. The direct **psychobiological pathways** are important as they help us understand how psychological factors can have a direct impact on physiological disease-related processes. The study of behavioural pathways can help us understand how psychological factors can indirectly influence disease-related processes by producing negative changes in health behaviours. This chapter will concentrate on describing the main psychobiological pathways, but first it is important that you understand some of the basic biological processes within the human body.

behavioural pathways the ways in which psychological factors can influence health indirectly by changing health behaviours.

psychobiological pathways the ways in which psychological factors directly impact on physiological disease-related processes.

8.2   BASIC FEATURES OF THE NERVOUS SYSTEM

The role of the **nervous system** is to allow us to adapt to changes within our body and environment by using our five senses (touch, sight, smell, taste, sound) to understand, interpret and respond to internal and external changes quickly and appropriately. The nervous system consists of the **brain**, the **spinal cord** and the **nerves** (bundles of fibres that transmit information in and out of the nervous system). The brain is the central part of the nervous system and it helps control our behaviour. It receives and sends messages to the rest of the body through the spinal cord.

nervous system the brain, the spinal cord and the nerves (bundles of fibres that transmit information in and out of the nervous system).

brain the central part of the nervous system which helps control our behaviour.

spinal cord the main neural axis in humans and other vertebrates.

nerves bundles of fibres that transmit information in and out of the nervous system.

8.2.1   Central Nervous System and Peripheral Nervous System

The nervous system is classified into various different sub-systems and sub-divisions, but these different components are all part of an integrated system that does not operate independently (see Table 8.1). The nervous system has two distinct parts:

- Central nervous system.
- Peripheral nervous system.

The **central nervous system** (CNS) comprises the brain and spinal cord and is protected by bone. The brain is encased within the skull and the spinal cord is enclosed in the spinal cavity and protected by the vertebrae. Both the brain and the spinal cord do not come into direct contact with the skull or the vertebrae, as they are further enclosed by a three-layered set of membranes called the meninges. Instead, they float in a clear liquid called cerebrospinal fluid.

The **peripheral nervous system** (PNS) is a network of nerves

central nervous system the brain and the spinal cord protected by bone.

peripheral nervous system a network of nerves that connects the brain and spinal cord to the rest of the body.

TABLE 8.1 *Overview of the Nervous System.*

Nervous system				
Central nervous system	**Peripheral nervous system**			
Brain Spinal cord	**Somatic nervous system**	**Autonomic nervous system**		
			Sympathetic division	**Parasympathetic division**

that connects the brain and spinal cord to the rest of the body. The PNS is further sub-divided, according to its function, into:

- Somatic nervous system.
- Autonomic nervous system.

somatic nervous system a sub-division of the peripheral nervous system concerned with coordinating the 'voluntary' body movements controlled by the skeletal muscles.

autonomic nervous system a sub-division of the peripheral nervous system concerned with regulating internal body processes that require no conscious awareness.

sympathetic division a sub-division of the ANS, it mobilises the body by increasing heart rate and blood pressure for example.

parasympathetic division a sub-division of the ANS, it restores the body's energy by reducing heart rate and respiration while increasing the rate of digestion.

The **somatic nervous system** (SNS) is concerned with coordinating the 'voluntary' body movements controlled by the skeletal muscles. The **autonomic nervous system** (ANS) regulates internal body processes that require no conscious awareness, for example the rate of heart contractions and breathing, or the speed at which food passes through the digestive tract.

The ANS is sub-divided into:

- Sympathetic division.
- Parasympathetic division.

The **sympathetic division** mobilises the body by increasing heart rate and blood pressure among other physiological changes, whereas the **parasympathetic division** generally restores the body's energy by reducing heart rate and respiration while increasing the rate of digestion. The changes in each of the divisions occur because the ANS triggers the endocrine system to react in the face of stress.

8.2.2 The Anatomy of the Brain

The brain has three major anatomic components: the **forebrain**, the **midbrain** and the **hindbrain**.

The forebrain consists of dense, elaborate masses of tissue and has two main sub-divisions:

- The **telencephalon**, which is composed of the cerebrum and limbic system.
- The **diencephalon**, which comprises the thalamus and hypothalamus.

The **cerebrum** is the largest part of the human brain, consists of a mass of intricate tissue and is divided into two halves – the left and right cerebral hemispheres – that are connected in the middle by a bundle of nerve fibres called the *corpus callosum*. The upper part of the cerebrum is the *cerebral cortex* (its outermost area). This is sub-divided into the frontal, parietal, occipital and temporal lobes and controls higher processes such as speaking, reasoning and memory (see Figure 8.1). More specifically, the frontal lobe (located towards the front of the cerebrum) is involved in speech, thought and emotion. Behind this is the parietal lobe, which perceives and interprets sensations such as touch, temperature and pain. The occipital lobe is at the centre back of the cerebrum and detects and interprets visual images. Finally, the temporal lobes located on either side are involved in hearing and aspects of memory storage.

The **limbic system** is evolutionarily older than other parts of the brain and consists of the amygdala and hippocampus, among other structures. This system interacts with the endocrine system (i.e. the network of glands that secrete hormones throughout the body, described later) and other bodily processes and plays an important role in motivational and emotional aspects of behaviours such as sex, eating, drinking and aggression. It is also involved in aspects of memory processes.

forebrain one of the three major anatomic components of the brain, situated towards the front.

midbrain one of the three major anatomic components of the brain which includes the brain stem, it regulates critical bodily functions such as breathing.

hindbrain part of the brain involved in coordinating the body's movements, sleep, arousal and regulation of the cardiovascular system and respiration.

telencephalon a sub-division of the forebrain which is composed of the cerebrum and limbic system.

diencephalon a sub-division of the forebrain which comprises the thalamus and hypothalamus.

cerebrum the largest part of the human brain consisting of a mass of intricate tissue divided into two halves, the left and right cerebral hemispheres.

limbic system evolutionarily old, this part of the brain interacts with the endocrine system, plays an important role in motivational and emotional aspects of behaviour and is involved in aspects of memory processes.

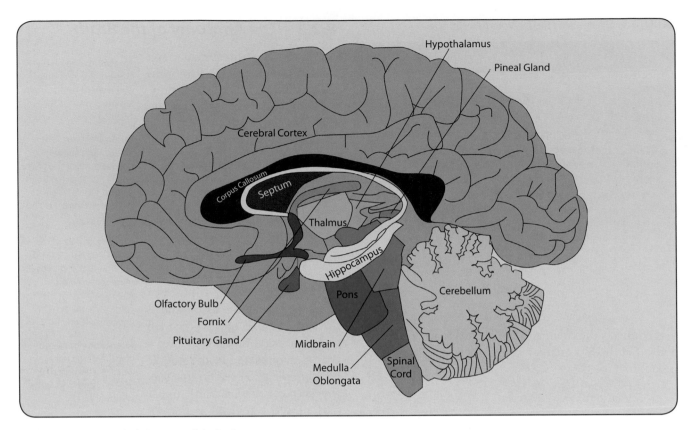

FIGURE 8.1 *Anatomical structure of the brain.*

Source: Shutterstock.

ACTIVITY BOX 8.1

You have just read that the brain has three major anatomic components and each has a number of sub-divisions. Can you list them? If not, it might be useful as a revision aid to draw a diagram of each component and its sub-divisions!

thalamus part of the forebrain, it plays an important role in regulating states of sleep, arousal and consciousness.

hypothalamus part of the forebrain, it regulates many of the body's systems, including controlling how an individual responds to stress.

The second major division of the forebrain is the diencephalon. Its two most important structures are the **thalamus** and the **hypothalamus** (see Figure 8.1). The thalamus is thought to have multiple functions and plays an important role in regulating states of sleep, arousal and consciousness. The hypothalamus is located below the thalamus and although it is a relatively small structure, it is very important, as it regulates many of the body's systems. As we will see later in this chapter, it controls how individuals respond to stressful encounters. In short, it oversees the basic behaviours associated with the survival of the species: fighting, feeding, fleeing and mating, often referred to as the four Fs!

The midbrain includes the brain stem, and regulates critical bodily functions such as breathing, swallowing, posture, movement and the rate at which the body metabolises food. The hindbrain comprises the cerebellum, medulla and the pons and is involved in coordinating the body's movements, sleep, arousal and the regulation of the cardiovascular system and respiration.

You may now want to try completing Activity Box 8.1.

8.2.3   The Spinal Cord and Nerve Cells

The spinal cord is a long, delicate structure that begins at the end of the brain stem and continues down to the bottom of the spine. It carries incoming and outgoing messages between the brain and the rest of the body. The brain communicates with much of the body through nerves that run up and down the spinal cord. As you will see later, the spinal cord plays an important role in responding to pain stimuli. The *nervous system* contains 100 billion or more nerve cells that run throughout the body. A nerve cell, called a neuron, is made up of a large cell body and a single, elongated extension (axon) for sending messages (see Figure 8.2). Neurons usually have many branches (dendrites) for receiving messages. Nerves transmit messages electrically from the axon of one neuron to the dendrite of another (at the synapse) by secreting a tiny amount of chemicals called *neurotransmitters*. These substances trigger the receptors on the next neuron's dendrite to start up a new electrical impulse.

8.2.4   Endocrine System

The **endocrine system** is central to all activities we engage in and represents an integrated system of small glands that work closely with the ANS. The most important components of this system are the *endocrine glands*, which secrete chemicals into the bloodstream to be transported to their point of use around the different parts of the body (see Figure 8.3). Unlike the nervous system, which uses nerves to send electrical and chemical messages, the endocrine system uses blood vessels to send chemical messages. Each of the endocrine glands (see Figure 8.3), once activated, secretes chemical substances called *hormones* into the bloodstream that carry messages to different parts of the body. Numerous endocrine glands are situated throughout the body such as the adrenal glands, pituitary gland, pineal gland, testis/ovary, pancreas, thyroid and thymus. However, the most important glands, in terms of understanding the influence of psychological stress on the development of disease, are the *adrenal* and *pituitary glands*.

> **endocrine system** an integrated system of small glands that work closely with the ANS.

8.2.4.1   The pituitary gland

The **pituitary gland** is situated just under the hypothalamus and is considered the 'master' gland, as it regulates the endocrine gland secretions. Overall the pituitary gland plays a significant role in the regulation of the growth of body tissues and the development of the gonads, ovum and sperm, as well as stimulating

> **pituitary gland** the 'master' gland regulating the endocrine gland secretions.

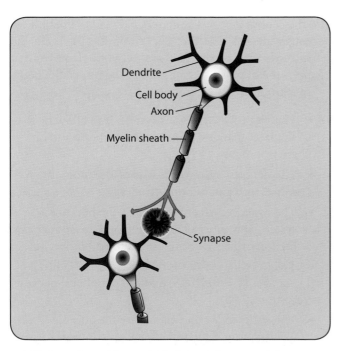

FIGURE 8.2 *Central features of a nerve cell or neuron. A neuron consists of a large cell body and a single, elongated extension (axon) for sending messages. Neurons have several dendrites (branches) for receiving messages.*

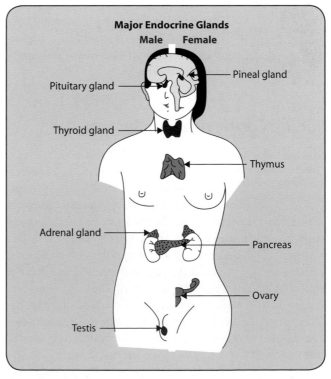

FIGURE 8.3 *Major endocrine glands. Each gland releases chemicals into the bloodstream to be used by different parts of the body.*

hypothalamic-pituitary-adrenal (HPA) axis response a physiological response to stress leading to the release of the stress hormone cortisol.

lactation and maintaining blood pressure. However, it also releases the important hormone adrenocorticotrophic hormone (ACTH) after stimulation by the hypothalamus. ACTH, in turn, stimulates the adrenal cortex. These processes are known as the **hypothalamic-pituitary-adrenal (HPA) axis response**. This is an extremely important response system that we describe in more detail later.

8.2.4.2 The adrenal glands

adrenal glands two glands within one located on the top of each kidney, secreting hormones and steroids.

The **adrenal glands** are best thought of as two glands within one that are located on the top of each kidney. Each has a central core, called the *adrenal medulla*, which secretes the hormones *adrenaline* and *noradrenaline* (also known as epinephrine and norepinephrine), which act to increase heart rate and mobilise glucose into the blood, among other things. When considered together, adrenaline, noradrenaline and a further hormone, dopamine, are known as *catecholamines*. The outer

cortisol commonly known as the 'stress hormone', it is secreted when a person encounters a stressful situation in order to help the body respond appropriately.

portion of the adrenal gland, called the adrenal cortex, secretes *glucocorticoids* when we encounter stressful situations in order to help the body respond appropriately. **Cortisol** (corticosterone in rodents) is the most important glucocorticoid and as a result it is now commonly referred to as the 'stress hormone'.

8.2.5 Cardiovascular System

cardiovascular system the circulatory system comprising the heart and blood vessels.

The heart, the centre of the **cardiovascular system**, is made of muscle and 'beats' or 'pumps' approximately 100 000 times per day. It has four chambers: the two upper chambers are known as *atriums* and the two lower ones are called *ventricles*. The main muscular outer part of the heart, which contains the cardiac *veins* and *arteries*, is called the *myocardium*. The central function of the cardiovascular system is to ensure that oxygen (and other nutrients) is transported to all the organs of the body and that carbon dioxide (as well as other waste products) is removed from each of the body's cells. The blood is used as the vehicle to transport the oxygen, with the heart and blood vessels allowing the blood to be carried around the body.

In the cardiovascular system, the arteries carry blood *from* the heart and myocardium and veins carry blood *to*

the heart and myocardium. Blood pressure is the force exerted by the blood on the artery walls and has two components:

- Diastolic blood pressure is the resting level in the arteries between contractions.
- Systolic blood pressure is the maximum pressure in the arteries when the heart pumps.

An individual's blood pressure is described using two numbers representing the systolic and diastolic components and is expressed in units known as millimetres of mercury (mmHg; e.g. 120 over 75 or 120/75 mmHg). Blood pressure levels are influenced by numerous factors, including temperature, weight, posture and food intake. However, psychological factors such as chronic stress have also been found to be associated with the development of high blood pressure (or hypertension), which can lead to serious damage to the heart and the arteries. The links between stress, blood pressure and cardiovascular disease will be revisited shortly.

8.2.6 Summary

The role of the nervous system is to allow us to adapt to changes within both our body and our environment. It consists of the brain, the spinal cord and billions of nerves. The brain is the central part of the nervous system and consists of three major components: the forebrain, the midbrain and the hindbrain. The nervous system is divided into the central nervous system (CNS) and the peripheral nervous system (PNS). The CNS comprises the brain and spinal cord, whereas the PNS is a network of nerves that connects the brain and spinal cord to the rest of the body.

To summarise:

- The role of the nervous system is to allow us to adapt to changes within both our body and our environment.
- The nervous system consists of the brain, the spinal cord and billions of nerves.
- The brain is the central part of the nervous system and consists of three major components: the forebrain, the midbrain and the hindbrain.
- The nervous system is divided into the central nervous system (CNS) and the peripheral nervous system (PNS).
- The main endocrine glands are the adrenal glands, pituitary gland, pineal gland, testis/ovary, pancreas, thyroid and thymus.
- The adrenal glands release adrenaline and noradrenaline (known as catecholamines) and cortisol.

8.3   WHAT HAPPENS WHEN YOU EXPERIENCE STRESS?

sympathetic adrenal medullary (SAM) system a physiological response to stress leading to the release of adrenalin and noradrenalin to put the body on alert.

Two biological systems are activated when you undergo stress: the **sympathetic adrenal medullary (SAM) system** and the *hypothalamic-pituitary-adrenal (HPA)* axis. Both systems are described below.

8.3.1   The Sympathetic Adrenal Medullary (SAM) Response System

When an individual is suddenly under threat or frightened, their brain instantly sends a message to the adrenal glands, which quickly release noradrenaline, which in turn activates the internal organs. This is the basic sympathetic division response to threat. At the same time, the adrenal medulla releases adrenaline, which is rapidly transported through the bloodstream in order to further prepare the body for its response. This system is known as the sympathetic adrenal medullary (SAM) system (see Figure 8.4). Within moments adrenaline and noradrenaline have the entire body on alert, a response sometimes called the 'fight or flight' response. As a result, breathing quickens, the heart beats more rapidly and powerfully, the eyes dilate to allow more light in, and the activity of the digestive system decreases to permit

more blood to go to the muscles. This effect is both rapid and intense.

8.3.2   The Hypothalamic-Pituitary-Adrenal (HPA) Axis Response System

Alongside the SAM response, when a person encounters an unpleasant event that they perceive as stressful, the hypothalamus (the H in HPA) releases a chemical messenger called *corticotrophin-releasing factor* (CRF). Once released, CRF is transported in the blood supply to the pituitary gland (the P) where it stimulates the release of adrenocorticotropic hormone (ACTH). Subsequently, the latter hormone travels through the circulatory system to the adrenal (the A) cortex, where it stimulates production of the glucocorticoid *cortisol* – known as the 'stress hormone' (see Figure 8.4).

8.3.3   Stress and Cardiovascular Disease

It is likely that our ancestors frequently encountered acute, short-lived stressors while out hunting for food. In such 'fight or flight' situations, the SAM and HPA response systems would prepare the body to respond appropriately. From an evolutionary perspective, these **stress response** processes are

stress response a bodily response to 'fight or flight' situations to prepare the body to respond appropriately to help ensure survival.

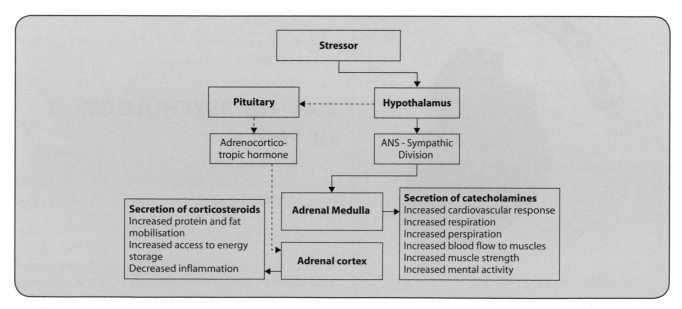

FIGURE 8.4 *Stress response: hypothalamic-pituitary-adrenal (HPA) axis response system (dashed line) and sympathetic adrenal medullary system (SAM) response system (full line).*

adaptive and help ensure survival. However, they are only adaptive in as much as they are short lived and the body's systems return to normal quickly. In reality, the stress of modern-day life rarely affords such infrequent, acute, life-threatening, stressful encounters. Instead, we are exposed to frequent daily hassles as well as long-lasting, chronic stressors (Lazarus & Folkman, 1984; O'Connor *et al.*, 2008). As a result, the stress response system is repeatedly activated and the cardiovascular system is potentially exposed to excessive wear and tear. In the longer term, repetitive activation of these bodily systems may contribute to future ill-health by increasing cardiovascular disease risk. In particular, repeated activation of the stress response systems may lead to the build-up of fatty plaques in the lining of the blood vessels that leads to the narrowing of the arteries. This is known as **atherosclerosis** (see Photo 8.1).

atherosclerosis the build-up of fatty plaques in the lining of the blood vessels which leads to narrowing of the arteries, partly caused by repeated activation of the stress response systems.

Recent studies conducted by psychologists in the US and the UK have provided good evidence linking stress with cardiovascular disease. For example, Matthews and Gump (2002) examined the impact of different work stressors and marital breakdown (a major stressor in its own right) on which people died from coronary heart disease during a nine-year follow-up period. Increasing numbers of different work stressors and being divorced were found to be associated with an increased risk of cardiovascular-related deaths during the study. Another study exploring the impact of an acute stressor found that admissions to hospitals in England increased on the day England lost to Argentina in a penalty shoot-out in the 1998 Football World Cup and the day following (Carroll *et al.*, 2002). The authors argue that their results suggest that **myocardial infarction** can be triggered by an emotional upset, such as watching your football team lose an important match. Nevertheless, it is important to remember that stress can have an indirect impact on cardiovascular disease by influencing our daily health behaviours (see Focus Point 8.1).

myocardial infarction destruction of heart tissue resulting from an interruption of blood supply to the area, possibly triggered by emotional upset.

8.3.4   *Summary*

Two response systems are activated when we experience stress. The first and easiest to activate is the sympathetic adrenal medullary (SAM) system; the second is the hypothalamic-pituitary-adrenal (HPA) axis response system. The SAM system leads to the release of the adrenaline and noradrenaline that put the body on alert; the HPA axis response system leads to the release of the stress hormone cortisol. The stress response has been found to have a negative impact on a number of health outcomes, such as cardiovascular disease.

To summarise:

- The sympathetic adrenal medullary (SAM) system and the hypothalamic-pituitary-adrenal (HPA) axis are activated when we experience stress.
- The SAM system leads to the release of adrenaline and noradrenaline.
- The HPA axis response system leads to the release of cortisol.
- The stress response is linked to the development of cardiovascular disease.

8.4   THE PSYCHOLOGY OF PAIN

Psychology has made a substantial impact in improving our understanding of how we experience pain and how best to manage pain (Horn & Munafo, 1998). It has long been recognised that psychological factors can influence how long we can tolerate pain. However, early theories of pain did not incorporate a role for psychological factors in explaining how we experience pain. This is surprising given that we can all think of episodes when someone's perception of pain has been influenced by cognitive, emotional or social factors. For example, we are less likely to

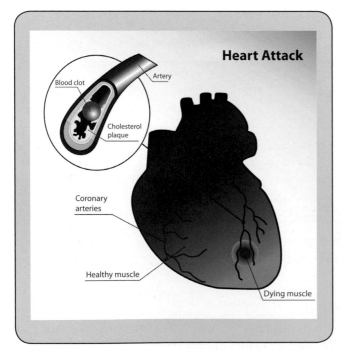

PHOTO 8.1 *The heart and atherosclerosis.*
Source: Shutterstock.

FOCUS POINT 8.1   VULNERABILITY TO STRESS-INDUCED EATING

A growing body of research has shown that psychological stress affects health directly by its impact on biological processes as well as indirectly through changes to health behaviours. Broadly speaking, this research has indicated that high levels of stress are associated with both increased and decreased overall food intake. However, a number of important vulnerability variables have been identified, which may explain why some people eat more in response to stress (Greeno & Wing, 1994; Newman, O'Connor & Conner, 2007; O'Connor et al., 2008, 2009a). These individual differences may be accounted for by variations in learning history, attitudes towards eating or biology. The main vulnerability variables are listed below together with the key findings.

Moderator	Key findings
Obese status	Obese individuals have been found to increase eating when stressed
Restraint	Individuals who restrict their food intake have been found to eat more when stressed
Gender	Women are more likely to eat more when stressed compared to men
Emotional eating	Individuals who have a tendency to eat more when anxious or emotionally aroused consumed more food when stressed compared to nonemotional eaters
External eating	Individuals who are more responsive to food cues in their environment eat more when stressed compared to internal eaters
Disinhibition	Individuals who have a tendency to over-eat generally eat more when stressed compared to those who do not

experience pain when we are distracted by the demands of taking part in a competitive sporting event or when we are concentrating on something in our immediate environment instead of the source of the pain.

8.4.1   The Role of Meaning in Pain

The meaning an individual attributes to pain has been found to affect their experience of it. An early example of this was discovered by Beecher (1956) in soldiers during the Second World War. Beecher was a physician who treated many soldiers who had been badly wounded and found that 49% reported being in 'moderate' or 'severe' pain, with only 32% requesting medication when it was offered. However, when he was treating civilians, many years later, with similar if not less severe wounds after having undergone surgery, he found that 75% of the civilians reported being in 'moderate' or 'severe' pain, with 83% of these requesting medication. He accounted for these marked differences in terms of the meaning the soldiers attributed to their injuries compared to the civilian surgical patients. For the soldiers, their injuries represented the 'end of their war' and they could look forward to getting on with their lives away from the dangers of war; whereas for the civilians, the surgery represented the beginning of a difficult, challenging and lengthy disruption to their lives.

8.4.2   Specificity Theory and Pattern Theory

Specificity theory and pattern theory are two of the early dominant theories of pain perception (Goldschneider, 1920; Von Frey, 1895). The former theory takes a very mechanistic view and assumes that we have a separate sensory system for perceiving pain, similar to hearing and vision. Moreover, specificity theory posits that the 'pain system' has its own set of special pain receptors for detecting pain stimuli and its own peripheral nerves, which communicate via a separate pathway to a designated area in the brain for the processing of pain signals.

In contrast, pattern theory suggests that the receptors for pain are shared with the other senses and that a separate sensory system does not exist. Central to this view is the notion that an individual will only experience pain when a certain pattern of neural activity reaches a critical level in the brain. Moreover, this theory suggests that only intense stimulation will produce a pattern of neural activity that will result in pain, given that mild and strong pain stimulation use the same sense modality.

However, there is a major problem with both of these early theories: they do not provide a role for psychological factors in pain perception. More specifically, they cannot account for how cognitive, emotional and social factors such as the meaning of pain can influence the experience of pain. Therefore, a new theory was required that incorporated psychological factors. We turn to such a theory next.

8.4.3 *Gate-Control Theory of Pain*

gate-control theory
the idea that a neural gate in the spinal cord can open and close thus modulating incoming pain signals

Melzack and Wall (1965) introduced the **gate-control theory** of pain perception. This theory represented a substantial step forward, as it included important aspects of earlier theories but at the same time provided a detailed description of the physiological mechanisms through which psychological factors could influence an individual's experience of pain. Briefly, gate-control theory proposes that a neural gate in the spinal cord can modulate incoming pain signals and that a number of factors influence the opening and closing of the gate. These are:

- The amount of activity in pain fibres.
- The amount of activity in other peripheral fibres.
- Messages that descend from the brain (or central nervous system).

When the neural gate receives information from each of these sources it decides whether to open or close the gate (see Table 8.2 and Photo 8.2). When the gate is open pain is experienced.

The theory postulates that the gating mechanism is located in the spinal cord. When we are exposed to a painful stimulus, the gating mechanism receives signals from pain fibres located at the site of the injury, other peripheral fibres that transmit information about harmless stimuli, and the brain (or central nervous system) to open the gate. The pain fibres then release a neurotransmitter that passes through the gating mechanism and stimulates nearby cells, which in turn transmit impulses to specific locations in the brain (e.g. thalamus, limbic system, hypothalamus). When this activity reaches a critical threshold level we will experience pain. Once the pain centres in the brain have been activated, we are able to respond quickly to remove ourselves from danger. There are different types of pain fibres with distinct functions.

It is worth noting that the three types of pain fibres have different functions. A group of fibres send information about sharp, brief pain, another group transmits information about dull, throbbing pain, and yet another sends information to the gate about harmless stimulation or mild irritation, such as a gentle touch or stroking or lightly scratching the skin. When the latter group of fibres is stimulated, the gate is likely to close and pain perception is subdued, thus explaining why people

TABLE 8.2 *Conditions that Can Open and Close the Pain Gate.*

Conditions that open the gate
- Physical conditions
  - Extent of the injury
  - Inappropriate activity level
- Emotional conditions
  - Anxiety or worry
  - Tension
  - Depression
- Mental conditions
  - Focusing on the pain
  - Boredom; little involvement in life activities

Conditions that close the gate
- Physical conditions
  - Medication
  - Counterstimulation (e.g. heat or massage)
- Emotional conditions
  - Positive emotions (e.g. happiness or optimism)
  - Relaxation
  - Rest
- Mental conditions
  - Intense concentration or distraction
  - Involvement and interest in life activities

Source: Adapted from Sarafino (2008), based on material by Karol *et al.* cited in Turk, Meichenbaum & Genest (1983).

PHOTO 8.2 *Anxiety and worry can open the gate leading to the experience of greater pain.*
Source: Shutterstock.

experience a reduction in pain during a gentle massage or when heat is applied to aching limbs.

As already outlined, early theories of pain were unable to account for how cognitive, emotional and social factors influenced the experience of pain. The gate-control theory suggests that such psychological factors have an impact on pain perception by influencing messages that descend from the brain. Neurons in different parts of the brain send impulses to the spinal cord. Various brain processes such as anxiety, distraction, hypnosis and pleasure have the capacity to influence this neural activity by releasing chemicals such as endorphins and therefore causing the opening and closing of the gate. Table 8.2 provides a summary of various conditions that individuals may experience that may open and close the gate.

8.4.4   Pain Management

Gate-control theory has been criticised by psychologists because it does not provide a detailed consideration of how psychological factors precisely influence pain processes (Horn & Munafo, 1998). Nevertheless, it has inspired researchers to develop various psychological and behavioural methods to manage pain and study how effective they are. We consider some of these approaches next.

Current treatment of pain focuses on a combination of approaches that include psychological as well as medical interventions (known as multidisciplinary programmes). Turk and Burwinkle (2000) highlighted the effectiveness and cost effectiveness of such programmes compared to traditional approaches to treating chronic pain. They list commonly used measures of pain assessment and show that multidisciplinary programmes are effective not only in reducing pain but in improving employment status and reducing medication and medical services usage. They also emphasise the role of psychologists both in designing and evaluating interventions within such multidisciplinary contexts.

There are numerous intervention techniques that may be used by psychologists working with individuals experiencing pain. As outlined earlier, the gate-control theory of pain perception (Melzack & Wall, 1965) helps us to understand how the brain is able to control the sensation of pain, providing a clear pathway for the psychological moderation of pain experience. Some of these important techniques are outlined next.

8.4.4.1   Cognitive techniques

Cognitive intervention techniques involve teaching individuals to identify and change cognitions and emotions that increase pain. So, for example, challenging catastrophic or hopeless thoughts may reduce anxiety and enhance self-efficacy. Such interventions have been shown to be efficacious, especially with chronic pain patients, and can be more effective than pharmacological interventions (Morley, Eccleston & Williams, 1999; see also Andrasik & Schwartz, 2006). Individuals may also be taught new coping strategies, including distraction (i.e. the patient focuses on a nonpainful stimulus in their nearby environment in order to distract attention away from pain); nonpainful imagery (i.e. the patient focuses on a positive, imagined event/scene unrelated to the pain); pain redefinition (i.e. the patient learns to redefine negative thoughts about the pain experience using positive self statements); and hypnosis (i.e. the patient experiences less pain while in a relaxed, hypnotic state). Each of these techniques has been found to be effective in reducing the pain experience (Horn & Munafo, 1998).

That said, the evidence is more convincing when applied to acute compared to chronic pain (Fernandez & Turk, 1989). In addition, in certain circumstances (e.g. headache pain) when combined with behavioural techniques, cognitive strategies have been found to be at least as effective as conventional analgesics (Holroyd *et al.*, 1991).

8.4.4.2   Operant techniques

An alternative group of **pain-management** techniques are based on the principles of operant conditioning. These focus directly on pain-related behaviour (and not pain reduction), with a view to enhancing activity and quality of life. The techniques that are mainly used relate to reinforcement and extinction and were pioneered by Fordyce (1976). In general terms, reinforcement refers to the presentation of a stimulus following a response that increases the frequency of subsequent responses (known as a conditioned response). Extinction refers to the occurrences of a conditioned response decreasing or disappearing when the stimulus is removed.

> **pain management** the treatment and management of pain using any combination of approaches – psychological, behavioural and medical.

Central to **operant techniques** is the assumption that pain behaviours (e.g. withdrawal, lying down, crying, limping, reliance on medication) are learned responses that become conditioned through reinforcement (e.g. receiving attention, sympathy and care in response to pain behaviour and avoiding anticipated pain by taking analgesic medication). Therefore, this approach seeks to:

> **operant techniques** in pain management, the idea that pain behaviours are learned responses which become conditioned through reinforcement.

- Reinforce adaptive 'well' behaviours such as walking without limping after a minor operation.
- Encourage family and friends not to attend to or reward pain behaviours.
- Provide analgesic medication on a fixed schedule (e.g. every 4 hours) and not when the individual requests it or is in pain.

Each of these techniques has been found to successfully reinforce new adaptive behaviour and to extinguish previous maladaptive behaviour (Horn & Munafo, 1998). For example, patients' reliance on medication can be reduced over a short period. By providing the medication

Think about the last time you visited the dentist. Was it a painful experience?

Based on your reading of the pain-management techniques described in this section, plan how you might use one or more of these techniques to reduce the pain experience. Which techniques would suit you best?

Think about which techniques are likely to be effective in different situations and individuals.

---

on a fixed schedule, receiving it becomes independent of their request for it and, as a result, reinforcing effects are eliminated. Over a couple of weeks, the dosage of medication can be reduced by mixing it with a flavoured syrup to mask the taste and then gradually reducing the amount of the analgesic in the mixture.

8.4.4.3 Biofeedback and progressive muscle relaxation

Stress is a well-known trigger for pain experiences such as headache pain and chronic back pain, as it leads to changes in physiological processes. As a result, patients are frequently taught to use **biofeedback** and relaxation techniques to help patients manage stress (Horn & Munafo, 1998). Biofeedback is a technique in which a patient learns to exert control over basic autonomic bodily processes such as blood pressure, heart rate and blood flow, as well as learning to gain increased control over voluntary processes such as muscle tension. Feedback is achieved by placing electrodes and transducers on the skin that can detect and convert bodily signals such as temperature, galvanic skin response and blood flow into electrical signals, which are then typically transmitted as a tone. Through training and hearing the tone change when a specific muscle group is relaxed, patients can learn to exert control over muscles previously not under their voluntary control.

> **biofeedback** in pain management, a technique taught to patients to help them manage stress by exerting control over autonomic and voluntary bodily processes.

> **progressive muscle relaxation** in pain management, a technique taught to patients to help them tighten and relax different muscle groups.

As mentioned above, patients can also be directed to use **progressive muscle relaxation** whereby they learn to relax and tighten different muscle groups in a quiet, comfortable environment for approximately 20 to 40 minutes in weekly sessions over an extended period. Subsequently, when a painful or stressful episode is developing, the patients are encouraged to use this technique to prevent or reduce the severity of the pain episode. Progressive muscle relaxation and biofeedback have both been found to be effective (e.g. Andrasik & Schwartz, 2006). However,

these techniques may have limited impact on patients suffering from severe chronic pain and therefore are often used in combination with other techniques (e.g. Holroyd *et al.*, 2001).

Activity Box 8.2 considers pain-management techniques.

8.4.5   Summary

Psychological factors can play a role in the perception of pain. The gate-control theory proposes that a neural gate in the spinal cord receives signals from pain fibres at the site of injury, other peripheral fibres and messages descending from the brain. The degree to which the gate opens (leading to the experience of pain) is determined by the combined effects of these three factors. The main psychological approaches to pain management are **cognitive techniques**, operant approaches, biofeedback and progressive muscle relaxation.

> **cognitive techniques** in pain management, interventions taught to individuals to identify and change cognitions and emotions which increase pain.

To summarise:

- Gain-control theory proposes that a neural gate in the spinal cord receives signals from pain fibres, peripheral fibres and messages descending from the brain.

- The main psychological approaches to pain management are cognitive techniques, operant approaches, biofeedback and progressive muscle relaxation.

- Cognitive techniques involve teaching individuals to identify and change cognitions and emotions that increase pain.

- Operant techniques are based on operant conditioning and use extinction and reinforcement methods.

- In biofeedback individuals learn to control basic bodily processes such as blood pressure.

- In progressive muscle relaxation individuals learn to relax and tighten different muscle groups in a comfortable environment.

8.5 PSYCHONEURO-IMMUNOLOGY

Can you get a cold as a result of being stressed? Is it true that an increased number of students report falling ill before important examinations? Is this simply bad luck or is there a biological explanation? Recent research suggests that there is a link between social and psychological factors and susceptibility to **respiratory infectious illness** such as the **common cold**.

respiratory infectious illness an illness caused by a virus that affects the respiratory system.

common cold a viral illness affecting the respiratory system.

psychoneuroimmunology an area of science that explores the interplay between psychological processes and the nervous and immune systems.

The term **psychoneuroimmunology** or PNI was coined by two American psychologists, Robert Ader and Nicholas Cohen, to describe this new area of science that explored the interplay between psychological processes and the nervous and immune systems. These researchers were some of the first to demonstrate the link between the brain and the immune system (Ader & Cohen, 1975). They used a paradigm called 'conditioned immunosuppression', based on Pavlov's classical conditioning, and found that the immune system of rats could be conditioned to respond to external stimuli unrelated to immune function. They found that after an artificially flavoured drink was paired with an immune-suppressive drug in rats, the introduction of the drink alone was able to suppress immune functioning. This particular study is important because it prompted researchers across the world to explore the effects of various psychological factors on human immunity. Considerable research now indicates that psychological stress affects immune functioning. Respiratory infectious illnesses and wound healing have received particular attention (cf. Cohen, 2005; Kiecolt-Glaser *et al.*, 1995). However, before turning to these findings we need to clarify how the **immune system** works.

immune system a network of organs and cells that protects the body from invading bacteria, viruses and other foreign substances.

8.5.1 The Different Types of Immunity

Broadly speaking, the human body has the capacity to mount two types of immune responses in order to defend the body against invaders. These are known as **cell-mediated immunity** and **antibody-mediated immunity**. The major difference between the different types of immunity is in terms of

cell-mediated immunity an immune reaction produced by T cells which attack and destroy infectious agents by triggering release of killer cells.

how they operate and the cells that are associated with them (see Table 8.3). Cell-mediated immune defence uses a particular type of white blood cell (i.e. lymphocyte) known as a T cell and, as the name suggests, works by attacking invaders directly at cell level; whereas antibody-mediated immune defence uses a different type of white blood cell known as a B cell and works via the bloodstream, whereby antibodies are released into the blood to attack and destroy invaders. It is noteworthy that these different types of white blood cells are named after where they formed in the body. T cells are formed in the bone marrow (i.e. in the tissue that fills the cavities of our bones) but are matured in one of the body's endocrine glands called the thymus (hence the T) (see Figure 8.3). B cells are formed and matured in the bone (the B) marrow. A brief summary of cell-mediated and antibody-mediated immunity is provided in Table 8.3.

antibody-mediated immunity an immune response produced by B cells which attack and destroy infectious agents by stimulating the release of antibodies.

8.5.2 Stress and the Immune System

People often say that they feel run down during stressful periods in their life (e.g. revising for exams, moving house, writing an important paper). Is this coincidental or can stressful experiences and events actually alter immune functioning? Interestingly, researchers have recently been able to show that stress can suppress cell-mediated immunity, although the data relating to antibody-mediated immunity is less convincing (see Cohen, Miller & Rabin, 2001; Rabin, 1999). For instance, several studies have shown that increased secretion of stress hormones such as cortisol can alter the production of important

TABLE 8.3 *Summary of Cell-Mediated and Antibody-Mediated Immunity.*

Cell-mediated immunity: T cells	Antibody-mediated immunity: B cells
Work directly at cell level	Work via the bloodstream
A type of lymphocyte (white blood cell)	A type of lymphocyte (white blood cell)
Formed in the bone marrow, but matured in the thymus (T)	Formed and matured in the bone (B) marrow
Attack and destroy infectious agents by triggering release of cytotoxic killer cells	Attack and destroy infectious agents by stimulating the release of antibodies

FOCUS POINT 8.2   DAILY PATTERNS IN CORTISOL RELEASE

Cortisol is known as the stress hormone and it has several important roles to play, such as increasing access to energy stores during time of stress as well as regulating aspects of immune function. However, it is also noteworthy because its release exhibits a distinct daily (or diurnal) pattern that is characterised by two well-defined components (shown in Figure 8.5): the peak levels after awakening (known as the cortisol awakening rise, CAR) and the diminishing levels throughout the rest of the day (known as diurnal levels) (Clow *et al.*, 2004; Fries, Dettenborn & Kirschbaum, 2009; Pruessner *et al.*, 1997). The levels of cortisol released after awakening typically jump to at least three times the levels when you wake up. Therefore, when you are next having a shower first thing in the morning, you can think that your body is exhibiting the cortisol awakening rise!

A relatively large amount of research has explored the links between daily cortisol levels and health outcomes. Different levels of cortisol secretory activity have been linked to numerous clinical and psychological endpoints such as hypertension, burnout, emotional distress, upper respiratory illness and eating behaviour. For

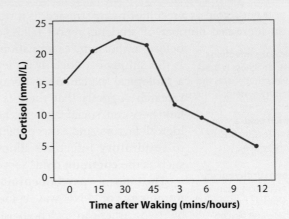

FIGURE 8.5 *Daily pattern in cortisol secretion.*

example, a recent study has shown that individuals who experience high levels of psychological stress may release less cortisol when they wake up in the morning compared to those who experience low stress (O'Connor *et al.*, 2009b).

---

cytokines chemicals in the body that play a crucial role in the functioning of the body's immunity.

immune chemicals known as **cytokines** (Kiecolt-Glaser *et al.*, 2002). These chemicals have been found to be vital when the body is trying to fight infections such as the common cold. Therefore, stress-induced changes in the production of these immune chemicals may represent an important mechanism through which stress compromises the body's response to infectious illness. For example, Kunz-Ebrecht and colleagues (2003) demonstrated that cortisol responses to stress were inversely associated with the production of two well-known cytokines, suggesting that psychological factors can influence important components of immune functioning (see Focus Point 8.2).

8.5.2.1 *Stress and the common cold*

Over the last 25 years, Sheldon Cohen, an American psychologist, has investigated the extent to which psychological and social factors influence susceptibility to infectious illnesses such as the common cold (see Cohen [2005] for a review). As part of the research programme, Cohen and his associates have developed an unusual prospective study design in which healthy participants are exposed to a virus that causes the common cold. Participants are then observed following exposure in order to examine who develops a respiratory illness

and reports cold-like symptoms. All participants also complete various psychological measures at baseline to assess their mood and whether they have had any recent stressful life events, and to measure their current level of perceived stress.

In 1991 Cohen and colleagues demonstrated for the first time that increases in psychological stress are associated with increases in risk for developing a cold after exposure to a cold virus. They also demonstrated that this association was independent of numerous other factors (such as season of the year, age, sex, education, allergic status and body mass index). In addition, they investigated whether this increased susceptibility was associated with changes in stress-related health behaviours such as smoking, exercise and diet. Their results showed that none of these factors explained the relationship (see Photo 8.3).

More recently, Cohen and colleagues (1998) turned their attention to identifying the *types* of stressful life events that were most strongly associated with increased risk of developing infectious illness. As part of this work, the researchers interviewed each of the participants who took part in their prospective studies and identified two types of stressful life events that were most important. The first type of event was enduring (one month or longer) interpersonal problems with family and friends. The second type was enduring problems associated with

PHOTO 8.3 *Psychological stress can increase the risk of developing the common cold.*
Source: Shutterstock.

work (such as under- or unemployment; see Chapter 9). They also found that the longer the stressful event had lasted, the greater was the risk of developing an infectious illness. Therefore, these results suggest that the effects of stress suppress the immune systems and, as a result, we are at greater risk of developing upper respiratory illnesses (see Cohen [2005] for a more detailed discussion).

8.5.2.2 Stress and wound healing

In this final section, we turn to the pioneering work conducted by Janice Kiecolt-Glaser and colleagues from Ohio State University in a different area of psychoneuroimmunology. In 1995, this group of researchers showed for the first time that psychological stress could slow the **wound healing** process. Kiecolt-Glaser and her associates also developed an unconventional methodology to examine the effects of stress on immune functioning. Using a punch biopsy, a 3.5-millimetre wound was created on the nondominant forearm (e.g. the left arm for a right-handed participant), approximately 4 centimetres below the elbow on each volunteer. Questionnaires were used to assess levels of perceived stress and the wound was photographed every day until it completely healed.

In their first investigation, the researchers focused on understanding the impact of chronic stress on immune function and wound healing. For that reason, they

wound healing the healing of wounds

recruited people who were caring for a relative with Alzheimer's disease (the high-stress group) and compared them to control participants (the low-stress group) matched for age and family income. The results of their study were startling. They found that complete wound healing took an average of 9 days or 24% longer in the care-giver group compared to the controls. They also found differences between the groups in the production of important immune chemicals (i.e. cytokines again), suggesting this as one of the immune mechanisms that may account for their findings.

Caring for a loved one with dementia is an exhausting, emotionally draining and labour-intensive duty extended over an indefinite period. Kiecolt-Glaser and colleagues wondered whether a more minor stressful experience such as preparing for an examination would also affect wound healing. Marucha, Kiecolt-Glaser and Favagehi (1998) inflicted a 3.5-millimetre punch biopsy wound in the mouths (i.e. on hard palate) of a sample of dental students, once during the summer vacation and again three days before a major examination. Consistent with the study predictions, all students took longer to heal before the examination compared to during the vacation, with complete healing taking an average of 3 days (or 40%) longer in the pre-examination condition. These findings indicate that even brief, predictable and relatively minor stressors can have significant consequences for wound healing.

Moreover, these data may have significant implications for treating patients who are recovering from surgery. It is well established that a more negative psychological response to surgery is associated with a slower and more complicated post-operative recovery, greater pain, longer hospital stays and worse treatment compliance (for more detailed discussion see Kiecolt-Glaser *et al.*, 1998). Therefore, the research described here suggests that if health psychologists (and other health professionals) prepare patients better psychologically in terms of stress and anxiety reduction, they may experience notable post-surgery health benefits. More generally, these findings also highlight that teaching individuals to cope better with stress may reduce its direct and indirect impact on health.

The next chapter will consider a number of the important methods used by people to cope with stress (see Focus Point 8.3 for an example of a stress management technique).

8.5.3 Summary

The term psychoneuroimmunology describes the new area of science that explores the interplay between psychological processes and the nervous and immune systems. When invaded, the human body has the capacity to mount two types of defence, known as cell-mediated immunity and antibody-mediated immunity.

In 1986, James Pennebaker developed the 'emotional writing paradigm' in which he explored the effects of writing for 15–20 minutes on three consecutive days about stressful or traumatic events on a range of health outcomes. In this paradigm, participants in the experimental group are asked to write about their deepest emotions and thoughts about the most upsetting experience(s) in their life. They are encouraged really to let go and to link their writing to other aspects of their life such as relationships, their childhood, their careers and who they would like to become, who they were in the past and who they are now. In the control group, individuals are asked to write about what they have done the previous day and to describe their plans for the following day. Research has found that emotional disclosure through expressive writing can produce clinically significant improvements in a number of physiological (e.g. lung function, blood pressure) and psychological (e.g. depression) health outcomes (see Frattaroli, 2006; O'Connor et al., 2008; Sloan & Marx, 2004).

How does emotional writing influence health? Several mechanisms have been suggested, but the most popular explanation suggests that the positive effect of emotional disclosure involves exposure and cognitive processing (Sloan & Marx, 2004). By accessing the emotions, feelings and cognitions linked to a stressful or traumatic event, memory begins to be restructured. Through such restructuring the individual becomes aware of the associated feelings and considers methods of coping with the traumatic or stressful encounter.

Psychological factors such as stress have been found to influence these immune functions. Kiecolt-Glaser, Cohen and colleagues have shown in numerous studies that stress is related to increased susceptibility to infectious illnesses such as the common cold and can slow down the wound-healing process.

To summarise:

- Psychoneuroimmunology explores the interplay between psychological processes and the nervous and immune systems.

- The human body has the capacity to mount two types of defence, known as cell-mediated immunity and antibody-mediated immunity.

- Stress has been found to influence the production of important immune chemicals such as cytokines.

- Stress is associated with increased susceptibility to infectious illnesses and the slowing down of wound healing.

8.6 A BIOPSYCHOSOCIAL APPROACH TO HEALTH PSYCHOLOGY REVIEWED

The role of the nervous system is to allow us to adapt to changes within both our body and our environment. It consists of the brain, the spinal cord and billions of nerves. The brain is the central part of the nervous system and consists of three major components: the forebrain, the midbrain and the hindbrain. The nervous system is divided into the central nervous system (CNS) and the peripheral nervous system (PNS). The CNS comprises the brain and spinal cord, whereas the PNS is a network of nerves that connects the brain and spinal cord to the rest of the body.

Two response systems are activated when we experience stress. The first and easier to activate is the sympathetic adrenal medullary (SAM) system; the second is the hypothalamic-pituitary-adrenal (HPA) axis response system. The SAM system leads to the release of the adrenaline and noradrenaline that put the body on alert; the HPA axis response system leads to the release of the stress hormone cortisol. The stress response has been found to have a negative impact on a number of health outcomes, such as cardiovascular disease.

Psychological factors can play a role in the perception of pain. Gain-control theory proposes that a neural gate in the spinal cord receives signals from pain fibres at the site of injury, other peripheral fibres and messages descending from the brain. The degree to which the gate opens (leading to experience of pain) is determined by the combined effects of these three factors. The main psychological approaches to pain management are cognitive techniques, operant approaches, biofeedback and progressive muscle relaxation.

The human body has the capacity to mount two types of defence, known as cell-mediated immunity and antibody-mediated immunity. Psychological factors such as stress have been found to influence these immune functions. In particular, research has shown stress to be associated with increased susceptibility to infectious illnesses and the slowing down of wound healing.

SELF-TEST QUESTIONS

- List the main components of the nervous system.
- List the main anatomic components of the brain and their sub-divisions.
- How does the endocrine system send electrical and chemical messages to different parts of the body?
- Give an example of a catecholamine.
- Describe the two main biological systems that are activated when we experience stress.
- In gate-control theory, what factors influence the opening and closing of the gate?
- Describe the main psychological techniques used in pain management.
- What are the two main types of immunity?

ESSAY QUESTIONS

- How can psychological factors influence health and illness processes?
- Evaluate the contribution that psychology has made to our understanding of pain and the perception of pain.
- Psychological factors are associated with increased risk of developing the common cold. Discuss.
- Describe the pathways through which stress can alter immune functioning.
- Outline the most common biological and behavioural responses to stress.

TEXTS FOR FURTHER READING

Abraham, C., Conner, M., Jones, F. & O'Connor, D. (2008) *Health Psychology: Topics in Applied Psychology*, London: Hodder Arnold.

Horn, S. & Munafo, M. (1997) *Pain: Theory, Research and Intervention*, Milton Keynes: Open University Press.

Kalat, J.W. (2004) *Biological Psychology*, Toronto: Thomson Wadsworth.

Lovallo, W.R. (2005) *Stress and Health: Biological and Psychological Interactions*, Beverly Hills, CA: Sage.

Sapolsky, R.M. (1998) *Why Zebras Don't Get Ulcers*, New York: W.H. Freeman.

Vedhara, K. & Irwin, M. (2005) *Human Psychoneuroimmunology*, Oxford: Oxford University Press.

RELEVANT JOURNAL ARTICLES

Cohen, S. (2005) The Pittsburgh common cold studies: Psychosocial predictors of susceptibility to respiratory infectious illness, *International Journal of Behavioral Medicine* 12: 123–31.

Eccleston, C., Morley, S., Williams, A., Yorke, L. & Mastroyannopoulou, K. (2002) Systematic review of randomized controlled trials of psychological therapy for chronic pain in children and adolescents, with a subset meta-analysis of pain relief, *Pain* 99: 157–65.

Kiecolt-Glaser, J.K., McGuire, L., Robles, T. & Glaser, R. (2002) Emotions, morbidity, and mortality: New perspectives from psychoneuroimmunology, *Annual Review of Psychology* 53: 83–107.

Matthews, K.A., Katholi, C.R., McCreath, H. *et al.* (2004) Blood pressure reactivity to psychological stress predicts hypertension in the CARDIA Study, *Circulation* 110: 74–8.

McEwen, B.S. (1998) Protective and damaging effects of stress mediators, *New England Journal of Medicine* 338: 171–9.

Melzack, R. (1999) From the gate to the neuromatrix, *Pain* 6: 121–6.

O'Connor, D.B., Hendrickx, H., Dadd, T. *et al.* (2009) Cortisol awakening rise in middle-aged women in relation to chronic psychological stress, *Psychoneuroendocrinology* 34: 1486–94.

Steptoe, A., Hamer, M., Chida, Y. (2007) The effects of acute psychological stress on circulating inflammatory factors in humans: A review and meta-analysis, *Brain Behavior & Immunity* 21: 901–12.

RELEVANT WEB LINKS

Bruce McEwen's laboratory, www.rockefeller.edu/labheads/mcewen/mcewen-lab.php
Janice Kiecolt-Glaser's laboratory, http://stressandhealth.org
Sheldon Cohen's laboratory, www.psy.cmu.edu/~scohen
UK Health and Safety Executive's stress website, www.**hse**.gov.uk/**stress**

REFERENCES

Ader, R. & Cohen, N. (1975) Behaviorally conditioned immunosuppression, *Psychosomatic Medicine* 37: 333–40.

Andrasik, F. & Schwartz, M.S. (2006) Behavioral assessment and treatment of pediatric headache, *Behavioural Modification* 30: 93–113.

Beecher, H.K. (1956) Relationship of significance of wound to pain experienced, *Journal of the American Medical Association* 161: 1609–13.

Carroll, D., Ebrahim, S., Tilling, K., Macleod, J. & Davey Smith, G. (2002) Admissions for myocardial infarction and World Cup football: Database survey, *British Medical Journal* 325: 1439–42.

Clow, A., Thorn, L., Evans, P. & Hucklebridge, F. (2004) The awakening cortisol response: Methodological issues and significance, *Stress* 7: 29–37.

Cohen, S. (2005) The Pittsburgh common cold studies: Psychosocial predictors of susceptibility to respiratory infectious illness, *International Journal of Behavioral Medicine* 12: 123–31.

Cohen, S., Miller, G.E. & Rabin, B.S. (2001) Psychological stress and antibody response to immunization: A critical review of the human literature, *Psychosomatic Medicine* 63: 7–18.

Cohen, S., Tyrrell, D.A.J. & Smith, A.P. (1991) Psychological stress and susceptibility to the common cold, *New England Journal of Medicine* 325: 606–12.

Cohen, S., Frank, E., Doyle, W.J., Skoner, D.P., Rabin, B.S. & Gwaltney, J.M., Jr. (1998) Types of stressors that increase susceptibility to the common cold in adults, *Health Psychology* 17: 214–23.

Fernandez, E. & Turk, D.C. (1989) The utility of cognitive coping strategies for altering pain perception: A meta-analysis, *Pain* 38: 123–35.

Fordyce, W.E. (1976) *Behavioural Methods for Chronic Pain and Illness*, St Louis, MO: Mosby.

Frattaroli, J. (2006) Experimental disclosure and its moderators: A meta-analysis, *Psychological Bulletin* 132: 823–65.

Fries, E., Dettenborn, L. & Kirschbaum, C. (2009) The cortisol awakening response (CAR): Facts and future directions, *International Journal of Psychophysiology* 72: 67–73.

Goldschneider, A. (1920) *Das Schmerz Problem*, Berlin: Springer.

Greeno, C.G. & Wing, R.R. (1994) Stress-induced eating, *Psychological Bulletin* 115: 444–64.

Holroyd, K., Nash, J., Pingel, J., Cordingley, G. & Jerome, A. (1991) A comparison of pharmacological (amitriptyline HCl) and nonpharmacological (cognitive-behavioral) therapies for chronic tension headaches, *Journal of Consulting and Clinical Psychology* 59: 387–93.

Horn, S. & Munafo, M. (1998) *Pain: Theory, Research and Intervention*, Buckingham: Open University Press.

Kiecolt-Glaser, J.K., Marucha, P.T., Malarkey, W.B., Mercado, A.M. & Glaser, R. (1995) Slowing of wound healing by psychological stress, *The Lancet* 346: 1194–6.

Kiecolt-Glaser, J.K., McGuire, L., Robles, T.F. & Glaser, R. (2002) Psychoneuroimmunology: Psychological influences on immune function and health, *Journal of Consulting and Clinical Psychology* 70: 537–47.

Kunz-Ebrecht, S.R., Mohamed-Ali, V., Feldman, P.J., Kirschbaum, C. & Steptoe, A. (2003) Cortisol responses to mild psychological stress are inversely associated with proinflammatory cytokines, *Brain, Behavior & Immunity* 17: 373–83.

Lazarus, R.S. & Folkman, S. (1984) *Stress, Appraisal and Coping*, New York: Springer.

Marucha, P.T., Kiecolt-Glaser, J.K. & Favagehi, M. (1998) Mucosal wound healing is impaired by examination stress, *Psychosomatic Medicine* 60: 362–5.

Matthews, K.A. & Gump, B.B. (2002) Chronic work stress and marital dissolution increase risk of posttrial mortality in men from the multiple risk factor intervention trial, *Archives of Internal Medicine* 162: 309–15.

Melzack, R. & Wall, P.D. (1965) Pain mechanisms: A new theory, *Science* 50: 971–9.

Morley, S., Eccleston, C. & Williams, A. (1999) Systematic review and meta-analysis of randomised controlled trials of cognitive behaviour therapy and behaviour therapy for chronic pain in adults, excluding headache, *Pain* 80: 1–13.

Newman, E., O'Connor, D.B. & Conner, M. (2007) Daily hassles and eating behaviour: The role of cortisol reactivity status, *Psychoneuroendocrinology* 32: 125–32.

O'Connor, D.B., Conner, M., Jones, F., McMillan, B. & Ferguson, E. (2009a) Exploring the benefits of conscientiousness: An investigation of the role of daily stressors and health behaviours, *Annals of Behavioral Medicine* 37: 184–96.

O'Connor, D.B., Hendrickx, H., Dadd, T. *et al.* (2009b) Cortisol awakening rise in middle-aged women in relation to chronic psychological stress, *Psychoneuroendocrinology* 34: 1486–94.

O'Connor, D.B., Jones, F., Conner, M., McMillan, B. & Ferguson, E. (2008) Effects of daily hassles and eating style on eating behavior, *Health Psychology* 27: s20–s21.

Pruessner, J.C., Wolf, O.T., Hellhammer, D.H. *et al.* (1997) Free cortisol levels after awakening: A reliable biological marker for the assessment of adrenocortical activity, *Life Sciences* 61: 2539–49.

Rabin, B.S. (1999) *Stress, Immune Function and Health: The Connection*, New York: John Wiley & Sons, Inc.

Sarafino, E. (2008) *Health Psychology: Biopsychosocial Interactions*, New York: John Wiley & Sons, Inc.

Sloan, D.M. & Marx, B.P. (2004) Taking pen to hand: Evaluating theories underlying the written disclosure paradigm, *Clinical Psychology: Science and Practice* 11: 121–37.

Turk, D.C. & Burwinkle T.M. (2000) Clinical outcomes, cost-effectiveness, and the role of psychology in treatments for chronic pain sufferers, *Professional Psychology: Research and Practice* 36: 602–10.

Turk, D.C., Meichenbaum, D. & Genest, M. (1983) *Pain and Behavioural Medicine: A Cognitive-Behavioral Perspective*, New York: Guilford.

Von Frey, M. (1895) *Untersuchungen über die Sinnesfuncionen der Menschlichen Haut Erste Abhandlung: Druckempfindung und Schmerz*, Leipzig: Hirzel.

9 Stress, Coping and Health

FIONA JONES, DARYL O'CONNOR, CHARLES ABRAHAM & MARK CONNER

LEARNING OUTCOMES

WHEN YOU HAVE COMPLETED THIS CHAPTER, YOU SHOULD BE ABLE TO:

1. Describe and evaluate key approaches to measuring stress.
2. Describe a range of coping strategies and discuss their effectiveness.
3. Describe key approaches to examining work stress and discuss the impact of work stress on health outcomes.
4. Discuss the pros and cons of a range of different approaches to intervening to reduce stress.

KEY WORDS

Allostasis • Appraisal • Benefit Finding • Coping • Daily Diaries • Daily Hassles • Effort–Reward Imbalance • Emotion-Focused Coping • Job Decision Latitude • Job Demand-Control Model • Job Design • Job Strain • Life Change Unit (LCU) • Life Events • Meta-analysis • Occupational Health Psychology • Over-commitment • Positive Reappraisal • Primary Appraisal • Problem-Focused Coping • Relaxation • Secondary Appraisal • Social Readjustment Rating Scale • Social Support • Stress • Stress-Diathesis Model • Stress-Management Training • Stressors • Transactional Approach • Work–Family Conflict • Work–Life Balance

CHAPTER OUTLINE

Greenhaus, J.H. & Beutell, N.J. (1985) Sources of conflict between work and family roles, *Academy of Management Review* 10: 76–80.

Helgeson, V.S., Reynolds, K.A. & Tomich, P.L. (2006) A meta-analytic review of benefit finding and growth, *Journal of Consulting and Clinical Psychology* 74: 797–816.

Hellerstedt, W. L. & Jeffrey, R.W. (1997) The association of job strain and health behaviours in men and women, *International Journal of Epidemiology* 26: 575–83.

Holmes, T.H. & Masuda, M. (1974) Life change and illness susceptibility, in B.S. Dohrenwend & B.P. Dohrenwend (eds) *Stressful Life Events: Their Nature and Effects*, London: John Wiley & Sons Ltd.

Holmes, T.H. & Rahe, R.H. (1967) The social readjustment rating scale, *Journal of Psychosomatic Research* 11: 213–18.

Johnson, J.V. & Hall, E.M. (1988) Job strain, work place social support and cardiovascular disease: A cross-sectional study of a random sample of the working population, *American Journal of Public Health* 78: 1336–42.

Kalichman, S.C., Benotsch, E.G., Weinhardt, L., Austin, J., Luke, W. & Cherry, C. (2003) Health-related internet use, coping, social support, and health indicators in people living with HIV/AIDS: Preliminary results from a community survey, *Health Psychology* 22: 111–16.

Karasek, R.A. (1979) Job demands, job decision latitude and mental strain: Implications for job design, *Administrative Science Quarterly* 24: 285–308.

Kiecolt-Glaser, J.K., Marucha, P.T., Malarkey, W.B., Mercado, A.M. & Glaser, R. (1995) Slowing of wound healing by psychological stress, *The Lancet* 346: 1194–6.

Kraut, R., Kiesler, S., Boneva, B., Cummings, J.N., Helgeson, V. & Crawford, A.M. (2002) Internet paradox revisited, *Journal of Social Issues* 58: 49–74.

Kraut, R., Patterson, M., Lundmark, V., Kiesler, S., Mukopadhyay, T. & Scherlis, W. (1998) Internet paradox: A social technology that reduces social involvement and psychological well-being, *American Psychologist* 53: 1017–31.

Lallukka, T., Ek, E., Sarlio-Lahteenkorva, S. *et al.* (2004) Working conditions and health behaviours among employed women and men: The Helsinki health study, *Preventive Medicine* 38: 48–56.

Landsbergis, P.A. & Vivona-Vaughan, E. (1995) Evaluation of an occupational stress intervention in a public agency, *Journal of Organizational Behavior* 16: 29–48.

Lazarus, R.S. (1966) *Psychological Stress and the Coping Process*, New York: McGraw Hill.

Lazarus, R.S. (1999) *Stress and Emotion: A New Synthesis*, New York: Springer.

Lazarus, R.S. & Folkman, S. (1984) *Stress, Appraisal and Coping*, New York: Springer.

LeShan, L. (1959) Psychological states as factors in the development of malignant disease, *Journal of the National Cancer Institute* 22: 1–18.

Liang, J., Krause, N.M. & Bennett, J.M. (2001) Social exchange and well-being: Is giving better than receiving? *Psychology and Aging* 16: 511–23.

Major, D.A. & Germano, L.M. (2006) The changing nature of work and its impact on the work home interface, in F. Jones, R.J. Burke & M. Westman (eds) *Work–Life Balance: A Psychological Perspective*, Hove: Psychology Press.

Marmot, M.G., Smith, G.M., Stansfield, S. *et al.* (1991) Health inequalities among british civil servants: The Whitehall II study, *The Lancet* 337: 1387–93.

McEwen, B.S. (1998) Protective and damaging effects of stress mediators, *New England Journal of Medicine* 338: 171–9.

McEwen, B.S. (2007) Physiology and neurobiology of stress and adaptation: Central role of the brain, *Physiological Reviews* 87: 873–904.

McEwen, B.S. & Stellar, E. (1993) Stress and the individual: Mechanisms leading to disease, *Archives of Internal Medicine* 153: 2093–101.

Michael, Y.L., Carlson, N.E., Chlebowski, R.T. *et al.* (2009) Influence of stressors on breast cancer incidence in the women's health initiative, *Health Psychology* 28: 137–46.

Moskowitz, J.T., Folkman, S., Collette, L. & Vittinghoff, E. (1996) Coping and mood during AIDS-related caregiving and bereavement, *Annals of Behavioral Medicine* 18: 49–57.

Murphy, L.R. (2003) Stress management at work: Secondary prevention of stress, in M.J. Schabracq, J.A.M. Winnubst & C.L. Cooper (eds) *The Handbook of Work and Health Psychology,* 2nd edn, Chichester: John Wiley and Sons, Ltd.

Niedhammer, I., Tek, M.L., Starke, D. & Siegrist, J. (2004) Effort–reward imbalance model and self-reported health: Cross-sectional and prospective findings from the GAZEL cohort, *Social Science and Medicine* 58: 1531–41.

Nielsen, N.R. & Brønbaek, M. (2006) Stress and breast cancer: A systematic update on the current knowledge, *Nature Clinical Practice Oncology* 3: 612–20.

NIOSH (2008) NIOSH safety and health topic: Occupational Health Psychology, retrieved from http://www.cdc.gov/niosh/topics/stress/ohp/ohp.html, accessed October 2010.

O'Connor, D.B., Jones, F., Conner, M., McMillan, B. & Ferguson, E. (2008) Effects of daily hassles and eating style on eating behavior, *Health Psychology* 27: s20–s21.

Paykel, E.S. & Rao, B.M. (1984) Methodology in study of life events and cancer, in C.L. Cooper (ed.) *Psychosocial Stress and Cancer*, Chichester: John Wiley and Sons, Ltd.

Payne, N., Jones, F. & Harris, P. (2002) The impact of working life on health behaviour: The effect of job strain on the cognitive predictors of exercise, *Journal of Occupational Health Psychology* 7: 342–53.

Peter, R., Geissler, H. & Siegrist, J. (1998) Associations of effort–reward imbalance at work and reported symptoms in different groups of male and female public transport workers, *Stress Medicine* 14: 175–82.

Petticrew, M., Fraser, J.M. & Regan, M.F. (1999) Adverse life events and risk of breast cancer: A meta-analysis, *British Journal of Health Psychology* 4: 1–17.

Pikhart, H., Bobak, M., Siegrist, J. *et al.* (2001) Psychosocial work characteristics and self rated health in four post-Communist countries, *Journal of Epidemiology and Community Health* 55: 624–30.

Rahe, R.H. & Paasikivi, J. (1971) Psychosocial factors and myocardial infarction: An outpatient study in Sweden, *Journal of Psychosomatic Research* 8: 35–44.

Reynolds, J.S. & Perrin, N.A. (2004) Mismatches in social support and psychosocial adjustment to cancer, *Health Psychology* 23: 425–30.

Richardson, K.M. & Rothstein, H.R. (2008) Effects of occupational stress management intervention programs: A meta-analysis, *Journal of Occupational Health Psychology* 13: 69–93.

Risch, N., Herrell, R., Lehner, T. *et al.* (2009) Interaction between the serotonin transporter gene (5-httlpr), stressful life events, and risk of depression: A meta-analysis, *Journal of the American Medical Association* 301: 2462–71.

Roos, E., Sarlio-Lahteenkorva, S., Lallukka, T. & Lahelma, E. (2007) Associations of work–family conflicts with food habits and physical activity, *Public Health Nutrition* 10: 222–9.

Schnall, P.L., Landsbergis, P.A. & Baker, D. (1994) Job strain and cardiovascular health, *Annual Review of Public Health* 15: 381–411.

Selye, H. (1956) *The Stress of Life*, New York: McGraw-Hill.

Siegrist, J. (1996) Adverse health effects of high-effort/low-reward conditions, *Journal of Occupational Health Psychology* 1: 27–41.

Siegrist, J. (2002) Effort–reward imbalance at work and health, *Historical and Current Perspectives on Stress and Health* 2: 261–91.

Siegrist, J.E. (2005) Effort–reward imbalance at work, retrieved from http://www.uni-duesseldorf.de/MedicalSociology/Effort-reward_imbalance_at_wor.112.0.html, accessed October 2010.

Skinner, E.A., Edge, K., Altman, J. & Sherwood, H. (2003) Searching for the structure of coping: A review and critique of category systems for classifying ways of coping, *Psychological Bulletin* 129: 216–69.

Snow, H. (1893) *Cancer and the Cancer Process*, London: J. & A. Churchill.

Strazdins, L., D'Souza, R.M., Lim, L.L., Broom, D.H. & Rodgers, B. (2004) Job strain, job insecurity, and health: Rethinking the relationship, *Journal of Occupational Health Psychology* 9: 296–305.

Theorell, T. & Rahe, R.H. (1971) Psychosocial factors and myocardial infarction, *Journal of Psychosomatic Research* 15: 25–31.

Tsutsumi, A., Kayaba, K., Theorell, T. & Siegrist, J. (2001) Association between job stress and depression among Japanese employees threatened by job loss in a comparison between two complementary job stress models, *Scandinavian Journal of Work, Environment & Health* 27: 146–53.

Uchino, B.N., Cacioppo, J.T. & Kiecolt-Glaser, J.K. (1996) The relationship between social support and physiological processes: A review with emphasis on underlying mechanisms and implications for health, *Psychological Bulletin* 119: 488–531.

Van der Doef, M. & Maes, S. (1998) The job demand-control (-support) model and physical outcomes: A review of the strain and buffer hypotheses, *Psychology and Health* 13: 909–36.

van der Klink, J.L., Blonk, R.W.B., Schene, A.H. & van Dijk, F.J.H. (2001) The benefits of interventions for work-related stress, *American Journal of Public Health* 91(2): 270–76.

van Hooff, M.L., Geurts, S.A., Taris, T.W. *et al.* (2005) Disentangling the causal relationships between work–home interference and employee health, *Scandinavian Journal of Work, Environment & Health* 31: 15–29.

Van Vegchel, N.V., De Jonge, J., Meijer, T. & Hamers, J.P.H. (2001) Different effort constructs and effort–reward imbalance: Effects on employee well-being in ancillary health care workers, *Journal of Advanced Nursing* 34: 128–36.

Vitaliano, P. P., Echeverria, D., Yi, J., Phillips, P. E., Young, H. and Siegler, I.C. (2005) Psychophysiological mediators of caregiver stress and differential cognitive decline, *Psychology and Aging* 20: 402–11.

10 Social Psychology and Health

MARK CONNER, CHARLES ABRAHAM, FIONA JONES & DARYL O'CONNOR

LEARNING OUTCOMES

WHEN YOU HAVE COMPLETED THIS CHAPTER, YOU SHOULD BE ABLE TO:

1. Describe the key personality traits related to health outcomes and potential mechanisms of effect.
2. Describe and compare and contrast important theories of how cognitions predict health behaviours.
3. Describe different ways of changing cognitions in order to change health behaviours.

KEY WORDS

Agreeableness ● Attitude Change ● Big Five Personality Model ● Central Route ● Cognitive Dissonance ● Conscientiousness ● Elaboration Likelihood Model ● Extraversion ● Graded Tasks ● Health Behaviours ● Health Belief Model ● Hostility ● International Personality Item Pool ● Major Theorists Model ● Mastery Experience ● Need for Cognition ● Negative Affect ● Neuroticism ● Openness to Experience ● Optimism ● Perception of Physiological Reactions ● Peripheral Route ● Terman Life-Cycle Personality Cohort Study ● Theory of Planned Behaviour ● Type A Behaviour Pattern ● Verbal Persuasion ● Vicarious Experience ● Western Collaborative Group Study

CHAPTER OUTLINE

ROUTE MAP OF THE CHAPTER

This chapter will show how health psychology has incorporated and applied models from social psychology, in particular personality models and social cognition models. The chapter considers the importance of personality factors such as optimism, impulsivity/neuroticism and hostility to various health outcomes. It will illustrate how personality can be considered from a developmental perspective by showing research indicating that personality measured at 3 years old can predict adult personality and adult health-risk behaviours, along with research on the effects of family relationships on the development of hostility. This discussion will argue that health-relevant personality characteristics show both stability and change over the life course. Finally, this section will introduce the Big Five model (OCEAN) of personality and highlight the importance of this model to health. Personality is also shown to be linked to more modifiable cognitions (e.g. attitudes and beliefs). A number of models of such cognitions including the health belief model, the theory of planned behaviour and Fishbein *et al.*'s integrative model will be introduced and discussed. The final section of this chapter will focus on changing cognitions and focus on persuasive communication, cognitive dissonance and the elaboration likelihood model.

10.1 INTRODUCTION

This chapter reviews research in health psychology that has drawn on theories and findings from social psychology, developmental psychology and personality and individual differences research. In particular, we first explore work on the relationship between personality and health outcomes such as longevity. Personality traits describe relatively stable and consistent patterns of acting across different situations. Developmental aspects are important in how and when such traits form. For example, some personality work emphasises how personality is fixed from an early age, with 'temperament' evident at

3 years of age predictive of adult personality traits and health outcomes. In contrast, other work shows how family relationships in the teenage years can have a major influence on other personality traits.

In the second part of the chapter we look at how thoughts and feelings about particular health behaviours influence who engages in them. This work illustrates the importance of a few key 'cognitions' in determining why we exercise, smoke or eat healthily. Important models of these key cognitions developed by social psychologists will be described. In the third and final section we look at research on how these cognitions might be altered in order to try to change health behaviour (see Focus Point 10.1).

FOCUS POINT 10.1 OUTCOMES OF BEING OPTIMISTIC

Individuals with high levels of optimism have fewer infectious illnesses and report fewer physical symptoms even during periods of stress (Peterson & Seligman, 1987). They are also more likely to recover from surgery more quickly and are less likely to be re-hospitalised (Scheier *et al.*, 1999). Peterson, Vaillant and Seligman (1988) showed that men who were highly optimistic at age 25 had better objective health at age 60 even when taking account of initial physical and mental health.

Even more impressively, Danner, Snowdon and Friesen (2001) coded the emotional content of what a sample of 180 Catholic nuns had written about themselves on entering the church as young women. The research then examined the survival rates of the same women when they were 75–95 years of age. Those who wrote sentences containing self-descriptions with the most positive emotions

(e.g. happiness, pride, love) were more likely to live longer than those who wrote about the fewest positive emotions. Comparison of the top and bottom 25% (quartiles) on this measure indicated that 24% of those in the top quartile had died at the time of the study compared to 54% of those in the bottom quartile.

Everson and colleagues (1996) showed similar effects in men on a measure of hopelessness (the opposite of optimism). Those with the highest hopelessness scores were 3.5 times more likely to die from all causes of death compared to those with the lowest scores. Similarly, men with AIDS who are optimistic live twice as long after diagnosis as men who are pessimistic (Reed *et al.*, 1994). More generally, among older individuals those with positive attitudes towards ageing live an average of 7.5 years longer than those with more negative attitudes (Levy *et al.*, 2002).

10.2 PERSONALITY AND HEALTH BEHAVIOUR

optimism an expectation that in the future good things will happen to you and bad things will not.

Type A behaviour pattern a pattern of behaviour characterised by a competitive drive, aggression, chronic impatience and a sense of time urgency.

hostility a negative attitude towards others, consisting, e.g., of enmity and unfriendliness.

neuroticism one of the dimensions of personality as suggested by the Big Five personality model.

extraversion one of the dimensions of personality as suggested by the Big Five personality model.

conscientiousness one of the dimensions of personality as suggested by the Big Five personality model.

Big Five personality model a model of personality sometimes known as the OCEAN model derived through taking the initial letter of each of the five key dimensions.

openness to experience one of the dimensions of personality as suggested by the Big Five personality model.

agreeableness one of the dimensions of personality as suggested by the Big Five personality model.

In this section we examine the idea that stable individual differences in the way people think, feel and behave (i.e. personality) are predictive of various health outcomes. We explore how these stable individual differences can pre-dispose individuals to respond to the challenges that life throws at us in a manner that, over time, damages or protects their health. First, we look at important research on **optimism**, **Type A behaviour pattern** and **hostility** as personality traits that have been found to be related to health. Next, we will look at research into **neuroticism**, **extraversion** and **conscientiousness** and how these relate to health behaviours and health outcomes.

These are three personality traits from the **Big Five personality model**, which has been the focus of much research into personality in recent years. This model suggests that personality can be viewed in terms of five broad personality types: **openness to experience**, conscientiousness, extraversion, **agreeableness** and neuroticism (Digman, 1990; McCrae & Costa, 1987). This is sometimes also known as the OCEAN model of personality. The Big Five model is based on the assumption that a range of more specific personality traits such as optimism and hostility can be understood as blends of Big Five traits (see Photo 10.1).

10.2.1 Optimism

Optimism refers to the expectation that in the future good things will happen to you and bad things will not. Most of us are optimistic in some areas of our lives while being more

PHOTO 10.1 *A face mask – showing different personality traits to the world.*
Source: Shutterstock.

pessimistic in others. For example, an individual might be optimistic about her chance of getting a serious illness but pessimistic about the chance of her football team winning. However, optimism taps the extent to which an individual is optimistic in general across a range of domains and across time. This can be measured by items such as 'In uncertain times, I usually expect the best' and 'I always look on the bright side of life' (Scheier & Carver, 1992). Those agreeing with such items are classified as optimists and research shows that they tend to experience increased psychological wellbeing and better physical health, and even that they live longer (see Focus Point 10.1). For example, those with high levels of optimism experience fewer infectious illnesses and report fewer physical symptoms even during periods of stress (Peterson & Seligman, 1987).

The precise explanation for the relationship between optimism and various health outcomes is still unclear. One interesting suggestion is that those high in optimism may be more likely to avoid certain high-risk situations. Some supporting evidence for this view comes from Peterson, Vaillant and Seligman (1988) who showed that optimists were less likely to die from accidental or violent causes than pessimists, while the two groups did not differ in respect of mortality from cancer or cardiovascular disease. A further explanation for the relationship between optimism and health is through the effects of optimism on coping strategies. Those high in optimism cope in seemingly more effective ways with the problems they face. For example, Scheier, Weintraub and Carver (1986) found that optimists were more likely to use strategies such as making a plan and sticking to it, focusing intently on the problem and seeking social support. Optimists were also less likely to distract themselves from thinking about the problem. The use of these more constructive coping strategies may lead to better health outcomes partly by helping individuals to avoid negative life events and also by helping them to confront and deal with problems earlier and more effectively.

10.2.2 Type A Behaviour and Hostility

Type A Behaviour Pattern is characterised by a competitive drive, aggression, chronic impatience and a sense of time urgency (Rosenman *et al.*, 1976). As discussed in Chapter 7, the observation of a Type A behaviour pattern originated from the work of two cardiologists, Meyer Friedman and Ray Rosenman, who realised that heart disease in their patients was not fully explained by conventional risk factors such as dietary cholesterol and smoking. They helped develop the **Western Collaborative Group study**, which examined risk factors for coronary heart disease (CHD) in a sample of over 3000 healthy, middle-aged men. They found that after 8.5 years those who were classified as Type A had around twice the risk of developing CHD as those not classified as Type A.

Western Collaborative Group study an examination of the risk factors for coronary heart disease (CHD) in a sample of over 3000 healthy middle-aged men.

However, subsequent research has suggested that perhaps only certain aspects of Type A behaviour represent a risk for CHD. In particular, hostility has emerged as the most toxic component of Type A behaviour and the one that predicts CHD (Miller *et al.*, 1996).

Hostility has been defined as 'a negative attitude towards others, consisting of enmity, denigration and ill will' (Smith, 1994, p. 26). Components of this characteristic are cynicism about others' motives, mistrust and hostile attributional style; that is, a tendency to interpret other people's actions as aggressive (Smith *et al.*, 2004). While this definition is mainly cognitive, the associated emotional and behavioural constructs of anger and aggression are often incorporated within the hostility construct (Miller *et al.*, 1996). The construct is measured using items such as 'Some of my family have habits that bother and annoy me very much' and 'It is safer to trust no one', with a response of 'true' indicating higher levels of hostility (Cook & Medley, 1954). Reviews of various studies examining hostility and CHD suggest that there is a small but consistent relationship between the two (Miller *et al.*, 1996). There are several possible mechanisms underlying the effects of hostility on CHD (Smith *et al.*, 2004). Individuals high in hostility may experience more stress through interpersonal conflict and show stronger physiological reactions to such stress (see Chapter 8). In addition, hostile people may be cynical about health warnings or resistant to medical advice and so might be less likely to engage in health behaviours such as exercise and not smoking (see Theory to Application Box 10.1).

More recent research is also now exploring how personality traits such as hostility develop. An interesting possibility in relation to the development of

---

BOX 10.1   **THEORY TO APPLICATION**

Reducing Hostility

There is now evidence suggesting that a hostility-reduction intervention aimed at CHD patients with high levels of hostility may reduce risks for heart disease. Gidron, Davidson and Bata (1999) randomly allocated 22 hostile male patients to either a treatment or a control group. The treatment condition involved eight 90-minute weekly group meetings using cognitive-behavioural techniques. Participants were taught skills to reduce antagonism, cynicism and anger. The control group had a one-session group meeting giving information about the risks of hostility and

about basic hostility-reduction skills. Participants in the intervention group were found to be less hostile at follow-up than the controls. They also had lower diastolic blood pressure. Furthermore, reductions in hostility were correlated with reductions in blood pressure. A follow-up (Davidson *et al.*, 2007) showed the intervention group to have fewer hospital admissions in the six months following the intervention involving significantly fewer days in hospital (a mean of 0.38 days compared with a mean of 2.15 days for the control group).

hostility is suggested by the work of Matthews and colleagues (1996). In this work, negative behaviours during parent–son discussions aimed at resolving disagreements were observed in 51 Caucasian adolescents (aged 12–13 years). Results showed that the frequency of negative behaviours in the family discussions predicted hostility and expressed anger assessed three years later, even after controlling for baseline hostility. This would suggest that hostility may be nurtured within particular family backgrounds that are characterised by negative behaviours during interactions; that is, a nurture explanation of personality.

This work shows how particular experiences and reactions during adolescence may be critical to how this unhealthy personality trait develops. This developmental perspective contrasts with other work on personality suggesting that aspects of personality are fixed from a very early age. For example, work by Caspi et al. (1997) shows that measures of temperament taken at 3 years of age predict later health-related risk behaviour in early adulthood and that this effect is mediated by personality measures taken in late adolescence; that is, temperament at 3 years predicts personality at 18 years, which in turn predicts behaviour. This would appear to be good evidence that personality traits are something we are born with or at least develop very early in life and remain stable throughout our lives.

Together these different studies suggest that while certain aspects of personality may be stable from a very young age, other aspects change and develop over time as a result of our interaction with our environment. This suggests the relevance of both a nature/genetic and a nurture/developmental explanation of personality development.

10.2.3 Neuroticism

Neuroticism is one of the Big Five personality traits from the OCEAN model. It refers to the tendency to experience negative emotions such as distress, anxiety, fear, anger and guilt (Watson & Clark, 1984). The focus on negative emotions means that it is sometimes referred to as **negative affect**. Those high in neuroticism or negative affect worry about the future, dwell on failures and shortcomings, and have less favourable views of themselves and others. Individuals high in neuroticism are more likely to consider statements such as 'worry a lot' and 'get upset easily' as good self-descriptions (**International Personality Item Pool**, http://ipip.ori.org/ipip).

negative affect affect is generally a loose term for emotion or mood, thus negative affect refers to negative or difficult emotion.

International Personality Item Pool a scientific collaboratory for the development of advanced measures of personality and other individual differences.

A variety of studies show that those high in neuroticism report themselves as experiencing more physical symptoms and that these symptoms are more intense (Affleck et al., 1992). For example, Costa and McCrae (1987) reported neuroticism to be related to frequency of illness, cardiovascular problems, digestive problems and fatigue across a sample of women with a wide variety of ages. Like hostility, a number of mechanisms by which neuroticism might influence health outcomes have been suggested. One way in which neuroticism may relate to health outcomes might be through perceived or actual stress experienced. For example, those high in negative affect tend to perceive events as more stressful and difficult to cope with than those who are low in negative affect (Watson, 1988). In addition, those high in negative affect may experience more prolonged psychological distress after a negative event (Ormell & Wohlfarth, 1991). High levels of neuroticism may also prompt people to notice and complain about symptoms without this influencing the symptoms that they experience. Indeed, studies find that neuroticism better predicts self-reported than objectively assessed physical health (Watson & Pennebaker, 1989).

Neuroticism may also influence individuals' health behaviours and in this way have an impact on health outcomes (see Focus Point 10.2). Neuroticism has been shown to relate to more smoking and alcohol abuse and less healthy eating and exercise (Booth-Kewley & Vickers, 1994). For example, in relation to smoking, longitudinal studies have found that those with higher neuroticism scores are both more likely to take up smoking and maintain the habit (e.g. Canals, Bladé & Domènech, 1997). A final mechanism by which neuroticism may influence health is through physiological changes. Research has highlighted that higher levels of neuroticism can reduce immune function (Kiecolt-Glaser et al., 2002).

10.2.4 Extraversion

Extraversion is also a Big Five personality trait in the OCEAN model. Those with high levels of the trait are referred to as extraverts and those with low levels as introverts. Extraverts tend to be outgoing, sociable, assertive and show high levels of energy; they also tend to seek stimulation and so enjoy new challenges but get easily bored. In contrast, introverts tend to be more cautious, serious and to avoid over-stimulating environments and activities (Costa & McCrae, 1992; Eysenck, 1967). Extraverts are more likely to agree with statements such as 'Are you usually carefree?' and 'Do you enjoy wild parties?' (Eysenck & Eysenck, 1964). Extraversion has been found to be associated with positive psychological wellbeing and better physical health.

FOCUS POINT 10.2   DEFINING HEALTH BEHAVIOURS?

All sorts of behaviours influence health, from health-enhancing behaviours such as exercise participation and healthy eating, to health-protective behaviours such as health-screening clinic attendance, vaccination against disease and condom use in response to the threat of AIDS, through to avoidance of health-harming behaviours such as smoking and excessive alcohol consumption, and sick-role behaviours such as compliance with medical regimens. A unifying theme across these behaviours has been that each has immediate or longer-term effects on the individual's health and is at least partially within the individual's control.

Several definitions of health behaviours have been suggested:

- 'Any activity undertaken by a person believing himself to be healthy for the purpose of preventing disease or detecting it at an asymptomatic stage.' (Kasl & Cobb, 1966)
- 'Any activity undertaken for the purpose of preventing or detecting disease or for improving health and well-being.' (Conner & Norman, 2005)

Behaviours encompassed in these definitions include medical service usage (e.g. physician visits, vaccination, screening), compliance with medical regimens (e.g. dietary, diabetic, anti-hypertensive regimens) and self-directed health behaviours (e.g. diet, exercise, breast or testicular self-examination, brushing and flossing teeth, smoking, alcohol consumption and contraceptive use).

For example, extraverts report more positive moods and higher levels of pleasure and excitement. Costa and McCrae (1980) showed that measures of extraversion could predict happiness 10 years later. In terms of physical health, extraverts tend to report lower rates of coronary heart disease, ulcers, asthma and arthritis (Friedman & Booth-Kewley, 1987). Some research has reported effects for extraversion on mortality. For example, Shipley *et al.* (2007), in their sample of over 5000 UK adults, reported extraversion to predict a reduced risk of respiratory disease 21 years later.

The exact explanation for the relationship between extraversion and health is not entirely clear. It is possible that this relationship is due to extraverts experiencing lower levels of stress, better coping strategies or more social support compared to introverts. However, there is as yet no strong evidence to support these explanations. Similarly, in relation to impacts on health behaviours, extraversion appears to be associated with both health-protective behaviours like exercise (Rhodes & Courneya, 2003) but also health-risking behaviours like smoking (Booth-Kewley & Vickers, 1994)!

10.2.5 *Conscientiousness*

Conscientiousness refers to the ability to control one's behaviour and to complete tasks. Highly conscientious individuals are more organised, careful, dependable, self-disciplined and achievement oriented than those low in conscientiousness (McCrae & Costa,

1987). Conscientious individuals are more likely to see statements such as 'I am always prepared' and 'I am exacting in my work' as good self-descriptors (International Personality Item Pool, http://ipip.ori.org/ipipo). A growing body of research shows conscientiousness to have impacts on health behaviours, health outcomes and even longevity. For example, the **Terman life-cycle personality cohort study** measured conscientiousness, optimism, self-esteem, sociability, stability of mood and energy level in around 1000 children from the age of 11 years. Friedman *et al.* (1993) reported that of these variables, only conscientiousness was significantly associated with lower mortality in later life. In fact, those high in conscientiousness were likely to live longer (by about two years) compared to those low in conscientiousness.

> **Terman life-cycle personality cohort study** a study measuring conscientiousness, optimism, self-esteem, sociability, stability of mood and energy level in around 1000 children from the age of 11 years.

An important mechanism by which conscientiousness may influence health is through health behaviours. Friedman *et al.* (1995) showed that the impact of conscientiousness on longevity in the Terman sample was partly accounted for by its effect on reducing smoking and alcohol use. A comprehensive review of work on the relationship between conscientiousness and behaviour (Bogg & Roberts, 2004) showed conscientiousness to be positively related to a range of protective health behaviours (e.g. exercise) and negatively related to a range of risky health behaviours (e.g. smoking) (see Table 10.1).

TABLE 10.1 *Relationship between Conscientiousness and Various Health Behaviours.*

In order to compare studies, psychologists look at the impact of one variable on another in terms of standardised effect sizes. The effect size for conscientiousness on health behaviours is small to medium, but can still be substantial enough to produce impacts on how long we live.

Behaviour	Effect size	Direction
Physical activity	Very small	Increase
Excessive alcohol use	Medium	Decrease
Drug use	Medium	Decrease
Unhealthy eating	Small	Decrease
Risky driving	Medium	Decrease
Risky sex	Medium	Decrease
Suicide	Small	Decrease
Tobacco use	Small	Decrease
Violence	Medium	Decrease

Source: Bogg & Roberts (2004). Copyright ©2004 by the American Psychological Association. Reproduced with permission.

10.2.6   Summary

Recent research has begun to examine how personality traits produce changes in health behaviours through shaping the way in which individuals think about these behaviours. This work suggests that our thoughts and feelings about performing a particular health behaviour (e.g. exercising) are a primary determinant of whether we perform that behaviour. That is, we tend to engage in behaviours about which we have positive thoughts and feelings (see Section 10.3). This would suggest that conscientiousness, for example, might influence the amount of exercise we do as a result of shaping our thoughts and feelings about exercising (Conner & Abraham, 2001).

We have reviewed relationships between key personality traits and health outcomes and considered some of the explanations of these relationships. Out of the Big Five personality framework there is as yet less evidence linking openness to experience to health outcomes, but more evidence in relation to conscientiousness, extraversion, neuroticism and agreeableness (when defined as low hostility), with better health outcomes associated with high conscientiousness, high extraversion, low neuroticism and high agreeableness (or low hostility).

We also noted that research supports a link between optimism and positive health outcomes. The negative impacts of Type A behaviour pattern and hostility on health were also examined, particularly in relation to the risk of coronary heart disease.

To summarise, this section has reviewed the relationships between key personality traits and health outcomes and considered some of the explanations of these relationships. The personality traits of conscientiousness, extraversion, neuroticism and agreeableness (when defined as high hostility) have all been linked to health outcomes, with better health outcomes associated with high conscientiousness, high extraversion, low neuroticism and high agreeableness (or low hostility). Optimism is also related to positive health outcomes, while Type A behaviour pattern and hostility are associated with risk of coronary heart disease.

10.3   PREDICTING HEALTH BEHAVIOUR

As well as personality factors, the thoughts and feelings we associate with **health behaviours** like smoking influences whether we smoke or not. In this section we discuss models of the key thoughts and feelings (or 'cognitions') that predict health behaviours.

health behaviours behaviours that affect one's health protectively (through prevention, detection and avoidance of health-harming behaviours) and positively (e.g. exercise participation and healthy eating).

10.3.1   The Health Belief Model

The **health belief model** (HBM) suggests that health behaviours are mainly determined by two aspects of individuals' cognitions about a *health behaviour* (Rosenstock, 1966): perceptions of illness threat (broken down into susceptibility and severity) and evaluation of behaviours (broken down into costs and benefits) to reduce this threat (see Figure 10.1). Threat perceptions are based on two beliefs: the perceived susceptibility of the individual to the illness – 'Am I likely to get it?' – and the perceived severity of the consequences of the illness for the individual – 'How bad would it be?' Together these influence the degree of threat that the individual perceives. Evaluation of possible responses to such a threat involves consideration of the potential benefits and barriers to acting to reduce this threat.

health belief model a model that considers that health behaviours are mainly determined by two aspects of an individual's cognitions about a health behaviour: perceptions of illness threat and evaluation of behaviours to reduce this threat.

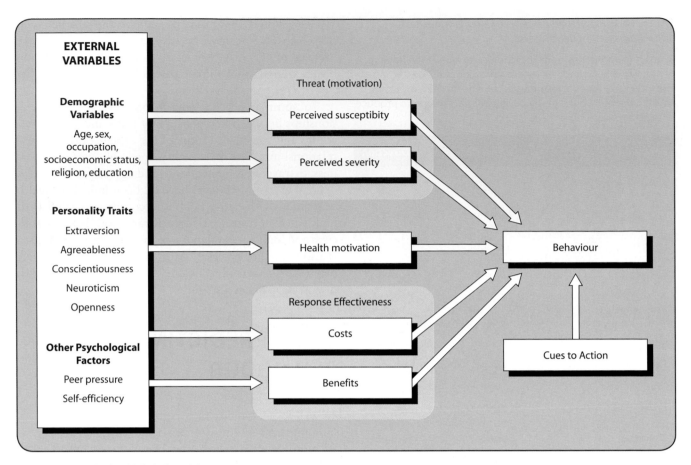

FIGURE 10.1 *The health belief model.*

The health belief model suggests that performing a health behaviour is determined by perceived susceptibility, perceived severity, cues to action, costs and benefits.

In the HBM these four beliefs determine the likelihood of the individual's performing a health behaviour. The action taken is determined by the evaluation of the available alternatives. This evaluation focuses on the benefits of the health behaviour and the perceived barriers to performing the behaviour. So individuals are more likely to perform a health behaviour if they believe themselves to be susceptible to a particular condition that they also consider to be serious, and believe that the benefits of the action taken to counteract the health threat outweigh the costs.

For example, Fred is 50 and he knows that his father and his grandfather before him both died of heart disease at the age of 50. Thus he perceives that he is likely to be *susceptible* to heart disease and he knows that heart disease is *serious*. He therefore recognises that he should try to reduce his risk by eating more healthily and giving up smoking. However, he finds this difficult because he very much likes sweet foods, does not enjoy fruit and vegetables and feels that he depends on smoking to cope with stress. Therefore changing his health-related behaviours represents a significant *cost*, which he has to weigh up against the *benefits*.

The HBM has provided a framework for investigating health behaviours and been widely used. It has been found to successfully predict a range of health behaviours. For example, Janz and Becker (1984) found that across 18 studies the four core beliefs were significant predictors of health behaviour in the majority of cases (82%, 65%, 81% and 100% of studies report significant effects for susceptibility, severity, benefits and barriers, respectively). The main strength of the HBM is the common-sense view it provides in including key beliefs related to decisions about health behaviours (see Abraham & Sheeran [2005] for a detailed review).

10.3.2   Theory of Planned Behaviour

The **theory of planned behaviour** (TPB) was developed by social psychologists and has been widely applied to health behaviours (Conner & Sparks, 2005). It sets out the key factors that

theory of planned behaviour a theory that sets out the key factors that determine the decision to act by an individual, these being intention to engage in that behaviour and perceived behavioural control over that behaviour.

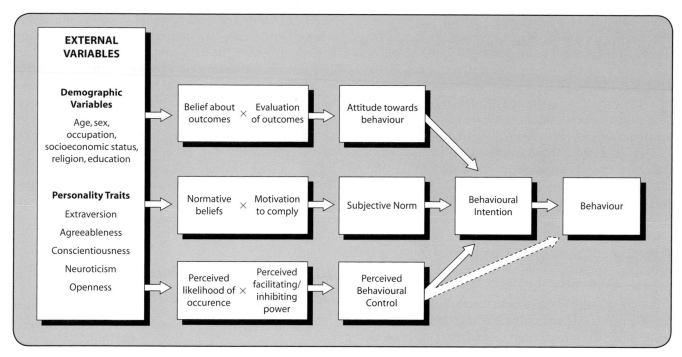

FIGURE 10.2 *The theory of planned behaviour.*

The theory of planned behaviour suggests that behaviour is determined by intentions. Intentions themselves are based on attitudes, subjective norms and perceived behavioural control.

determine an individual's decision to act (see Figure 10.2). The key factors determining behaviour are intention to engage in that behaviour and perceived behavioural control over that behaviour. Intentions here are a plan or decision to exert effort to perform the behaviour (e.g. 'I intend to exercise'). Perceived behavioural control (PBC) is a person's confidence that they can perform the behaviour (e.g. 'I am confident I can exercise no matter what the obstacles') and is similar to Bandura's (1982) concept of self-efficacy (see Section 10.4.3).

In the TPB, intention is then based on three factors: attitudes, subjective norms and PBC. Attitudes are the overall evaluations of the behaviour by the individual as positive or negative (e.g. 'It is good for me to exercise'). Subjective norms are perceptions of what others think (e.g. 'People who are important to me think I should exercise'). PBC also influences intentions and is the confidence that we can perform the behaviour. So, according to the TPB, smokers are likely to quit smoking if they intend to do so. An intention to quit is likely if you have a positive attitude towards quitting, if you believe that people who are important to you think you should quit smoking, and if you feel that you have control over quitting smoking.

Figure 10.2 shows that attitudes, subjective norms and PBC are all based on sets of beliefs about the behaviour. Attitudes are based on beliefs about the outcome of performing the behaviour (e.g. 'My exercising will

protect me against getting CHD') and are called behavioural beliefs or outcome expectancies. It is assumed that an individual will have a limited number of outcomes in mind when considering a behaviour. A positive attitude towards quitting smoking would be the result of thinking that more positive than negative consequences would follow from quitting. In measuring behavioural beliefs we assess how likely each outcome is perceived to be and how positive or negative each outcome is for that individual.

Subjective norms are based on beliefs about whether others approve of your engaging in a behaviour (e.g. 'Would my family approve?', 'Would my best friend approve?'). These are called normative beliefs (e.g. 'My family would approve of me exercising') and are weighted by the 'motivation to comply' with each group (e.g. 'Do I care what my sexual partner/best friend thinks about this?'). So the more people (whose approval is seen to be important) are thought to approve of the action, the more positive the subjective norm.

Finally, judgements of PBC are influenced by control beliefs. Control beliefs tap the extent to which various factors make the behaviour easier or more difficult (e.g. 'Having friends who regularly exercise makes my exercising more likely'). These are weighted by the perceived frequency of these control factors (e.g. 'I have friends at work who regularly exercise at lunchtime'). Control factors include both internal (information, personal deficiencies, skills, abilities, emotions) and external (opportunities, dependence on others, barriers) factors. As for the other types of beliefs, it is assumed that an individual will only consider a limited number of control factors when considering a particular behaviour. So, for example, in relation to quitting smoking, a strong PBC to quit smoking would be expected when a smoker believes there are more factors that facilitate quitting smoking than inhibit it.

PBC is closely related to the concept of self-efficacy (SE). SE is the belief that one has the ability and resources to succeed in achieving a goal despite environmental barriers (and PBC and SE can be thought of as referring to the same underlying behaviour-relevant cognitions). Those with high SE in relation to a behaviour (or sequence of behaviours) are more likely to engage in that behaviour, and this is true across a range of behaviours, from academic performance to health-related behaviours (Bandura, 1997). SE affects behaviour indirectly by changing intentions. SE influences intention because we generally cease to be motivated to achieve things that seem impossible or beyond our reach. So SE helps maintain motivation. In addition, those who believe that they can succeed set themselves more challenging goals. They exert more effort, use more flexible problem-solving strategies and are more persistent because they believe that they will eventually succeed. High SE facilitates concentration on the task rather than concerns about personal deficiencies or exaggeration of task demands (Wood & Bandura, 1989), thereby minimising anxiety during performance. By contrast, low SE undermines efforts to reach goals. Thus SE affects how people conceptualise a task, how confident they feel during performance, how persistent they are in the face of setbacks, how much effort they invest and how they feel about themselves during performance (see Photo 10.2).

PHOTO 10.2 *A key psychologist influencing work on health behaviours: Albert Bandura.*
Source: Getty Images.

A large number of studies support the use of the TPB in relation to predicting various health behaviours (Armitage & Conner, 2001). The TPB contains the most important determinants of behaviour. Although other factors are assumed to influence behaviour, they do so through changing one of the components of the model (e.g. intentions; Figure 10.2). For example, differences in behaviour by demographic factors (e.g. men being more likely to exercise) or personality (e.g. those high in conscientiousness being less likely to smoke) are assumed to be explained by differences in the model (e.g. men having more positive behavioural beliefs about exercising; those high in conscientiousness perceiving more control over smoking).

10.3.3 Integrated Models of the Determinants of Health Behaviours

Models such as the HBM and the TPB show several similarities but also a number of key differences. One approach to this problem is to consider developing an integrated model. This may be valuable given the overlap in cognitions considered by different models. For example, experts agree that the key cognitions influencing behavior are intention, self-efficacy and outcome expectancies (or attitudes). An important attempt at integration was conducted in order to 'identify a finite set of variables to considered in any behavioral analysis' by Martin Fishbein and a number of other major theorists (Fishbein *et al.*, 2001, p. 3). For this reason it is often called the **major theorists model**.

> **major theorists model**
> a model developed by Martin Fishbein and colleagues which suggests that behaviour is determined by intentions, environmental constraints and skills.

This integrated model included eight variables that determine behaviour. The variables are organised into two groups. First are those variables that were viewed as necessary and sufficient determinants of behaviour. Thus, for behaviour to occur an individual must:

- Have a strong intention.
- Have the necessary skills to perform the behaviour.
- Experience an absence of environmental constraints that could prevent the behaviour.

The second group of variables was seen primarily to influence intention, although it was noted that some of the variables may also have a direct effect on behaviour. Thus, a strong intention is likely to occur when an individual:

- Perceives the advantages (or benefits) of performing the behaviour to outweigh the perceived disadvantages (or costs).

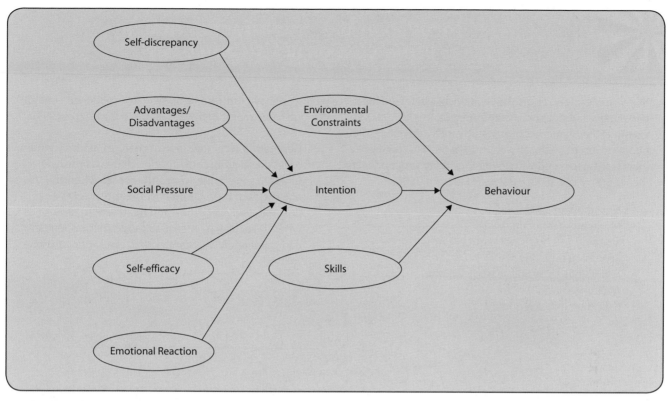

FIGURE 10.3 *The major theorists model.*

The 'major theorists' model was developed by Martin Fishbein and colleagues. It suggests that behaviour is determined by intentions, environmental constraints and skills. Intentions are then determined by five other factors: self-discrepancy, advantages/ disadvantages, social pressure, self-efficacy and emotional reaction.

PHOTO 10.3 *Self-efficacy is a prerequisite to success.*

Source: From Newsweek 11/2/2009. ©2009 Harman Newsweek LLC, Inc.

- Perceives the social (normative) pressure to perform the behaviour to be greater than that not to perform the behaviour.
- Believes that the behaviour is consistent with their self-image.
- Anticipates the emotional reaction to performing the behaviour to be more positive than negative.
- Has high levels of self-efficacy.

Figure 10.3 illustrates this integrated ('major theorists') model. Although this model represents a useful integration of the main predictors of health behaviours such as exercising and health eating, it has not as yet been as widely applied as models such as the HBM or TPB.

10.3.4 Summary

We have reviewed three important models of the key cognitions (i.e. thoughts and feelings) that predict health behaviours. There is growing consensus that the key cognitions include intention, self-efficacy and outcome expectancies (or attitudes). So, for example, if Jane, a

FOCUS POINT 10.3   THE IMPACT OF HEALTH BEHAVIOURS ON HEALTH OUTCOMES

Many studies now report the relationship between health behaviours and health outcomes (e.g. Doll *et al.*, 1994). For example, the Alameda County study followed nearly 7000 people over 10 years and found that seven key behaviours were associated with lower morbidity and longer life (Belloc & Breslow, 1972; Breslow & Enstrom, 1980):

- Not smoking
- Moderate alcohol intake
- Sleeping 7–8 hours per night
- Exercising regularly
- Maintaining a desirable body weight
- Avoiding snacks
- Eating breakfast regularly

Health behaviours are assumed to influence health through three major pathways (Baum & Posluszny, 1999):

- Generating direct biological changes, such as when excessive alcohol consumption damages the liver.
- Changing exposure to health risks, as when the use of a condom protects against the spread of HIV.
- Ensuring early detection and treatment of disease, as when testicular or breast self-examination leads to early detection of a cancer that can more easily be treated.

CHANGING HEALTH BEHAVIOURS   ACTIVITY BOX 10.1

Pick one important health behaviour (e.g. physical activity).

Think about what might be the key determinants of this behaviour from what you have read in this chapter.

Plan how you might go about changing this behaviour by targeting one of these determinants of this behaviour.

How might you go about evaluating the effectiveness of your attempts to change this behaviour?

20-year-old woman, has a strong intention to eat healthily and feels confident that she can eat healthily, and she also perceives that mainly positive outcomes will result from eating healthily, she should be highly likely to eat healthily. In the next section we review how cognitions like these might be changed in order to increase the likelihood of an individual engaging in health behaviours such as exercising or avoiding unhealthy behaviours like smoking (see Focus Point 10.3 and Activity Box 10.1).

To summarise, this section has reviewed three important models of the key cognitions that predict health behaviours: the health belief model, the theory of planned behaviour and the major theorists model. There is growing consensus that the key cognitions prominently include intention, self-efficacy and outcome expectancies (or attitudes).

10.4   CHANGING HEALTH BEHAVIOUR

The work on predicting health behaviour reviewed in Section 10.3 attempted to provide a better understanding of the determinants of health behaviours. The assumption is that this understanding can be used to promote health-inducing behaviour patterns (e.g. exercising) and decrease unhealthy ones (e.g. smoking) – see Chapter 7. Our review identified a number of key predictors of health behaviours that could be targeted for change in order to promote health. For example, promoting intentions and self-efficacy not to smoke could be helpful in reducing smoking and so contribute to improving individuals' health outcomes. Section 10.4 reviews work on changing health behaviours through cognitive dissonance, attitude change and self-efficacy change.

10.4.1   *Cognitive Dissonance*

cognitive dissonance an unpleasant feeling arising in an individual when two or more cognitions are inconsistent or when the person's behaviour is inconsistent with their underlying attitudes.

Cognitive dissonance theory (Festinger, 1957) proposes that we are motivated to maintain a consistent view of the world because cognitive inconsistency creates dissonance, which is inherently unpleasant. This idea has inspired a whole range of social psychology research showing that getting individuals to act in a way that is inconsistent with their attitudes can change those attitudes and behaviour. This is assumed to happen because acting not in accord with our attitudes makes us feel uncomfortable. This feeling of discomfort is labelled cognitive dissonance. We are then motivated to reduce this dissonance by changing our attitudes to bring them into line with our behaviour.

For example, Zanna and Cooper (1974) showed that writing an essay that went against their views could lead individuals to change their attitudes in the direction of what was written in the essay. Importantly, this effect was strongest when individuals believed that they had freely chosen to write the essay (i.e. taken responsibility for the action). The study also showed that the individual must experience some discomfort (i.e. dissonance) that they attribute to the behaviour (i.e. writing the essay) for the effect to occur. In the Zanna and Cooper study participants were given a pill that had no active ingredients but were informed that it would make them either aroused or relaxed. In the aroused condition, the participants had a ready-made explanation for why they felt aroused (i.e. it was the pill) after writing the essay. In this case, there was little attitude change because changing their attitude was thought unlikely to reduce the feelings of discomfort. In contrast, in the condition where the pill was expected to make you feel relaxed, the effect of writing the essay on attitude change was even stronger. In this case the feeling of discomfort after writing the essay could not be explained by the pill (indeed, the pill should be making them relaxed, so writing the essay must be the reason). The best way to reduce that discomfort was to change their attitude to make it more in line with what was written in the essay. This work shows that attitude change resulting from cognitive dissonance is most likely when people perceive negative consequences of the attitude-inconsistent action, they take personal responsibility for the action and they attribute unpleasant arousal (i.e. dissonance) to the action.

It should be possible to motivate change in health behaviours by generating salient contradictions between beliefs and actions. In an experiment conducted by Stone and colleagues (1994) participants were randomly allocated to one of four conditions:

- Receiving information about condom use (information only).
- Receiving information and giving a talk promoting condom use that might be used in school health education (commitment).
- Being made aware of past failures to use condoms by recalling these failures (failure awareness).
- A combination of the commitment and failure awareness conditions.

All participants were then given an opportunity to buy condoms cheaply. The findings showed that significantly more people in the combined commitment and failure-awareness condition bought condoms (82%) than in the failure-awareness condition (50%) or the commitment condition (34%). The study also emphasised that information alone is often not enough to prompt behaviour change because significantly fewer people in the information-only condition bought condoms (44%). This study illustrates how, applying cognitive dissonance theory, a cognitive contrast was created between people's view of what is appropriate behaviour (to which they were committed by becoming an advocate of that position for school students) and their own health behaviour. This technique does not rely on a direct appeal, as in the case of persuasive argument (see Section 10.4.2) designed to change people's perceptions of the outcomes of their action, but depends instead on the power of the salient contradiction between beliefs and the person's own past actions (i.e. cognitive dissonance).

10.4.2   *Attitude Change*

Changing your attitudes after hearing a particularly persuasive message is a common experience. The amount of **attitude change** in these circumstances has been found to be influenced by your reaction to the message. Recent models of attitude change suggest that a persuasive message can be processed in two different ways (Petty & Cacioppo, 1986). These are usually called different routes to persuasion. In one route, the information is systematically and carefully considered. Here attitude change is determined by the extent to which the message produces favourable thoughts about the message. So if after reading a message

attitude change a shift in a person's hypothetical construct in one or more of its three components: cognition, affect and behaviour.

about the benefits of exercising you have mainly positive thoughts, your attitude towards exercising is likely to become more positive. This route to persuasion is called the central or systematic route. It is what we traditionally think of as persuasion and requires quite a bit of effort. In the other route to persuasion, information in the message is not carefully scrutinised or thought about. Here persuasion depends on the presence of peripheral cues. These include whether the message comes from an expert. A message from an expert is judged to be more persuasive and is more likely to produce attitude change. This route to persuasion is called the peripheral or heuristic route and requires little effort.

Petty and Cacioppo (1986) argue that we all want to have attitudes that help us make reliable predictions about our reality. However, we can have more or less motivation and ability to devote to the processing of messages that we receive. We simply have not got the time and energy to process systematically all the persuasive messages that we receive. Petty and Cacioppo refer to the amount of systematic processing devoted to a message as 'cognitive elaboration' and, consequently, their model is known as the **elaboration likelihood model** (ELM). High elaboration is associated with **central route** (effortful) processing of messages, while low elaboration is associated with **peripheral route** (effortless) processing.

elaboration likelihood model a model by Petty and Cacioppo that considers the amount of systematic processing devoted to a message, known as 'cognitive elaboration'.

central route the term for high (effortful) processing of messages according to the elaboration likelihood model of Petty and Cacioppo.

peripheral route the term for low (effortless) processing of messages according to the elaboration likelihood model of Petty and Cacioppo.

The likelihood of elaboration is determined by motivation and the ability to think about the messages. When we are highly motivated because the message is about an issue of interest to us, we are more likely to elaborate and so engage in central-route processing (Petty & Cacioppo, 1986). Ability to think about a message is determined by factors such as not having time pressure or distraction and again increases the likelihood of elaboration (Petty & Cacioppo, 1986). When motivation or ability is low, elaboration will be less likely and persuasion can occur only through the peripheral route. Central-route processing involves greater cognitive elaboration and the strength of the arguments in the message is critical to the amount of persuasion that occurs (via making us think positive thoughts about the message). So here the amount of attitude change is dependent on the arguments being strong. This is consistent with traditional views of how persuasion works: strong arguments will persuade us to change our views; weak arguments will be dismissed and have little impact on attitude change.

By contrast, peripheral-route processing involves little systematic processing (low cognitive elaboration) and other characteristics of the message are more likely to determine whether or not it is persuasive. For example, people use simple rules or decision-making heuristics to evaluate messages (Chaiken, 1980). These include 'expertise = accuracy' – that is, 'She's an expert so what she says must be right' – or 'consensus = correctness' – that is, 'If so many people agree they must be right' – and 'length = strength' – that is, 'There are lots of arguments so it must be true'. Sometimes situational constraints force people into peripheral-route processing. For example, the message may be presented quickly amid distractions, as is the case in many television advertisements. In addition, individual differences mean that some people are more or less likely than others to engage in systematic processing. For example, Chaiken (1980) identified people who agreed or disagreed with the 'length = strength' heuristic (using agreement with questionnaire items such as 'The more reasons a person has for some point of view the more likely he/she is correct'). These people were then presented with a message containing six arguments in favour of cross-course, end-of-year examinations for students. However, the message was described to participants as either containing ten or two arguments (although it always contained the same six arguments). The results showed that those who endorsed the length = strength heuristic were more likely to be persuaded when the message was described as having ten arguments than were those who did not endorse the heuristic.

When people have time to process messages or make time because they see the message as personally relevant, they are more likely to engage in systematic processing so that the meaning of the message is more important than other characteristics. Figure 10.4 shows how perceiving the message source to be an expert has different effects depending on whether recipients regard a message as high or low in personal relevance. The low-relevance participants are strongly affected by perceived expertise and are more persuaded by an expert (rather than inexpert) source whether strong or weak arguments are used. However, for those who see the message as personally relevant (and so engage in systematic processing), only the quality of the argument determines persuasion. Strong arguments are persuasive for this group, regardless of source expertise, and even an expert cannot persuade this group with weak arguments. This does not mean that source expertise is unimportant, but rather that for those with the ability and motivation to engage in systematic processing, poor-quality arguments cannot be compensated for by the impression of expertise.

Overall, then, research suggests that if you do *not* have strong arguments you are better to discourage systematic

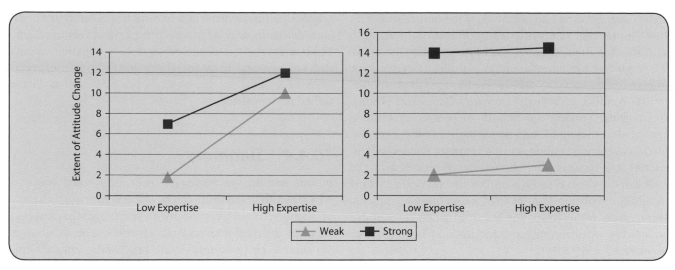

FIGURE 10.4 *The impact of expertise on persuasion.*

The impact of expertise on persuasion by strong and weak arguments under conditions of low (left) and high (right) personal relevance (Petty & Cacioppo, 1986). Strong arguments produce the most attitude change under conditions of high personal relevance.

USING PERSUASION TO CHANGE HEALTH BEHAVIOURS

ACTIVITY BOX 10.2

Design a short set of arguments that could be used to persuade young people to use condoms, drawing on evidence-based principles of persuasion.

---

processing and rely instead on numerous arguments, consensus and perceived expertise. Perhaps fortunately, attitude changes resulting from peripheral-route processing are less likely to be stable (that is, long lived) and more likely to change further due to other persuasive messages, whereas attitude change resulting from systematic (central-route) processing is more likely to be stable and to influence behaviour. Consequently, health promoters should encourage systematic processing by ensuring appropriate prior knowledge, emphasising personal relevance, providing distraction-free presentations, using repetition and encouraging confidence in people's own judgement.

Activity Box 10.2 considers the role of persuasion.

10.4.3 Enhancing Self-Efficacy

Bandura (1997) and colleagues have demonstrated that self-efficacy can be enhanced through mastery experiences, vicarious experience, verbal persuasion or changing perception of physiological and affective states. First,

and most powerful, **mastery experiences** (i.e. experience of successfully performing the behaviour) give people confidence that they can tackle new tasks because they know they have previously succeeded with similar challenges. This recommends that teachers and trainers guide learners towards success by identifying manageable tasks and only increasing difficulty as confidence and skill grow; that is, by the use of **graded tasks**. Moreover, helping someone practise a manageable task and providing feedback can consolidate skills and enhance SE. Failure undermines SE and focusing on past failure can be self-handicapping.

Second, SE can also be enhanced through observation of others' success (i.e. **vicarious experience**), especially if we categorise

mastery experience past experience of successfully performing a behaviour thus giving a person confidence that he or she can tackle a new task providing a similar challenge.

graded tasks manageable tasks that are only increased in difficulty as confidence and skill in task performance grow.

vicarious experience a term generally used to indicate experience that has not been direct but rather observation of another's experience.

the models as being like ourselves. For example, Bandura (1997) notes that observing failure in a model judged to have less skill than ourselves has little or no impact on SE, but observing the same failure in a model judged to have similar skills is likely to undermine SE. Health promoters should conduct preliminary research into when positive and negative models are helpful to people establishing new goals, building SE and acquiring new skills. Positive models occur when there is observation of successful others; negative models when there is use of models failing to establish the desired behaviour. Positive models are likely to be SE enhancing (e.g. in the case of physical fitness), although in some cases, for example when undesirable body image is salient, negative models may be motivating (Lockwood *et al.*, 2005).

> **verbal persuasion** influencing someone by what is said, often enhanced by maximising the trustworthiness and expertise of the speaker.

Third, when direct experience and modelling are not available, SE can be enhanced through **verbal persuasion**. People can be persuaded by arguments demonstrating that others (like them) are successful in meeting challenges similar to their own (thereby changing descriptive norms), as well as persuasion highlighting individuals' own skills and past success. Tailoring communication to enhance persuasiveness (as discussed in this chapter), including for example maximising source trustworthiness and expertise, is likely to enhance the effectiveness of such interventions.

> **perception of physi-ological reactions** one's performance can be affected positively or negatively depending on how one perceives and interprets one's physical and emotional responses during performance.

Finally, our own **perception of physiological reactions** and our interpretation of these reactions affect SE. Mood, stress and anxiety during performance can bolster or undermine self-efficacy. For example, although arousal is normal during demanding performances, it can be interpreted as a sign of panic or incompetence. Such interpretations are likely to disrupt and undermine performance. By contrast,

acknowledging arousal as a natural response to performance demands may add to excitement and commitment. Thus interventions designed to reduce negative moods and anxiety and to re-interpret destructive interpretations of arousal are likely to enhance SE and facilitate skilled performance.

10.4.4 Summary

In this section we reviewed three important ways in which health behaviours can be changed: through the use of cognitive dissonance to promote change; the employment of different messages to promote attitude change via central- or peripheral-route processing; and self-efficacy change. Combinations of these techniques might be particularly effective in promoting health behaviours. However, there are many other techniques that are used to change health-related behaviour (Abraham & Michie, 2008). Research on personality traits such as **need for cognition** suggests that messages may be more effective if they are tailored to maximise health behaviour in groups with different personality traits. Those low in need for cognition may be less likely to be persuaded by messages relying on strong messages that require central-route processing, because such individuals tend to use peripheral-route processing. For example, Conner *et al.* (2011) showed that messages promoting exercise through targeting affective attitudes (e.g. suggesting the fun involved in exercising) was more effective for those low in need for cognition.

> **need for cognition** a tendency to enjoy thinking.

To summarise, three important ways in which health behaviours can be changed were reviewed: through use of cognitive dissonance to promote change, use of different messages to promote attitude change via central or peripheral route processing and self-efficacy change. Combinations of these techniques might be particularly effective in promoting health behaviours.

10.5 CONCLUSION

The chapter has shown a number of ways in which social psychology has contributed to understanding issues in health psychology. The first part of the chapter showed how various aspects of personality are related to health outcomes. This included work on optimism, impulsivity/neuroticism, hostility and more general personality traits such as conscientiousness. The second part of the chapter looked at a number of models of the cognitions about specific

health behaviours that influence whether we engage in such behaviours. These models include the health belief model, the theory of planned behaviour and Fishbein *et al.*'s integrative model. The final part of the chapter examined how behaviour might be changed through changing cognitions. The focus here was on persuasive communication, cognitive dissonance and the elaboration likelihood model. Together the chapter helps to show the numerous important ways by which knowledge in health psychology has developed out of important perspectives from social psychology and other areas of psychology.

SELF-TEST QUESTIONS

- List key personality traits shown to be related to health outcomes.
- List the components of the health belief model.
- List the components of the theory of planned behaviour.
- List the determinants of behaviour in the major theorists model.
- List the determinants of intentions in the major theorists model.
- What are the two routes to persuasion in the elaboration likelihood model?
- How can self-efficacy be changed?

ESSAY QUESTIONS

- Describe the evidence relating key personality traits to different kinds of health outcomes.
- Critically evaluate the mechanisms by which personality traits might have impacts on health.
- Compare and contrast the health belief model and the theory of planned behaviour as explanations of why people do and do not perform a range of health behaviours.
- What do we know about the predictors of intention?
- What lessons can health promoters learn from the psychology of attitude change?
- How might we change self-efficacy to help change health-related behaviour?

TEXTS FOR FURTHER READING

Abraham, C. & Sheeran, P. (2005) Health belief model, in M. Conner & P. Norman (eds) *Predicting Health Behaviour: Research and Practice with Social Cognition Models*, 2nd edn, Buckingham: Open University Press.

Conner, M. & Norman, P. (2005) Predicting health behaviour: A social cognition approach, in M. Conner & P. Norman (eds) *Predicting Health Behaviour: Research and Practice with Social Cognition Models,* 2nd edn, pp. 1–27, Maidenhead: Open University Press.

Conner, M. & Sparks, P. (2005) Theory of planned behaviour and health behaviour, in M. Conner & P. Norman (eds) *Predicting Health Behaviour: Research and Practice with Social Cognition Models*, 2nd edn, Buckingham: Open University Press.

Petty, R.E. & Cacioppo, J.T. (1986) The elaboration likelihood model of persuasion, in L. Berkowitz (ed.) *Advances in Experimental Social Psychology, 19*, pp. 123–205, New York: Academic Press.

RELEVANT JOURNAL ARTICLES

Ajzen, I. & Fishbein, M. (2004) Questions raised by a reasoned action approach: Reply on Ogden (2003), *Health Psychology* 23: 431–4.

Bandura, A. (1999) Health promotion from the perspective of social cognitive theory, *Psychology & Health* 13: 623–50.

Caspi, A., Roberts, B.W. & Shiner, R.L. (2005) Personality development: Stability and change, *Annual Review of Psychology* 56: 453–84.

Cialdini, R.B. (1995) Principles and techniques of social influence, in A. Tesser (ed.) *Advanced Social Psychology* (pp. 257–81), New York: McGraw Hill.

Coulter, A., Entwistle, V. & Gilbert, D. (1999) Sharing decisions with patients: Is the information good enough? *British Medical Journal* 318: 318–22.

Matthews, K.A., Woodall, K.L., Kenyon, K. & Jacob, T. (1996) Negative family environment as a predictor of boys' future status on measures of hostile attitudes, interview behavior and anger expression, *Health Psychology* 14: 30–37.

Ogden, J. (2003) Some problems with social cognition models: A pragmatic and conceptual analysis, *Health Psychology* 22: 424–8.

Peterson, C., Vaillant, G.E. & Seligman, M.E.P. (1988) Pessimistic explanatory style is a risk factor for physical illness: A thirty-five-year longitudinal study, *Journal of Personality and Social Psychology* 55: 23–7.

Pressman, S.D. & Cohen, S. (2005) Does positive affect influence health? *Psychological Bulletin* 131: 925–71.

Smith, T.W., Glazer, K., Ruiz, J.M. & Gallo, L.C. (2004) Hostility, anger, aggressiveness, and coronary heart disease: An interpersonal perspective on personality, emotion, and health, *Journal of Personality* 72: 1217–70.

RELEVANT WEB LINKS

Developing a Theory of Planned Behaviour Questionnaire, http://people.umass.edu/aizen
Personality measures, http://ipip.org
Self-efficacy, www.learning-theories.com/social-learning-theory-bandura.html

REFERENCES

Abraham, C. & Michie, S. (2008) A taxonomy of behavior change techniques used in interventions, *Health Psychology* 2: 379–87.

Abraham, C. & Sheeran, P. (2005) The health belief model, in M. Conner & P. Norman (eds) *Predicting Health Behaviour: Research and Practice with Social Cognition Models*, 2nd edn, pp. 28–80, Maidenhead: Open University Press.

Affleck, G., Tennen, H., Uroows, S. & Higgins, P. (1992) Neuroticism and the pain-mood relation in rheumatoid arthritis: Insights from a prospective daily study, *Journal of Counsulting and Clinical Psychology* 60: 119–26.

Armitage, C.J. & Conner, M. (2001) Efficacy of the theory of planned behaviour: A meta-analytic review, *British Journal of Social Psychology* 40: 471–99.

Bandura, A. (1982) Self-efficacy mechanism in human agency, *American Psychologist* 37: 122–47.

Bandura, A. (1997) *Self-efficacy: The Exercise of Control,* New York: Freeman.

Baum, A., & Posluszny, D.M. (1999) Health psychology: Mapping biobehavioral contributions to health and illness, *Annual Review of Psychology* 50: 137–63.

Belloc, N.B. & Breslow, L. (1972) Relationship of physical health status and health practices, *Preventive Medicine* 1: 409–421.

Bogg, T. & Roberts, B.W. (2004) Conscientiousness and health-related behaviors: A meta-analysis of the leading behavioral contributors to mortality, *Psychological Bulletin* 130: 887–919.

Booth-Kewley, S. & Vickers, R.R. (1994) Associations between major domains of personality and health behavior, *Journal of Personality* 62: 281–98.

Breslow, L. & Enstrom, J.E. (1980) Persistence of health habits and their relationship to mortality, *Preventive Medicine* 9: 469–83.

Canals, J., Bladé, J. & Domènech, E. (1997) Smoking and personality predictors in young Spanish people, *Personality and Individual Differences* 23: 905–8.

Caspi, A., Begg, D., Dickson, N. *et al.* (1997) Personality differences predict health-risk behaviour in young adulthood: Evidence from a longitudinal study, *Journal of Personality and Social Psychology* 73: 1052–62.

Chaiken, S. (1980) Heuristic versus systematic information processing and the use of source versus message cues in persuasion, *Journal of Personality and Social Psychology* 39: 752–66.

Conner, M. & Abraham, C. (2001) Conscientiousness and the Theory of Planned Behavior: Towards a more complete model of the antecedents of intentions and behavior, *Personality and Social Psychology Bulletin* 27: 1547–61.

Conner, M.T. & Norman, P. (eds) (2005) *Predicting Health Behaviour: Research and Practice with Social Cognition Models*, 2nd edn, Maidenhead: Open University Press.

Conner, M. & Sparks, P. (2005) The theory of planned behaviour and health behaviours, in M. Conner & P. Norman (eds) *Predicting Health Behaviour: Research and Practice with Social Cognition Models*, 2nd edn, pp. 170–222, Maidenhead: Open University Press.

Conner, M., Rhodes, R., Morris, M., McEachan, R. & Lawton, R. (2011) Changing exercise through targeting affective or cognitive attitudes, *Psychology & Health* 26: 154–70.

Cook, W.W. & Medley, D.M. (1954) Proposed hostility and pharisaic-virtue scores for the MMPI, *Journal of Applied Psychology* 38: 414–18.

Costa, P.T., Jr. & McCrae, R.R. (1980) Influence of extraversion and neuroticism on subjective well-being: Happy and unhappy people, *Journal of Personality and Social Psychology* 40: 19–28.

Costa, P.T., Jr. & McCrae, R.R. (1987) Neuroticism, somatic complaints, and disease: Is the bark worse than the bite? *Journal of Personality* 55: 299–316.

Costa, P.T., Jr. & McCrae, R.R. (1992) Four ways five factors are basic, *Personality and Individual Differences* 13: 653–65.

Danner, D.D., Snowdon, D.A. & Friesen, W.V. (2001) Positive emotions in early life and longevity: Findings from the nun study, *Journal of Personality and Social Psychology* 80: 804–13.

Davidson, K.W., Gidron, Y., Mostofsky, E. & Trudeau, K.J. (2007) Hospitalization cost offset of a hostility intervention for coronary heart disease patients, *Journal of Consulting and Clinical Psychology* 75: 657–62.

Digman, J.M. (1990) Personality structure: Emergence of the five-factor model, *Annual Review of Psychology* 41: 417–40.

Doll, R., Peto, R., Wheatley, K., Gray, R. & Sutherland, I. (1994) Mortality in relation to smoking: 40 years' observations on male British doctors, *British Medical Journal* 309: 901–11.

Everson, S.A., Goldberg, D.E., Kaplan, G.A. & Cohen, R.D. (1996) Hopelessness and risk of mortality and incidence of myocardial infarction and cancer, *Psychosomatic Medicine* 58: 103–21.

Eysenck, H.J. (1967) *The Biological Basis of Personality*, Springfield, IL: Charles Thomas.

Eysenck, H.J. & Eysenck, S.B.G. (1964) *Eysenck Personality Inventory*, San Diego, CA: Education and Industry Testing Service.

Festinger, L. (1957) *A Theory of Cognitive Dissonance*, Palo Alto, CA: Stanford University Press.

Fishbein. M., Triandis, H.C., Kanfer, F.H., Becker, M., Middlestadt, S.E. & Eichler, A. (2001) Factors influencing behavior and behavior change, in A. Baum, T.A. Revenson & J.E. Singer (eds) *Handbook of Health Psychology*, pp. 3–17, Mahwah, NJ: Lawrence Erlbaum Associates.

Friedman, H.S. & Booth-Kewley, S. (1987) The disease-prone personality, *American Psychologist* 42: 539–55.

Friedman, H.S., Tucker, J.S., Schwartz, J.E. et al. (1995) Childhood conscientiousness and longevity: Health behaviors and cause of death, *Journal of Personality and Social Psychology* 68: 696–703.

Friedman, H.S., Tucker, J.S., Tomlinson-Keasay, C., Schwartz, J.E., Wingard, D.L. & Criqui, M.H. (1993) Does childhood personality predict longevity? *Journal of Personality and Social Psychology* 65: 176–85.

Gidron, Y., Davidson, K. & Bata, I. (1999) The short-term effects of a hostility-reduction intervention on male coronary heart disease patients, *Health Psychology* 18: 416–20.

Janz, N.K., & Becker, M.H. (1984). The health belief model: a decade later. *Health Education Quarterly* 11: 1–47.

Kasl, S.V. & Cobb, S. (1966) Health behavior, illness behavior and sick role behavior, *Archives of Environmental Health* 12: 246–66.

Kiecolt-Glaser, J.K., McGuire, L., Robles, T.F. & Glaser, R. (2002) Psychoneuroimmunology: Psychological influences on immune function and health, *Journal of Consulting and Clinical Psychology* 70: 537–47.

Levy, B.R., Slade, M.D., Kunkel, S.R. & Kasl, S.V. (2002) Longevity increased by positive self-perceptions of aging, *Journal of Personality and Social Psychology* 83: 261–70.

Lockwood, P., Wong, C., McShane, K. & Dolderman, D. (2005) The impact of positive and negative fitness exemplars on motivation, *Basic and Applied Social Psychology* 27: 1–13.

Matthews, K.A., Woodall, K.L., Kenyon, K. & Jacob, T. (1996) Negative family environment as a predictor of boys' future status on measures of hostile attitudes, interview behaviour and anger expression, *Health Psychology* 15: 30–37.

McCrae, R.R. & Costa, P.T. (1987) Validation of the five-factor model of personality across instruments and observers, *Journal of Personality and Social Psychology* 54: 81–90.

Miller, T.Q., Smith, T.W., Turner, C.W., Guijarro, M.L. & Hallet, A.J. (1996) A meta-analytic review of research on hostility and physical health, *Psychological Bulletin* 119: 322–48.

Ormell, J. & Wohlfarth, T. (1991) How neuroticism, long-term difficulties, and life situation change influence psychological distress: A longitudinal model, *Journal of Personality and Social Psychology* 60: 744–55.

Peterson, C. & Seligman, M.E.P. (1987) Explanatory style and illness, *Journal of Personality* 55: 237–65.

Peterson, C., Vaillant, G.E. & Seligman, M.E.P. (1988) Pessimistic explanatory style is a risk factor for physical illness: A thirty-five-year longitudinal study, *Journal of Personality and Social Psychology* 55: 23–7.

Petty, R.E. & Cacioppo, J.T. (1986) The elaboration likelihood model of persuasion, in L. Berkowitz (ed.) *Advances in Experimental Social Psychology*, 19, pp. 123–205, New York: Academic Press.

Reed, G.M., Kemeny, M.E., Taylor, S.E., Wang, H.-Y.J. & Vissher, B.R. (1994) Realistic acceptance as a predictor of decreased survival time in gay men with AIDS, *Health Psychology* 13: 299–307.

Rhodes, R.E. & Courneya, K.S. (2003) Investigating multiple components of attitude, subjective norm, and perceived control: An examination of the theory of planned behaviour in the exercise domain, *British Journal of Social Psychology* 42: 129–46.

Rosenman, R.H., Brand, R.J., Sholtz, R.I. & Friedman, M. (1976) Multivariate prediction of coronary heart disease during 8.5 year follow-up in the western collaborative group study, *American Journal of Cardiology* 37: 903–10.

Rosenstock, I.M. (1966) Why people use health services, *Millbank Memorial Fund Quarterly* 44: 94–124.

Scheier, M.F. & Carver, C.S. (1992) Effects of optimism on psychological and physical well-being: Theoretical overview and empirical update, *Cognitive Therapy and Research* 16: 201–28.

Scheier, M.F., Matthews, K.A., Owens, J. *et al.* (1999) Optimism and rehospitalization after coronary artery bypass graft surgery, *Archives of Internal Medicine* 159: 829–35.

Scheier, M.F., Weintraub, J.K. & Carver, C.S. (1986) Coping with stress: Divergent strategies of optimists and pessimists, *Journal of Personality and Social Psychology* 51: 1257–64.

Shipley, B.A., Weiss, A., Der, G, Taylor, M.D. & Deary, I.J. (2007) Neuroticism, extraversion, and mortality in the UK health and lifestyle surviery: A 21-year prospective cohort study, *Psychosomatic Medicine* 69: 923–31.

Smith, T.W. (1994) Concepts and methods in the study of anger, hostility, and health, in A.G. Seigman & T.W. Smith (eds) *Anger, Hostility and the Heart*, pp. 23–42, Hillsdale, NJ: Lawrence Erlbaum Associates.

Smith, T.W., Glazer, K., Ruiz, J.M. & Gallo, L.C. (2004) Hostility, anger, aggressiveness, and coronary heart disease: An interpersonal perspective on personality, emotion, and health, *Journal of Personality* 72: 1217–70.

Stone, J., Aronson, E., Crain, A.L., Winslow, M.P. & Fried, C.B. (1994) Inducing hypocrisy as a means of encouraging young adults to use condoms, *Personality and Social Psychology Bulletin* 20: 116–28.

Watson, D. (1988) Intra-individual and inter-individual analyses of positive and negative affect: Their relation to health complaints, perceived stress, and daily activities, *Journal of Personality and Social Psychology* 54: 1020–30.

Watson, D. & Clark, L.A. (1984) Negative affectivity: The disposition to experience aversive emotional states, *Psychological Bulletin* 96: 465–90.

Watson, D. & Pennebaker, J.W. (1989) Health complaints, stress and distress: Exploring the central role of negative affectivity, *Psychological Review* 96: 234–54.

Wood, R.E. & Bandura, A. (1989) Impact of conceptions of ability on self-regulatory mechanisms and complex decision making, *Journal of Personality and Social Psychology* 56: 407–15.

Zanna, M.P. & Cooper, J. (1974) Dissonance and the pill: An attribution approach to studying the arousal properties of dissonance, *Journal of Personality and Social Psychology* 29: 703–9.

11 Training and Working as a Health Psychologist

CHARLES ABRAHAM, DARYL O'CONNOR, FIONA JONES,
MARK CONNER & KAREN RODHAM

LEARNING OUTCOMES

WHEN YOU HAVE COMPLETED THIS CHAPTER, YOU SHOULD
BE ABLE TO:

1. Provide a brief description of the work that health psychologists do in different settings and give some examples.

2. List the six key roles that all professional psychologists are expected to be able to perform in the UK and provide illustrations of these roles in everyday work settings.

3. List and explain the four areas of expertise that a UK trainee health psychologist is expected to have attained once they have passed their Stage 1 Qualification in Health Psychology.

4. Assess what areas of health psychology you have been introduced to in this book and identify which areas specified at Stage 1 you have not yet studied.

5. List and explain the five groups of competencies that a UK trainee health psychologist is expected to have attained once they have passed their Stage 2 Qualification in Health Psychology. In addition, explain what kinds of projects and assessments Stage 2 candidates must undertake in order to demonstrate these competencies.

KEY WORDS

Assess • Competencies • Conduct Research • Consult • Coping Strategies • European Federation of Professional Psychologists Associations (EFPA) • Generic Professional Competencies • Health Trainers • Health-Enhancing Behaviour Patterns • Intervene • Key Roles • Multidisciplinary Settings • National Occupational Standards • Psychological Wellbeing • Stage 1 Qualification in Health Psychology • Stage 2 Qualification in Health Psychology • Supervise and Manage • Train and Supervise

CHAPTER OUTLINE

ROUTE MAP OF THE CHAPTER

In this chapter we will discuss what health psychologists do. We will consider different settings in which they work and the various roles they play in these settings. We will describe and illustrate how a psychology student can become a trained health psychologist, focusing on the UK training route but also showing how this relates to training in Europe. We will explain how a psychology student can gain Graduate Basis for Chartered Membership of the British Psychological Society by being awarded an accredited degree in psychology. We will then describe how a student with this qualification can acquire a Stage 1 Qualification in Health Psychology, so becoming a trainee health psychologist. This can be done by passing a one-year MSc in Health Psychology and we will discuss the content of such a qualification. A trainee health psychologist can become a trained and chartered health psychologist by completing a Stage 2 qualification recognised by the Health Professionals Council. We will explain what this entails. Finally, one of the chapter authors will briefly characterise her work across two settings, a university and a hospital.

11.1   WHAT DO PROFESSIONAL HEALTH PSYCHOLOGISTS DO?

health-enhancing behaviour patterns behaviours that have an immediate or long-term positive affect on an individual's health and are at least partially within the individual's control.

coping strategies ways of coping that are problem-focused or emotion-focused.

We noted in Chapter 7 that the primary aim of health psychology is to promote health and prevent illness. Practising health psychologists apply research findings to further this aim. For example, practising health psychologists may intervene to promote **health-enhancing behaviour patterns** and/or **coping strategies** that promote health, reduce stress and offer protection against disease and illness. Health psychologists work with individuals, families and organisations (e.g. job redesign) as well as advising local and national governments on health-promoting policy options (see the social ecological model described in Chapter 7). Focus Point 11.1 illustrates questions that health psychologists may address in their everyday practice, including questions that have been worked on by the authors of this chapter.

So generally, those who choose to work as health psychologists have a strong interest in people, in promoting health and in how interaction organisations affect people and their health. Unlike clinical psychologists, health psychologists do not focus on psychological problems or mental illness but rather on physical health and **psychological wellbeing**. However, both health and clinical

psychological wellbeing includes feeling happy and contented, maintaining good social relationships and using one's time to achieve realistic goals.

FOCUS POINT 11.1   WHAT SORT OF QUESTIONS DO HEALTH PSYCHOLOGISTS ADDRESS IN THEIR EVERYDAY PRACTICE?

- Why is patient X not taking the medication recommended?
- How can stress at work be reduced for client X?
- What kind of rehabilitation programme will work best to help patient X get back to work after an illness (e.g. a heart attack)?
- How can we reduce stress at work for a group of professionals, e.g. nurses in a particular hospital?
- How can we help patients with chronic pain who are visiting a pain clinic?
- How can we promote physical activity within a senior school?

- How can we best train front-line professionals to change health-related behaviours among the clients who consult them?
- How can a company reduce stress among its employees without reducing productivity?
- How can a city reduce the prevalence of teenage pregnancies?
- What health-promotion policies should the government adopt to reduce the prevalence of health-risk behaviours such as over-eating and excessive alcohol consumption?

psychologists may help patients suffering from stress and/or depression and seek to change their perceptions, attitudes and behaviours.

Health psychologists conduct and draw on a range of health psychology research in their everyday practice. For example, health psychologists may be involved in developing or applying research into:

- Individual differences (e.g. personality characteristics; see the five-factor model described in Chapter 10).
- Cognitions (e.g. beliefs, attitudes, perceived norms and self-efficacy; see Chapters 7 and 10).
- Stress reduction (see Chapters 8 and 9).
- How these factors shape health-related behaviours (see Chapter 7).

Health psychologists aim to understand the processes that explain psychological characteristics and tendencies (see Chapter 7) in order to develop effective interventions that can change cognitions, the experience of stress and health-related behaviour patterns.

multidisciplinary settings health psychologists work in a variety of settings in which a variety of professionals work together.

Health psychologists work in a variety of **multidisciplinary settings**. In a discussion of the health psychologist's role in health-care services, Hallas (2004) notes that health psychologists may be involved in direct patient care, assessing and enhancing individuals' psychological adjustment to illness and treatment, minimising distress associated with medical procedures, delivering health education, facilitating patient decision making and implementing psychological interventions. Health psychologists may be involved in designing and improving screening programmes, training health-care professionals, running stress-management courses and advising on job redesign.

The British Psychological Society, Division of Health Psychology (BPS DHP), illustrates the career paths open to health psychologists using a series of case studies (see http://www.bps.org.uk/dhp/career-paths-in-health-psychology/career-paths-in-health-psychology.cfm). Case History 11.1 includes two brief case studies based on the BPS DHP illustrations.

To summarise:

- Health psychologists work in a variety of settings. These include academic settings such as a university, health-care environments such as a hospital and industrial contexts.

- In addition to research (e.g. into adherence – see Chapter 7), health psychologists may care for patients and provide advice and consultancy to individuals, companies and government. Health psychologists also usually teach and train others.

- At senior levels, health psychologists manage research, professional and clinical staff.

- Health psychologists' work focuses on psychological and behaviour change, which promotes wellbeing and health. Practising health psychologists often work in multidisciplinary settings, so they need to be able to work with other professionals.

11.2 CORE COMPETENCIES REQUIRED BY PROFESSIONAL HEALTH PSYCHOLOGISTS

Health psychology training programmes must ensure that their graduates have key skills or **competencies** that will enable them to practise effectively

competencies skills that are essential to perform certain functions and roles, acquired during a professional's training.

CASE HISTORY 11.1

WHAT DO HEALTH PSYCHOLOGISTS DO? TWO EXAMPLES

Julie is a Chartered Health Psychologist who is head of a 'Stop Smoking' service funded by the National Health Service. She decides how many smoking-cessation groups are needed in order to respond to local demand and manages a multidisciplinary team of stop-smoking advisors. She ensures that there is appropriate training available for health professionals and others regarding smoking cessation. She also evaluates services and applies changes where necessary. Finally she liaises with other services to provide coordinated local and national service provision.

Anne is a Consultant Health Psychologist responsible for developing, leading, managing and providing a psychology service to Cardiac Medicine and Renal Medicine. Her service provides specialist psychological care (including individual and group interventions, consultative advice and supervision of colleagues) for patients with renal disease and coronary heart disease. She and her colleagues work in multidisciplinary teams. She also contributes to budgetary planning for the renal and cardiac rehabilitation services.

National Occupational Standards identified levels of knowledge, skill and performance expected after professional qualification, enabling professionals and employers to match acquired skills or competencies against job demands.

and safely. In the UK, **National Occupational Standards** have been developed for a variety of professional roles, including psychologists. These standards identify the knowledge, skills and levels of competent performance expected after qualification from training programmes and so allow professionals and employers to match acquired skills or competencies against job demands. The 'Key Purpose Statement' from the National Standards for Psychology is as follows:

> to develop, apply and evaluate psychological principles, knowledge, theories and methods in an ethical and appropriate way (i.e. systematic, evidence-based and reflective) in order to promote work-related issues. This includes the development, well-being and effectiveness of organisations, groups and individuals for the benefit of society. (http://www.bps.org.uk/professional-development/nos/nos_home.cfm)

key roles professional psychologists are expected to be able to fulfil six key roles, four achieved with qualification, a further two with post-qualifying work experience.

This over-arching definition of professional practice in psychology is sub-divided into six **key roles**. Professional psychologists are expected to:

1. Develop, implement and maintain personal and professional standards and ethical practice.

2. Apply psychological and related methods, concepts, models, theories and knowledge derived from reproducible research findings.

3. Research and develop new and existing psychological methods, concepts, models, theories and instruments in psychology.

4. Communicate psychological knowledge, principles, methods, needs and policy requirements.

5. Develop and train in the application of psychological skills, knowledge, practices and procedures.

6. Manage the provision of psychological systems, services and resources.

All professional psychologists are expected to attain key roles 1–4 on qualification. The competencies required to fulfil key roles 5 and 6 may, however, only be attained through work experience. Each of these key roles is, in turn, sub-divided into many standards of performance. These standards were derived from a series of workshops and consultations that involved a range of applied psychologists.

Health psychologists have used this framework to define core competencies that are essential to health psychology (see Michie & Abraham, 2004). Below are six core areas of competency that identify what it is that health psychologists need to be able to do in their everyday work:

1. **Assess** – that is, understand, describe and explain psychological and behavioural processes that result in individual differences, including individual strengths and vulnerabilities. This may involve applying measures to characterise personality, stress levels, attitudes, patient satisfaction, adherence or health behaviours (see Chapters 7–10).

   assess understand and explain the determinants of an individual's health or wellbeing problems.

2. **Conduct research**, including developing theory and methods relevant to health-related behaviour. This could involve applying for research funding, conducting an interpretative analysis of interview data, a systematic review, a meta-analysis, a prospective survey or randomised control trial. Once health psychologists have completed a piece of research they want to inform others who could benefit from their findings. This may include working with the media to publicise their research.

   conduct research for example, developing theoretical understandings, collecting data and interpreting the meaning of findings for theory and intervention.

3. **Intervene** – that is, generate changes in psychological and behavioural processes that result in improved health-care and health outcomes. This could involve applying social cognition theories to design an intervention for an individual in a health-care setting, in a school or among a group of workers in a private company (see Chapter 7).

   intervene designing, implementing and evaluating any programme or materials to promote psychological or behavioural change.

4. **Train and supervise** – other health professionals – that is, facilitate others acquiring the skills of psychological theorising, assessment, consultancy and intervention, for example teaching nursing and medical students (e.g. in communication skills) as well as colleagues (e.g. by running training workshops). This will involve designing, delivering and evaluating training using materials appropriate to the student audience.

   train and supervise facilitate the development of health psychology competencies in others.

5. **Consult**, with both individuals and organisations. This would include being able to manage effective one-to-one consultations (see Chapter 7) and to accept a commission for a larger piece of work, such as evaluating an in-house stress-management programme within a company or assisting a local authority with the reduction of unplanned teenage pregnancies. This work requires highly developed communication and negotiation skills.

consult to negotiate the nature of a piece of work requested by a client and then undertake this competently, delivering what has been agreed to a good standard and on time.

6. **Supervise and manage** – that is, guide others with less psychological training or experience in psychological practice. Assessing, training and management are overlapping and complementary skills. Even a newly qualified professional health psychologist will be able to monitor, train and report on the design and implementation of psychological research by colleagues with less training in this area. More experienced health psychologists will be able to manage and supervise teams of psychologists.

supervise and manage to monitor directly and develop the work of others.

Intervening (core competency 3 above) may involve attempting to change cognitions or behaviour patterns. In 2007, the UK National Institute of Clinical and Public Health Excellence (NICE) guidance on behaviour change (discussed in Chapter 7) emphasises the importance of high-quality, evidence-based training for health promoters to design, evaluate and deliver behaviour-change interventions. In particular, the guidance notes that specialist training is required to ensure that health promotion teams are able to competently:

1. Identify and assess evidence related to behaviour change.

2. Understand evidence relating to psychological, social, economic and cultural determinants of behaviour.

3. Interpret relevant data on local or national needs and characteristics.

4. Design and plan, implement and evaluate interventions.

5. Work in partnership with members of the target population(s) and those with local knowledge.

These five behaviour-change competencies are central to health psychology training, allowing health psychologists

to adopt key roles in services involved in health behaviour change. Health psychologists are able to apply behaviour-change competencies and also train, assess and supervise colleagues in this area.

To summarise:

- Looking after patients and helping them change, conducting research, providing advice and training to others are very responsible roles.

- In order to perform these roles effectively and safely, health psychologists need particular skills or competencies. Six key areas of competence have been identified: assessment, research, intervention, teaching and training, consultation and management of other staff.

11.3   TRAINING AS A HEALTH PSYCHOLOGIST

The UK National Standards for Psychology have been adopted by the British Psychological Society and the Health Professionals Council, who are involved in developing and accrediting training for health psychologists in the UK. Similar standards have also been adopted by the **European Federation of Professional Psychologists Associations (EFPA)** in developing common standards across European psychology training courses. EFPA represents 32 European national psychological associations, including all European Union Member States. EFPA has declared that independent practice as a psychologist requires university training equivalent to at least five years of full-time study, at least one year of supervised practice and a commitment to specified standards of ethical practice (see http://www.efpa.eu/professional-development/efpa-declaration-on-the-european-standards-of-education-and-training-in-professional-psychology-europsy and http://www.efpa.eu/professional-development/standards-for-professional-training-in-psychology-higher-than-the-bologna-declaration). The title 'psychologist' is regulated in most European countries. In the UK psychologists have to be registered by the Health Professionals Council (www.hpc-uk.org) before they can use the title 'health psychologist' (see Chapter 1).

European Federation of Professional Psychologists Associations (EFPA) the representative body for 32 European national psychological associations, including all European Union Member States.

11.3.1 Graduate Basis for Chartered Membership of the BPS

The British Psychological Society (BPS) has developed a competency-based training course for UK health psychologists. To follow this route a student must first gain a qualification that will make them eligible for Graduate Basis for Chartered Membership of the BPS. This is usually a three-year Bachelor's degree in psychology, but may be a one-year conversion course in psychology following an undergraduate degree in another discipline.

11.3.2 Stage 1 Qualification in Health Psychology

Having acquired Graduate Basis for Chartered Membership of the BPS, students proceed to study for a **Stage 1 Qualification in Health Psychology**. Normally, students do this by taking a one-year, accredited Master's course in Health Psychology, which covers a specified, essential knowledge base and postgraduate research skills. However, some students study independently and take a Stage 1 examination that is set and assessed by the BPS.

Focus Point 11.2 lists the core knowledge and skills base that a Stage-1-qualified health psychologist must acquire. This may seem to be a long list, but most candidates will have been studying psychology for at least four years before they reach Stage 1 standard. The Stage 1 standard in health psychology includes four areas of expertise:

- Health-related behaviour: Cognitions and individual differences.
- Psychological processes in illness and health-care delivery.
- Research and development in health psychology.
- Context and related issues.

Stage 1 Qualification in Health Psychology
having acquired Graduate Basis for Chartered Membership of the BPS students proceed to study for a one-year, accredited Master's course in Health Psychology or they may study independently and take a Stage 1 examination set and assessed by the BPS.

FOCUS POINT 11.2   AREAS OF EXPERTISE REQUIRED TO ATTAIN A STAGE 1 QUALIFICATION IN HEALTH PSYCHOLOGY

1. **Health-related behaviour: Cognitions and individual differences**

Health-related behaviour:
- Theoretical models
- Protective/promotional behaviour
- Behavioural risk factors
- Sociocultural factors

Health-related cognitions:
- Efficacy and control beliefs
- Attributions
- Social and individual representations
- Health beliefs
- Symptom perception; the perception of pain
- Perceptions of risk
- Decision making by health-care psychologists; by patients/clients etc.
- Mood and cognition

Individual differences, health and illness:
- Personality factors in health and illness
- Dispositional optimism/pessimism
- Locus of control
- Self-efficacy
- Negative affectivity
- Emotional expression and health

2. **Psychological processes in illness and health-care delivery**

Stress, health and illness:
- Causes/consequences of stress
- Models of stress
- Stress management
- Stress moderators
- Social support
- Models of coping

Chronic illness/disability:
- Coping with chronic illness/disability
- Pain: theories of pain, management of pain
- Interventions of chronic illness/disability
- Issues in caring for the chronically ill

Health-care contexts:
- Communication in health-care settings
- The impact of screening
- The impact of hospitalisation on adults and children
- Preparation for stressful medical procedures
- Giving bad news
- Adherence
- Communication and patient satisfaction
- Placebos

Lifespan, gender and cross-cultural perspectives of health psychology:

- Cross-cultural perspectives
- Gender and health
- Children's perceptions of illness
- The role of the family in health and illness
- Lifespan changes in health and illness
- Death, dying and bereavement

3. **Research and development in health psychology**

Applications of health psychology:

- Designing interventions and evaluating outcomes
- Health education/promotion: (i) worksite interventions; (ii) community-based interventions; (iii) public health/media campaigns
- Specific applications/interventions, e.g. in the management of cardiovascular disease, cancer, HIV etc.

Research methods:

- Experimental designs; cross-sectional and longitudinal designs; single case-study designs
- Advanced qualitative and quantitative data analysis
- The development of theories, models and hypotheses
- Health services research
- Common pitfalls in research

Measurement issues:

- Measurement of process
- Measurement of outcome

- Individual differences
- Health-related quality of life

Professional issues:

- Ethical codes of conduct
- Legal and statutory obligations and restrictions
- Inter-professional relations
- European and international perspectives on health psychology

4. **Context and related issues**

Context and perspectives in health psychology:

- Historical overview and current theories and approaches to health psychology
- Awareness of related disciplines (medical sociology; medical ethics; medicine; behavioural medicine; health policy; health economics; medical anthropology)
- Social, cultural and organisational factors

Epidemiology of health and illness:

- Causes of mortality/morbidity
- Behavioural epidemiology
- Bio-statistics
- Inequalities of health

Biological mechanisms of health and disease:

- Immune, neuroendocrine and cardiovascular systems
- Genes

The first of these areas (*Health-related behaviour: Cognitions and individual differences*) requires the student to have a good knowledge of cognition and personality theories, the evidence supporting current models and an ability to apply these to practical problems. We have introduced some of the models in Chapter 10.

The second area of expertise in Stage 1 training (*Psychological processes in illness and health-care delivery*) includes a knowledge of stress and coping models and an ability to interpret relevant evidence and apply the models to practical problems. We have introduced some of these models in Chapter 9. In addition, this area includes expertise in understanding gender, developmental and cross-cultural perspectives, for example understanding how health and health inequalities (see Chapter 7) may affect men and women differently; how development may affect health (see Chapter 10); and the special challenges facing those with long-term illnesses and their carers. In addition, Stage-1-trained health psychologists need to have a good understanding of communication in health-care settings, including the impact of communication on patient adherence (see Chapter 7).

The third area of expertise in Stage 1 training (*Research and development in health psychology*) include gaining expertise in the design and evaluation of behaviour-change interventions. We have introduced some of the key ideas in this area in Chapter 7 (see Abraham *et al.*, 2008 for further details). In addition, Stage-1-trained health psychologists will have a high level of expertise in designing and conducting research methods applying both qualitative and quantitative methods. These skills will be further developed in Stage 2 training, but at Stage 1 health psychologists will be expected to undertake an independent research project. For example, Abraham and Graham-Rowe (2009) report a systematic review that was begun as an empirical project focusing on behaviour-change interventions as part of an accredited, Stage 1 MSc programme. We have introduced some measures used in health psychology in Chapters 9 and 10 (e.g. our discussion of how best to measure levels of stress in an individual's life). Stage 1 health psychologists need a much more comprehensive and detailed knowledge of psychological measures and how to use them.

Stage 1 training also involves studying professional issues. Skills in these areas, including understanding and managing ethical, legal and professional issues, are extended in Stage 2 training.

The fourth area of Stage 1 expertise training (*Context and related issues*) includes understanding the context of psychological research as well as the organisational, national and international context of health and health behaviour patterns (see Chapter 7 for an introduction). In addition, this area of expertise requires students to have a knowledge of the causes of mortality/morbidity, including an understanding of human biology. We have introduced some of these ideas in relation to the immune and cardiovascular systems and an explanation of pain in Chapter 8.

Now have a look at Activity Box 11.1.

11.3.3 Stage 2 Qualification in Health Psychology

Having completed Stage 1 training, students must gain a **Stage 2 Qualification in Health Psychology**, which may be taken as a stand-alone qualification or as part of a doctoral programme. Below we outline the content of the UK Stage 2 training and the evidence that candidates must submit to demonstrate their competency. All these competencies are acquired by practising under supervision. Focus Point 11.3 provides a summary of what health psychologists do and Focus Point 11.4 summarises what health psychologists are able to do once they finish their training. Have a look at these boxes before you read on.

Case History 11.2 presents a case study briefly outlining the training experiences of a fictional student based on the real experiences of some of our own students. Thinking about Chris's Stage 2 training will help you understand what a Stage 2 candidate needs to do to become a trained health psychologist, so read Chris's story now.

The UK Stage 2 health psychology training specifies five groups of competencies. These reflect the jobs that health psychologists are required to do in their everyday work (see above). They are:

- **Generic professional competencies**
- Behaviour-change competencies

> **Stage 2 Qualification in Health Psychology** the qualification gained after completing Stage 1 training, this may be taken as a stand-alone qualification or as part of a doctoral programme.

> **generic professional competencies** everyday skills that all psychologists need, e.g., the ability to talk to clients and keep accurate records in a confidential manner.

WHAT HAVE YOU LEARNED ABOUT HEALTH PSYCHOLOGY?   ACTIVITY BOX 11.1

Once you have finished reading Chapters 7–10, have a look at Focus Point 11.2 and tick those topics to which you have been introduced in this book. There are quite a few of these topics that you now know about!

This book provides an introduction, but if you are interested to learn more (and tick off more of these topics), have a look at more advanced health psychology textbooks (e.g. Abraham *et al.*, 2008).

FOCUS POINT 11.3   WHERE DO HEALTH PSYCHOLOGISTS WORK – AND WHAT DO THEY DO?

Health psychologists work in academic health care and industrial settings. They:

- Teach students and health professionals
- Conduct research
- Assess patients
- Manage clinical interventions
- Supervise and manage other staff
- Inform health promotion and public policy

Health psychologists are well placed to meet the challenges of the modern NHS, with its commitment to flexibility and the need to improve service delivery, to improve health and to reduce inequalities.

Source: Adapted from BPS Division of Health Psychology.

FOCUS POINT 11.4 AT THE END OF TRAINING

At the end of training a health psychologist will:

- Have a core knowledge base of health psychology theory, research and methods.
- Be able to develop, deliver and evaluate evidence-based health interventions.
- Maintain ethical and professional standards throughout their work.

- Have consultancy skills enabling them to work with individuals, teams and organisations.
- Be competent in designing and evaluating training programmes in health psychology.
- Have professional skills such as teaching patients and staff skills in stress management, or preparing patients for surgery.

Source: Adapted from BPS Division of Health Psychology.

CASE HISTORY 11.2

STAGE 2 HEALTH PSYCHOLOGY TRAINING

Chris is a trainee health psychologist. He was awarded his MSc Health Psychology with merit from a university accredited by the UK Health Professional Council, thereby achieving his Stage 1 Qualification in Health Psychology. He is now working and studying for his Stage 2 qualification. His Stage 2 supervisor is a chartered health psychologist who teaches and conducts research in a university, but also practises as a health psychologist. Chris's supervisor provides consultancy and undertakes research for government departments, industry and local authorities. This consultancy and research focuses on behaviour change, including, for example, improving adherence of young diabetic patients and increasing physical activity among teenagers (see Chapter 7).

Chris is working in a Health Care Trust helping to manage a team of health trainers. Health trainers are lay people recruited from the community and given brief training on behaviour change. Health trainers then provide advice to others in the community on how to change their health behaviour patterns (Chapter 7). There are many health trainer services in the UK (e.g. see Scorer, 2007). These services apply the core competencies of assessment, consultation, intervention, training and management for which health psychologists are trained.

Chris's manager at work is keen that he completes his Stage 2 training and has built Stage 2 training and study into Chris's weekly work timetable. Working together, Chris, his supervisor and his work manager hope that he will be able to pass his Stage 2 qualification in two years. Chris is conducting an evaluation of his local health trainer service under supervision as part of his Stage 2 training. He is also providing the Trust with consultancy on how to improve the health trainer service, again under supervision. His consultancy includes advice on how to improve the training of health trainers in order to enhance their effectiveness as facilitators of behaviour change. The advice he is offering is based on his own evaluation of the local service and on a broader systematic review of the literature on the training and effectiveness of lay facilitators who have received brief training.

- Research
- Consultancy
- Teaching and training

Generic competencies are needed by all psychologists. These ensure that psychologists have sufficient professional experience to practise autonomously and are able to make professional judgements in accordance with current codes of professional legal and ethical conduct (see Chapter 1). Candidates must submit a logbook of

professional practice maintained over two years of full-time supervised practice. This lists and reflects on experiences that have enabled candidates to gain generic skills, including communicating with patients and colleagues and managing secure information so as to demonstrate compliance with ethical and legal standards. In addition, candidates must submit a self-reflective report summarising their personal and professional development as a health psychologist.

Behaviour-change competencies ensure that health psychologists can assess behaviour-change needs in people, groups and organisations, design appropriate interventions and evaluate those interventions rigorously. Candidates must submit two reports. The first must describe a case study of a behaviour-change intervention they have implemented, including assessment, design, application and evaluation. For example, Chris (in the case study above) could describe how he, acting in the role of a **health trainer**, had assisted a client in her goal of losing weight over five or six consultations. He might include a brief description of a follow-up interview with his client in which she describes her progress four months after he first saw her.

health trainer lay people recruited from the community and given brief training on facilitating health behaviour change in others in the community.

The second report must compare the application of two psychological models (see Chapter 10) in relation to an assessment and intervention design task conducted by the candidate. For instance, Chris might discuss how useful the major theorists' model of motivation (see Chapter 10) was in understanding his work with this client and compare this to the information, motivation and behavioural skills model (see Chapter 7).

Research competencies ensure that the candidate is an independent researcher able to undertake research design, sampling, data collection and data analysis, evaluate methods and discuss the implications of data and the relationship of data to previously published research. Candidates must submit two pieces of research: first, a systematic review of literature relevant to health psychology; second, a rigorous study of a question relevant to health psychology. Both of these must be written to a standard acceptable for publication in peer-reviewed academic journals relevant to health psychology. For example, Chris could undertake a systematic review of what has been found to work best in enhancing the effectiveness of services in which lay people receive brief training and then facilitate others in changing their behaviour. There are many such services that have been evaluated worldwide. He could then discuss the implications for his own health trainer service. In addition, he could undertake an evaluation of how effective his local service has been using both quantitative and qualitative data.

Consultancy competencies ensure that health psychologists understand and can apply theories regarding communication (see Chapter 7) and organisational change (see Photo 11.1). Candidates must demonstrate that they can assess offers of consultancy, plan what to do and deliver an evidence-based service to individuals, groups or organisations. Candidates must also demonstrate their ability to monitor and review consultancy work. Candidates must submit a case study describing a request for consultancy, the planning of consultancy work and what theoretical frameworks were applied, a consultancy contract, a timetable of work, budget and

minutes, as well as evidence of formal evaluation, where appropriate. Chris could offer his local Trust advice on how to improve its health trainer service based on the finding of his two research studies. This could include specific advice on additional training and practice for health trainers on how to use behaviour-change techniques that clients found easy to use and are associated with clients achieving their goals.

Teaching and training competencies ensure that health psychologists can employ a range of teaching approaches, including lectures, seminars and discussion groups, and the use of educational packages and distance-learning programmes, including booklets, video- and audio-taped information (see Photo 11.2). Health psychologists need to be able to teach and train members of the

PHOTO 11.1 *Health psychologists conduct consultations with clients and patients.*
Source: Shutterstock.

PHOTO 11.2 *Health psychologists teach and train others.*
Source: Shutterstock.

general public, patients and professionals. Candidates must also demonstrate the ability to select teaching techniques appropriate to the characteristics of the person or group they are training and the setting in which this training will take place. Candidates must have experience of teaching health psychology to two populations (e.g. undergraduate students and practising nurses). They must also have experience of both large and small group teaching. Candidates must submit a case study based on observed and supervised teaching sessions, to be submitted together with the observer's report. The case study should include a teaching plan and evaluation and a reflective commentary of the teaching session/s. For example, Chris could give a lecture and seminar to a group of final-year undergraduates on understanding the processes of behaviour change (see Chapter 7), including helping undergraduates understand key papers published in this field. In addition, he could provide a one-day training session for his health trainer colleagues on motivating others and assisting them in goal setting and goal review. Chris could use the Health Trainer Handbook as the basis of this training session (http://www.dh.gov.uk/en/Publicationsandstatistics/Publications/PublicationsPolicyAndGuidance/DH_085779).

To summarise:

- All psychologists need the basic training provided by a good undergraduate degree, which usually takes three years of study, although graduates in other areas may be able to complete such study in a one-year conversion degree. In the United Kingdom many such degrees are accredited to provide Graduate Basis for Chartered Membership of the British Psychological Society.

- Once a UK graduate has this qualification they can begin training for a Stage 1 Qualification in Health Psychology. Stage 1 study can be completed by taking an accredited one-year, full-time MSc in Health Psychology.

- In this section we describe the four areas of expertise that a Stage 1 trainee will study. These are health-related behaviour; psychological processes in illness and health-care delivery; research and development in health psychology; and the context of health psychology practice and related issues.

- A Stage-1-qualified health psychologist is able to go on to further training in health psychology in the form of a professional doctorate or take up employment (e.g. within health services) under

supervision. In either case the trainee must demonstrate the core competencies required by a health psychologist in a work setting (over two years) before they can be awarded their Stage 2 Qualification in Health Psychology and so become fully qualified.

- The five key areas of competency that are assessed during Stage 2 training are generic professional competencies (required by all professional psychologists); behaviour change competencies; research competencies; consultancy competencies; and teaching and training competencies.

11.4 WORKING AS A PROFESSIONAL HEALTH PSYCHOLOGIST: AUTHOR'S EXPERIENCE

Many health psychologists work in an academic setting such as a university, in a health-care environment such as a hospital or in an industrial setting where they might conduct research into patient experiences and adherence to a new drug or behaviour-change programme. Karen Rodham, one of the authors of this chapter, is a UK health psychologist who works in a university and a health-care setting simultaneously. On Mondays she works at the Royal National Hospital for Rheumatic Diseases and from Tuesday to Friday she is a lecturer in health psychology in the Department of Psychology at the University of Bath. Below Karen provides a brief overview of what her job entails, focusing on her practising health psychologist role.

11.4.1 Academic Work

As with most academics, my work at the university involves three main areas: teaching at undergraduate and postgraduate levels, research in my area of expertise (health psychology) and administration.

My teaching on the Master's in Health Psychology focuses on the process of developing and writing research proposals, explaining how to employ qualitative approaches to data collection and analysis, and explaining the theory and practice underlying the application of health psychology to health interventions. My administrative role is that of admissions tutor for the

Master's in Health Psychology, so I deal with queries and applications for our programme throughout the academic year.

My current research includes investigating how people cope with difficult situations (see Chapter 9). In particular, I have published work on how people use Internet message boards to help themselves cope with traumatic episodes in their lives. I have also conducted research on stress at work and adolescent deliberate self-harm. It was my interest in coping that led me to my current NHS role. One aspect of being a researcher is dealing with media interest in your findings. The media may often want to know about the findings of health research;

psychologists need to take time to explain research to journalists and to ensure that media coverage accurately reflects research results. For more details see Theory to Application Box 11.1.

11.4.2 Work as a Practising Psychologist

I am based in the Rheumatology Department at the Royal National Hospital for Rheumatic Diseases. The department offers a specialist service for adults who have complex regional pain syndrome (CRPS).

BOX 11.1 THEORY TO APPLICATION

Health Psychology and the Media

Acquiring research knowledge and skills is a core competency required by health psychologists and conducting research studies and evaluations is often a feature of their work in both academic and professional contexts. The research they conduct can provide important information that may be useful in helping health professionals (in their work with patients), health promoters (producing campaign materials) and members of the general public who wish to maintain a healthy lifestyle. An important part of the job of health psychologists is therefore to ensure that their results are not merely published in academic journals but reach much wider audiences. In fact, most research funding bodies now require that researchers plan how they will publicise their findings. One way to achieve this is via newspapers, magazines, broadcast media and the Internet. Fortunately, there is considerable public interest in health psychology research.

Large organisations such as the British Psychological Society (BPS), the Economic and Social Research Council (ESRC) and individual universities employ press officers who will work with psychologists to produce press releases of their research findings. Journalists also frequently attend psychology conferences to look for interesting news items. As a result, health psychologists often get the opportunity to discuss their research with journalists. This is likely to result in newspaper and magazine articles or,

sometimes, radio or television interviews. These are all important ways of making sure that the relevant audiences get to hear about research findings.

The opportunities to publicise our findings have rapidly increased with the growth of the Internet. Research conducted by some of the authors of this chapter (Jones *et al.*, 2007; O'Connor *et al.*, 2008) provides a good example of how this can work. The researchers undertook a large study in which 400 people completed daily diary questionnaires about stress, health behaviour and individual differences. Interesting results related to the negative effects of hassles on people's eating behaviours and the negative effects of long work hours on a range of health behaviours. These findings led to a number of press releases issued by the BPS and the ESRC (which funded the research). This resulted in the researchers conducting interviews with a range of journalists, including radio interviews, and included a summary of findings appearing on the BBC news website. There was also further coverage of aspects of the research in newspapers and women's magazines. As a result of the initial wave of publicity, findings from the study have gradually appeared in a much wider range of health-related websites worldwide, including sites concerning women's health, health in employment and self-help sites. This can be a very valuable and enduring way of ensuring that our research has impact.

CRPS (which is also known as reflex sympathetic dystrophy) is a collection of symptoms where pain is the major problem. Other symptoms found in the affected site can include swelling, temperature and colour changes, increased sweating, hair and nail growth changes and sensory changes (such as allodynia, where a person experiences pain in response to things that are not normally painful). Commonly affected areas are the hands, feet, knees and elbows, although it can be seen in other parts of the body too.

I work in a multidisciplinary team that consists of physiotherapists, occupational therapists, a consultant rheumatology nurse, a research fellow and a clinical research practitioner. The service includes a two-week in-patient programme offering a full multidisciplinary team assessment, patient-centred goal setting, concentrating on providing good information on the condition and helping patients learn new skills to assist them in optimising what they can do despite their condition; that is, providing support for physical rehabilitation.

My day at the hospital is always very busy. Once I arrive I catch up with the post and e-mails that have accumulated throughout the week. Next I meet with the consultant nurse, the physiotherapist and the occupational therapist, who brief me about current and incoming patients. Together we are able to share our different perspectives, experiences and concerns about each patient. This allows for good communication between the different members of the team and also ensures that the individual needs of the patients are being met.

My psychology clinic runs all afternoon and I see patients from across the UK. In clinic I aim to explore how CRPS has affected the patient's life and assess how well they are coping. The consultations can be emotionally draining for the patients, as the appointment is often the first opportunity they have had to reflect on and talk at length with a health professional about their feelings. Therefore, my listening skills are incredibly important.

Each week I see a minimum of two out-patients and two in-patients. Out-patients are either being assessed for their suitability to attend the in-patient programme, or are returning having completed the in-patient programme three months earlier for a further assessment of their progress. The in-patients are attending the intensive two-week CRPS in-patient programme. Each appointment lasts approximately 50 minutes. Much of the consultation is spent helping the patients to explore how well their current coping strategies are working, and how they can identify alternative strategies.

Another part of my role is to prepare patients for their return home on completion of the intensive in-patient programme. To this end, I study the patients attending the in-patient programme to find out which factors facilitate or prevent CRPS patients from implementing skills they have learned as they transfer from the hospital to the home setting.

11.5   CONCLUSION

Health psychologists work to promote health and prevent illness. They work in academic contexts such as universities, in health-care environments such as hospitals and clinics and in industrial settings, where they might conduct research into patient experiences and adherence to a new drug or behaviour-change programme. In order to perform these roles effectively and safely, they need to able to (i) assess, (ii) conduct research, (iii) intervene to change motivation and behaviour, (iv) train and supervise others, (v) conduct consultations with clients and patients and (vi) manage other staff. To acquire these skills takes some time; most health psychologists will have studied at university for at least four years and trained under supervision for at least two years before they are fully trained. In the United Kingdom this will involve them in acquiring the Graduate Basis for Chartered Membership of the British Psychological Society by being awarded an accredited degree in psychology and, usually, an MSc in Health Psychology. Following this (which might involve four years' study at university) they will go on to take a Stage 2 qualification, which will involve two years of supervised practice. During their Stage 2 training they will acquire skills or competencies in five areas: (i) generic professional, (ii) behaviour change, (iii) research, (iv) consultancy and (v) teaching and training competencies. Once trained, health psychologists have a sophisticated skills base that allows them to work on psychological and behaviour change in relation to a variety of problems and challenges.

See Table 11.1 for more information about a career in health psychology.

TABLE 11.1 *Frequently Asked Questions about a Career in Health Psychology.*

What income can I expect while I am training?	This will vary depending on the training route you chose. Stage 2 funded and PhD route trainees can expect an income circa £14K (for year 2010).
What salary can I expect when I am fully trained?	Chartered health psychologists work in various different settings (e.g. universities, hospitals), therefore the salary will vary.
What job opportunities are there?	Health psychologists can work in university, hospital, research and primary care settings.
What unique skills will I learn?	See Focus Point 11.4.
What qualifications and experience should I have prior to training?	A BPS accredited degree in psychology.
What further training and development can I do once I have qualified?	All applied psychologists should engage in continuing professional development (e.g. attending courses on motivational interviewing, cognitive-behavioural therapy).
What particular qualities will employers look for?	Again, this will vary job by job. Most employers will look for clinical, teaching, research and consultancy skills.
What career progression opportunities are there?	In the NHS, health psychologists can progress to Consultant grade. In academia, health psychologists can progress to Professorial grade.
Will my training make me an attractive proposition for other careers? If so, which careers?	Any that involve research, teaching and consultancy.
What are the hours of work?	Again, this will vary by job, but generally health psychologists work conventional working hours (9 a.m. to 5 p.m.).
Will I have a job for life?	Yes, if you get a permanent job.
Where can I go for further information?	http://www.health-psychology.org.uk/dhp_home.cfm

SELF-TEST QUESTIONS

- What are the six key roles that professional psychologists are expected to be able to perform according to UK National Occupational Standards?
- List the four broad areas of expertise required to qualify as a Stage-1-trained health psychologist.
- List the five groups of competencies specified in UK Stage 2 health psychology training.

ESSAY QUESTIONS

- Describe the competencies that health psychologists need to develop and explain why they need these particular skills.
- Describe a job for a UK trainee health psychologist who wished to gain their Stage 2 Qualification in Health Psychology. Explain how this job would allow them to acquire essential Stage 2 competencies.

TEXT FOR FURTHER READING

Michie, S. & Abraham, C. (eds) (2004) *Health Psychology in Practice*, Oxford: Blackwell.

RELEVANT JOURNAL ARTICLES

Abraham, C. & Gardner, B. (2009) What psychological and behaviour changes are initiated by 'expert patient' training and what training techniques are most helpful? *Psychology & Health* 10: 1153–65.

Bassman, L.E. & Uellendahl, G. (2003) Complementary/alternative medicine: Ethical, professional, and practical challenges for psychologists, *Professional Psychology: Research and Practice* 34: 264–70.

Friedman, R., Sobel, D., Myers, P., Caudill, M. & Benson, H. (1995) Behavioral medicine, clinical health psychology and cost offset, *Health Psychology* 14: 509–18.

Kaplan, R.M. (1990) Behavior as the central outcome in health care, *American Psychologist* 45: 1211–20.

Turk, D.C. & Burwinkle T.M. (2000) Clinical outcomes, cost-effectiveness, and the role of psychology in treatments for chronic pain sufferers, *Professional Psychology: Research and Practice* 36: 602–10.

West, R., McNeill, A. & Raw, M. (2000) Smoking cessation guidelines for health professionals: An update, *Thorax* 55: 987–99.

RELEVANT WEB LINKS

For information about careers in health psychology:
http://www.bps.org.uk/careers/what-do-psychologists-do/areas/health.cfm
http://www.bps.org.uk/dhp/career-paths-in-health-psychology/career-paths-in-health-psychology.cfm

For further information about health psychology:
http://www.bps.org.uk/dhp/php/php_home.cfm

For examples of press releases on psychology research (including health psychology research):
http://www.bps.org.uk/media-centre/press-releases/press-release-archive$.cfm

REFERENCES

Abraham, C. & Graham-Rowe, E. (2009) Are worksite interventions effective in increasing physical activity? A systematic review and meta-analysis, *Health Psychology Review* 3: 108–44.

Abraham, C., Conner, M., Jones, F. & O'Connor, D. (2008) *Health Psychology: Topics in Applied Psychology*, London: Hodder Education.

Hallas, C.N. (2004) Health psychology within health service settings, in S. Michie and C. Abraham (eds) *Health Psychology in Practice*, pp. 353–71, Oxford: Blackwell.

Jones, F., O'Connor, D.B., Conner, M., McMillan, B. & Ferguson, E. (2007) Effects of daily hassles and eating style on eating behavior, *Journal of Applied Psychology* 92: 1731–40.

Michie, S. & Abraham, C. (eds) (2004) *Health Psychology in Practice*, Oxford: Blackwell.

O'Connor, D.B., Jones, F., Conner, M., McMillan, B. & Ferguson, E. (2008) Effects of daily hassles and eating style on eating behavior, *Health Psychology* 27: s20–s21.

Scorer, C. (2007) Health Trainers implementing a new public health role, *Journal of the Royal Society for the Promotion of Health* 127: 258–59.

Part III
Forensic Psychology

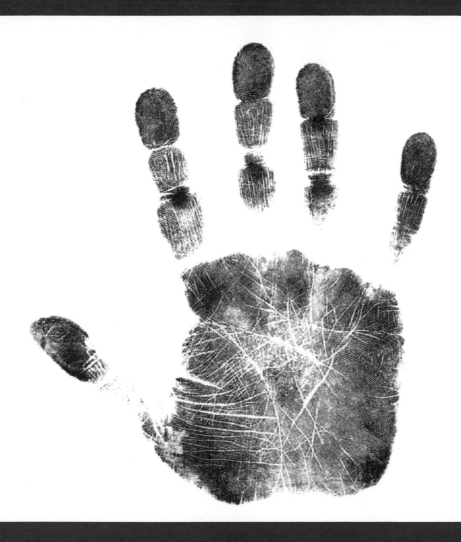

12 Introduction to Forensic Psychology: Working with Organisations and Offenders

Carol Ireland

LEARNING OUTCOMES

WHEN YOU HAVE COMPLETED THIS CHAPTER
YOU SHOULD BE ABLE TO:

1. Understand the importance of scientific practice in forensic psychology.
2. Compare the role of the media against the actual work of a forensic psychologist.
3. Compare and contrast the different types of work a forensic psychologist engages in when working with organisations and perpetrators.
4. Understand the importance of ethical decision making in the role of applied psychology, including that of the forensic psychologist.

KEY WORDS

Conflict ● Crisis ● Diagnostic Assessment ● Dynamic Risk ● Habitual Aggression ● Integrated ● Protective Factors ● Psychodynamic ● Risk Assessment ● Sex Offenders ● Static Risk ● Systemic

CHAPTER OUTLINE

So, when you talk about a forensic psychologist, does that mean you talk to all those crazy offenders, those mad serial killers? Does that not really scare you? Do you actually have to talk to them? If so, what do you talk to them about? I would think it was really scary, and I don't know how you do it. Yet, then again, I suppose with all your training it is a bit like reading their minds. I would think you were good at that; that is obviously part of your training. It does sound really exciting though, to spend your days doing that. It sounds much better than my day job, that's for sure. (John, a member of the general public, talking to a forensic psychologist)

12.1 WHAT DO FORENSIC PSYCHOLOGISTS DO?

Forensic psychologists work within a range of forensic settings, including HM Prison Service, NHS forensic hospitals, Youth Offending Teams, Probation, private forensic health care, private prisons, Scottish and Irish Prison Systems, the Police and to a lesser extent the Foreign Office. Forensic psychologists may work independently or in private practice, and they can also be found in academic institutions, either full time or more usually combining academic work with part-time practitioner work. It is a profession that continues to develop. For example, the Division of Forensic Psychology as part of the British Psychological Society has grown significantly. In 1977 there were only 105 members; this had grown to 1996 members by 2008.

The work of forensic psychologists can vary, and this chapter will focus solely on the forensic psychologist's role as a consultant when working with perpetrators. Forensic psychologists also work with victims of crime, the general public in relation to their anxieties around crime, and with government bodies and universities as part of postgraduate teaching and research. One of the many challenges facing forensic psychology is to offer a realistic interpretation of what it does in contrast to the often 'glamorised' media and journalistic portrayals.

For example, television programmes such as *Cracker*, starring Robbie Coltrane, or more recently *Wire in the Blood*, starring Robson Green (which portrays a clinical psychologist working in the forensic arena), are popular and entertaining but far removed from the day-to-day work of a forensic psychologist. In this respect, Focus Point 12.1 describes some recent examples of how forensic psychology can be portrayed in the media.

To further illustrate the work of a forensic psychologist, Focus Point 12.2 describes the work of a forensic psychologist who works with sexual offenders and is involved in risk assessment, intervention and research.

12.2 THE ROLE OF THE FORENSIC PSYCHOLOGIST IN AN ORGANISATION

The consultancy role of the forensic psychologist is varied and wide-ranging. It can include:

- Working with management on the assessment, initiation and evaluation of change within an organisation.
- Initiating or supporting policy development.
- Helping to alleviate stress in an organisation.

FOCUS POINT 12.1   FORENSIC PSYCHOLOGY IN THE NEWS

On 12 December 2006 (http://news.bbc.co.uk/1/hi/england/suffolk/6171571.stm), the BBC reported on a police investigation into the death of a woman in a city in the UK. The media reported that a consultant forensic psychologist who had 'worked on previous serial killer cases' was asked to advise. There was further reference to this psychologist having 'advised the makers of the TV drama *Cracker*'. It is noted in the media excerpt that the psychologist stated:

> He said although there was little information to build up a clear profile of who may have killed these women, it was possible to hypothesise about what the person may be like … the suspect was probably male, white, in his late 20s, 30s or 40s, and is someone who probably had been let down by women in his past … He maybe had a mother who has let him down, or a mother who has abandoned him . . . in some sense he may have idolised women and then they let him down . . . He also said the killer might believe he is on some kind of Christian mission … clearing the world of prostitutes.

Such claims are likely to be no more than guesswork and not grounded in scientific theory. Also, there is every possibility that the forensic psychologist was misquoted, their discussions with the media misinterpreted, and that they probably did not explicitly state their involvement with the television drama *Cracker*.

It is just these types of media stories that misleadingly glamorise the role of a forensic psychologist. Terms such as 'serial killer' can be unnecessarily emotive, and the knowledge relating to psychological profiling probably cannot yet be said to meet the stringent criteria necessary to represent a scientific theory. Furthermore, there is little scientific evidence from a psychological perspective that predicts characteristics of the potential offender in circumstances such as this – other than the more general ones. For example, in this case the offender has been estimated to be anywhere between 20 and 40 years of age. Such estimations are rarely based on theories of forensic psychology, nor does this type of activity represent what

Source: Courtesy of ITV limited.

forensic psychologists usually do in their professional life. Yet, this aside, the situation is not all negative and there can be a range of examples where the role of a forensic psychologist is presented more accurately within the media, certainly over the last few years. For example, there have been many reports of forensic psychologists assisting the courts in high-profile cases, where their work has been regarded as crucial in helping the judge and jury to consider the offender's risk and the protection of the public from harm.

- Advising on critical incidents within an organisation.
- Advising on government projects.
- Assisting in the auditing of government initiatives in agencies such as Her Majesty's Inspectorate of Prisons.

12.2.1   The Role of Consultancy within an Organisation

Consultancy is 'an advisory service … to identify management problems, analyse such problems, recommend solutions to these problems and help when requested in the implementation of solutions' (Greiner & Metzger, 1983).

FOCUS POINT 12.2 A WEEK IN THE LIFE OF A FORENSIC PSYCHOLOGIST

WORKING WITH INDIVIDUALS WHO COMMIT SEXUAL OFFENCES – A FORENSIC PSYCHOLOGIST'S EXPERIENCE

I have worked with individuals who have committed sexual offences for over 15 years, both in HM Prison Service, and for the last eight years in the NHS. One of the real positives of my job is that my work can be quite varied, and I can work with a variety of clients. Yet for this example I have just focused on my work with individuals who have committed sexual offences. I suppose even the term I use, 'individuals who have committed sex offences', gives an idea of my kind of views and experiences. When working in therapy with individuals, labelling can be unhelpful, and to label someone a 'sex offender' is no exception. When working with such individuals, to be called clients from now on, labelling can be unhelpful as it can prevent therapy from progressing. It can be challenging to inform a client that you are keen to move them towards an offence-free lifestyle when you label them as a 'sex offender', and to do so indicates they have little potential for change. Yet realistically, this is not necessarily about 'curing' **sex offenders**, but assisting them to manage their areas of risk. Importantly as a forensic psychologist, you need to work with offenders in therapy because you feel they have the potential to change for the better, and because you want to change them positively as individuals.

> **sex offenders** individuals who have committed crimes of a sexual nature and who may be characterised by: sexual pre-occupation; deviant sexual interests; conflicts in intimate relationships and intimacy deficits; hostility; the use of sex as a coping strategy.

When exploring my day-to-day work with clients who have sexually offended across my working week, I am currently involved in supervising a team of three therapists who deliver a sex offender therapy group to seven group members. This therapy encourages group members to discuss their offending, particularly the lead-up to their offences, and to initially encourage them to take responsibility, to reduce any minimisation around their offending, and to begin some preliminary work in the understanding and then management of their risk.

When I am not involved in the group, I tend to see around two clients per week, usually seeing each client twice per week for around one hour at a time. This is usually a combination of work, such as individual therapy to address outstanding needs around sexual offending, the completion of risk assessments for court, undertaking personality assessments or encouraging clients to engage in therapy. One of my areas of expertise is motivational work. Here I look to explore the potential barriers to some individuals who would be best placed in therapy for their sexual offending, but find it difficult to undertake this work.

As with all applied psychologies there is the hidden work, such as writing up case notes and the writing of reports. I probably spend around one day per week writing up notes after seeing clients, drafting reports and preparing for my intervention work with them, both group work and individual. This is a vital part of our work, as accurate record keeping is a requirement for a psychologist, and is needed in order to maximise a true reflection of our engagement with them.

I also spend time conducting research, although I do not do as much of this as I would like at present. My current piece of research is looking at the effectiveness of the sex offender therapies in a population where clients have a mental disorder. This is a substantial task, not only in the collection of data, but its input and analysis. Yet, I love research, and I can still feel that sense of anticipation when I run statistical analyses, and when determining the significance (or nonsignificance) of my results.

The examples I have given here focus on my work with individuals who commit sexual offences, yet I also do a lot of consultancy work with organisations, looking at cultural issues or how various management strategies can be implemented. I am also involved in a lot of training, not only in the area of sex offending, but also **crisis** and **conflict** management, violent offending, personality assessment and supervision skills. I really love my job, and although it can at times be challenging in regard to the workload and the demands made of me, the rewards far outweigh these challenges.

> **crisis** a crisis situation is one in which the individual concerned has no clear goals and his or her emotional distress is high.

> **conflict** a conflict situation is one in which an individual has orchestrated a hostile situation of some kind with a clear plan and focus in mind.

The forensic psychologist can be pivotal in encouraging the organisation or individuals within the organisation to explore and define relevant problems or issues and to consider a management plan. Importantly, the consultant's role is not to direct the management of any problem, but to encourage creative thinking around the issue, to support and encourage learning, to develop the necessary skills if they are lacking and to enhance the organisation's responsibility for managing and resolving problems. For example, if the forensic psychologist in a prison is to encourage discussions around the management of a potentially challenging prisoner, they may encourage the governor of the prison to consider a detailed understanding of the prisoner's motivations, different options for managing the prisoner and what the consequences of these changes might be.

12.2.2 Competencies of the Consultant

Importantly, the forensic psychologist as a consultant to an organisation is expected to have the following competencies (Kakabadse, Louchart & Kakabadse, 2006):

- *Experience*: It is expected that the forensic psychologist as the consultant will have the necessary experience and knowledge of the area under discussion. For example, if a governor in a prison is seeking support in the management of self-harm and suicide in the prison population, it would be expected that the psychologist would have a good knowledge of the scientific theories and models of self-harm and suicide. It is further important that the forensic psychologist understands the forensic setting in which the consultancy is to take place and should not assume that each forensic organisation is identical in set-up, structure and culture.

- *Ability to listen and question*: A poor consultant is a forensic psychologist who fails to attend in detail to the material they are being given and is unable to explore the relevant issues effectively. The psychologist needs to listen actively to what is being said and check their understanding of the issue with the client organisation and its members. A failure to do so may lead to assumptions about the issue that may prove incorrect or lead to a failure to separate facts from opinions. For example, the consultant forensic psychologist may be brought in to consider issues of conflict within a team. They may then decide to introduce

methods to manage such conflict. Yet the issue may not be conflict, but something entirely different. It may be that the senior manager has labelled the issue as one of conflict when closer scrutiny suggests it is more a breakdown in communication. In this example, the consultant may have failed to explore all the relevant issues and accepted the senior manager's opinion as fact.

- *Objectivity*: It is important for the consultant forensic psychologist to be able and confident enough to express views that the client organisation may not always wish to hear. As a result, the forensic psychologist must communicate issues in a clear, yet sensitive way. This may mean that the forensic psychologist can often be at odds with the client's own views, yet the key is skilful negotiation to encourage wider thinking in the client. This also extends to the psychologist being comfortable with their own area of expertise and competency and being able to indicate when this expertise and competence may have been exceeded.

- *Self-awareness*: It is important for the consultant forensic psychologist to be reflective about their role in the management of an issue. This reflection requires that they be aware of their own thoughts and feelings as they progress through the areas of concern and management of a problem, and of the impact of these thoughts and feelings on their own interactions with the client and the decisions they may make.

- *Environmental awareness*: It is important for the consultant forensic psychologist to consider the more general cultural and environmental challenges for the client organisation. For example, when the forensic psychologist is encouraging solutions to the management of the issue, it is important to consider the overall culture of the organisation. Encouraging staff to be open in discussing an issue may need careful consideration if the culture is one where blaming each other is prevalent and may prevent staff from revealing their true views on a problem. For example, the culture of an organisation may not recognise the potential for staff to be bullied, which sends an implicit message to staff that bullying does not exist in the organisation and that any discussion of this with external individuals will be viewed negatively. If the forensic psychologist is not aware of this culture, they are unlikely to get a complete picture of the organisation and the views of its staff.

12.2.3 *Types of Consultancy Work*

Consultancy work undertaken by forensic psychologists can be very varied. It can include working with senior management on high-level organisational and strategic issues. It can also include working with staff who are engaged directly with forensic clients (e.g. perpetrators, prisoners) and working within organisational teams to maximise their performance and engagement. Some examples include:

- *Management of self-harm and suicide*: A forensic psychologist may be asked for advice on a policy or procedure for an organisation's management of its forensic client's risk of self-harm or attempted suicide. This may involve the implementation of structures to support those most as risk, the development of awareness in staff about the psychological function of self-harm and attempted suicide, and the development of policies to monitor and minimise risk.

- *Management of bullying and harassment*: A forensic psychologist may be asked to advise on a policy or procedure for the management of bullying within an organisation, including staff–staff bullying, staff–client bullying and client–client bullying.

This may include help in defining bullying and harassment to help with the management of such incidents, including the support of victims.

- *Development of new policies and procedures*: A forensic psychologist can be asked to advise on a wide variety of organisational policies and procedures, from the developmental stages through to implementation and later review and evaluation. This can include issues such as the management of work stress, staff burnout, sickness and even strategy development and implementation.

- *Crisis negotiator adviser*: A forensic psychologist may be asked to train negotiators, to set up negotiator protocols and to advise the command structure in a crisis or conflict situation (such as a roof-top protest, barricade or hostage-taking incident). Such forensic psychologists are trained as consultants, but with specialised knowledge of crisis and conflict incidents, which requires a detailed knowledge of negotiation strategies.

A detailed summary of the key theoretical approaches and applications is presented in Theory to Application Box 12.1.

BOX 12.1 THEORY TO APPLICATION

An Example of the Theoretical Approaches of the Forensic Psychologist as an Adviser in a Crisis/Conflict Incident, and Their Application

Crisis and Conflict Situations

An example of a *crisis situation* is when a prisoner may have barricaded themselves into their room because they are distressed and wish to end their life. This situation is one where negotiators make attempts to calm the situation down and to increase the rational thinking of the person in crisis. A *conflict situation* can be regarded as one where a prisoner takes another prisoner hostage with a clear purpose, such as demanding to see the governor, or requesting a move to another establishment. In summary, a crisis situation is where there are no clear goals and emotional distress is high; a conflict situation is where the individual has orchestrated the situation with a clear plan and focus in mind. Yet this can still be simplistic as situations can change, and it is beneficial to consider crisis and conflict on a continuum, with a crisis situation at one end and a conflict situation at the other. The forensic psychologist as the adviser can be critical in assessing this, and in supporting the negotiators in their negotiations.

Introducing the Psychological Theory

The approach to the management of crisis and conflict situations has a strong basis in core psychological theory. For example, the work of Ryan and Deci (2000) on motivational theory underlies some of the core principles. Ryan and Deci (2000) identified three basic human needs that we all seek: competence, relatedness and autonomy. They argue that we all have a desire to feel competent at what we do, with a sense of effectiveness in our relationships with others, while having the freedom of choice and control that autonomy offers. Such motivational theory underpins

Source: Getty Images.

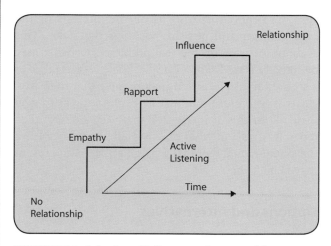

FIGURE 12.1 *Behavioural influence stairway model.*

the negotiation approach to a crisis and conflict situation, and is illustrated below.

Steps to Managing Crisis and/or Conflict

One of the fundamental approaches to crisis or conflict situations is first to make efforts to develop a relationship with the person in conflict or crisis, and by doing so encouraging competence, relatedness and autonomy in the individual. The most utilised approach for this is the behavioural influence stairway model, developed by the Federal Bureau of Investigation, the FBI (Vecchi, Van Hasselt & Romano, 2005), where the ultimate aim is a peaceful settlement (Dalfonzo, 2002). The emphasis on the relationship-building process highlights the importance of having a positive and trusting relationship between the person in crisis and a negotiator if behavioural change and peaceful resolution are to take place (Ireland & Vecchi, 2009). This model and a definition of each step are presented below, using the example of hostage taking.

Active Listening

Here the negotiator attempts to calm the situation by listening carefully to what the individual is stating. This involves checking for understanding and repeating back the 'gist' of what has been stated, in the negotiator's own words. The negotiator may summarise as part of this, such as stating:

> So let me get this straight [making an announcement], you are feeling upset because you feel that staff are not listening to you, and stopping Paul [a nurse] from leaving the room is the only way you feel you can achieve this? [summarises the discussion] Have I got that right? [checks for any errors in understanding] Okay, so tell me some more about what we can do here [opening up a question for further dialogue].

Empathy

Here the negotiator demonstrates an appreciation for the difficult situation in which the hostage taker feels that they have found themselves, such as the above example. This is not about demonstrating sympathy, but appreciating how they may feel, such as stating:

> I obviously don't know how you feel, but I can only imagine that this whole situation must be frustrating for you. I hope I have got this right, but you sound frustrated when you were talking to me just then.

Rapport

Here the negotiator is attempting to build trust between themselves and the hostage taker, primarily developed by a clear emphasis on active listening and empathy. The negotiator and forensic psychologist monitor for signs that may indicate that trust is developing.

Influence

Here the negotiator is testing to see if they are at a stage where they can influence the behaviour of the hostage taker, seeing this as a sign that rational thinking on the part of the hostage taker is increasing and the relationship is developing in a positive direction. Such influence begins at a low level and may increase as the situation continues. For example:

> I'm wondering if you would mind coming to the door so I can see if you are okay. I'm keen to make sure you are okay, is that alright?... It is? That's great, thanks very much for that.

(Continued)

Forensic Psychologist as the Adviser

The forensic psychologist as an adviser would be monitoring the progress of these negotiations and advising the negotiator on the most beneficial tactics and approaches. Importantly, each of these steps in the relationship-building process need to be developed. For example, it is not a simple case that the negotiator begins with active listening, then stops this to move on to empathy. All of the steps build on one another, each laying the foundation for the next. It may even be that the individual is already at a stage where their behaviour can be influenced. The role of the forensic psychologist as an adviser is to ensure that the stairway is implemented effectively by the negotiation team.

Moving to a Problem-Solving Approach

Once rational thinking has been facilitated, the forensic psychologist as an adviser supports the negotiation team in the next stage of negotiation – principled negotiation.

Principled Negotiation

This approach was developed by Fisher, Ury and Patton (1993) and aims to negotiate a means of reaching an agreement that is acceptable to all. This form of negotiation was developed with a focus on day-to-day business negotiations, which was then applied to the crisis or conflict situation. It focuses on four objectives:

- Personalities must be separated from the problem.
- The focus should be on interests and not positions.
- Options and alternatives must be discussed.
- The criteria must be objective.

Each is taken in turn and related to a crisis and/or conflict situation.

Personalities must be Separated from the Problem

This acknowledges that, as human beings, we all have emotions. When dealing with the issue, such as a barricade, it is important for the forensic psychologist as the adviser to ensure that the negotiators focus on the problem and that any emotions do not get in the way of this. A failure to do so can only lead to confrontation. For example, the aim here is not about 'winning', 'defeating' or 'scoring points' with the hostage taker.

Focus on Interests and not Positions

Here the forensic psychologist as an adviser encourages the negotiator to focus on the interests of the hostage taker and not the positions they take. This is about focusing on the real problem, not what may be initially stated. For example, the hostage taker in a secure forensic hospital may request that their psychiatrist be present. On further exploration as to why they ask for this, it is revealed that they are fearful of repercussions and what may happen when they leave the situation and feel that a psychiatrist being present may benefit them.

Options and Alternatives

Here the forensic psychologist as adviser encourages the negotiator to identify with the hostage taker all the possible options for dealing with the current situation, and to search for some of the most effective options that lead to a safe and peaceful resolution for all.

Criteria must be Objective

The forensic psychologist must advise the negotiator to be clear with the hostage taker about what is negotiable and what is not. For example, the negotiator must be clear on what they can negotiate on, and what is nonnegotiable.

Hatcher et al. (1998) emphasise that the forensic psychologist must be aware of the limits of their role. They also emphasise the importance of a consultant's ability to function in a stressful environment, such as a crisis/conflict situation.

12.3 THE ROLE OF THE FORENSIC PSYCHOLOGIST WHEN WORKING WITH OFFENDERS

12.3.1 Types of Engagement

diagnostic assessment a forensic psychologist who has some professional mental health experience and training can diagnose mental health problems and personality disorders in individuals.

Another important focus for the forensic psychologist is working with perpetrators of offending. This can range from **diagnostic assessment**, assessing the risk that such individuals pose, and formulating an understanding of their offending, along with the identification and management of their areas of treatment through intervention work and therapy. Each of these aspects is discussed in turn below.

12.3.2 Diagnostic Assessment

The forensic psychologist who has experience in mental health matters can be involved in the diagnosis of *mental health problems* and *personality disorders*. For example, forensic psychologists can be trained to use the International Personality Disorder Examination (IPDE; Loranger, 1999), which is an assessment tool designed to diagnose the presence of a personality disorder (see Chapter 3).

12.3.3 Risk Assessment

risk assessment an appraisal by a forensic psychologist who will consider the dangers posed to others by an offender, as well as attempt to understand the individual offender.

static risk factors influencing an offender that are historical and cannot be changed.

dynamic risk factors influencing an offender that may be open to change through therapy.

The forensic psychologist also has to consider the areas of risk presenting in the offender. **Risk assessment** focuses on the potential risk the offender may present to others, such as the general population, were they to be released. It also aims to understand the individual's offending. This assessment most usually focuses on a combination of **static** and **dynamic risk** factors. Static risk factors are historical and cannot be changed, such as their age when first convicted or a history

of childhood abuse that may have been one of many potential factors leading to their later offending. It can offer a useful guide to an individual's risk historically, although it is not designed to consider the changing nature of risk, as well as factors that can increase and decrease for an individual over time and in regard to their vulnerabilities. It can be helpful as a starting point of assessment, yet it does not attempt to understand the reasons behind the individual's risky behaviours.

As there continues to be a more developed understanding of risk and how it presents, greater attention has been paid to the changing nature of risk. Examples of such factors that influence risk, which may be more susceptible to change through therapy, can include:

- Offending attitudes and values (e.g. violence is okay, rape is acceptable in the right circumstances – a victim can 'ask' to be raped).
- Unhelpful beliefs of the world that promote offending (e.g. the world is an untrusting and hostile place – you need to look out for yourself, people are just out to ridicule you).
- A lack of knowledge in the effective development and management of relationships with others (e.g. poor communication skills, poor expression of emotion and negotiation in an intimate relationship).

Hanson and Bussiere (1998) argue that there are a number of dynamic risk factors that are common to both sex offenders and non sex offenders. These include:

- Unstable employment.
- Abuse of alcohol and drugs.
- Holding unhelpful pro-offending attitudes.
- Associating with criminal peers.

To use sex offending as an example, Hanson and Morton-Bourgon (2004) identified a number of dynamic factors that were predictive of sexual re-offending rates. These included:

- An unstable lifestyle.
- Sexual preoccupation.
- Deviant sexual interests.
- Conflicts in intimate relationships and intimacy deficits.
- Hostility.
- The use of sex as a coping strategy.

There are a range of risk assessments that assist the forensic psychologist in determining both static and dynamic risk that are based on structured professional guidelines. These include the Sexual Violent Risk-20 (SVR-20; Boer *et al.*, 1997), the Risk for Sexual Violence Protocol (RSVP; Hart, Kropp & Laws, 2004) and the Assessment of Future Violence (HCR-20; Webster *et al.* (1997).

As with all areas of forensic psychology, risk assessments continue to evolve. For example, there is a continuing emphasis on the importance of **protective factors** in offending. These are factors that effectively buffer against risk and reduce risk. For example, a range of re-offending risk factors may have been identified in an offender, but these may be minimised if the offender is in an appropriate intimate relationship where their partner can present as a positive influence and a consequent protective factor against risk. When exploring risk and protective factors in young people, the Youth Justice Board (2005) identified a range of individual, social and health factors that can help protect young people from engaging in criminal activity. These include the following (all identified from research by the Youth Justice Board, 2005).

> **protective factors** factors which effectively buffer against risk and reduce risk.

12.3.3.1 *Individual protective factors*

- Being female (females are generally involved in fewer criminal activities).
- Resilient temperament.
- Sense of self-efficacy (e.g. our ability to feel we can succeed, and our confidence in doing so).
- Positive, outgoing disposition.
- High intelligence.

12.3.3.2 *Social protective factors*

- Stable, warm, affectionate relationship with one or both parents.
- Link with teachers, other adults and peers who hold positive attitudes, modelling positive social behaviour.

12.3.3.3 *Healthy standards*

- Prevailing attitudes across a community.
- Views of parents.
- Promotion of healthy standards within school.
- Opportunities for involvement, social and reasoning skills, recognition and due praise.

12.3.4 *Formulation of Offending*

While risk assessments help forensic psychologists to consider the factors that make an individual vulnerable to re-offending, drawing these into a detailed understanding of how they link together for the individual who has committed the offence/s is paramount. A *formulation* aims to draw together the core issues for the offender, trying to link together how all of these issues are inter twined, making reference to appropriate theory and science. For example, a formulation aims to:

- Understand the motivation and reasoning behind the offending.
- Identify the elements that reinforce their offending.
- Identify when any vulnerabilities to offending may be heightened.
- Note any protective factors that may serve to buffer or minimise offending.

It aims to 'tell the story' about how the individual began to offend as well as what appears to be maintaining any future risk of re-offending. For example, an individual may have been exposed to poor parenting as a child, which meant they were unable to learn effective ways of dealing with problems and emotions. Such poor parenting may have led to them learning that aggression is a helpful way to meet their needs and to manage their emotions and, as they became older, they may have used aggression to meet their needs. As a result, the use of aggression has become a crucial factor in meeting their needs and managing their emotions. A formulation is often seen as a 'work in progress', and is open to continual revision and reconsideration as further information or ideas are explored and considered (Johnstone & Dallos, 2006).

There are many approaches to formulation, including cognitive-behavioural, **psychodynamic**, **systemic** and **integrated** (see also Chapter 6). All formulations should be undertaken collaboratively with the client, with the latter required to take ownership of the formulation wherever possible. The formulation can then be used to consider a clear path of intervention for the client that focuses on how risk factors can be managed (Tarrier & Calam, 2004).

Formulation has been defined as 'the tool used by clinicians to relate theory to practice. . . Formulations can be best understood as hypotheses to be

> **psychodynamic** a psychotherapeutic approach concerned with the impacts of past relationships on a person's present, and that of an active unconscious.

> **systemic** a psychotherapeutic approach concerned with the system(s) in which the client lives and how changes in relationships within the system may lead to improvement in the client's wellbeing.

> **integrated** a model of information processing outlined by Huesmann in 1998.

tested' (Butler, 1998; Eells, 1997). They are 'essentially a hypothesis about the causes, precipitants and maintaining influences of a person's psychological, interpersonal and behavioural problems' (Eells, 1997). Hence, the key aspects of formulation are hypotheses about the causes of a person's problems, such as in their violent offending, while referring to relevant theoretical models. So, for example, a formulation would explore the origin of risk factors, their development and the current factors that may maintain these risks.

Butler (1998) argues that formulation can help to identify the most crucial factors in offending. For example, a forensic client who has committed sexual offences may make efforts to sit close to members of staff, and on some occasions touch their hair. This may initially be formulated as being sexually preoccupied and actively seeking victims. However, as evidence for such a hypothesis is considered, the formulation would also explore alternative explanations. For example, following further exploration, there may be clearer evidence to suggest that the offender actually presents with a substantial brain injury, which affects their ability to engage effectively with others. They may be impulsive, rigid in their thinking and struggle to understand social rules such as respecting an individual's personal space. In this case, sitting close to staff can be reformulated as more likely a result of cognitive impairment where the client is struggling to understand boundaries. Furthermore, the stroking of staff's hair is more likely to be a form of social engagement,

but the client does not have the capacity to determine this to be inappropriate. Such an example illustrates that what may initially be regarded as an explanation for a behaviour may not always be accurate, and when pursuing a formulation the forensic psychologist has to test such hypotheses for accuracy.

12.3.5   Intervention Work/Therapy

Forensic psychologists are involved in the delivery and development of a range of interventions and therapies, both individual and group based. This can include developing interventions, engaging as a therapist delivering such work and/or supervising others to do so. Such interventions/therapies can be wide ranging and focus on supporting an offender to manage areas of outstanding risk. All intervention/therapies undertaken by forensic psychologists follow the 'what works' literature of the key principles for effective treatment with offenders (e.g. McGuire & Priestley, 1995). The nine key principles for effective treatment are listed in Table 12.1.

Examples of the types of therapies a forensic psychologist can be involved in include:

- *Coping and problem-solving skills*: Some offenders' vulnerability factors for offending are linked to their inability to cope with stress. Many

TABLE 12.1 *Key Principles for Effective Treatment.*

Principle	Requirement for effective treatment
1	Therapy/intervention must be empirical and grounded in theory.
2	Therapy/intervention must target 'criminogenic needs' that are relevant for the offence population.
3	Therapy/intervention must use methods that are responsive to the learning styles of the client.
4	Therapy/intervention must use methods that are known to be effective.
5	Therapy/intervention must teach skills (when appropriate).
6	Therapy/intervention must address a range of criminogenic factors.
7	Therapy/intervention must use the right dosage of treatment.
8	There must be focus on a clear care pathway for the client, such as focusing on future needs following therapy.
9	A programme must have treatment integrity (i.e. aims are linked to grounded theory and approaches; there are adequate resources to run it; there should be training, support and evaluation in place).

interventions can teach the offender skills to cope with their stress and how to deal effectively with common stressful situations (Ross & Fabiano, 1991).

- *Social engagement skills*: This type of intervention can help an offender acquire the skills they may need to engage successfully with others. These skills may include interacting appropriately with others in a social context, negotiation and communication skills, and the effective expression of their needs (Ross & Fabiano, 1991).

- *Intimacy-deficit intervention*: Some offenders present with a difficulty in developing and maintaining effective intimate relationships. This type of intervention attempts to address a range of areas that may be relevant to the offender, such as the effective expression of emotion, effective listening, negotiation skills with a partner and tolerance of differences (O'Brien, 2004).

- *Attitudinal intervention*: Some offenders have views of the world, themselves and others that can generate offending (O'Brien, 2004). These may include attitudes that the world is a hostile environment where there is little respect, that others are deceitful and cannot be trusted, and that an individual is entitled to whatever they desire. Cognitive therapies can be employed that will effectively address these dysfunctional beliefs.

- *Violent offender therapies*: This type of intervention aims to manage offenders who have a history of **habitual aggression**. The type of therapies here can vary, although one of the more important approaches is known as the Life Minus Violence Therapy (LMV-Enhanced; Ireland, 2008). While utilising a wide range of therapies, its main approaches are social cognition (in particular the integrated model of information processing outlined by Huesmann, 1998), social learning theory (e.g. Bandura, 1973), emotional intelligence (e.g. Matthews, Zeidner & Roberts, 2002) and the good lives model of offender rehabilitation and self-determination theory (Ryan & Deci, 2000; Ward, 2002). The LMV-Enhanced therapy consists of nine treatment modules, comprising around 125 sessions of around 2.5 hours per session. It further utilises around 14 individual sessions of around 1 hour per session, where offenders are encouraged to rehearse and consolidate their learning. This is further supported by regular between-session

habitual aggression frequently or continually occurring behaviour that results in harm.

work. The core components of the therapy explore motivation; stress and coping; exploration of aggression across the life span; recognition and effective management of unhelpful emotions; the role of beliefs, thoughts, emotions and the environment in processing information; exploration of the consequences of their actions for both themselves and others; issues around empathy and interpersonal skills; and working towards an offence-free and quality future (Ireland, 2008).

- *Sex offender therapies*: This type of intervention attempts to manage the risk posed by an offender who has committed sexual offences, with a view to further enhancing an offence-free quality of life. The type of therapies can vary, yet they are routinely run as group therapies. For an individual who presents with a range of problems, the initial group therapy is cognitive-behavioural in its general approach, and may last for around 90 sessions of 2 hours per session, with around eight group members per therapy. For those who present with fewer problems, the therapy length may be a little shorter. The initial therapies will focus on the development of trust and encouraging an offender to feel part of the group. This will then focus on encouraging them to develop insight into their offending and to take responsibility for their offending. This is undertaken in a supportive and motivational manner, where any difficulties the offender has in exploring this are considered in a collaborative and encouraging way. Empathy may well form a component of this therapy, where the offender is encouraged to consider the impact of their offences on their victims and the victims' immediate friends and family. Efforts may then be spent encouraging the offender to consider their past behaviours and how they wish to change in the future, and for the better. This is then explored in detail, and the skills required for a better future are considered and implemented as part of the therapy. Such therapies also encourage an offender to prepare themselves for setbacks and possible re-offending. The management of treatment needs linked to sexual offending is generally seen as long-term work, where an offender may spend at least a few years addressing some of the most pertinent issues.

For greater illustration, a detailed summary of the key theoretical approaches and application of sex offender therapy is presented in Theory to Application Box 12.2.

BOX 12.2 THEORY TO APPLICATION

An Example of the Theoretical Approaches of the Forensic Psychologist When Engaging with a Client as Part of Sex Offender Therapies

Source: Getty Images.

Paul has committed a range of sexual offences against girls aged 12–14 years. These offences ranged from gross indecency and indecent assault to rape. He was charged with these offences last year, and is currently serving a seven-year sentence for them. Paul has only recently come out of denial and is now undertaking the sex offender group therapy, of which he is partway through. The forensic psychologist discussed with Paul the barriers initially stopping him from acknowledging what he had done, and from engaging in sex offender therapies. When this was discussed, Paul reported:

> I just could not face up to it, I had too much to lose. Besides, I just had too much going on, with the drugs and everything I was taking, I just needed to get my life in order.

The model of barriers to change (Burrowes & Needs, 2009) was used, which explores what may prevent individuals who have committed offences from moving forward. It was noted that the initial difficulty for Paul was a conflict in important goals; while therapists felt that undertaking work to address his sex offending was paramount, Paul had actually thought that addressing his substance-use difficulties was indeed the priority for him. He first felt that, from doing a cost–benefit analysis of change, the benefits for change were initially outweighed by the costs of undertaking such change. He discussed how his family had initially supported him in his denial of the offending, and had

further indicated that if he was ever to acknowledge that he had indeed committed the offence, they would disown him. This was felt to be a huge cost for Paul, which far outweighed him undertaking sex offender therapy. Following some really effective work by Social Services, his family was now able to see the importance of supporting Paul, and had more recently encouraged him to undertake sex offender therapy.

Once Paul had begun to undertake the sex offender therapies, time was spent in the group discussing the way in which individuals who had committed sex offences may choose to discuss information that was difficult for them. This was then reviewed some months into the group. This was made with particular reference to the Disclosure Management Model (Frost, Daniels & Hudson, 2006). This model was developed through research on individuals who had committed sexual offences and describes four main styles that an individual may adopt. These four styles were presented to the group as follows:

- *Exploratory style*: Here an individual is keen to move forward and to set goals that prioritise their needs.
- *Oppositional style*: Here an individual is seen as resistant to making progress.
- *Placatory style*: Here an individual attempts to present a good impression of themselves and be seen in a favourable light.
- *Evasive style*: Here an individual presents with a fear of being evaluated negatively by the forensic psychologist and their peers, and can present with an overwhelming sense of shame around their offending.

Paul reported feeling that he was initially evasive in therapy:

> When I first started the group, I had already decided that I did not want to be here. I felt exposed, like I was on show. I was so desperate for people to believe my distorted view of things. When I really think about this, it was because I felt I had to put on a show to my family that I was innocent, but also it was because I was so

(Continued)

ashamed of what I had done, I hated myself, and I did not want to own up to being that person. I felt humiliated. I'd guess you'd say I was the evasive style to begin with.

When Paul was encouraged to discuss his current style of disclosure, he reported:

As time went on, I realised that no matter what was discussed in the group, the therapists or my fellow group members did not seem to judge me. I began to realise that I got out of the group only what I was putting in. I decided just to 'go for it', to discuss how I really saw things. I'd guess you'd say I was feeling more comfortable with being exploratory in my style.

As time progressed, a formulation of Paul's offending was discussed within the group. This was based on one of the more developed and influential models, one that first began to explore developmental factors in sexual offending, namely Marshall and Barbaree's integrated theory of child sexual abuse (Marshall, Anderson & Fernandez, 1999; Marshall & Barbaree, 1990). This model draws on a range of psychological theories, such as attachment (Bowlby, 1969), and argues that individuals can develop vulnerability factors from early childhood that make them vulnerable to committing a sexual offence.

As part of the therapy, Paul's formulation was discussed. It described how Paul experienced *poor parenting* as a child and was regularly exposed to his mother being beaten by his father. He further reported how his father would tell him that 'women are no good, they are only good for one thing'. As a result, Paul had not learned how to deal with his emotions very well and this led to problems in his *mood management*. He had never been taught how to disclose his feelings to others, and when he became older he struggled to develop appropriate relationships with others, including his intimate partners. Consequently he reported a number of failed intimate relationships. He was therefore *regularly met with rejection*. He reported that he was keen to have a close relationship but did not know how to go about this. It was also noted that he had *low self-worth* at the time of his offending, with feelings of inadequacy and an inability to undertake any meaningful intimate relationships. He reported meeting one of his victims when she was 13 years of age and that she was the daughter of a colleague at work. He reported that he offered to babysit for the family and did so on a regular basis. He indicated that, while he knew the victim was under age, he tried to convince himself that it was okay. He reported that the victim was the first female he had met who did not seem to reject him; she would laugh when in his company and appeared genuinely interested in him. He then reported that he started to develop sexual feelings about her, feeling that she was *less likely to reject him*.

This Theory to Application Box demonstrates the complexity of offending behaviour, as well as the need for the forensic psychologist to show sensitivity when engaging with forensic clients. The success of sex offender therapy can be partly achieved by a careful understanding of each individual's path towards offending, and the challenges they may face when discussing their offences with others.

12.4 ETHICAL ISSUES ASSOCIATED WITH FORENSIC PSYCHOLOGY

Ethical considerations underpin the work of all psychologists, and forensic psychology is no exception. In the United Kingdom all forensic psychologists' conduct is regulated by the Health Professions Council (HPC). The HPC offers guidance to applied psychologists about their expected conduct and ethical considerations. It identifies 14 expected standards to which a psychologist is expected to adhere, in order for the general public to continue to have confidence in the expertise of the psychologist. Ultimately the HPC is focused on the protection of the public from harm. The British Psychological Society (BPS) is the learned society that an applied psychologist is encouraged to join and supports them in their practice, including their continuing professional development. A brief summary of each of the 14 expected standards from the HPC is presented in Table 12.2, with links to the type of ethical considerations relevant to forensic psychologists.

In order to draw together some of the factors discussed above, Focus Point 12.4 identifies a forensic psychologist's ethical decision-making process when considering an ethical dilemma.

TABLE 12.2 *HPC's Standards for Psychologists.*

Standard 1: You must act in the interests of service users (your clients)

That is, you must not abuse your relationship with them, you must not discriminate and you are responsible for your professional conduct, any care/advice you offer, and any failure to act.

Considerations for the forensic psychologist: It is important that a forensic psychologist does not ridicule, punish or discriminate a client based on their offence history. It is important that they do not abuse their position of power with the client, such as making inappropriate requests and expectations of them. Importantly, a forensic psychologist is accountable for all their decisions. For example, if a client presents as suicidal and a forensic psychologist makes a judgement as to the level of care needed, they are accountable for that decision.

Standard 2: You must respect the confidentiality of service users (your clients)

That is, client information must be treated as confidential and used only for the purposes for which it was originally provided.

Considerations for the forensic psychologist: It is important that a forensic psychologist does not divulge confidential information to individuals who should not have access to this. For example, a risk assessment report would be expected to be disclosed to the client's care team and/or the court, but not to a member of staff who has no involvement in their care. Also, if a forensic psychologist collects data as part of a research project, such data cannot then be used to inform a particular client's type of care, unless of course the client consented to this in the first instance and it formed part of the research consent form agreed by the organisation's ethics and research governance.

Standard 3: You must keep high standards of personal conduct

Considerations for the forensic psychologist: As with all psychologists, a forensic psychologist must uphold appropriate conduct outside of their work environment. For example, it would be regarded as failing the standards of personal conduct if a forensic psychologist engaged in criminal activity outside of work, which may lead to their removal as a practising psychologist.

Standard 4: You must provide any important information about your conduct and competence

That is, the HPC must be provided with any details of criminal convictions and employment tribunals where the forensic psychologist has been found to have acted improperly. The forensic psychologist is expected to inform the HPC of an issue that affects their conduct and competence to practice.

Considerations for the forensic psychologist: As with all psychologists, there is the obligation to inform the HPC of any conduct or competency issues. For example, if a forensic psychologist has been found guilty at an employment tribunal for misconduct, such as bullying and harassing staff and/or clients, this is a serious matter to be considered by the HPC. More extreme and rare examples may involve forensic psychologists engaging in improper relationships with clients. Other examples may include a forensic psychologist failing to complete their work without appropriate explanation, work of a poor standard, or being found guilty at an organisation's capability hearing for not meeting the job's requirements. Such examples would be expected to be forwarded to the HPC.

Standard 5: You must keep your professional knowledge and skills up to date

Considerations for the forensic psychologist: The work that a forensic psychologist undertakes, particularly those with forensic clients, has the potential to have a substantial impact on their care, and in many ways can assist the judge in court when deciding on sentencing or continued detainment. As such, it is vital that a forensic psychologist ensures they are at an appropriate level of competence for the work they undertake. For example, it would be inappropriate for a forensic psychologist to undertake a personality assessment without the appropriate training, or to conduct a risk assessment based on clinical judgement alone, without the use of a validated risk assessment tool.

Standard 6: You must act within the limits of your knowledge, skills and experience and, if necessary, refer the matter to another practitioner

Considerations for the forensic psychologist: It is important for the forensic psychologist to ensure that they are aware of their limits of knowledge and expertise. For example, a forensic psychologist is not a neuropsychologist, and does not possess the same level of expertise. So, for example, if they were asked to conduct and interpret a detailed neuropsychological assessment on a very specific disorder, it is more appropriate that they decline.

Standard 7: You must communicate properly and effectively with service users (clients) and other practitioners

That is, the psychologist must ensure they are cooperative and share their expertise and knowledge with others.

Considerations for the forensic psychologist: It is important that the forensic psychologist openly shares their knowledge and expertise with a wide range of practitioners, including the client. The aim is to ensure that the client receives the necessary benefits. For example, in forensic services, a team of professionals may recommend a certain type of therapy to address a client's offending behaviour. It is important for the forensic psychologist to ensure that the team of professionals have the right level of understanding when making this decision, and that the suggested therapy best meets the needs of the client.

(Continued)

TABLE 12.2 *(Continued)*

Standard 8: You must effectively supervise tasks that you have asked other people to carry out

That is, all the work you supervise you must be competent to do yourself, and to supervise effectively.

Considerations for the forensic psychologist: It is important that the appropriate level of supervision is offered, as well as that supervision is adequate for the task at hand. The aim is that the supervisor should ensure that all of the work of others they supervise is done to an acceptable standard.

Standard 9: You must obtain informed consent in order to provide treatment (except in an emergency)

That is, a psychologist must seek consent from a client to engage in assessment and interventions.

Considerations for the forensic psychologist: It is important that the forensic psychologist always seeks *informed consent* from their client in order to conduct any work with them. Importantly, it is vital that they make the client aware of the risks of engagement and nonengagement. For example, with regard to therapy engagement, the client may experience emotional risks as a result of discussing topics that are difficult for them. As part of gaining informed consent, the client has the right to refuse assessment and treatment, and it is important for the forensic psychologist to record the decision made by the client. A brief example of a consent form is presented in Focus Point 12.3.

Standard 10: You must keep accurate records

Considerations for the forensic psychologist: As with all applied psychology, it is vital that a forensic psychologist ensures that all records on clients are completed promptly, such as case notes and records of any interviews. All records and notes made need to be dated, signed and clearly legible. If corrections need to be made, they should be drawn through with a line so they are still recognisable but easily noted as an error. This not only applies to the forensic psychologist but staff they supervise, such as forensic psychologists in training.

Standard 11: You must deal fairly and safely with the risks of infection

That is, a psychologist must not refuse treatment to an individual with an infection, and must take the necessary precautions to protect themselves.

Considerations for the forensic psychologist: Although less routine with forensic clients, it is not unusual for some clients to present with infections and disease, such as Hepatitis B. Psychologists working with risks in this area are usually provided with vaccinations to promote immunity. A forensic psychologist cannot refuse to treat a client simply due to an infection or disease, provided that reasonable precautions against risk of infection can be managed. Importantly, the forensic psychologist is expected to ensure confidentiality guidelines are followed, such as not disclosing the details of the infection to unnecessary parties.

Standard 12: You must limit your work or stop practising if your performance or judgement is affected by your physical and mental health

Considerations for the forensic psychologist: If, as a forensic psychologist, you experience an episode of mental or physical health problems that significantly affects your ability to work, you must suspend your practice. For example, if a forensic psychologist has a history of mental illness and they suffer a relapse, they should remove themselves from work until such time as it is appropriate to return. This is in order to ensure that the client receives the best possible treatment, not by a psychologist who has an impairment in their abilities.

Standard 13: You must behave with honesty and integrity and make sure that your behaviour does not damage the public's confidence in you or your profession

That is, you must ensure that all of your work is conducted in an appropriate and professional manner, with scientific integrity.

Considerations for the forensic psychologist: It is important for a forensic psychologist to present their work with honesty and integrity. For example, a forensic psychologist would be regarded as falling below the required standards if they chose to present someone else's work as their own. Further, if a forensic psychologist chose to work based on outdated models of treatment as this was where their familiarity lay, this would also be noted as falling below the standard expected.

Standard 14: You must make sure that any advertising you do is accurate

For example, any advertisements of services must not be misleading, and there should be no financial benefits for agreeing a particular course of action.

Considerations for the forensic psychologist: As with all applied psychologists, it is important that a forensic psychologist does not misrepresent their services, such as claiming 'sex offenders can be cured' where the scientific literature points to the management and not the curing of behaviours. Crucially, it is important for a forensic psychologist not to make recommendations for the treatment of a client that has a financial benefit for themselves. For example, a forensic psychologist should not make recommendations for the therapy a client should undertake as part of a risk assessment, and then agree to undertake such an intervention themselves. While the identification of recommendations is important, it would not be appropriate for the forensic psychologist to undertake such work, because it can potentially appear that such recommendations may have been generated for the financial benefit of the forensic psychologist.

FOCUS POINT 12.3   CONSENT FORMS – CONSENTING TO ASSESSMENT

CONSENT TO UNDERTAKE PSYCHOLOGICAL ASSESSMENT (FORM A)

NAME OF CLIENT:_____.

DATE CONSENT FORM WAS PROVIDED:_____.

INFORMATION

The purpose of the assessment will be to focus on your offending and factors that may contribute or link to your offending or overall risk. This information will then be used to contribute to a risk management plan and to make some recommendations to assist you and other professionals involved in your case to manage your risk.

The assessment process will involve interviews and you may be asked to complete some questionnaires. If you are asked to complete questionnaires you will be given information on these and asked to sign a separate consent form before completing these.

CONSENT AGREEMENT

1. I agree to participate in a psychological assessment with

    _____

2. I understand that the results of this assessment may be used as part of an overall assessment to identify appropriate work to address my offending and risk.

3. I understand that this assessment requires access to reports and documents written about me to assist in completing the assessment.

4. I understand that a report will be written following the assessment and this will be available to individuals involved in my case for the purpose of public protection, risk assessment and management. This report will be placed in my file. If any treatment is recommended in the report I will be asked to complete a separate consent form before starting any work.

5. I understand that if I disclose any offences for which I have not been charged that the professional has a duty to report these to the hospital and other relevant agencies or their representatives.

AGREEMENT

I confirm that I have read all the information provided to me and have had the opportunity to ask any questions. I confirm that I will consent to the assessment process on the above basis.

Name of Client_____.

Signed _____.

Date _____.

I have explained the above consent form to the client. The client has signed this form in my presence:

Signature of Psychologist

Name   Paul Smith

                             Chartered Psychologist, Forensic Psychologist

Signed _____   Date _____

FOCUS POINT 12.4   FORENSIC PSYCHOLOGY IN ACTION – AN ETHICAL DILEMMA

I have recently qualified as a forensic psychologist, and a lot of my experience has involved therapy work with clients and some research. I currently work in a prison. Last week when I was at work, a prisoner had barricaded themselves into their room, taking another prisoner with them against their will, and was threatening to harm themselves and the other prisoner. The governor from the prison asked for psychological support and needed a psychologist who was skilled in these types of negotiation to advise the command team and the negotiators. The psychologist with skills in this area was on leave, and this left only me. I had never done anything like this before, and I was aware that any psychologists who did this work tended to have received a lot of training. I had done some initial awareness training, but nothing substantive. A lot of pressure was put on me to attend. Really they were just keen for support. The governor asked to see me and I had to be clear, despite the pressure put on me, that I could not assist as an adviser because I was not trained as one. I did though say that I would find someone who was, and quickly went away to phone other prisons for support. I was lucky and found someone who came and assisted.

When I reflected on this, I thought of the ethical decision-making process I had gone through. I considered the work of Koocher and Keith-Spiegel (1998), who described a range of considerations to be made when working through an ethical decision. This included determining whether the issue was an ethical one and consulting professional guidelines, through to evaluating the rights, responsibilities and vulnerabilities of those affected by the dilemma, to implementing the decision made. The following are the considerations I made based on the advice of Koocher and Keith-Spiegel (1998):

- When *determining whether the issue is an ethical one*, I decided it clearly was: the prisoner in crisis was at potential risk, as well as their hostage and other people involved.
- When I *consulted my professional guidelines* it was clear that, as a qualified psychologist, you work only within your area of expertise. I did not have knowledge of crisis situations such as this. I did not have sufficient expertise, and it was important that I made other professionals aware of this.
- When I *considered all the sources that may influence the decision I was to make*, I did consider my relationship with the governor. I did not feel that I wanted to let him down. I had a good relationship with him. I also felt awkward as I did not like to see him under pressure. I felt that my good relationship

Source: Shutterstock.

could potentially affect my decision, such as wanting to assist, but I had to put this to one side. I also considered the Health Professions Council (HPC) and its views on this situation, namely the risks posed to the client and also my lack of expertise. I also wanted to demonstrate that psychological services were helpful and supportive, yet I had to make sure that this did not then direct me to agreeing to help in an area I was unfamiliar with.

- I did manage to *locate a trusted colleague whom I could consult with*. This was reassuring, as they reminded me of the expertise needed to undertake an advisory role, as well as my need to work within my area of expertise.
- When I then explored the *rights, responsibilities and vulnerability of all affected parties*, I considered that for me to undertake this role could potentially place individuals at risk. This would not be intentional, but unintentionally I may offer advice that is not based on theory and models of crisis and conflict negotiation. As such, I was potentially placing the person in crisis, their hostage and the staff at risk if I was to agree. This could also have a negative impact on the organisation, especially if the crisis situation was managed poorly as a result of my support, leading to an inquiry. The person in crisis and the hostage, for example, had the right to expect a

psychologist qualified in the area to assist in managing the crisis.

- When looking to *generate alternative decisions* I quickly discounted a decision to assist as an adviser. Other decisions could include not supporting the team at all, or I could look to identify a forensic psychologist skilled in the area.
- When then considering the *consequences of each decision*, to assist as an adviser would place both myself and all others at potential risk. Not to support the team and effectively to 'walk away' would not place myself or psychological services in a positive light, and could damage future working relationships. To be honest with everyone about the limits of my expertise could probably gain the respect of them and other colleagues. If I was to suggest supporting them by seeking out a forensic psychologist qualified to assist, that would support my role in the organisation as a team player and help at a time of crisis. I decided this was the best way forward.
- I therefore *made my decision* to inform them of the limits of my skill in this area, but to offer an alternative.
- I therefore *implemented this decision* by telling the governor and then quickly arranging for a forensic psychologist skilled in the area to come and assist.

12.5   CONCLUSION

It is hoped that this chapter has illustrated the role of the forensic psychologist who works with organisations and perpetrators. Forensic psychology, as with all applied psychologies, is a detailed and engaging area of work. Forensic psychology as a profession is a demanding and at times stressful endeavour. Yet the value and sense of achievement obtained by such work ensure that it is a positive and extremely valuable profession of which to be part.

SELF-TEST QUESTIONS

- Name four of the competencies a forensic psychologist as a consultant is expected to have and why.
- Can you describe the difference between a crisis and a conflict situation?
- Can you describe one theory of motivation and apply this to a forensic situation?
- Why is it important to encourage a person in crisis to become more rational in their thinking?
- What are the key elements of principled negotiation and when would you use it during a conflict and/or crisis situation?
- What is the difference between static and dynamic risk?
- Name three areas on which a forensic psychologist may work when engaged with an offender.
- Compare and contrast the difference between diagnostic and risk assessment.
- Name five out of the nine key principles for all intervention/therapies undertaken by forensic psychologists, as part of the 'what works' literature for effective treatment with offenders.
- Name three different types of therapy in which a forensic psychologist may engage when working with an offender.
- Referring back to the Disclosure Management Model (Frost, Daniels & Hudson, 2006), compare and contrast two of the different disclosure styles.
- Name and describe five of the key ethical standards a psychologist is expected to meet as part of their registration under the Health Professions Council (HPC).
- Identify three key considerations when attempting to consent an offender to engage in work with a forensic psychologist.

ESSAY QUESTIONS

- Compare and contrast the role of the forensic psychologist as an adviser in a crisis incident and that of the forensic psychologist who engages in therapy with an offender.
- Critically evaluate the following statement: 'Motivational and collaborative engagement does not work with offenders, it is unethical and a waste of time.'
- Critically evaluate the following statement: 'Risk assessments are all the same – there is no difference between dynamic and static risk. They all tell you the same thing.'
- Ethics in psychology is straightforward and often the ethical issues are obvious and easily managed. Discuss.

TEXTS FOR FURTHER READING

Bartol, C.R. & Bartol, A. (2008) *Introduction to Forensic Psychology: Research and Application*, Beverly Hills, CA: Sage.

Francis, R.D. (2009) *Ethics for Psychologists*, Chichester: Wiley-Blackwell.

Ireland, C.A. & Fisher, M. (2010) *Consultancy and Advising in Forensic Practice: Empirical and Practical Guidelines*, Chichester: Wiley-Blackwell.

Ireland, J.L., Ireland, C.A. & Birch, P. (2008) *Violent and Sexual Offenders: Assessment, Treatment and Management*, Abingdon: Willan Publishing.

McMains, M.J. & Mullins, W.C. (2006) *Crisis Negotiations: Managing Critical Incidents and Hostage Situations in Law Enforcement and Corrections*, 2nd edn, Cincinnati, OH: Anderson.

RELEVANT JOURNAL ARTICLES

Applebaum, S.H. & Steed, A.J. (2005) The critical success factors in the client–consulting relationship, *Journal of Management Development* 24(1/2): 68–93.

Beech, A.R. & Ward, T. (2004) The integration of etiology and risk in sexual offenders: A theoretical framework, *Aggression and Violent Behavior: A Review Journal* 10: 31–61.

Blud, L., Travers, R., Nugent, F. & Thornton, D. (2003) Accreditation of offending behaviour programmes in HM Prison Service: 'What Works' in practice, *Legal and Criminological Psychology* 8: 69–81.

Douglas, K., Cox, D. & Webster, C. (1999) Violence risk assessment: Science and practice, *Legal and Criminological Psychology* 4: 149–84.

Giebels, E., Noelanders, S. & Vervaeke, G. (2005) The hostage experience: Implications for negotiation strategies, *Clinical Psychology and Psychotherapy* 12: 241–53.

Ireland, J.L. (2004a) Anger management therapy with male young offenders an evaluation of treatment outcome, *Aggressive Behavior* 30: 174–82.

Ireland, J.L. (2004b) Compiling forensic risk assessment reports, *Forensic Update* April(77): 15–22.

Kakabadse, N.K., Louchart, E. & Kakabadse, A. (2006) Consultant's role: A qualitative inquiry from the consultant's perspective, *Journal of Management Development* 25(5): 416–500.

Mann, R.E. & Rollnick, S. (1996) Motivational interviewing with a sex offender who believed he was innocent, *Behavioural and Cognitive Psychotherapy* 24: 127–34.

Vecchi, G.M., Van Hasselt, V.B. & Romano, S.J. (2005) Crisis (hostage) negotiation: Current strategies and issues in high-risk conflict resolution, *Aggression and Violent Behavior* 10: 533–51.

RELEVANT WEB LINKS

British Psychological Society, www.bps.org.uk
Division of Forensic Psychology, www.bps.org.uk/sub-sites$/dfp
Health Professions Council: www.hpc-uk.org

REFERENCES

Bandura, A. (1973) *Aggression: A Social Learning Analysis,* New York: Holt.

Boer, D.P., Hart, S.D., Kropp, P.R. & Webster, C.D. (1997) *Manual for the Sexual Violence Risk-20: Professional Guidelines for Assessing Risk of Sexual Violence,* Burnaby, BC: Mental Health, Law, and Policy Institute, Simon Fraser University.

Bowlby, J. (1969) *Attachment and Loss, Vol. 1,* 2nd edn, New York: Basic Books.

Burrowes, N. & Needs, A. (2009) Time to contemplate change? A framework for assessing readiness to change with offenders, *Aggression and Violent Behavior* 14: 39–49.

Butler, G. (1998) Clinical formulation, in A.S. Bellack & M. Hersen (eds) *Comprehensive Clinical Psychology,* Oxford: Pergamon.

Dalfonzo, V. (2002) *National Crisis Negotiation Course,* Quantico, VA: FBI Academy.

Eells, T.D. (1997) Psychotherapy case formulation: History and current status, in T.D. Eells (ed.) *Handbook of Psychotherapy Case Formulation,* New York: Guilford Press.

First, M.B., Spitzer, R.L., Gibbon, M. & Williams, J.B.W. (1997) *SCID-1:Structured Clinical Interview for DSM-IV Axis I Disorders,* Arlington, VA: American Psychiatric Publishing.

Fisher, R., Ury, W. & Patton, B. (1993) *Getting to Yes: Negotiating Agreement without Giving In,* 2nd edn, New York: Penguin.

Frost, A., Daniels, K. & Hudson, S.K. (2006) Disclosure strategies among sex offenders: A model for understanding the engagement process in groupwork, *Journal of Sexual Aggression* 12(3): 227–44.

Greiner, L. & Metzger, R. (1983) *Consulting to Management,* Englewood Cliffs, NJ: Prentice-Hall.

Hanson, R.K. & Bussiere, M.T. (1998) Predicting relapse: A meta analysis of sexual offender recidivism studies, *Journal of Consulting and Clinical Psychology* 66(2): 348–62.

Hanson, R.K. & Morton-Bourgon, K. (2004) *Predictors of Sexual Recidivism: An Updated Meta Analysis,* Ottawa: Public Safety and Emergency Preparedness Canada.

Hart, S.D., Kropp, P.R. & Laws, R.L. (2004) *The Risk for Sexual Violence Protocol (RSVP),* Burnaby, BC: Mental Health, Law, and Policy Institute, Simon Fraser University.

Hatcher, C., Mohandie, K., Turner, J. & Gelles, M. (1998) The role of the psychologist in crisis/hostage negotiations, *Behavioral Sciences and the Law* 16: 455–72.

Huesmann, L.R. (1998) The role of social information processing and cognitive schemas in the acquisition and maintenance of habitual aggressive behavior, in R.G. Green & E. Donnerstein (eds), *Human Aggression: Theories, Research, and Implications for Policy,* pp. 73–109, New York: Academic Press.

Ireland, C.A. & Vecchi, G.M. (2009) The Behavioral Influence Stairway Model (BISM): A framework for managing terrorist crisis situations? *Behavioral Sciences of Terrorism and Political Aggression* 1(3): 203–18.

Ireland, J.L. (2008) *Life Minus Violence Manual,* Liverpool: Mersey Care NHS Trust.

Johnstone, L. & Dallos, R. (2006) *Formulation in Psychology and Psychotherapy: Making Sense of People's Problems,* Routledge: London.

Kakabadse, N.K., Louchart, E. & Kakabadse, A. (2006) Consultant's role: A qualitative inquiry from the consultant's perspective, *Journal of Management Development* 25(5): 416–500.

Koocher, G.P. & Keith-Spiegel, P. (1998) *Ethics in Psychology: Professional Standards and Cases,* 2nd edn, Oxford: Oxford University Press.

Loranger, A.W. (1999) *IPDE: International Personality Disorder Examination,* Lutz, FL: PAR Inc.

Marshall, W.L., Anderson, D. & Fernandez, Y. (1999) *Cognitive Behavioural Treatment of Sexual Offenders,* Chichester: John Wiley & Sons, Ltd.

Marshall, W.L. & Barbaree, H.E. (1990) An integrated theory of sexual offending, in W.L. Marshall, D.R. Laws & H.E. Barbaree (eds) *Handbook of Sexual Assault: Issues, Theories, and Treatment of the Offender,* New York: Plenum Press.

Matthews, G., Zeidner, M. & Roberts, R. (2002) *Emotional Intelligence: Science and Myth,* Cambridge, MA: MIT Press.

McGuire, J. & Priestley, P. (1995) Reviewing what works: Past, present and future, in J. McGuire (ed.) *What Works: Reducing Reoffending. Guidelines from Research and Practice,* Chichester: John Wiley and Sons, Ltd.

Megargee, E.I. (1966) Undercontrolled and overcontrolled personality types in extreme antisocial aggression, *Psychological Monographs* 80(611).

O'Brien, M.D. (2004) *HSFP (Healthy Sexual Functioning Program),* London: Correctional Services Accreditation Panel.

Ross, R. & Fabiano, E. (1991) *Reasoning and Rehabilitation: A Handbook for Teaching Cognitive Skills,* Ottawa: T3 Associates.

Ryan, R.M. & Deci, E.L. (2000) Self-determination theory and the facilitation of intrinsic motivation, social development and well-being, *American Psychologist* 55(1): 68–78.

Tarrier, N. & Calam, R. (2004) New developments in cognitive behavioural case formulation, *Behavioural and Cognitive Psychotherapy* 30: 311–28.

Tremblay, R.E. & Côté, S. (2005) The developmental origins of aggression: Where are we going?, in R.E. Tremblay, W.W. Hartup & J. Archer (eds) *Developmental Origins of Aggression,* pp. 447–64, New York: Guilford Press.

Vecchi, G.M., Van Hasselt, V.B. & Romano, S.S. (2005) Crisis (hostage) negotiation: Current strategies and issues in high-risk conflict resolution, *Aggression and Violent Behaviour* 10: 533–51.

Ward, T. (2002) Good lives and the rehabilitation of offenders: Promises and problems, *Aggression and Violent Behaviour* 7: 513–28.

Ward, T., Polaschek, D. & Beech, T. (2006) *Theories of Sex Offending*, Chichester: John Wiley and Sons, Ltd.

Webster, C.D., Douglas, K.S., Eaves, D. & Hart, S.D. (1997) *HCR-20: Assessing risk for violence (version 2)*, Burnaby, BC: Mental Health Law and Policy Institute, Simon Fraser University.

Youth Justice Board (2005) *Risk and Protective Factors*, London: Home Office.

13 Working with Child and Adult Victims

MICHELLE DAVIES

KEY WORDS

Acute Stress • Aftermath • Attitudes • Attributions • Attribution Theory • Child Sexual Abuse • Chronic Stress • Counterfactual Thinking • Cycle of Abuse • Defensive Attribution Hypothesis • Feminist • Hindsight Bias • Homophobia • Hypothetical Scenario • Just World Theory • Multiple Victimisation • Rape • Repeat Victimisation • Resilience • Routine Activities Theory (RAT) • Sexual Assault • Social Psychology • Society • Stereotypes • Trauma • Traumagenic Model • Victim Proneness • Vulnerability Hypothesis

CHAPTER OUTLINE

ROUTE MAP OF THE CHAPTER

This chapter discusses theoretical and practical issues to do with working with child and adult victims of crime. The first section describes psychological reactions of victims in the immediate aftermath of criminal victimisation. We then move on through the experiences of victims in the longer term, as they come to terms with their victimisation experience. We spend some time studying social psychological principles of recovery after crime, and issues relating to post-traumatic stress disorder. Further, in this chapter we consider how negative societal attitudes towards crime influence recovery after criminal victimisation, giving particular attention to attitudes towards rape and child sexual abuse. We explore theoretical principles in the explanation of negative attitudes towards rape and sexual assault. Finally, we consider the effects of crime on victims, when victims are victimised on more than one occasion. We investigate how some people abused as children might be vulnerable to multiple victimisation in adulthood, and how such abuse cycles might be broken by those who work with victims of crime.

Up to the mid 1970s, victimology was a small sub-field of criminology. Since the 1990s there has been a shift in focus from traditional victimological perspectives to encompass the study of victimisation in wider social contexts. This chapter aims to introduce the reader to studying victimology in the wider social context. We will consider how victims of crime are affected by social attitudes about crime and victimisation; how, for example, victims' recovery after crime can be hampered by lack of support from people who work with crime; and how many victims never tell anyone about their experiences through fear that they will be disbelieved or blamed. Indeed, many victims blame themselves for being victimised, which can have negative effects on their lives in the future. We will explore theoretical aspects of working with victims of crime, within a wide societal framework.

The theoretical underpinnings of this chapter are based on social psychological theories of attribution. We will consider how social psychological principles relate to the effects of crime, both in the immediate aftermath and later, in the longer term, as the victim comes to term with their experience. As we are exploring victimology in the wider social context, we will consider in some depth how society feels and acts towards victims of crime. We will focus on negative attitudes towards rape and sexual abuse. We will see that such negative attitudes are not only detrimental to individual victims but to society as a whole. I will ask you to consider your own attitudes towards crime in this chapter.

Finally, we will consider one aspect of victimisation that is often forgotten in the literature. Some victims are not only victimised once: they are victimised again and again in a cycle of violence called multiple victimisation. We will consider the theoretical reasons why certain people might be vulnerable to victimisation all through their life. We will finalise the chapter by considering if there is anything that psychologists can do to break this cycle of abuse.

13.1 THE EFFECTS OF CRIMINAL VICTIMISATION

13.1.1 The Immediate Aftermath of Crime

Being the witness to, or a victim of, a traumatic event leads to physiological and psychological effects on the body. Physiological reactions are similar regardless of the nature of the **trauma**. However, psychological reactions after criminal victimisation tend to be more severe than to other types of trauma. Psychological reactions include shock, numbness, denial and severe anxiety. Reactions after sexual assault are particularly bad and specific ways of reacting to victimisation can depend on whether the victim is male or female (Frazier, 1993). Negative psychological reactions to being victimised can occur even if the victim has not been threatened directly by the perpetrator. For example, Mawby and Walklate (1997) found that one third of burglary victims had severe negative reactions, even though they had not confronted the perpetrator in person (also see Mawby [2001] for a detailed discussion about burglary and its victims).

> **trauma** in psychology, the term used for a psychological injury caused by a physical or emotional shock or wound.

13.1.2 Gender Differences in Response to Rape

Frazier (1993) investigated the psychological effects of **rape** on male and female victims in the immediate **aftermath**. She recruited the help of one emergency room

> **rape** foreful and unlawful sexual intercourse with another person without their consent.

> **aftermath** later consequences of a particular incident or occurrence.

in the United States (the equivalent of the accident and emergency department in UK hospitals). Every adult who attended this emergency room who reported that they had been raped within the last three days was given the opportunity to take part in the study. If they agreed to take part, they were given a series of questionnaires to complete. These included questionnaires about depression, anxiety, hostility and anger. Frazier found significant differences in the results on some of the questionnaires. Male victims of rape were more likely to feel hostile, anxious and depressed than female victims (see Figure 13.1).

At first glance it might appear that men are more negatively affected by rape than are women. However, this might not be the case. Frazier suggested that both men and women are negatively affected by rape, but that they deal with those effects differently. Due to societal stereotyping, men are more likely to have been socialised to respond to stresses such as attacks on the person in a hostile way. They may have been socialised not to show pain, or to cry or to respond to trauma in an emotional way. In short, they are more likely than women to bottle up their emotions and become depressed. Women may have been socialised in a way that allows them to show their emotions, to cry, and thus their reactions might be to show an outward emotional reaction, rather than bottling it up. Thus, could we conclude that women recover from rape more quickly than men? No, not necessarily. The reaction of both sexes to rape tends to be very severe. Further, Frazier's study had some methodological problems. For example, there were many more females in the study than males. However, it does give an indication that gender is one issue to consider when working with victims of rape. Treatment for female victims may not necessarily work for men and men may become alienated by some treatments.

It may even be the case that men and women have different reasons for reporting rape. Pino and Meier (1999), for example, showed that men are less likely to report rape if they feel that their core self would be put into question – what we mean here is their fundamental sense of who they are, their masculinity. In a study by Walker, Archer and Davies (2005a), male rape victims were asked to talk about the effects of rape on them in their own words. One man said, 'It was a shock to find that a so called strong man could become a helpless victim at the hands of another man. My sense of who I was (ex army) was lost for about 10 years' (Walker, Archer & Davies, 2005a, p. 76). Men are not only victimised by other men. Some men are sexually assaulted by women, which in society is considered not as serious a crime as a similar offence committed by a man. However, female perpetration of sexual assault can be every bit as bad for a man. The following excerpt is a quote by a male victim who was sexually abused at the age of 14 on a number of occasions, by a 21-year-old woman.

> I was abused by a female when I was 14. She was 21 and up to that point I was a virgin. She used me for sex among other depraved acts. I'd often feel worthless and never really realised what she was doing was abusing my innocence at that age. There are often feelings that you need someone to blame and in my case I chose to blame myself for what happened . . . Ever since my experience I have been shy around females, if I want to talk to them in a personal sense and I feel it has made me think of sex as being worthless . . . and didn't really care for anyone's feelings as my own had already been shattered. (Davies & Rogers, 2004, p. 22)

This victim's testimony shows how blaming oneself can be detrimental to one's recovery, and shows why we, as psychologists working with victims, need to be aware of wider societal attitudes towards victims of crime.

13.1.3 Coming to Terms with Criminal Victimisation from a Social Psychological Perspective: Counterfactual Thinking and the Hindsight Bias

We are now going to consider from a social psychological perspective how victims come to terms with their experience. All human beings are 'programmed' to seek the causes of events, especially when those events are unusual, unexpected or traumatic. Because it is a traumatic and often unexpected experience, criminal victimisation

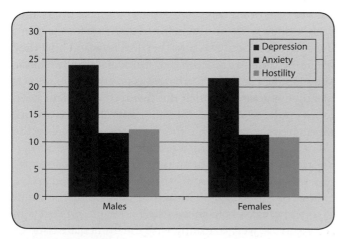

FIGURE 13.1 *Male and female victim scores on depression, anxiety and hostility.*

Source: Based on Frazier (1993), p. 71.

is the perfect type of experience to inspire us to seek its causes; that is, regardless of whether we are the actual victim of the crime, whether we are a witness to it or whether we hear about a crime from a third-party source, such as a newspaper article.

Much of the turmoil involved in coming to terms with a victimisation experience could be characterised in terms of **attribution theory**. Those working in treatment settings, such as therapists conducting cognitive therapy or crisis counselling, use the basic tenets of attribution theory in their practice. For example, working on alleviating a client's faulty thinking processes about their assault involves making judgements about what **attributions** they currently hold about the assault, which might be holding them back from reaching a more positive place in their life, and working with the client on how to change those faulty thinking patterns (see also Section 13.1.4).

> **attribution theory** an explanation of the ways in which people assess the causes of their own or the behaviour of others.

> **attributions** assessments about our own or the behaviour of others.

Attributional processes, such as counterfactual thinking, are common after victimisation (Frazier & Schauben, 1994). These types of attributions are 'if only' thoughts. We all make counterfactual judgements sometimes, even over relatively trivial matters. For example, you may forget to set your alarm clock one morning, and as a result miss the bus and consequently are late for the important examination you are sitting that day. As you realise you are late and the whole day is going to be a disaster, you may say to yourself, '*If only* I had remembered to set my alarm clock . . .' In a similar way, victims of crime may try to make sense of what has happened by using **counterfactual thinking**. A victim of burglary, for example, whose perpetrator gained entry by an unlocked window, might say, '*If only* I had remembered to lock that window, this would not have happened.'

> **counterfactual thinking** an attributional process commonly used by victims to make sense of their victimisation, it is characterised by the phrase, "If only . . . ".

Another attributional phenomenon that is used to make sense of events is what we call the **hindsight bias** (Frazier & Schauben, 1994). Thinking in hindsight how you might have prevented or avoided an event is similar in some ways to counterfactual thinking, but is more generalised. These types of attributional styles are related to self-blame. People might use these negative attributions in a way that hinders their recovery. Indeed, those who are more likely to blame themselves take longer to recover after a victimisation experience than those who are not. However, attempting to make sense

> **hindsight bias** an attributional phenomenon related to self-blame that is used to make sense of events.

of a negative event can be positive. For example, a victim might make themselves feel better by 'looking on the bright side'. This is a quote from a victim of burglary:

> Well in a way I was very much aware that it could have been much worse. So I was relived there wasn't any damage . . . They'd been in my house, they could have touched my little girl. (Mawby, 2001, p. 39)

Certain types of people have different attributional styles, which may influence the way they come to terms with events such as criminal victimisation. Those working with victims need to consider social psychological issues and how attributions might be used in coming to terms with victimisation.

13.1.4   Cognitive Therapy

Cognitive therapy deals with thinking styles and changing attributions. A cognitive therapist would set up with the client, via a number of sessions, a series of achievable goals in order to work on their issues (Resick & Schnicke, 1993). The goal of the first session would be both to lay out the course of treatment and to educate the client about issues that may be affecting them, such as post-traumatic stress disorder (see the next section) and depression. Compliance at this stage is important, as avoiding issues that the client might find painful and thus might not want to tackle is not conducive to a good treatment outcome.

Further sessions might look at the situation of the crime itself and what that means for the client. The client might be guided how to re-evaluate their perceptions of what happened to them in order for them, for example, to be less self-blaming. Identifying thoughts and feelings and re-educating the client are key issues in cognitive therapy. The therapist might set the client a series of written tasks or ask them to make notes after each session, with the aim being to discuss with the client the differences between how they feel now and how they felt at the time of the crime, or immediately afterwards. Showing the client their progress is positive in itself, as is identifying areas on which the therapist and client need to do more work. The therapist and client may work through what faulty thinking patterns are holding the client back from reaching a resolution of the issues relating to being a victim of crime. They might also work on issues such as developing trust, self-esteem and taking control over one's life. The aim of developing the client as a person is to help them gain better life prospects in the future, as well as dealing with the immediate issue of the victimisation experience.

More information about cognitive therapy is given in Chapter 15.

13.1.5 Focus on Post-Traumatic Stress Disorder (PTSD)

In this section we consider how victims of crime might be negatively affected in the longer term by considering what post-traumatic stress disorder (PTSD) is, how it is diagnosed and other negative effects that may be experienced alongside PTSD.

Several models have been forwarded to explain why people develop PTSD. Some have focused on the types of trauma that might induce PTSD, while others have investigated the symptomology involved in this disorder. No research to date fully explains why some people develop PTSD after trauma while others do not, though we may assume that multiple factors are involved in the development of PTSD (Lee & Turner, 1997).

We do know that rape is one trauma that commonly induces symptoms of PTSD (Mezey, 1997), therefore in the following section we will focus on findings from victims of that crime, and in particular on the work of Walker *et al.* (2005a).

13.1.5.1 Diagnosing PTSD

Before making a diagnosis of PTSD issues, such as the nature of the trauma, the presentation of symptoms and their duration, as well as personal, family and medical history, might be investigated (Newman & Lee, 1997).

The DSM IV indicates that PTSD may be presenting when three behavioural clusters are apparent (see also Chapter 3):

- Re-experiencing the event. This may include flashbacks, intrusive thoughts or nightmares.
- Avoidance. This can include avoiding talking about the trauma, or avoiding situations whereby they could be reminded of it.
- Generalised increased arousal or anxiety.

The use of questionnaires, such as the Impact of Events Scale (Horowitz *et al.*, 1979), or semi-structured interviewing techniques are the usual methods of investigating traumatic distress in adults or older children. Identifying the effects of trauma in very young children is extremely problematic, especially if the child is so young that they do not understand nuances of language that are necessary to facilitate diagnosis.

Diagnosing PTSD is not straightforward due to its diversity of symptomology and the number of comorbid conditions that might be apparent, which might overshadow or mask the underlying issue relating to trauma. For example, Walker *et al.* (2005a) found that over 90%

of the 40 male rape victims in their sample who showed signs of PTSD also reported depressive symptoms. In addition, 27.5% of this sample reported developing bulimia after being raped, 62.5% reported increased use of alcohol and 52.5% reported abusing drugs after their assault. All of these situations are worthy of treatment in their own right (see also Table 13.1).

Moreover, it is important to distinguish PTSD from other psychological conditions, such as obsessive

TABLE 13.1 *Long-term Effects of Rape on Male Survivors.*

Reaction	N	%
Depression	39	97.5
Fantasies about revenge and retaliation	38	95
Flashbacks of the assault	37	92.5
Feelings of anxiety	37	92.5
Loss of self-respect/damaged self-image	36	90
Increased sense of vulnerability	36	90
Emotional distancing from others	34	85
Fear of being alone with men	33	82.5
Guilt and self-blame, e.g. for not being able to prevent the assault	33	82.5
Increased anger and irritability	32	80
Low self-esteem	31	77.5
Intrusive thoughts about the assault	30	75
Withdrawal from family and friends	29	72.5
Impaired task performance	28	70
Long-term crisis with sexual identity	28	70
Damaged masculine identity	27	68
Increased use of tobacco	27	67.5
Abuse of alcohol	25	62.5
Increased security consciousness	23	57.5
Suicide ideation	22	55
Abuse of drugs	21	52.5
Self-harming behaviours	20	50
Suicide attempts	19	47.5
Eating disorders, e.g. bulimia, anorexia	11	27.5

Source: Walker, Archer & Davies (2005a), p. 75.

compulsive disorder, which may require different, specific treatments, and also to isolate organic conditions that may require medical treatment in addition to psychological intervention (Newman & Lee, 1997).

It is well known in the medical literature that chronic stress can influence physical health. This area is under-researched in psychology, though one interesting study by Britt (2001) indicates a link between criminal victimisation and negative health consequences. In this study, physical wellbeing was negatively affected by victimisation when demographics such as age and occupation were controlled for. Future work is needed in this regard to investigate its possible interaction with the development of disorders such as PTSD.

Those working with victims also need to consider that those close to the victim might also be seriously negatively affected by the event. This may be particularly the case when the victim is a child. Nonoffending parents of child victims suffer greatly, often experiencing post-traumatic stress disorder themselves. In cases involving abduction and murder, the media interest that these crimes bring can be extremely traumatic for the families of such victims. In some cases, family members may be police suspects in the case, as well as being thrust into a media spotlight that they simply do not know how to handle.

In less media-worthy cases it may still be the case that negative judgements are made about the parents and other care givers of child victims. See Focus Point 13.1.

FOCUS POINT 13.1   FAMILIES AFFECTED BY CRIME

Madeleine McCann, a 3-year-old British girl, disappeared on the evening of 3 May 2007, while on holiday with her family in the Algarve region of Portugal. She has never been found. Madeleine's parents, Kate and Gerry McCann, left Madeleine and her two younger siblings unsupervised in a ground-floor bedroom while they ate at a restaurant close by the apartment.

Source: Press Association.

The initial investigation focused on the belief that Madeleine had been abducted. It was also considered that she might have died in the apartment and the body removed. During the investigation there were a number of unconfirmed claimed sightings of Madeleine in Portugal and further afield. Kate and Gerry McCann were also named as suspects by the Portuguese police, but this line of enquiry was later dropped.

Madeleine's disappearance and the unusual circumstances whereby she was left unsupervised while her parents were socialising were scrutinised by the media. The immense publicity was initially due to the active involvement of the parents, to several awareness-raising campaigns by international celebrities, and later to Kate and Gerry being named as suspects. Kate and Gerry were criticised heavily by the press because they left their children alone. This was seen as a causal factor in Madeleine's disappearance, which elicited blame attributions towards them because it is generally considered to be the role of parents to protect their children. We may also see negative attributions elicited to the nonoffending parents of other types of crime, such as child sexual abuse.

Source: Press Association.

High-profile, very unusual events such as the McCann case highlight the way in which the media deals with crime, and also can illustrate how people think about crime generally. When a crime is committed against a child, it is often the parents who take at least some of the blame. However, we must also consider how parents are seriously and negatively affected when their child becomes a victim of crime.

One way in which parents might deal with crime that affects their children is to become an active supporter of campaigns that seek to protect children. For example, Sara Payne, the mother of 8-year-old Sarah who was abducted and murdered in 2000, has campaigned heavily for children's rights since her daughter's death and has now been awarded an MBE for her work.

13.2 ATTITUDES TOWARDS CRIME

Many people who have been criminally victimised do not tell anyone about their experience. Many suffer in silence, never reporting their experience to the police, medical or psychological services, or even friends and family, out of fear that they will not be believed or will be blamed, or because they feel ashamed about what happened to them. We shall see in this section how detrimental not receiving the appropriate help can be to victims. Not reporting crime means that many perpetrators go unpunished, even for very serious crimes such as rape (Davies, 2002). Rape and **sexual assault** are crimes that victims are particularly not likely to report to officials such as the police (Temkin & Krahe, 2008). Central to explaining what Temkin and Krahe called the 'justice gap' is the fact that negative societal **attitudes** about rape, rape victims and rapists affect those who are involved at every stage of the justice process.

When confronted with an account of rape, people tend to look at it from a backdrop of their own personal beliefs and **stereotypes**, as we see next.

sexual assault an indecent attack, attempted rape or rape.

attitudes a hypothetical construct with three components: cognition, affect and behaviour.

stereotypes fixed and often simplistic generalisations about particular groups or classes of people.

13.2.1 How Do Societal Attitudes towards Crime Influence Recovery and Reporting?

Researchers believe that negative attitudes about rape contribute to the special difficulties that victims have in coming to terms with this crime. **Society** endorses negative attitudes about both female and male rape victims. Many victims endorse these negative attitudes and use them to make negative judgements about themselves. They may blame themselves for what has happened; if they do, it is likely that they will take longer to recover than those who do not blame themselves. In a study of 40 adult male rape victims recruited from the UK general public, Walker, Archer and Davies (2005b) found that when compared to a control group of non-raped men, who were matched closely on demographic variables such as age, ethnicity, sexuality and educational

society a term that is often used to mean the collective citizenry of the country in which a person lives.

level, men who had been raped in the past were more likely to suffer from depression, anxiety and other psychological disorders as much as 10 years after their assault. Nearly half had never received help from psychological services. Those who did receive help were less likely to attempt suicide, showing how important seeking psychological help can be. It is very important for those working with victims to remember this and make their service as available as possible to victims, because not receiving help can literally be a matter of life and death.

Some men in Walker *et al.*'s study reported that they did not seek help because they felt that they would be negatively evaluated. Only 5 out of the 40 men had reported their rape to the police, and only one of these cases resulted in a conviction. However, there is good news. Recent changes in police training may have influenced police officers to endorse more positive views about victims. If this is the case, victims in future will receive better treatment. Davies, Smith and Rogers (2009), in a sample of UK police officers, found that these workers were not negative to victims, regardless of their gender or sexuality. The effects found in this study were much more positive than people in the general public.

So, why are people negative towards rape victims? We will consider this issue next.

13.2.2 Why Does Society Think Badly of Rape Victims?

In the 1970s, **feminist** researchers such as Brownmiller (1975) theorised that negative societal attitudes about women were the reason that people were negative towards rape victims. These ideas were tested empirically through the 1980s, beginning with the hugely influential work of Martha Burt. Burt (1980) coined the term *rape myth*. She conceptualised rape myths as prejudicial and false beliefs that people hold about rape, rape victims and rapists. These negative beliefs about rape correlate with other negative attitudes about women, such as the endorsement of violence against women. Basically, if someone has negative views about women they are also negative about rape. These findings therefore support the feminist view that negative attitudes about rape are influenced by general negative attitudes about women.

Further investigation by Lonsway and Fitzgerald (1995) showed that both men and women accept myths about rape, but do so for different reasons. Men endorse rape myths because they feel hostile towards women. However, women endorse rape myths because they want to deny their own vulnerability to rape; they want

feminist an advocate for women's social, economic and legal equality with men.

to be negative towards people who are raped because they do not like to think about themselves becoming a victim. Consider Activity Box 13.1 to explore your own feelings about crime.

Although feminists have done much to aid the understanding of how rape victims are viewed, their theoretical principles did not allow for the consideration of male victims. Indeed, it was estimated by Rogers (1998) that help, support and understanding towards male rape victims were 20 years behind those of female victims. Fortunately, in recent years a flurry of research into the experience, effects of and attitudes towards male rape has made this subject much less of a taboo. A number of empirical studies have been conducted to investigate how people think and feel about male rape. For example,

Davies, Pollard and Archer (2001) asked participants to read a short story that depicted rape. Two variables – victim gender and victim sexual orientation – were varied between subjects. Participants were then asked to complete a series of questions about the story, which focused on how much they thought the victim was to blame for the rape and how serious they thought the assault was. Results showed that female participants did not blame the victim, and they thought that the assault was very serious, regardless of the victim's gender or sexual orientation. Male participants' responses were, however, influenced by both the victim's gender and sexual orientation. In short, men were more blaming and considered the assault to be less serious when the victim was depicted as a gay male.

ACTIVITY BOX 13.1

When social psychologists investigate how people think and feel about crime, they often use the hypothetical scenario paradigm. That is, they present participants with a hypothetical story that depicts a criminal event. They then get participants to answer questions about how they think and feel about this incident.

Read the following depiction of a rape scene and consider the questions that follow.

> Sarah is a 21-year-old student, in the final year of her English degree. She lives with her boyfriend near the university. She works several evenings a week at the local leisure centre. At weekends she enjoys going to pubs and the cinema. She is also an active member of the university drama society and is a member of the squash club.
>
> After finishing at work Sarah made her way to her car that was parked in the nearby car park. The surrounding streets were quiet, but as Sarah walked through the car park towards her car a man approached her and asked her for a light. As Sarah reached into her pocket the man suddenly grabbed her by the arm, pushing her roughly towards the bushes at the darkened rear of the car park. Sarah at first resisted, but the man told her threateningly that she would be very sorry if she did not do what she was told. Sarah was very scared as the man forced her to the ground. Still issuing threats, the man then raped her. Afterwards the man ran away, leaving Sarah on the ground, bruised and shaken. (Adapted from Davies, Pollard & Archer [2001], p. 619)

Think about how you felt when you read that story. Were there aspects of it that you identified with? For instance you may be of the same gender as Sarah, or you may be a student who works evenings and has to go home alone in the dark. Do you think that identifying with the person in the story makes you more likely to think negatively about them for what happened, or less?

Take a few moments to consider those issues. Perhaps you could write a few notes about how you feel about the victim in this story.

Now consider the following questions about Sarah (adapted from Davies, Pollard & Archer [2001], p. 611):

- Do you think Sarah can be blamed for not putting up enough of a fight?
- Do you think Sarah can be blamed because she did not try hard enough to escape?
- How much do you think Sarah's behaviour was to blame for the attack?

These questions ask about how blameworthy the victim could be considered to be. They particularly focus on how the victim's behaviour (or lack thereof) could be considered blameworthy. Sometimes participants' blame judgements differ when the victim is portrayed as male versus when the victim is portrayed as female. Look at the story again, but this time imagine how you would have felt about the victim if he had been a man called Steve, rather than a woman called Sarah. Do you think your feelings would be different if you had read a story about a male victim? Take a few moments to consider this issue.

Davies, Polland and Archer's (2001) finding that rape victims are more negatively evaluated when depicted as a gay male has been replicated several times, and is now considered a robust finding (see Davies & Rogers [2006] for a detailed review). Next we will explore what theories have been developed to explain blame towards rape victims.

13.2.2.1 Is blaming male victims all about homophobia?

Is it the homosexual (albeit nonconsensual) nature of male rape that makes people who endorse homophobic attributions negative towards male rape victims? There are various lines of enquiry we can use to investigate this question.

Heterosexual men, on average, are more homophobic than women (Davies, 2004) and as we know that men are more blaming than women, we can suppose that this is because they are more homophobic. However, even the most homophobic men do not blame male victims who are clearly portrayed as heterosexual. Burt and DeMello (2002) found that homophobic participants attributed more blame to gay male victims than towards heterosexual victims.

This research pertains to heterosexual men's judgements towards male rape victims. Davies & McCartney (2003) furthered this work and investigated gay men's judgements towards male rape. Gay men may perceive themselves as more similar to a gay male rape victim than heterosexual men do, thus, in line with Shaver's (1970) defensive attribution hypothesis (as we will see shortly), should not blame him. It could also be that gay men are more aware of male rape issues than heterosexual men are. Thus, they should not resort to using false beliefs about male rape in order to make negative attributions about a victim. Davies and McCartney found that only heterosexual men in a general population sample of young people in Manchester, England blamed a gay male rape victim or endorsed myths about male rape. Gay men and heterosexual women did not express negative views about the victim.

homophobia fear and/ or a strong dislike of homosexual men.

We can conclude that **homophobia** does influence how people react towards gay male rape victims, though we need to know more about this issue in order to be able to combat it. We next look at more general motivations that people have to attribute blame to victims.

13.2.2.2 Motivational theories of victim blame

Motivational theories assert that people blame victims for two basic reasons: to maintain control over their environment, and to maintain self-esteem. Two theories have emerged in the literature on victim blame: the **defensive attribution hypothesis** (Shaver, 1970) and the **just world theory** (Lerner, 1980).

13.2.2.2.1 Defensive attribution hypothesis Shaver's (1970) defensive attribution hypothesis emphasised the role of 'relevance'. Relevance is perceived by the observer when they can perceive personal similarities with the victim (e.g. perceived similarities in personality, attitudes, age, gender etc.) or situational similarities (that one day the observer might be in the same situation as the victim). When sufficient relevance exists, the observer is motivated to engage in defensive attributions to deny the possibility of the same fate happening to them.

Studies have investigated the defensive attribution hypothesis in relation to gender differences in blame towards rape victims. For example, Fulero and Delara (1976) in a student sample manipulated the type of rape victim – student victim (similar victim) or 45-year-old housewife (dissimilar victim) – and rated attributions of responsibility towards these victims. Results showed that the type of victim did not affect the responsibility ratings of males (their scores were relatively low in both conditions), but the type of victim did affect the females' ratings. The victim seen as most similar to the observer (the student) was assigned less responsibility than the dissimilar victim (the housewife).

In relation to perceptions of male rape, the defensive attribution hypothesis predicts that if the male observer can see personal similarities between himself and the victim, he should attribute no blame to the victim. Perhaps this is one reason why heterosexual men do not blame heterosexual male victims, and why gay men do not blame gay male victims? This research is still ongoing and we do not have definitive answers to these questions yet.

13.2.2.2.2 Just world theory The basic assumption of the just world theory is that individuals are motivated to believe that the world is a fair and just place (Lerner, 1980). When a bad event occurs, to maintain their belief in the just world people are motivated to believe that the victim must have done something to deserve it.

Although numerous studies have investigated just world principles in relation to how people blame rape victims, doubts have been cast on the usefulness of the just world theory as a sole explanation of victim blame. Evidence suggests that the just world theory is part of a broader construct of attributional defences (Muller, Caldwell & Hunter, 1995). Muller, Caldwell and Hunter found that

defensive attribution hypothesis a motivational theory of victim blame in which the role of relevance is emphasised.

just world theory a belief that individuals are motivated to believe that the world is a fair and just place.

when the defensive attribution hypothesis was compared with the just world theory, no variance was explained by the just world theory and it appeared to be completely subsumed by the defensive attribution hypothesis.

13.2.3 Attitudes towards Child Sexual Abuse

child sexual abuse abuse of a child by an adult or older adolescent for sexual stimulation.

Child sexual abuse (CSA) has generated much public and media interest in recent years. It is difficult to believe that negative societal attitudes about victims would be used in order to make negative evaluations about CSA cases. Unfortunately, studies have shown that in some situations child victims are indeed negatively evaluated after being sexually victimised.

The age of the victim influences attributions towards the victim, perpetrator and nonoffending family members in CSA cases. Because children are generally considered to be sexually naïve, the younger the child, the more trustworthy a child's account of CSA is deemed to be (Bottoms & Goodman, 1994). Bottoms and Goodman found support for this assumption in a series of **hypothetical scenario** studies depicting sexual abuse victims of various ages. A victim depicted as a young child (aged 6 years) was seen as a more credible witness to a sexual assault than an older child (aged 14) or an adult victim (aged 22). Other studies have shown that in cases where the child is approaching adulthood, they may be attributed some responsibility in all the same ways and for the same reasons that adult victims are (Back & Lips, 1998; Rogers & Davies, 2007).

hypothetical scenario a tool used by social psychologists to investigate how people think and feel about something by presenting participants with a hypothetical story and asking them how they think and feel about the contents of the story.

13.2.4 Evaluation

Although several theoretical perspectives have been proffered as sole explanations of why people negatively evaluate victims, it is perhaps more useful to consider victim blame as being influenced by multiple psychological processes. Crome and McCabe (2001), for example, considered victim blame to be a product of attributional processes, motivational biases and stereotypes about male and female rape victims. We need to consider all of these factors when assessing how victims might be evaluated.

Regardless of the theoretical reasons for such negative evaluations, it is important for those working with victims to be aware that they may have been subject to victim blaming judgements or other negative evaluations by those to whom they may have disclosed in the past. It is important for those working with victims to understand that certain types of victim may have been subject to very negative and very specific attributions just because of the person they are. It is also important for those working with victims to remember that even some children are subject to negative evaluations. Further work is needed to consider how the negative evaluation of victims should be reduced in future.

See also Focus Point 13.2, which details how the media views rape.

13.3 REPEAT AND MULTIPLE VICTIMISATION

In this next section we consider why it is that some people seem to be more vulnerable to becoming a victim of crime than others. We go on to consider how psychologists might attempt to break this **cycle of abuse**.

cycle of abuse a term with a variety of meanings including multiple victimisation whereby an individual is victimised again and again throughout his or her life.

13.3.1 The Victim-Prone Person?

Cohen and Felson (1979) theorised that criminal victimisation is not randomly distributed in society. They argued, for example, that certain routine activities in which people engage make them more vulnerable to becoming victims. They formulated the **routine activities theory (RAT)** based on this premise, and theorised that proneness to victimisation occurs in the presence of the following three factors:

routine activities theory (RAT) the theory that certain routine activities engaged in by people make them more vulnerable to becoming victims.

- Exposure to motivated offenders.
- Suitability as a target.
- Lack of adequate guardianship.

A major advantage of this theory is that it can be applied to many different types of criminal situation. However, it must be considered that the term **victim proneness** is

victim proneness a somewhat controversial term that suggests that some people are more prone than others to victimisation.

FOCUS POINT 13.2   MEDIA PERCEPTIONS OF RAPE

A survey conducted for the Havens service (a sexual assault referral centre) hit the national headlines in the United Kingdom on 15 February 2010 because of its findings regarding rape. Although the report covered issues relating to other crimes than rape, it was the findings regarding how people think and feel about rape on which the press seemed to focus. For example, over half of participants said that if someone had gone to bed with a person who went on to rape them, the victim should take some responsibility. Although findings like this have been discussed by academics for many years, it is noteworthy that the media considers findings such as these particularly interesting. It is also noteworthy that despite many years of academic study on the subject, the views of the general population tend to remain negative.

It is also the case that many rape victims blame themselves for what happened. Women might blame themselves and other rape victims for not following 'the rules' – don't go out alone at night, don't get too drunk, don't wear anything too revealing and don't flirt too much – that way, they can stay safe from becoming victims (or becoming a victim again, if it has already happened once).

Most women are told how to avoid sexual assault from the time they start going through puberty (if not sooner), in ways that men are not. Women might be cautious about how they dress, may monitor their drinks more than men, may be more likely not to go out alone at night and so on. This of course has implications for women's freedom, but also for the safety of men, who may also be at risk of crime.

Many women reason, sometimes unconsciously, that if rape victims have done something 'wrong' that makes them responsible, they themselves are protected. If rape victims are viewed as stupid and irresponsible, every woman who thinks of herself as smart and level-headed is reassured that she won't become a victim. Indeed, rape is often one of a woman's biggest fears. And if they are raped, many women are sure that they would not report it out of a fear of negative reactions from the police.

Here are a couple of quotes from women from the Havens survey (p. 6) as they talk about whether or not they would report rape:

> I would be afraid of being demoralised by the police and society during court proceedings, why bother when they are just going to get off the charges anyway?
>
> I am not sure whether I would be taken seriously and the follow through procedure would be thorough.

As psychologists working with forensic issues, we must be very aware of how the general public thinks and feels about crimes like rape, how forensic services like the police are viewed and how the media portrays such issues. As academics, even if we work with victims on a regular basis, it is sometimes difficult to see issues as people generally do. Nevertheless, we must remember that it is the views of the many that may have negatively influenced how victims react to their victimisation.

---

somewhat controversial, in that considering someone as prone to crime could be seen as making them responsible for it. This is not the intention of this research, but it is a subject of study that must be handled very sensitively. The fact is that some people are more prone to victimisation than others, and we seek to investigate the theoretical reasons for this next.

13.3.2   Theories of Multiple Victimisation – from Child to Adult Victimisation

For some crimes being re-victimised by the same perpetrator is common, for example domestic violence and child sexual abuse, as these may be situations where the victim may not be able to remove themselves from the victimising

situation. Being re-victimised by the same perpetrator is known as **repeat victimisation**. However, further to this situation, some victims appear to be prone to **multiple victimisation**, which is where an individual is victimised on more than one occasion by different perpetrators over a period of time. In some situations an individual is abused as a child and then goes on to be re-victimised as an adult, and in these cases it appears that the individual has become a vulnerable person prone to victimisation.

Finkelhor and Browne (1985) developed the **traumagenic model** of sexual re-victimisation to explain

repeat victimisation
the term for the process whereby a person is re-victimised by the same perpetrator.

multiple victimisation
the term for the process in which an individual is victimised on more than one occasion by different perpetrators over a period of time.

traumagenic model a model of sexual re-victimisation explaining how some child victims become further victimised in adulthood.

how some child victims go on to become victims of further victimisation in adulthood. This model highlights that the negative effects of child abuse, which can include traumatic sexualisation, betrayal, powerlessness and the stigma of being a victim of abuse, make them psychologically vulnerable to other victimisation experiences as they grow up. For example, feelings of stigmatisation predict low self-esteem and suicide ideation, and powerlessness predicts depression, dissociation and somatic complaints. Such vulnerability may then create situations where further victimisation occurs in the future.

Although the traumagenic model is a good starting point for understanding multiple victimisation, it has been criticised by various sources. For example, Arata (2000) found only partial support for the traumagenic model, when considered alongside another model of multiple victimisation, the **vulnerability hypothesis** (Koss & DeNiro, 1989; see Arata [2000] for a detailed discussion). The traumagenic model is also problematic when considering *resilient* victims. Resilient victims are those who do not appear to suffer greatly after abuse. They may not, for example, show severe negative effects, such as depression, anxiety or **acute stress**. They do not go on to suffer from PTSD and do not appear to be vulnerable to future abuse (see Boardman & Davies [2009] for a further discussion). Resilient victims are particularly difficult for those working with victims to treat, in part because they tend not to come forward for treatment, but also because they report no or few negative effects. However, theoretically speaking, resilient victims may be the key to understanding how the cycle of abuse that some people appear to experience may be broken, which is why it is particularly important for anyone working in this area to be aware of them. We consider this issue in the final section of this chapter.

vulnerability hypothesis a model of multiple victimisation.

acute stress an urgent and usually distressing bodily response to 'fight or flight' situations to prepare the body to respond appropriately to help ensure survival.

13.3.3   *Breaking the Cycle of Abuse*

Researchers have investigated a variety of individual differences that may protect resilient victims against the development of negative symptomology after being victimised. Factors such as high self-esteem, effective coping strategies and positive disclosure have been implicated as promoting positive outcomes in children following sexual abuse (Collishaw *et al.*, 2007; Hershkowitz, Lanes &

Lamb, 2007). Other studies aiming to explain the variance in symptomology after child sexual abuse have focused on variables related to the abuse, such as severity and type of abuse, duration of abuse, age of onset of abuse, and the effect these variables had on future mental health. Spaccarelli (1994) suggested that no one model can predict negative symptomology after child sexual abuse and no sole factor can predict **resilience**.

resilience the ability to withstand and recover from harmful experiences.

As a result of the variety of avenues of research, it is perhaps best to view symptom expression and the chances of a positive outcome after victimisation as unique to each victim and the individuating circumstances of the victimisation experience. A wide range of individual, environmental and abuse factors could influence whether the victim recovers well, or not, after their victimisation experience. For those working with victims, it is important to consider the factors that may make them vulnerable to future abuse, perhaps by working on issues such as developing effective coping strategies, increasing self-esteem and reducing symptoms of depression. With both child and adult victims, it is also important to consider the victim's personal circumstances and family environment in order to increase the support that could be made available through this route. It is furthermore important to consider that those close to the victim, such as partners, parents or other family members, could also be experiencing negative effects as a result of the victimisation experience, even though they were not an actual victim of crime. Research indicates that family members of victimised people can suffer from both acute and **chronic stress**, and even go on to develop symptoms of PTSD. Therefore it is important for those working with victims not to see family members as a support service for the victim, but to consider them as worthy of support in their own right. Many support services in the United Kingdom now offer independent help to family members of victims for this reason.

chronic stress a long-term, ongoing bodily response to 'fight or flight' situations to prepare the body to respond appropriately to help ensure survival.

To conclude this chapter, we should note that considering criminal victimisation in a wide social context shows us that issues relating to victimisation are very complex, encompassing many psychological and societal factors. It is important for those working with victims to take a broad theoretical stance in understanding the effects of victimisation, and to take into account the wide range of factors that will affect the possibility of a positive outcome for each individual.

SELF-TEST QUESTIONS

- What kinds of psychological effects can occur in the immediate aftermath of criminal victimisation?
- How are social psychological principles important when investigating how victims might be affected by crime?
- Can you describe how victims use counterfactual thinking and hindsight biases when coming to terms with their victimisation experience?
- Can you describe the diagnosis of post-traumatic stress disorder?
- Can you explain what the difficulties might be of diagnosing someone presenting with symptoms of post-traumatic stress disorder?
- Can you explain how victim-blaming attributions can negatively affect the recovery of victims?
- Can you discuss how people might use negative stereotypes to think badly about victims of rape?
- How have psychologists explained why some men blame male rape victims more than women do?
- Can you describe and evaluate two motivation theories of victim blame?
- Can you discuss what factors have been shown to influence judgements about child sexual abuse victims?
- Can you define the concepts of repeat and multiple victimisation?
- Can you discuss the three factors implicated in routine activities theory?
- Can you critically evaluate the traumagenic model and explain how it might contribute to the cycle of abuse?
- How must psychologists consider multiple victimisation when working with victims?
- What can psychologists do to stop the cycle of abuse?

ESSAY QUESTIONS

(These bullet points can also be used by the teacher or instructor to lead class discussion on victimological issues.)

- Are factors relating to gender stereotypes relevant to understanding gender differences in effects of rape?
- How can those working with victims utilise social psychological principles as effective treatments?
- How does diagnosing post-traumatic stress disorder present problems to the psychologist?
- What factors could extend the work on victim blame to understand negative reactions to victims?
- How might psychologists work to reduce negative societal attitudes towards victims?
- How might investigation of attitudes towards victims be improved?
- How might the effects of multiple victimisation differ from the effects of one sole victimisation experience?
- How might vulnerability to crime differ across individuals or situations?
- What additional factors should psychologists consider when researching the cycle of abuse?

TEXTS FOR FURTHER READING

Abdullah-Khan, N. (2008) *Male Rape: The Emergence of a Social and Legal Issue*, London: Palgrave Macmillan.
Corby, B. (2006) *Child Abuse: Towards a Knowledge Base*, 3rd edn, Milton Keynes: Open University Press.

Fergusson, D.M. & Mullen, P.E. (1999) *Childhood Sexual Abuse: An Empirical Based Perspective*, Thousand Oaks, CA: Sage.

Goodey, J. (2005) *Victimology: Research, Policy and Practice*, London: Pearson.

Kernshall, H. & Pritchard, J. (2000) *Good Practice in Working with Victims of Violence*, London: Jessica Kingsley.

Mawby, R.I. (2001) *Burglary*, Abingdon: Willan.

Petrak, J. & Hedge, B. (2002) *The Trauma of Sexual Assault: Treatment, Prevention, and Practice*, Chichester: John Wiley & Sons, Ltd.

Resick, P.A. & Schnicke, M.K. (1993) *Cognitive Processing Therapy for Rape Victims*, London: Sage.

Temkin, J. & Krahe, B. (2008) *Sexual Assault and the Justice Gap: A Question of Attitude*, Oxford: Hart.

Walklate, S. (2007) *Handbook of Victims and Victimology*, Abingdon: Willan.

Williams, B. (2005) *Victims of Crime and Community Justice*, London: Jessica Kingsley.

RELEVANT JOURNAL ARTICLES

Arata, C.M. (2000) From child victim to adult victim: A model for predicting sexual revictimisation, *Child Maltreatment* 5: 28–38.

Collishaw, S., Pickles, A., Messer, J., Rutter, M., Shearer, C. & Maughan, B. (2007) Resilience to adult psychopathology following childhood maltreatment: Evidence from a community sample, *Child Abuse and Neglect* 31: 211–29.

Crome, S.A. & McCabe, M.P. (2001) Adult rape scripting within a victimological perspective, *Aggression and Violent Behavior* 6: 395–413.

Davies, M. & Rogers, R. (2006) Perceptions of male victims in depicted sexual assaults: A review of the literature, *Aggression and Violent Behavior* 11: 367–77.

Frazier, P. & Schauben, L. (1994) Causal attributions and recovery from rape and other stressful life events, *Journal of Social and Clinical Psychology* 13: 1–14.

Frazier, P.A. (1993) A comparative study of male and female rape victims seen at a hospital based rape crisis program, *Journal of Interpersonal Violence* 8: 64–76.

Pino, N.W. & Meier, R.F. (1999) Gender differences in rape reporting, *Sex Roles* 40: 979–90.

Shaver, K.G. (1970) Defensive attributions: Effects of severity and relevance on the responsibility assigned for an accident, *Journal of Personality and Social Psychology* 14: 101–13.

Spaccarelli, S. (1994) Stress, appraisal and coping in child sexual abuse: A theoretical and empirical review, *Psychological Bulletin* 116: 340–62.

Walker, J., Archer, J. & Davies, M. (2005a) Effects of rape on male survivors: A descriptive analysis, *Archives of Sexual Behavior* 34: 69–80.

Walker, J., Archer, J. & Davies, M. (2005b) Effects of male rape on psychological functioning, *British Journal of Clinical Psychology* 44: 445–51.

REFERENCES

Arata, C.M. (2000) From child victim to adult victim: A model for predicting sexual revictimisation, *Child Maltreatment* 5: 28–38.

Back, S. & Lips, H.M. (1998) Child sexual abuse: Victim age, victim gender, and observer gender as factors contributing to attributions of responsibility, *Child Abuse & Neglect* 22: 1239–52.

Boardman, M. & Davies, M. (2009) Asymptomatic victims of child sexual abuse: A critical review, *Forensic Update*, 99: 6–12.

Bottoms, B.L. & Goodman, G.S. (1994) Perceptions of children's credibility in sexual assault cases, *Journal of Applied Social Psychology* 24: 702–32.

Britt, C.L. (2001) Health consequences of criminal victimisation, *International Review of Victimology* 8: 63–73.

Brownmiller, S. (1975) *Against Our Will: Men, Women and Rape*, Toronto: Bantam.

Burt, D.L. & DeMello, L.R. (2002) Attributions of rape blame as a function of victim gender and sexuality, and perceived similarity to the victim, *Journal of Homosexuality* 43: 39–57.

Burt, M. (1980) Cultural myths and support for rape, *Journal of Personality and Social Psychology* 38: 217–30.

Cohen, L.E. & Felson, M. (1979) Social change and crime rate trends: A routine activity approach, *American Sociological Review* 44: 588–608.

Collishaw, S., Pickles, A., Messer, J., Rutter, M., Shearer, C. & Maughan, B. (2007) Resilience to adult psychopathology following childhood maltreatment: Evidence from a community sample, *Child Abuse and Neglect* 31: 211–29.

Crome, S.A. & McCabe, M.P. (2001) Adult rape scripting within a victimological perspective, *Aggression and Violent Behavior* 6: 395–413.

Davies, M. (2002) Male sexual assault victims: A selective review of the literature and implications for support services, *Aggression and Violent Behavior* 7: 203–14.

Davies, M. (2004) Correlates of negative attitudes towards gay men: Sexism, male role norms and male sexuality, *Journal of Sex Research* 41: 259–66.

Davies, M. & McCartney, S. (2003) Effects of gender and sexuality on judgements of victim blame and rape myth acceptance in a depicted male rape, *Journal of Community and Applied Social Psychology* 13: 391–8.

Davies, M., Pollard, P. & Archer, J. (2001) The influence of victim gender and sexual orientation on judgements of the victim in a depicted stranger rape, *Violence and Victims* 16: 607–19.

Davies, M. & Rogers, P. (2004) Attributions towards the victim and perpetrator in a child sexual abuse case: Roles of participant, perpetrator and victim gender, *Forensic Update* 79: 17–24.

Davies, M. & Rogers, R. (2006) Perceptions of male victims in depicted sexual assaults: A review of the literature, *Aggression and Violent Behavior* 11: 367–77.

Davies, M., Smith, R. & Rogers, P. (2009) Police perceptions of rape as a function of victim gender and sexuality, *The Police Journal,* 82: 4–12.

Finkelhor, D. & Browne, A. (1985) The traumatic impact of child sexual abuse: A conceptualization, *Journal of Orthopsychiatry* 55: 530–41.

Frazier, P.A. (1993) A comparative study of male and female rape victims seen at a hospital based rape crisis program, *Journal of Interpersonal Violence* 8: 64–76.

Frazier, P. & Schauben, L. (1994) Causal attributions and recovery from rape and other stressful life events, *Journal of Social and Clinical Psychology* 13: 1–14.

Fulero, S.M. & Delara, C. (1976) Rape victims and attributed responsibility: A defensive attribution approach, *Victimology* 1: 551–63.

Hershkowitz, I., Lanes, O. & Lamb, M. (2007) Exploring the disclosure of child sexual abuse with alleged victims and their parents, *Child Abuse & Neglect* 31: 111–23.

Horowitz, M.J., Wilner, N. & Alvarez, W. (1979) Impact of Events Scale: A measure of subjective stress, *Psychosomatic Medicine* 41: 209–18.

Koss, M.P. & Dinero, T. (1989) Discriminant analysis of risk factors for sexual victimization among a national sample of college women, *Journal of Consulting and Clinical Psychology* 57: 242–50.

Lee, D. & Turner, S. (1997) Cognitive behavioural models of PTSD, in D. Black, M. Newman, J. Harris-Hendriks & G. Mezey (eds) *Psychological Trauma: A Developmental Approach*, London: Royal College of Psychiatrists.

Lerner, M. (1980) *The Belief in a Just World: The Fundamental Delusion*, London: Plenum Press.

Lonsway, K.A. & Fitzgerald, L.F. (1995) Attitudinal antecedents of rape myth acceptance: A theoretical and empirical re-examination, *Journal of Personality and Social Psychology* 68: 704–11.

Mawby, R.I. (2001) *Burglary*, Abingdon: Willan.

Mawby, R.I. & Walklate, S. (1997) The impact of burglary: A tale of two cities, *International Review of Victimology* 4: 267–95.

Mezey, G. (1997) Psychological responses to interpersonal violence, in D. Black, M. Newman, J. Harris-Hendriks & G. Mezey (eds) *Psychological Trauma: A Developmental Approach*, London: Royal College of Psychiatrists.

Muller, R.T., Caldwell, R.A. & Hunter, J.E. (1995) The construct dimensionality of victim blame: The situations of physical child abuse and rape, *Personality and Individual Differences* 19: 21–31.

Newman, M. & Lee, D. (1997) Diagnosis and treatment, in D. Black, M. Newman, J. Harris-Hendriks & G. Mezey (eds) *Psychological Trauma: A Developmental Approach*, London: Royal College of Psychiatrists.

Pino, N.W. & Meier, R.F. (1999) Gender differences in rape reporting, *Sex Roles* 40: 979–90.

Pollard, P. (1992) Judgements about victims and attackers in depicted rapes: A review, *British Journal of Social Psychology* 31: 309–26.

Resick, P.A. & Schnicke, M.K. (1993) *Cognitive Processing Therapy for Sexual Assault Victims: A Treatment Manual*, Newbury Park, CA: Sage.

Rogers, P. (1998) Call for research into male rape, *Mental Health Practice* 1: 9–34.

Rogers, P. & Davies, M. (2007) Perceptions of victims and perpetrators in a depicted child sexual abuse case, *Journal of Interpersonal Violence* 22: 566–84.

Shaver, K.G. (1970) Defensive attributions: Effects of severity and relevance on the responsibility assigned for an accident, *Journal of Personality and Social Psychology* 14: 101–13.

Spaccarelli, S. (1994) Stress, appraisal and coping in child sexual abuse: A theoretical and empirical review, *Psychological Bulletin* 116: 340–62.

Temkin, J. & Krahe, B. (2008) *Sexual Assault and the Justice Gap: A Question of Attitude*, Oxford: Hart.

Walker, J., Archer, J. & Davies, M. (2005a) Effects of rape on male survivors: A descriptive analysis, *Archives of Sexual Behavior* 34: 69–80.

Walker, J., Archer, J. & Davies, M. (2005b) Effects of male rape on psychological functioning, *British Journal of Clinical Psychology* 44: 445–51.

14 Eyewitnesses and the Use and Application of Cognitive Theory

CHARLIE FROWD

LEARNING OUTCOMES

WHEN YOU HAVE COMPLETED THIS CHAPTER YOU SHOULD BE ABLE TO:

1. Explain how good we are at describing unfamiliar people, objects and events.

2. Describe what the main differences are between familiar and unfamiliar face recognition, and how this relates to eyewitness memory.

3. Describe how effective facial composites are and what can be done to improve their effectiveness.

4. Outline why eyewitness evidence can be unreliable.

5. List the main techniques used in the enhanced cognitive interview.

KEY WORDS

Caricatured Composite ● Cognitive Interview (CI) ● Context ● Conversational Management (CM) ● Cued Recall ● Description–Identification Relationship ● E-FIT-V ● Encode ● Enhanced Cognitive Interview (ECI) ● EvoFIT ● External Facial Features ● Eyewitness ● Facial Composite ● Facial Configuration ● False Memory ● Familiar Face Recognition ● Feature Composite Systems ● Free Recall ● Group Identification ● Hair ● Holistic Cognitive Interview ● Identification Parade ● Individual Facial Features ● Internal Facial Features ● Line-up ● Memory ● Miscarriages of Justice ● Mock Witness Paradigm ● Morphed Composite ● PEACE Interview ● Person Descriptions ● Photofit ● PRO-fit ● Picture Matching ● Prototype ● Rapport Building ● Recall ● Recognition ● Reinstating the Context ● Repeated Recall ● Report Everything ● Retrograde Amnesia ● Sequential Line-up ● Simultaneous Line-up ● Sketch Artist ● Standard Interview ● Structural Code ● Suspect ● Unfamiliar Face Recognition ● Victim ● Video Identification ● VIPER (Video Identification Parade Electronic Recording) ● Weapon Focus ● Witness

CHAPTER OUTLINE

14.4   SUMMARY: EVIDENCE AND EYEWITNESSES

Evidence collected from eyewitnesses is just one of many different sources available in a criminal investigation. Criminals may unknowingly leave their DNA at a crime scene, having touched objects and left fingerprints; even fibres from clothing may fall and be collected for analysis. These sources may also produce false leads, since we naturally leave behind such physical materials: hairs fall off, we make footprints and CCTV cameras record our presence. As with the case of Laszlo Virag and others, any one piece of evidence is not sufficiently reliable as a basis on which to convict. The Crown Prosecution Service in the United Kingdom is acutely aware of this issue and will not allow a case to be brought before the courts if it is based on insufficient or potentially unreliable evidence.

In spite of the unreliable nature of human memory, eyewitnesses can be very valuable to a police investigation. There are many situations where they are the only observers, and so their memory of what happened is of importance. Each of our senses produces memories that are potentially valuable, even personal feelings. Eyewitnesses can provide a range of evidence to assist in an investigation. They can provide descriptions of events and people, take part in identification procedures and construct a likeness of the offender's face. Each area of their evidence has potential problems, but research has attempted to limit bias and maximise the value of a memory. Each piece of evidence is potentially unreliable but, when combined, can provide a reliable system for identifying and convicting criminals.

As a final summary:

- There are many types of evidence available to a criminal investigation, but some of these can be misleading.
- There have been many cases of wrongful conviction that have occurred due to errors of eyewitness identification.
- Convictions can be rendered more reliable by combining evidence from different sources.

SELF-TEST QUESTIONS

- Describe the various sources of evidence available in a police investigation.
- What is a suspect?
- How well do eyewitnesses recall information?
- Describe the kinds of inaccuracies that eyewitnesses suffer from.
- What factors affect what we recall?
- Describe the cognitive interview and say how it has been enhanced.
- The UK police use a special kind of interview. What is this called and what are the techniques it contains?
- What is weapon focus?
- How does state anxiety affect information recall?
- Do we recall different parts of a human face in different ways? If so, how?
- What cues do we use to recognise a person? Which of these is the most effective?
- How are familiar and unfamiliar face recognition different to each other and how does this issue relate to eyewitnesses?
- Describe the different types of identification procedures.
- What are the potential problems with constructing line-ups and how can these be overcome?
- What kinds of errors are made when recognising unfamiliar faces?
- What is a facial composite?
- Describe the traditional systems that the police use to construct faces with eyewitnesses.
- How effective are composite systems?
- When do feature system run into difficulty?
- Various developments have improved the effectiveness of traditional feature composites. What are these?

- Describe the alternative approach to construction by individual features.
- How effective is one of these 'holistic' systems? What has been done to improve its performance even further?
- What is the problem with evidence collected at a crime scene?
- What happened in the investigation of Laszlo Virag?
- Can eyewitness evidence be reliable? If not, why?

ESSAY QUESTIONS

(This section can also be used by teachers/instructors to lead class discussions on eyewitness research and forensic issues.)

- What are the different sources of evidence collected in a criminal investigation?
- What is the difference between recall and recognition?
- What type of errors do eyewitnesses make when they recall information?
- What do witnesses recall the best about another person's face and why?
- Why might it be possible to accurately describe details of a crime but not details of a person's face?
- Why is facial distinctiveness an important factor for face perception?
- What are the techniques that assist information recall in the PEACE interview?
- What sources of information do we use when we try to recognise a person? Which one is likely to be the most important?
- What is the consequence of becoming familiar with a person's appearance?
- What kinds of errors do eyewitnesses make with face recognition?
- There is a consequence of constructing line-ups directly from a picture of a suspect's face. Describe what this is.
- Suggest good procedures for building line-ups.
- What are the three main methods used to construct a facial composite?
- What is the 'cognitive' approach and why is it effective?
- How useful are facial composites?
- When building a composite system's database, why must only a *sample* of facial features be taken from each photographic subject?
- Why might composite quality be poor when a person constructs a composite two days after seeing the face?
- Which region of the face is important when recognising a composite, and why?
- Why are recent techniques likely to be effective for improving the performance of facial composites?
- How reliable is eyewitness evidence?
- What methods can be used to improve their effectiveness?
- Should evidence be collected from an eyewitness in any order? If so, what might this be?
- What normally happens to information in our memory over time, and does this occur in real crimes?
- What is a false memory and how is it created?
- Why might it be possible to accurately describe details of a crime but not details of a person's face?
- Why might hair be the easiest to describe?
- What techniques are used to maximise the recall of information?
- What type of face perception do eyewitnesses normally engage in and why might this be a problem?
- What is a major source of error in person recognition?
- Why is it best to use line-ups with a large number of foils?
- What problem occurs if an offender substantially changes their hair between the crime and a line-up?

- Which techniques are used in the cognitive interview with eyewitnesses for obtaining a description of an offender's face? Which are not used?
- What do the Frowd *et al.* (2005a) naming data imply for police practice?
- When is it permissible for a composite to be constructed and when is it not?
- What are the implications of an offender's face being distinctive?
- In what way can good-quality composites be constructed from traditional systems, and what techniques are available to improve their performance?
- Does an eyewitness need to have good face recall to use EvoFIT?
- What is the main reason for miscarriages of justice?

TEXTS FOR FURTHER READING

Baddeley, A. (2004) *Human Memory: A User's Guide*, New York: Firefly Books.

Matlin, M. (2009) *Cognitive Psychology*, Chichester: John Wiley & Sons, Ltd.

Milne, R. & Bull, R. (1999) *Investigative Interviewing: Psychology and Practice*, Chichester: John Wiley & Sons, Ltd.

Sporer, S.L., Malpass, R.S. & Koehnken, G. (2006) *Psychological Issues in Eyewitness Identification*, Hillsdale, NJ: Lawrence Erlbaum Associates.

Williamson, T. (2005) *Investigative Interviewing: Rights, Research, Regulation*, Abingdon: Willan.

Young, A. & Ellis, H.D. (1989) *Handbook of Research on Faces*, Amsterdam: North-Holland.

RELEVANT JOURNAL ARTICLES

Bruce, V. (1998) Fleeting images of shade: Identifying people caught on video. President's Award lecture, *The Psychologist* July: 331–7. Available at www.bps.org.uk.

Bruce, V. & Young, A.W. (1986) Understanding face recognition, *British Journal of Psychology* 77: 305–27.

Deffenbacher, K.A., Bornstein, B.H., Penrod. S.D. & McGorty, E.K. (2004) A meta-analytic review of the effects of high stress on eyewitness memory, *Law and Human Behavior* 28: 687–706.

Devlin, P. (1976) *Report to the Secretary of State for the Home Department of the Departmental Committee on Evidence of Identification in Criminal Cases*, London: HMSO.

Ellis, H.D. & Shepherd, J.W. (1996) Face recall methods and problems, in S.L. Sporer, R.S. Malpass & G. Koehnken (eds) *Psychological Issues in Eyewitness Identification*, Hillsdale, NJ: Lawrence Erlbaum Associates.

Frowd, C.D., Bruce, V. & Hancock, P.J.B. (2008) Changing the face of criminal identification, *The Psychologist* 21: 670–72.

George, P.A. & Hole, G.J. (2000) The role of spatial and surface cues in the age-processing of unfamiliar faces, *Visual Cognition* 7: 485–509.

Griffiths, A. & Milne, R. (2005) Will it all end in tiers? Police interviews with suspect in Britain, in T. Williamson (ed.) *Investigative Interviewing: Rights, Research, Regulation*, Abingdon: Willan.

McQuiston-Surrett, D., Malpass, R.S. & Tredoux, C.G. (2006) Sequential vs. simultaneous line-ups: A review of methods, data, and theory, *Psychology, Public Policy and Law* 12: 137–69.

Meissner, C.A. & Brigham, J.C. (2001) Thirty years of investigating the own-race bias in memory for faces: A meta-analytic review, *Psychology, Public Policy and Law* 7: 3–35.

Meissner, C.A., Sporer, S.L. & Susa, K.J. (2007) A theoretical review and meta-analysis of the description–identification relationship in memory for faces, *European Journal of Cognitive Psychology* 20: 414–55.

Rattner, A. (1988) Convicted but innocent: Wrongful conviction and the criminal justice system, *Law and Human Behavior* 12: 283–93.

Steblay, N.M. (1992) A meta-analytic review of the weapon focus effect, *Law and Human Behavior* 16: 413–24.

Wells, G., Memon, A. & Penrod, S.D. (2007) Eyewitness evidence: Improving its probative value, *Psychological Sciences in the Public Interest*, 7: 45–75.

Wells, G.L. & Olson, E.A. (2003) Eyewitness testimony, *Annual Review of Psychology* 54: 277–95.

REFERENCES

ACPO (2009) Facial Identification Guidance, produced by the National Policing Improvement Agency, unpublished document.

Baddeley, A. (2004) *Human Memory: A User's Guide*, New York: Firefly Books.

Berman, G.L. & Cutler, B.L. (1998) The influence of processing instructions at encoding and retrieval on face recognition accuracy, *Psychology, Crime & Law* 4: 89–106.

Brace, N.A., Pike, G.E., Kemp, R.I. & Turner, J. (2009) Eye-witness identification procedures and stress: A comparison of live and video identification parades, *International Journal of Police Science & Management* 11: 183–92.

Brigham, J.C., Ready, D.J. & Spier, S.A. (1990) Standards for evaluating the fairness of photograph lineups, *Basic and Applied Social Psychology* 11: 149–63.

Bruce, V. (1982) Changing faces: Visual and non-visual coding processes in face recognition, *British Journal of Psychology* 73: 105–16.

Bruce, V. & Young, A. (1998) *In the Eye of the Beholder: The Science of Face Perception*, New York: Oxford University Press.

Bruce, V., Henderson, Z., Greenwood, K., Hancock, P.J.B., Burton, A.M. & Miller, P. (1999) Verification of face identities from images captured on video, *Journal of Experimental Psychology: Applied* 5: 339–60.

Bruce, V., Ness, H., Hancock, P.J.B, Newman, C. & Rarity, J. (2002) Four heads are better than one. Combining face composites yields improvements in face likeness, *Journal of Applied Psychology* 87: 894–902.

Burton, A.M., Wilson, S., Cowan, M. & Bruce, V. (1999) Face recognition in poor quality video: Evidence from security surveillance, *Psychological Science* 10: 243–8.

Cabeza, R., Bruce, V., Kato, T. & Oda, M. (1999) The prototype effect in face recognition: Extension and limits, *Memory & Cognition* 27: 139–51.

Cutler, B.L., Penrod, S.D. & Martens, T.K. (1987) Improving the reliability of eyewitness identifications: Putting context into context, *Journal of Applied Psychology* 72: 629–37.

Cutshall, J.L. & Yuille, J.C. (1989) Field studies of eyewitness memory of actual crime scenes, in D.C. Raskin (ed.) *Psychological Methods in Criminal Investigation and Evidence*, pp. 97–124, New York: Springer.

Davies, G.M. (1983) Forensic face recall: The role of visual and verbal information, in S.M.A. Lloyd-Bostock and B.R. Clifford (eds) *Evaluating Witness Evidence*, pp. 103–23, Chichester: John Wiley & Sons, Ltd.

Davies, G.M. & Christie, D. (1982) Face recall: An examination of some factors limiting composite production accuracy, *Journal of Applied Psychology* 67: 103–9.

Davies, G.M., & Griffiths, L. (2008) Eyewitness identification and the English courts: A century of trial and error, *Psychiatry, Psychology and Law* 15: 435–49.

Davies, G.M. & Milne, A. (1982) Recognizing faces in and out of context, *Current Psychological Research* 2: 235–46.

Davies, G.M., Shepherd, J.W. & Ellis, H.D. (1977) Similarity effects in face recognition, *American Journal of Psychology* 92: 507–23.

Deffenbacher, K.A., Bornstein, B.H., Penrod. S.D. & McGorty, E.K. (2004) A meta-analytic review of the effects of high stress on eyewitness memory, *Law and Human Behavior* 28: 687–706.

Dehon, H. & Bredart, S. (2001) An 'other-race' effect in age estimation from faces, *Perception* 30: 1107–13.

Devlin, P. (1976) *Report to the Secretary of State for the Home Department of the Departmental Committee on Evidence of Identification in Criminal Cases*, London: HMSO.

Doob, A.N. & Kirshenbaum, H.M. (1973) Bias in police line-ups – partial remembering, *Journal of Police Science and Administration* 1: 287–93.

Ekman, P. (1978) Facial signs: Facts, fantasies and possibilities, in T. Sebeok (ed.) *Sight, Sound and Sense*, pp. 124–56, Bloomington: Indiana University Press.

Ellis, H.D. (1986) Face recall: A psychological perspective, *Human Learning* 5: 1–8.

Ellis, H.D. & Shepherd, J.W. (1996) Face recall methods and problems, in S.L. Sporer, R.S. Malpass & G. Koehnken (eds) *Psychological Issues in Eyewitness Identification*, Hillsdale, NJ: Lawrence Erlbaum.

Ellis, H.D., Shepherd, J.W. & Davies, G.M. (1979) Identification of familiar and unfamiliar faces from internal and external features: Some implications for theories of face recognition, *Perception* 8: 431–9.

Ellis, H.D., Shepherd, J.W. & Davies, G.M. (1980) The deterioration of verbal descriptions of faces over different delay intervals, *Journal of Police Science and Administration* 8: 101–6.

Fisher, R.P., Geiselman, R.E. & Amador. M. (1989) Field test of the cognitive interview: Enhancing the recollection of actual victims and witnesses of crime, *Journal of Applied Psychology* 74: 722–7.

Fisher, R.P., Geiselman, R.E., Raymond D.S., Jurkevich, L.M. & Warhaftig, M.L. (1987) Enhancing enhanced eyewitness memory: Refining the cognitive interview, *Journal of Police Science and Administration* 15: 291–7.

Flin, R.H. & Shepherd, J.W. (1986) Tall stories: Eyewitnesses' ability to estimate height and weight characteristics, *Human Learning: Journal of Practical Research & Applications* 5: 29–38.

Frowd, C.D. & Hepton, G. (2009) The benefit of hair for the construction of facial composite images, *British Journal of Forensic Practice* 11: 15–25.

Frowd, C.D., Bruce, V. & Hancock, P.J.B. (2008) Changing the face of criminal identification, *The Psychologist* 21: 670–72.

Frowd, C.D., Bruce, V., McIntyre, A. *et al.* (2006) Implementing holistic dimensions for a facial composite system, *Journal of Multimedia* 1: 42–51.

Frowd, C.D., Bruce, V., McIntyre, A. & Hancock, P.J.B. (2007a) The relative importance of external and internal features of facial composites, *British Journal of Psychology* 98: 61–77.

Frowd, C.D., Bruce, V., Ness, H. *et al.* (2007b) Parallel approaches to composite production, *Ergonomics* 50: 562–85.

Frowd, C.D., Bruce, V., Ross, D., McIntyre, A. & Hancock, P.J.B. (2007c) An application of caricature: How to improve the recognition of facial composites, *Visual Cognition* 15: 1–31.

Frowd, C.D., Bruce, V., Smith, A. & Hancock, P.J.B. (2008a) Improving the quality of facial composites using a holistic cognitive interview, *Journal of Experimental Psychology: Applied* 14: 276–87.

Frowd, C.D., Carson, D., Ness, H. *et al.* (2005a) Contemporary composite techniques: The impact of a forensically-relevant target delay, *Legal & Criminological Psychology* 10: 63–81.

Frowd, C.D., Carson, D., Ness, H. *et al.* (2005b) A forensically valid comparison of facial composite systems, *Psychology, Crime & Law* 11: 33–52.

Frowd, C.D., McQuiston-Surrett, D., Anandaciva, S., Ireland, C.E. & Hancock, P.J.B. (2007d) An evaluation of US systems for facial composite production, *Ergonomics* 50: 1987–98.

Frowd, C.D., Park., J., McIntyre, A. *et al.* (2008b) Effecting an improvement to the fitness function. How to evolve a more identifiable face, in A. Stoica, T. Arslan, D. Howard, T. Higuchi & A. El-Rayis (eds) *2008 ECSIS Symposium on Bio-inspired, Learning, and Intelligent Systems for Security*, pp. 3–10, Edinburgh: CPS.

Frowd, C.D., Pitchford, M., Bruce, V. *et al.* (2010) The psychology of face construction: Giving evolution a helping hand, *Applied Cognitive Psychology* DOI: 10.1002/acp.1662.

Geiselman, R.E., Fisher, R.P., MacKinnon, D.P. & Holland, H.L. (1985) Eyewitness memory enhancement in the police interview: Cognitive retrieval mnemonics versus hypnosis, *Journal of Applied Psychology* 70: 401–12.

George, P.A. & Hole, G.J. (2000) The role of spatial and surface cues in the age-processing of unfamiliar faces, *Visual Cognition* 7: 485–509.

Gibson., S.J., Solomon, C.J. & Pallares-Bejarano, A. (2003) Synthesis of photographic quality facial composites using evolutionary algorithms, in R. Harvey & J.A. Bangham (eds) *Proceedings of the British Machine Vision Conference*, pp. 221–30, Malvern: British Machine Vision Association.

Goldstein, A.G. & Chance, J.E. (1971) Visual recognition memory for complex configurations, *Perception & Psychophysics* 9: 237–41.

Griffiths, A. & Milne, R. (2005) Will it all end in tiers? Police interviews with suspect in Britain, in T.Williamson (ed.) *Investigative Interviewing: Rights, Research, Regulation*, Abingdon: Willan.

Hill, H. & Bruce, V. (1996) Effects of lighting on the perception of facial surfaces, *Journal of Experimental Psychology: Human Perception and Performance* 22: 986–1004.

Hulse, L.M. & Memon, A. (2006) Fatal impact? The effects of emotional arousal and weapon presence on police officers' memories for a simulated crime, *Legal and Criminological Psychology* 11: 313–25.

Kemp, R.I., Pike, G.E. & Brace, N.A. (2001) Video-based identification procedures: Combining best practice and practical requirements when designing identification systems, *Psychology, Public Policy, and Law* 7: 802–7.

Lander, K., Bruce, V. & Hill, H. (2001) Evaluating the effectiveness of pixelation and blurring on masking the identity of familiar faces, *Applied Cognitive Psychology* 15: 101–16.

Laughery, K.R., Duval, C. & Wogalter, M.S. (1986) Dynamics of facial recall, in H.D. Ellis, M.A. Jeeves, F. Newcombe, & A. Young (eds) *Aspects of Face Processing*, pp. 373–87, Dordrecht: Martinus Nijhoff.

Levi, A.M. (1998) Protecting innocent defendants, nailing the guilty: A modified sequential lineup, *Applied Cognitive Psychology* 12: 265–75.

Levi, A.M. (2002) Up to forty: Lineup size, the modified sequential lineup, and the sequential lineup, *Cognitive Technology* 7: 39–46.

Levi, A.M. (2006) An analysis of multiple choices in MSL lineups, and a comparison with simultaneous and sequential ones, *Psychology, Crime & Law* 12: 273–85.

Levi, A.M. (2007) Research note: Evidence for moving to an 84-person photo lineup, *Journal of Experimental Criminology* 3: 377–91.

Loftus, E.F. (1992) When a lie becomes memory's truth, *Current Directions in Psychological Science* 1: 121–3.

Loftus, E. F. (1997) Creating false memories, *Scientific American* 277: 70–75.

Loftus, E.F. & Burns, T.E. (1982) Mental shock can produce retrograde amnesia, *Memory & Cognition* 10: 318–23.

Loftus, E.F., Loftus, G.R. & Messo, J. (1987) Some facts about weapon focus, *Law and Human Behavior* 11: 55–62.

Loftus, E. F. & Palmer, J.C. (1974) Reconstruction of automobile destruction: An example of the interaction between language and memory, *Journal of Verbal Learning and Behavior* 13: 585–9.

McQuiston-Surrett, D., Malpass, R.S. & Tredoux, C.G. (2006) Sequential vs. simultaneous line-ups: A review of methods, data, and theory, *Psychology, Public Policy and Law* 12: 137–69.

Meissner, C.A. & Brigham, J.C. (2001) Thirty years of investigating the own-race bias in memory for faces: A meta-analytic review, *Psychology, Public Policy and Law* 7: 3–35.

Meissner, C.A., Sporer, S.L. & Susa, K.J. (2008) A theoretical review and meta-analysis of the description-identification relationship in memory for faces, *European Journal of Cognitive Psychology* 20: 414–55.

Meissner, C.M., Tredoux, C.G., Parker, J.F. & MacLin, O. (2005) Investigating the phenomenological basis for eyewitness decisions in simultaneous and sequential line-ups: A dual-process signal detection theory analysis, *Memory & Cognition* 33: 783–92.

Milne, R. & Bull, R. (1999) *Investigative Interviewing: Psychology and Practice*, Chichester: John Wiley & Sons, Ltd.

Olsson, N. & Juslin, P. (1999) Can self-reported encoding strategy and recognition skill be diagnostic of performance in eyewitness identification? *Journal of Applied Psychology* 84: 42–9.

PACE Code D (2008) Code of Practice for the Identification of Persons by Police Officers, http://police.homeoffice.gov.uk/operational-policing/powers-pace-codes/pace-code-intro/, accessed 6 December 2009.

Rattner, A. (1988) Convicted but innocent: Wrongful conviction and the criminal justice system, *Law and Human Behavior* 12: 283–93.

Read, J.D., Hammersley, R., Cross-Calvert, S. & McFadzen, E. (1989) Rehearsal of faces and details in action events, *Applied Cognitive Psychology* 3: 295–311.

Shapiro, P.N. & Penrod, S.D. (1986) Meta-analysis of facial identification rates, *Psychological Bulletin* 100: 139–56.

Shepherd, J.W. (1983) Identification after long delays, in S.M.A. Lloyd-Bostock & B.R. Clifford (eds) *Evaluating Witness Evidence*, pp. 173–87. Chichester: John Wiley & Sons, Ltd.

Shepherd, J.W., Davies, G.M. & Ellis, H.D. (1978) How best shall a face be described?, in M.M. Gruneberg, P.E. Morris & R.N. Sykes (eds) *Practical Aspects of Memory*, New York: Academic Press.

Skelton, F. & Frowd, C.D. Facial context and composites, manuscript in preparation.

Sondhi, V. & Gupta, A. (2007) The quality of suggested memories, *International Journal of Psychology* 42: 116–23.

Sörqvist, P. & Eriksson, M. (2007) Effects of training on age estimation, *Applied Cognitive Psychology* 21: 131–5.

Sporer, S.L. (1996) Psychological aspects of person descriptions, in S.L. Sporer, R.S. Malpass & G. Koehnken (eds) *Psychological Issues in Eyewitness Identification*, pp. 53–86. Hillsdale, NJ: Lawrence Erlbaum Associates.

Steblay, N.M. (1992) A meta-analytic review of the weapon focus effect, *Law and Human Behavior* 16: 413–24.

Tanaka, J.W. & Farah, M.J. (1993) Parts and wholes in face recognition, *Quarterly Journal of Experimental Psychology: Human Experimental Psychology* 46A: 225–45.

Valentine, T. & Heaton, P. (1999) An evaluation of the fairness of police line-ups and video identifications, *Applied Cognitive Psychology* 13: S59–S72.

Valentine, T. & Mesout, J. (2009) Eyewitness identification under stress in the London Dungeon, *Applied Cognitive Psychology* 23: 151–61.

Valentine, T., Pickering, A. & Darling, S. (2003) Characteristics of eyewitness identification that predict the outcome of real line-ups, *Applied Cognitive Psychology* 17: 969–93.

Wells, G.L. (1985) Verbal descriptions of faces from memory: Are they diagnostic of identification accuracy? *Journal of Applied Psychology* 70: 619–26.

Wells, G.L. & Hryciw, B. (1984) Memory for faces: Encoding and retrieval operations, *Memory & Cognition* 12: 338–44.

Wells, G.L., Olson, E.A. & Charman, S.D. (2002) The confidence of eyewitnesses in their identifications from line-ups, *Current Directions in Psychological Science* 11: 151–4.

Wells, G.L. & Turtle, J.W. (1988) What is the best way to encode faces?, in M.M. Gruneberg, P. Morris & R. Sykes (eds) *Practical Aspects of Memory: Current Research and Issues*, Vol. 1, pp. 163–8, Chichester: John Wiley & Sons, Ltd.

Yuille, J.C. & Cutshall, J.L. (1986) A case study of eyewitness memory of a crime, *Journal of Applied Psychology* 71: 291–301.

ANSWERS

Composites in Figure 14.6 are of England footballer Michael Owen. The images in Figure 14.12 are based on an EvoFIT composite of media mogul Simon Cowell.

ACKNOWLEDGEMENT

The author would like to thank Dr Faye Skelton, University of Central Lancashire, Preston, for her insightful comments on a draft of this chapter, and Emma Walker for proofreading a near-final version.

15 Violence Assessment and Intervention

JANE L. IRELAND

LEARNING OUTCOMES

WHEN YOU HAVE COMPLETED THIS CHAPTER, YOU SHOULD BE ABLE TO:

1. Outline the problems in defining and describing aggression.
2. Identify and describe the best methods for assessing aggression.
3. Compare and contrast explicit and implicit methods of measurement.
4. Describe at least four psychological theories that underpin our understanding of aggression.
5. Understand the best approaches to assessing violence, including the value in using functional assessment, explicit and implicit tests.
6. Understand the different approaches to managing risk.
7. Describe at least two essential components for aggression therapy, including being able to describe two models applied to information processing.

KEY WORDS

ABC • Actuarial Risk Assessment • Aggression Function • Antecedents • Broken Leg Problem • B-SAFER • Cognitive Script • Cognitive Restructuring • Clinical Risk Assessment • Direct Aggression • Disputation Techniques • Distraction Techniques • Effect–Danger Ratio Theory • Emotional Acceptance • Emotional Reactivity • Emotional Regulation • Explicit Tests • Expressive Aggression • False Positives • 4-What Assessment • Functional Assessment • General Aggression Model • HCR-20 • Hostile Attribution Bias • Implicit Association Test • Implicit Cognition • Implicit Tests • Impression Management • Indirect Aggression • Information Processing • Instrumental Aggression • Mixed-Motive Aggression • Organism Variables • Over-controlled Aggression • Negative Reinforcement • Parallel Development Models • Positive Reinforcement • Proactive Aggression • Punishment • Reactive Aggression • Reinforcers • SAVRY • Schema • Sequential Development Models • Social Information Processing • Social Learning Models • Stroop Test • Structured Clinical Assessment • Triggers • Under-controlled Aggression • Unified Model of Social Information Processing • V-RAG

CHAPTER OUTLINE

PHOTO 15.2 *Which of these pictures are acts of aggression?*
Source: Shutterstock.

The learning point here is that *all* of the behaviours indicated in Activity Box 15.1 are forms of aggression. The subtle behaviours are referred to as **indirect aggression** and the more overt behaviours (likely to appear in the 'most likely to be aggression' column) as **direct aggression**. This distinction was first reported by Kai Björkqvist (1994), who described how the two can be distinguished on the basis of overt intent and perpetrator identification. When you are aggressed towards directly you will know who the perpetrator(s) is and it will be clear that their intention is aggressive; indirect aggression is more subtle, with the identity of the aggressor often not known or the intent hidden via rationalising or trying to explain the behaviour away (e.g. 'no we were not ignoring you, don't be so sensitive, we were just busy'). Indirect aggression is, however, harmful, particularly with regard to promoting psychological distress and adjustment

indirect aggression subtle aggression in which the victim is harmed but the perpetrator is protected from social or official retribution by virtue of the subtle nature of the aggression.

direct aggression overt aggression.

difficulties (Crick & Grotoper, 1996; Prinstein, Boergers & Vernberg, 2001).

The value of indirect aggression as a strategy to be adopted by a perpetrator is also well recognised. The **effect–danger ratio theory** (Björkqvist, 1994) indicates that when a perpetrator chooses an aggressive strategy, they will adopt one that carries the least cost for them but yet still has an impact on the victim. Indirect aggression is one such strategy, since it can harm the victim but protect the perpetrator from social or official retribution by virtue of its subtle nature and rationalisation (e.g. 'I was not picking on them, it is all in their head'). There are also developmental reasons that can explain the use of indirect aggression, particularly among children. Developmentally girls will employ indirect aggression much earlier than boys, who will focus on using direct aggression to resolve conflict (Björkqvist, Österman & Kaukiainen, 1992). The developmental theory proposed by Björkqvist, Österman and Kaukiainen (1992) suggests that this is a result of the advanced development of social skills in girls, in comparison to boys, during childhood and adolescence, further stating that by late adolescence sex differences in indirect and direct aggression begin to disappear as men, like women, begin to supplement their use of direct aggression with indirect. Indeed, some studies conclude that there is an absence of sex differences in indirect aggression (e.g. Ireland & Ireland, 2008) and a preference by adults for indirect aggression as it is more protective for the perpetrator, again in keeping with the effect–danger ratio theory. The social retribution for using aggression as adults is much higher and thus if you can find a strategy where you can hide your identity or intent then you are likely to choose this.

Although the indirect/direct distinction continues to represent one of the most robust methods of categorising aggression, its value only lies in informing on *how* aggression may manifest itself, not *why*. It is the latter question that has concerned researchers and practitioners more in recent years, namely the *motivation* for aggression (Ireland, 2008a).

effect–danger ratio theory a theory indicating that when a perpetrator chooses an aggressive strategy he or she will adopt one that carries the least cost for the perpetrator but still has an impact on the victim.

15.1.2.2   The importance of aggression motivation

One of the most published motivational distinctions is that of the afore-mentioned reactive and proactive aggression (e.g. Bushman & Anderson, 2001). Reactive aggression has been described as an uncontrolled form of aggression occurring in the context of provocation, frustration or threat. It is generally perceived to be

social learning models models that define aggression as an acquired behaviour driven and reinforced by the actual or anticipated rewards of aggression that an individual receives or observes being received by those he or she respects or admires.

'emotional' aggression. Proactive aggression, however, is more in keeping with **social learning models** of aggression (Bandura, 1973), which describe aggression as an acquired behaviour driven and reinforced by the actual or anticipated rewards that you receive *or* observe in those you respect or admire. Social learning theory argues that you can learn the value of aggression not just by your own actions but by observing others using aggression 'successfully'. If you identify with the observed aggressor and consider them to be a role model, you are likely to be influenced by their use of aggression even more. Proactive aggression is also largely planned.

However, the distinction between proactive and reactive was not designed to be dichotomous and in recent years the concept of mixed-motive aggressors is increasingly being accepted. Indeed, there is recognition that a true 'proactive' aggressor is extremely rare (e.g. Bushman & Anderson, 2001) and that there may be emotional goals to a range of aggressive acts, as illustrated earlier in relation to the case examples of Michael Stone and Jamie Mark Watkins. The advancement of developmental models, designed to understand aggression, have certainly begun to move away from **parallel development models**, which viewed proactive and reactive aggression as originating from different background factors and developing almost independently in parallel; that is, with reactive aggressors exposed to a threatening and unpredictable environment and/or abusive parenting. Proactive aggressors, by contrast, are exposed to a supportive environment that fosters the use of aggression as goal-seeking behaviour (Dodge, 1991; Vitaro & Brendgen, 2005).

Instead, there is increasing focus on the **sequential development model** (Vitaro & Brendgen, 2005). This stresses the role of temperamental and neurophysiological elements in reactive aggression but not proactive, with environmental factors emphasised with proactive aggression. It argues that children with specific temperamental or neurophysiological characteristics are initially disposed to display aggression as they interact with their environment. If their reactive aggression is successful in alleviating stress and in doing so obtaining a goal, learning should take place (Vitaro & Brendgen, 2005; Ireland, 2008a). It is argued that gradually

parallel development models a model that understands proactive and reactive aggression as originating from different background factors and developing almost independently in parallel.

sequential development model a developmental model that suggests that reactive aggression develops first and proactive aggression develops after this.

purely proactive aggression may be used to obtain goals, particularly in a permissive familial or peer environment. Thus this model suggests that reactive aggression comes first and proactive aggression develops after this. It is arguable that every proactive aggressor is underpinned at some point by reactive aggression. The sequential development model therefore begins to provide an explanation as to why there is **mixed-motive aggression**.

mixed-motive aggression aggression that can be considered to be reactive as well as proactive.

15.1.2.3   Is aggression controlled?

Connected to the notion of motivation underlying aggression is the concept of **over-controlled** and **under-controlled aggression**, a model proposed by Megargee (1966) to explain how emotion, specifically anger, can relate to expressions of aggression. The original 1966 conceptualisation described 'over-controlled' aggressors as those for whom a strategy for ignoring emotions had developed, resulting in emotions only being identified when they had become overwhelming for them. 'Under-controlled' aggressors, by contrast, over-attend to emotion, resulting in an inability to manage even minor emotional fluctuations. Put simply, they react more to their emotions and are classically the individuals on whom traditional 'anger-management' programmes focus (Ireland, 2008b). To illustrate this, consider the following three examples:

over-controlled aggression a strategy whereby an individual tries, ultimately unsuccessfully, to inhibit and repress his or her negative emotions.

under-controlled aggression a strategy whereby an individual is unable to manage even minor emotional fluctuation and reacts strongly to their own negative emotions.

- Kai is convicted of a serious assault towards his ex-wife's new partner. He talks about a 'red mist descending' prior to the assault. He does not have a history of previous aggression and there are no reports of frequent anger loss. His victim sustained 25 stab wounds, leading to a punctured lung.

- Charlotte has been on the ward for five months. In this time she has averaged four incidents of verbal aggression a week, with eight counts of physical aggression. Charlotte reports feeling that she has to protect herself against other patients and thus 'attacks first'. She reports that her verbal aggression is always motivated by anger, whereas her physical aggression is sometimes motivated by a wish to leave a situation as she feels unsafe.

PHOTO 15.3 *Is this who we need to complete our violence risk assessments?*

Source: Getty Images.

TABLE 15.1 *V-RAG and HCR-20 Compared.*

Factors considered on the V-RAG – an actuarial risk assessment	
Clinical psychopathy score	Marital status
Elementary school maladjustment	Diagnosis of schizophrenia
Diagnosis of personality disorder	Victim injury
Age at index offence	History of alcohol abuse
Lived with both parents till 16	Female victim
Failure on prior conditional release	
Nonviolent offence score	

Factors considered on the HCR-20 – a structured clinical risk assessment	
HISTORICAL ITEMS	**CLINICAL ITEMS**
Previous violence	Lack of insight
Young age at first violent incident	Negative attitudes
Relationship instability	Active symptoms of major mental illness
Employment problems	
Substance-use problems	Impulsivity
Major mental illness	Unresponsive to treatment
Psychopathy	**RISK-MANAGEMENT ITEMS**
Early maladjustment	Plans lack feasibility
Personality disorder	Exposure to destabilisers
Prior supervision failure	Lack of personal support
	Noncompliance with remediation attempts
	Stress

according to the V-RAG they remain at the same level of risk. Put simply, it does not account for change, something referred to as the **broken leg problem** (Dawes, Faust & Meehl, 1989). Dawes illustrates this by posing the following scenario. Imagine that a college lecturer goes to the cinema every week without fail. What is their likelihood of attending this week? Actuarially you would say something close to 100%. However, what if the lecturer breaks their leg that week? What then? It is at this point that the actuarial approach fails.

> **broken leg problem** the term given to the failure of actuarial approaches to risk to account for unexpected change.

In addition, there have been further problems raised over the validity of the final actuarial score. More recently researchers have been arguing that the 'score' produced by such measures only tells you the extent to which a *group* of individuals with the same profile as Prisoner X will commit a violent offence, not Prisoner X as an *individual* (Hart, Michie & Cooke, 2007). Such approaches also do not account sufficiently for *social, cognitive* or *developmental theory*, unlike the *structured clinical* approaches.

Moving on to looking at the clinical approaches to risk assessment, first a distinction needs to be drawn between the *structured* and the *unstructured clinical* approaches. Unstructured approaches are where you consider the aggressor's offence and their background and use this to determine the extent to which you think they will commit a further act of aggression. You do this purely using your existing experience and without a list of what factors the research tells you to look for. It is very much the 'Sherlock Holmes' approach, and is only slightly better than chance with regard to producing a correct judgement. *Structured clinical approaches*, however, force the researcher and the clinician to focus only on those factors that are empirical (i.e. researched) risk factors. For violence there are a number of structured clinical tools, such as the **HCR-20** (Historical, Clinical and Risk Management Guide; Webster *et al.*, 1997); **SAVRY** (Structured Assessment for Violence Risk in Youth; Borum, Bartel & Forth, 2003); and the **B-SAFER** (Brief Spousal Assault Form for the Evaluation of Risk;

> **HCR-20** a structured clinical risk assessment for violence.

> **SAVRY** an acronym for Structured Assessment for Violence Risk in Youth.

> **B-SAFER** the acronym for Brief Spousal Assault Form for the Evaluation of Risk.

Kropp, Hart & Belfrage, 2005). All have the advantage of accounting for factors that are related to psychological theory explaining aggression.

To focus on one – the *HCR-20* – this considers a range of factors relevant to the risk of future violence. Historical factors are static and not expected to change. The clinical and risk management factors are dynamic and expected to change over time. Clinical factors focus on recent presentation and risk management on future behaviours. Structured clinical assessments such as the

HCR-20 are also helpful with regard to identifying what should be incorporated in therapy and, like the other structured assessments, account for *change*.

Table 15.1 illustrates each of these HCR-20 factors. Structured assessments avoid using numbers; all HCR-20 risk factors are thus described using qualitative statements of 'definitely present', 'possibly present' and 'not present/no evidence'. Practitioners developing treatment plans for aggressors will then determine the risk factors that require particular attention by accounting for those factors rated as 'definite' or 'possible', with the clinical and risk management items particularly valuable, since these are the factors most likely to change in a positive direction. Treatment issues will be addressed later in the chapter, but you will see there how a number of the risk factors picked up in treatment can be traced back to empirical risk factors such as those assessed by these structured clinical approaches (go to Case History 15.1 for an example).

CASE HISTORY 15.1

FOCUSING ON STRUCTURED CLINICAL APPROACHES

LINKING RISK ASSESSMENT INTO TREATMENT: THE CASE OF BARRY

THE BACKGROUND

Barry is married with two children: Kelly who is aged 3 and Tom who is aged 4. He has been losing his temper on a frequent basis with his children for quite a while and things have become really bad since he was made redundant from a job he had worked at for over 20 years. Barry and his wife Julie have been worrying about how they will pay their bills and this has resulted in Julie having to take a part-time job, leaving Barry to spend all day at home with the children. Julie has reported to her friends that she is worried about doing this as she does not feel Barry will be able to cope. Julie is unhappy at how frequently he loses his temper. Barry has also started to drink excessively and has started drinking from early morning through to early evening.

One Tuesday morning Barry loses his temper after Tom hits his sister Kelly with a toy car, causing a cut to Kelly's face. Kelly starts to cry uncontrollably and Barry responds by hitting Tom so hard on his back that he leaves a large welt and significant bruising to his face. He then locks Tom under the stairs to 'teach him a lesson'. This is all completed in front of Kelly, who becomes increasingly distressed. There is so much noise during this incident that the neighbours call the police. The police attend the family home, discovering Tom under the stairs with marked facial injuries and a significant injury to his back. Both children are taken into emergency care and court proceedings are issued to determine how safe the children are. As part of these proceedings a risk assessment of Barry is ordered.

THE RISK ASSESSMENT

Barry is assessed using the *HCR-20* (see Table 15.1) and this indicates that he presents with definite evidence for the following risk factors:

- *Employment problems*.
- *Substance-use problems*.
- *Lack of insight*, with Barry reporting that his alcohol use was wholly responsible for the aggression, feeling that he does not have a problem with his temper and holding the opinion that the children will not be affected by the aggression as they are too young for it to have a lasting effect on them.
- *Exposure to destabilisers*, with negative emotions (i.e. anger), managing challenging behaviour with children and alcohol use identified as factors most likely to increase his risk for being aggressive.
- *Stress*.

THE TREATMENT PLAN

Based on the above risk factors, Social Services develop a treatment plan for Barry that includes:

- Involving him in *vocational counselling*, where Barry can obtain some support to get him back into employment.
- Referring him to a local *substance misuse service* for some short-term psychological intervention to explore his management of alcohol and also his management of stress.
- Referring him to the NSPCC (a charity that assists with children who are neglected) for some brief *educational parenting work* that will explore the management of challenging behaviour in children, and the impact on children of exposure to conflict.
- Referring him to an *anger-management therapy* group that is run at his local GP's surgery.

15.2.2 Addressing the Function of Aggression

Earlier in the chapter the importance of aggression motivation was noted and the focus here will be on *how* we assess this motivation. One of the approaches most commonly used by psychologists is **functional assessment** (see Ireland, 2008a). The current chapter will not provide a comprehensive outline of this approach, it will merely indicate the core principles on which such assessments are based.

functional assessment a way of assessing motivation based on learning theory.

Functional assessment is based on learning theory, where we know that behaviour can be driven by what goes before it (i.e. *antecedents*) and what goes after (i.e. *consequences*). Indeed, these were the focus of classic psychological theories such as operant and classical conditioning, which argue that what goes before an event can produce a specific conditioned response (i.e. classical conditioning), with an individual learning to associate an antecedent with a specific likely consequence (i.e. operant conditioning). So imagine an individual with a history of losing their temper when they are told what to do by others as they feel this loses them respect. Imagine that they are then told what to do. This antecedent (trigger) may generate a conditioned (learned) response of 'feeling angry' (classical conditioning), and they may have learned that shouting at the person in an angry tone will make them feel better (operant conditioning). So they shout at the person believing that this will give them respect. This is a simple example, but it begins to illustrate how antecedents and consequences become important.

Functional assessment represents one of the oldest methods of psychological assessment (e.g. Goldiamond, 1975) and although there are a number of approaches, the most useful is one referred to as the *SORC* (Lee-Evans, 1994). This stands for:

triggers in learning theory, an antecedent, something that begins the behavioural sequence.

reinforcers those responses that happen after a behaviour which strengthens the likelihood of the behaviour reccuring in the future.

- Setting conditions (i.e. antecedents/**triggers**).
- Organism variables (i.e. learning history, previous experiences of the individual).
- Response variable (i.e. behaviour displayed, in this instance aggression).
- Consequences (i.e. **reinforcers**, namely what happens afterwards that strengthens the likelihood of the behaviour reccuring).

It is worth noting at this point the importance of reinforcers. In learning theory these are separated into two – **positive reinforcement** and **negative reinforcement**. Each is separate from the concept of **punishment**, which is designed to *weaken* behaviour, and instead are focused on what is likely to *strengthen* behaviour. Positive reinforcement refers to a gain and negative reinforcement to a removal of something an individual considers aversive (i.e. unpleasant). In the example given earlier of an individual shouting at someone when they were told what to do, learning theory would suggest that the negative reinforcement would represent the removal of angry feelings (e.g. removal of something unpleasant), whereas the positive reinforcement would be the perception that their behaviour gave them respect. Both would strengthen the likelihood that the individual would choose to use this behaviour again, namely to be aggressive.

The SORC is also helpful because it identifies the developmental and learning history of the individual and how this may contribute to their interpretation of the antecedents/triggers and their choices to be aggressive. It does this by incorporating what are termed **organism variables**, which simply refer to an individual's history and existing skills. So considering the example again of the individual shouting when they were told what to do, you may find they have a history of responding in this way, that they have a dislike or fear of being controlled, and that they lack the skill to respond in a nonaggressive fashion. They may also hold the belief, based on their learning history, that being aggressive is a method of obtaining respect in some circumstances.

Once the psychologist has identified the **S**etting conditions, **O**rganism variables, **R**esponse variable and **C**onsequences, they can then determine *why* the behaviour occurred, specifically its *function*. Based on the example provided here, a psychologist may conclude that the reason for the display of aggression could be due to the following functions:

- A need to retain control.
- A need to be respected by others.
- A way of coping with negative emotion (e.g. anger).

positive reinforcement in learning theory, something that is intended to strengthen behaviour by 'adding' something an individual perceives as a gain following their behaviour.

negative reinforcement in learning theory, something that is intended to strengthen behaviour by removing something an individual considers unpleasant.

punishment in learning theory, something that, when it follows a response, has the effect of reducing the probability of that event occurring again in the future, i.e. it weakens behaviour.

organism variables in functional assessment the 'O' of SORC which includes, e.g., the previous experiences of the individual and his or her learning experience.

Treatment would then focus on these areas, thus moving away from the aggression typology (i.e. the fact that the person shouted) to the function/motivation for aggression. SORC analyses are also being used increasingly in a broader range of clinical practices (e.g. Nelson-Gray & Farmer 1999a, 1999b) and are being applied more routinely to aggression (e.g. Daffern, Howells & Ogloff, 2007). There are other versions of functional assessments available such as the **ABC** model (Antecedents, Behaviour and Consequences; e.g. Leslie & O'Reilly, 1999). These do not explicitly incorporate developmental history, which as you can see from earlier elements of this chapter are of considerable significance

ABC A functional psychological model involving: Antecedents, Behaviour and Consequences.

when you are trying to explore and understand aggression. To help you see how we would put the theory indicated here into practice, illustrated in Theory to Application Box 15.1 is an abridged version of a treatment session that is delivered on a long-term aggression treatment programme (Life Minus Violence – Enhanced™; Ireland, 2009a). In this session clients are encouraged to develop their own version of the SORC so that they can begin to understand the function of their aggression. This is simplified for them and referred to as the '**4-what**' **assessment**. Theory to Application Box 15.1 illustrates this.

4-what assessment a simplified SORC functional assessment of four questions beginning with 'what' that a client asks when considering his or her negative emotional reaction.

| **BOX 15.1** | **THEORY TO APPLICATION** |

Example of a '4-what' treatment session taken from the Life Minus Violence – Enhanced™ 2009 group therapy programme. It illustrates how functional assessment can be put into practice.

*Treatment Session Content**	*Facilitator Note(s) – Theory*
Introduce the '4-what' assessment. Inform the group that it refers to 4 'what' questions that they should ask themselves when considering a negative emotional reaction such as anger.	The aim of this section is to assist group members to identify their own individual indicators that their emotion levels are increasing. Once these are identified, group members will be encouraged to increase their ability to self-monitor emotions and implement strategies to reduce arousal.
1. **What** in your individual background encourages you to become angry on occasion (e.g. learning history, experiences etc.)? 2. **What** happened beforehand? 3. **What** happened during? 4. **What** happened afterwards?	This is a SORC functional assessment (Setting conditions/triggers; Organism variables; Response; Consequences) i.e.: 1. ORGANISM [individual] VARIABLES: Learning history, experiences. 2. TRIGGERS: Should include thoughts, feelings, behaviour and the context [i.e. what was going on around them]. 3. RESPONSE: The behaviour shown. 4. CONSEQUENCES: Should include the positive and negative reinforcers.
Go through a brief example with the group just to illustrate how this will work in practice. Next, give each group member some flipchart paper and some pens. Ask them to individually complete a SORC on 'A time when you felt a negative emotion such as anger'. Once completed, the '4-what' assessments should be put on display. Learning points should be pulled out by asking the following questions and flipcharting their responses:	
• What have you learned about your history which can help you to understand why you find it difficult to manage emotions on occasion? • What have you now noticed happens as you become emotional? • What is the reason for your behaviour?	The first '4-what' question, i.e. 'What did you bring in terms of learning history, experiences?', should focus on areas likely to increase their risk for the mismanagement of emotion [e.g. observing those that they looked up to not coping with negative emotions; having a history of coping poorly with negative emotion].

Source: © Life Minus Violence – Enhanced™ 2009.

15.2.3 Using Explicit vs Implicit Tests for Assessment

Any good psychologist will tell you that collecting accurate client data can be challenging, particularly when you are trying to assess sensitive areas, such as an individual's proneness to be aggressive. Self-report is our most commonly used method of assessment, but it is challenged by the fact that individuals either over- or under-report their tendencies, either because they are trying to project an image of 'toughness' (i.e. over-report) or because they fear the consequences if they are too honest about their difficulties (i.e. under-report). The self-report tests that

explicit tests self-report tests administered by psychologists that measure tendencies overtly so that their purpose is clear to participants.

psychologists use are most commonly **explicit tests** – by this we mean they overtly measure tendencies, and thus their purpose to clients is very clear. They also address tendencies of which a client is likely to be aware.

To illustrate this, consider one of the most commonly used aggression measures – the Buss & Perry Aggression Questionnaire (AQ; Buss & Perry, 1992). This includes questions such as:

- I am an even-tempered person.
- I have trouble controlling my temper.

Clients are asked to rate each question on a scale of 1 to 5, with 1 representing 'totally unlike me' and 5 'very like me'. Those who are concerned about how they are likely to present to others, particularly to professionals, are likely to under-report their difficulties, thus rating their presentation on the above items as less problematic than they actually are (Ireland, 2009b). Indeed, this tendency is sometimes called **impression management**, which refers to how individuals strive to present

impression management an attempt by an individual to present himself favourably to others.

themselves in a good light to others. Imagine, for example, that you are attending a job interview and the interviewer asks you: 'Do you have trouble controlling your temper?' Are you going to say: 'Yes, that is very like me.' Clearly this would be an unfavourable response to make.

It is not being suggested, though, that such explicit tests

implicit tests assessments of an individual's tendencies towards being aggressive without the individual knowing what the tests are designed to assess.

are unhelpful. They are certainly valuable in measuring the more overt tendencies that an individual presents with. However, there is a developing drive in the aggression literature towards the use of **implicit tests**. These latter tests

assess tendencies towards being aggressive by 'hiding' the reason for the test. Essentially, individuals complete them without realising or being able to tell which answers are the right answers. The role of implicit tests is also to address the cognitive processes involved in aggression, with several theories of aggression acknowledging cognition as a central process (e.g. Huesmann, 1998; Richetin & Richardson, 2008). One of the

most valuable of these theories – **information processing** – will be outlined later. In essence, what they suggest is that cognition can

information processing a theory that suggests that cognition can be explicit or implicit.

be at an explicit level (i.e. a level at which the individual is aware of their cognitions) or at an implicit level (i.e. a level at which an individual is largely unaware of their cognitions).

One of the tests most commonly applied is the **implicit association test** (IAT; Greenwald, McGhee & Schwartz, 1998). IAT is designed to access a partici-

implicit association test a test designed to measure in a non transparent way underlying aggressive attitudes.

pant's attitudinal unconscious and is a computerised test requiring participants to associate categories, combining selection with response times. In short, the test is measuring underlying attitudes but in a nontransparent fashion. Another example is the classic **Stroop test**, where participants are shown a range of words in dif-

Stroop test a classic implicit association test which uses words in different colours, designed in some instances to assess the participant's unconscious aggression.

ferent colours and they must indicate the colour in which the word is presented. Again, this is timed and it is argued that the more aggressive individuals will take longer to identify the colour of aggressive words, as their cognitive interpretation of an aggressive word begins to stimulate an aggressive script (i.e. they start to think of aggression). This results in a slower response time in comparison to neutral words.

It is difficult to convey an implicit test without actually demonstrating one. As indicated by Ireland (2009b), 'In a nutshell they are best thought of as self-report tests in which the true variable of measurement is hidden. Thus they are not transparent.' Figure 15.1 presents a question from one such implicit test – the Puzzle Test (© Ireland, 2009c). The basic premise is that those with higher levels of trait aggression will complete the test using words more closely associated with aggression than those with lower levels of trait aggression. Thus if you want to ensure a comprehensive assessment of an individual's aggressive tendencies, you should incorporate both explicit and implicit measures. Only then can we be most assured that we have a more accurate assessment of an individual's presentation.

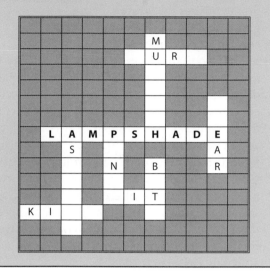

FIGURE 15.1 *Example item from the Puzzle Test.*

15.2.4 Summary

This section commenced by highlighting the real human consequences of not assessing and understanding aggression correctly. Cases such as Peter Bryan illustrate the most serious consequences that can occur if risk assessment procedures for aggression are out of date or are not followed. As indicated, risk assessment is a complex business to complete, but it represents one of the core duties of a forensic psychologist in practice. Running alongside risk assessment is the importance of assessing in detail *why* aggression occurs using theoretically grounded approaches such as functional assessment. The theoretical grounding underlying this was emphasised and it led into a discussion of how we can utilise self-report versus other measures. The value of using a range of methods – both explicit methods (e.g. self-report) and implicit methods (e.g. subtle processing biases) – was outlined and its utility can be linked back to risk assessment: if we rely solely on self-report then we rely on an offender's personal perception of risk, their level of insight and their desire for a positive personal outcome (e.g. release from prison or hospital).

To summarise:

- Assessing the risk for aggression can use *actuarial* (e.g. feeding information on a client into a formula), *unstructured clinical* (the 'Sherlock Holmes' approach) and *structured clinical* approaches (e.g. using guides such as the *HCR-20*).

- *Structured clinical* approaches are the best approach to aggression assessment if the focus is on management, treatment and recognising dynamic change.

- *Actuarial* approaches do not account for change in a client and can fail therefore to provide current and accurate assessments of violence risk.

- To assess aggression we have to understand its *function*, and this is best achieved using a *functional assessment*.

- *Functional assessment* was developed on the basis of *learning theory* and it includes a focus on the **antecedents** (triggers) and *consequences* associated with the behaviour.

  antecedents things that go before, namely triggers.

- *SORC* assessments where the focus is on the triggers (*Setting conditions*), *Organism variables* (learning history), *Response* (behaviour) and Consequences (*reinforcers*) are the most useful methods of *functional assessment*.

- *Reinforcers* can be *positive* (i.e. gains) and *negative* (i.e. removal of something unpleasant) and are designed to strengthen behaviour.

- Self-report measures are the most common approaches to assessing risk and are *explicit* (i.e. overt and transparent) methods of assessment. *Implicit* measures are, by contrast, less commonly used. They are helpful since they explore more hidden and less obvious beliefs.

15.3 PSYCHOLOGICAL TREATMENTS FOR AGGRESSION: SOME KEY COMPONENTS

The most effective treatment for aggression is cognitive-behavioural therapy, where an individual's emotions, thoughts, beliefs and behaviour can be addressed. Group-based therapy is the most effective, since this is a means by which you can challenge the attitudes and beliefs underpinning aggression by using the views of other group members (see Ireland, 2008b). It is much more effective if clients are challenged by their peers than by a therapist alone.

The next section will explore some of the core elements that need to be considered in such therapy and will illustrate the points using a long-term violence therapy programme (Life Minus Violence – Enhanced™) as an example (Ireland, 2008b, 2009a, 2009b). Regardless of the exact nature or emphasis of violence therapy, there are two key areas that *all* aggression treatment should have in common if it is to begin to address the treatment needs of habitual aggressors, namely *emotions* and *cognitions*. These are just sample areas and in no way represent the full range of content that should be covered in an aggression-treatment programme. Space restrictions prevent a detailed review of all the areas.

15.3.1 Emotions: Reactivity, Regulation and Acceptance

Emotions are an important concept to account for within aggression-management programmes since they can represent triggers, amplifiers, goals and/or moderators of aggression (Steffgen & Gollwittzer, 2007). There are a number of important points that can be identified from the literature, but the three key areas are as follows:

- *A need to recognise the developmental changes that can occur with the experiencing of aggression.* There has been an over-focus on emotion as a 'static' concept, while research suggests that age may influence the nature of the emotion and its expression (Ireland, 2008b). For example, the older the client the longer it may take for them to become emotionally aroused to something, particularly in more advanced age, but once aroused their emotions may be experienced more intensely (Schultz, 1985). Aggression treatment cannot therefore presume that individuals have generic needs; their individual development needs to be accounted for with a recognition that change in presentation will inevitably occur over time (Ireland, 2008b).

emotional acceptance
accepting rather than inhibiting or suppressing emotion and the cognitions underpinning the emotion.

- *The importance of recognising that treatment focusing on emotions should attend to* **emotional acceptance, emotional regulation** *and* **emotional reactivity** (Steffgen & Gollwittzer, 2007), not merely regulation (Ireland, 2008b). Acceptance refers to the importance of not trying to inhibit or suppress emotion and particularly the cognitions underpinning this; regulation describes the strategies an individual employs consciously or subconsciously to manage emotion; and reactivity is the extent to which an individual reacts to a negative or positive event. These are important concepts to attend to and can also be related to the earlier descriptions of over-controlled and under-controlled aggression. Those placed more towards the 'under-controlled' end of the spectrum present with treatment needs focused more on the control of emotion (i.e. the classic emotional regulation component), whereas those towards the 'over-controlled' end have treatment needs focused more on emotional acceptance (Ireland, 2008b).

emotional regulation
the strategies an individual employs, consciously or subconsciously, to manage his or her emotion.

emotional reactivity
the extent to which an individual reacts to a negative or positive event.

- *Looking beyond the concept of anger.* The link between anger and aggression has been studied extensively (e.g. Baumeister & Bushman, 2007; Davey, Day & Howells, 2005). It is certainly the case that the subjective experience of anger is closely related to the expression of aggression, although the importance of not over-stating the association is recognised (Baumeister & Bushman, 2007). There are also a range of further emotions important to account for in any understanding of aggression, such as fear, anxiety, pain, shame, guilt, jealousy, envy, excitement, pleasure, frustration, stress and humiliation (Baumeister & Bushman, 2007; Ireland, 2008b; Montada, 2007), to name but a few. Indeed, all emotions are important since all are associated with physiological arousal, either high or low arousal, which in turn can interfere with an individual's ability to process information (Huesmann, 1998).

To address emotional regulation, reactivity and acceptance, aggression-treatment programmes have to employ a range of strategies. The Life Minus Violence – Enhanced™ programme uses the following methods to do this: behavioural and cognitive relaxation; **distraction techniques** and

distraction techniques
methods for disturbing one's thoughts using attention-shifting or physical distraction.

cognitive restructuring the process of learning to challenge distortions in thinking by, e.g. using disputation techniques.

disputation techniques methods in which a client can learn to argue, debate or negotiate with their own thoughts.

cognitive restructuring (such as **disputation techniques**) to encourage clients not to suppress thoughts likely to promote negative emotion; developing effective coping skills; and raising awareness of *implicit* cognition. Case History 15.2 provides an example of how we may employ **disputation techniques**.

15.3.2 Cognitions: Information Processing

How individuals process information is a crucial component to how we respond to a range of social situations.

There are a number of different models, influenced by social cognition and often referred to as **social information-processing models**, which psychologists utilise to try to explain aggressive responses, including those that have attempted to incorporate a range of models to explain the large variance in aggressive behaviour. This includes the **general aggression model** (GAM; Anderson & Bushman, 2002; Anderson, Gentile & Buckley, 2007), which places important emphasis on aggression as a product of multiple interacting factors, integrates social cognition

social information-processing models influenced by social cognition, there are a variety of models used by psychologists to try and explain aggressive responses.

general aggression model a social information processing model which places emphasis on aggression as a product of multiple interacting factors, including: social cognition, emotional aggression, predisposition and factors based on learning and developmental history.

CASE HISTORY 15.2

CLIENT L: Presents with a history of experiencing negative thoughts that she finds difficult to control. She reports that these thoughts make her feel very angry. Whenever she feels angry she states that she has thoughts of wanting to harm the person who has caused her to feel annoyed and that often she loses sleep thinking about how much they have made her angry. Client L identifies the following thoughts as the ones most likely to may her feel angry: 'What have I done to deserve this?'; 'Why do people always try and annoy me?'; 'Everyone has it in for me'.

Client L reports that she will spend a lot of time thinking about the last thought, stating that this can keep her awake for hours, even though she knows that it is not true and that she has some good friends. Her current strategy for managing these thoughts is to try and stop thinking about them. This is not working.

APPROACH: Therapists recognise that encouraging a client to try and suppress thoughts is an impossible task since this only serves to make the thoughts reappear. Instead, therapists may try to use:

1. **Distraction techniques,** such as encouraging the client to shift their attention to something else while also using physical distraction. This would include asking the client to snap an elastic band on their wrist each time they had the thought and then to immediately shift attention to something else, to something absorbing like a puzzle.

2. **Disputation techniques,** where you would encourage the client to negotiate with themselves. In this particular example disputation was chosen as the best approach for Client L and this is illustrated below.

What Client L was advised to do*	Therapist notes*
Think about how you could manage the thought 'Everyone has it in for me' by working through the **RICE** formula, i.e.: - **R**easons? Why did I/do I think this? - **I**s it useful to think like this? - **C**atastrophe? What is really the worst that can happen? - **E**vidence? What is the real evidence for this? Go through each part and think about a positive thing you could say to yourself that would help you. If you struggle with this imagine what a good friend of yours may suggest to you for each part.	This is an example of disputation (i.e. self-negotiation). Each section stands for the following: **R**easons – Why did it happen? What were the reasons? Focus on specific nonpersonal examples. **I**s it useful – Does this thought help me? Does it have a functional value? *NB: If the answer to the last point is NO then a distraction technique should be used.* **C**atastrophe – What are the implications? De-catastrophise. **E**vidence – What are the real facts here?

Source: *Life Minus Violence – Enhanced™, 2009.

and emotional aggression, and was designed originally for application. It also emphasises the importance of predisposition and interactional factors, based on learning and developmental history (Anderson & Bushman, 2002). It shares many conceptualisations, however, with Huesmann's (1998) **unified model of social information processing**. Indeed, the general aggression model is perhaps best considered as an endorsement of many of the elements of Huesmann's model, which should be considered the core underpinning model for understanding aggression in terms of information processing.

> **unified model of social information processing** a model devised by Huesmann (1998) that focuses on understanding the acquisition and maintenance of repeated aggressive behaviour.

Huesmann's model focused on how we can understand the acquisition and maintenance of repeated aggressive behaviour. It integrates an earlier model outlined by Huesmann and a reformulated model of Crick and Dodge (1994), highlighting the role of cognitive processes and affect at each element of information processing. Such models classically consider aggressive behaviour to be a maladaptive behaviour produced by difficulties in processing situations and in responding effectively to them. More recent academic opinion, as noted earlier, considers some aggression to be adaptive and an example of well-developed social cognitive skills (e.g. Bennett, Farrington & Huesmann, 2005). In addition, although there has been a distinction drawn between proactive and reactive aggression, an examination of the information processes underlying each has indicated that many of the same mechanisms are involved in both types of aggression (Huesmann, 1998).

Earlier models, such as that of Dodge (1986, 1991) view an individual's behavioural responses to a social situation as following a series of information-processing steps that generally occur outside conscious awareness. The steps, in order, included:

A. Encoding social cues in the environment.
B. Forming a mental representation and interpretation of these cues.
C. Searching for a possible behavioural response.
D. Deciding on a response.
E. Enacting the chosen response.

Models such as these are popular within therapy and Table 15.2 illustrates how this may look in practice. In therapy you would begin to explore these steps with clients and focus on how they are interpreting each of them. Although these are popular models, they have been reformulated to account for the complexities in how humans process information. In a reformulation of the social information-processing model, Crick and Dodge

TABLE 15.2 *Employing a Step-by-Step Information-Processing Model of Aggression.*

Problem-Solving Step (Dodge, 1986, 1991)	How It May Work With An Individual Who Is Aggressive
	SITUATION: Someone calls them an offensive name and threatens them.
Encoding social cues in the environment	Looking at what is going on around them – e.g. Who else is present? Who has heard them say this to me?
Forming a mental representation and interpretation of these cues	This person is doing this to try and humiliate me; they are doing it in front of others to try to look better than me.
Searching for a possible behavioural response	What are my options? I can walk away; I can tell them how I feel in a polite way; I can threaten them; I can hit them.
Deciding on a response	If I hit them this will really show them that I cannot be messed with; threatening them is not going to do this; being polite does not work with people like this; walking away will make me look like I cannot look after myself.
Enacting the chosen response	Choosing to hit them.

(1994) proposed that although information processing logically follows a sequence of steps, it should not be viewed as being rigidly sequential with each step following on from the previous one. Instead, they argue that the actual processing of information at each step should be seen as occurring in simultaneous parallel paths and that in reality individuals will be engaged in multiple social information-processing activities at the same time. So a client could be engaging in Step C (searching for a behavioural response) at the same time as engaging in Step A (encoding social cues).

The *unified model of information processing* put forward by Huesmann (see Huesmann, 1998) attempted to take these models one step further by integrating all previous models of information processing into one. This model argued for more inclusion of emotions and normative beliefs (i.e. beliefs an individual holds that they feel are representative of society beliefs, one example of which may be 'It's okay to hit someone if they threaten you'). Emotions were largely neglected in the earlier models, although as we have seen in the earlier section emotions should be key elements, and we know that they can have a negative impact on information-processing ability (Harper, Lemerise & Caverly, 2009). The Huesmann model favours an information-processing approach as opposed to a 'problem-solving' approach. The latter is based on the premise that certain social interactions are labelled as a 'problem' by the individual involved when this may not be the case. The *unified model of information processing* also places greater emphasis on the role of **schema** (e.g. organised knowledge about self, events and beliefs), emotions and the interpretation of environmental responses (i.e. how individuals interpret the responses of others/society influences, and how this serves to maintain an aggressive script; see later).

schema an individual's organised knowledge about self, events and beliefs.

Adopting an information-processing approach to understanding and managing aggression is important, as it allows for a focus on the processes involved and helps us to break down aggressive responding for clients. One of the most important elements of the *information-processing* approach are the concepts of *hostile attribution biases* and **cognitive scripts**. **Hostile attribution biases** are really a tendency that an individual has to see hostility where it may not exist. They are most likely to occur in ambiguous situations. An aggressive individual, for example, is more likely to interpret someone looking at them, or someone bumping into them in a queue, in a hostile fashion than is a nonaggressive individual. These biases can also trigger *cognitive scripts* focused on aggression. Such scripts are 'guides' a client has that will tell them how to respond in certain situations, based on their previous experience and learning.

cognitive script based on previous experience and learning, mental 'guides' which a client has which will tell him or her how to respond in certain situations.

hostile attribution bias a tendency that an individual has to see hostility where it may not exist.

Go to Activity Box 15.2 and work through the two script examples there. This should illustrate that it is harder to generate steps to a script that you are less familiar with – you should have fewer steps and it should take

---

ACTIVITY BOX 15.2

Going to a restaurant	Flying a plane
Write below all of the steps that you would have to go through in order to purchase a meal at a restaurant. Try to work as quickly as you can and think of as many steps as you can. Time yourself!	Write below all of the steps that you would have to go through in order to fly a plane. Try to work as quickly as you can and think of as many steps as you can. Time yourself.
1. 6. 2. 7. 3. 8. 4. 9. 5. 10.	1. 6. 2. 7. 3. 8. 4. 9. 5. 10.

What have I just done?

The first exercise is an example of a script that you have retained in your memory for visiting restaurants, whereas the second one relates to a script for flying a plane.

Which took you longer and why?

Which script were you able to complete without much thought? Why?

you longer. This allows for more errors to be made. When someone has a history of aggression their responses to conflict can work in a very similar way – if they are not used to using nonaggression or they have few positive experiences of the use of a nonaggressive option, *social information-processing* theories tell us that they will be less likely to access such scripts and, if they do access them, they will not implement them correctly. This can lead aggressive individuals to opt for an aggressive response to the conflict as they are more used to employing this and are confident of its outcome (Ireland, 2008b). What the research also suggests is that aggressive individuals do have nonaggressive scripts to use during conflict situations; the problem is that they lack a *range* of nonaggressive scripts. In therapy we can spend a lot of time teaching aggressive individuals a range of nonaggressive scripts to conflict and encouraging them to over-learn these scripts so that they become like a habit.

Within therapy it can be challenging to talk clients through all of the theory and so it has to be presented in a way that is accessible but at the same time does not compromise the underpinning theory. Table 15.2 has illustrated a very simple example of a step-by-step processing model and how this may appear in practice. The *unified model of information processing* (Huesmann, 1998), which is the preferred model, is also applied within therapy and Figure 15.2 illustrates how this may be presented to clients. You will see from this figure that the focus is on

removing the 'step-by-step' approach of earlier models by presenting the model in a circular fashion and trying to incorporate emotions and cognitions more clearly. Within therapy sessions clients would be talked through this model and they would complete a number of these 'circles' for their incidents of aggression.

15.3.3 Summary

The focus in this section has been on the value of applying psychological theory to the therapy that we provide. Earlier sections have illustrated clearly the importance of managing and treating aggression, particularly if the focus is on risk management and public protection. We cannot therefore take any 'chances' with our therapy. There is no room within forensic psychology practice for poorly developed, dated and atheoretical work. The therapy we deliver has to be of the highest quality and forensic psychologists have very much led with this specific area of work. The section has highlighted in particular the importance of accounting for a range of emotions, not just anger, and incorporating information processing. The latter is a particularly important area to include since it combines the importance of cognition, experience, individual differences and emotions. In essence, it can be seen to 'pull together' the earlier sections into a comprehensive academic theory that has application to the real world.

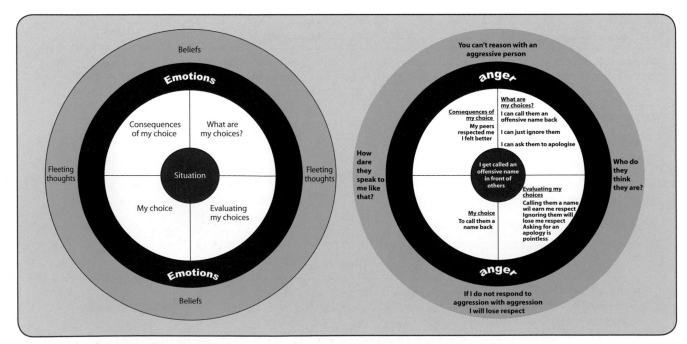

FIGURE 15.2 *Information-processing circle.*
Example of a blank and a completed information-processing circle – called a 'choice chain' in therapy.
Source: Life Minus Violence – Enhanced™, Ireland (2009a), first appearing in Ireland (2008b).

To summarise:

- *Cognitive behavioural therapy* is the most effective method of addressing aggression, since it allows you to challenge the beliefs underpinning aggression using peers.

- *Emotions* can alter over time – the older the client, the longer it will take them to become aroused but the more intense the final arousal will be.

- Treatment has to address *emotional acceptance, emotional regulation* and *emotional reactivity,* specifically the extent to which a client accepts negative emotions, can manage these and how they react to them across various situations.

- Anger is not the only emotion of importance when you are considering aggression. You need also to consider emotions such as fear, anxiety, pain, shame, humiliation, guilt, jealousy, envy, excitement, pleasure, frustration and stress, to name but a few.

- *Distraction techniques* that include both attention shifting and a physical distraction can be very useful in stopping thought rumination. *Disputation techniques* where a client 'negotiates' with themselves are also invaluable.

- *Social information-processing models* are particularly helpful in assisting us to understand how aggression is developed, with the *unified information-processing* model particularly valuable.

- *Information processing* places emphasis on the role of *schemas, scripts, normative beliefs* and *hostile attribution biases.*

15.4 CONCLUSION

The current chapter highlights the complexities involved in understanding, assessing and treating aggression. The importance of adopting an individual approach to formulating and treating a client's aggression is clear: you cannot assume that all aggressors are the same with equal motivations and similar backgrounds. You also have to be sensitive to what aggression can include, attending to both *direct aggression* and *indirect aggression* so that you cover the full spectrum of aggressive behaviours. The assessments that we use, including **risk assessment** and *functional assessments,* also serve to illustrate how different one client can be from another. These differences are then addressed in therapy, which explores, among other topics, individual responses and reactions to emotions, individual cognitions including *normative beliefs,* tendencies toward *hostile attributions* and the development of *scripts.* The assessments and treatments arc underpinned by a range of psychological theories including *parallel developmental models, sequential developmental models, learning theory* and *information-processing theory* to name but a few, leading to therapy that is closely aligned to theory and enhancing its effectiveness in treating a behaviour as complex as aggression.

risk assessment an appraisal by a forensic psychologist who will consider the dangers posed to others by the person being assessed, whether that is in terms of risk of offending, risk of violence etc.

SELF-TEST QUESTIONS

- What important elements should a definition of aggression include?
- What different types of aggression are there?
- Describe the different motivations for aggression – what do these include?
- Name two things that are essential to consider when you look at aggression motives.
- Describe two models that explain the development of proactive and reactive aggression.
- If we say someone is an over-controlled aggressor, what do we mean?
- What is the effect–danger ratio theory?
- What does social learning theory tell us about the development of aggression?
- What is actuarial assessment?
- In what way do unstructured and structured clinical assessment differ?
- What are some examples of structured clinical assessments?

- What does learning theory tell us are the crucial elements to consider when we assess the function of behaviour? Which specific learning theories are most important?
- What are the four components of the SORC assessment?
- How does positive reinforcement differ from negative reinforcement?
- What weakens behaviour – punishment or reinforcement?
- What is explicit assessment?
- Which method of assessment is more transparent and easily faked – explicit or implicit?
- Which method of assessment is most related to information-processing theories – explicit or implicit?
- What is the most effective method of therapy for addressing aggression and why?
- Other than exploring how an individual responds to emotions, what else should we consider in therapy with regard to emotions?
- What other emotions are important to account for with aggression other than anger?
- What are the five steps of Dodge's (1986) social information-processing model?
- How does the unified information-processing model differ from Dodge's (1986) model and the reformulated model of Crick and Dodge (1994)?
- What techniques can be applied to prevent rumination?
- What components constitute disputation?
- What is a script?
- What is the difference between a normative belief and a hostile attribution bias?

ESSAY QUESTIONS

- Critically evaluate the following statement: 'Aggressive individuals are either emotionally driven or well planned.'
- Describe the developmental and learning models that can help us to understand aggressive behaviour.
- Compare and contrast two approaches for assessing the risk for aggression, indicating which is preferred.
- With attention to theory, describe the different steps you would take to complete a functional assessment of a client.
- Outline at least two components that should be included in aggression therapy, with reference to psychological theory.
- Describe at least one information-processing model, illustrating how it can be related to aggression treatment.

(The following can also be used by the teacher or instructor to lead a class discussion on issues of contemporary relevance to the understanding, explanation or treatment of aggression.)

- Can we really define aggression?
- If we ask someone 'have you been aggressive?' what do we need to account for?
- Is indirect aggression as serious as direct aggression?
- Are males more aggressive than females once we take into account age and aggression type?
- Can aggression really have more than one motivation?
- Which model offers a better explanation of the development of reactive and proactive aggression – sequential or parallel?
- Is structured clinical assessment really better at predicting risk than unstructured and actuarial assessment?
- Is unstructured judgement really a poor judgement of risk or does the hypo-deductive method work well in some circumstances?
- Which elements of functional assessment are most useful in determining the behaviour function?

- How valid and reliable are functional assessments?
- Do implicit tests outperform explicit terms in predicting aggression?
- How valid and reliable are implicit tests?
- Does our experiencing of emotions really change with age? How could we test this?
- What types of normative beliefs are most likely to be challenged effectively by group therapy?
- Is there a difference between proactive and reactive aggressors with regard to their level of emotional acceptance, emotional regulation or emotional reactivity?
- Do disputation and distraction techniques work for all types of aggressor? How could we evaluate this?
- Are normative beliefs and hostile attribution biases similar across aggressor type?
- Do the information-processing models fit all the different types of and motivations for aggression?
- If we want to treat or assess aggression, why should we not focus on how it looks?
- Will clients always recognise that they have been aggressive? If not, why not?
- Exploring aggression motivation is important for what reason(s)?
- Tracing back the development of proactive aggression is essential when you want to explore where it commenced and how it was reinforced socially. Discuss.
- Should we treat males with aggression problems any differently than women? Why?
- Why should we account for dynamic (changing) risk factors with clients? What do such factors recognise?
- Why are functional assessments valuable in developing clinical rapport with a client?
- What are the most useful elements of functional assessment to bring into treatment?
- What value do implicit tests have in developing a formulation of a client?
- Looking at risk assessment, functional assessment and testing, which are the most valuable in assessing a client's risk and why?
- Why should we look at emotional acceptance as well as regulation and reactivity?
- If a client is described as having 'anger-management' problems, on what would we focus?
- If we wanted to develop a number of attention-shifting and physical distraction techniques for a client, what could we suggest?
- How can disputation techniques help a client and when might they best be used?
- If you were developing a clinical session for a client that intended to incorporate an information-processing approach, which areas would you look at?

TEXTS FOR FURTHER READING

Ireland, J.L., Ireland, C.A. & Birch, P. (2008) *Violent and Sexual Offenders: Assessment, Treatment and Management*, Abingdon: Willan.
Steffgen, G. & Gollwitzer, M. (2007) *Emotions and Aggressive Behavior*, Göttingen: Hogrefe.
Tremblay, R., Hartup, W. & Archer, J. (eds) *Developmental Origins of Aggression*, New York: Guilford Press.

RELEVANT JOURNAL ARTICLES

Anderson, C.A. & Bushman, B.J. (2002) Human aggression, *Annual Review of Psychology* 53: 27–51.

Anderson, C.A., Gentile, D.A. & Buckley, K.E. (2007) *Violent Video Game Effects on Children and Adolescents: Theory, Research and Public Policy*, New York: Oxford University Press.

Bennett, S., Farrington, D. & Huesmann, R. (2005) Explaining gender differences in crime and violence: The importance of social cognitive skills, *Aggression and Violent Behavior* 10(3): 263–88.

Björkqvist, K. (1994) Sex differences in physical, verbal, and indirect aggression: A review of recent research, *Sex Roles* 30: 177–88.

Bushman, B.J. & Anderson, C.A. (2001) Is it time to pull the plug on the hostile versus instrumental aggression dichotomy? *Psychological Review* 108: 273–9.

Crick, N.R. & Dodge, K.A. (1994) A review and reformulation of social information processing mechanisms in children's social adjustment, *Psychological Bulletin* 115: 74–101.

Daffern, M., Howells, K. & Ogloff, J. (2007) What's the point? Towards a methodology for assessing the function of psychiatric inpatient aggression, *Behaviour Research and Therapy* 45: 101–11.

Davey, L., Day, A. & Howells, K. (2005) Anger, over-control and serious violent offending, *Aggression and Violent Behavior* 10: 624–35.

Dawes, R.M., Faust, D. & Meehl, P.E. (1989) Clinical versus actuarial judgment, *Science* 243: 1668–74.

Douglas, K.S., Cox, D.N. & Webster, C.D. (1999) Violence risk assessment: Science and practice, *Legal and Criminological Psychology* 4: 149–84.

Harper, B.D., Lemerise, E.A. & Caverly, S.L. (2009) The effect of induced mood on children's social information processing: Goal clarification and response decision, *Journal of Abnormal Child Psychology* 38(5): 575–86.

Hart, S.D., Michie, C. & Cooke, D.J. (2007) Precision of actuarial risk assessment instruments: Evaluating the 'margins of error' of group v. individual predictions of violence, *British Journal of Psychiatry*, 190: s60–s65.

Megargee, E.I. (2009) A life devoted to crime, *Journal of Personality Assessment* 91(2): 95–107.

Richetin, J. & Richardson, D.S. (2008) Automatic processes and individual differences in aggressive behaviour, *Aggression and Violent Behavior* 13: 423–30.

RELEVANT WEB LINKS

Center for the Study of Violence, http://www.psychology.iastate.edu/faculty/caa/csv/index.htm

Harry Frank Guggenheim Foundation, www.hfg.org

International Society for Research on Aggression, www.israsociety.com

REFERENCES

Anderson, C.A. & Bushman, B.J. (2002) Human aggression, *Annual Review of Psychology* 53: 27–51.

Anderson, C.A., Gentile, D.A. & Buckley, K.E. (2007) *Violent Video Game Effects on Children and Adolescents: Theory, Research and Public Policy*, New York: Oxford University Press.

Bandura, A. (1973) *Aggression: A Social Learning Analysis*, New York: Holt.

Baumeister, R.F. & Bushman, B.J. (2007) Angry emotions and aggressive behaviours, in G. Steffgen & M. Gollwittzer (ed.) *Emotions and Aggressive Behavior*, pp. 61–75, Cambridge, MA: Hogrefe & Huber.

Bennett, S., Farrington, D. & Huesmann, R. (2005) Explaining gender differences in crime and violence: The importance of social cognitive skills, *Aggression and Violent Behavior* 10(3): 263–88.

Björkqvist, K. (1994) Sex differences in physical, verbal, and indirect aggression: A review of recent research, *Sex Roles* 30: 177–88.

Björkqvist, K., Österman, K. & Kaukiainen, A. (1992) The development of direct and indirect aggressive strategies in males and females, in K. Björkqvist & P. Niemela (eds) *Of Mice and Women: Aspects of Female Aggression*, pp. 51–64, San Diego, CA: Academic Press.

Borum, R., Bartel, P. & Forth, A. (2003) *Manual for the Structured Assessment of Violence Risk in Youth (SAVRY)*, Tampa: University of South Florida.

Bushman, B.J. & Anderson, C.A. (2001) Is it time to pull the plug on the hostile versus instrumental aggression dichotomy? *Psychological Review* 108: 273–9.

Buss, A.H. & Perry, M. (1992) The Aggression Questionnaire, *Journal of Personality and Social Psychology* 63: 452–9.

Crick, N.R. & Dodge, K.A. (1994) A review and reformulation of social information processing mechanisms in children's social adjustment, *Psychological Bulletin* 115: 74–101.

Crick, N.R. & Grotoper, J.K. (1996) Children's treatment by peers: Victims of relational and overt aggression, *Development and Psychopathology* 8: 367–80.

Daffern, M., Howells, K. & Ogloff, J. (2007) What's the point? Towards a methodology for assessing the function of psychiatric inpatient aggression, *Behaviour Research and Therapy* 45: 101–11.

Davey, L., Day, A. & Howells, K. (2005) Anger, over-control and serious violent offending, *Aggression and Violent Behavior* 10: 624–35.

Dawes, R.M., Faust, D. & Meehl, P.E. (1989) Clinical versus actuarial judgment, *Science* 243: 1668–74.

Dodge, K.A. (1986) A social information processing model of social competence in children, in M. Perlmutter (ed.) *Minnesota Symposia on Child Psychology, Vol. 18*, pp. 77–125, Hillsdale: Lawrence Erlbaum Associates.

Dodge, K.A. (1991) The structure and function of reactive and proactive aggression, in D.J. Pepler & K.H. Rubin (eds) *The Development and Treatment of Childhood Aggression*, pp. 201–18), Hillsdale, NJ: Lawrence Erlbaum Associates.

Dollard, J., Doob, L.W., Miller, N.E., Mowrer, O.H. & Sears, R.R. (1970) Frustration and aggression, in E.I. Megargee & J.E. Hokanson (ed.) *The Dynamics of Aggression*, pp. 22–32), New York: Harper & Row.

Douglas, K.S., Cox, D.N. & Webster, C.D. (1999) Violence risk assessment: Science and practice, *Legal and Criminological Psychology* 4: 149–84.

Goldiamond, I. (1975) Alternate sets as a framework for behavioural formulation and research, *Behaviorism* 3: 49–86.

Greenwald, A.G., McGhee, D.E. & Schwartz, J.K.L. (1998) Measuring individual differences in implicit cognition: The Implicit Association Test, *Journal of Personality and Social Psychology* 74: 1464–80.

Harper, B.D., Lemerise, E.A. & Caverly, S.L. (2009) The effect of induced mood on children's social information processing: Goal clarification and response decision, *Journal of Abnormal Child Psychology* 38(5): 575–86.

Harris, G.T., Rice, M.E. & Quinsey, V.L. (1993) Violent recidivism of mentally disordered offenders: The development of a statistical prediction instrument, *Criminal Justice and Behavior* 20: 315–35.

Hart, S.D., Michie, C. & Cooke, D.J. (2007) Precision of actuarial risk assessment instruments: Evaluating the 'margins of error' of group v. individual predictions of violence, *British Journal of Psychiatry*, 190: s60–s65.

Hay, D.F. (2005) The beginnings of aggression in infancy, in R. Tremblay, W. Hartup & J. Archer (eds) *Developmental Origins of Aggression*, New York: Guilford Press.

Huesmann, L.R. (1998) The role of social information processing and cognitive schema in the acquisition and maintenance of habitual aggressive behaviour, in R.G. Geen & E. Donnerstein (ed.) *Human Aggression: Theories, Research, and Implications for Social Policy*, pp. 73–109, London: Academic Press.

Ireland, J.L. (2008a) Conducting individualised theory-driven assessments of violent offenders, in J.L. Ireland, C.A. Ireland & P. Birch (2008) *Violent and Sexual Offenders: Assessment, Treatment and Management*, Abingdon: Willan.

Ireland, J.L. (2008b) Treatment approaches for violence and aggression: Essential content components, in J.L. Ireland, C.A. Ireland & P. Birch (2008) *Violent and Sexual Offenders: Assessment, Treatment and Management*, Abingdon: Willan.

Ireland, J.L. (2009a) *Life Minus Violence – Enhanced*, Liverpool: Mersey Care NHS Trust.

Ireland, J.L. (2009b) Some reflections on understanding and assessing aggression: Lessons from half a century, *Forensic Update*, 100.

Ireland, J.L. (2009c) *Puzzle Test*, Preston: University of Central Lancashire.

Ireland, J.L. & Ireland, C.A. (2008) Intra-group aggression among prisoners: Bullying intensity and exploration of victim-perpetrator mutuality, *Aggressive Behavior* 34: 76–87.

Ireland, J.L., Ireland, C.A., Morris-King, S., Turner, P., Graham-Kevan, N. & Xuereb, S. (2009) Life Minus Violence-Enhanced™, Liverpool: Psychological Services, Mersey Care NHS Trust.

Kropp, R., Hart, S. & Belfrage, H. (2005) *Manual for the Brief Spousal Assault Form for the Evaluation of Risk: B-Safer*, Toronto: Proactive Solutions, Inc.

Lee-Evans, J.M. (1994) Background to behavioural analysis, in M. McMurran & J. Hodge (ed.) *The Assessment of Criminal Behaviours of Clients in Secure Settings*, pp. 6–33, London: Jessica Kingsley.

Leslie, J.C. & O'Reilly, M.F. (1999) Assessing behavior in applied settings, in J.C. Leslie & M.F. O'Reilly, *Behaviour Analysis: Foundations and Applications to Psychology*, pp. 151–81, Newark, NJ: Harwood Academic Publishers.

Megargee, E.I. (1966) Undercontrolled and overcontrolled personality types in extreme antisocial aggression, *Psychological Monographs* 80(3), whole issue.

Megargee, E.I. (2009) A life devoted to crime, *Journal of Personality Assessment* 91(2): 95–107.

Montada, L. (2007) Emotion-based aggression motives, in G. Steffgen & M. Gollwitzer (eds) *Emotions and Aggressive Behavior*, pp. 19–37, Göttingen: Hogrefe.

Nelson-Gray, R.O. & Farmer, R.F. (1999) Behavioral assessment of personality disorders, *Behaviour Research and Therapy* 37: 347–68.

Nelson-Gray, R.O. & Farmer, R.F. (1999) Functional analysis and response covariation in the assessment of personality disorders: A reply to Staats and to Bissett and Hayes. *Behaviour Research and Therapy* 37: 385–94.

Prinstein, M.J., Boergers, J. & Vernberg, E.M. (2001) Overt and relational aggression in adolescents: Social-psychological adjustment of aggressors and victims, *Journal of Clinical Child Psychology* 30: 479–91.

Richetin, J. & Richardson, D.S. (2008) Automatic processes and individual differences in aggressive behaviour, *Aggression and Violent Behavior* 13: 423–30.

Schulz, R. (1985) Emotion and affect, in J.E. Birren & K.W. Schaie (eds) *Handbook of the Psychology of Aging*, 2nd edn, pp. 531–43, New York: Van Nostrand Reinhold.

Steffgen, G. & Gollwitzer, M. (2007) *Emotions and Aggressive Behavior*, Göttingen: Hogrefe.

Sturmey, P. (1996) *Functional Analysis in Clinical Psychology*, Chichester: John Wiley & Sons, Ltd.

Vitaro, F. & Brendgen, M. (2005) Proactive and reactive aggression: A developmental perspective, in R. Tremblay, W. Hartup & J. Archer (eds) *Developmental Origins of Aggression*, New York: Guilford Press.

Webster, C.D., Douglas, K.S., Eaves, D. & Hart, S.D. (1997) *HCR-20: Assessing Risk for Violence (Version 2)*, Burnaby, BC: Mental Health Law and Policy Institute, Simon Fraser University.

16 Training in Forensic Psychology and Professional Issues

Neil Gredecki & Polly Turner

LEARNING OUTCOMES

WHEN YOU HAVE COMPLETED THIS CHAPTER YOU SHOULD BE ABLE TO:

1. Describe the process for training as a forensic psychologist.
2. Describe the four core roles of forensic psychology training.
3. Apply ethical principles to the work of a forensic psychologist in training.
4. Describe and evaluate different methods and models of reflective practice.

KEY WORDS

Diploma in Forensic Psychology • Exemplar • Experiential Learning Theory • Forensic Psychologist in Training • Mental Health Review Tribunal (MHRT) • Practice Diary • Reflective Practice • Training Needs Analysis

CHAPTER OUTLINE

TABLE 16.4 (*Continued*)

What further training and development can I do once I have qualified?	HM Prison Service: There are a range of avenues for progression, depending on your qualifications, competencies and experience. Trainee psychologists have the chance to apply for qualified posts once they are eligible to do so, while qualified psychologists can take on a number of roles, including policy, management or direct delivery of services.
What particular qualities will employers look for?	HM Prison Service: see website, http://www.hmprisonservice.gov.uk/careersandjobs/psychologists/therole/
What career progression opportunities are there?	HM Prison Service: There are also opportunities to move into general management and policy positions, such as a reducing reoffending lead, or into more specialised posts, such as policy lead for sex offender strategy. Roles in consultancy and research are also available.
Will my training make me an attractive proposition for other careers? If so, which careers?	Yes – Civil Servant, NHS, private practice.
What are the hours of work like?	HM Prison Service: 37 hours a week, 25 days' leave rising to 30 days' after 10 years. 10.5 days' public holidays.
What are the working conditions like?	Challenging. See website, http://www.hmprisonservice.gov.uk/careersandjobs/psychologists/therole/
Will I have a job for life?	HM Prison Service: subject to performance and competence the Civil Service is relatively stable, however on 1 April 2010 the terms and conditions for Civil Servants altered, meaning that for the first time redundancy in times of constraint may be a reality.
Where can I go for further information?	http://www.hmprisonservice.gov.uk/careersandjobs/psychologists/therole/ http://www.bps.org.uk/careers/what-do-psychologists-do/areas/forensic.cfm http://www.nhscareers.nhs.uk/details/Default.aspx?Id=451

SELF-TEST QUESTIONS

- What is the core aim of Stage I?
- What might be important to consider when embarking on Stage I?
- What is the focus of Stage II?
- What are the four core roles in which a trainee needs to evidence competency?
- How might a trainee evidence competency in one of the four core roles (e.g. what activities might they engage in?)
- Describe how reflection enhances learning and professional practice.
- What tools can be helpful to reflection?
- How can positive psychological approaches assist trainees?

ESSAY QUESTIONS

- Discuss the role of reflective practice in relation to Stage II training.
- Evaluate the apprenticeship model for Forensic Psychology training.
- Discuss the role of applied forensic research to forensic practice.
- Explore how ethical standards can be applied to the practice of core role 1.

TEXTS FOR FURTHER READING

Adler, R.B. & Rodman, G. (1994) *Understanding Human Communication*, 5th edn, London: Harcourt Brace.

British Psychological Society (n.d.) *Ethical Principles for Conducting Research with Human Participants*, www.bps.org.uk.

British Psychological Society (2006) *Code of Conduct and Ethical Guidelines*, Leicester: British Psychological Society.

British Psychological Society (2008) *Diploma in Forensic Psychology: Candidate Handbook*, Leicester: BPS.

Crighton, D.A. & Towl, G.J. (2008) *Psychology in Prisons*, 2nd edn, London: BPS Blackwell.

Health Professionals Council (2008) *Standards of Conduct, Performance and Ethics*, London: Health Professionals Council.

Ireland, C.A. & Fisher, M. (in press) *Consultancy and Advising in Forensic Practice: Empirical and Practical Guidelines*, Abingdon: Willan.

Ireland, J.L., Ireland, C.A. & Birch, P. (2008) *Violent and Sexual Offenders: Assessment, Treatment and Management*, Abingdon: Willan.

Jupp, V., Davies, P. & Francis, P. (eds) (2000) *Doing Criminological Research*, London: Sage.

Miller, W.R. & Rollnick, S. (1991) *Motivational Interviewing: Preparing People to Change Addictive Behaviour*, London: Guilford Press.

Prins, H. (2005) *Offenders, Deviants or Patients?*, 3rd edn, London: Routledge.

Rae, L. (1997) *Planning and Designing Training Programmes*, Aldershot: Gower.

Reece, I. & Walker, S. (2007) *Teaching, Training and Learning: A Practical Guide*, 6th edn, Sunderland: Business Education.

Towl, G.J. (2006) *Psychological Research in Prisons*, Oxford: Blackwell.

Towl, G.J., Farrington, D.P., Crighton, D.A. & Hughes, G. (2008) *Dictionary of Forensic Psychology*, Abingdon: Willan.

RELEVANT JOURNAL ARTICLES

Anderson, C.A. & Bushman, B.J. (2002) Human aggression, *Annual Review of Psychology* 53: 27–51.

Atkins, S. & Murphy, K. (1995) Reflective practice, *Nursing Standard* 9: 31–7.

Beech, B. & Leather, P. (2006) Workplace violence in the health care sector: A review of staff training and integration of training evaluation models, *Aggression and Violent Behaviour* 11: 27–43.

Burrowes, N. & Needs, A. (2009) Time to contemplate change? A framework for assessing readiness to change with offenders, *Aggression and Violent Behavior* 14(1): 39–49.

Kuiper, R.A. & Pesut, D.J. (2004) Promoting cognitive and meta-cognitive reflective reasoning skills in nursing practice: Self-regulated learning theory, *Journal of Advanced Nursing* 45: 381–91.

Lake, N., Solts, B. & Preedy, K. (2008) Developing skills in consultation 4: Supporting the development of consultation skills – a trainer's and a manager's perspective, *Clinical Psychology Forum* 186: 29–33.

Ryan, R.M. & Deci, E.L. (2000) Self-determination theory and the facilitation of intrinsic motivation, social development, and well-being, *American Psychologist* 55(1): 68–78.

Tannenbaum, S.I. & Yukl, G. (1992) Training and development in work organisations, *Annual Review of Psychology* 43: 399–41.

Tversky, A. & Kahneman, D. (1981) The framing of decisions and the psychology of choice, *Science* 211: 453–8.

Ward, T. & Beech, A. (2006) An integrated theory of sexual offending, *Aggression and Violent Behaviour* 11: 44–63.

REFERENCES

Atkins, S. & Murphy, K. (1995) Reflective practice, *Nursing Standard* 9: 31–7.

Borders, L.D. & Leddick, G.R. (1987) *Handbook of Counselling Supervision*, Alexandria, VA: Association for Counsellor Education and Supervision.

British Psychological Society (2008) *Diploma in Forensic Psychology: Candidate Handbook*, Leicester: BPS.

Burrowes, N. & Needs, A. (2009) Time to contemplate change? A framework for assessing readiness to change with offenders, *Aggression and Violent Behaviour* 14: 39–49.

Cohen, G. (1996) *Memory in the Real World*, 2nd edn, Hove: Psychology Press.

Deci, E.L., & Ryan, R.M. (1985) *Intrinsic Motivation and Self-Determination in Human Behaviour*, New York: Plenum.

Duckworth, A.L., Steen, T.A. & Seligman, M.E.P. (2005) Positive psychology in clinical practice, *Annual Review of Clinical Psychology* 1: 629–51.

Fredrickson, B.L. (2001) The role of positive emotions in positive psychology, *American Psychologist* 56: 218–26.

Gibbs, G. (1988) *Learning by Doing: A Guide to Teaching & Learning Methods*, Oxford: Further Education Unit, Oxford Polytechnic.

Gredecki, N. & Turner, P. (2009) Positive psychology and forensic clients: Applications to relapse prevention in offending behaviour interventions, *British Journal of Forensic Practice* 11: 50–59.

Hancock, P. (1998) Reflective practice – using a learning journal, *Nursing Standard* 13: 36–9.

Ireland, C. (2009a) The reality of work as a Forensic Psychologist, *The Psychologist* 22(6): 538–9.

Ireland, C. (2009b) Notes from the Chair, *Forensic Update* 98: 2–6.

Ireland, J.L. (2009c) Life Minus Violence-Enhanced, Liverpool: Mersey Care NHS Trust.

Johns, C. (2000) *Becoming a Reflective Practitioner: A Reflective and Holistic Approach to Clinical Nursing, Practice Development and Clinical Supervision*, London: Blackwell Science.

Kirkpatrick, D.L. (1959) Techniques for evaluating training programmes, *Journal of the American Society for Training and Development* 13: 3–9.

Kirkpatrick, D.L. (1976) Evaluation of training, in B. Beech & P. Leather (2006) Workplace violence in the health care sector: A review of staff training and integration of training evaluation models, *Aggression and Violent Behaviour* 11: 27–43.

Kolb, D. (1984) *Experiential Learning as the Science of Learning and Development*, Englewood Cliffs, NJ: Prentice Hall.

Kuiper, R.A. & Pesut, D.J. (2004) Promoting cognitive and meta-cognitive reflective reasoning skills in nursing practice: Self-regulated learning theory, *Journal of Advanced Nursing* 45: 381–91.

Larrivee, B. (2000) Transforming teaching practice: Becoming the critically reflective teacher, *Reflective Practice* 1: 293–307.

Locke, E.A. (1996) Motivation through conscious goal setting, *Applied & Preventative Psychology* 5: 117–24.

Locke, E.A. & Latham, G.P. (2002) Building a practically useful theory of goal setting and task motivation, *American Psychologist* 57: 705–17.

McCulloch, A., McMurran, M. & Worley, S. (2005) Assessment of clinical change: A single case study of an intervention for alcohol-related aggression, *Forensic Update* 82: 4–9.

McGehee, W. & Thayer, P.W. (1961) *Training in Business and Industry*, New York: John Wiley & Sons, Inc.

Miller, W.R. & Rollnick, S. (1991) *Motivational Interviewing: Preparing People to Change Addictive Behaviour*, London: Guilford Press.

Neenan, M. (2009) *Developing Resilience: A Cognitive Behavioural Approach*, London: Routledge.

Nickerson, R.S. (1977) cited in Cohen, G. (1996) *Memory in the Real World*, 2nd edn, Hove: Psychology Press.

Ong, A., Bergeman, C.S., Bisconti, T.L. & Wallace, K.A. (2006) The contours of resilience and the complexity of emotions in later life, *Journal of Personality and Social Psychology* 91: 730–49.

Padesky, C. & Mooney, K. (2008) Uncover Strengths & Build Resilience with CBT: A 4 Step Model, workshop delivered May, London.

Peterson, C. (2000) The future of optimism, *American Psychologist* 55: 44–55.

Rolfe, G., Freshwater, D. & Jasper, M. (2001) *Critical Reflection for Nursing and the Helping Professions: A User's Guide*, London: Palgrave Macmillan.

Ryan, R.M. & Deci, E.L. (2000) Self-determination theory and the facilitation of intrinsic motivation, social development and well-being, *American Psychologist* 55(1): 68–78.

Schön, D. (1983) *The Reflective Practitioner*, New York: Basic Books.

Seligman, M.E.P. (2002) *Authentic Happiness: Using the New Positive Psychology to Realise Your Potential for Lasting Fulfilment*, London: Nicholas Brealey Publishing.

Tannenbaum, S.I. & Yukl, G. (1992) Training and development in work organisations, *Annual Review of Psychology* 43: 399–41.

Thorpe, K. (2004) Reflective learning journals: From concept to practice, *Reflective Practice* 5: 327–43.

Ward, T. (2002) Good lives and the rehabilitation of offenders: Promises and problems, *Aggression and Violent Behavior* 7: 513–28.

Wilkinson, J. (1999) Implementing reflective practice, *Nursing Standard* 13: 36–40.

Part IV
Educational Psychology

17 Educational Psychology: History and Overview

Robin Banerjee, Andy Tolmie & Jim Boyle

LEARNING OUTCOMES

WHEN YOU HAVE COMPLETED THIS CHAPTER, YOU SHOULD BE ABLE TO:

1. Describe the history of educational psychology, both as a field of academic research and as professional practice.
2. Compare and contrast different approaches to childhood and education in the past and today.
3. Describe different approaches to the nature and measurement of intelligence.
4. Describe and evaluate research on classroom management, the potential impact of class size and the role of self-regulation in learning at school.
5. Compare and contrast different research methodologies utilised in educational psychology research.

KEY WORDS

Ability Grouping • Apprentices • Associations • Behavioural Data • Bullying • Cause-and-Effect Relations • Child-Centred Education • Classroom Management • Control Group • Controlled Conditions • Cross-Sectional Design • Dependent Variable • Dialogic • Didactic • Discovery Learning • Ecologically Valid • Electro-Encephalography (EEG) • Emotional Intelligence (EQ) • Experimental Conditions • Experimental Group • Experimental Methods • Factorial Designs • Functional Magnetic Resonance Imaging (fMRI) • Group Work • Inclusive Education • Independent Variable • Intelligence • Intelligence Quotient (IQ) Tests • Interaction Effects • Interview Schedule • Interviews • Item Selection • Longitudinal Studies • Main Effects • Microgenetic Designs • Multiple Intelligence • Near Infra-Red Spectroscopy (NIRS) • Nonexperimental Methods • Observational Methods • Pedagogy • Psychometric Measures • Quasi-Experimental Designs • Questionnaire • Random Assignment • Randomised Design • Repeated Measures Design • Socratic Method • Structural MRI • Survey Methods • Triarchic Theory of Intelligence

CHAPTER OUTLINE

In this chapter, we will introduce the topic of educational psychology, considering the historical origins of this field of work, both as an academic discipline and as professional practice. Next, we will examine different views on education, with attention to the historical changes in our perspectives on children and schooling, and to the diverse approaches to education today. The subsequent section will provide some examples of how psychology is relevant to understanding aspects of individual pupils' functioning, as well as the dynamics of the classroom as a whole. Finally, we will examine some of the common research methods utilised in educational psychology research.

I have a sign in my classroom that says, 'Education is either to calm the disturbed or disturb the calm.' This has profoundly affected the way I teach. I discuss this saying with my classes on the first day of school, asking them whether they classify themselves as among the calm or among the disturbed. This usually creates a lively discussion, and I get some immediate insights into some of my students. I point out that many of them have drifted through school for years, sitting quietly, doing whatever was required, questioning nothing, and waiting for the bell to ring. These are the 'calm' and my job is to disturb them. I need to make them take charge of their own education, analyzing information rather than just regurgitating it. I work with them in small groups so that they cannot hide in the back of the class; each of them has to defend an answer. I let them know that in my class there is a great tolerance for differences of opinion, but everyone must have an opinion and be able to back it up. Then, I address the 'disturbed.' These are the students who have what I call 'noisy minds.' Perhaps their personal lives are in such chaos, they feel the school has nothing to offer of any use. Others are extremely bright students who have become openly hostile to the mediocrity of most classwork. My job is to show them how the skills I'm teaching can help them take control of their lives and futures. My job is to make them think something they have never thought before. My job is to help them turn down the noise in their minds so they can concentrate on the academic skills that will make them successful. (Gill, 2001, pp. 10–11)

There are thirty plus of them in every class and I see them twice a week and I have to be honest, with seven different classes, that's over two hundred kids. Even three months into the term I still don't know all of their names, but I do get to know the SEN [special educational needs] kids very quickly as they take up most of my attention. It seems like hardly have they all settled in and quietened down and dealt with all the cries for help, it is time to do all the winding up and leaving again. Some of these SEN kids are just bewildered by it all and just shuffle off to the next crazy episode. (Secondary school teacher, in MacBeath *et al.*, 2006, p. 33)

17.1 WHAT IS EDUCATIONAL PSYCHOLOGY?

The excerpts at the beginning of this chapter remind us of how complex the dynamics of the school environment are, and how challenging it can sometimes become to achieve the basic goal of promoting learning at school, both for teachers and for pupils. Teachers have to support the learning of a large number of pupils, each of whom has a unique profile of abilities, personality characteristics, goals, values and interests – all of which colour the way they behave, feel and think at school. At the same time, pupils not only have to handle the academic side of school life – acquiring new knowledge and skills across a wide range of subjects, and persisting with tasks at school and at home even when they find the subject matter difficult or uninteresting – but also must manage the countless interpersonal interactions they have with other pupils and the adults at school. Successful navigation of these many challenges can make the experience of education incredibly rewarding and fulfilling both for teachers and for learners, but it is not hard to see how problems can arise.

Educational psychology is concerned with the application of psychological theories and research to help us understand how teachers and learners behave, perform, think, feel and relate to each other in various educational settings. By shedding light on these processes, work in this area has the important function of helping us to bring about positive changes in the educational context, particularly in order to support those individuals who are experiencing difficulties – whether to do with academic performance, social behaviour and relationships, or emotional wellbeing. In the following five chapters, we will be exploring the many different facets of psychological theory, research and practice in the educational context. We will begin with an introduction to some of the different ways in which psychology has been applied to education, before moving on to an account of the different kinds of 'special educational needs' that might be encountered by psychologists in the school context. Then, we will turn to core areas of psychological theory and research to help us understand different aspects of teaching, learning and psychological adjustment in educational settings. Finally, we will consider the details of what is involved in training and then working as an educational psychologist.

17.2 HISTORICAL ORIGINS OF EDUCATIONAL PSYCHOLOGY

In the UK, the earliest teachers of psychology were philosophers such as Alexander Bain (1818–1903) and James Sully (1842–1923), who highlighted the relevance of psychology for education. The founding of the new science of experimental psychology in Germany in the mid-nineteenth century coincided with marked population growth in Europe and elsewhere, increased emigration, particularly to the United States, and the development of an international reform movement in education (Probst, 1997). This led to an expansion in the demand for schools and teacher training, which in the 1890s in the United Kingdom was met by the establishment of new day training colleges for teachers. Led by Sir John Adams (1857–1934), first professor of education at London University, and Sir Percy Nunn (1870–1944), principal of the London Day Training College (which later became the Institute of Education), these colleges built on the pioneering work of Wilheim Rein (1847–1929) and Ernst Meumann (1862–1915) in Germany and William James (1842–1910) and G. Stanley Hall (1844–1924) in the United States in applying the theory and methodology of the new science to schooling and education. This in turn led to the emergence of educational psychology as an academic research field in its own right, with a strong emphasis on 'mental testing' (Thomas, 1996; Wooldridge, 1994).

Educational psychology as an academic discipline developed rapidly during the twentieth century, particularly in the United States. The Educational Division of the American Psychological Association identified 16 psychologists who made significant contributions to educational psychology over the course of the twentieth century (Zimmerman & Schunk, 2002). Focus Point 17.1 provides brief summaries of their contributions. Find out more about these and also about some of the controversies that were associated with their work at http://academic.udayton.edu/gregelvers/hop/welcome.asp.

17.2.1 Emergence of Educational Psychology as Professional Practice

When in the quiet experimental working place of the psycho-educational scholar, through the steady co-operation of specialists, a real system of acknowledged facts is secured, then the practical attempts of the consulting school psychologist and of the leader of experimental classrooms have a safer basis, and their work will help again the theoretical scholar until the co-operation of all these agents produces a practical education which the teacher will accept without his own experimenting. (Munsterberg, 1898, pp. 131–2)

Hugo Munsterberg (1863–1916), the founder of the psychology department at Harvard University, was the first to coin the term 'school psychologist' (Kagan, 2005) and to distinguish such a specialist, school-based post from the academic educational psychologists based in teacher-training institutions. The first such professional educational psychologist was Cyril Burt (1883–1971), who was appointed by the London County Council in 1913, at a time when there were only 11 posts in psychology in total at universities in the United Kingdom. This was followed in 1923 by the appointment of David Kennedy Fraser (1888–1962) by the Glasgow Education Committee to the post of 'psychological adviser'.

The number of child psychologists in the United Kingdom grew throughout the late 1920s and 1930s, often under the aegis of the multidisciplinary Child Guidance model that was introduced from the US at that time (Sampson, 1980). Early development was, however, hampered by lack of funding and the view that the psychology courses in teacher training equipped teachers to deal with classroom-based problems (Wooldridge, 1994). There was also tension between the first professional educational psychologists (EPs) working in education

FOCUS POINT 17.1   CONTRIBUTIONS TO RESEARCH AND THEORY IN EDUCATIONAL PSYCHOLOGY

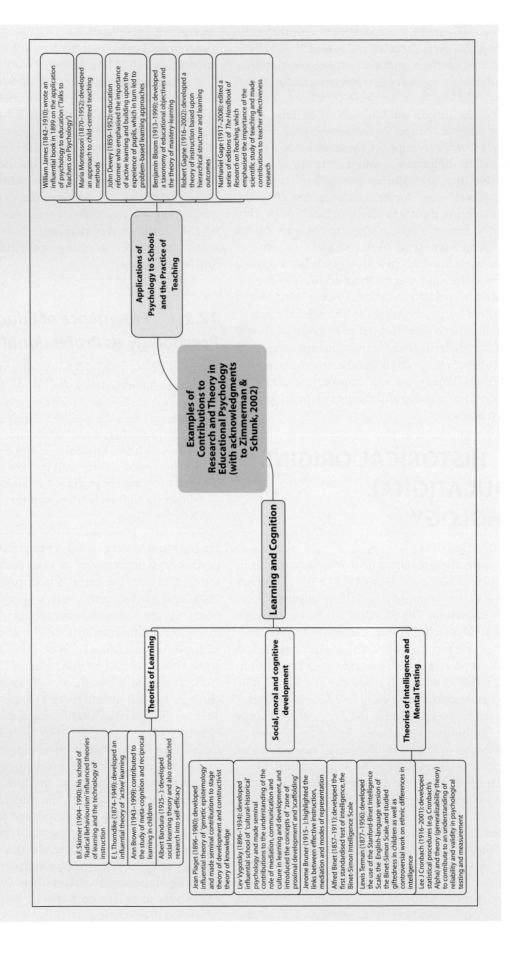

Examples of Contributions to Research and Theory in Educational Psychology (with acknowledgments to Zimmerman & Schunk, 2002)

Applications of Psychology to Schools and the Practice of Teaching

William James (1842–1910): wrote an influential book in 1899 on the application of psychology to education ('Talks to Teachers on Psychology')

Maria Montessori (1870–1952): developed an approach to child-centred teaching methods

John Dewey (1859–1952): education reformer who emphasised the importance of active learning and building upon the experience of pupils, which in turn led to problem-based learning approaches

Benjamin Bloom (1913–1999): developed a taxonomy of educational objectives and the theory of mastery-learning

Robert Gagne (1916–2002): developed a theory of instruction based upon hierarchical structure and learning outcomes

Nathaniel Gage (1917–2008): edited a series of editions of *The Handbook of Research on Teaching*, which emphasised the importance of the scientific study of teaching and made contributions to teacher effectiveness research

Learning and Cognition

Theories of Learning

B.F. Skinner (1904–1990): his school of 'Radical Behaviourism' influenced theories of learning and the technology of instruction

E L Thorndike (1874–1949): developed an influential theory of 'active' learning

Ann Brown (1943–1999): contributed to the study of meta-cognition and reciprocal learning in children

Albert Bandura (1925–): developed social learning theory and also conducted research into self-efficacy

Social, moral and cognitive development

Jean Piaget (1896–1980): developed influential theory of 'genetic epistemology' and made seminal contributions to stage theory of development and constructivist theory of knowledge

Lev Vygotsky (1896–1934): developed influential school of 'cultural-historical' psychology and made seminal contributions to the understanding of the role of mediation, communication and culture in learning and development, and introduced the concepts of 'zone of proximal development and scaffolding'

Jerome Bruner (1915–): highlighted the links between effective instruction, mediation and modes of representation

Theories of Intelligence and Mental Testing

Alfred Binet (1857–1911): developed the first standardised test of intelligence, the Binet-Simon Intelligence Scale

Lewis Terman (1877–1956): developed the use of the Stanford-Binet Intelligence Scale, the English-language version of the Binet-Simon Scale, and studied giftedness in children as well as controversial work on ethnic differences in intelligence

Lee J Cronbach (1916–2001): developed statistical procedures (e.g. Cronbach's Alpha) and theory (generalizability theory) to contribute to an understanding of reliability and validity in psychological testing and measurement

authorities and in Child Guidance Clinics and their academic colleagues in universities and teacher-training institutions, who often had higher academic qualifications. But EPs began to make their mark, not least by influencing government policy making (Boyle, Mackay & Lauchlan, 2008), which led to steady expansion from the 1970s to the present day. In Chapter 21, we will look in more detail at the kind of work undertaken by educational psychologists today.

17.3 APPROACHES TO EDUCATION

In order to understand how psychological theory can inform the educational process, we need to start by considering views of children and education. We will do this by looking first at historical changes in ideas about the nature of childhood and the role of education in preparing children for adulthood, and then move on to examine contemporary approaches to education, especially in the United Kingdom.

17.3.1 Historical Changes in Approaches to Children and Schooling

While childhood is nowadays seen by most societies as a very distinct period of preparation for adult life, historically speaking this is a recent conception (Cunningham, 2005; Koops, 2004; Mintz, 2004). In earlier cultures, once children were no longer infants and began to be capable of independent action, they were regarded increasingly as adults in miniature, and expected to play a full role in the daily work needed to maintain the family and wider community. This was still a commonplace conception in the Victorian era (as is evident from the novels of Dickens), especially for the children of poorer parents. Until the end of the Second World War, the majority of children in the United Kingdom continued to leave school to begin work at 14, an age that seems inconceivable now.

This does not mean that there was no notion that children had to *learn* things in the pre-Victorian era, but in general there was no explicit **pedagogy**. The focus was on learning practical skills or trades and learning in situ as **apprentices**, in much the same way as an adult would learn any new skill (Lave, 1988; Lave & Wenger, 1991). Apprenticeship is an apparently culturally universal form of informal learning (see Section 20.2.2), suggesting that it has evolutionary origins in forms of observational learning (Tomasello, 2009; see also Chapter 19), and simply relies on 'natural' behaviour on the part of both the model and the learner (see Case History 17.1).

> **pedagogy** the art and science of teaching.
>
> **apprentices** individuals who learn a craft or trade through the guidance of a more skilled or competent person.

Education as we understand it now *was* provided for a very few individuals (Cunningham, 2005): basic literacy and numeracy skills were taught to the children of wealthier families, in order to support the work they had to do. More embellished forms of these skills (including some aspects of science) were taught to (male) children of those in positions of influence, to provide them with

---

CASE HISTORY 17.1

Lave and Wenger (1991) describe the widespread nature of apprenticeship processes in a range of different work contexts, and use the term *legitimate peripheral participation* to capture a key element of these processes. What they mean by this is that those who are learning a particular trade or craft are specifically allowed to stand on the boundaries of the activity of a skilled worker, observing how they carry out specific aspects of their work, and gradually assisting, initially in a peripheral way, as their knowledge and understanding get better.

A good example would be the plumber and the plumber's mate. When the plumber's mate first goes out on jobs with the plumber, they will appear to do little more than carry the tools, but in fact even at this point they are gaining a sense of how the work is organised, how clients are treated and so on, by being effectively walked through the process. They will also spend a lot of time just watching how the plumber goes about the job in hand – how the problem is examined, and when the water supply is turned off and actual work commences. They will gradually begin to be assigned specific tasks within the activity, such as locating the stopcock, and handing over specific tools as requested. The key moment comes when they have gained sufficient experience of how a particular task is managed that they no longer need to be told to do something, but do it spontaneously, because they can anticipate the need – for instance, having a tool ready for use without having to be asked for it. Once this point has been reached, they will be given greater responsibility for aspects of the task, with the role of plumber and observed reversing, and the plumber intervening when uncertainties or errors arise. In this way the plumber's mate acquires the expertise to become an actual plumber themselves – *but without any form of actual instruction*, just by taking part in the work itself, in a very specific way.

access to the 'refined' culture of this grouping so that they could participate fully within it. Fully developed and specialised education was reserved for the members of religious communities (where most learning resided) and for those with sufficient wealth and interest to attend the universities established by those communities, especially those going into specific professions such as the law. Where formal education existed, though, it was provided on a one-to-one or one-to-few basis, and utilised forms of instruction and guidance that owed much to classical philosophy, such as the **Socratic method** of learning through dialogue and asking questions. This was essentially just a form of *intellectual* apprenticeship.

Socratic method learning through dialogue and asking questions.

The principal catalyst for change was the industrial revolution (Cunningham, 2005). In terms of demand, the altered nature of work that came with industrial-scale production required a more educated workforce to maintain the record keeping and correspondence that it necessitated. At the same time, the general increase in wealth (in relative terms) meant that more families had the money to pay for education for their children, and reason to invest in it because of the increased social mobility and opportunity to which it led. Similarly, increased political organisation on the part of those involved in industrial work meant that they seized on the value of education – and their *right* to it – for the same reasons. In terms of provision, this increased demand for education meant that it made economic sense for people to set up and run schools (Tooley, 2000). Increased wealth also meant that there were a number of philanthropists prepared to support free or subsidised education as a means to wider social improvement, either via independent foundations or church schools. Churches and religious groupings of various kinds played a major role in organising schools for similar reasons, and as a means of ensuring that communities were brought up in the knowledge of their precepts (Cunningham, 2005).

In terms of curriculum content, there was a particular emphasis within these burgeoning schools on the 'three Rs' (reading, 'riting, 'rithmetic), the basic skills needed for work, supplemented with religious instruction, some basic history, geography, science, and perhaps foreign languages. The increased scale of demand meant, however, that provision was only possible on the basis of large classes, resulting in a fundamental shift to **didactic**, instructional modes of pedagogy, with a great deal of rote learning, repetition and recitation. This had practical benefits, but also corresponded to some extent with empiricist philosophy

didactic designed to instruct.

that became dominant in the nineteenth century, which saw humans as blank slates and children by extension as empty vessels into which knowledge had to be poured (Koops, 2004). This kind of patchwork quilt arrangement covered the majority of children, in the United Kingdom at least, by the start of the twentieth century, and continued to operate until the 1944 Education Act, which aimed to set up an *ideal* system for the post-war era.

17.3.2 *Perspectives on Education Today*

The 1944 Act and parallel changes elsewhere in the United Kingdom established universal free education on the basis of state provision for children up to the age of 15, while leaving the content of school curricula open (Barber, 1996). This apparent freedom was constrained, though, by the framework of educational structures that it introduced. From 5 to 7 children were to be taught in infant schools, and then from 7 to 11 in junior schools, both focused on developing basic skills and competencies. At age 11 they were to transfer to one of three types of secondary school: grammar, technical or secondary modern (see Table 17.1). Technical schools never really got off the ground in the way that they did in Germany after the war, leaving a division between grammar and secondary modern schools split roughly 20:80 in terms of numbers.

Despite its idealism, the Act was still primarily concerned with serving the needs of industry and the economy, and the only involvement of psychology was the IQ testing that took place at the end of junior school to decide which secondary route children took. Shifts in the perception of what education was for, and how it should be provided, came instead from philosophers and from within the teaching profession itself. Herbart (1841) began to articulate a role for psychology in scientifically determining effective pedagogy. This was later taken up by Dewey (1903), who emphasised the importance of child-directed education that took as its starting point the interests and capabilities of the child, not least as part of the democratic development of society (see also the independent school systems set up by Maria Montessori and Rudolf Steiner). Dewey's work was highly influential within the teaching profession and among those training teachers, and this in turn fuelled an interest in developmental psychology, especially the work of Jean Piaget. This interest culminated in the Plowden Report (CACE, 1967) on primary education in England, and similar reports in Wales and Scotland. These made a firm recommendation to government in

TABLE 17.1 *The Three Types of Secondary School Introduced in England by the 1944 Education Act.*

Grammar schools	Technical schools	Secondary modern schools
Focus: broad range of **academic** disciplines (arts and languages, maths, sciences), preparation for working life as a **professional**	Focus: **knowledge and skills** required for specific **industrial** occupations	Focus: **basic provision** in arts and sciences, coupled with **practical skills** for **office work or manual labour** (e.g. typing, woodwork)

child-centred education approach to education which focuses on the needs, abilities, and other attributes of the child.

discovery learning an enquiry-based form of learning in which the student explores and finds answers rather than merely receives instruction.

group work a way of organising students into groups to actively engage them in study.

dialogic using talk between partners to enhance learning.

inclusive education a policy to provide access to mainstream education for those with disabilities unless good reason can be shown that this is counterproductive.

favour of **child-centred education**, including **discovery learning**, in which children actively constructed an understanding of the world (see Section 20.2.1).

This emphasis on evidence-based provision in primary schools (and its extension down to nursery schools) has continued since then, driven most recently by the perception that this provides the fundamental platform for later achievement, and by the need to improve children's performance in literacy, numeracy and science (DfEE, 1998). At the same time, discovery learning as such has been replaced by a broader emphasis on active engagement by children, especially via the use of student **group work** and **dialogic** pedagogies in which children discuss and solve carefully structured problems, an approach with established effects on learning (Alexander, 2004; Royal Society, 2010). The emphasis on scientific approaches is much less evident at secondary level, however, despite the shift to comprehensive schools in which more diverse provision is made. This was primarily politically inspired rather than being based on research evidence; this politicisation of secondary education, for good or ill, is also reflected in the content and structure imposed by the National Curriculum under the 1988 Education Act, and equivalents in Scotland and Northern Ireland. It is also reflected in the adoption of **inclusive education** policies, following anti-discrimination legislation in both the United Kingdom and United States that compels schools and education authorities to provide access to mainstream education for those with disabilities unless good reason can be shown that this is counterproductive.

These changes have meant that schools and teachers have experienced an increased need for understanding learning and pedagogical processes, including those involving children with a range of special needs. Despite this, though, formal psychological input to teacher training, in the United Kingdom at least, has more or less disappeared over the same period, due to time and resource pressures (Tomlinson, 2002). There are exceptions to this in a few areas, notably visual impairment, where the mandatory training that teachers have to undergo to work with such populations has a psychological component. Otherwise, most psychological understanding is gained by teachers voluntarily taking courses (and receiving recognition for this in salary increments in Scotland) or working alongside EPs.

17.3.3 Summary

The concept of childhood as a period universally spent in formal education and preparation for adult life is not yet 150 years old. Prior to this, virtually all learning that took place among children was acquired through direct experience of work alongside adults; where 'book learning' did occur, there was no explicit pedagogy to inform teaching methods. The shift to centrally structured universal provision, summarised in Table 17.2, was largely driven by economic and political concerns, and the interest in trying to define effective pedagogies came primarily from those working within education as a consequence of their experience of the structures that were put in place. Psychological input to educational provision itself has never been more than patchy, though its role in shaping evidence-based practice, especially in nursery and primary schools, has become considerably stronger over the past 40 years.

17.4 UNDERSTANDING PUPIL AND CLASSROOM FUNCTIONING

Over the course of the next few chapters, we will consider how psychology has a role to play in helping us understand both the functioning of individual pupils, and the functioning of the classroom as a whole. We will see that educational psychology sheds light not only

TABLE 17.2 *Summary of Key Shifts in Educational Provision within the United Kingdom.*

Time point	Nature of/change in provision
Mediaeval to pre-industrial period	Apprenticeship and situated learning for vast majority Tutors and early forms of university education for wealthy and those in religious communities, using Socratic methods
Industrial Revolution	Patchwork quilt of privately run, philanthropic and church schools, gradually building up to cover most children Focus on three Rs plus religious instruction, elements of other subjects, use of didactic pedagogies
End of Second World War	Introduction of universal provision up to age 15 in infant and junior schools, followed by grammar or secondary modern school according to result of 11 plus intelligence test
1960s	Growth of interest in child-centred, evidence-based provision in primary schools particularly
1970s	Replacement (largely) of grammar and secondary modern schools with comprehensive schools
1980s	Introduction of National Curriculum or its equivalent
1990s	National Strategies to support early literacy teaching via evidence-based practice
2000s	Growth of inclusive provision and dialogic pedagogies

on the cognitive abilities that influence pupils' academic outcomes, but also on the broader social, emotional and motivational context of schooling. Below, we introduce some examples of important educational issues – many of them controversial – that highlight the significance of these psychological dimensions of school life.

17.4.1 Assessing Pupils' Functioning

One of the important roles of an educational psychologist is to provide expert assessments of pupils, which might cover cognitive, academic, behavioural and socio-emotional characteristics. The aim of this assessment work is to help shed light on difficulties pupils may be having at school and – importantly – to identify any pupil

needs that require particular educational provisions (e.g. additional small-group or individual teaching, specialist facilities and so on). In Chapter 18, we will look in more detail at the different kinds of 'special educational needs' that might become apparent to an educational psychologist, as well as the process for responding to those needs. However, it is important to recognise that the assessment process is itself a subject of complex psychological theory and research.

A good example of this can be found in the case of psychometric tests of **intelligence**. As we noted above, educational psychology has historically included a major focus on mental testing. To this day, the expertise of educational psychologists in evaluating intellectual functioning can be a crucial starting point for work with a pupil. For example, in determining the needs of a pupil suspected of having learning difficulties, it would be very common for an educational psychologist to be involved in profiling the general intelligence of the pupil – using a measure such as the Wechsler Intelligence Scale for Children (WISC) – as well as more specific abilities in academic subjects such as reading and writing. The idea of testing the intellectual functioning of pupils at school is in fact one of the starting points of modern developmental psychology. The work of Alfred Binet and his collaborator Theodore Simon in the early twentieth century (Binet & Simon, 1916) led to the development of **intelligence quotient (IQ) tests**, such as the WISC, that compare a given individual pupil's overall test performance with an average or standard performance (scored as 100).

> **intelligence** a complex concept which incorporates intellectual capability, reasoning and understanding.

> **intelligence quotient (IQ) tests** means of comparing the mental age of a child with their chronological age, to determine the child's current intellectual capacity.

Yet the concept of intelligence is itself a controversial one. Early in the twentieth century, Spearman (1927) argued that there is a single general mental ability (labelled *g*) that is involved in completing any mental test, and that this is the key to intelligence. Thus, many people assume that the IQ score derived from an intelligence test such as the WISC is essentially a measure of this general ability. However, educational psychologists know that individuals very often have 'spiky' profiles, whereby they perform well on some sub-tests but poorly on others. In fact, while the precise nature and meaning of *g* is still a matter of considerable debate, many theories of intelligence today focus on multiple components that exist alongside each other or within a hierarchy. For example, Gardner's (1983, 2000) theory of **multiple intelligence** distinguishes between various distinct intelligences, including a

> **multiple intelligence** a theory that distinguishes between various distinct intelligences, including logical-mathematical, spatial, musical, interpersonal, and kinaesthetic components.

triarchic theory of intelligence a theory that distinguishes three components of intelligence: analytic, creative, and practical.

emotional intelligence (EQ) intelligence relating to the perception, understanding, and management of emotions.

logical-mathematical component but also spatial, musical, interpersonal and kinaesthetic components (see Table 17.3). Meanwhile, Sternberg (1985) refers to a **triarchic theory of intelligence**, involving analytic, creative and practical abilities. And in recent years, considerable attention has been paid to the notion of **emotional intelligence (EQ)** – involving the perception, understanding and management of emotions – as being an essential part of human functioning (Goleman, 1995; Mayer & Salovey, 1997).

Debate about these multifaceted approaches to intelligence includes concerns about what really counts as 'intelligence' (as opposed to a preferred 'learning style', a talent or a personality trait), as well as arguments about overlap between different components. Furthermore, besides the broad questions about the nature of intelligence, we have additional controversies about such issues as: the use and implications of psychometric assessments in different populations, for instance children from eth-nic minorities (e.g. Brooks-Gunn, Klebanov & Duncan, 1996); the degree to which cognitive ability is inherited and/or shaped by environmental experiences (e.g. Grigorenko, 2000); and the relative importance of psychometric measures of intelligence – alongside various other psychosocial factors – in predicting long-term educational outcomes (e.g. Jimerson *et al.*, 2000).

So where does this leave the pupil assessment process? In fact, educational psychologists rarely rely on a single test to evaluate pupils' abilities and determine their needs. Rather, they often work to collate evidence from multiple sources – teachers, other professionals, families, the pupils themselves, as well as direct observation in the classroom – to arrive at a comprehensive and fully informed portrait of the pupils' current functioning, as well as the factors that may have influenced the pupils' development (Association of Principal Educational Psychologists, 2005). As we will see in Chapters 19 and 20, psychologists have convincingly demonstrated that a multitude of cognitive, motivational, social and emotional processes are involved in pupils' functioning at school. Thus, in order to design effective intervention programmes and promote positive change – whether this relates to academic learning and achievement or to behavioural and emotional adjustment – the assessment process clearly must go beyond a single psychometric test.

17.4.2 Organising and Managing the Classroom

The role of the educational psychologist is by no means limited to assessing individual pupils' needs and designing effective interventions for those selected pupils, important though that may be. Educational psychologists also work in a more general capacity to support teachers' everyday classroom activities, in order to enhance the universal provision offered to all pupils. In doing so, psychologists need to be mindful of the many factors that influence how successful a teacher is in promoting the learning of their pupils. One key task is **classroom management**, which involves the approaches and strategies used by teachers to create a positive learning environment. A way to think about this is to ask how much of the time *allocated* to learning at school is time where pupils are really *engaged* in learning. The size of the gap between allocated time and engaged time is critical: according to Brophy (1986, p. 1070), 'High task-engagement rates attained through successful classroom management are among the most powerful correlates of student achievement.'

classroom management the approaches and strategies used by teachers to create a positive learning environment.

TABLE 17.3 *Gardner's Theory of Multiple Intelligences.*

Intelligence	Description
Linguistic	Sensitivity to sounds, rhythm and meanings of words and language
Logical-mathematical	Ability to see and reason about logical and numerical patterns
Spatial	Accurate perception of the physical, spatial world, and capacity to transform those perceptions
Musical	Ability to appreciate and produce rhythm, pitch and timbre in musical expressions
Bodily/kinaesthetic	Controlling one's body movements and handling physical objects in a skilful way
Interpersonal	Ability to identify and respond to the emotional states, goals and desires of other people
Intrapersonal	Awareness and knowledge of one's own feelings, strengths and weaknesses, and ability to use this to guide behaviour
Naturalist	Sensitivity to patterns in the natural world (e.g. plants and animals)

Source: Adapted from Gardner (1983, 2000).

Many people might assume that ensuring greater task engagement simply depends on having smaller class sizes, so that behaviour can be monitored and controlled more easily; in fact, pledges about reducing class size are frequently made by political parties. However, the research on the topic is far from straightforward. Although some research has indeed shown that smaller class sizes are associated with more individual teacher contact, higher-quality instruction, better pupil support and less off-task behaviour, there are also indications that larger class sizes can sometimes lead to children being more engaged in group activities directed by the teacher (e.g. Blatchford *et al.*, 2003; NICHD Early Child Care Research Network, 2004). In fact, rather than making a blanket judgement about the optimal size of a class, it seems reasonable to conclude that the effects of class size are most likely to depend on a whole host of factors relating to how teachers organise their instructional practices and manage their classrooms to meet the needs of their pupils (see Figure 17.1).

The task of creating an orderly learning environment with a class of pupils who vary on multiple dimensions – ability, behaviour, personality, emotional adjustment, motivation and so on – is highly complex. Much of the educational psychology research on this topic has focused on specific teacher attributes, behaviours and practices that are conducive to a positive learning environment, such as explicit teaching of classroom rules and procedures, effective planning and monitoring of classroom activities, and consistent systems of feedback and consequences (e.g. see Brophy, 1986). This at least partly has involved the application of behaviourist perspectives concerning the way in which desirable behaviours can be reinforced and undesirable behaviours extinguished (see Landrum & Kauffman, 2006; see also Section 19.2 for more information about behavioural approaches to learning). Yet, increasingly, psychological research has led to greater consideration of teacher cognitions, interpersonal relationships and emotional dynamics within the classroom (e.g. Emmer & Stough, 2001). For example, some approaches to classroom management focus on strategies to build a sense of community, enhancing classroom management not by authoritarian enforcement of rules but instead by creating a joint sense of ownership and self-regulation among both the pupils and the staff (see Focus Point 17.2). In Chapter 20, we will consider more carefully how related social-motivational processes play a role in shaping the educational experience of pupils and teachers at school.

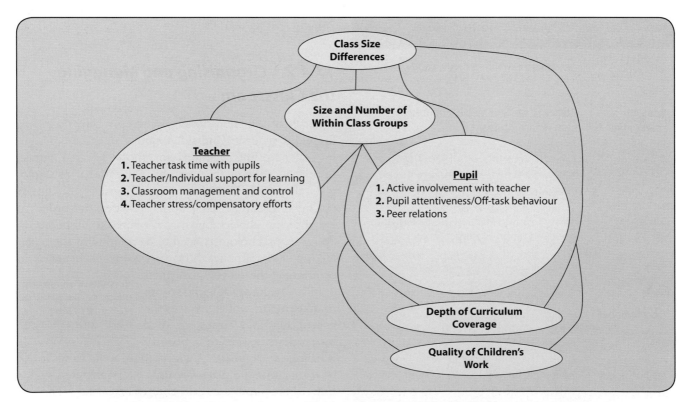

FIGURE 17.1 *Relationships between class size and various aspects of classroom processes.*

This diagram shows how differences in class size are connected to numerous variables related to organisational structures within the class, teacher behaviours and pupil experiences. Blatchford *et al.* (2003, p. 719) conclude, 'Class size effects are … *not singular but multiple.* there may be not only multiple effects, but different effects themselves affect each other.'

Source: Blatchford et al. (2003, p. 720).

FOCUS POINT 17.2   BUILDING COMMUNITY IN THE CLASSROOM – A TEACHER'S PERSPECTIVE

I began with my first-period class. We started slowly, with my asking them about what it would take for the class to work for them. I then told them what it would take for the class to work for me. I was amazed at the overlap ... We talked about the best classes and the worst classes. We talked about respect and the need to respect ideas and each other. ... Well, this was five months ago and I am amazed at the level of cooperation ... We have class meetings once a week to see how things are going and adjust as needed ... I didn't believe it would make a difference, the students really surprised me with their level of maturity and responsibility ... I have been teaching for fourteen years and this has been my best year. I feel supported by my students and my students told me they feel supported by me. (Seventh-grade teacher, cited in Freiberg, 1999, p. 171)

Importantly, the idea that pupils can learn to *regulate themselves* is a cornerstone of contemporary psychological approaches to classroom management. In other words, rather than conceiving of classroom management in terms of making pupils obey the authority of the teacher, we can argue that enabling pupils to monitor and control their *own* behaviour, emotional reactions and cognition is the critical goal. In fact, one account of what pre-school children need in order to be 'ready' for school suggests:

> Whether defined as the regulation of emotion in appropriate social responding or the regulation of attention and selective strategy use in the execution of cognitive tasks, self-regulatory skills underlie many of the behaviors and attributes that are associated with successful school adjustment. (Blair, 2002, p. 112)

This kind of perspective maps on to evidence that teachers see characteristics such as sensitivity to others' feelings, capacity to follow directions and ability to take turns and share – all of which clearly require you to regulate what you are doing and thinking – as far more important for school readiness than knowledge of the alphabet or counting skills (National Center for Education Statistics, 1993).

Focusing on pupils' self-regulation skills does not mean that we can afford to neglect the social dimensions of school life. As we will see in Chapter 20, theories of developmental psychology make it clear that children's capacity to regulate themselves in many ways emerges out of their interactions with others. In fact, educational psychologists frequently contribute insights into the social dynamics of pupils' learning experience at school. One of the most controversial issues in this area is the practice of **ability grouping**, where pupils are grouped with other pupils at school on the basis of their ability

ability grouping pupils are grouped with other pupils at school on the basis of their ability in a given subject or task.

in a given subject or task. This may include systematic streaming of pupils into different classes (or even schools) based on general ability, setting of pupils into different classes depending on abilities in particular subjects (e.g. in mathematics or English) or the allocation of pupils into different ability groups within the same class. Intriguingly, although grouping on the basis of ability is common practice in many schools, the research evidence on the benefits of these practices is far from clear. One recent report showed that the overall impact of setting on GCSE attainment was actually negligible, although it seems clear that pupils placed in a higher set end up achieving significantly better results than those of the same ability who are placed in a lower set (Ireson, Hallam & Hurley, 2005). Thus, it seems likely that ability-grouping practices can potentially lead to greater divergence between the more and less able pupils: higher-attaining pupils are typically placed in higher sets, which in turn enables further growth in attainment, making those pupils increasingly superior to lower-attaining pupils who are typically placed in lower sets.

Ireson, Hallam and Hurley (2005) explain that these kinds of effects often reflect differences in teacher practices:

> They convey high expectations of students in top sets through work that proceeds at a fast pace and is challenging, whereas students in low sets receive teaching that tends to proceed more slowly and covers less of the curriculum. The students in lower sets receive more structured work, more repetition and fewer opportunities for discussion. (Ireson, Hallam & Hurley, 2005, p. 455)

Furthermore, different ways of grouping by ability can influence the way in which pupils think and feel about their own ability by providing different frames of reference for pupils to judge themselves (e.g. Reuman, 1989).

We will see in Chapter 20 that the social comparisons made by pupils, along with differences in teacher beliefs and expectations, can have a powerful effect on the pupils' motivation to learn.

17.4.3 Links between Pupil and Classroom Functioning

It is very important to recognise that in many cases, educational psychologists' work will involve close attention to the links between individual pupil functioning and the dynamics of the class (or even the school) as a whole. A good example of this is pupils' involvement in **bullying** –

bullying aggressive acts by individuals or groups that are directed, repeatedly and over time, towards victims in order to hurt them emotionally or physically.

aggressive acts or behaviours by individuals or groups that are directed, repeatedly and over time, towards victims in order to hurt them emotionally or physically. Bullying is known to be associated with negative psychological and social adjustment outcomes for all parties involved, including not only the victims, but also the bullies themselves as well as those who witness the incidents (e.g. Hawker & Boultons, 2000; O'Connell, Pepler & Craig, 1999; Storch & Ledley, 2005). Thus, an individual pupil's difficulties in functioning as a consequence of being victimised cannot be separated from the wider social context of the classroom.

So imagine a case where concerns have been raised about a pupil who has been underperforming for some time – despite the best efforts of her teacher – and who has shown a recent increase in unauthorised absences from school. An educational psychologist might initially become involved in assessing the pupil's intellectual and cognitive functioning (e.g. evaluating the possibility of specific learning difficulties), but in the course of a more comprehensive assessment could find that the pupil has been involved in a significant bullying problem within her class. In such a situation, the educational psychologist will have to grapple not just with the difficulties of the individual pupil, but also with the broader social problems within the class (or even the school) as a whole. For example, an educational psychologist in this situation might help schools to implement a range of intervention strategies operating at a much broader level, beyond support for the individual pupil. This could include peer-support strategies, whole-class curriculum activities, school awareness-raising events, and even changes in the school environment and adult supervision patterns (see DCSF, 2007).

Focus Point 17.3 gives one pupil's story about her experiences of being bullied – what could be done to support the pupil and to reduce or even prevent such problems in the school? In the next chapter, we will see that school-based work to meet pupils' needs often involves multiple waves of intervention, ranging from universal educational provision for all pupils in a school to intense one-to-one work with the individual pupil.

FOCUS POINT 17.3   JAX'S STORY ABOUT BULLYING

I don't know whether it has ever happened to you? It started when Justine came into our class. I was friends with Joanne and Justine wanted to hang round with us. It was OK at first but then she and Jo began laughing about things and I didn't know what was funny. They had secrets they wouldn't tell me. They started nicking my things and pretending I had lost them. I stopped hanging around with them and sat next to Lucy in English and Science. She was my friend from primary school.

Then they started spreading rumours about me. They said I was a slag and slept with Pete Smithson. They said I was pregnant. They started sending me horrible text messages. They got everyone against me. I didn't want to tell her – but my Mum found out when I told her because she found me crying in my room.

I wouldn't go to school. Mum went to school and spoke to Miss Ratcliffe but she said they, the teachers, hadn't seen anything and they couldn't do anything about it. I got really down. My Mum went to school and got angry because I was missing so much school. They got everyone together and changed my form. They also gave me a mentor. Things are better now but I still don't speak to Jo and Justine – although they aren't friends anymore.

Discussion: Think about Jax's situation. What else could have been done to support Jax at school? What could be done to reduce the likelihood of similar problems occurring at the school in the future?

Source: http://www.rcpsych.ac.uk/mentalhealthinfo/
mentalhealthandgrowingup/bullyingandemotion/jaxsstory.aspx

17.4.4   Summary

We have seen that one area of educational psychology research is concerned with the important task of assessing individual pupils' needs. In most cases, it is clear that the assessment process must be multifaceted and comprehensive in order to be truly informative. Even measurement of intellectual functioning is likely to require a consideration of several different areas of skill. Furthermore, the work of educational psychologists also includes close examination of processes operating at a broader level, such as the way in which the classroom is being managed. In many cases, individual pupils' needs are inextricably tied up with patterns of social relationships, behaviour and learning within the class as a whole.

17.5   RESEARCH METHODS IN EDUCATIONAL PSYCHOLOGY

nonexperimental methods methods of research using questionnaires, interviews, or observations in order to provide descriptions of the 'real world' that are as far as possible complete, accurate, and ecologically valid.

experimental methods methods of research using tightly controlled studies to identify cause-and-effect relations.

The examples considered above show how research in educational psychology has tackled a diverse range of issues connected with the functioning of pupils and the classroom as a whole. But how is research on these topics conducted? In this section, we consider the methodologies employed by researchers in educational psychology, focusing on the key distinction between **nonexperimental** and **experimental methods**.

17.5.1   Nonexperimental Methods

Nonexperimental research attempts to provide descriptions of the 'real world' that are as far as possible complete, accurate and **ecologically valid** (true to the context they are intended to describe). It does this by collecting data out in the field, rather than in 'cleaned-up' experimental environments, where there may be a risk of artificial contexts producing unrepresentative results. Such research commonly employs **survey methods** or observational methods, which are less likely to distort the nature of the data that is collected than

ecologically valid when research accurately describes psychological functioning in the 'real world'.

survey methods research methods utilising questionnaires, reports on children's behaviour by parents or teachers, or systematic observations of behaviour by researchers.

methods that require participants to behave in ways that they would not ordinarily do (e.g. by asking them to respond under test conditions).

What these different types of research have in common is a focus on uncovering **associations** between variables, such as the relationship between pupil attainment and the incidence of disruptive behaviour in the classroom. Many survey studies employ a **cross-sectional design**, where the same survey instrument is completed at one point in time by individuals within different groups, such as different types of school or children of different ages. The actual *method* of conducting the survey may vary, the most commonly employed alternatives being self-completed written **questionnaire** and **interviews**. The first involves respondents being provided with a printed form containing a number of questions or items designed to measure the key variables. Interviews involve a conversation between respondents and a researcher, in which the respondents are asked a similar series of questions defined by an **interview schedule**, and respond to these verbally. Interviews allow greater depth of response and are used where detailed information is important, for example, in examining children's understanding of concepts such as emotions (Harris, Olthof & Meerum Terwogt, 1981).

Psychometric measures such as those of intelligence, personality, or academic abilities are also a form of survey method, since they employ fixed questions. They are often administered on a one-to-one basis under time limitations, however, so in this sense are more like interviews. Psychometric measures also differ from other survey methods in the attention that is paid to **item selection**, which usually takes place through one or more cycles of design, testing and weeding out.

Longitudinal studies measure the same characteristics in a single

associations in research methodology, links between variables.

cross-sectional design a research design where the same task or questionnaire is completed at the same point in time by individuals within different groups.

questionnaire a nonexperimental method of research using a prepared set of written questions for self-completion.

interviews a nonexperimental method of research using a prepared set of questions delivered via conversation between respondent and researcher.

interview schedule the sequence of questions in an interview.

psychometric measures a form of survey method employing fixed questions, and giving rise to quantitative scores of psychological or intellectual functioning.

item selection The method of choosing the items included in a survey, determined by going through one or more cycles of design, testing and weeding out.

longitudinal studies research which takes measures from the same participants at two or more different times in order to specify the relationships between variables over time. This may extend over months or years or even over a participant's whole lifetime.

sample at repeated intervals over an extended period (typically a year or more), in order to map the profile of change and determine how far later characteristics (e.g. achievement levels at school) are related to earlier ones (e.g. degree of engagement in studying). They make it possible to attribute changes with age much more confidently to real shifts in the participants. In cross-sectional designs comparing children in separate age groups, apparent differences might simply be due to the different individuals involved in each group and the different experiences they have had. For example, if an older group benefited from a teaching intervention that had not been available to younger groups, it might make it seem as if there was a bigger change with age than was really the case.

observational methods in research, observation and recording of behaviour exhibited by a participant.

Observational methods are used in both cross-sectional and longitudinal studies, though they have greater power in the latter. One commonly used type of measure that relies on observation is parental or teacher reports on children, employing questionnaires focused on key aspects of behaviour. An example of this is the Strengths and Difficulties Questionnaire (Goodman, 1997), which is designed to assess the areas in which children appear to be doing well and those in which they show problems. Systematic researcher observations, made at fixed intervals, perhaps in classroom contexts, are also frequently used. In this type of approach, children targeted for observation will be watched by an observer for a predefined period of time, possibly as long as an hour, as far as possible under broadly representative and comparable circumstances. During this period, the occurrence of predetermined categories of behaviour (e.g. number of contributions to classroom discussion) will be recorded. One example is the research on use of group work in science lessons reported by Baines, Rubie-Davies and Blatchford

cause-and-effect relations in experimentation, the relations between the independent variable that is manipulated (hypothesised as the cause) and the dependent variable or resultant change in behaviour (the effect).

(2009), which recorded the incidence of different types of dialogue in student groups, such as collaborative discussion, disagreement and off-task talk.

17.5.2 Experimental Methods

Experimental research is used to identify **cause-and-effect relations**, through the use of tightly controlled studies. **Quasi-experimental designs** examine the effects of a variable that is not directly under the researcher's control (e.g. student age or gender)

quasi-experimental designs experiments that examine the effects of a variable that is not directly under the researcher's control (e.g., student age or gender) on outcomes such as achievement or performance level.

on outcomes such as achievement or performance level. These designs are like genuine experiments in the use of **controlled conditions**, where the circumstances surrounding data collection will be kept as comparable as possible across participants, rather than being left free to vary, as is usually the case in survey research. The focus is normally on relatively brief observational or performance measures so that data can be collected within a narrow time window, to make controlling conditions somewhat easier.

Genuine experiments employ the further principle of **random assignment** of participants to **experimental conditions** (levels of an **independent variable** that is hypothesised to have a causal influence on the outcome or **dependent variable**). It is only by exerting direct control over the independent variable in this way that we can be confident that variations in the dependent variable are attributable to its influence, rather than something else. The most basic form of experimental design is the **randomised design**, in which participants are randomly assigned to a number of experimental conditions, each of which is carefully defined by the circumstances under which a specific task or problem is to be carried out, such as different types of prior training. **Factorial designs** manipulate two or more independent variables (e.g. length *and* type of prior training) at the same time, by combining or *crossing* the levels of each. These designs enable us to look not only at the effects of each independent variable by itself (what are termed the **main effects**), but also at any effects they have in combination with each other (the **interaction effects**). For instance, we might be interested in whether some forms of training require much less time to be effective.

Another very common form of experimental study in education is when an intervention,

controlled conditions in experimental survey research, the circumstances surrounding data collection are kept as comparable as possible across participants.

random assignment the allocation, according to chance not design, by experimenters of participants into the different experimental conditions so that there is no bias in the distribution of participant characteristics.

experimental conditions the various groups used in an experiment, to which participants are assigned.

independent variable in an experiment, the variable that is manipulated by the experimenter as a means of determining cause-and-effect relations.

dependent variable in an experiment, the variable that is measured to demonstrate whether its value was affected by the independent variable.

randomised design the most basic form of experimental design, in which participants are randomly assigned to a number of experimental conditions.

factorial designs a form of experimental design that manipulates two or more independent variables at the same time, by combining or crossing the levels of each.

main effects the effects of each independent variable by itself.

interaction effects any effects independent variables have in combination with each other.

repeated measures design a very common form of experimental study in education using tests before and after introducing an intervention.

control group in an experiment, the group in which an intervention is not applied, making it possible to assess how far any change that occurs in the experimental group is attributable to the intervention itself, rather than something that would have happened anyway over that period of time.

experimental group in an experiment, the group exposed to a particular value of the independent variable, which has been manipulated by the experimenter.

microgenetic designs a specialised form of experimental study, the key characteristic of which is the use of a small sample and many more observations than would be employed in an ordinary repeated measures design with these being densely packed together.

such as a new teaching method, is evaluated via the use of pre- and post-tests (a **repeated measures design**, also known as a before-and-after design). In practice, there is usually an accompanying **control group** in such studies, for whom the intervention is not applied, making it possible to assess how far any change that occurs in the **experimental group** is attributable to the intervention itself, rather than something that would have happened in any case over that period of time. An example of such a design is outlined in Research Methods Box 17.1. **Microgenetic designs** are a more specialised form of the same idea. The key characteristic of these is the use of a small sample and many more observations than would be employed in an ordinary repeated measures design (perhaps as many as 10 or 12 points of testing), with these being densely packed together (every two to three days is not uncommon). This allows us to examine in detail how performance changes, and how the pattern of change varies from individual to individual (see Section 20.2.3 for more information about microgenetic methodologies). Philips and Tolmie (2007), for example, used this approach to look at how parents helping their children solve balance problems affected those children's performance on similar problems over the following week, compared to controls.

Randomised control trials (RCTs) are a different kind of specialised intervention study. In an RCT, no pre-test is used to establish a baseline since the sample is drawn from a population that is known to be homogeneous (for instance, they have all been identified as suffering from a particular kind of learning difficulty). Once the sample has been identified, the participants are randomly allocated to a treatment condition – either alternative forms of intervention or treatment versus control conditions. The intervention is then applied, and the outcome monitored, usually for a period of time. These data are used to determine whether the treatment (or one specific form of it) has worked, and therefore might be more widely applied.

RCTs are relatively uncommon in educational research, however, since assignment to interventions often has to be managed at class or even school level: it may simply not be feasible to apply it to individual members of a class without affecting others. For instance, in the research on group work described in Research Methods Box 17.1, the group-work programme could not easily have been introduced for only some children in each class, since this would have meant the teachers running parallel lessons, and these would have been bound to influence each other.

RESEARCH METHODS BOX 17.1

Howe *et al.* (2007) report research testing the effects of implementing a programme of group work within the upper primary school age range. Teachers and pupils of 24 classes were recruited to take part in the programme, which involved two days of professional development activity for the teachers, followed by the training of pupils in group-work skills. Classes subsequently worked through four weeks of pre-designed group activities in each of two areas of science, forces and evaporation. Three further classes, broadly representative of the intervention sample, were recruited as controls. These classes were studying similar topics during the intervention period but received no aspect of the group-work support programme.

A variety of measures were collected as part of the study, including data from pre- and post-tests relating to understanding of forces and of evaporation, focused on grasp of the factors that affect how fast objects travel and how fast water evaporates. Separate multiple-choice tests were used for these two topic areas, these being administered in the intervention classes immediately prior to starting work on each topic, and then two weeks after completion. Control classes used a similar schedule for testing.

Examination of pre- and post-test scores showed that the intervention classes exhibited gains in understanding of both forces and evaporation that were absent in the control classes. These gains were uniform across different classes (single-age group and mixed-age group) in different types of school (rural and urban). Post-test scores for both forces and evaporation were found to be significantly correlated to pupils' discussions during group work, but not during whole-class lessons, confirming that the group-work activity was directly responsible for the gains.

17.5.3 Educational Neuroscience

behavioural data in educational psychology research, data relating to students' observable behaviour or task performance.

Until recently, research in educational psychology had to rely on **behavioural data** (e.g. the type of word on which reading errors were made) to work out what was happening at a psychological level. However, developments in neuroscience now make it possible to look more directly at what is happening in the brain, and researchers have begun to apply these techniques to education and learning (see Section 19.5.2). In **functional magnetic resonance imaging (FMRI)**, the flow of blood to different areas of the brain is monitored, telling us which regions are active. Comparison between activated regions in different individuals working on the same task allows us to see, for instance, how a dyslexic reader differs from a nondyslexic one (Demonet, Taylor & Chaix, 2004). **Structural MRI** provides data on the organisation of cells in different areas of the brain, and again, can allow us to see how one group of children differs from another. Watkins *et al.* (2008), for example, used structural mappings to investigate differences between children who stutter and those who do not. **Near infra-red spectroscopy (NIRS)** is a much newer technique that provides similar information to functional MRI, but has the advantage that participants do not need to be placed in a large scanner: they simply wear a cap arrangement on their head and can engage in normal activity. **Electro-encephalography (EEG)** also provides information about brain activation, but in this case in terms of changes over time rather than in location. Campbell (2010), for example, discusses how changes in brain activation measured by EEG can be used to examine changes in processing associated with learning in mathematics. It is important to note that none of these techniques provides

functional magnetic resonance imaging (FMRI) a means of visually monitoring the flow of blood to different areas of the brain showing which regions are active.

structural MRI a means of gathering data on the organisation of cells in different areas of the brain.

near infra-red spectroscopy (NIRS) a means of gathering similar data to that gained by a functional MRI, but with the participant wearing a cap-like arrangement and acting normally rather than being placed in a large scanner.

electro-encephalography (EEG) a means of gathering information about brain activation in terms of changes over time.

very clear evidence *on its own*; however, when combined with behavioural data, they can offer us crucial new insights into why educational problems might be happening, and what types of intervention might be effective.

17.5.4 Summary

Research methods used by psychologists in education fall into two main types: nonexperimental methods (questionnaires, interviews and observations) used to collect data on behaviour and perceptions in everyday settings, including the classroom; and experimental methods, usually but not always employed in controlled settings, where it is possible to establish different conditions and directly examine the effect of these on performance. Before-and-after designs, examining the impact of a particular educational intervention, are commonly used by researchers in this field as a means of establishing potentially important new educational techniques. The past 10 years have seen increasing interest in neuroscientific data on brain activity as an important additional source of information about educational difficulties, which can help us understand better the source of differences in performance between children with and without problems.

17.6 CHAPTER SUMMARY

This chapter has shown that educational psychology has emerged as an important field of academic research as well as having a distinctive contribution in terms of professional practice. Research in educational psychology is connected to broad themes arising from different approaches to childhood and schooling – which themselves have changed over the course of history – and has important contributions to make in terms of identifying and assessing individual pupil needs as well as illuminating processes operating at the whole-class or even whole-school level. Academic work in this area is based on the use of robust and rigorous research methodologies to yield insights into various aspects of teaching, learning and psychological adjustment at school.

SELF-TEST QUESTIONS

- Describe the history of educational psychology as an academic research field and as a professional practice.
- Compare and contrast different approaches to childhood and schooling.
- Compare and contrast contemporary viewpoints on the nature of intelligence.
- What are some of the factors that promote effective classroom management?
- Compare and contrast different methodologies utilised by researchers in educational psychology.

ESSAY QUESTIONS

- Critically discuss how approaches to childhood and schooling have changed over the course of the last 150 years.
- What is intelligence and how should it be measured?
- What are the implications of psychological research for effective classroom management?

TEXTS FOR FURTHER READING

Gardner, H. (2000) *Intelligence Reframed: Multiple Intelligences for the 21st* Century, New York: Basic Books.

Kelly, B., Woolfson, L. & Boyle, J. (eds) (2008) *Frameworks for Practice in Educational Psychology: A Textbook for Trainees and Practitioners*, London: Jessica Kingsley.

Martin, J., Sugarman, J. & McNamara, J. (2000) *Models of Classroom Management: Principles, Practices and Critical Consideration*, 3rd edn, Calgary: Detselig Enterprises.

Sternberg, R.J. (1985) *Beyond IQ: A Triarchic Theory of Human Intelligence*, New York: Cambridge University Press.

RELEVANT JOURNAL ARTICLES

Blair, C. (2002) School readiness: Integrating cognition and emotion in a neurobiological conceptualization of children's functioning at school entry, *American Psychologist* 57: 111–27.

Blatchford, P., Bassett, P., Goldstein, H. & Martin, C. (2003) Are class size differences related to pupils' educational progress and classroom processes? *British Educational Research Journal* 29: 709–30.

Brooks-Gunn, J., Klebanov, P.K. & Duncan, G.J. (1996) Ethnic differences in children's intelligence test scores: Role of economic deprivation, home environment, and maternal characteristics, *Child Development* 67: 396–408.

Brophy, J. (1986) Teacher influences on student achievement, *American Psychologist* 41: 1069–77.

Jimerson, S., Egeland, B., Sroufe, L.A. & Carlson, B. (2000) A prospective longitudinal study of high school dropouts examining multiple predictors across development, *Journal of School Psychology* 38: 525–49.

Thomas, J.B. (1996) The beginnings of educational psychology in the Universities of England and Wales, *Educational Psychology* 16(3): 229–44.

RELEVANT WEB LINKS

British Educational Research Association, http://www.bera.ac.uk

British Psychological Society, educational psychology information, http://www.bps.org.uk/careers/what-do-psychologists-do/areas/educational.cfm

History of Psychology website, http://academic.udayton.edu/gregelvers/hop/welcome.asp

Indiana University website on human intelligence, http://www.indiana.edu/~intell/index.shtml

Teaching and Learning Research Programme's capacity-building resources, http://www.tlrp.org/capacity/rm/resource_index.html

Teaching Expertise, guide to classroom management, http://www.teachingexpertise.com/topic/classroom-management

REFERENCES

Alexander, R.J. (2004) *Towards Dialogic Teaching: Rethinking Classroom Talk*, York: Dialogos.

Association of Principal Educational Psychologists (2005) Educational Psychology assessment in Scotland, http://www.bps.org.uk/sdep/publications/assessment.cfm, accessed November 2010.

Baines, E., Rubie-Davies, C. & Blatchford, P. (2009) Improving pupil group work interaction and dialogue in primary classrooms: Results from a year-long intervention study, *Cambridge Journal of Education*, 39: 95–118.

Barber, M. (1996) *The Learning Game: Arguments for an Education Revolution*, London: Victor Gollancz.

Binet, A. & Simon, T. (1916) *The Development of Intelligence in Children*, Baltimore, MD: Williams & Wilkins.

Blair, C. (2002) School readiness: Integrating cognition and emotion in a neurobiological conceptualization of children's functioning at school entry, *American Psychologist* 57: 111–27.

Blatchford, P., Bassett, P., Goldstein, H. & Martin, C. (2003) Are class size differences related to pupils' educational progress and classroom processes? *British Educational Research Journal* 29: 709–30.

Boyle, J., Mackay, T. & Lauchlan, F. (2008) The legislative context and shared practice models, in B. Kelly, L. Woolfson & J. Boyle (eds) *Frameworks for Practice in Educational Psychology: A Textbook for Trainees and Practitioners*, pp. 33–51, London: Jessica Kingsley.

Brooks-Gunn, J., Klebanov, P.K. & Duncan, G.J. (1996) Ethnic differences in children's intelligence test scores: Role of economic deprivation, home environment, and maternal characteristics, *Child Development* 67: 396–408.

Brophy, J. (1986) Teacher influences on student achievement, *American Psychologist* 41: 1069–77.

CACE (1967) *Children and their Primary Schools* (Plowden Report), London: HMSO.

Campbell, S.R. (2010) Embodied minds and dancing brains: New oppportunities for research in mathematics education, in B. Sriraman & L. English (eds) *Theories of Mathematics Education: Seeking New Frontiers*, pp. 309–31, Berlin: Springer.

Cunningham, H. (2005) *Children and Childhood in Western Society since 1500*, 2nd edn, Harlow: Pearson Education.

Demonet, J.-F., Taylor, M.J. & Chaix, Y. (2004) Developmental dyslexia, *Lancet* 363: 1451–60.

Department for Children, Schools and Families (2007) *Secondary National Strategy, Social and Emotional Aspects of Learning for Secondary Schools: Guidance Booklet*, London: DfES Publications.

Department for Education and Employment (1998) *The National Literacy Strategy: Framework for Teaching*, London: HMSO.

Dewey, J. (1903) Democracy in education, *The Elementary School Teacher* 4: 193–204.

Emmer, E.T. & Stough, L.M. (2001) Classroom management: A critical part of educational psychology, with implications for teacher education, *Educational Psychologist* 36: 103–12.

Freiberg, H.J. (1999) Sustaining the paradigm, in H.J. Freiberg (ed.) *Beyond Behaviorism: Changing the Classroom Management Paradigm*, pp. 164–173, Boston: Allyn & Bacon.

Gardner, H. (1983) *Frames of Mind: The Theory of Multiple Intelligences*, New York: Basic Books.

Gardner, H. (2000) *Intelligence Reframed: Multiple Intelligences for the 21st Century*, New York: Basic Books.

Gill, V. (2001) *The Eleven Commandments of Good Teaching*, 2nd edn, Thousand Oaks, CA: Corwin.

Goleman, D. (1995) *Emotional Intelligence*, New York: Bantam.

Goodman, R. (1997) The Strengths and Difficulties Questionnaire: A research note, *Journal of Child Psychology and Psychiatry* 38: 581–6.

Grigorenko, E.L. (2000) Heritability and intelligence, in R.J. Sternberg (ed.) *Handbook of Intelligence*, pp. 53–91, New York: Cambridge University Press.

Harris, P.L., Olthof, T. & Meerum Terwogt, M. (1981) Children's knowledge of emotion, *Journal of Child Psychology and Psychiatry* 22: 247–61.

Hawker, D.S.J. & Boultons, M.J. (2000) Twenty years' research on peer victimization and psychosocial maladjustment: A meta-analytic review of cross-sectional studies, *Journal of Child Psychology and Psychiatry* 41: 441–55.

Herbart, J.F. (1841) *Umriss Paedagogischer Vorlersungen*, Berlin.

Howe, C., Tolmie, A., Thurston, A. et al. (2007) Group work in elementary science: Towards organisational principles for supporting pupil learning, *Learning and Instruction* 17: 549–63.

Ireson, J., Hallam, S. & Hurley, C. (2005) What are the effects of ability grouping on GCSE attainment? *British Educational Research Journal* 31: 443–58.

Jimerson, S., Egeland, B., Sroufe, L.A. & Carlson, B. (2000) A prospective longitudinal study of high school dropouts examining multiple predictors across development, *Journal of School Psychology* 38: 525–49.

Kagan, T.K. (2005) Literary origins of the term 'School Psychologist' revisited, *School Psychology Review* 34(3): 432–34.

Koops, W. (2004) Imaging childhood in European history and developmental psychology, *European Journal of Developmental Psychology* 1: 1–18.

Landrum, T.J. & Kauffman, J.M. (2006) Behavioral approaches to classroom management, in C.M. Evertson & C.S. Weinstein (eds) *Handbook of Classroom Management: Research, Practice, and Contemporary Issues*, Mahwah, NJ: Lawrence Erlbaum Associates.

Lave, J. (1988) *Cognition in Practice*, Cambridge: Cambridge University Press.

Lave, J. & Wenger, E. (1991) *Situated Learning: Legitimate Peripheral Participation*, Cambridge: Cambridge University Press.

MacBeath, J., Galton, M., Steward, S., MacBeath, A. & Page, C. (2006) *The Costs of Inclusion*, Cambridge: University of Cambridge.

Mayer, J.D. & Salovey, P. (1997) What is emotional intelligence?, in P. Salovey & D. Sluyter (eds) *Emotional Development, Emotional Literacy, and Emotional Intelligence*, New York: Basic Books.

Mintz, S. (2004) *Huck's Raft: A History of American Childhood*, Cambridge MA: Harvard University Press.

Munsterberg, H. (1898) Psychology and education, *Educational Review* 16: 105–32.

National Center for Education Statistics (1993) *Public School Kindergarten Teachers' Views on Children's Readiness for School*, Report for the US Department of Education, Number 93–410, Washington, DC: NCES.

NICHD Early Child Care Research Network (2004) Does class size in first grade relate to children's academic and social performance or observed classroom processes? *Developmental Psychology* 40: 651–64.

O'Connell, P., Pepler, D. & Craig, W. (1999) Peer involvement in bullying: Insights and challenges for intervention, *Journal of Adolescence* 22: 437–52.

Philips, S. & Tolmie, A. (2007) Children's performance on and understanding of the Balance Scale problem: The effects of parental support, *Infant and Child Development* 16: 95–117.

Probst, P. (1997) The beginnings of educational psychology in Germany, in W.G . Bringmann, H.E. Luck, R. Miller & C. Early (eds) *A Pictorial History of Psychology*, pp. 315–21, Hanover Park, IL: Quintessence Publishing.

Reuman, D.A. (1989) How social comparison mediates the relation between ability-grouping practices and students' achievement expectancies in mathematics, *Journal of Educational Psychology* 81(2): 178–89.

Royal Society (2010) *Science and Mathematics Education 5–14: A State of the Nation Report*, London: Royal Society.

Sampson, O. (1980) *Child Guidance: Its History, Provenance and Future*, British Psychological Society Division of Educational and Child Psychology, Occasional Papers, Vol. 3, No 3, London: BPS.

Spearman, C. (1927). *The Abilities of Man*, New York: Macmillan.

Sternberg, R.J. (1985) *Beyond IQ: A Triarchic Theory of Human Intelligence*, New York: Cambridge University Press.

Storch, E.A. & Ledley, D.R. (2005) Peer victimization and psychosocial adjustment in children: Current knowledge and future directions, *Clinical Pediatrics* 44: 29–38.

Thomas, J.B. (1996) The beginnings of educational psychology in the Universities of England and Wales, *Educational Psychology* 16(3): 229–44.

Tomasello, M. (2009) *Why We Co-operate*, Boston, MA: MIT Press.

Tomlinson, P. (2002) Series preface, in R. Stainthorp & P. Tomlinson (eds) *British Journal of Educational Psychology Monograph Series II: Psychological Aspects of Education – Current Trends: Learning and Teaching Reading*, Leicester: BPS.

Tooley, J.N. (2000) *Reclaiming Education*, London: Cassell.

Watkins, K.E., Smith, S.M., Davis, S. & Howell, P. (2008) Structural and functional abnormalities of the motor system in developmental stuttering, *Brain* 131: 50–59.

Wooldridge, A. (1994) *Measuring the Mind: Education and Psychology in England c1860–1990*, Cambridge: Cambridge University Press.

Zimmerman, B.J. & Schunk, D.H. (eds) (2002) *Educational Psychology: A Century of Contributions. A Project of Division 15 (Educational Psychology) of the American Psychological Society*, Mahwah, NJ: Lawrence Erlbaum Associates.

18 Educational Psychology: Problems and Interventions

Robin Banerjee, Andy Tolmie & Jim Boyle

LEARNING OUTCOMES

WHEN YOU HAVE COMPLETED THIS CHAPTER, YOU SHOULD BE ABLE TO:

1. Describe the 'graduated response' to the identification of special educational needs in the current code of practice on SEN in England and Wales.

2. Evaluate the core features of the difficulties and disorders commonly encountered by educational psychologists, including learning difficulties, behavioural, emotional and social difficulties, communication and interaction difficulties, and sensory and physical disabilities.

3. Describe and evaluate the concept of inclusion.

4. Describe different 'waves of intervention' and see how they relate to special educational needs.

5. Understand the purpose and value of an Individual Education Plan.

KEY WORDS

Attention Problems • Developmental Coordination Disorder (DCD) • Developmental Dyslexia • Dyscalculia • Executive Dysfunction • Hearing Impairment • Inclusion • Individual Education Plan • Moderate Learning Difficulties (MLD) • P Scales • Physical Disabilities • Profound and Multiple Learning Difficulties (PMLD) • School Action • School Action Plus • SEN Code of Practice • Severe Learning Difficulties (SLD) • Specific Language Impairment (SLI) • Specific Learning Difficulties • Statutory Assessment • Theory of Mind • Visual Impairment • Waves of Intervention Model • Weak Central Coherence

CHAPTER OUTLINE

ROUTE MAP OF THE CHAPTER

This chapter introduces the current codes of practice on special educational needs in the United Kingdom, before turning to a description of key areas of need that educational psychologists are likely to encounter. For each area, we will look at the kinds of difficulties that children and young people might have, as well as some of the basic research on the origins of those difficulties. The chapter concludes with an examination of issues relating to the inclusion of pupils with special educational needs, and how interventions can be designed, implemented and reviewed in order to support pupils with such needs.

18.1   INTRODUCTION

Many people become interested in educational psychology as a potential career because of a desire to help children and teenagers who are experiencing difficulties at school. Research in educational psychology can help us to understand how and why problems in pupils' learning and in their general social and emotional adjustment can occur, and this in turn can help us to develop effective strategies to intervene in the development of such problems – or even to prevent them from occurring in the first place. It is also important to remember that this work of educational psychologists contributes to a broader goal of encouraging *all* children and young people to flourish at school. In other words, by shedding light on the ways in which difficulties can arise at school, work in the area of educational psychology has clarified the key factors that promote the best outcomes for pupils.

In this chapter, we will examine a range of characteristics and difficulties that lead some pupils to have 'special educational needs', and will consider the role of educational psychology research and practice in understanding

and supporting these pupils. In the course of doing so, we will see how educational psychologists have to pay attention to an array of biological, cognitive, social and emotional processes that influence the educational experience of children and young people. At the end of the chapter, we will consider the different approaches to intervention, with particular attention to the role of psychological research and practice in helping us to choose, design and review the strategies used to meet the needs of pupils at school.

18.1.1   The Special Educational Needs Code of Practice

Understanding what is meant by 'special educational needs' is an important first step before embarking on our journey into the difficulties and problems encountered by educational psychologists. Schools in England and Wales are guided by the **SEN Code of Practice** (DfES, 2001a), which sets out a definition of SEN (see Focus Point 18.1).

> **SEN Code of Practice** a code of practice in England and Wales concerning the provision of education for those with special educational needs.

FOCUS POINT 18.1   DEFINITION OF SPECIAL EDUCATIONAL NEEDS IN THE 2001 CODE OF PRACTICE

Children have special educational needs if they have a learning difficulty that calls for special educational provision to be made for them.

Children have a learning difficulty if they:

(a) have a significantly greater difficulty in learning than the majority of children of the same age; or

(b) have a disability which prevents or hinders them from making use of educational facilities of a kind generally provided for children of the same age in schools within the area of the local education authority

(c) are under compulsory school age and fall within the definition at (a) or (b) above or would so do if special educational provision was not made for them.

Children must not be regarded as having a learning difficulty solely because the language or form of language of their home is different from the language in which they will be taught.

Special educational provision means:

(a) for children of two or over, educational provision which is additional to, or otherwise different from, the educational provision made generally for children of their age in schools maintained by the LEA, other than special schools, in the area

(b) for children under two, educational provision of any kind.

Northern Ireland has a Code of Practice similar to that in England and Wales, but in Scotland the Education (Additional Support for Learning) (Scotland) Act 2004 replaced the term SEN with the broader concept of 'Additional Support Needs' (ASN), bringing with it new responsibilities for local authorities in regard to the introduction of Coordinated Support Plans and transition planning and more rights for parents.

As you can see from Focus Point 18.1, the way in which SEN has been conceptualised – focusing on a pupil profile that leads that pupil to have greater difficulties in learning than the majority of their peers, or a disability that prevents or inhibits access to the usual educational facilities – means that a very wide range of difficulties and attributes could fall under this heading. In fact, the national statistical releases relating to special educational needs in England and Wales (e.g. DCSF, 2009) list 12 different 'types of need', as in Table 18.1.

Given this rather all-encompassing definition of special educational needs, it is not surprising that many different kinds of problem can bring a pupil to the attention of an educational psychologist. But how do schools know when a pupil's problems merit a referral to an educational psychologist? The SEN Code of Practice (DfES, 2001a) provides guidelines for how schools should handle pupil difficulties. Although the

> **School Action** as laid down in the SEN Code of Practice guidelines for a graduated response to pupil difficulty, this is the first phase of response, which uses existing school resources.

precise details vary depending on the age of the child, the guidelines essentially call for a 'graduated response' involving three phases. In the first phase, labelled **School Action**, the focus is primarily on strategies delivered using the school's existing resources (e.g. some extra small-group or individual tuition by existing staff, deployment of special equipment within the school). Educational psychologists may be consulted for advice and support in the case of pupils in this phase. However, their involvement often becomes more direct and substantial for pupils who display continued difficulties and inadequate progress. Such pupils will typically be moved on to the second phase of response, labelled **School Action Plus**. In this phase, external support services are brought in, and educational psychologists can play a key role in providing specialist assessments of the pupil's abilities, difficulties and attributes, as well as in designing, implementing and monitoring intervention strategies to help the pupils. Finally, where there is continuing significant cause for concern, pupils move into a third phase of response, involving a **statutory assessment**. This is a comprehensive assessment of the pupil's history, characteristics and needs. It can potentially give rise to a Statement of Special Educational Need, which specifies in detail the nature of the pupil's special educational needs, and the particular arrangements for special educational provisions that are necessary in order to meet those needs. Educational psychologists frequently have a central role in contributing to this process. Some of the possible triggers for identifying a pupil at each of these phases, as well as the typical actions involved in each phase, are listed in Table 18.2.

> **School Action Plus** the SEN Code of Practice second phase of response for pupils who display continued difficulties and inadequate progress, involving external support services including those of educational psychologists.

> **statutory assessment** the third phase of response for pupils about whom there is continuing cause for concern, involving a comprehensive assessment of the pupil's history, characteristics and needs and can potentially give rise to a Statement of Special Educational Need.

Towards the end of this chapter, we will look at some broader issues relating to the intervention process at school. But first, let us consider some of the major areas of problems and difficulties that educational psychologists may encounter, with attention to research on the nature of those problems and the factors that play a role in their development. Throughout this chapter, it is worth remembering that the numbers of pupils we are talking about are substantial: the national statistical release based on the School Census in January 2009 (DCSF, 2009) showed that over 220 000 pupils in England and Wales were listed as having a statement of SEN and over 1 400 000 pupils were listed as having SEN without a statement (i.e. School Action or School Action Plus) – amounting to around 20% of the school population in total.

TABLE 18.1 *Types of Need.*

• Specific learning difficulty	• Moderate learning difficulty
• Severe learning difficulty	• Profound and multiple learning difficulty
• Behavioural, emotional and social difficulties	• Speech, language and communication needs
• Hearing impairment	• Visual impairment
• Multisensory impairment	• Physical disability
• Autism spectrum disorder	• Other difficulty/disability

TABLE 18.2 *Graduated Approach to Special Educational Provision.*

Phase	Possible triggers	Actions
School Action	<ul><li>Little or no progress even when teaching directly targets the pupil's area of weakness</li><li>Continued emotional or behavioural difficulties despite use of the school's usual behaviour-management and support strategies</li><li>Sensory or physical problems that seem to be interfering with progress despite existing support and equipment</li><li>Communication and/or interaction difficulties that lead to continued problems with making progress</li></ul>	<ul><li>The school's Special Educational Needs Coordinator (SENCo) leads further assessment, planning of future support and review of progress</li><li>Record of short-term targets, strategies, provisions and outcomes, in the form of an Individual Education Plan (IEP)</li><li>Interventions can involve extra tuition by existing staff, deployment of specialist equipment, and new teaching strategies</li><li>Advice may be sought from external professionals, but there is no ongoing intervention by outside agencies</li></ul>
School Action Plus	<ul><li>Continued difficulties in specific curriculum areas over a lengthy period, despite School Action</li><li>Emotional or behavioural difficulties have significant impact on the pupil's own learning or that of their classmates, despite an individualised programme of behaviour management and support</li><li>Sensory or physical needs that require additional specialist support or facilities</li><li>Communication and/or interaction difficulties continue to be a significant obstacle to learning</li></ul>	<ul><li>External support services (including educational psychologists) may conduct specialist assessments and provide ongoing support and intervention</li><li>Coordinated efforts to foster progress by class teacher, SENCo and external professionals</li></ul>
Statutory Assessment	<ul><li>Significant cause for concern despite School Action Plus</li><li>Strategies or programmes previously implemented have not been successful</li></ul>	<ul><li>Detailed investigation of the pupil's abilities, difficulties and progress, often involving assessments from multiple external professionals (including educational psychologists)</li><li>May lead to a Statement of Special Educational Needs, which sets out the pupil's characteristics and needs in detail and lists the specific special provisions that must be put in place for meeting those needs</li></ul>

18.2 DIFFICULTIES ASSOCIATED WITH COGNITIVE FUNCTIONING

Educational psychologists and teaching professionals distinguish between two broad categories of difficulty with cognitive functioning: *pervasive* learning difficulties of varying levels of severity, which manifest as deficits in ability across many or all areas of performance; and **specific learning difficulties**, which relate to a deficit of a particular type, though the impact of this on achievement may be wider. What both categories have in common is that the principal impairment is first and foremost one of thinking and learning rather than behaviour or communication: children with difficulties of this kind often exhibit no particular problems with spoken communication, nor any very problematic behaviour. In this section, we look at both of the two broad categories in turn, and at the main sub-classifications within them.

18.2.1 Moderate and Severe Learning Difficulties

The categorisation and labelling of different levels of pervasive learning difficulty vary considerably from

specific learning difficulties impairment in one narrowly defined area of a pupil's learning, accompanied by normal or near-normal ability in other areas.

one country to another (Farrell, 2009; Norwich, 2008), but the internationally recognised *Diagnostic and Statistical Manual of Mental Disorders* (DSM-IV to denote its fourth edition; American Psychiatric Association, 2002) distinguishes between *mild, moderate, severe* and *profound* mental retardation, with boundaries set partly by IQ levels. This reflects the notion of a *general* level of impairment that extends across the range of abilities assessed by IQ tests (see Section 17.4.1). Scores on IQ tests are standardised so that 100 represents average performance. The majority of individuals fall into the band of scores 30 points either side of this (i.e. between 70 and 130). Levels of retardation or learning difficulty are therefore defined in relation to bands of scores below 70.

Within the DSM-IV scheme, mild retardation is associated with IQ scores in the range of 55 to 70. Children with this level of difficulty have problems with independent activity and learning, but acquire social, communication and motor skills fairly normally, and by adulthood may have learned academic skills up to the later primary school level. Slightly confusingly, this equates with **moderate learning difficulties (MLD)** as defined by government guidance in the United Kingdom. This states that pupils with MLD 'will have attainments well below expected levels in all or most areas of the curriculum, despite appropriate interventions' (DfES, 2005, p. 6). In particular, they have much greater difficulty with literacy, numeracy and conceptual understanding than their peers, though there may be other associated problems with social skills and self-esteem, perhaps as a consequence of their academic difficulties (this is a pattern that has been clearly established for children with other forms of difficulty; see Conti-Ramsden & Botting, 2008).

Moderate to severe retardation is associated with IQ scores in the range from 25 to 55, though again it is also marked by levels of academic progress, and to some extent slower acquisition of language and communication skills. Those in the upper half of this range still tend to acquire the latter skills in early childhood, but those in the lower half may not do so until they reach school age. The key marker, though, is that at best children in this range will progress academically to no more than early primary school levels, and may not be able to do more than master simple counting and sight reading of a few words (see Section 19.4.1 on the pre-alphabetic stage of reading).

In terms of the UK system, children in this range are defined as having **severe learning difficulties (SLD)**,

moderate learning difficulties (MLD) as defined by government guidance in the UK, difficulties by pupils in all or most areas of the curriculum, particularly literacy, numeracy and conceptual understanding, despite appropriate intervention.

and as in need of support 'in all areas of the curriculum' (DfES, 2005, p. 6). In terms of attainment, England and Wales operate a measurement system for levels below the basic rungs of the National Curriculum, known as the **P scales** (P for 'performance'). The P scales have eight levels, which define target performance in all curriculum areas, though the focus is primarily on the core areas of English, mathematics, science and personal, social and health education (PSHE). In terms of the P scales, children with SLD are expected to reach the upper levels, where for instance they have to show some recognition of reading as an activity and of what written words represent, and similarly understand something of counting, perhaps being able to count up to 10 (Ndaji & Tymms, 2009).

Both DSM-IV and the DfES guidelines recognise a level below this, termed profound mental retardation, or in UK terms, **profound and multiple learning difficulties (PMLD)**. This is associated with IQ scores of below 25 and is marked by severe and complex needs evident from infancy, often accompanied by physical disabilities and sensory impairments (DfES, 2005; Farrell, 2009). In terms of learning, they may require basic sensory stimulation before all else, and any more structured learning needs to be broken down into small steps. Progress is unlikely to be beyond the lower levels of the P scales, where they can show awareness of activities and can communicate preferences by use of expression and gesture, but may not have use of language.

What these descriptive systems leave open is the cause of these different levels of difficulty. In the case of PMLD, this is typically associated with some form of genetic or pre-natal/peri-natal neurological impairment, hence the association with sensory problems. This may also be true at higher levels of functioning, where some impairments may be associated with conditions such as Down's syndrome. In general, though, relatively little is known about the underlying causes of the more moderate pervasive difficulties. It is possible that to some extent these represent part of the naturally occurring range of variation, and therefore have no specifically identifiable origin.

severe learning difficulties (SLD) a diagnostic term in the UK applied to those children who at best will progress academically to no more than early primary school levels, and may not be able to do more than master simple counting and sight-reading of a few words.

P scales operating in England and Wales, a system for measuring performance falling below the basic levels of the National Curriculum.

profound and multiple learning difficulties (PMLD) a diagnostic term for those with IQ scores of below 25 who have severe and complex needs, evident from infancy, often accompanied by physical disabilities and sensory impairments.

18.2.2 Dyslexia and Other Specific Learning Difficulties

Specific learning difficulties involve a very different profile, in which impairment in one narrowly defined area is characteristically accompanied by normal or near-normal ability in others. In terms of reading problems, for instance, DSM-IV defines a child with a *reading disorder* as having reading achievement substantially below that expected for their age, IQ and education. In other words, their general level of ability is typically appropriate to their chronological age, and the deficit only appears in relation to reading. It should be noted that the DSM's reading disorder category is not in fact the same as dyslexia, or more accurately **developmental dyslexia** (to mark it out from reading problems that appear later in life due to specific neurological damage), since it defines reading achievement in terms of both accuracy *and* comprehension. In fact, impaired comprehension is regarded by psychologists as a different condition, separate from dyslexia, which relates in particular to problems with reading accuracy. So, for example, Lyon, Shaywitz and Shaywitz (2003) say that dyslexia is marked by problems with accurate and fluent word recognition, and by poor spelling (see Section 19.4.1 on the differences between reading and writing; Figure 18.1 shows an example of a piece of writing from a dyslexic pupil).

> **developmental dyslexia** a specific learning difficulty involving problems in reading accuracy and spelling, related to a number of cognitive and neurobiological processes.

This still begs the question of how far out of step with other aspects of ability reading has to be before a child is regarded as dyslexic. This might in a sense seem to be an odd question, especially given that our understanding of the cognitive and neurological causes of dyslexia has advanced to the point where it is possible to identify those at risk during infancy, long before they actually start to read (see Section 19.5.2). Surely, then, it is merely a matter of looking for these underlying symptoms and the precise level of deficit is of no concern? In fact, though, research is still ongoing, and it is therefore necessary to have some *external* performance-based criterion for defining those children who appear to have problems, so that these can be compared, cognitively and neurologically, with children who do not show problems, in order to identify *what* the sources of difference might be. Similarly, in terms of educational provision, the resources simply do not exist to conduct brain-imaging tests of all children at risk of dyslexia, so again behavioural and performance-based criteria are needed in order to identify those in need of special assistance.

Having said this, though, there is no great consensus on where the cut-off should be. Using the same scale of

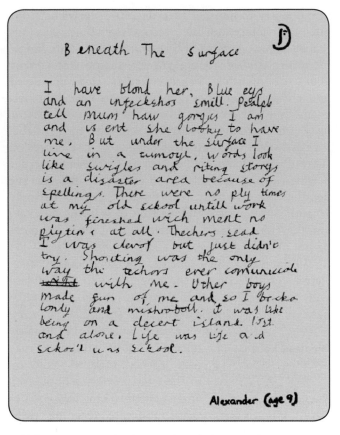

FIGURE 18.1 *Example of writing by a dyslexic pupil.*
Source: http://www.dyslexia-inst.org.uk/what.htm

measurement as for IQ (see above), some studies (e.g. Yule *et al.*, 1974) have defined it as being reading scores of below 70, coupled with IQ in the normal range (70 to 130). Studies of this kind suggest that between 3% and 6% of children have sufficient problems in learning to read to be classed as dyslexic, with problems being more apparent in boys than in girls. More recent studies (e.g. Shaywitz *et al.*, 1992) have used a less stringent cut-off of reading scores below 77.5, and found prevalence to be somewhere between 5% and 7%. Furthermore, the process of assessing a pupil thought to have specific reading difficulties typically involves careful profiling of various dimensions of cognitive and behavioural functioning, particularly in order to identify specific deficits thought to be responsible for the difficulties in reading (see Section 19.4). Although the precise prevalence – and cognitive profile – therefore remains a matter of some debate, the evidence certainly indicates that dyslexia is a relatively common disorder, and more common than would be expected simply in terms of natural variation.

The DSM-IV definition of a *mathematics disorder* follows exactly the same pattern as that for reading disorders: mathematical ability below that which would be expected, given the child's age, IQ and education. The same issues about cut-off therefore arise, though there has been rather less dispute about where this should be set, with most studies adopting a less stringent criterion than has been the case for reading. For example, Lewis, Hitch and Walker (1994) defined the cut-off as a mathematics score of 85, coupled with a reading score and nonverbal IQ above 90. This identified 1.3% of children as having a specific problem in mathematics, though a further 2.3% had both mathematics and reading problems coupled with normal nonverbal IQ, and this kind of comorbidity – more than would be expected simply by chance overlap – presents a further challenge to our understanding of the causes of these specific problems.

It is important to note that, as with reading, mathematics disorder is not necessarily exactly the same

dyscalculia a term used to describe specific difficulties in recognising and working with numbers.

thing as **dyscalculia**. This term was first used by Kosc (1974) to classify children who showed problems in learning arithmetic (the basic computational abilities required to work with numbers – see Section 19.4.2), and it has only gradually become apparent that there may be distinctions among these, between those who have problems managing the computational conventions (Passolunghi & Siegel, 2001) and those with a more fundamental impairment in the capacity to recognise number (Landerl, Bevan & Butterworth, 2004). It is the latter grouping for whom the term dyscalculia is now typically reserved.

A third major category of specific learning difficulty is what is now termed **developmental coordination disorder (DCD)**, though it has also been known as the *clumsy child syndrome* and as *developmental dyspraxia*.

developmental coordination disorder (DCD) a specific learning difficulty involving problems with movement and motor coordination, characterised by difficulties in object recognition and planning of movement.

DCD is distinct from problems with movement and motor skills that arise from particular conditions such as cerebral palsy, and, like reading and mathematics disorder, it is defined instead in terms of the absence of these more general impairments and a level of difficulty that is out of line with the child's age and IQ (Hulme & Snowling, 2009). It may not be immediately apparent why problems with movement come under the broad category of problems with cognitive functioning, but in fact DCD is marked by problems in object recognition and the *planning* of movement, bringing it squarely into cognitive territory. Children with these problems are likely to have difficulty with writing and drawing, but also with physical sports and even with dressing themselves.

Tests for measuring motor skill have received less attention than those for reading and mathematics, but the Movement Assessment Battery for Children (2nd edn,

Henderson, Sugden & Barnett, 2007) has become increasingly widely used in the United Kingdom. This assesses manipulative skills, ball skills and balance skills, and can be used to generate an overall standardised score of impairment for children between 4 and 12 years old. However, the relative novelty of these assessments means that there is as yet little consensus on where to draw the cut-off in terms of the level of impairment that is regarded as defining DCD. Many studies have used scores equivalent to 85 on the IQ scale (Geuze et al., 2001), whereas others have used scores closer to 70 (Mon-Williams, Pascal & Wann, 1994), which may be more appropriate. Prevalence figures vary between 5% and 18% as a result, but only 5% tend to exhibit severe problems, with these being four times as likely in boys as in girls (Kadesjo & Gillberg, 1999). These authors also report high levels of comorbidity with autism and ADHD (considered below). The causes of DCD are not well understood as yet, but may be due to deficits in specific neural functions (see Section 19.5.1).

18.2.3   Summary

Difficulties with cognitive functioning fall into two types: pervasive learning difficulties of moderate, severe and profound levels of severity, which affect many or all areas of performance; and specific learning difficulties, which are marked by impairments in reading, mathematics or motor coordination, typically accompanied by a normal profile in other areas, though comorbidity between two areas of difficulty is not uncommon. Understanding of the causes of these different difficulties is inconsistent, with dyslexia the best researched, but there is increasing evidence of a central role for different forms of neural deficit.

18.3   BEHAVIOURAL, EMOTIONAL AND SOCIAL DIFFICULTIES

In 2009, over 150 000 pupils in England were identified as having 'behavioural, emotional, and social difficulties' as the primary aspect of their special educational needs (either at School Action Plus or with a Statement of SEN; DCSF, 2009). This category of difficulties is second only to learning difficulties in terms of prevalence in the UK. The government's Code of Practice for Special Educational Needs (DfES, 2001a) includes a wide range of characteristics under this umbrella heading, including:

- Being withdrawn or isolated.
- Being disruptive or disturbing.

- Being hyperactive and lacking concentration.
- Having immature social skills.

If we think about these characteristics in terms of individual differences in psychological functioning, we can see that a range of internalising disorders (disorders primarily involving emotional disturbances, such as anxiety and depression), externalising disorders (disorders primarily involving problems in behaviour and conduct, such as excessive aggression and defiance) and **attention problems** (disorders primarily involving difficulties in concentration, such as attention-deficit/hyperactivity disorder) are relevant here. Some examples of the psychological disorders that create behavioural, emotional and social difficulties at school are listed in Table 18.3.

attention problems
disorders involving difficulties in concentration, such as attention deficit/ hyperactivity disorder (ADHD).

18.3.1 Internalising Disorders

We have already seen in Chapter 5 that depression and anxiety can be debilitating conditions for many people. Increasing attention is now being paid to the emergence of these kinds of symptoms much earlier in life. As shown in Table 18.3, there are a number of different disorders relating to anxiety and mood, but it is apparent that one common theme linking all of these is negative emotion. Thus, it is not surprising that anxiety and mood disorders often co-occur: in a review of studies using DSM criteria, Brady and Kendall (1992) found that many of the youths identified as anxious or depressed in fact met criteria for both conditions.

There continues to be considerable debate about the ways in which anxiety and depressive disorders converge and diverge (e.g. see Anderson & Hope, 2008), but it is clear that these are important conditions that affect a significant proportion of children and young people. Arriving at definitive prevalence rates regarding anxiety disorders and depressive disorders in young people is not easy because of differences in measurement and diagnosis across different studies, but we are certainly not dealing with isolated cases. Verhulst (2001) concludes on the basis of his review that around 6% to 10% of children and adolescents have some kind of anxiety disorder. In the case of depression, the proportion of children who have experienced a major depressive episode is low – below 3% – but the lifetime prevalence rate increases to around 14% by late adolescence, with a markedly greater prevalence in this period for girls than for boys (Hammen & Rudolph, 2003). Moreover, besides those who meet the

TABLE 18.3 *Examples of DSM-IV Disorders Relating to Behavioural, Emotional and Social Difficulties at School.*

Category	Type	Key symptoms
Anxiety Disorders	Separation anxiety disorder	Anxiety and distress regarding separation from home or from attachment figures (e.g. parents)
	Generalised anxiety disorder	Anxiety and distress regarding various events, activities, and settings
	Social phobia (social anxiety disorder)	Anxiety and distress regarding exposure to social or performance situations
	Specific phobia	Anxiety and distress regarding exposure to a specific class of objects or situations (e.g. heights, spiders)
	Panic disorder	Anxiety and distress involving sudden and acute physiological symptoms and accompanying fear
	Obsessive-compulsive disorder	Persistent or repetitive thoughts or behaviours
Mood Disorders	Major depressive disorder	Depressed mood, involving decreased interest or pleasure in everyday activities
	Bipolar disorder	Significant mood swings from hopeless depression to manic 'highs'
Disruptive Behaviour Disorders	Conduct disorder	Repetitive violations of others' rights or social norms, including aggression, theft, destruction of property etc.
	Opposition-defiant disorder	Uncooperative, resistant and hostile behaviour towards authority figures
	Attention-deficit hyperactivity disorder	Persistent difficulties in attention and/or significant hyperactivity and impulsivity

criteria for psychiatric diagnoses, there are many others who display 'sub-clinical' levels of anxiety or depression that can be picked up in simple self-report measures of anxiety and depressive symptoms (e.g. Birmaher *et al.*, 1997; Kovacs, 2003; La Greca & Stone, 1993).

Evidence suggests that genetic and environmental factors play a role in the emergence of both types of conditions during childhood. Both depressive and anxiety symptoms seem to have a common genetic basis, which appears to account for the correlation between the two types of symptoms (Eley & Stevenson, 1999). On the other hand, environmental factors play a key role in the particular manifestation of symptoms; for example, life events related to threat (danger, psychological challenges) have been found to be more strongly predictive of anxiety than of depression (Eley & Stevenson, 2000). Both depressive and anxious symptoms in children have also been linked to aspects of parenting and family processes, although again the precise dimensions of interest may vary across the different disorders (e.g. Hammen & Rudolph, 2003; McLeod, Wood, & Weisz, 2007; Rapee & Spence, 2004). But one further issue that has attracted a considerable amount of research attention is the role of cognition. In the case of both depression and anxiety, it seems likely that negative thinking patterns – such as negative self-perceptions and biased beliefs about events that occur in one's life (e.g. blaming yourself for bad events but not taking the credit for your successes) – play a key role in creating and maintaining feelings of emotional distress (Banerjee, 2008; Kyte & Goodyer, 2008). Thus, a range of biological, social and cognitive factors are likely to play a role in the development of internalising difficulties (also see Section 20.4).

The extent to which internalising problems could affect pupils' experience at school will of course vary from one individual to the next, but there is good evidence that these kinds of difficulties are often associated with poorer social adjustment and peer relations, and sometimes even poorer academic performance (e.g. Schwartz *et al.*, 2008). Moreover, these school difficulties are likely to have reciprocal effects in terms of escalating the internalising problems, thus creating a vicious cycle where anxiety and depression cause problems at school that make the emotional difficulties even more severe. A good example of this kind of interplay can be found in the case of peer victimisation, where early internalising problems can lead a child to be socially withdrawn and isolated at school, which in turn can make the child more vulnerable to bullying, which finally can lead to further increases in internalising difficulties (e.g. Hodges *et al.*, 1999; Sweeting *et al.*, 2006; see Figure 18.2). It is therefore not surprising that a combination of emotional distress (possibly including anxiety about separation from

FIGURE 18.2 *Bullying.*
Problems with bullying at school can often lead to or escalate internalising difficulties such as depressive symptoms.

parents) and peer problems at school can often be a critical factor in extreme anxious reactions to school, which in turn can potentially lead to refusals to attend school altogether (Elliott, 1999).

18.3.2 Externalising and Attention-Deficit Difficulties

Pupils with externalising and attention-deficit difficulties attract a great deal of attention from educational psychologists because of the disruption they can cause to their own learning, the learning of their peers, and interactions at school more generally. As we can see in Table 18.3, conduct disorder, oppositional-defiant disorder (ODD) and attention-deficit/hyperactivity disorder (ADHD) all have the potential to create disturbances in the classroom, because they involve symptoms that can interfere with academic tasks as well as with positive social relationships. The behaviour of a small number of pupils with externalising difficulties – on top of the more widespread low-level disruptive behaviours such as talking out of turn – certainly contributes to the sense of frustration reported by many teachers and even by other pupils (Activity Box 18.1). Moreover – as was the case with internalising disorders – we are not dealing with isolated instances here. In one study where youths were assessed for DSM disorders annually between 9 and 16 years of age (Costello *et al.*, 2003), the average prevalence rate for behavioural disorders was approximately 7%. Over the course of the seven-year project, nearly a quarter of youths at some point met the criteria for a behavioural disorder, with the figure much higher for boys than for girls.

FRUSTRATIONS ABOUT BEHAVIOUR IN SCHOOLS   ACTIVITY BOX 18.1

According to a report by MacBeath and Galton (2004), secondary school teachers regard 'poor pupil behaviour' as the single biggest obstacle to teaching, regardless of their years of experience in schools. Here are a few examples of comments from teachers:

> My biggest negative thing is behaviour management. You've gone in and prepared every last second of the lesson and you've gone in thinking, 'It's going to be fantastic'. Then somebody at break time, somebody has fallen out with someone else and there's absolutely nothing you can do about it and your lesson falls to pieces. That's soul destroying. It really is. (Head of Science, 8 years' experience)

> It's the abuse you get really . . . no one else would go to work in an office and be told to * * * * off and be expected to put up with it. It's what really drags you down. (Head of History, 4 years' experience)

> It takes an awful amount of time. And you don't have the environment where you can sit them down

and say, 'Go sit down over there and tell me what happened.' You can't do that in the teaching area. (Head of Design and Head of Year, 5 years' teaching experience)

Pupils themselves recognise how a small number of disruptive pupils can create difficulties for the general learning environment.

> If they've got a really disruptive pupil they have to be really stern just to keep one bad behaving pupil in line but not all pupils need that level of stern (response) and then they suffer and they sometimes …get it and get treated as if they're the problem pupil. (Girl, year 10)

Discussion: Read the rest of this chapter and think about where disruptive behaviour in the classroom might come from. How do you think teachers should respond to such problems? Can they do anything to reduce the disruption caused by pupils with externalising problems?

Just as researchers have pointed to a range of factors as contributing to the development of internalising disorders, studies of conduct disorder, ODD and ADHD have also revealed a number of biological, social and cognitive factors that are involved in problem behaviour. First, out of the three types of behavioural disorder examined here, we have the greatest knowledge about specific neurophysiological factors involved in ADHD. In line with research pointing to specific differences in brain functioning among youths with ADHD (see Smith, Barkley & Shapiro, 2007), studies have revealed that certain medications that stimulate particular parts of the brain responsible for attention can be helpful in countering ADHD problems; these include studies with placebo controls showing that methylphenidate treatment (the most famous brand name being Ritalin) can lead to significant improvements in behaviour at school (e.g. Pelham *et al.*, 2002).

However, apart from the fact that the effectiveness of medication cannot be guaranteed and in any case depends on accurate diagnosis (which cannot always be assumed), there seems little doubt that a *combination* of biological and social-environmental factors must be considered in order to understand this and other behaviour disorders fully. One intriguing study by Burt *et al.* (2001) examined the genetic and environmental contributions

to conduct disorder, ODD and ADHD, with particular attention to why these three disorders seem to cooccur so frequently. By studying the characteristics of a very large sample of twins and their mothers, the researchers were not only able to determine that each disorder was explained by both genetic and environmental factors, but also found that a common 'shared' environmental factor accounted for the co-occurrence of the various disorders. In other words, some aspect of the children's environment seems to be responsible for a *general* tendency to exhibit disruptive behaviour problems. Drawing on evidence from other research, Burt *et al.* suggest:

> psychosocial adversity within the family system [e.g. parental discipline, family conflict, parents' mental health] appears to be a prime candidate for the shared environmental vulnerability revealed in this study. (Burt *et al.*, 2001, p. 524)

As we will see in Section 20.4, however, this kind of family influence on externalising problems is probably not a direct one, whereby children simply copy the aggressive behaviour they see around them. Rather, psychologists have shown how family problems such as harsh punishment can first bring about biases and distortions in the way children think about themselves and the things that happen to them, which in turn lead to problems in behaviour at school and in other settings. And, just as we saw in the case of internalising disorders, problems at school such as academic under-performance and difficulties in peer relations can serve to reinforce and exacerbate the biased thinking and problem behaviours (Dodge & Pettit, 2003). Therefore, the advice and support of educational psychologists is often critical in helping schools to intervene in these kinds of vicious cycle.

18.3.3 Summary

Behavioural, emotional and social difficulties include a wide range of difficulties, including internalising, externalising and attention-deficit disorders. Although clinical problems in this area affect only a minority of pupils, a sizeable proportion of pupils can be expected to experience behavioural, emotional and social difficulties at some point during their life at school. A variety of biological, social and cognitive factors have been identified as playing a role in these disorders.

18.4 COMMUNICATION AND INTERACTION DIFFICULTIES

Most children develop communication skills without difficulty, but some with hearing impairment, severe learning difficulties or other conditions such as cerebral palsy, Down's syndrome and autism may experience problems in the development of language. In addition, there is a further group of children, around 6% of pupils of school age, with **specific language impairment (SLI)** (Stark & Tallal, 1981): delays in language development that cannot be explained by these factors (Law *et al.*, 2000).

Educational psychologists work closely with speech and language therapists to meet the needs of children with communication difficulties. We will consider first those experiencing speech and language difficulties associated with SLI and second the problems experienced by those with autism, or, more accurately, those with autistic-spectrum conditions, where delays in language development are associated with additional problems in social development and interaction.

specific language impairment (SLI) specific delays in language development which cannot be explained by other conditions such as hearing impairment, severe learning difficulties, cerebral palsy, Down's syndrome or autism.

18.4.1 Speech and Language Difficulties

Children with SLI form a heterogeneous group, but in general there are more boys than girls (2.8 boys:1 girl) and there is evidence of familial concentrations that are suggestive of underlying genetic factors (Tomblin, 1989). Those with SLI can present with problems in any of the five sub-systems of language indicated in Focus Point 18.2, or indeed, in combinations of these areas. The most common difficulties, however, are those of expressive language, the language produced by the child (see Case History 18.1). These can involve problems in understanding and applying the rules in areas such as sound production (articulation), phonology, syntax

FOCUS POINT 18.2 'SUB-SYSTEMS' OF LANGUAGE

Language is central to communicative competence and is used not only to represent objects, events and states of affairs in the real world, but also to express ideas, feelings and beliefs. Language is highly complex and children must acquire competence in five 'sub-systems' (Hoff, 2008):

* *Phonology*: organisation of sounds and the rules regulating usage.
* *Syntax*: rules that determine relationships between words and the organisation of words in phrases and sentences.

* *Morphology*: word forms and inflections (e.g. word endings indicating time or number).
* *Semantics*: meanings of words (in isolation and in phrases and sentences).
* *Pragmatics*: the social and functional use of language in relation to the perspectives of both speaker and listener, which underpins conversation and narrative, and indeed all social interaction.

Find out more about the 'milestones' of typical language development in these areas. How do they help us understand 'atypical' development?

A CHILD WITH LANGUAGE IMPAIRMENT

Nicholas was a communicative baby, babbling by 1 year, but he relied on pointing and gesture and produced his first words at 22 months. By 30 months, he could follow instructions but was frustrated by his lack of vocabulary and often had tantrums. By the time he went to nursery at 42 months, he had a reasonable single-word vocabulary but had just started using two-word utterances, such as 'more ball' and 'daddy car'. He found it hard to combine words and to use tenses and plurals correctly. As a result, he was difficult to understand and was very self-conscious about speaking.

Educational psychologists and speech and language therapists were involved in assessing the extent and severity of Nicholas's difficulties and in advising his parents and nursery staff. They confirmed that his understanding of language was typical for his age and that the problems were specific to grammar. When he moved to school, Nicholas found it easier to engage in 'rough-and-tumble' play rather than to express himself verbally. He made a slow start in reading, particularly in phonics, 'sounding out' words. His teachers were concerned that he would have problems on the assessment tasks for speaking and listening in the National Curriculum. However, speech and language therapy was helpful to him in developing his use of syntax (grammar) and his overall confidence in communication. But at 14 years, he continues to have some problems in written language, particularly in spelling.

and morphology. However, these areas are responsive to speech and language therapy (Boyle *et al.*, 2009) and indeed to remission (Law *et al.*, 2000). Around half of the pre-school children who present with specific delays in expressive language may 'catch up' with their typically developing peers without treatment by 5 years of age. But this also means that half continue to experience problems after school entry that can be associated with persistent difficulties in reading and spelling (Stothard *et al.*, 1998) and also with secondary problems of behaviour and social adjustment (Baker & Cantwell, 1987), which may have an impact on mental health in later life. Risk factors for persistent problems include:

- The initial severity of the delay: the more severe, the more likely the problems are to persist and be resistant to intervention.

- The extent to which the difficulties are generalised across areas of speech and language (e.g. problems in more than one domain, particularly where understanding of language is involved, as in 'mixed receptive-expressive' delay).

- The extent to which other cognitive and developmental skills are also delayed (secondary difficulties).

In addition to these linguistic and genetic explanations, there are also explanations based on underlying cognitive processing (see Boyle *et al.* [2010] for a discussion). Children with SLI have slower reaction times on a wide range of verbal and nonverbal tasks, giving rise to the possibility that they may have a more limited general processing capacity than their typically developing peers. Problems with executive functions, such as working memory and inhibition, and with auditory processing are also reported in the literature.

Systematic reviews of the literature regarding intervention for SLI (Law, Garrett & Nye, 2003) reveal that there have been few published controlled studies of intervention for those with speech and language difficulties, and most of these are based on monolingual, English-speaking children. However, while there is evidence for a range of effective treatment approaches for specific problems in speech production and phonology and expressive language more generally, there is less evidence for effective intervention for problems in receptive language (understanding of language; see also Boyle *et al.*, 2009).

18.4.2 Autistic Spectrum Conditions

The term 'autism' was introduced by Kanner (1943) and is characterised by a 'triad' of impairments in reciprocal social interaction, verbal and nonverbal communication, and 'behavioural flexibility' (American Psychiatric Association, 2002; see also Chapter 4). Children with autism have delays in language development and, in the most severe cases, may fail to develop verbal language. Delays in starting and maintaining conversations are typically due to repetitive and unusual use of language, and children with autism commonly have problems with pretend or imitative play in social settings (see Case History 18.2). Children with Asperger's syndrome have the impairments in social interaction and in restricted, repetitive behaviours, but do not have significant early problems in language.

CASE HISTORY 18.2

A CHILD WITH AUTISTIC SPECTRUM DISORDER

Richard was extremely slow to develop language and his parents were concerned about his lack of responsivity to others and about obsessive and repetitive play. Following assessments by educational psychologists, speech therapists and paediatricians, Richard was diagnosed with ASD. At the age of 5, his expressive language is restricted to single words and stereotypic phrases, which are often used inappropriately. He also has difficulties in understanding even simple verbal instructions and has problems in interacting and playing with his peers. He is very attached to his mother, although he often seeks attention from her in inappropriate ways. He becomes very anxious about even small changes in his daily routine. His special educational needs have been identified and he has responded to a highly structured, visually based approach in his classroom, TEACCH – Treatment and Education of Autistic and Communication Handicapped Children (Schopler & Mesibove, 1995).

Autism and Asperger's syndrome are conceptualised using a dimensional approach as autism-spectrum disorder (ASD), which reflects current thinking that such a 'spectrum' approach is preferable to the more traditional categorical approach. More males are affected than females (3:1 or 4:1) and around three-quarters of those with ASD have marked learning difficulties, although some of these individuals have savant skills, special abilities in memory, calculation or art. In general, however, global cognitive delays are a risk factor for a poor prognosis of longer-term progress.

As in the case of SLI, there are problems in establishing the prevalence of ASD, but there have been recent rises in the reported prevalence, currently held to be around some 100 per 10 000 (Baird *et al.*, 2006). However, it is unclear whether these rises are due to better case finding or to an actual increase in the numbers with ASD. Like SLI, ASD is developmental – that is, present from birth – and twin studies show underlying genetic influences. Problems in sensory processing are common, with those with ASD often either highly sensitive or highly insensitive to auditory, visual or tactile stimulation.

Three cognitive theories have been developed by psychologists to account for the characteristic impairments of ASD, including social problems (see Rajendran and Mitchell [2007] for a review):

theory of mind the ability to understand one's own and other people's mental states.

- **Theory of mind** can account for difficulties in social interaction. Many, although by no means all, of those with ASD have problems in 'mentalising' or making correct attributions of the intentions and beliefs of others, which are central to predicting how they will react in interaction.

executive dysfunction impairment of the cognitive skills involved in problem-solving, planning and engaging in goal-directed behaviour.

- The notion of **executive dysfunction** can account for the repetitive and sometimes inappropriate behaviours of those with ASD in terms of deficits in executive functions such as planning, monitoring and inhibition.

- **Weak central coherence** can account for the special abilities of some of those with ASD. In contrast to typically developing individuals, those with ASD process information in a 'detail-focused' manner, rather than as a meaningful whole.

weak central coherence an atypical way of processing information focusing on individual details rather than on the meaningful whole.

Systematic reviews of the literature (Howlin, Magiati & Charman, 2009; Reichow & Volkmar, 2010) reveal that there have been few randomised control trials (see Section 17.5.2) of intervention for children with ASD, and that many studies have methodological weaknesses. However, there is evidence of positive outcomes for intensive early intervention based on behavioural theory, such as applied behavior analysis (Lovass, 1987), and also for less intensive interventions that focus on communication skills and joint interaction (Howlin *et al.*, 2007). There is also evidence that training in perspective taking may be effective, although further research is needed (Gray, 1998; Howlin, Baron-Cohen & Hadwin, 1999).

18.4.3   Summary

Specific difficulties in communication and interaction are present in a small but significant minority of pupils at school. Pupils with specific language impairments and autistic-spectrum conditions form heterogeneous groups, with a range of skills, abilities and weaknesses evident across different pupils. Various explanations for the origins of these problems have been suggested, and continued research on both aetiology and approaches to intervention is needed in order to better understand and support pupils with these difficulties.

18.5 DIFFICULTIES ASSOCIATED WITH SENSORY AND PHYSICAL NEEDS

Sensory and physical difficulties cross the boundary from primarily psychological conditions (though they may have physiological or neurological origins) into conditions that are primarily physiological in character, though they typically have a range of psychological consequences. **Visual impairment** covers a spectrum of differing degrees of loss of sight including blindness, and even there it is important to recognise that total loss of vision – which is what people generally understand by the term – is relatively unusual. 'Blindness' is used technically to refer to a severe level of sight loss, which leaves children reliant on learning by touch. There are in fact a variety of conditions giving rise to loss of sight, with various characteristics relating to these. Short- and long-sightedness result from the eyeball being sufficiently misshapen to make it impossible to focus, though even fairly extreme degrees of this can be corrected by the use of spectacles or contact lenses (Farrell, 2009). Retinitis pigmentosa affects the sensitivity of the retina to light and is a condition that progressively worsens, creating pronounced loss of vision in low light levels and in the periphery of the visual field (tunnel vision).

> **visual impairment** loss of sight of various degrees including blindness.

The more common source of pronounced difficulty, however, is neurological impairment to the visual system, which prevents proper processing of visual information. Such impairments are commonly associated with wider genetic or pre-natal/peri-natal problems, with the consequence that visual impairment is very typically found alongside a range of other difficulties, including autism, SLD and PMLD, and various types of emotional and behavioural difficulty (Jan, 1993). Given the dominance of vision in typical human functioning, children with visual impairments are at a particular disadvantage even if other aspects of cognition are unimpaired, and educational provision in the United Kingdom is therefore still primarily with special schools, where the emphasis is on learning to carry out a range of everyday tasks – mobility and hygiene being the most obvious – as well as learning cognitive skills.

Hearing impairment similarly covers a range of hearing loss, with total deafness again being uncommon. To some extent, loss can be defined in terms of the degree of reduced sensitivity to sound, measured in decibels (Westwood, 2003). In this scheme, *slight*, *mild* and *moderate* loss mean a reduction of 15 to 25, 25 to 40 and 40 to 65 decibels respectively. *Severe* and *profound* loss are defined as loss above 65 and 95 decibels respectively, taking it into the range where speech would be inaudible. This has particular implications where the loss is *pre-lingual* (i.e. before language has been acquired). Volume alone is not the only issue, however, since sounds of different frequency or *pitch* are typically affected in different ways. As human speech covers a range of frequencies, the consequence is that it can seem distorted even to someone with less severe hearing loss, possibly to the point of incomprehensibility. This is particularly likely where the loss is in the higher frequency range, since this has an impact on the ability to detect the consonants that help us divide up sounds into words (Farrell, 2009).

> **hearing impairment** loss of hearing of various degrees including total deafness.

As with visual impairment, hearing impairment is most often the result of neurological damage, which creates a variety of comorbidities. In addition, while hearing is less dominant in human perception than vision, hearing loss can still affect safe mobility – we rely heavily on sound for moving around traffic environments, for instance (van der Molen, 1981) – and the effects of the loss of hearing before language is acquired have a profound impact on communicative ability and social understanding. Peterson and Siegal (2003), for instance, found that children with pre-lingual deafness and parents who were unable to compensate via early use of sign language showed lags of five years or more in performance on simple tasks of social understanding and theory of mind. Compensating for loss of oral communication is therefore now recognised as a key priority for these children, whether via the use of hearing aids, cochlear implants that actually restore hearing to some degree, or the creation of environments in which normal levels of communication can be maintained through sign language (see Figure 18.3).

Physical disabilities again have multiple causes that are often neurological in origin, as with *cerebral palsy*. As noted above, conditions of this type are often associated with comorbid problems with vision or hearing, but even where this is not the case, the loss of physical control may make sensory perception more difficult, creating problems of the same kind (Farrell, 2009). Disabilities of this type are perhaps the hardest of all to define, unless they stem from a specific medical condition, since there is

> **physical disabilities** difficulties or impairments in normal physical functioning.

FIGURE 18.3 *Hearing-impaired children using sign language in a classroom.*

Source: Ann Senghas (2004)

considerable dispute about the kind of classification system that is appropriate, and much contention on the part of disability rights groups that such systems are typically based on social perceptions of normality (Johnstone, 2001). Severity is perhaps a little easier to define, since it can be assessed in terms of degree of impairment in performing everyday tasks, and the P scales provide some yardstick for defining the relative capabilities of severely disabled here (see also Section 18.2.1 on PMLD). In general, though, educational provision for children with physical disabilities has to be determined on a case-by-case basis.

18.5.1 Summary

Visual, hearing and physical impairments are extremely variable in both character and severity, and are usually comorbid with a range of other difficulties. For this reason, educational provision remains typically focused on special schools with the capacity to provide individualised arrangements for both assessment of needs and teaching.

18.6 APPROACHES TO INTERVENTION

Once a child or adolescent has been identified as having special educational needs, it is not always obvious what course of action is going to be most effective in enhancing the educational experience and bringing about positive change. At the beginning of this chapter, we reviewed the 'graduated response' prescribed in the Code of Practice for SEN in England and Wales (DfES, 2001a), moving from (i) support strategies within school; to (ii) additional support from external professionals and agencies; to (iii) a full statutory assessment, potentially giving rise to a formal commitment to implement special educational provisions. We cannot do justice here to the enormous literature on the range of intervention strategies for pupils with particular difficulties or areas of need. However, in this section we will consider some general issues relating to the support provided for pupils with SEN.

18.6.1 Inclusion

One big issue, and perhaps one of the most controversial questions concerning education, relates to the notion of **inclusion**. The National Union of Teachers defines inclusion in these terms:

inclusion a process focused on fulfilling each child's entitlement to high quality education.

> It is about adequate provision to meet each pupil's needs with the most appropriate provision and reasonable adjustments made to enable each pupil to access fully education and the life of his or her school or college. The provision and adjustments may be different for each pupil. Inclusion is a process focussed on fulfilling each child's entitlement to high quality education. This is the essence of inclusion. (NUT, 2006, p. 3)

This approach to inclusion is consistent with a 2004 policy statement from the government, which sets out a key goal of having special schools not only to provide education for 'children with the most severe and complex needs', but also to work alongside other local authority and health services to 'share specialist skills and knowledge to support inclusion in mainstream schools' (DfES, 2004, p. 26). Thus, although it is clear that special schools still have a key role to play in the education of pupils with SEN, policies over the last decade have clearly focused on how the integration of such pupils into mainstream education can be made more effective. This is a pressing matter of concern, as mainstream primary and secondary schools have had to contend with an overall rise in the number of pupils listed as having special educational needs (from 1 171 700 in 2005 to 1 362 350 in 2009, a rise of 16%). Indeed, a clear majority of pupils receiving statements of SEN in 2008 were placed in mainstream schools, rather than special schools (DCSF, 2009).

The inclusion of pupils with SEN in mainstream education is a highly complex issue. Even though teachers are broadly positive about the concept of inclusion in mainstream schools, researchers have reported potential risks relating to the resourcing of support (in terms of both staff time and special facilities), the impact on teaching practices (e.g. attention to pupils with SEN at the expense of other pupils' learning) and inadequacies in staff expertise and knowledge (MacBeath *et al.*, 2006). Added to this is the difficulty of knowing what kind of school context is most conducive to the social and emotional wellbeing of pupils with SEN. For example, Stinson, Whitmire and Kluwin's (1996) study of hearing-impaired adolescents showed that greater integration into mainstream classes led to more participation in activities with hearing peers, but did not imply greater emotional security about social relationships; in fact, in the last year of school, hearing-impaired pupils who had spent more time in mainstream classes were significantly *less* positive about their own social skills. The results imply that although inclusion in mainstream classes can expand the social (as well as academic) activities of pupils with SEN, the sense of 'being different' in comparison with one's 'normal' peers can potentially have negative consequences. We will explore the role of social comparison in pupils' development in more detail in Chapter 20.

18.6.2   Intervention, Planning and Review

Regardless of how we view the pros and cons of integrating pupils with SEN into mainstream schools, what seems abundantly clear is that virtually all teachers working in mainstream schools will have to support the learning and development of at least some pupils with SEN. So what could be done to support pupils with SEN in school? The nature of intervention and support strategies obviously varies a great deal depending on the particular profile and needs of the pupil, but we can think about all educational interventions – whether concerned with academic learning, social behaviour or psychological wellbeing – in terms of a tiered pyramid. For example, the DCSF's (2006) **waves of intervention model** sets out three waves of intervention, from universal provisions intended to benefit all pupils, to additional support for some groups of pupils, to intense individual support for pupils with severe difficulties (see Figure 18.4). In practice, provision often takes the form of:

waves of intervention model a three-tiered model of intervention to support pupils' learning: universal provisions intended to benefit all pupils; additional support for some groups of pupils; intense individual support for pupils with severe difficulties.

- General teaching and behaviour-management strategies, and universal curriculum lessons/activities.

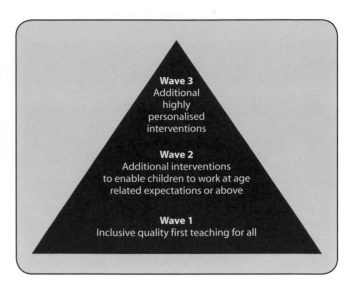

FIGURE 18.4 *The 'waves of intervention' model: Tiered support for inclusive education.*
Source: DCSF (2006).

- Small-group work to support pupils with particular difficulties (e.g. pupils with dyslexia, pupils on the autistic spectrum), possibly with input from external professionals and agencies.

- One-to-one support by specialist staff to help pupils with severe disabilities (e.g. pupils with profound hearing or visual impairments).

All of these strategies can involve complex psychological processes and are closely connected to academic research topics as well as to input from practising clinical and educational psychologists. For example, research on universal provisions to foster social and emotional development – whole-class curriculum approaches, such as the Promoting Alternative Thinking Strategies programme (PATHS; Greenberg *et al.*, 1995) – have been studied carefully and utilised in school-based projects that include children at risk of developing behavioural problems (e.g. Conduct Problems Prevention Research Group, 1999). In addition, research on strategies to prevent aggressive behaviour problems in high-risk inner-city samples has also included small-group social skills training programmes, in combination with the universal provision (e.g. Metropolitan Area Child Study Research Group, 2002). This kind of psychological research has therefore informed the development of DCSF's own Wave 1 and Wave 2 resources within the 'Social and Emotional Aspects of Learning' programme (DCSF, 2005, 2007).

In a similar way, psychological research has been invaluable in providing a foundation for designing intervention work across all the other domains of SEN, from cognitive deficits to sensory impairments to communication difficulties. For example, research on the key factors involved in reading development (e.g. Muter *et al.*, 2004) has informed policies concerning universal approaches to teaching early reading (e.g. Rose, 2006). At the same time, research on group-based support strategies has also been critical for shaping the nature of small-group work for pupils with reading delays (e.g. Hatcher *et al.*, 2006). Thus, psychological research in schools not only has been important for improving our understanding of key aspects of cognitive, social and emotional development, but also has directly influenced the way in which teachers and other practitioners work with pupils with SEN.

One key ingredient in all of this work is a framework for identifying needs, profiling strengths and weaknesses, setting targets, planning the specific intervention work and reviewing progress. In many countries, including the UK, this framework is manifested in an **individual education plan** (IEP; see example in Focus Point 18.3). Effective work involves a collaboration between the Special Educational Needs Coordinator (SENCo) at the school, the other school staff and any external professionals providing support. It is important to stress that work at this level often includes direct work with parents (e.g. parent group meetings, regular telephone contact, homework assignments), in recognition of research showing that parents often have a key role to play in successful

> **individual education plan** in the UK, an individualised plan for a child in education that identifies the child's needs, profiles his or her strengths and weaknesses, sets targets for the child, plans specific intervention to achieve those targets, and reviews the child's progress towards those targets.

FOCUS POINT 18.3   SAMPLE INDIVIDUAL EDUCATION PLAN

Individual Education Plan

Pupil	F.
Year group	6
Placement on SEN Record	Statement
Area of need	Autistic Spectrum Disorder

Summary of Main Aspect(s) of Pupil's Special Needs:	*Inappropriate social interaction with adults* *Communication difficulties* *Difficulties forming relationships with peers* *Lack of imagination.*
Summary of Main Aspect(s) of Pupil's Relative Strengths:	*Friendly* *Good vocabulary* *Excellent presentation skills* *Excellent drawing skills*
Contribution of School Staff (Teaching/Ancillary) to Arrangements for Pupil:	*5 hrs teaching assistant support* *3.5 hrs teacher support* *Involved in 'Circle of Friends'* *Teaching assistant involved in playtimes to encourage appropriate interaction* *Supported during Literacy Hour for comprehension.*
Contribution of External Agencies/ Support Services to Arrangements for Pupil:	*Termly visits from Austism Outreach Team:* • *Social story approach* • *Use of Social Communication Skills Programme* *Support from Speech Therapy* • *Use of 'Language Pack' for teaching assistant*
Contribution of Parents/Carers to Arrangements for Pupil:	*Mum to refer to contact book on a regular basis and respond, as appropriate.*
Contribution of Pupil:	*Attends games club on Thursday lunchtimes.* *F. will try hard not to 'take over' during lessons.* *F. enjoys school and particularly likes art.*

Individual Education Plan

Duration of IEP – From: *January*   **To:** *April*

IEP TARGETS (LEARNING/ BEHAVIORAL/ DEVELOPMENTAL, etc.)	SUCCESS CRITERIA	TEACHING STRATEGIES AND SUPPORT	OUTCOMES FOR PUPIL (with dates)
1. *To listen to the other children during 'Circle of Friends' time.*	*To listen to 2 other children speak before contributing himself during a 'Circle of Friends' session.*	*'Circle of Friends' approach. Passing of pebble to indicate when to speak.*	
2. *To answer factual comprehension questions based on a story/ play/ poem.*	*To be able to answer 3 questions correctly after guided reading sessions.*	*Guided reading within a group Use of role models through asking others in the group first.*	
3. *To understand a non-verbal signal to 'be quiet' when given by class teacher.*	*To respond appropriately to the signal consistently.*	*Role modelling of signal from teacher and peers Use of social story approach.*	
4. *To be able to understand idioms identified in 'Language Pack'.*	*To be able to explain the meaning of an idiom with understanding on 3 occasions.*	*Use of 'Language Pack' from speech therapist during withdrawal with teaching assistant on a weekly basis.*	
Monitoring Arrangements: *Home-school contact book Teaching assistant monitoring sheet for 'Language Pack' work Observation.*			

Source: http://www.leics.gov.uk/pupil_f.pdf

therapeutic interventions with children (e.g. Barrett, Dadds & Rapee, 1996). A critical element of the intervention work is the commitment to monitoring and reviewing progress – including formal updates to IEPs at least twice a year – and adjusting outcomes accordingly (and possibly planning for 'exit' from the extra support strategies). This may involve use of standardised assessment tools – which themselves have often been developed through psychological research – as well as informal measurements and observations of progress. Educational psychologists have an important role to play in liaising with staff as part of this monitoring and review process, by directly assessing pupils' functioning themselves, and/ or by providing expert consultation and advice on the choice of interventions and teaching approaches that would best meet the needs of the pupil.

18.6.3 Summary

Work to support pupils with special educational needs demands a careful consideration of how to promote genuine inclusion. Integration into mainstream classes can potentially have major benefits, but also carries risks.

Intervention to meet the needs of pupils with SEN can take place at multiple levels, from work to enhance universal provision for all pupils, to small-group work for pupils needing additional support, to intensive one-to-one work for selected pupils. In all cases, a robust system of assessment, planning, monitoring and reviewing is required in order to implement intervention strategies effectively.

18.7 CHAPTER SUMMARY

This chapter has provided an overview of the current code of practice regarding the 'graduated response' to the identification of pupils with special educational needs in England and Wales. We have seen that there are a number of areas of difficulty that might be encountered by an educational psychologist, and that a range of causal explanations for the development of such difficulties have been suggested. Having a rigorous system of assessment, planning and monitoring is essential in order to make interventions at whole-school, small-group and individual levels as effective as possible.

SELF-TEST QUESTIONS

- Describe the 'graduated response' to the identification of special educational needs in the SEN Code of Practice.
- Describe the definition of moderate, severe and profound and multiple learning difficulties.
- How does dyslexia differ from reading disorder?
- How does dyscalculia differ from mathematics disorder?
- Describe one example each of an internalising disorder, an externalising disorder and an attention-deficit disorder.
- What are the key features of a specific language impairment?
- What are three cognitive theories of autistic spectrum disorders?
- What are the main characteristics of visual, hearing and physical impairment?
- What are the three 'waves of intervention' in the DCSF model?
- What are the potential benefits and risks of integrating pupils with SEN/additional support needs into mainstream classes?
- What is an IEP?

ESSAY QUESTIONS

- Critically evaluate the role of biological and social factors in the development of behavioural, emotional and social difficulties.
- How and to what extent can intervention strategies be effective in helping children with specific language impairments?
- Compare and contrast alternative explanations of autistic spectrum disorders. Are they mutually exclusive?
- To what extent should pupils with SEN be integrated into mainstream school classes?

TEXTS FOR FURTHER READING

Farrell, M. (2009) *Foundations of Special Education: An Introduction*, Chichester: Wiley-Blackwell.

Frith, U. (2003) *Autism: Explaining the Enigma*, 2nd edn, Oxford: Blackwell.

Hoff, E. (2008) *Language Development*, 4th edn, Belmont, CA: Wadsworth/Thomson Learning.

Mash, E.J. & Barkley, R.A. (eds) (2001) *Child Psychopathology*, 2nd edn, New York: Guilford Press.

Silverman, W.K. & Treffers, P.D.A. (eds) (2001) *Anxiety Disorders in Children and Adolescents: Research, Assessment and Intervention*, Cambridge: Cambridge University Press.

RELEVANT JOURNAL ARTICLES

Barrett, P.M., Dadds, M.R. & Rapee, R.M. (1996) Family treatment of childhood anxiety: A controlled trial, *Journal of Consulting and Clinical Psychology* 64(2): 333–42, doi:10.1037/0022-006X.64.2.333.

Boyle, J., McCartney, E., O'Hare, A. & Forbes, J. (2009) Direct versus indirect and individual versus group modes of language therapy for children with primary language impairment: Principal outcomes from a randomized controlled trial and economic evaluation, *International Journal of Language and Communication Disorder* 44(6): 826–46.

Costello, E.J., Mustillo, S., Erkanli, A., Keeler, G. & Angold, A. (2003) Prevalence and development of psychiatric disorders in childhood and adolescence, *Archives of General Psychiatry* 60: 837–44.

Dodge, K.A. & Pettit, G.S. (2003) A biopsychosocial model of the development of chronic conduct problems in adolescence, *Developmental Psychology* 39: 349–71.

Eley, T.C. & Stevenson, J. (2000) Specific life events and chronic experiences differentially associated with depression and anxiety in young twins, *Journal of Abnormal Child Psychology* 28(4): 383–94.

Lovass, O.I. (1987) Behavioral treatment and normal intellectual and educational functioning in autistic children, *Journal of Consulting and Clinical Psychology* 55: 3–9.

Pelham, W.E., Hoza, B., Pillow, D.R. *et al.* (2002) Effects of methylphenidate and expectancy on children with ADHD: Behavior, academic performance, and attributions in a summer treatment program and regular classroom settings, *Journal of Consulting and Clinical Psychology* 70: 320–35.

Rajendran, G. & Mitchell, P. (2007) Cognitive theories of autism, *Developmental Review* 27: 224–60.

Reichow, B. & Volkmar, F. (2010) Social skills interventions for individuals with autism: Evaluation for evidence-based practices within a best evidence synthesis framework, *Journal of Autism and Developmental Disorders* 40: 149–66.

Schwartz, D., Gorman, A., Duong, M. & Nakamoto, J. (2008) Peer relationships and academic achievement as interacting predictors of depressive symptoms during middle childhood, *Journal of Abnormal Psychology* 117: 289–99.

USEFUL WEBSITES

Afasic, http://www.afasic.org.uk

British Dyslexia Association, http://www.bdadyslexia.org.uk

Department for Children, Schools, and Families: Inclusion, http://nationalstrategies.standards.dcsf.gov.uk/inclusion

Dyslexia Action, http://www.dyslexiaaction.org.uk

I-Can, http://www.ican.org.uk

Linden Lodge School, Wimbledon, http://www.lindenlodge.wandsworth.sch.uk/Welcome/welcome.html

National Autistic Society, http://www.nas.org.uk

Scottish Government: Autism Toolbox, http://www.scotland.gov.uk/Publications/2009/07/06111319/0

Teachernet Special Educational Needs, http://www.teachernet.gov.uk/wholeschool/sen

REFERENCES

American Psychiatric Association (2002) *Diagnostic and Statistical Manual of Mental Disorders*, 4th edn, Washington, DC: APA.

Anderson, E.R. & Hope, D.A. (2008) A review of the tripartite model for understanding the link between anxiety and depression in youth, *Clinical Psychology Review* 28: 275–87.

Baird, G., Simonoff, E., Pickles, A. *et al.* (2006) Prevalence of disorders of the autistic spectrum in a population cohort of children in South Thames: The Special Needs and Autism Project (SNAP), *Lancet* 368: 210–15.

Baker, L. & Cantwell, D.P. (1987) A prospective psychiatric follow-up of children with speech/language disorders, *Journal of the American Academy of Child and Adolescent Psychiatry* 26: 546–53.

Banerjee, R.A. (2008) Social cognition and anxiety in children, in C. Sharp, P. Fonagy & I. Goodyer (eds) *Social Cognition and Developmental Psychopathology*, pp. 239–69, Oxford: Oxford University Press.

Barrett, P.M., Dadds, M.R. & Rapee, R.M. (1996) Family treatment of childhood anxiety: A controlled trial, *Journal of Consulting and Clinical Psychology* 64(2): 333–42, doi:10.1037/0022-006X.64.2.333.

Birmaher, B., Khetarpal, S., Brent, D. *et al.* (1997) The Screen for Child Anxiety Related Emotional Disorders (SCARED): Scale construction and psychometric characteristics, *Journal of the American Academy of Child and Adolescent Psychiatry* 36: 545–53.

Boyle, J., McCartney, E., O'Hare, A. & Forbes, J. (2009) Direct versus indirect and individual versus group modes of language therapy for children with primary language impairment: Principal outcomes from a randomized controlled trial and economic evaluation, *International Journal of Language and Communication Disorder* 44(6): 826–46.

Boyle, J., McCartney. E., O'Hare, A. & Law, J. (2010) Intervention for receptive language disorder, *Developmental Medicine and Child Neurology* 52(11): 994–9.

Brady, E.U. & Kendall, P.C. (1992) Comorbidity of anxiety and depression in children and adolescents, *Psychological Bulletin* 111(2): 244–55.

Burt, S.A., Krueger, R.F., McGue, M. & Iacono, W.G. (2001) Sources of covariation among attention-deficit/hyperactivity disorder, oppositional defiant disorder, and conduct disorder: The importance of shared environment, *Journal of Abnormal Psychology* 110: 516–25.

Conduct Problems Prevention Research Group (1999) Initial impact of the Fast Track prevention trial for conduct problems: I. The high-risk sample, *Journal of Consulting and Clinical Psychology* 67: 631–47.

Conti-Ramsden, G.M. & Botting, N. (2008) Emotional health in adolescents with and without a history of specific language impairment (SLI), *Journal of Child Psychology and Psychiatry* 49: 516–25.

Costello, E.J., Mustillo, S., Erkanli, A., Keeler, G. & Angold, A. (2003) Prevalence and development of psychiatric disorders in childhood and adolescence, *Archives of General Psychiatry* 60: 837–44.

Department for Children, Schools and Families (2005) *Primary National Strategy, Social and Emotional Aspects of Learning: Guidance*, London: DfES Publications.

Department for Children, Schools and Families (2006) *Waves of Intervention Model*, London: DfES Publications, http://nationalstrategies.standards.dcsf.gov.uk/node/41795, accessed November 2010.

Department for Children, Schools and Families (2007) *Secondary National Strategy, Social and Emotional Aspects of Learning for Secondary Schools: Guidance Booklet*, London: DfES Publications.

Department for Children, Schools and Families (2009) *Statistical First Release: Schools, Pupils, and Their Characteristics, January 2009*, London: DCSF, http://www.dcsf.gov.uk/rsgateway/DB/SFR/s000843/index.shtml, accessed November 2010.

Department for Education and Skills (2001a) *Special Educational Needs: Code of Practice*, London: DfES Publications.

Department for Education and Skills (2001b) *Removing Barriers to Achievement: The Government's Strategy for SEN*, London: DfES Publications.

Department for Education and Skills (2004) *Removing barriers to achievement: The government's strategy for SEN*. Nottingham, UK: DfES Publications.

Department for Education and Skills (2005) *Data Collection by Special Educational Need*, 2nd edn, London: DfES.

Dodge, K.A. & Pettit, G.S. (2003) A biopsychosocial model of the development of chronic conduct problems in adolescence, *Developmental Psychology* 39: 349–71.

Eley, T.C. & Stevenson, J. (1999) Using genetic analyses to clarify the distinction between depressive and anxious symptoms in children, *Journal of Abnormal Child Psychology* 27(2): 105–14.

Eley, T.C. & Stevenson, J. (2000) Specific life events and chronic experiences differentially associated with depression and anxiety in young twins, *Journal of Abnormal Child Psychology* 28(4): 383–94.

Elliott, J.G. (1999) School refusal: Issues of conceptualisation, assessment, and treatment, *Journal of Child Psychology and Psychiatry* 40: 1001–12.

Farrell, M. (2009) *Foundations of Special Education: An Introduction*, Chichester: Wiley-Blackwell.

Geuze, R.H., Jongmans, M., Schoemaker, M. & Smits-Englesman, B. (2001) Clinical and research diagnostic criteria for developmental coordination disorder: A review and discussion, *Human Movement Science* 20: 7–47.

Gray, C.A. (1998) Social stories and comic strip conversations with students with Asperger's Syndrome and high functioning autism, in E. Scholper & G. Mesibov (eds) *Asperger's Syndrome or High Functioning Autism? Current Issues in Autism*, pp. 167–98, New York: Plenum Press.

Greenberg, M.T., Kusche, C.A., Cook, E.T. & Quamma, J.P. (1995) Promoting emotional competence in school-aged children: The effects of the PATHS curriculum, *Development and Psychopathology* 7(1): 117–36.

Hammen, C. & Rudolph, K.D. (2003) Childhood mood disorders, in E.J. Mash & R.A. Barkley (eds) *Child Psychopathology*, Vol. 2, pp. 233–78, New York: Guilford Press.

Hatcher, P.J., Hulme, C., Miles, J.N.V. *et al.* (2006) Efficacy of small group reading intervention for beginning readers with reading-delay: A randomised controlled trial, *Journal of Child Psychology and Psychiatry* 47: 820–27.

Henderson, S.E., Sugden, D.A. & Barnett, A.E. (2007) *Movement Assessment Battery for Children – 2nd Edition (Movement ABC-2)*, London: Pearson Education.

Hodges, E.V.E., Boivin, M., Vitaro, F. & Bukowski, W.M. (1999) The power of friendship: Protection against an escalating cycle of peer victimization, *Developmental Psychology* 35: 94–101.

Hoff, E. (2008) *Language Development*, 4th edn, Belmont, CA: Wadsworth/Thomson Learning.

Howlin, P., Baron-Cohen, S. & Hadwin, J. (1999) *Teaching Children with Autism to Mind-Read: A Practical Guide for Teachers and Parents*, London: John Wiley & Sons, Ltd.

Howlin, P., Gordon, K., Pasco, G., Wade, A. & Charman, T. (2007) A group randomised, controlled trial of the Picture Exchange Communication System for children with autism, *Journal of Child Psychology and Psychiatry* 48: 473–81.

Howlin, P., Magiati, I. & Charman, T. (2009) Systematic review of early intensive behavioral interventions for children with autism, *American Association on Intellectual and Developmental Disabilities* 114(1): 23–41.

Hulme, C. & Snowling, M.J. (2009) *Developmental Disorders of Language Learning and Cognition*, Chichester: Wiley-Blackwell.

Jan, J. (1993) Neurological causes of visual impairment and investigation, in A. Fielder, A. Best & M.C.O. Bax (eds) *The Management of Visual Impairment in Childhood*, London: Mackieth.

Johnstone, D. (2001) *An Introduction to Disability Studies*, 2nd edn, London: David Fulton.

Kadesjo, B. & Gillberg, C. (1999) Developmental coordination disorder in Swedish 7-year-old children, *Journal of the American Academy of Child and Adolescent Psychiatry* 42: 487–92.

Kanner, L. (1943) Autistic disturbances of affective contact, *Nervous Child* 2: 217–50.

Kosc, L. (1974) Developmental dyscalculia, *Journal of Learning Disabilities* 7: 159–62.

Kovacs, M.K. (2003) *Children's Depression Inventory (CDI) Technical Manual Update*, New York: Multi-Health Systems.

Kyte, Z. & Goodyer, I. (2008) Social cognition in depressed children and adolescents, in C. Sharp, P. Fonagy & I. Goodyer (eds) *Social Cognition and Developmental Psychopathology*, pp. 201–37, Oxford: Oxford University Press.

La Greca, A.M. & Stone, W.L. (1993) Social Anxiety Scale for Children – Revised: Factor structure and concurrent validity, *Journal of Clinical Child Psychology* 22(1): 17–27.

Landerl, K., Bevan, A. & Butterworth, B. (2004) Developmental dyscalculia and basic numerical capacities: A study of 8–9 year old students, *Cognition* 93: 99–125.

Law, J., Garrett, Z. & Nye, C. (2003) *Speech and Language Therapy Interventions for Children with Primary Speech and Language Delay or Disorder* (Cochrane Review), in The Cochrane Library Issue 3, Oxford: Update Software.

Law, J., Boyle, J., Harris, F., Harkness, A. & Nye, C. (2000) Prevalence and natural history of primary speech and language delay: Findings from a systematic review of the literature, *International Journal of Language and Communication Disorder* 35(2): 165–88.

Lewis, C., Hitch, G. & Walker, P. (1994) The prevalence of specific arithmetic difficulties and specific reading difficulties in 9- and 10-year-old boys and girls, *Journal of Child Psychology and Psychiatry* 35: 283–92.

Lovass, O.I. (1987) Behavioral treatment and normal intellectual and educational functioning in autistic children, *Journal of Consulting and Clinical Psychology* 55: 3–9.

Lyon, R., Shaywitz, S.E. & Shaywitz, B.A. (2003) A definition of dyslexia, *Annals of Dyslexia* 53: 1–14.

MacBeath, J., & Galton, M. (2004). *A life in secondary teaching: Finding time for learning.* Cambridge: University of Cambridge.

MacBeath, J., Galton, M., Steward, S., MacBeath, A. & Page, C. (2006) *The Costs of Inclusion*, Cambridge: Cambridge University Press.

McLeod, B.D., Wood, J.J. & Weisz, J.R. (2007) Examining the association between parenting and childhood anxiety: A meta-analysis, *Clinical Psychology Review* 27: 155–72.

Metropolitan Area Child Study Research Group (2002) A cognitive-ecological approach to preventing aggression in urban settings: Initial outcomes for high-risk children, *Journal of Consulting and Clinical Psychology* 70: 179–94.

Mon-Williams, M., Pascal, A.E. & Wann, J.P. (1994) Opthalmic factors in developmental coordination disorder, *Adapted Physical Activity Quarterly* 11: 170–78.

Muter, V., Hulme, C., Snowling, M.J. & Stevenson, J. (2004) Phonemes, rimes, vocabulary, and grammatical skills as foundations of early reading development: Evidence from a longitudinal study, *Developmental Psychology* 40: 665–81.

Ndaji, F. & Tymms, P. (2009) *The P Scales: Assessing the Progress of Children with Special Educational Needs*, Chichester: Wiley-Blackwell.

Norwich, B. (2008) Dilemmas of difference and the identification of special educational needs/disability: International perspectives, *British Educational Research Journal* 35: 447–68.

NUT (2006) *National Union of Teachers Policy Statement on Meeting the Needs of Pupils with Special Educational Needs,* London: National Union of Teachers.

Passolunghi, M.C. & Siegel, L.S. (2001) Short-term memory, working memory, and inhibitory control in children with difficulties in arithmetic problem solving, *Journal of Experimental Child Psychology* 80: 44–57.

Pelham, W.E., Hoza, B., Pillow, D.R. *et al.* (2002) Effects of methylphenidate and expectancy on children with ADHD: Behavior, academic performance, and attributions in a summer treatment program and regular classroom settings, *Journal of Consulting and Clinical Psychology* 70: 320–35.

Peterson, C.C. & Siegal, M. (2003) Deafness, conversation and Theory of Mind, *Journal of Child Psychology and Psychiatry* 36: 459–74.

Rajendran, G. & Mitchell, P. (2007) Cognitive theories of autism, *Developmental Review* 27: 224–60.

Rapee, R.M. & Spence, S.H. (2004) The etiology of social phobia: Empirical evidence and an initial model, *Clinical Psychology Review* 24: 737–67.

Reichow, B. & Volkmar, F. (2010) Social skills interventions for individuals with autism: Evaluation for evidence-based practices within a best evidence synthesis framework, *Journal of Autism and Developmental Disorders* 40: 149–66.

Rose, J. (2006) *Independent Review of the Teaching of Early Reading*, London: DfES Publications.

Schopler, E. & Mesibove, G. (1995) *Learning and Cognition in Autism*, New York: Plenum Press.

Schwartz, D., Gorman, A., Duong, M. & Nakamoto, J. (2008) Peer relationships and academic achievement as interacting predictors of depressive symptoms during middle childhood, *Journal of Abnormal Psychology* 117: 289–99.

Shaywitz, S.E., Escobar, M.D., Shaywitz, B.A., Fletcher, J.M. & Makugh, R. (1992) Evidence that dyslexia may represent the lower tail of a normal distribution of reading ability, *New England Journal of Medicine* 326: 145–50.

Smith, B.H., Barkley, R.A. & Shapiro, C.J. (2007) Attention-deficit/hyperactivity disorder, in E.J. Mash & R.A. Barkley (eds) *Assessment of Childhood Disorders*, 4th edn, pp. 53–131, New York: Guilford Press.

Stark, R.E. & Tallal, P. (1981) Selection of children with specific language deficits, *Journal of Speech and Hearing Disorders* 46: 114–80.

Stinson, M.S., Whitmire, K. & Kluwin, T.N. (1996) Self-perceptions of social relationships in hearing-impaired adolescents, *Journal of Educational Psychology* 88: 132–43.

Stothard, S.E., Snowling, M.J., Bishop, D.V.M., Chipchase, B.B. & Kaplan, C.A. (1998) Language-impaired preschoolers: a follow-up into adolescence. *Journal of Speech, Language, and Hearing Research* 41: 407–18.

Sweeting, H., Young, R., West, P. & Der, G. (2006) Peer victimization and depression in early-mid adolescence: A longitudinal study, *British Journal of Educational Psychology* 76: 577–94.

Tomblin, J.B. (1989) Familial concentration of developmental language impairment. *Journal of Speech and Hearing Disorders* 54: 287–95.

van der Molen, H.H. (1981) Blueprint of an analysis of the pedestrian task 1: Method of analysis, *Accident Analysis and Prevention* 13: 175–91.

Verhulst, F.C. (2001) Community and epidemiological aspects of anxiety disorders in children, in W.K. Silverman & P.D.A. Treffers (eds) *Anxiety Disorders in Children and Adolescents: Research, Assessment and Intervention*, pp. 273–92, Cambridge: Cambridge University Press.

Westwood, P. (2003) *Commonsense Methods for Children with Special Educational Needs: Strategies for the Regular Classroom*, 4th edn, London: Routledge Falmer.

Yule, W., Rutter, M., Berger, M. & Thompson, J. (1974) Over and under achievement in reading: Distribution in the general population, *British Journal of Educational Psychology* 44: 1–12.

19 Educational Psychology: Research on Cognitive and Biological Factors

ANDY TOLMIE

LEARNING OUTCOMES

WHEN YOU HAVE COMPLETED THIS CHAPTER, YOU SHOULD BE ABLE TO:

1. Distinguish between different types of learning process, and identify the ways in which they might apply to humans and other animals.

2. Describe the main aspects of cognitive functioning that relate to human learning.

3. Outline the key processes involved in learning to read, do arithmetic and develop scientific understanding.

4. Describe the main problems underlying conduct disorder, dyslexia, dyscalculia and autism, and the contribution to these of neural and cognitive systems.

KEY WORDS

Applied Behaviour Analysis (ABA) • Attention • Behaviourism • Central Executive • Ethology • Imitation • Imprinting • Metacognition • Motivation • Neural Networks • Observational Learning • Perception • Phonological Awareness • Psychology of Education • Self-Regulated Learning • Sensitive Period • Social Referencing • Stimulus–Response (SR) Mechanisms • Top-Down Processing • Vicarious Learning • Working Memory

CHAPTER OUTLINE

ROUTE MAP OF THE CHAPTER

This chapter focuses on research in the psychology of education, what this research tells us about typical learning processes, and how it helps explain some of the learning difficulties discussed in Chapter 18. We start by looking at forms of learning that exist in animals generally and consider how far these apply to humans. We then move on to examine processes within the brain that appear to be unique to humans, and how these apply to the learning of literacy, mathematics and science. The chapter finishes by looking at how deficits in these processes may contribute to socioemotional difficulties, dyslexia, dyscalculia and autism.

19.1   INTRODUCTION

A distinction is often drawn between *educational psychology* – the professional practice focused on helping children with difficulties in school – and **psychology of education** – research concerned with processes of learning and adaptation to schooling. Researchers are usually interested in *general* theories of learning and education that deal with *typical* development and, when they address educational difficulties, it is in terms of breakdowns in more general processes. This chapter focuses on this wider research, and the understanding that it has produced about the biological and cognitive factors that affect learning outcomes.

psychology of education the application of psychological knowledge to the processes of learning.

was built up in layers, with a set of primitive biological urges, the *id*, energising behaviour. These urges were controlled by the *ego*, which learned practical methods for satisfying needs, and this was in turn controlled by the *super-ego*, which internalised rules about appropriate behaviour. His theory implied that the driving force of behaviour, its **motivation**, is biological in origin, and that one fundamental form of learning involves adaptation of motivation to the real world. It also implied that humans exhibit a further layer of learning, *not* widely shared with other animals: adaptation to *socialised* patterns of behaviour. These ideas crystallised psychological thinking at that time and provided a reason to study other animals: biological influences and basic forms of learning may be discerned more easily there, making it possible to examine how far these help explain human behaviour and disentangle their influence from socialised forms of learning.

motivation an internal force pushing behaviour in certain directions.

19.2   BEHAVIOURAL APPROACHES TO LEARNING

Processes of learning are observable across most living organisms. Animals' genetic inheritance provides them with innate and complex patterns of behaviour – for example the ritual displays of aggression exhibited by stags to establish dominance and mating rights. However, if an animal's behaviour was *completely* predetermined, it is unlikely that their species would survive long, because effective behaviour always has to be adapted to prevailing environmental conditions. Learning therefore has distinct evolutionary advantages.

Human beings exhibit a great capacity for learning, with complex outcomes, but early psychologists recognised that such complexity *might* simply be an extension of biologically driven processes governing behaviour and learning in other animals. Sigmund Freud (1910), for instance, argued that human psychological functioning

19.2.1   Behaviourism

Subsequent research within **ethology** (the study of animal behaviour) regarded **stimulus–response (SR) mechanisms** as the basic building blocks of behaviour. When an animal encounters an object (the stimulus) marked out as significant for survival during evolution (e.g. an opportunity for food), this triggers a specific response that has proved effective for dealing with it. A good example is the stalk-and-pounce behaviour exhibited by cats in response to certain movement patterns. SR mechanisms were never regarded as completely automated, though, but as modifiable through experience (Hull, 1943; Miller & Dollard, 1941; Tinbergen, 1951). This idea was fundamental to

ethology the study of animal behaviour, particularly its function and evolution.

stimulus–response (SR) mechanisms the basic building blocks of behaviour in which an object (the stimulus) marked out as significant for survival triggers a specific effective response.

behaviourism an approach to the study of psychology which focuses entirely on observable events and the behaviours associated with them, without referring to the mind and emotions.

behaviourism, which aimed to apply models of animal learning to human behaviour.

According to Watson (1925), all human behaviour could be analysed in terms of SR reflexes, with learning coming about through the process of classical conditioning identified by Pavlov (1927). This involves presenting a previously neutral stimulus at the same time as an innate one (*pairing*), so that eventually the first provokes the innate response even when presented on its own. The innate response is therefore transferred to a new stimulus, though the response itself is not modified (see the description of the Little Albert study in Chapter 28).

Watson's claims were problematic, however, since human behaviour is characterised by the invention of *new* ways of acting on the world. The work of Thorndike

(1898) on *instrumental conditioning* was more promising. Thorndike placed a hungry cat in a 'puzzle box' that required a simple action to release the catch, allowing access to food. It initially took cats a long time to make the correct response. Over successive trials, though, the correct behaviour occurred more and more rapidly. The shift was always gradual, however, so could not be due to sudden insight. Thorndike argued that the successful response became slowly *stamped in*. This led him to propose his *law of effect*: the strength of a response is a function of its past consequences – the more successful it is, the more dominant it will become.

The idea that new forms of behaviour might be created in this way was taken up by Skinner (1938), who renamed the approach operant conditioning (see Focus Point 19.1). In this, the animal was seen as *emitting* responses to operate on the world, trying things to find out what worked, with behaviours altering according to their consequences. Skinner saw no need to analyse behaviour in terms of

FOCUS POINT 19.1   SKINNER'S WORK ON OPERANT CONDITIONING

Skinner developed the *Skinner box* for use with rats and pigeons as an extension of Thorndike's puzzle box. An animal was placed in the box, and a simple lever-press or key-peck device delivered a reward of food automatically, provided that the preceding behaviour was the one selected for *reinforcement*. Complex patterns of behaviour could be produced if successively closer approximations to these were reinforced – a process termed *shaping*.

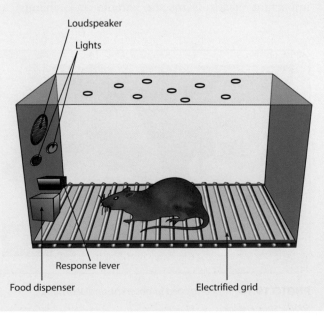

The Skinner box made it possible to examine how the *reinforcement schedule* (how often the behaviour had to be performed to generate a reward) affected response strength, with the lever-press or key-peck rate providing direct information on this. A *fixed ratio* schedule provides rewards for performance a set number of times, while a *variable ratio* changes the number across trials. Responses are most resistant to extinction when rewarded randomly – what is known as *superstitious* behaviour.

The effects of different types of behavioural consequence have also been explored: *positive reinforcers* (rewards), *negative reinforcers* (termination of something unpleasant) and *punishers* (*occurrence* of something unpleasant when a behaviour is performed). Punishers work in the same way as reinforcers, except that they lead to *avoidance* of a behaviour. Operant conditioning may also use the pairing of a neutral event (e.g. a light coming on) with a reinforcement. The event serves as *discriminative stimulus*, signalling that the reinforcer is due – and that response strength and sensitivity to what behaviour is effective should both increase.

Discussion: How far can shaping be used to explain human learning? What kinds of reinforcers and punishers might operate for us? Does the fact that much human learning does not require a *behavioural* response create problems for this explanation?

unobservable internal states such as motivation, though, claiming that changes could be explained solely via observable reinforcements.

19.2.2 Behaviourism in Education

The educational applications of operant conditioning were held by Skinner (1971) to be of profound importance. Culture at present is largely the product of *unplanned* reinforcements, he argued, and better outcomes would be achieved if these were deliberately *designed* and built into education. This notion has been taken up in various ways, but the most significant is applied behaviour analysis or **ABA** (Baer, Wolf & Risley, 1968). ABA researchers and practitioners apply behaviourist principles of learning to behaviour such as parenting and industrial safety, as well as education. The start point is *functional behaviour assessment*, detailed analysis of the focal behaviour within its environment, to determine what reinforcers influence its occurrence. On the basis of this, changes to the pattern of reinforcement are introduced, to nudge behaviour in the desired directions.

> **applied behaviour analysis (ABA)** applying the principles of behaviourism and operant conditioning to the assessment of treatment of those exhibiting behavioural difficulties.

However, although ABA has strong adherents, its usage in education has been largely restricted to promoting learning of productive behaviours among children with autism (Dillenburger & Keenan, 2009) and to counteracting disruptive classroom behaviour (e.g. Dufrene *et al.*, 2007). Despite claims of positive outcomes, these are only achievable with small numbers, because the effort required is intensive. This begs the question of why ABA is *not* needed to produce learning for the vast majority of children. Meard, Bertone and Flavier (2008), for instance, describe how regulated classroom behaviour is learned under normal conditions by children internalising social rules and using them to control their own behaviour (see Chapter 20 on Vygotsky). The implication is that even behavioural learning among children is usually the result of cognitive and social processes, and that ABA – and behaviourism more generally – only applies where normal learning mechanisms are disabled.

19.2.3 Observational Learning

> **observational learning** learning through imitation.

Ethological work on **observational learning** shows better correspondence with human processes. Lorenz (1950) observed that newly hatched ducklings would follow any moving stimulus and form an attachment to this object. This process of **imprinting** helps the duckling identify its mother (usually the first moving object it encounters) and it only operates for a brief **sensitive period** of about two days (Hess, 1959). Once imprinting has taken place, though, the duckling goes on to acquire other forms of behaviour from its mother via **imitation**. Human infants do not exhibit imprinting, but they do form strong attachments to their care givers and show similar forms of observational learning. One example is the acquisition of emotional reactions via **social referencing**. When infants encounter a novel object, they exhibit a characteristic pattern of looking at the object, then at their care giver and then back at the object. Klinnert (1984) found that if the care giver showed a distinct emotional reaction to a new toy during this sequence, either smiling or looking fearful, infants used this to guide their own reaction, advancing or retreating accordingly.

Forms of observational learning are present among older children too, where they take the form of **vicarious learning**. This involves the child learning how to behave by observing important *models* (same-sex parents and siblings) and

> **imprinting** an instinctive process of learning the features of other members of the same species that occurs shortly after hatching or birth, usually focused on the mother.

> **sensitive period** a specific and usually short period of time in early development during which learning of a particular type is especially active.

> **imitation** the direct copying of another organism's behaviour.

> **social referencing** the acquisition by infants of emotional reactions through using as a guide the emotional reactions of others, notably their care giver.

> **vicarious learning** learning how to behave by observing important models and imitating what they do.

PHOTO 19.1 *Infant engaged in observational learning.*
Source: Shutterstock.

imitating what they do, provided that it does not result in punishment (Bandura, Ross & Ross, 1963). Bandura's *social learning theory* combines ideas from operant conditioning and observational learning, therefore, and has been argued to carry implications for the depiction of unpunished violence on television (Lefkowitz *et al.*, 1977). However, if models are usually those who are close to the child, television portrayals should have little impact. This also ignores actual interactions with parents, in which the child is shown or told more actively how to behave and their *own* behaviour is corrected. As with learning classroom rules, then, *induction* into acceptable behaviour seems the more usual process.

19.2.4   Summary

Early recognition that learning processes occurred in other animals led to extensive research on the nature of such processes and how far they applied to humans. The most notable aspects of this research are Skinner's work on operant conditioning and the effects of reinforcement on behaviour, and research on learning by observation and imitation. However, both provide only a limited account of human learning, and tend to assume particular importance only under unusual circumstances or early in development.

19.3   COGNITIVE PERSPECTIVES ON LEARNING

Behavioural approaches to learning provide us with useful insights, but research suggests that the forms of learning that appear so dominant in other species have limited explanatory value within education. Animal learning is heavily *external* in nature – with stimulus and response characteristics and overt consequences playing a major role – whereas human learning is more *internal* and is often concerned with evaluation and *understanding* rather than actual behaviour. This suggests that internal processing within the brain *between* stimulus and behaviour is more critical among humans.

19.3.1   The Neural Basis of Learning

The brain is essentially a simple organ, comprised primarily of one type of cell, the *neuron*, which is linked via branches called *dendrites* to other neurons. These allow very small electric currents to be passed from neuron to neuron, activating each in turn. These currents are not passed directly, however: there is a small

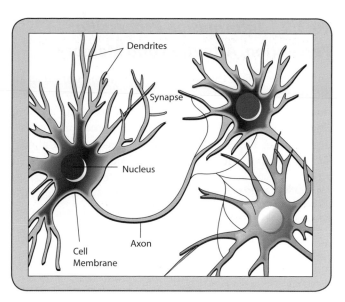

FIGURE 19.1 *The basic structure of a neuron.*

gap between the dendrites of one neuron and the body of the next, called a *synapse* (see Figure 19.1). When a neuron is activated, it causes chemical changes at the synapses that can be of two basic types: *excitatory*, activating the adjacent neuron, or *inhibitory*, suppressing activation. In simple brain structures, neural activation begins with *sensory input* – the firing of receptors in the eyes, ears, nose, mouth or skin brought about by different forms of stimulus – and ends with *behavioural output* – the firing of nerves to direct muscle movement. Neural activity in humans and other mammals is more complex than this, but the basic division of activity into input, processing and output still makes sense.

The complexity of the brain's activity derives not from its basic processes, but from the number of neurons involved – as many as a trillion in humans, with each linked to up to 10 000 others (Nauta & Feirtag, 1986). These are organised to some extent into distinct structures with specific functions, such as the *visual cortex*, responsible for processing the visual input. However, many are unspecialised, and capable of building up new connections and new ways of processing input *information* into output *decisions*. This capacity provides the neural foundation for learning, whether through conditioning and observation (adding to or changing the connections between input and output) or through development of more complex **neural networks**, which perform detailed information processing.

neural networks a set of interconnected neurons producing complex patterns of inhibitory and excitatory activation.

19.3.2 Information Processing: Perception, Attention and Memory

During the 1960s, the concept of the human brain as an information-processing system superseded animal-based theories of learning. Much effort went into refining understanding of different types of information-processing routine, focusing on the basic phases noted above. As far as the input phase is concerned, interest centred on **perception** (especially vision, the dominant sensory *modality* for humans). Early work on perception started with the notion that the main goal of this phase is to map out the features of objects in the *perceptual field*, a crucial first step towards identifying *what* is actually being perceived. Research such as that by Hubel and Wiesel (1959) with cats isolated groups of neurons in the visual cortex that were activated by the presence of certain features (e.g. edges, straight lines, motion of particular kinds). This suggested that feature extraction is an automated process built into the biological structure of the brain.

However, research on visual illusions and context effects (see Focus Point 19.2) indicates that much of the time, perception is influenced by interpretative biases – we tend to look only to confirm what we *expect* to see, making use of **top-down processing** (Neisser, 1976). Processing of this kind operates through a number of different mechanisms, including some that seem to be automatic and very hard to override, such as *constancy scaling*.

Top-down processing indicates that our perceptual system is not designed to capture all available information, but to direct **attention** to things that are salient because we expect to see them, or because it is important that we notice them. One implication of this is that some form of *pre-processing* of information takes place and we use this to switch attention. Some process of this kind appears to be used by skilled readers, for instance, to determine where to make eye movements when reading text. A skilled reader does not look at each word in turn, but only at the key elements of the text necessary to extract meaning – as can be seen from fact that less important words can missed out without us noticing (check this sentence again!). Where the important words fall can be anticipated to

> **perception** a two-part process integrating physiological sensory input and processing within the brain by which information in the environment is 'translated' into a recognition of objects, sounds, etc.

> **top-down processing** direction of information processing by pre-existing neural and cognitive structures aimed at confirming the presence of expected features.

> **attention** part of the information-processing system of the human brain related to taking notice and observing.

FOCUS POINT 19.2   ILLUSIONS AND TOP-DOWN PROCESSING

A huge range of visual illusions and context effects have been documented, but we focus here on two examples.

The first is the *moon illusion*. When we see the moon rising above the horizon, especially when it is full, we see it as being abnormally large – much larger than when it is higher in the sky. The apparent increase is illusory: the actual size of the image remains constant. The effect is due to a process called *constancy scaling*, in which our perception of the relative size of objects is influenced by our knowledge of their *actual* size. When the moon is close to the horizon, we see it alongside buildings, trees and so on. Since we *know* the moon is bigger than these, our visual system increases our sense of its relative size to reflect this. The illusion is reduced when the moon is higher in the sky, since there are no objects to compare it with. It does not disappear, though, as anyone who has taken a photograph of a 'glorious full moon' will know – its size in the resulting image is disappointingly small.

The second example is a demonstration of our tendency to interpret identical visual information differently according to context, and what this implies about what we are probably seeing. Selfridge's (1955) classic example is shown below:

TAE CAT

The configuration of lines in the middle of these two words is identical, and yet people have no difficulty in reading the first as *h* in 'the' and the second as *a* in 'cat' – because these are the interpretations that make most sense in each context.

Discussion: What might be the advantage in our perceptual system being influenced by prior knowledge in this way?

some extent, but even unpredictable sentences can be read without much extra effort, indicating a role for pre-processing (Rayner, 1978).

Attention is involved in the operations most central to learning, the *encoding*, *storage* and *retrieval* of information within different types of memory systems. In general, a distinction is made between *long-term* and *short-term* memory stores (Atkinson & Shiffrin, 1968). Material in long-term memory survives over a long period and forms a kind of background knowledge store that can be used in a variety of ways. While long-term memory has extended duration, the information contained in it is typically stored in less than exact detail, preserving only the gist or the main elements. The process of encoding extracts and organises material into a form where storage is possible (Miller, 1956), by arranging it into meaningful units or *chunks* or by mapping it on to existing knowledge (Bartlett, 1932). In contrast, short-term memory stores retain high levels of more readily recallable detail (encoding is more exact), but for much shorter durations.

consisting of four interrelated mechanisms: the *phonological loop*, which deals with auditory material and rehearsal; the *visuospatial sketch pad*, which provides a processing space for manipulating information in visual form; the *episodic buffer*, which manages the transfer of information to and from long-term memory; and a **central executive** for directing operations within the other three elements (see Figure 19.2).

> **central executive** the key part of the working memory system which directs the manipulation and transformation of information.

It is working memory that arguably provides the core system for conscious awareness and attention to information, since this is where we deliberately work on it, as can be seen in *problem solving* (see Focus Point 19.3). The *manipulation* and *transformation* of information within working memory, as part of *hierarchical decomposition* of tasks into sub-problems and sub-goals, appear to be central features of human problem solving (Newell & Simon, 1972). However, the example of the multiplication sum in Focus Point 19.3 illustrates that the operation

19.3.3   *Working Memory, Problem Solving and Metacognition*

In the early stages of memory research, short-term memory was seen as just a 'loading platform' for long-term memory – a transitional stage during which items were rehearsed (implicating attention, since rehearsed items had to be attended to) to prepare them for transfer (Murdock, 1962). Incoming information was stored very briefly in precise detail in an *iconic memory* buffer (see the points about pre-processing) before salient aspects were extracted for rehearsal. Current theories see short-term memory as serving the much more crucial role of principal mental working space, reflected in the term **working memory** (Baddeley, 1986; Baddeley & Hitch, 1974). Working memory is seen as

> **working memory** a short-term store for visual and verbal information which allows that information to be actively manipulated and transformed.

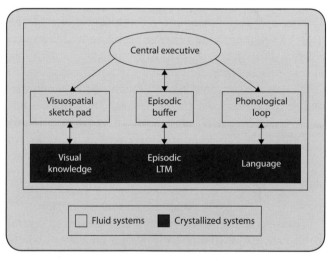

FIGURE 19.2 *Baddeley's working memory model.*

Source: Adapted from Baddeley, A.D. (2003) Working memory: Looking back and looking forward, Nature Reviews Neuroscience 4: 835. © Nature Publishing Group.

FOCUS POINT 19.3   WORKING MEMORY OPERATION

Suppose that you have to work out the sum 27×465 in your head. One characteristic way of going about this would be to break the sum down into components (central executive): 20×400 and so on. As each component is computed (visuospatial sketch pad), its answer has to

be retained (phonological loop) until all of them have been worked out, when the operation has to shift (central executive) to adding them up (visuospatial sketch pad) and encoding the final result (phonological loop) for later reporting.

of working memory is also heavily influenced by learning. For instance, in decomposing the sum into sub-problems, it helps substantially if you know in advance which components are likely to be easiest to compute and in what sequence, in order to avoid taxing the sketch pad and the phonological loop.

This makes the role of the central executive yet more critical: where possible, it has to retrieve from long-term *procedural* memory past examples of similar problems and the *algorithms* or strategies used to solve these, and then enact them. Where there has been substantial relevant experience, the problem-solving process will be near automatic. Where past experience provides no direct help, the central executive has to search for ways to proceed, perhaps using *analogies* to provide clues (Gentner & Jeziorski, 1989). When the solution has been arrived at, it is also important that it checks how it has been arrived at to make sure that the steps are sound, and that the end product looks plausible. In the multiplication sum example, you might start by estimating what size of answer you would expect and checking the answer you get against this.

This process of *monitoring* the effectiveness of the strategies that are used to solve problems and the suitability of their output is obviously important for learning, so that mistakes can be avoided the next time a similar problem is encountered. This highlights a further dimension to the function of the central executive: it does not just organise the manipulation of information within the tasks we have to perform, it watches its own operation and attempts to correct itself when it goes wrong – what we call **metacognition**.

metacognition the awareness of one's own thought processes, enabling effective learning through correction.

This overseeing of activity is now regarded as central to human learning, especially within education, where tasks typically involve the internal manipulation of information and output in the form of an answer to a question rather than a series of external behaviours that can be regulated by others. **Self-regulated learning** (Pintrich, 2000) comprises the deliberate application of known *strategies* to tasks, planning their use in advance, monitoring them in action and evaluating their output. It also involves *metacognitive* awareness of the cognitive and *motivational* factors that affect personal performance (e.g. distractibility, the importance of being interested in the outcome) and how to adjust for these. There is good evidence that self-regulated learning ability is at least as strong a predictor of educational achievement as measures of intelligence (Blair & Diamond, 2008).

self-regulated learning comprises the deliberate application of known strategies to tasks, planning their use in advance, monitoring them in action, evaluating their output, and modifying subsequent behaviour on the basis of performance.

19.3.4 Summary

Internal changes in neural organisation and cognitive function are critical characteristics of human learning. Even such basic operations as visual perception and the direction of attention show clear effects of learning over time, with knock-on effects on memory, both long term and short term. Current theories place working memory at the core of human cognitive functioning, with this system directing ongoing mental activity, drawing on existing knowledge and creating new knowledge as part of its operation. The working memory system even becomes self-regulating as children develop, taking a central role in planning activity, monitoring feedback and ultimately directing further learning.

19.4 COGNITIVE PROCESSES IN THE CURRICULUM

Learning within school curricula engages a range of cognitive and neural processes. In many instances these seem to rest initially on dedicated brain systems, which recruit more general functions as ability develops. In what follows, we look at aspects of the processes that are involved in three major strands of the school curriculum: reading, mathematics and science.

19.4.1 Learning to Read

As discussed in Section 19.3.2, reading is a complex process, with skilled readers exhibiting refined use of pre-attentional processes to direct eye movements to pick up information from written symbols in organised fashion. This information then needs to be integrated on an ongoing basis within working memory, suitably manipulated and processed for meaning, and the key elements extracted and encoded for storage within long-term memory. Given that there is so much involved, where does the learner begin?

Learning to decode written forms of language rests in fundamental ways on the child's earlier acquisition of oral language, especially where the writing system or *orthography* is alphabetic in character. Even where children grow up with a character-based orthography such as Chinese, initial language acquisition provides them with an important sense of the structure of the language (if only an implicit one). This includes the division of sounds into meaningful word units or *morphemes* ('word' is one morpheme, whereas 'words' is two – 'word' plus 's' indicating the plural), the basic *vocabulary* encoded in this way, and acceptable ways of organising this into sequences to create combined meaning – the *grammar* of the language. There is good evidence that children have an apparently innate sensitivity to these structures as they manifest in their local language community, and that imitative observational learning plays an important role in acquiring use of them (Saxton, 2010).

This prior knowledge provides the child with a valuable tool for learning to read, since it makes it possible to map orthographic forms that they encounter on to known elements of language. Initially at least, this mapping seems to happen at whole-word level and in rote fashion (what Hulme & Snowling [2009] call the *pre-alphabetic stage*), with children simply learning the association between a given written symbol or set of symbols and a spoken word or morpheme that is significant to them (Ehri, 2002, 2005). Rote learning of this kind is inefficient, however, and where the language uses alphabetic orthography, a further level of mapping is possible, at the *grapheme – phoneme* (i.e. letter – sound) level. Use of this allows the child to begin to decode writing into known words without needing the assistance of others to tell them what each word is (Byrne, 2002).

According to Ehri (1992), as soon as children have begun to acquire basic letter – sound and letter – name knowledge (usually by 5 years), they use this mapping to learn the relationship between letter strings and their pronunciation (the *alphabetic stage*). At first, they are better able to work with larger units than single letters and phonemes, with syllables ('crust') and *onset – rime structures* ('cr' and 'ust') marking important points of transition to the use of full phonological strategies, in which letters are sounded out and blended to arrive at the pronunciation of unknown words. Finally, as these strategies become more familiar, they become more automated, so that sounding out is no longer necessary. At this point, the child starts to extract the spelling rules that they encounter (the *orthographic stage*) and in a sense return to whole-word recognition – but on the basis of

explicit knowledge about word composition and strategies for decoding unknown words.

Phonological awareness – the ability (possibly innate) to identify sound values in speech, and to decompose spoken words into these – has been shown to be a key precursor of learning to read, since it underpins the shift to the alphabetic stage (see Focus Point 19.4). There has therefore been a gradual shift in the United Kingdom towards the use of *phonics teaching* for reading in primary schools, enshrined in the 1998 National Literacy Strategy (Stainthorp, 2002). Phonics teaching involves working directly in the early years to promote awareness of phonemes. However, it is also accompanied in the United Kingdom by work on whole-word recognition for high-frequency words. This is needed because of the number of *irregular* spellings in English, which limit the value of grapheme – phoneme conversion as a method of learning to read – children need to recognise where these mappings do not apply and words are not pronounced as they are written ('yacht').

> **phonological awareness** in learning to read, the ability (possibly innate) to identify sound values in speech, and to decompose spoken words into these.

This outline only tells us how children come to be able to read *words*. While this is obviously a crucial step (Ehri, 2002) it is not the whole story, as anyone who has heard a young child reading out loud will recognise – even if the words are accurately pronounced, they are spoken as if disconnected from each other. Skilled readers put them together and *read for meaning*, and are probably able to do this because they no longer need to use working memory to put together letter – sound strings and can move up to a higher level of integration. Perhaps for this reason, comparison of different methods indicates that phonics teaching produces better *comprehension* of text than teaching for meaning (Torgesen, 2002): getting children past decoding helps them begin to work on comprehension sooner. What else might help children to acquire these

FOCUS POINT 19.4   PHONOLOGICAL AWARENESS AND READING

Bradley and Bryant (1983) conducted a longitudinal study in which 400 children were followed from age 4 to 8, and found that reading and spelling skills at age 8 were strongly related to phonological awareness (as measured by sensitivity to rhymes and alliteration) at age 4. Subsequent work by Muter *et al.* (2004) found that of the different types of phonological awareness that are possible,

it was *phoneme segmentation* (i.e. recognition of individual sound values) that mattered most, especially where this was accompanied by good letter knowledge to facilitate grapheme–phoneme mapping. There have even been suggestions (Wolf, 2008) that the human brain has become innately receptive, not only to spoken language but to these particular kinds of mappings.

meta-level reading skills is less clear, but one answer seems to be exposure to text, and there is some evidence that being read to at an early age has an influence on later reading ability (Davis-Kean, 2005). This may help children develop more effective working memory strategies for processing *narrative* structures: differences between children in working memory are certainly associated with differences in reading (Hulme & Snowling, 2009).

Learning to read is also *not* the same as learning to *write*, because spelling and reading involve different constraints (Fayol, Zorman & Lété, 2009). In reading the primary task is to recognise the *pattern* of letters present in a word, whereas in spelling the *order* of letters is crucial. This creates different demands, and the memory for a word when it is read may not be the same as the memory of that word when it has to be written, since the latter involves the *action* of writing (Galbraith, 2009). Learning to write therefore involves other skills, including learning how to manipulate a pencil or pen, and also learning how to structure and compose text to be meaningful and interesting to readers (Myhill, 2009). At the moment, less is known about how these skills develop.

19.4.2   *Learning Mathematics*

As with reading, it is the earlier stages of mathematics learning that are best understood. The focus of most research is on the growth of children's understanding of number and *arithmetic* (the concrete use of number within the basic operations of addition, subtraction, multiplication and division) in the pre-school and primary years, since, as with word reading, this basic level underpins later achievement (Cowan & Saxton, 2010).

There is good evidence (Dehaene, 1997; Starkey, Spelke & Gelman, 1990) that infants (in common with other primates) possess two *innate perceptual systems* for recognising number. One system enables them to distinguish without counting small, exact quantities up to 3 (Wynn, 1992) – what is termed *subitization*. The other allows them to judge relative differences in large quantities (e.g. 16 vs 32; Xu & Spelke, 2000). These systems are thought to provide a foundation for the acquisition of verbal counting skills in the same way that phonological awareness provides a starting point for reading (Dehaene, 1997).

The linkage between perception of number and counting may be less exact, however, since children have to grasp new principles that only apply to the latter (Gelman & Gallistel, 1978). These include the *one-to-one principle* (each object to be counted only gets *one* count word), the *stable order principle* (*count words* get used in fixed order), the *order irrelevance principle* (the order in which *objects* are counted makes no difference to the total) and the *cardinality principle* (the last count word

used represents the total number of things in the set). Current evidence suggests that grasp of these principles is relatively hard won on the basis of prolonged practice (Rittle-Johnson & Siegler, 1998) and that children move more easily from the innate systems to *estimation* (Gilmore, McCarthy & Spelke, 2007).

Basic counting ability is usually in place by the time children go to school and forms the foundation for the growth of arithmetic skills (Hulme & Snowling, 2009). These skills are more disparate than those involved in reading and are more appropriately compared to the component skills of writing. They comprise a rough hierarchy (Dowker & Sigley, 2010), which includes single- and then multiple-digit addition, subtraction, multiplication and division, along with varying *strategies* for carrying out these computations (Verschaffel *et al.*, 2010); understanding of tens and units and the role of *place value* in distinguishing between these; translation between arithmetical problems presented in *concrete, verbal and numerical formats*; knowledge of *number facts* (e.g. any number multiplied by 10 is equal to the original number shifted a place leftwards with a 0 on the end); and *derived fact strategies* (e.g. use of the multiplication by 10 fact to decompose sums into workable sub-problems, as earlier in Focal Point 19.3).

There appears to be no consistent order for the emergence of these components, or any particularly strong relationship between them as they are acquired (Dowker & Sigley, 2010; Geary, 2010), so children may show surprising gaps. Though there is some evidence that variation in the efficiency of innate perceptual abilities is associated with later arithmetic skills (Landerl, Bevan & Butterworth, 2004), the relationship between skills and such abilities appears to be weaker than it is for reading. Achievement in arithmetic appears to be more strongly and consistently related to knowledge of number facts and working memory ability (Cowan & Saxton, 2010; Cowan *et al.*, 2009). Given the role of attention and executive control in counting and computation noted earlier, and the impact that knowledge has on the strategies used for solving problems, this is unsurprising. It does, however, make it harder to tell what kinds of teaching strategy might be most effective.

19.4.3   *Understanding in Science*

As with number, the cognitive capacities on which science understanding depends originate in the pre-school period, and again some aspects seem to be innate. There are three elements of learning in science: factual knowledge (evidence); grasp of scientific procedure (generation of evidence); and conceptual grasp (understanding of phenomena). Despite the emphasis in much teaching on the first two, it is conceptual grasp that is central (Wellington

& Osbourne, 2001). Concepts are the unifying frameworks that help us make sense of experience (Mareschal, Quinn & Lea, 2009) and are especially critical in science, because of their focus on capturing understanding of *causal processes*.

There is some evidence that infants have an innate sensitivity to causal information, so that when one object strikes another and the second object moves, this is naturally perceived as the first object *causing* the second to move (Gopnik *et al.*, 2004; Michotte, 1963). Neuroscientific evidence supports this claim, indicating a basis in the brain for the organisation of causal perceptions (Satpute *et al.*, 2005). Consistent with this, children develop an understanding of the behaviour of their 'common-sense' world before encountering science in the classroom (Driver, Guesne & Tiberghien, 1985; Howe, 1998).

However, as with number, this understanding may hinder subsequent science learning as much as it helps (Howe & Tolmie, 1998). While innately organised perceptions may provide a starting point, they are based on implicit sensitivity to *covariation*, the association between events. They are therefore not the same as *explicit* concepts, broken down into elements that can be described in language and subjected to analysis and discussion. Implicit perceptions can readily give rise to misconceptions, especially since innate systems have a bias towards detecting *simple* patterns of causation (Lu *et al.*, 2008), even when events have multiple causes. Explicit concepts, especially if founded in systematic scientific procedures for collecting observations, help remove such misconceptions.

As with number, then, the crucial step in development is the mapping of implicit perceptions on to explicit concepts and the recognition of particular principles that accompany this change. According to Piaget (1974), true causal understanding involves coordination of the knowledge of the different stages involved in an event

PHOTO 19.2 *Young children's ability to play with balls demonstrates they have an implicit understanding of object motion long before they can express this in language.*
Source: Shutterstock.

(e.g. the motion of one ball bearing, the point of contact with a second, the transfer of energy to the second and the second moving) into a mental sequence that captures both the evident and *invisible* aspects of the phenomenon (you cannot *see* the transfer of energy, for instance). Explicit causation is cognised and projected rather than directly perceived, therefore.

The development of these explicit concepts appears to be *domain specific*. Howe (1998), for instance, reports little sign of integration between different areas of physics such as heating and cooling or forces, and understanding in one area may be considerably more advanced than another. There is also wide agreement that conceptual growth involves the *coordination* of implicit knowledge from very specific events, based on actions and their consequences, into increasingly explicit, generally applicable ideas (Karmiloff-Smith, 1992). This suggests it is important that primary school teachers provide children with concrete experiences that involve manipulation of causal events and draw attention to the exact sequence within these (e.g. what happens when an object that barely floats is dropped into a tank of water?), providing descriptions to help make this sequence explicit. This should then be followed by testing and re-testing of the emerging concepts in different contexts to help them become more generally applicable.

19.4.4 Summary

Learning to read, to do arithmetic and to develop scientific understanding all begin with innate capacities of one kind or another, which then have to be adapted and applied to culturally generated systems. In reading, phonological awareness of oral language provides the starting point for learning letter–sound relationships, which are the foundation for word recognition and comprehension. Learning to count and to use number has its origin in innate recognition of certain number patterns, though various other principles have to be understood before arithmetic is firmly grasped. Scientific understanding begins with apparently innate recognition of causal effects, but again this has to be developed into more explicit concepts before it becomes secure. For both reading and arithmetic at least, working memory appears to play a central role in later developments.

19.5 LEARNING DIFFICULTIES

As noted in Section 19.1, the psychology of educational research on learning difficulties attempts to understand these in terms of breakdowns in the processes of typical development. In this section, we consider how knowledge of the behavioural, neural and cognitive aspects of learning looked at in the preceding sections informs our understanding of some of the types of learning difficulty outlined in Chapter 18. We focus in particular on conduct problems, dyslexia, dyscalculia and autism, the areas where current understanding is greatest.

19.5.1   Problems Involving Behavioural Learning

We concluded at the start of Section 19.3 that behavioural approaches to learning had limited applicability to humans. However, ABA techniques based on operant conditioning *do* work with children who have emotional and behavioural difficulties, for whom more typical processes of learning social rules seem not to work. As noted in Section 19.2.4, there is a well-documented role for observational and imitative learning in the growth of emotional and social understanding. *Social referencing* provides the young child with guidance on how to react to novel events, and also a means of learning about the reactions of *others*, apparently via a primitive system that is less reliant on cognition, initially at least (Izard, 1977). Is it when *this* system goes wrong that reinforcement-based methods provide an effective fall-back?

Recent research on the underlying sources of *conduct problems* suggests that it might indeed be the case. This research (Viding *et al.*, 2009, in press; Rijsdijk *et al.*, in press) used a combination of behavioural, genetic and brain-imaging methods (see Section 17.5), and found that there are two important sub-groups of children with conduct problems. Those with *callous – unemotional* traits have genetically linked problems in recognising the emotions of others, and experience little emotional reaction to events themselves (the classic idea of a *psychopath*). Children without these traits show no deficit in recognising emotions, but are typically traumatised and emotionally *over-aroused*, and exhibit blindness to the reactions of others because of this overload.

The key point is that different types of intervention are effective with these two groups of children. For those without callous – unemotional traits, what appears to work best is providing a calm and safe space, which leads to the restoration of more normal functioning. This approach is completely ineffective with the callous – unemotional group, but reward-based systems where they receive benefits for positive behaviour do appear to work, since the capacity to value these rewards remains intact – hence the success of ABA methods, at least in these instances.

What is less clear as yet is the source of the callous – unemotional group's underlying deficit in emotional processing, but one possibility may be malfunctioning or under-development of the *mirror neuron system*. Mirror neurons are a specialised set of brain cells, first discovered in macaque monkeys, which become activated both when an animal acts *and* when it observes the *same* action performed by another – the neuron literally 'mirrors' the activity of the other, as though the observer were itself acting (Iacobani & Dapretto, 2006). A similar system has been found in humans, which becomes activated not only by witnessing the actions of others, but also by *imagining* an action (Daecety *et al.*, 1994). Damage to this system in patients with brain injury is associated with an inability to imitate hand actions (Buxbaum, Kyle & Menon, 2005).

While much more work remains to be done, the existence of the mirror neuron system helps to explain the imitative abilities (especially as regards *facial expressions*) that have been found to be present from birth in infants (Meltzoff & Moore, 1976), providing a foundation for observational learning. Deficits in this system would help explain insensitivity to social referencing processes in learning about emotions, and might also account for aspects of difficulty in language acquisition. Such deficits may also be implicated in *developmental coordination disorder* (see Section 18.5), given the potential role of the mirror neuron system in mapping between an intended (imagined) movement and an actual action (Hulme & Snowling, 2009).

19.5.2   The Contribution of Other Forms of Neural Deficit

Other forms of neural deficit related to information processing rather than to behaviour have been identified as playing a role in dyslexia and dyscalculia. There is also evidence that problems in the visual processing system contribute to autism.

With regard to *dyslexia*, as discussed in Section 19.4.1, research has identified the importance of being able to segment words into their component sounds (phonemes) when learning to read, at least when using an alphabetic writing system. Neuroscience studies using functional brain imaging have identified the neural pathways involved in reading and the anomalies found in children with dyslexia (Demonet, Taylor & Chaix, 2004; Paulesu *et al.*, 2001). These studies reveal that the main problem is a deficit in the emergence of phonological awareness. This work has also demonstrated that the differences that separate nonimpaired from impaired readers also predict individual differences in typically developing children, implying that dyslexia is not a qualitatively different syndrome but a more pronounced degree of deficit.

It is important to note, though, that how far this deficit has an impact is also affected by the nature of the letter–sound relationship in the child's native language. Reading disorders are less apparent where there is a consistent relationship between letters and phonemes, as in Spanish or German, or in writing systems that do not require segmentation into phonemes, such as Chinese or Japanese (Wydell & Butterworth, 1999; Ziegler & Goswami, 2005). Computer modelling also highlights the importance of regularity in determining how difficult it is to build up stable representations of letter–sound relationships (Harm, McCandliss & Seidenberg, 2003; Zorzi, Houghton & Butterworth, 1998).

Such modelling has been able to explore how the underlying deficit might be corrected for in an irregular language such as English, as well as identifying the stage at which remediation of different sorts is likely to be successful (Ziegler *et al.*, 2007). This has led to the development of phoneme practice as a form of remediation and evaluation of the brain-activation changes in children who respond positively, compared to those who do not (Eden *et al.*, 2004). Moreover, studies using EEG have made it possible to identify children at risk of dyslexia before they begin to learn to read (Lyytinen *et al.*, 2001), so that remediation can begin at an early age. Similarly, while it has long been known that reading difficulties tend to run in families, candidate genes that may affect brain development have now been found (Fisher & DeFries, 2002; Paracchini *et al.*, 2006; Schulte-Körne *et al.*, 2007). Such understanding makes it possible to contemplate yet earlier forms of remediation.

In the case of *dyscalculia*, a basic deficit in the ability to learn arithmetic was identified over 30 years ago (Kosc, 1974), but the advent of research showing that humans have the inherited 'number sense' (Nieder, 2005) discussed in Section 19.4.2 has led to recent progress in understanding. The neural pathways involved in typical numerical capacities are now relatively well understood (Castelli, Glaser & Butterworth, 2006; Dehaene, Molko & Cohen, 2004) and dyscalculia appears to be due to a deficit in this number sense. This is reflected in poor performance on tasks such as saying how many dots there are in a visual display, or comparing two displays (Butterworth, 2008; Landerl, Bevan & Butterworth, 2004). Less is known as yet about the precise nature of this deficit than is the case for dyslexia, but research has led to interventions that are aimed at strengthening

number sense via practice with the kinds of displays used to diagnose problems (Butterworth & Yeo, 2004). These appear to be more effective than more traditional interventions for children with number problems, which focus on simple repetition of number–object correspondences: it is not *counting* as such that is the source of the problem.

With regard to *perceptual problems in autism*, it has long been clear that sensory processing in children with autism is very unusual. Atypical processing in visual perception has been reported for a wide range of stimuli, including moving dots (Milne *et al.*, 2002), social stimuli such as faces (Dalton *et al.*, 2005) and the motion of living creatures (Blake *et al.*, 2003). Despite this, progress in understanding the nature and causes of these atypicalities has been slow. However, one recent idea is that *adaptive processes* in the visual system of the kind discussed in Section 19.3.2 malfunction in autism.

When functioning is normal, these processes are fundamental to helping us maintain stable representations of the world despite variations in viewing conditions. For instance, although *constancy scaling* may trip us up sometimes, it is generally crucial in allowing us to recognise that a tin of baked beans viewed from 10 metres is still the same object when seen close up. Other adaptive processes of this kind allow us to discount constant – or redundant – information in the visual environment and instead focus attention on picking up information about the *changing* aspects of the world around us. This makes it possible to notice the novel features that we are more likely to need to know about, and maximise the efficiency of the brain's activity.

Recent research has found that children diagnosed with an autism spectrum condition show significantly weaker visual adaptation than typically developing children of the same age or the same ability levels (Pellicano *et al.*, 2007). If these effects are borne out by further research, it seems likely that they would have a profound impact on the way in which children with autism view the world. For instance, a failure in constancy scaling would lead to perceptions that are fragmented and confusing, with reduced stability of object perception and recognition. Similarly, increased transmission of unimportant, redundant information about sensory events would interfere with picking up novel, salient information, making it harder to distinguish between the two. Such effects might plausibly lead to the repeated stereotypical behaviours and apparent fascination with certain objects characteristic of autism. If these problems with sensory adaptation extended to the auditory system, this might also explain the difficulties that those with autism experience in processing language.

19.5.3 *The Role of Cognitive Deficits*

It is unlikely that any single deficit or problem is the cause of a disorder as complex as autism, however, and earlier research has identified a range of other *cognitive* deficits that also appear to be prevalent. These focus on attempts to explain two common characteristics of those with autism, a better than normal ability to attend to the detail of objects and visual displays, coupled with a poorer ability to integrate this detail into whole object perception; and an impaired ability, even where language use is well developed, to recognise the mental states of other people (see Section 18.4.2).

One explanation of these characteristics is that children with autism suffer from deficits in *executive function* (Pennington & Ozonoff, 1996), or more generally what is termed *weak central coherence* (Frith, 1989; Frith & Happé, 1994). The first focuses on the notion that there is a failure in the *central executive* aspect of working memory, which makes it difficult to integrate perceptions and to engage in planning or monitoring of behaviour (Hughes, Russell & Robbins, 1994). One consequence may be the known difficulties that children with autism have with social perception. In particular, to understand the perceptions and beliefs of *other* people (e.g. about where an object is located), it is necessary actively to direct attention *away* from one's own knowledge, and build up a picture of the beliefs that might result from the information available to those others (e.g. they are unaware the object was moved because they were out of the room). If executive control is impaired, such re-direction and integration would be harder (Hughes & Russell, 1993).

The weak central coherence hypothesis proposes more generally that the *cognitive style* of children and adults with autism leads them to attend more to details and not to integrate information to extract more general patterns. This might certainly explain the performance of children with autism on nonsocial tasks, such as their superior performance at identifying hidden patterns in drawings (Shah & Frith, 1983) and their inability to take context into account when reading ambiguous words (Frith & Snowling, 1983). However, it provides less explanation as to why they exhibit problems in deciphering the mental states of others. Moreover, other research (Pellicano *et al.*, 2005) has found little evidence of a *general* style, since the performance of children with autism across different tasks of the kind used by Frith and colleagues appears to be largely uncorrelated, whereas it ought to be consistent.

Issues with regard to working memory, and especially the central executive, do recur frequently, though, across research on different types of learning difficulty, indicating that this system is especially sensitive to disruption. So, for instance, while dyslexia is associated with a neural deficit above and beyond any influence of working memory, less extreme instances of problems with reading, such as reading comprehension impairment, *are* associated with poor working memory (Hulme & Snowling, 2009). Indeed, children with autism (for whom executive control is an identified issue) have impaired comprehension that is very similar in form to that exhibited by poor readers (Nation, 1999). Similarly, nondyscalculic learners who exhibit number problems appear to suffer from specific impairments in executive function (McLean & Hitch, 1999; Passolunghi & Siegel, 2001). Problems with executive control are also by definition associated with difficulties in metacognition and self-regulated learning (Blair & Diamond, 2008).

One difficulty with the focus on executive control, however, is that this term covers a variety of functions (Zelazo *et al.*, 1997). Logically, the precise aspects involved in any given form of learning difficulty must be to some extent different, otherwise there would be extensive *comorbidity*, or overlap in conditions. Comorbidities are in fact found. For instance, there appears to be a greater overlap between reading and number difficulties than might be expected by chance (31% in one study by Lewis, Hitch & Walker, 1994). Nevertheless, the rate is smaller than would be expected if the same impairments in executive function were involved in both cases, so the picture is obviously more complex than this.

Some greater attempt to specify the nature of potential problems has been made in research on ADHD (see Section 18.3.2), where difficulties with attention and executive control are central. Wilcutt *et al.* (2005) examined the performance of children with ADHD on 13 different kinds of task, involving *response inhibition* (resisting making an automatic but incorrect response), *updating* (integrating new information with old), *task switching* (shifting on a given signal from one form of a task to another with different rules) and *interference control* (ignoring irrelevant information). In fact, the ADHD children performed significantly worse than controls on all 13 tasks, but this is still useful in indicating that they have *pervasive* difficulties, where poor readers and children with number problems may have more specific problems with updating or interference control. These various relationships underline how critical the working memory system is to cognitive functioning in its many different forms: deficits here will have an impact in some way or another on learning.

19.5.4 Summary

Some of the key types of learning difficulty can be attributed to problems in the functioning of the basic neural and cognitive mechanisms that underpin typical learning. Certain types of conduct disorder appear to stem from deficits in the recognition of emotion, and potentially the mirror neuron system connected with imitative learning. Dyslexia is brought about in part by weaknesses in phonological awareness, though this is exacerbated by irregularity of spelling. Dyscalculia has its origins in impaired number sense, and autism may be connected with poor visual and auditory adaptation. Problems in different aspects of working memory are associated in one way or another with a very wide range of learning difficulties, underlining further its central role in cognitive activity.

19.6 CHAPTER SUMMARY

Learning processes provide animals with a crucial mechanism of adaptation to alterations in environmental conditions, but the mechanisms of learning by reinforcement and imitation that are crucial for other animals appear to have limited applicability to humans. Instead, human learning depends much more centrally on changes in neural organisation and cognition that allow increasingly sophisticated and self-directing methods of information processing to emerge. The operation and refinement of the working memory system play a crucial role in this, and in the learning of the main elements of the primary school curriculum. Problems with working memory lead to a variety of learning difficulties, though the failure of more basic neural mechanisms for recognising speech, number and objects is also an important contributory factor.

SELF-TEST QUESTIONS

- Describe a basic stimulus–response mechanism.
- What are the main characteristics of classical conditioning?
- What is applied behaviour analysis (ABA) and what are its limitations?
- What is social referencing?
- What are the main phases of neural activation?
- What is meant by top-down processing?
- What is the difference between long-term and short-term memory?
- What are the main elements of working memory?
- What is metacognition?
- What are the main stages in learning to read?
- Why is phonological awareness important for learning to read?
- Describe the innate perceptual systems relating to number.
- What principles does a child have to grasp in order to count and do arithmetic?
- What aspects of science understanding have been argued to be innate?
- In what way do children with callous – unemotional traits differ from other children with conduct problems?
- What is the mirror neuron system?
- What factors contribute to dyslexia?
- What factors contribute to dyscalculia?

ESSAY QUESTIONS

- How is operant conditioning different from classical conditioning?
- What is the difference between observational learning and vicarious learning?
- How does an information-processing account of learning differ from a behaviourist one?
- Why might self-regulation be important to learning?
- What are the similarities and differences between learning to read and learning to write?
- What is the difference between implicit perception and explicit concepts of causation?
- What neural and cognitive factors might contribute to the problems of children with autism?
- Why does disruption to working memory have so much of an impact on learning?

TEXTS FOR FURTHER READING

Alloway, T.P. & Gathercole, S.E. (2006) *Working Memory in Neurodevelopmental Conditions*, Hove: Psychology Press.
Dehaene, S. (1997) *The Number Sense: How the Mind Creates Mathematics*, Oxford: Oxford University Press.
Frith, U. (2003) *Autism: Explaining the Enigma*, 2nd edn, Oxford: Blackwell.
Hulme, C. & Snowling, M.J. (2009) *Developmental Disorders of Language Learning and Cognition*, Chichester: Wiley-Blackwell.

RELEVANT JOURNAL ARTICLES

Blair, C. & Diamond, A. (2008) Biological processes in prevention and intervention: The promotion of self-regulation as a means of preventing school failure, *Development and Psychopathology* 20: 899–91.
Bradley, L. & Bryant, P.E. (1983) Categorising sounds and learning to read – a causal connection, *Nature* 301: 419–21.
Dufrene, B.A., Doggett, R.A., Henington, C. & Watson, T.S. (2007) Functional assessment and intervention for disruptive classroom behaviors in preschool and Head Start classrooms, *Journal of Behavioral Education* 16: 368–88.
Muter, V., Hulme, C., Snowling, M.J. & Stevenson, J. (2004) Phonemes, rimes, vocabulary and grammatical skills as foundations of early reading development: Evidence from a longitudinal study, *Developmental Psychology* 40: 663–81.
Passolunghi, M.C. & Siegel, L.S. (2001) Short-term memory, working memory, and inhibitory control in children with difficulties in arithmetic problem solving, *Journal of Experimental Child Psychology* 80: 44–57.
Viding, E., Simmonds. E., Petrides, K.V. & Frederickson, N. (2009) The contribution of callous-unemotional traits and conduct problems to bullying in early adolescence, *Journal of Child Psychology and Psychiatry* 50: 471–81.

RELEVANT WEB LINKS

Centre for Brain and Cognitive Development at Birkbeck College London, www.cbcd.bbk.ac.uk
Centre for Reading and Language at the University of York, http://www.york.ac.uk/psychology/research/groups/crl
Centre for Research in Autism and Education at the Institute of Education, http://www.ioe.ac.uk/study/departments/phd/28036.html
Centre for Working Memory and Learning at the University of York, http://www.york.ac.uk/res/wml

REFERENCES

Atkinson, R.C. & Shiffrin, R.M. (1968) Human memory: A proposed system and its control, in K.W. Spence & R.T. Spence (eds) *The Psychology of Learning and Motivation, Vol. 2*, pp. 89–105, New York: Academic Press.

Baddeley, A.D. (1986) *Working Memory*, Oxford: Clarendon Press.

Baddeley, A.D. & Hitch, G.J. (1974) Working memory, in G. Bower (ed.) *The Psychology of Learning and Motivation: Advances in Research and Theory*, pp. 47–90, New York: Academic Press.

Baer, D.M., Wolf, M.M. & Risley, T.R. (1968) Some current dimensions of applied behavior analysis, *Journal of Applied Behavior Analysis* 1: 91–7.

Bandura, A., Ross, D. & Ross, S.A. (1963) Imitation of film-mediated aggressive models, *Journal of Abnormal and Social Psychology* 66: 3–11.

Bartlett, F.C. (1932) *Remembering: A Study in Experimental and Social Psychology*, Cambridge: Cambridge University Press.

Blair, C. & Diamond, A. (2008) Biological processes in prevention and intervention: The promotion of self-regulation as a means of preventing school failure, *Development and Psychopathology* 20: 899–91.

Blake, R., Turner, L.M., Smoski, M.J., Pozdol, S.L. & Stone, W.L. (2003) Visual recognition of biological motion is impaired in children with autism, *Psychological Science* 14: 151–7.

Bradley, L. & Bryant, P.E. (1983) Categorising sounds and learning to read – a causal connection, *Nature* 301: 419–21.

Butterworth, B. (2008) State-of-science review SR-D4: Dyscalculia, in J. Beddington (ed.) *Foresight Mental Capital and Wellbeing*, London: Government Office for Science.

Butterworth, B. & Yeo, D. (2004) *Dyscalculia Guidance*, London: nferNelson.

Buxbaum, L.J., Kyle, K.M. & Menon, R. (2005) On beyond mirror neurons: Internal representations subserving imitation and recognition of skilled object-related actions in humans, *Cognitive Brain Research* 25: 226–39.

Byrne, B. (2002) The process of learning to read: A framework for integrating research and educational practice, in R. Stainthorp & P. Tomlinson (eds) *British Journal of Educational Psychology Monograph Series II: Psychological Aspects of Education – Current Trends: Learning and Teaching Reading*, Leicester: British Psychological Society.

Castelli, F., Glaser, D.E. & Butterworth, B. (2006) Discrete and analogue quantity processing in the parietal lobe: A functional MRI study, *Proceedings of the National Academy of Science* 103: 4693–98.

Cowan, R. & Saxton, M. (2010) Understanding diversity in number development, in R. Cowan, M. Saxton & A. Tolmie (eds), *British Journal of Educational Psychology Monograph Series II: Psychological Aspects of Education – Current Trends: Number Development and Difficulty*, Leicester: British Psychological Society.

Cowan, R., Donlan, C., Shepherd, D. & Cole-Fletcher, R. (2009) Variation in number proficiency is not just a matter of fact, BPS Developmental Psychology Section Annual Conference, Nottingham.

Daecety, J., Perani, D., Jeannerod, M. *et al.* (1994) Mapping motor representations with positon emission tomography, *Nature* 371: 600–2.

Dalton, K.M., Nacewicz, B.M., Johnstone, T. *et al.* (2005) Gaze fixation and the neural circuitry of face processing in autism, *Nature Neuroscience* 8: 519–26.

Davis-Kean, P.E. (2005) The influence of parent education and family income on child achievement: The indirect role of parental expectations and the home environment, *Journal of Family Psychology* 19: 294–304.

Dehaene, S. (1997) *The Number Sense: How the Mind Creates Mathematics*, Oxford: Oxford University Press.

Dehaene, S., Molko, N. & Cohen, L. (2004) Arithmetic and the brain, *Current Opinion in Neurobiology* 14: 218–24.

Demonet, J.-F., Taylor, M.J. & Chaix, Y. (2004) Developmental dyslexia, *The Lancet*, 363: 1451–60.

Dillenburger, K. & Keenan, M. (2009) None of the As in ABA stand for autism: Dispelling the myths, *Journal of Intellectual and Developmental Disabilities* 34: 193–5.

Dowker, A. & Sigley, G. (2010) Targeted interventions for children with arithmetical difficulties, in R. Cowan, M. Saxton & A. Tolmie (eds) *British Journal of Educational Psychology Monograph Series II: Psychological Aspects of Education – Current Trends: Number Development and Difficulty*, Leicester: British Psychological Society.

Driver, R., Guesne, E. & Tiberghien, A. (1985) *Children's Ideas in Science*, Buckingham: Open University Press.

Dufrene, B.A., Doggett, R.A., Henington, C. & Watson, T.S. (2007) Functional assessment and intervention for disruptive classroom behaviors in preschool and Head Start classrooms, *Journal of Behavioral Education* 16: 368–88.

Eden, G., Jones, K., Cappell, K. *et al.* (2004) Neural changes following remediation in adult developmental dyslexia, *Neuron* 44: 411–22.

Ehri, L.C. (1992) Reconceptualising the development of sight word reading and its relationship to recoding, in P.B. Gough, L.C. Ehri & R. Trieman (eds) *Reading Acquisition*, pp. 107–43, Hillsdale, NJ: Lawrence Erlbaum Associates.

Ehri, L.C. (2002) Phases of acquisition in learning to read words and implications for teaching, in R. Stainthorp & P. Tomlinson (eds) *British Journal of Educational Psychology Monograph Series II: Psychological Aspects of Education – Current Trends: Learning and Teaching Reading*, Leicester: British Psychological Society.

Ehri, L.C. (2005) Development of sight word reading: Phases and findings, in M.J. Snowling & C. Hulme (eds) *The Science of Reading: A Handbook*, pp. 135–54, Oxford: Blackwell.

Fayol, M., Zorman, M. & Lété, B. (2009) Associations and dissociations in reading and spelling French: Unexpectedly poor and good spellers, in V. Connelly, A. Barnett, J. Dockrell & A. Tolmie (eds) *British Journal of Educational Psychology Monograph Series II: Psychological Aspects of Education – Current Trends: Teaching and Learning Writing*, Leicester: British Psychological Society.

Fisher, S. & DeFries, J. (2002) Developmental dyslexia: Genetic dissection of a complex cognitive trait, *Nature Review of Neuroscience* 3: 767–80.

Freud, S. (1910) The origin and development of psychoanalysis, *American Journal of Psychology* 21(2): 196–218.

Frith, U. (1989) *Autism: Explaining the Enigma*, Oxford: Blackwell.

Frith, U. & Happé, F. (1994) Autism: Beyond 'theory of mind', *Cognition* 50: 115–32.

Frith, U. & Snowling, M.J. (1983) Reading for meaning and reading for sound in autistic and dyslexic children, *British Journal of Developmental Psychology* 1: 329–42.

Galbraith, D. (2009) Writing as discovery, in V. Connelly, A. Barnett, J. Dockrell & A. Tolmie (eds) *British Journal of Educational Psychology Monograph Series II: Psychological Aspects of Education – Current Trends: Teaching and Learning Writing*, Leicester: British Psychological Society.

Geary, D. (2010) Missouri longitudinal study of mathematical development and disability, in R. Cowan, M. Saxton & A. Tolmie (eds) *British Journal of Educational Psychology Monograph Series II: Psychological Aspects of Education – Current Trends: Number Development and Difficulty*, Leicester: British Psychological Society.

Gelman, R. & Gallistel, C.R. (1978) *The Child's Understanding of Number*, Cambridge, MA: Harvard University Press.

Gentner, D. & Jeziorski, M. (1989) Historical shifts in the use of analogy in science, in B. Gholson, W. Shadish, R. Neimeyer & A. Houts (eds) *Psychology of Science: Contributions to Metascience*, Cambridge: Cambridge University Press.

Gilmore, C.K., McCarthy, S.E. & Spelke, E. (2007) Symbolic arithmetic knowledge without instruction, *Nature* 447: 589–91.

Gopnik, A., Glymour, C., Sobel, D.M., Schulz, L.E., Kushnir, T. & Danks, D. (2004) A theory of causal learning in children: Causal maps and Bayes nets, *Psychological Review* 111: 1–31.

Harm, M.W., McCandliss, B.D. & Seidenberg, M.S. (2003) Modeling the successes and failures of interventions for disabled readers, *Scientific Studies of Reading* 7: 155–82.

Hess, E.H. (1959) Imprinting, *Science* 130: 133–41.

Howe, C. (1998) *Conceptual Structure in Childhood and Adolescence*, London: Routledge.

Howe, C.J. & Tolmie, A. (1998) Productive interaction in the context of computer-supported collaborative learning in science, in K. Littleton & P. Light (eds) *Learning with Computers: Analysing Productive Interaction*, pp. 24–45, London: Routledge.

Hubel, D.H. & Wiesel, T.N. (1959) Receptive fields of single neurons in the cat's visual cortex, *Journal of Physiology* 148: 574–91.

Hughes, C. & Russell, J. (1993) Autistic children's difficulty with mental disengagement from an object: Its implications for theories of autism, *Developmental Psychology* 29: 498–510.

Hughes, C., Russell, J. & Robbins, T. (1994) Evidence for executive dysfunction in autism, *Neuropsychologia* 32: 477–92.

Hull, C. (1943) *Principles of Behavior*, New York: Appleton-Century-Crofts.

Hulme, C. & Snowling, M.J. (2009) *Developmental Disorders of Language Learning and Cognition*, Chichester: Wiley-Blackwell.

Iacobani, M. & Dapretto, M. (2006) The mirror neuron system and the consequences of its dysfunction, *Nature Neuroscience Reviews* 7: 942–51.

Izard, C.E. (1977) *Human Emotions*, New York: Plenum.

Karmiloff-Smith, A. (1992). *Beyond Modularity: A Developmental Perspective on Cognitive Science*, Cambridge, MA: MIT Press.

Klinnert, M.D. (1984) The regulation of infant behaviour by maaternal facial expression, *Infant Behavior & Development* 7: 447–65.

Kosc, L. (1974) Developmental dyscalculia, *Journal of Learning Disabilities* 7: 159–62.

Landerl, K., Bevan, A. & Butterworth, B. (2004) Developmental dyscalculia and basic numerical capacities: A study of 8–9 year old students, *Cognition* 93: 99–125.

Lefkowitz, M.M., Eron, L.D., Walder, L.O. & Huesmann, L.R. (1977) *Growing Up to Be Violent*, Oxford: Pergamon.

Lewis, C., Hitch, G. & Walker, P. (1994) The prevalence of specific arithmetic difficulties and specific reading difficulties in 9- and 10- year old boys and girls, *Journal of Child Psychology and Psychiatry* 35: 283–92.

Lorenz, K. (1950) Part and parcel in animal and human societies, in K. Lorenz (ed.) *Studies in Animal and Human Behaviour, Vol. II*, pp. 115–95, London: Methuen.

Lu, H., Yuille, A.L., Liljeholm, M., Cheng, P.W. & Holyoak, K.J. (2008) Bayesian generic priors for causal learning, *Psychological Review* 115: 955–84.

Lyytinen, H., Ahonen, T., Eklund, K. *et al.* (2001) Developmental pathways of children with and without familial risk for dyslexia during the first years of life, *Developmental Neuropsychology* 20: 535–54.

Mareschal, D., Quinn, P.C. & Lea, S.E.G. (2009) *The Making of Human Concepts*, Oxford: Oxford University Press.

McLean, J.F. & Hitch, G.J. (1999) Working memory impairments in children with specific arithmetic learning difficulties, *Journal of Experimental Child Psychology* 74: 240–60.

Meard, J., Bertone, S. & Flavier, E. (2008) How second-grade students internalize rules during teacher–student transactions: A case study, *British Journal of Educational Psychology* 78: 395–410.

Meltzoff, A.N. & Moore, M.K. (1976) Imitation of facial and manual gestures by human neonates, *Science* 198: 75–8.

Michotte, A. (1963) *The Perception of Causality*, Oxford: Basic Books.

Miller, G.A. (1956) The magical number seven plus or minus two: Some limits in our capacity for processing information, *Psychological Review* 63: 81–97.

Miller, N. & Dollard, J. (1941) *Social Learning and Imitation*, New Haven, NJ: Yale University Press.

Milne, E., Swettenham, J., Hansen, P., Campbell, R., Jeffries, H. & Plaisted, K. (2002) High motion coherence thresholds in children with autism, *Journal of Child Psychology and Psychiatry* 43: 255–63.

Murdock, B. (1962) The serial position effect of free recall, *Journal of Experimental Psychology* 64: 482–8.

Muter, V., Hulme, C., Snowling, M.J. & Stevenson, J. (2004) Phonemes, rimes, vocabulary and grammatical skills as foundations of early reading development: Evidence from a longitudinal study, *Developmental Psychology* 40: 663–81.

Myhill, D. (2009) From talking to writing: Linguistic development in writing, in V. Connelly, A. Barnett, J. Dockrell & A. Tolmie (eds) *British Journal of Educational Psychology Monograph Series II: Psychological Aspects of Education – Current Trends: Teaching and Learning Writing*, Leicester: British Psychological Society.

Nation, K. (1999) Reading skills in hyperlexia: A developmental perspective, *Psychological Bulletin* 125: 338–55.

Nauta, W.J.H. & Feirtag, M. (1986) *Fundamental Neuroanatomy*, New York: Freeman.

Neisser, U. (1976) *Cognition and Reality: Principles and Implications of Cognitive Psychology*, New York: Freeman.

Newell, A. & Simon, H.A. (1972) *Human Problem Solving*, Englewood Cliffs, NJ: Prentice-Hall.

Nieder, A. (2005) Counting on neurons: The neurobiology of numerical competence, *Nature Neuroscience Reviews* 6: 1–14.

Paracchini, S., Thomas, A., Castro, S. *et al.* (2006) The chromosome 6p22 haplotype associated with dyslexia reduces the expression of KIAA0319, a novel gene involved in neuronal migration, *Human Molecular Genetics* 15: 1659–66.

Passolunghi, M.C. & Siegel, L.S. (2001) Short-term memory, working memory, and inhibitory control in children with difficulties in arithmetic problem solving, *Journal of Experimental Child Psychology* 80: 44–57.

Paulesu, E., Démonet, J.-F., Fazio, F. *et al.* (2001) Dyslexia: Cultural diversity and biological unity, *Science* 291: 2165.

Pavlov, I. (1927) *Conditioned Reflexes*, Oxford: Oxford University Press.

Pellicano, E., Gibson, L., Maybery, M., Durkin, K. & Badcock, D. (2005) Abnormal global processing along the dorsal visual pathway in autism: A possible mechanism for weak visuospatial coherence? *Neuropsychologia* 43: 1044–53.

Pellicano, E., Jeffery, L., Burr, D. & Rhodes, G. (2007) Abnormal adaptive face-coding mechanisms in children with autism spectrum disorder, *Current Biology* 17: 1508–12.

Pennington, B.F. & Ozonoff, S. (1996) Executive function and developmental psychopathology, *Journal of Child Psychology and Psychiatry* 37: 51–87.

Piaget, J. (1974) *The Principles of Genetic Epistemology*, London: Routledge & Kegan Paul.

Pintrich, P.R. (2000) The role of goal orientation in self-regulated learning, in M. Boekaerts, P.R. Pintrich & M. Zeidner (eds) *Handbook of Self-Regulation*, pp. 451–502, San Diego, CA: Academic Press.

Rayner, K. (1978) Eye movements in reading and information processing, *Psychological Bulletin*, 85: 618–60.

Rijsdijk, F.V., Viding, E., DeBrito, S. *et al.* (in press) Heritable variations in gray matter concentration as a potential endophenotype for psychopathic traits, *Archives of General Psychiatry*.

Rittle-Johnson, B. & Siegler, R.S. (1998) The relation between conceptual and procedural knowledge in learning mathematics, in C. Donlan (ed.) *The Development of Mathematical Skill*, pp. 75–110, Hove: Psychology Press.

Satpute, A.B., Fenker, D.B., Waldmann, M.R., Tabibnia, G., Holyoak, K.J. & Lieberman, M.D. (2005) An fMRI study of causal judgments, *European Journal of Neuroscience* 22: 1233–8.

Saxton, M. (2010) *Child Language: Acquisition and Development*, London: Sage.

Schulte-Körne, G., Ziegler, A., Deimel, W. *et al.* (2007) Interrelationship and familiality of dyslexia related quantitative measures, *Annals of Human Genetics* 71: 160–75.

Selfridge, O.G. (1955) Pattern recognition and modern computers, in *Proceedings of Western Joint Computer Conference*, Los Angeles.

Shah, A. & Frith, U. (1983) An islet of ability in autistic children: A research note, *Journal of Child Psychology and Psychiatry* 24: 613–20.

Skinner, B.F. (1938) *The Behavior of Organisms*, New York: Appleton-Century-Crofts.

Skinner, B.F. (1971) *Beyond Freedom and Dignity*, Harmondsworth: Penguin.

Stainthorp, R. (2002) Reading for the 21st century, in R. Stainthorp & P. Tomlinson (eds) *British Journal of Educational Psychology Monograph Series II: Psychological Aspects of Education – Current Trends: Learning and Teaching Reading*, Leicester: British Psychological Society.

Starkey, P., Spelke, E.S. & Gelman, R. (1990) Numerical abstraction by human infants, *Cognition* 36: 97–127.

Thorndike, E.L. (1898) Animal intelligence: An experimental study of the associative processes of animals, *Psychological Monographs*, 2.

Tinbergen, N. (1951) *The Study of Instinct*, Oxford: Clarendon.

Torgesen, J.K. (2002) Lessons learned from intervention research in reading: A way to go before we rest, in R. Stainthorp & P. Tomlinson (eds) *British Journal of Educational Psychology Monograph Series II: Psychological Aspects of Education – Current Trends: Learning and Teaching Reading*, Leicester: British Psychological Society.

Verschaffel, L., Torbeyns, J., De Smedt, B., Peters, G. & Ghesquière, P. (2010) Solving subtraction problems flexibly by means of indirect addition, in R. Cowan, M. Saxton & A. Tolmie (eds) *British Journal of Educational Psychology Monograph Series II: Psychological Aspects of Education – Current Trends: Number Development and Difficulty*, Leicester: British Psychological Society.

Viding, E., Fontaine, N.M.G., Oliver, B.R. & Plomin, R. (in press) Negative parental discipline, conduct problems and callous-unemotional traits: A monozygotic twin differences study, *British Journal of Psychiatry*.

Viding, E., Simmonds. E., Petrides, K.V. & Frederickson, N. (2009) The contribution of callous-unemotional traits and conduct problems to bullying in early adolescence, *Journal of Child Psychology and Psychiatry* 50: 471–81.

Watson, J.B. (1925) *Behaviourism*, New York: Norton.

Wellington, J. & Osbourne, J. (2001) *Language and Literacy in Science Education*, Buckingham: Open University Press.

Wilcutt, E.G., Doyle, A.E., Nigg, J.T., Faraone, S.V. & Pennington, B.F. (2005) Validity of the executive function theory of attention deficit/hyperactivity disorder: A meta-analytic review, *Biological Psychiatry* 57: 1336–46.

Wolf, M. (2008) *Proust and the Squid: The Story and Science of the Reading Brain*, New York: Icon.

Wydell, T.N. & Butterworth, B. (1999) A case study of an English-Japanese bilingual with monolingual dyslexia, *Cognition* 70: 273–305.

Wynn, K. (1992) Addition and subtraction by human infants, *Nature* 458: 749–50.

Xu, F. & Spelke, E. (2000) Large number discrimination in 6-month old infants, *Cognition* 74: B1–B11.

Zelazo, P.D., Carter, A., Reznick, J.S. & Frye, D. (1997) Early development of executive function: A problem-solving framework, *Review of General Psychology* 1: 198–226.

Ziegler, J. & Goswami, U. (2005) Reading acquisition, developmental dyslexia, and skilled reading across languages: A psycholinguistic grain size theory, *Psychological Bulletin* 131: 3–29.

Ziegler, J., Castela, C., Pech-George, C., Georgel, F., Alarioa, F.-X. & Perry, C. (2007) Developmental dyslexia and the dual route model of reading: Simulating individual differences and subtypes, *Cognition* 107: 151–78.

Zorzi, M., Houghton, G. & Butterworth, B. (1998) The development of spelling–sound relationships in a model of phonological reading, *Language & Cognitive Processes* 13: 337–71.

20 Educational Psychology: Research on Developmental and Social Factors

ROBIN BANERJEE

LEARNING OUTCOMES

WHEN YOU HAVE COMPLETED THIS CHAPTER, YOU SHOULD BE ABLE TO:

1. Describe, evaluate and compare the educational implications of Piagetian, Vygostkyan and information-processing approaches to cognitive development.

2. Describe and evaluate the role of self-determination, goal orientation, self-efficacy, attribution and values in pupils' academic achievement motivation.

3. Describe, evaluate and compare the effects of social agents – teachers, parents and peers – on pupils' motivation to achieve at school.

4. Describe and evaluate research on the causes of behavioural, emotional and social difficulties of young people at school, and consider the implications for prevention and intervention.

KEY WORDS

Accommodation ● Achievement Goal Orientations ● Assimilation ● Big Fish–Little Pond Effect ● Causal Attribution ● Classroom Goal Structures ● Constructivist ● Culturally Mediated ● Cultural Tools ● Developmental Psychology ● Disequilibrium ● Domain-Specific ● Elementary Mental Functions ● Expectancy–Value Account ● Extrinsic Motivation ● Generalising ● Higher Mental Functions ● Information-Processing Accounts ● Intrinsic Motivation ● Mastery or Learning Goals ● Microgenetic Methodologies ● Over-justification Effect ● Overlapping Waves ● Parenting Style ● Peer Relationships ● Performance or Ego Goals ● Performance-Approach Orientation ● Performance-Avoidance Orientation ● Private Speech ● Scaffolding ● Schemes ● Self-Determination Theory ● Self-Fulfilling Prophecies ● Self-Presentation ● Self-Regulation ● Social Comparison ● Social Information Processing ● Sociocultural or Cultural–Historical Theory of Cognitive Development ● Strategies ● Subjective Values ● Zone of Proximal Development

CHAPTER OUTLINE

This chapter focuses on the developmental and social processes that influence the learning, achievement, motivation and behaviour of children and young people in educational settings. We will begin with an examination of core theories and research regarding cognitive development, which have important implications for the educational context. Then, we will describe and evaluate the importance of a range of motivational factors (e.g. academic goal orientation) that are related to academic learning, behaviour and achievement, and will consider the role of socialising agents (teachers, parents and peers) in influencing these factors. We will conclude the chapter with a discussion of individual differences, with attention to the 'behavioural, emotional and social difficulties' (BESD) that some pupils exhibit at school.

20.1   INTRODUCTION

We saw in Chapter 19 that a study of psychological processes in the educational context helps us understand more about the cognitive and biological factors that play a role in learning. However, other areas of psychology need to be considered in order to understand more fully how children and young people think, feel and behave in various educational contexts. The area of psychology that has the most obvious relevance to these processes is of course **developmental psychology**, which addresses the ways in which psychological processes develop through the lifespan. In the course of our examination of these developmental processes, we will see that a range of cognitive, emotional, motivational and social factors play a role in both the differences *between* age groups (e.g. what could be responsible for differences between 7 year olds and 14 year olds in their attitudes to learning?) and the differences *within* age groups (e.g. why might two 10 year olds differ greatly in their level of disruptive behaviour in the classroom?).

developmental psychology the branch of psychology concerned with change and development over the lifespan, often focused on development during childhood and adolescence.

20.2   THEORIES OF COGNITIVE DEVELOPMENT

Our exploration of approaches to learning in Chapter 19 showed how research over the past 100 years has stimulated a substantial interest in the cognitive processes that underpin effective learning, from attention and memory to problem solving and metacognition. But it is important for us to recognise also that simply applying models of human cognition based on research with adults is probably inadequate for understanding the way in which thinking changes in complexity, sophistication and

flexibility over the course of development. In this section we examine three major approaches to cognitive development, where theorists have taken on the challenge of explaining how thinking changes over the course of child and adolescent development.

20.2.1   Piaget's Cognitive-Developmental Theory

When we were introduced to different philosophical and pedagogical approaches to education in Chapter 17, we noted that the rise in 'child-centred' education in the late 1960s was intimately connected to the work of Jean Piaget. This Swiss psychologist transformed the way many people thought about children. He rejected the 'blank slate' view of the child as a passive respondent to the influences of people in the environment (such as

PHOTO 20.1 *Jean Piaget (1896–1980), the Swiss psychologist known for his theory of cognitive development.*
Source: Press Association.

teachers), and instead portrayed the child as an active agent in his or her own development.

constructivist an approach in cognitive-development theory focusing on how children construct their knowledge and understanding based on their experiences.

Piaget's cognitive-developmental theory is often thought of as a **constructivist** approach because it focuses on how children construct their knowledge and understanding based on their experiences. Coming from a background of early work in zoology, Piaget was interested in how the developing organism adapts to the surrounding environment. Knowledge, he argued, is not something that is simply delivered to the child by parents and teachers, but rather is generated by the children themselves on the basis of their actions within the environment. In particular, he emphasised the role of **schemes**,

schemes in Piagetian theory, an organised structure of knowledge (of self, beliefs and events) or abilities that change with age or experience.

or mental structures, which he believed were 'progressively constructed by continuous interaction between the subject and the external world' (Piaget, 1970, p. 703). These schemes are fundamentally concerned with action, whether this involves very basic motor activities (e.g. sucking, pushing, grasping) or sophisticated intellectual activities (e.g. putting ideas for an essay in a logical order). Within this theoretical view, children become something like 'mini-scientists', continually testing out their expectations and hypotheses based on their existing schemes. Sometimes a child can encounter new experiences (e.g. a

disequilibrium a state experienced by a child when encountering new experiences that do not map onto his or her existing schemes.

new toy) that does not map on to their existing schemes. This places the child in a state of **disequilibrium**, which Piaget saw as a critical starting point for growth. Piaget argued that existing schemes can

assimilation in Piagetian theory, a means of extending existing schemas by incorporating a new experience.

sometimes be extended by **assimilation** (incorporating, a new experience, e.g. when a baby incorporates a new toy into an existing 'sucking' scheme). But at other times, schemes must be created or changed for the **accommodation**

accommodation in Piagetian theory, a type of adaptation in which a child creates or makes changes to existing schemas.

of a new experience (e.g. when a baby first works out how to grasp a hard and spiky plastic toy in a different way compared to a soft cuddly toy). The crucial point is that a child's growing knowledge does not arise directly from the objects they encounter, but rather emerges out of the *interactions that they have with those objects*.

Piaget certainly did not set out to create a model of effective classroom instruction, but the impact of his theory within the educational context has been very

strong. In fact, Piagetian ideas played a critical role in the movement away from a 'chalk-and-talk' model of teaching, where the child is viewed as an empty vessel to be filled up with information from teachers, to a more 'discovery-based' approach to teaching, where the child is given opportunities to construct their own knowledge through active learning (see Bruner, 1960). A further element of Piaget's theory that had major implications for education was the emphasis on a developmental progression of stages in children's cognition, based on the idea of major qualitative shifts in logical thought occurring at around the ages of 2, 7 and 11 years. The four stages, and the principal cognitive features thought to be associated with them, are summarised in Table 20.1. The notion of an invariant sequence of stages in children's cognition immediately raised questions about the 'readiness' of children to cope with various aspects of the school curriculum at different ages; as the 1967 Plowden report on primary school education in England puts it, 'Until a child is ready to take a particular step forward, it is a waste of time to try to teach him to take it' (Plowden, 1967, p. 25).

This kind of bald conclusion about what in the curriculum is and is not appropriate for a child at a given 'stage' masks a deeper issue, namely the extent to which the child's social environment can facilitate their cognitive growth. One idea taken up by the so-called social Genevans, a group of Swiss psychologists who extended Piaget's approach, focused on the ways in which exposure to different perspectives on a problem from one's peers could trigger a state of disequilibrium and thereby lead to cognitive growth. They found, for example, that children who worked with peers on standard Piagetian tasks (e.g. conservation and perspective taking, as described in Focus Point 20.1) came to exhibit a greater understanding than children who worked with the task materials on their own (Doise, Mugny & Perret-Clermont, 1975). This kind of evidence highlights the potential value of peer-group work in classroom learning, which relates to a major historical shift in classroom organisation, from traditional arrangements of desks in front-facing horizontal rows, to the common contemporary arrangement of work areas in group-based clusters.

Despite the very significant impact of Piaget's theory of cognitive development, particularly within the educational context, it is important to stress that this approach has been criticised on a number of fronts. First, questions have been raised about many of the cognitive limitations that Piaget saw as characterising children's cognition at each stage. For example, considerable experimental evidence, involving methodological techniques much more sophisticated than the child observations, tasks and interviews used by Piaget, has shown that children often demonstrate knowledge and skills with regard to object permanence, conservation and perspective taking at a considerably younger age

TABLE 20.1 *Piaget's Stages of Cognitive Development.*

Stage	Approximate age range	Key cognitive features
Sensori-motor	Birth–2 years	○ Initial growth from simple reflexes towards goal-directed actions (e.g. reaching for an object) ○ Early difficulties in understanding 'object permanence' (i.e. that objects exist independently of one's own immediate perceptual experience) ○ Emergence of internal mental representations (e.g. having an idea in your head about something that cannot actually be seen) towards the end of this stage
Pre-operational	2–7 years	○ Growth in language and increased use of mental representations ○ Difficulties with transformations (e.g. recognising that the volume of water is conserved when it has been poured from a tall and narrow glass into a short and wide glass) ○ Focused on one dimension in various perceptual problems, with difficulties in seeing the world from any perspective other than your own (egocentrism)
Concrete operations	7–12 years	○ Ability to perform mental operations and transformations (e.g. ordering, sorting, reversing, combining), which helps children to understand conservation and overcome egocentrism ○ Difficulties with abstract reasoning and consideration of multiple possibilities
Formal operations	12 years +	○ Capacity to understand abstract concepts and engage in systematic logical reasoning and problem solving

FOCUS POINT 20.1 SOCIAL INTERACTION AND THE UNDERSTANDING OF CONSERVATION

Although Piaget is often regarded as having given insufficient attention to the role of the social environment, he did make the point that 'cooperation is the first of a series of forms of behaviour which are important for the constitution and development of logic' (Piaget, 1950, pp. 162–3). This idea was taken forwards by Doise, Mugny and Perret-Clermont (1975) in an experiment on children's capacity for understanding conservation. The researchers first tested 6- and 7-year-old children, individually, with a standard task to see if the children understood that the amount of juice remains the same when poured from one glass to another glass with a different shape. On the basis of this performance, children were classified into three levels:

- ○ *Nonconservers*: These children were able to compare the amounts of juice in identical glasses, but when juice was poured into a different-shaped glass, they believed that the amount of liquid increased or decreased.
- ○ *Intermediates*: These children sometimes stated that the amount of juice was the same despite being poured into a different-shaped glass, but did not understand that this logically had to be the case.
- ○ *Conservers*: These children understood that the amount of juice always stays the same no matter how many times it is poured out in different-shaped containers, and could explain their answers logically.

In the next part of the experiment (about two weeks later), children were brought together in groups of three – two

Conservers and one Intermediate or Nonconserver – to play another game with juice. The children had to cooperate in a task whereby the Nonconserver or Intermediate had to share out juice among the group using several different-shaped glasses. Crucially, he or she had to secure the agreement of the other children that the sharing was fair and equal. After completing this cooperation task, approximately a week later, children individually completed a post-test to assess their understanding of conservation. A control group of children completed the pre-test and the post-test at the same times but without the cooperation task in between.

Results showed that in the control group, only 17% of the children who were initially found to be Nonconservers or Intermediates showed any progress at the post-test in their understanding of conservation. However, among those who completed the cooperation task, 65% of the children who had initially been classed as Nonconservers or Intermediates showed that they had made significant progress in their understanding. The authors concluded that the peer interaction in the cooperation task encouraged cognitive growth. However, they also recognised that the study could not explain *why* the cooperation task resulted in greater progress.

Discussion: Read the rest of this chapter and think of several possible explanations for why the cooperation task led to an improved understanding of conservation. How would you go about testing these alternative hypotheses?

PHOTO 20.2 *A traditional 'chalk-and-talk' classroom layout.*
Source: Getty Images.

PHOTO 20.3 *A contemporary classroom layout facilitating group-based learning.*
Source: Getty Images.

than would be predicted on the basis of Piaget's theory (e.g. Baillargeon & DeVos, 1991; Borke, 1975; Donaldson, 1978). But perhaps more important are the deeper questions about the theoretical framework itself. Some theorists were concerned about the extent to which Piaget adequately accounted for the active role of social agents – particularly adults – in guiding children's cognitive development (Gauvain, 2001). Others objected to Piaget's emphasis on qualitatively distinct stages of thought in children's development (Gelman & Baillargeon, 1983). Below, we examine two different approaches to cognitive development that address these issues.

20.2.2 *Vygotsky's Sociocultural Theory*

At around the same time that Piaget was beginning to develop his theory of children's cognition, a Soviet psychologist named Lev Vygotsky was also working on a theoretical approach to cognitive development. In a substantial programme of work that shaped the intellectual

PHOTO 20.4 *Lev Vygotsky (1896–1934), a Soviet psychologist known for his sociocultural theory of cognitive development.*

context of Soviet psychology, Vygotsky (1978) illuminated the role played by culture and the social environment in children's thinking. His theoretical perspective is therefore frequently referred to as a **sociocultural or cultural–historical theory of cognitive development**. Unlike the Piagetian emphasis on children as 'mini-scientists' whose experiences lead them to construct, modify and refine their schemes about the world, the Vygotskyan approach focuses on the way in which people such as parents and teachers play an active role in transmitting cultural knowledge to the child. For this reason, many researchers use the analogy of the child as an 'apprentice' to describe the Vygotskyan approach.

Of course, Vygotsky recognised that children are likely to have some basic cognitive capacities such as attention, perception and memory, which are independent of any cultural learning. These **elementary mental functions**, however, are significantly expanded by the social interactions in which a child participates. Most importantly, Vygotsky argued that interactions with others provide a forum for the transmission of **cultural tools** that enable and stimulate cognitive growth. These tools can take many different forms, from entire symbolic systems for writing and

> **sociocultural or cultural–historical theory of cognitive development** a theory developed by Vygotsky that focuses on the way in which people, such as parents and teachers, play an active role in transmitting cultural knowledge to the child.

> **elementary mental functions** according to Vygotsky, mental capacities that are independent of any cultural learning, such as attention, perception, and memory.

> **cultural tools** products of human culture that are passed on to children in order to promote and extend their cognitive development.

counting, to objects such as computers and clocks, to abstract concepts such as time itself. Children's grow-ing experience with these tools enables them to develop **higher mental functions** that allow them to control their attention, build a conceptual understanding of the world and engage in logical prob-lem solving. For example, our elementary capacity for memory is significantly enhanced by having a writing system that allows us to write down a list of things to remember. In a similar way, reasoning about the logic of a sequence of statements, or about the abstract category that binds a certain array of objects together, may become possible for children through their experi-ences of formal schooling (see Focus Point 20.2).

Thus, for Vygotsky, all higher mental functions emerge in a child's development within the context

higher mental func-tions mental capacities developed through the use of 'cultural tools' enabling a child to control his or her atten-tion, build a conceptual understanding of the world and engage in logical problem solving.

of social interactions with oth-ers who are more experienced in the use of psychological tools; hence, children's cognitive devel-opment is said to be **culturally mediated**. In one famous quota-tion, Vygotsky explained:

culturally mediated according to Vygotsky, a child's mental func-tions emerge within the context of social interac-tions, particularly with others who are more competent in the use of cultural tools.

> Every function in the child's cultural development appears twice: first, on the social level, and later on the individual level; first, between people (interpsychological), and then inside the child (intrapsychological).
>
> (Vyogtsky, 1978, p. 57)

A major implication of this theoretical perspective, which continues to influence educational approaches today, is that cognitive development involves a shift in regulation. Initially, a child's understanding of a given task is regulated by a more knowledgeable other (e.g. a

---

FOCUS POINT 20.2   FORMAL SCHOOLING AND LOGICAL REASONING – LURIA'S RESEARCH IN UZBEKISTAN

One of Vygotsky's students and collaborators, Alexander Luria, conducted research in the villages of Uzbekistan during the 1930s in order to examine the impact of social and cultural change – including the introduction of for-mal schooling – on people's logical reasoning. Because this was a transitional period, Luria was able to observe and interact with illiterate peasants who had not experi-enced any sociocultural shifts as well as groups that had experienced formal schooling and 'modern life'.

In the excerpt below, Luria (1979, pp. 69–71) describes how the basic idea of using an abstract category to group objects and find the odd one out seemed to be completely alien to the illiterate villagers who had not encountered formal schooling:

Rakmat, a thirty-year-old illiterate peasant from an outlying district, was shown drawings of a hammer, a saw, a log, and a hatchet.

'They're all alike,' he said. 'I think all of them have to be here. See, if you're going to saw, you need a saw, and if you have to split something, you need a hatchet. So they're all needed here.' . . .

'Look,' we said, 'here you have three wheels and a pair of pliers. Surely, the pliers and the wheels aren't alike in any way, are they?'

'No, they all fit together. I know the pliers don't look like the wheels, but you'll need them if you have to tighten something in the wheels.'

'But you can use one word for the wheels that you can't for the pliers – isn't that so?'

'Yes, I know that, but you've got to have the pliers. You can lift iron with them and it's heavy, you know.'

'Still, isn't it true that you can't use the same word for both the wheels and the pliers?'

'Of course you can't.'

We returned to the original group, including ham-mer, saw, log, and hatchet. 'Which of these could you call by one word?'

'How's that? If you call all three of them a "hammer," that won't be right either.'

'But one fellow picked three things – the hammer, saw, and hatchet – and said they were alike.'

'A saw, a hammer, and a hatchet all have to work together. But the log has to be here too!' . . .

This tendency to rely on operations used in practi-cal life was the controlling factor among uneducated and illiterate subjects. . . . The somewhat more educated group of subjects employed categorical classification as their method of grouping objects even though they had had only a year or two of schooling. . . . When given the series of camel, sheep, horse, and wagon, they responded, 'The wagon doesn't belong. All the others are animals.'

Discussion: What kinds of cognitive skills do we acquire as a result of our experience of formal schooling? What does Luria's work tell us about cognitive development?

teacher). At this time, the child needs the support and assistance of the social partner in order to progress with the task. However, with the other person's guidance and support, the child can gradually move towards **self-regulation**; that is, regulating his or her own behaviour and thinking.

self-regulation the ability of an individual to regulate his or her own behaviour and thinking.

A good example of this process can be found when we study children's use of language, one of the most important cultural tools of all. Any interested observer will find that pre-school children quite often appear to talk to themselves while going about their various activities. Within a Piagetian framework, this could be dismissed as immature, 'egocentric' speech, but Vygotsky saw things differently. He argued that this **private speech** played a crucial role in the shift from other-regulation to self-regulation. Specifically, children here are using language as a tool to regulate their own thinking and behaviour. In line with this, it seems to be the case that when children – or even adults – find a task particularly challenging or difficult, they use private speech to guide themselves through the activity (Patrick & Abravanel, 2000). Thus, private speech plays a critical role in enabling the child to move from being regulated by others (e.g. being talked through a task by an adult) to internalising the knowledge and performing the task independently.

private speech talking to oneself as a child which, according to Vygotsky, plays a critical role in enabling a child to develop from being regulated by others to self-regulation.

This shift in regulation can be seen as occurring on an ongoing basis in children's school learning, as they encounter and eventually come to master an ever-increasing range of tasks and problems. According to Vygotsky (1978), this process of learning is taking place within what he called the **zone of proximal development**, the distance between what a child can do unaided and what he or she can achieve with the guidance and support of a more competent other (see Figure 20.1). Exactly how educators can best work within a child's zone of proximal development, and thereby help a child achieve his or her potential, is a question that has provoked a great deal of discussion.

zone of proximal development the distance between what a child can do unaided and what he or she can achieve with the guidance and support of a more competent other

One instructional approach that has found its way into mainstream educational thinking is **scaffolding**. This notion was first introduced by Bruner in the 1950s with regard to language acquisition, and was developed and refined by Wood and other colleagues in the 1970s. It refers to the way in which a child's efforts to master a new or challenging task can be supported in a flexible and

scaffolding the way in which a child's efforts to master a new or challenging task can be supported in a flexible and contingent way by adults or more competent partners

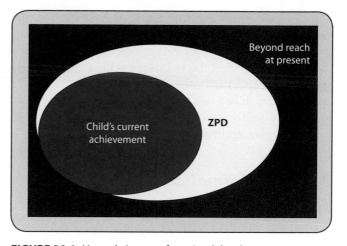

FIGURE 20.1 *Vygotsky's zone of proximal development.*

Many educators talk about how important it is to work within the child's zone of proximal development – the area of development that lies beyond the child's current level of achievement (what they can do without support from someone else), but that falls within the child's grasp when they have support and guidance from a more competent or experienced partner, such as an adult or a peer tutor.

contingent way by adults or more competent partners. The existence of contingency in the scaffolding process is critical: children have been shown to learn best when the level of support provided is finely tuned to their emerging successes and difficulties. In a study by Wood, Wood and Middleton (1978), for example, mothers who had been taught the contingency strategy when supporting their child with a pyramid-building task – 'If the child succeeds, when next intervening offer less help. If the child fails, when next intervening take over more control' – were more successful in stimulating learning than mothers who had been taught other, less flexible strategies such as just giving general encouragement or modelling every single action.

It appears that adults are often more effective than peers in the process of providing this kind of guidance and support to children. In experimental studies of 'guided participation', where children have to work with a partner to complete a task or solve a puzzle, children seem to perform better after having been paired with an adult than with a peer, even when the peers have been trained to have exactly the same level of expertise as the adults (Radziszewska & Rogoff, 1991). However, this does not mean that children are unable to be effective partners for one another in collaborative activities. Rather, studies investigating Vygotskyan approaches to peer collaboration have shown that with training in the process of providing support and guidance, effective learning can take place. For example, in one study of peer tutoring by King and colleagues (1998), 13-year-old science students were given opportunities to be both tutors and tutees, and were taught to use specific tutoring techniques, including ways of asking thought-provoking questions in a particular sequence. With this training – and even without greater expertise in the particular task at hand – students in the tutor role had the necessary skills to scaffold the learning of students in the tutee roles. This underlines the fact that, in line with Vygotskyan theory, particular qualities of social interaction are important for stimulating children's cognitive development.

20.2.3 Information-Processing Theories

Although we might adopt a sociocultural perspective in order to explain how children's ability to solve an arithmetic problem can be scaffolded by guidance from a more competent other, such an approach would not help us to explain the precise nature and sequence of changes in children's reasoning that are taking place here. Piagetian theory offers one way of thinking about changes in children's cognition, but there are alternatives that do not emphasise the kinds of stage-like qualitative shifts in thinking that Piaget described.

information-processing accounts an array of theories that seek to describe cognitive development in terms of changes in the processing of information

Information-processing **accounts** include an array of theories that seek to describe cognitive development in terms of changes in the processing of information (Siegler & Alibali, 2005). Some researchers use the computer as a metaphor for human cognition (see Klahr, 1992). Just as computers have hardware with specifiable information-processing limits, we can think of the brain as our hardware, with specifiable limits regarding speed of processing and memory capacity. And just as computers may be loaded with software in order to perform certain functions, we

strategies in information processing accounts of cognitive development, particular ways of performing information-processing tasks, especially those related to memory and problem-solving.

can acquire knowledge of a range of **strategies** that we use in order to perform different information-processing tasks. Some theorists, such as Case (1985), have tried to integrate key concepts from information-processing theories into the kind of stage approach favoured by Piaget. However, careful studies of changes in children's knowledge and use of strategies have raised questions about whether children's cognitive development can really be said to take place in

microgenetic methodologies a research approach whereby measurements of a child's problem-solving are made repeatedly over the period of change being studied.

a sequence of discrete stages at all. Siegler's approach to cognitive development allows us to integrate quantitative and qualitative changes in children's problem solving. He pioneered the use of **microgenetic methodologies**

(Siegler & Crowley, 1991), whereby measurements of a child's problem solving are made repeatedly over the period of change being studied (Research Methods Box 20.1). This methodological approach has given us a number of new insights into developmental processes, in particular showing us that there is a great deal of variability in how children approach a given problem. Rather than being restricted to one strategy for solving a problem – as might be implied by a stage approach to cognitive development – the same child can often use multiple strategies for solving a particular kind of problem (see Focus Point 20.3). In addition, children often show 'regressions' – switching to a less efficient or less

---

RESEARCH METHODS BOX 20.1

The Microgenetic Methodology

Siegler and Crowley's (1991) explanation of the microgenetic methodology explains why this approach is so vital for understanding the process of cognitive change. The researchers point out that the very widely found comparisons of different age groups in developmental research (e.g. comparing a group of 6 year olds, a group of 8 year olds and a group of 10 year olds) can only give us 'snapshots' of development. But in order really to understand exactly how changes take place, we need something that is more like a 'movie' of what is happening as the changes occur. The microgenetic approach has three key features:

- Observations span the entire period from the beginning of the change to the time at which it reaches a relatively stable state.

- The density of observations is high relative to the rate of change of the phenomenon.

- Observed behaviour is subjected to intensive trial-by-trial analysis, with the goal of inferring the processes that give rise to . . . change. (Siegler & Crowley, 1991, p. 606)

Thus, if we can identify the specific period of time when children are making a transition in their learning or problem-solving strategies, and study in detail their responses to problems on a trial-by-trial basis, we can begin to shed light on the process of cognitive development. Look at Focus Point 20.3 to see one example of how this kind of trial-by-trial analysis of children's problem solving can give us valuable insights into how children approach cognitive tasks.

FOCUS POINT 20.3   STRATEGY USE IN SOLVING ARITHMETIC PROBLEMS

Siegler's research has provided important insights into children's use of strategies to solve different kinds of problems. In one paper (Siegler, 1987), he concentrated on simple addition problems such as 6 + 3. The assumption in earlier research was that young children solve a problem like this by starting at the larger addend and counting up (i.e. they start at 6 and then count '7, 8, 9'). This conclusion was based on studies that looked at children's performance over a large number of trials, which found that the size of the smaller addend was the best predictor of the children's solution times.

In Siegler's study, the experimenter presented 5 to 7 year olds with 45 addition problems. Using the traditional approach of examining solution times across all the problems, Siegler replicated previous results: once again, the size of the smaller addend was the best predictor of solution time, implying that children were using the strategy of starting at the larger addend and counting up. But, as Siegler (1987) went on to show us, concluding that the

children are using this strategy on most of the problems is simply wrong.

By looking at children's performance on each individual trial carefully, and also speaking with the child about the way they had solved each problem, Siegler showed that 99% of the children used at least two strategies, and 62% used at least three strategies. By the age of 6, it was apparent that most children knew of five different strategies for solving the problems: as well as counting on the larger addend, children sometimes counted both addends, retrieved the answer from memory, decomposed the problem into two simpler or more familiar problems (e.g. 7 + 8 became 7 + 7 = 14 and 14 + 1 = 15) or just guessed. In fact, the 'counting-on' strategy was used on just 36% of trials!

Discussion: Siegler's report on this study is titled, 'The perils of averaging data over strategies'. Why did he choose this title? How have his results influenced your ideas about cognitive development?

---

sophisticated strategy for solving a problem even when they know and can explain a better strategy (Siegler, 2005). By mapping out the kinds of strategies used by children of different ages, we arrive at a model of development that implies neither a gradual linear improvement in sophistication nor a stepwise stage progression. Rather, Siegler (2005) charac-

overlapping waves a theory of child development suggesting that as a child develops, different strategies that are available to the child rise and fall in frequency of use.

terises development in terms of a series of **overlapping waves**, whereby different strategies rise and fall in frequency of use as the child gets older; of course, different strategies can become dominant at different ages, but at any given age there are multiple strategies available to the child (see Figure 20.2).

Thinking about children's cognitive development in terms of changes in the knowledge of different strategies raises another important issue. Rather than assuming that cognitive development involves broad changes in logical thought, as emphasised by Piaget, it seems more appropriate to think about children acquiring strategies in a more **domain-specific** way; that is, learning strategies for reasoning or problem solving within a particular domain of activity (e.g. instruction in arithmetic at school).

domain-specific applicable to a specialised area of knowledge or activity.

Some psychologists have sought to test this hypothesis directly. For example, Chi (1978) examined the memory of children who were

chess experts and of adults who were chess novices. She tested memory performance in two tasks, one that simply involved repeating increasingly lengthy sequences of digits (a 'digit span' task), and another that involved remembering

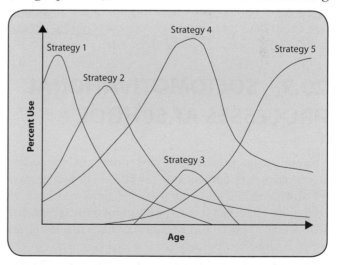

FIGURE 20.2 *Siegler's (2005) 'overlapping waves' model.*

Siegler's metaphor of overlapping waves reminds us that a student at any given age is likely to have multiple strategies for solving a particular kind of problem. Rather than thinking about developmental change in terms of abrupt shifts from one strategy to another, we can examine how the use of different strategies rises and falls as students increase in age.

Source: Siegler (2005). Copyright ©2005 by the American Psychological Association.

the positions of pieces on a chessboard. She found a clear pattern of results: although the child chess experts had a poorer 'digit span' than the adult chess novices, they were far superior in remembering the positions of chess pieces. Clearly, the children's greater experience and expertise in working with chess pieces had provided them with domain-specific knowledge that helped them to process and remember their precise locations on chessboards more efficiently and effectively. This kind of evidence implies that educators need to think about how they can support children in taking strategies they have acquired in one domain and **generalising** them to other domains.

> **generalising** in information-processing theory, taking a strategy applicable to one specific domain and applying it to other domains.

20.2.4 Summary

Our overview of approaches to cognitive development has revealed some very different perspectives on the way in which pupils at school think and learn as they grow older. However, it is important to recognise that many of the contributions from these different perspectives not only coexist but actually complement each other. Piaget highlighted the active role of children in constructing their own knowledge and understanding of the world. Vygotskyan theory adds to this significantly by showing how social partners with greater cultural knowledge and experience (including parents, teachers and trained peer tutors) can guide children in their efforts to master new concepts and skills. And finally, information-processing approaches remind us of how important it is to be precise about the strategies children discover, select and utilise in order to tackle a problem or learn a new skill.

20.3 SOCIOMOTIVATIONAL PROCESSES AT SCHOOL

The previous section has identified some basic approaches to cognitive development that can shed light on the ways in which children and young people think and learn as they grow older. But it is also important to recognise that school is an important *social* context, which in turn relates to, or is embedded within, other social contexts (e.g. the family, the culture). In fact, we have already seen from our overview of Vygotskyan theory that the development of cognition is intimately connected to the social interactions that children and young people have with other people. However, we can go further than this. Developmental psychologists have for many decades studied the ways in which children and adolescents are socialised by a range of different social agents, including the family, the peer group, schools and other institutions, and even the media.

In the context of education, studying these social processes not only gives us important additional insights into how students think and learn, but also helps to explain and predict their behaviour and feelings at school. Many of these insights relate to the way in which socialisation agents influence students' motivation at school. Therefore, before turning to the specific effects of parents, peers, teachers and schools, we will first review a number of key issues relating to students' academic motivation.

20.3.1 Academic Motivation

As in other domains of life, we can think about students' academic activities at school not just in terms of abilities, skills and performance, but also in terms of the underlying motivation to engage with – and successfully master or complete – the activities. We can also apply the commonly made distinction between **intrinsic motivation** – being driven to complete schoolwork simply for the interest and enjoyment it provides to you – and **extrinsic motivation** – doing your schoolwork because of pressure put on you by others or because of the rewards and sanctions that result from success or failure on the tasks.

> **intrinsic motivation** doing something because of one's own internal drives and the interest and enjoyment that it brings.

> **extrinsic motivation** doing something because of incentives and pressures applied to the individual from outside.

Interestingly, developmental research suggests that students at school tend to follow an age-related trend in the kinds of motivation they have with regard to their academic work. In work reported by Harter (1981), children were asked to respond to a range of statements reflecting a number of key dimensions relating to intrinsic and extrinsic motivations. Harter's findings suggested that as children grew older, there seemed to be a developmental shift from an intrinsic orientation (e.g. being motivated by curiosity and interest and preferring challenging work) to an extrinsic orientation (e.g. being motivated by teacher approval and preferring easy work). More recent work has more clearly shown that it is specifically the agreement with statements indicating intrinsic motivation that tends to decline between around 9 and 14 years of age (Lepper, Corpus & Iyengar, 2005).

In order to understand whether a given student will display a strong intrinsic motivation to perform academic tasks, we need to consider what kinds of psychological prerequisites there might be for this. One prominent account of human motivation that provides an important perspective on this is **self-determination theory**. According to this theory (Ryan & Deci, 2000), human motivation,

> **self-determination theory** a theory that conceptualises human motivation in terms of three needs: need for competence; need for relatedness; need for autonomy.

including students' academic motivation at school, can be understood in terms of three fundamental needs:

- The need for competence (the perception that one is effective in dealing with the surrounding environment).
- The need for relatedness (the subjective experience of belonging and feeling connected to others).
- The need for autonomy (the sense of volition in one's own actions, as opposed to being controlled by other people or external circumstances).

Ryan and Deci (2000) go on to argue that environmental circumstances that meet these basic needs are likely to provide a strong foundation for intrinsically motivated behaviour. In the educational context, then, a school environment that promotes children's sense of competence, relatedness and autonomy ought to be one in which children are more likely to engage with academic work and learning for the intrinsic interest and enjoyment it elicits (see Activity Box 20.1). In seeking to explain the troubling developmental decline in intrinsic motivation noted earlier, Lepper, Corpus and Iyengar (2005) comment that our school system often seems to become more focused on tightening control and reducing personal choice, ironically just at a time of transition (from pre-adolescence to early adolescence) when young people are displaying increased needs for autonomy. However, these researchers also highlight the increased emphasis that students place – and are encouraged to place – on performance outcomes as they get older, and suggest that this could detract from the intrinsic enjoyment and interest in learning. In fact, a large literature on achievement goal orientations supports the idea that the kinds of goals students have with regard to their schoolwork have important consequences for learning and motivation.

20.3.1.1 *Achievement goal orientations*

One important line of research on this topic began in the 1970s when researchers began to document two very different responses to failure. In one study (Diener & Dweck, 1978), some 'helpless-oriented' children responded to failure with self-blame, negative emotions and deteriorations in performance, whereas other 'mastery-oriented' children focused on new strategies for solving the difficulties on the task and sustained a positive attitude towards coping with the challenge. Subsequently, researchers showed that these different responses to failure map on to fundamentally different **achievement goal orientations** (Elliott & Dweck, 1988). The distinction that is now very widely used in educational research refers to engaging in a task in order to:

- Maintain a positive judgement of yourself by proving or demonstrating your ability (known as **performance or ego goals**); or
- Master the task and/or increase one's ability and knowledge (known as **mastery or learning goals**).

Broadly speaking, those who hold a performance goal orientation are focused on the end product of learning and are especially concerned about comparisons

achievement goal orientations in education research, theory of goals in which those who hold a performance goal orientation are focused on the visible end product of learning, while those who hold a mastery goal orientation are focused on the process of learning itself and progress in mastering the task at hand.

performance or ego goals in education, goals whereby an individual is motivated to maintain a positive judgement of self by proving or demonstrating ability.

mastery or learning goals in education, goals whereby an individual is motivated to master the task and/or increase his or her ability and knowledge

---

AN IDEAL SCHOOL?   ACTIVITY BOX 20.1

Self-determination theory suggests that three fundamental human needs are 'essential for facilitating optimal functioning of the natural propensities for growth and integration, as well as for constructive social development and personal well-being' (Ryan & Deci, 2000, p. 68). As discussed in the text, these have been identified as the needs for *autonomy*, *competence* and *relatedness*.

Discussion: Think back to your school life. Did the schools you attended foster a sense of autonomy, competence and

relatedness? What would an 'ideal' school that satisfied young people's fundamental needs look like? Think about:

- The school and classroom environment
- Approaches to discipline
- The behaviour of the staff and the pupils at the school
- Structures for pupils to have a voice in the operation of the school
- The academic curriculum
- Approaches to assessment
- Extracurricular activities and community involvement

between their own performance and that of others. In contrast, those who hold a mastery goal orientation are focused on the process of learning itself, are tolerant of mistakes, and are more concerned with their own personal progress and improvement in mastering the task at hand.

In one important study of children's goal orientations, Elliott and Dweck (1988) elicited a performance goal orientation in some children by telling them that their performance would be video-recorded and evaluated by experts. Under such conditions, children were far less likely to select tasks that were described as challenging. Moreover, particularly among those children who had also been led to believe that their ability at the experimental task was low, there was a distinctive 'helpless' response to difficulties on the task, including blaming themselves for their failures, deteriorations in problem-solving performance and negative verbalisations (e.g. 'This is boring', 'My stomach hurts'). This has led researchers to conclude that the combination of a focus on performance outcomes, together with low perceived ability, is a particularly problematic motivational orientation (see Elliott & Church, 1997). This has

performance-avoidance orientation a goal orientation leading to withdrawal from a task that is perceived to carry a risk of negative evaluation of performance.

performance-approach orientation a focus on performance goals leading to a desire to demonstrate competence in front of others.

been labelled the **performance-avoidance orientation** and is associated with withdrawal from any task that is perceived to carry a risk of negative evaluation of one's performance. In contrast, a focus on performance goals when perceived ability is high is likely to lead to a desire to demonstrate competence in front of others (even though this might be done at the expense of learning anything new) and is therefore known as a **performance-approach orientation**.

It is important to recognise that goal orientations can be thought of not only at the level of the individual pupil, but also at the level of the classroom learning environment. For example, Kaplan, Gheen and Midgley (2002) examined the extent to which secondary school classrooms were seen as environments where mastery goals were emphasised (e.g. a focus on learning, understanding and personal progress) or as environments where performance goals were emphasised (e.g. a focus on good grades, comparisons of pupil performance, competition).

classroom goal structures orientations within classrooms that can parallel personal goal orientation as being either performance or mastery focused.

Research results concerning such **classroom goal structures** fall neatly in line with the work on personal goal orientation, in that classrooms with an orientation to mastery goals tended to be

associated with more positive patterns of learning. In fact, in the study by Kaplan and colleagues referred to above, a mastery goal structure within the classroom was associated with a lower incidence of disruptive behaviour among the students.

20.3.1.2 Self-efficacy, attributions and values

Other theorists have particularly emphasised the crucial role played by students' views of themselves and their ways of explaining the events that have occurred in their academic lives such as success or failure on a test (see Eccles & Wigfield, 2002). Turning first to students' perceptions of their own ability, we must recognise the large literature on the importance of self-efficacy – the perception of one's own ability to do what is needed to achieve desired outcomes on a given activity or task – for understanding human behaviour. Bandura (1977, 1986) laid out a broad conceptual framework explaining how self-efficacy predicts the capacity to cope with challenging circumstances. The concept of self-efficacy overlaps substantially with the need for competence, identified earlier in our discussion of self-determination theory (Ryan & Deci, 2000). Thus, the emphasis on self-efficacy can be brought into a very wide range of analyses, from research on the impact of psychological therapies through to investigations of academic learning and performance at school.

Closely related to the concept of self-efficacy is the question of **causal attribution**: how a particular event or outcome may be explained. In Weiner's (1985)

causal attribution an explanation by an individual of the cause of a particular behaviour.

widely used model of attribution, three dimensions are emphasised: locus (is the causal factor responsible for success or failure located within the individual or external to the individual?), stability (is the causal factor likely to endure over time?) and controllability (is the causal factor under the control of the individual?). For example, if you explained your high score on a test by thinking that the teacher happened to be in a good mood that day, you would be making an external, unstable and uncontrollable attribution. Clearly, those who have higher self-efficacy with regard to a given task are more likely to attribute success on the task to an internal cause, which in turn should reinforce their positive expectations and make them more likely to attempt similar tasks in the future. Moreover, the kinds of attributions a student makes are likely to be linked to emotional consequences; for example, blaming an internal and stable factor for failure often leads to guilt and hopelessness.

A final component of academic motivation that needs to be considered before we can turn to the impact of socialising contexts and agents concerns the subjective importance that students attach to their academic activities. Eccles and colleagues have conducted a major programme of research on the **subjective values** attached by students to their academic work. According to Eccles-Parsons *et al.* (1983), a given task's subjective value comprises four distinct components: intrinsic value (the interest and enjoyment that are attached to doing the activity), attainment value (the personal importance of doing well on the task), utility value (the importance of doing well on the task for accomplishing specific achievement or career goals) and perceived cost (the perceived risks of engaging in the task, in terms of effort, anxiety and so on). Research suggests that people's subjective values interact with, and are closely associated with, their competency beliefs and efficacy expectations. According to this kind of **expectancy–value account**, your engagement in a given academic task will depend on both your estimated probability of success and the subjective value you attach to the task. As we will see below, these conceptual constructs have been of great value in helping us to make sense of the impacts of various socialising agents – teachers, parents and peers – in shaping students' academic development.

> **subjective values** the worth to an individual of doing a task , which can be categorised into intrinsic value, attainment value, utility value and perceived cost.

> **expectancy–value account** a theory whereby an individual's engagement in a given academic task will depend on both estimated probability of success as well as the subjective value attached to the task.

20.3.2 Socialisation of Academic Motivation

Now that we have examined some of the key aspects of students' academic motivation, we can begin to consider the ways in which socialising agents – particularly teachers, parents and peers – can play a role in psychological processes at school. Of course, we must recognise that teachers, parents and peers can have direct influences on students' knowledge, reasoning and academic performance (e.g. through direct instruction and collaboration, conversations and other social interactions concerning school-related tasks). In addition, as we will see later in this chapter, these socialising agents could play a role in the emergence of (and also in the therapeutic response to) behavioural, emotional and social difficulties at school. However, the research described below shows that many findings regarding variability in students' behaviour, learning and performance at school can be explained at least partly in terms of the influence that socialising agents have on students' motivation.

20.3.2.1 Teachers

The role of teachers in the socialisation of children and adolescents has of course been given special attention in investigations of academic achievement, motivation and adjustment. Eccles and Roeser's (2005) review of the effects of schools on development highlights numerous levels of influence, from the nature of the academic tasks and instruction within the classroom right through to the linkages between schools and the broader communities within which they are situated. Below, we examine several examples of research studies showing how student outcomes can be linked to specific teacher behaviours, expectations and classroom practices.

One of the most famous investigations within the educational context was Rosenthal and Jacobson's (1966) work on the impact of teacher expectations. In their classic study, primary school teachers were led to believe that 20% of their students were 'intellectual bloomers' who would be likely to show unusual intellectual gains, when in fact these students had been randomly selected to receive this label. The study gained prominence because of the finding that simply raising teachers' expectations about this group of students seemed to lead to significantly greater gains in intellectual performance over the course of the ensuing school year, at least among the youngest children, aged 6–8 years. Although questions can be and have been asked about the methodology and analysis used in this particular study, subsequent research has supported the idea that teacher expectations can serve as **self-fulfilling prophecies**, whereby those who are expected to do well indeed end up with superior performance.

> **self-fulfilling prophecies** a prediction that causes itself to become true because people respond to it in such a way that they bring about the prophecy.

The next step in understanding the impact of teacher expectations on pupil outcomes is to identify the mechanism by which this impact occurs. Numerous studies have considered the ways in which teachers' expectations influence their behaviour as well as the kinds of tasks and activities (i.e. learning opportunities) that they provide for the students. For example, high expectations could lead to positive nonverbal cues such as smiles and eye contact, specific instructional practices such as teaching more difficult material or asking more questions, and globally warmer interpersonal interactions (Harris & Rosenthal, 1985). More recently, Rubie-Davies (2007) has shown that some teachers in general approach their class with significantly higher or lower expectations than would be expected from the children's actual achievement levels. In this observational work, those teachers with significantly lower expectations were found to provide less instructional support in terms of linking teaching material with prior knowledge and previous lessons, asking questions, giving feedback and managing behaviour positively.

It is important to stress that teacher expectations have the most potent effects on students' learning and achievement when the teacher is also perceived by their students to treat low- and high-achieving students differently. For example, one recent study set out to explain the role of biased teacher expectations in the achievement gap between different ethnic groups. With an ethnically diverse sample of nearly 2000 primary school students and their teachers, McKown and Weinstein (2008) showed that biased teacher expectations played a significant role in the poorer achievement of African American and Latino students, especially in classrooms where low and high achievers were seen by students to be treated differently.

The impact of teacher behaviours can also be understood in terms of the extent to which they satisfy the kinds of basic needs emphasised in self-determination theory. For example, Assor, Kaplan and Roth (2002) focused specifically on teacher behaviours classified as either supporting or suppressing pupil autonomy. The former category included behaviours such as making the teaching material personally relevant to the students' goals and interests, and providing choices. The latter category included suppressing criticism and independent opinions, and being intrusive and controlling with regard to pupil activities. In line with self-determination theory, this study showed that teachers' autonomy-supportive behaviours were associated with significantly more positive pupil attitudes and engagement, whereas teachers' autonomy-suppressive behaviours were associated with more negative pupil attitudes. Other research confirms that students' perceptions of autonomy support could have significant implications for life-course trajectories: one prospective study of over 4000 French-Canadian teenagers from Montreal showed that the 6% of the sample who dropped out of school early had previously reported low levels of intrinsic motivation, which in turn could be tracked back to lower levels of perceived autonomy support from schools, teachers and parents (Vallerand, Fortier & Guay, 1997).

Particularly problematic is the finding that for those students who appear least engaged in their schooling (and for whom teacher expectations might be low to begin with), teachers – perhaps not surprisingly – use more coercion to try to secure desired behaviours and display a less positive emotional connection with the pupils. According to Skinner and Belmont (1993), these kinds of patterns indicate a vicious cycle whereby students who are disengaged from learning receive teacher responses that do not satisfy their basic needs for competence, autonomy and relatedness, and therefore serve to undermine their motivation still further.

Finally, one particular aspect of teacher behaviour that deserves special attention is the provision of rewards for pupils' activities and achievements at school. The idea of reinforcing desired behaviour to increase its frequency is a basic tenet of behaviourist learning theories, but a number of researchers have raised important questions about the impact of rewards on levels of intrinsic motivation for engaging with a particular task. In a famous study by Lepper, Greene and Nisbett (1973), children who had previously shown intrinsic motivation to engage in a target activity were placed in an experimental condition where they completed that same activity in order to receive a tangible reward. Subsequently, the researchers observed a significant decline in the level of interest in the target activity, in comparison with control conditions (see Focus Point 20.4). At the time, this so-called **over-justification effect** was interpreted in terms of an attributional account: the children in the experimental condition were re-attributing their completion of the target activity to an extrinsic reward rather than the intrinsic interest they had regarding the activity. However, more recent accounts explain these kinds of findings as evidence that rewards – at least sometimes – can have a detrimental effect on individuals' sense of autonomy and personal control, and thereby lead to lower intrinsic motivation (Deci, Koestner & Ryan, 1999).

> **over-justification effect** an effect whereby the existence of an extrinsic reward can lower intrinsic motivation to complete a task.

Although the provision of verbal praise – which ought to boost an individual's sense of competence – would generally not be expected to reduce intrinsic motivation, research suggests that certain kinds of teacher praise are less effective than others in promoting positive learning attitudes and behaviours. Researchers have established that praising children for their ability and intelligence – aspects of self that are not obviously under their direct control – could have negative consequences for future motivation, in comparison with praising children for their effort, which of course is more controllable. Children receiving the former kind of praise were more likely to display an orientation towards performance goals; thus, when later confronted with failure on a task, they showed the familiar 'helpless' pattern of self-blame, low task persistence, low task enjoyment and poorer task performance (Mueller & Dweck, 1998).

20.3.2.2 Parents

In general, parents are often regarded as the most important socialising agents in child development. There is therefore a large literature concerning the role of parents in influencing developmental outcomes, including those relating to behaviour and achievement at school. One of the most common approaches to studying the effects of parents on children involves the classification of **parenting style**. The seminal

> **parenting style** according to Baumrind (1967) there are three major parenting styles: authoritarian, authoritative and permissive.

FOCUS POINT 20.4   THE DANGERS OF REWARDS? TESTING THE 'OVERJUSTIFICATION' EFFECT

Several decades ago, social psychologists put forward the hypothesis that a person's intrinsic interest in an activity could be undermined by getting them to engage in that activity in order to achieve some extrinsic goal (like getting a reward). Probably the most famous test of this prediction was Lepper, Greene and Nisbett's (1973) study of nursery school children's involvement in a drawing activity.

In that study, the researchers selected nursery children who had shown an initial intrinsic interest in a drawing activity. During a baseline observation period over three days, these children had spontaneously, and without any prompting, chosen to spend time at a new drawing table equipped with a set of magic markers and white drawing paper. After this baseline period, children were told that they were going to do some drawings for a man or a woman (one of the experimenters) who was visiting the nursery school to see what kinds of pictures children liked to draw. When the visitor arrived, each child was given six minutes to draw pictures for them. However, the children were randomly allocated to one of three conditions:

○ *Expected award*: These children were told in advance that the visitor would give Good Player Awards (a certificate with a big gold star and bright red ribbon) to the children who helped him out by drawing pictures for them. At the end of the drawing session, the children were thanked for their help and received the awards as promised.

○ *Unexpected award*: These children were not told in advance about the awards, but at the end of the drawing session they were thanked for their help and also received the awards.

○ *No award*: These children were thanked for their help but did not receive any awards.

One or two weeks after this, another observation period took place to measure how often each child spontaneously chose to spend time at the drawing table. The researchers found that only the children in the 'expected award' condition showed a significant drop in interest, compared to the time spent on drawing before the experimenters' visit. In fact, the children in this condition were now spending about half as much time at the drawing table as children in the 'no award' and 'unexpected award' conditions. As an aside, the authors also noted that the pictures drawn for the experimenters by the 'expected award' children were also significantly poorer in quality than those of the other children, as rated by three judges who did not know which condition the children were in.

Discussion: What does this study tell you about the effect of rewards on intrinsic motivation? Think about the different kinds of rewards students might encounter in school. What effects do you think they could have on students' motivation?

---

work of Baumrind (1967) identified three major parenting styles: authoritarian (high on control and demands for strict obedience, with significant restrictions on the child's autonomy); authoritative (firm and adaptive control but with rational explanations and affirmation of the child's perspective); and permissive (acceptant attitude towards the child, with low control and few demands). Research has suggested that, at least in Euro-American samples, authoritative parenting is associated with more positive developmental outcomes than either authoritarian or permissive child-rearing styles (see Rothbaum & Trommsdorff, 2007). It is not difficult to see a connection between these parenting styles and the kinds of need fulfilment described within self-determination theory. For example, whereas the responsive and communicative approach of authoritative parents provides support for children's autonomy, the kind of coercion implied by authoritarian parenting is likely to undermine the need

for autonomy. Drawing on this conceptual link, Grolnick and Ryan (1989) showed that low levels of parental support for a child's autonomy, as predicted, were associated with poorer school adjustment, competence and academic self-regulation.

Even more direct evidence of parents' role in the socialisation of academic motivation can be found when we examine the impact of parental beliefs and expectations on children's self-perceptions and attitudes to learning. A good example of how this works can be found when investigating gender differences in attitudes to mathematics and science. Numerous studies have shown that even when the actual average performance of boys and girls is at the same level, there are still substantial differences in self-perceptions and expectations, attribution patterns and affective states regarding these academic subjects. For example, one study by Stipek and Gralinski (1991) assessed 8- and 14-year-old students before they took a standard classroom mathematics test, and after they received their results. Even after controlling for actual performance, girls' self-perceptions of ability were significantly lower than those of boys, they were more likely to attribute perceived failure to low ability than boys, and they were less likely to attribute perceived success to high ability than boys. Moreover, girls reported less pride in success and were more likely to feel like hiding their papers following failure. Is it possible that these kinds of patterns are connected, at least to some extent, to parents' attitudes and expectations?

In fact, over 25 years ago, researchers had already begun to show that parental expectations and attributions influence boys' and girls' attitudes and choices regarding mathematics and science. In one study (Parsons, Adler & Kaczala, 1982), 11- to 17-year-old students and their parents completed questionnaires regarding mathematics. Remarkably, parents' expectations and ability perceptions regarding their sons and daughters were better predictors of the students' self-perceptions and expectations than was the students' own past performance in mathematics. More recent longitudinal evidence has supported the prediction that these patterns play a role in career choices in young adulthood. Bleeker and Jacobs (2004) showed that mothers' expectations of their 13-year-old daughters' success in a mathematics-related career significantly predicted actual career choices by age 24, even after controlling for teachers' ratings of actual mathematics performance and ability.

Finally, it is important to remember that the family is itself situated within a broader socioeconomic and cultural context with normative beliefs and values that may influence students' academic learning and behaviour outcomes. In line with this, superior mathematics performance in East Asian cultural groups, compared with Euro-American groups, has been linked to broad sociocultural value orientations regarding the significance of effort for achievement outcomes, which in turn are reflected in parental attitudes and expectations (Chen & Stevenson, 1995). Similarly, Wigfield and Eccles (2002) discuss the ways in which cultural stereotypes, expectations and values can play a role in the educational aspirations and outcomes of students from ethnic minorities, particularly under conditions of socioeconomic deprivation. In fact, overcoming the sociocultural factors that lead to disengagement from school and learning in these demographic groups is a key objective of pre-school intervention programmes, such as Head Start in the United States and Sure Start in the United Kingdom. It is noteworthy that these programmes are considered most likely to succeed where they are clearly embedded within a well-defined system of support for the family and the broader community (e.g. Love et al., 2005; Melhuish et al., 2008).

20.3.2.3 Peers

One further socialisation context that also plays a major role within the educational domain is the peer-group context. We can think of this peer-group impact not only in terms of the classroom interactions that directly influence academic learning and motivation, but also in terms of the broader role of peer relations in shaping students' emotional and behavioural characteristics. With regard to the former, we have already encountered some accounts of how peer interactions can foster cognitive development. From a Piagetian perspective, the exposure to multiple perspectives often brought about by peer collaboration can provide an important stimulus for cognitive growth, while from a Vygotskyan perspective, peers – with the relevant expertise and skills in guidance – can help each other to progress in their learning through the zone of proximal development.

Classroom interactions between peers are also important in other ways. For example, we have already referred briefly to the potential importance of **social comparison** between peers. In fact, social psychologists have recognised for many decades that our tendency to compare ourselves with other people and with external norms and standards is an essential part of how we evaluate ourselves (Festinger, 1954). The relevance to education is obvious, as there is so much opportunity for a student to compare himself or herself with a peer group in virtually every domain of academic activity. Moreover, there is good evidence that children begin to use such comparisons in order to evaluate themselves from a fairly young age, particularly from around 7–8 years of age (e.g. Ruble et al., 1980). In fact, a consideration of social comparison can help us understand some of the key patterns of results regarding students' academic motivation that we have discussed earlier in this chapter. For example, developmental declines in intrinsic motivation for school tasks might be traced back to decreases in self-perception of ability as children begin to make less positive (and often more realistic) appraisals of their own performance through social comparison (Wigfield et al., 2006).

The effect of social comparison on students' self-perception, motivation and behaviour clearly depends on who is selected as a target for comparison. For example, we have already seen the negative impact of a performance goal orientation on children with low self-perception of ability, and this is obviously connected to the unfavourable social comparisons those children are making with their better-performing peers. Research has shown that this kind of social comparison is likely to be particularly problematic in school contexts where

> **social comparison**
> comparison made by individuals regarding their abilities and attributes relative to those of others.

children are explicitly grouped within a classroom on the basis of their ability (Reuman, 1989). In a similar way, research on the **big fish–little pond effect** (Marsh & Hau, 2003) has shown that moving into academically selective schools – where peer performances set a high standard – can often lead to lower academic self-concept. For example, a high-achieving child at the top of her class in a small primary school (a 'big fish in a little pond') can experience a significant decline in self-perception after moving into a very high-ability secondary school. However, the choice of targets for social comparison, and the consequences for academic motivation and behaviour, are not solely dependent on school characteristics and classroom practices. In fact, the importance of social comparison becomes even more apparent when we consider students' **peer relationships** – their friendships, their peer group affiliations and their status within the broader peer network.

> **big fish–little pond effect** the effect whereby students' academic self-perception depends on comparison with the ability of peers in their school.

> **peer relationships** relationships with friends, in peer group affiliations, and within the broader peer network.

A consideration of students' peer relationships reminds us that achievement goals are not the only goals that might influence students' behaviour and learning at school. Researchers have shown that the pursuit of social goals – such as maintaining friendly and cooperative relationships with peers or gaining approval from others – can play a key role in determining classroom behaviours (Urdan & Maehr, 1995; Wentzel, 1996). However, these kinds of social goals do not always encourage a stronger academic motivation. Some studies, for example, have shown that as students get older, academic diligence may be regarded as leading to *dis*approval from peers (Juvonen & Murdock, 1995). In fact, Banerjee (2002) showed that by the end of primary school, pupils clearly distinguish between their **self-presentation** to peers and to adults, and in particular are less likely to recommend focusing on academic skills when interacting with peers.

> **self-presentation** efforts to control the way one presents oneself, in order to convey desired images of the self to others.

Of course, the impact of peer relationships on academic behaviour and motivation will depend on the nature and characteristics of the particular peer group with whom the student interacts. Thus, if the peer group consists of high-achieving students who value hard work and academic performance, the goal of gaining social approval could provide an additional incentive for academic work. Ryan (2001) carefully studied the transition from primary to secondary school with attention to students' peer networks. Even after controlling for the fact that students selected friends of a similar achievement

level to themselves, Ryan found evidence clearly suggesting that students were affected by their peer group: those in low-achieving peer groups showed greater declines in academic achievement, whereas those in high-achieving peer groups showed relatively better achievement outcomes. Similarly, students who 'hung out' with a group of friends who disliked school were likely to show decreases in their own enjoyment of school. In addition, the impact of the peer group extends to specific social behaviours that could influence interactions at school. Wentzel, Barry and Caldwell (2004) showed that 12 year olds whose friends displayed more pro-social behaviour (based on students' nominations of who is cooperative, sharing and helpful towards others) themselves became more pro-social over the following two years.

But what about those students who do not have any friends at all, or who experience significant peer victimisation and rejection at school? Wentzel, Barry and Caldwell's (2004) study showed that students without any friends displayed less pro-social behaviour, poorer achievement and poorer emotional wellbeing. There is also a considerable research literature suggesting that those students who have experienced problems with bullying at school could suffer a wide range of psychosocial problems as a consequence (e.g. Storch & Ledley, 2005). It is important to stress that these kinds of difficulties within the peer group can have a very negative impact on adjustment within the classroom context. One major longitudinal investigation that followed children from 5 to 12 years of age strongly indicated that peer rejection inhibits children's participation in normal classroom tasks and activities (Ladd, Herald-Brown & Reiser, 2008). However, it was not the case that peer rejection resulted in a permanent inability to engage in classroom learning activities; when the rejection by the peer group ceased, children became more able to participate. This underlines the importance of addressing students' social difficulties not only to improve their levels of wellbeing, but also to bring about positive opportunities to learn and achieve academically. Interestingly, work on anti-bullying interventions suggests that the solution for peer problems may often be found within the peer group itself: peer mentoring and other forms of peer support are increasingly being seen as an important part of schools' efforts to reduce bullying and victimisation (e.g. Naylor & Cowie, 1999; Smith & Watson, 2004).

20.3.3 Summary

This section has highlighted the need for psychologists to go beyond cognitive aspects of development in order to understand pupils' learning, achievement and behaviour at school. We have seen that these outcomes depend critically on pupils' motivations, which in turn relate to the goals they have, the beliefs and feelings they have about themselves, the way they explain the events that occur in their academic lives, and the values they attach to their academic work. Perhaps most importantly, psychologists have shown that all of these features are shaped in powerful ways by our social interactions with teachers, parents and peers.

20.4 BEHAVIOURAL, EMOTIONAL AND SOCIAL DIFFICULTIES IN THE CLASSROOM: AETIOLOGY AND INTERVENTION

The previous section highlighted the broad range of social–motivational processes that play a role in students' adjustment at school, and also showed that some students who have significant social difficulties are at risk of a wide range of both behavioural and academic problems. In this section, we briefly examine psychological research on a range of behavioural, emotional and social difficulties in children and young people in order to identify the causal factors involved and to consider the implications for how we can try to prevent or reduce such difficulties.

20.4.1 Nature and Aetiology of Behavioural, Emotional and Social Difficulties

We saw in Chapter 18 that a wide range of psychological disorders can fall under the umbrella heading of 'behavioural, emotional and social difficulties', and it is beyond the scope of this chapter to review all of these. However, it is possible to identify some key issues concerning the causal factors responsible for individual differences in students' behavioural, emotional and social functioning at school. One good example of a relevant theoretical framework is Dodge and Pettit's (2003) biopsychosocial model of conduct problems. According to this model, early social experiences combine with biological dispositions to put some children at risk of developing chronic problems in anti social behaviour. These risks can then lead to, and be amplified

by, a wide range of life experiences as well as cognitive and emotional processes that can make conduct problems even more likely (see Figure 20.3). The authors show how children growing up in severe socioeconomic disadvantage, and who have a temperamental disposition towards aggressive behaviour, are already at greater risk of developing conduct difficulties. This can then be exacerbated by physically harsh and cold parenting, and by the peer rejection that follows from the children's emerging behavioural problems. Importantly, these researchers have shown that the children also start to display distinctive ways of thinking about the social experiences and encounters they have. These biases in **social information processing** include features such as interpreting ambiguous events as reflecting hostility from others (e.g. tripping over someone's foot and thinking 'he tripped me on purpose') and over-estimating the success of aggressive responses in resolving a conflict. These kinds of cognitive processes make aggressive behaviours even more likely, and therefore are a key mechanism by which early risk factors lead to chronic behavioural problems.

> **social information processing** as used in models of psychological and interpersonal functioning, cognitive processes whereby events in the social world are encoded and interpreted, and possible responses are identified and evaluated.

Interestingly, exactly the same kind of model can be applied to understanding internalising disorders such as

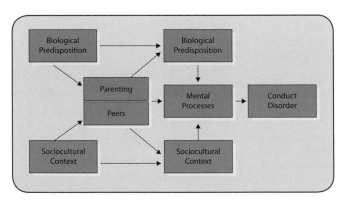

FIGURE 20.3 *Dodge and Pettit's (2003) biopsychosocial model of conduct problems.*

The biopsychosocial model of conduct problems shows the complex interweaving of influences that can give rise to behavioural problems in young people at school. Social factors (including parents and peers) can shape the way young people think about themselves and the world around them, which in turn has an impact on how they behave. These factors are also influenced by the wider sociocultural context (e.g. poverty) as well as by each individual's inherited predispositions (e.g. temperament).

Source: Dodge & Pettit (2003). Copyright ©2003 by the American Psychological Association.

anxiety and depression. For example, Banerjee (2008) has reviewed evidence showing that a combination of genetic predispositions and parenting factors can place children at greater risk of developing anxiety disorders. These risks in turn are carried forward by a number of cognitive characteristics – such as greater attention to negative social cues, overinterpretation of threats, and unrealistic and overly negative self-evaluation – which amplify the feelings of anxiety. Similar arguments have also been made about the development of depressive symptoms in children and young people (Dodge, 1993). Thus, a wide range of emotional and behavioural difficulties that become apparent within the school setting can be better understood through use of a theoretical framework that incorporates biological, social and cognitive dimensions.

20.4.2 Strategies for Preventing and Reducing Behavioural, Emotional and Social Difficulties

The psychological models discussed above make it clear that a range of factors are involved in the development of behavioural and emotional problems. Accordingly, a range of different approaches have been taken to the question of how best to prevent and reduce such problems in children and adolescents. However, of the many psychological therapies that could be used to address these difficulties, one approach – cognitive-behavioural therapy (CBT) – has gained a great deal of prominence in recent years. Reviews of this therapeutic approach, which focuses on the connections between cognitive, emotional and behavioural processes that maintain and exacerbate pathological difficulties, have shown that CBT is effective in addressing a wide range of difficulties, including internalising disorders such as anxiety and depression, as well as behavioural problems relating to aggression and attention difficulties (e.g. Butler *et al.*, 2006; Kendall, 1993). One line of important work has also begun to examine how direct work with parents can be integrated into CBT approaches in order to make the therapy even more effective for children (e.g. Barrett, Dadds & Rapee, 1996; Cobham, Dadds & Spence, 1998).

As well as playing a role in the identification and initial assessment of children who could benefit from this kind of individual therapy, educational psychologists often become involved in school-based strategies to prevent and reduce difficulties in whole groups or classes of children. For example, the Fast Track Project (see Focus Point 20.5) is a major intervention project designed to prevent anti social behaviour problems emerging in high-risk communities with low income and high crime levels. In line with the conceptual models regarding the aetiology of conduct problems, discussed in the previous section, this project involves a classroom curriculum to support all students' social and emotional understanding

FOCUS POINT 20.5   THE FAST TRACK PROJECT

The Fast Track Project is a major intervention designed to break into the negative cycle of influences that leads to anti social behaviour and other conduct problems in childhood and adolescence. The project began in the early 1990s with the identification of young children at high risk of developing conduct problems – children whose teachers and parents were reporting high levels of aggressive and disruptive behaviour. The project team introduced a comprehensive prevention programme including classroom work on social and emotional skills, tutoring and social skills training groups for the children, as well as home visits and parent-support activities. The project recruited 891 children, half of whom were randomly assigned to experience the intervention and half of whom were in a control group, and the developmental outcomes for these children were monitored through to the age of 16 years.

The research revealed various positive impacts of the prevention programme, including improvements in children's social-cognitive and academic skills, positive changes in family interactions and reduced aggressive behaviour. You can read more about this project at http://www.fasttrackproject.org, where you will also find a comprehensive list of all the research publications emanating from the study.

Discussion: How much of an impact can psychologists have in reducing anti social behaviour in young people? If you were a policy maker, what would you put in place in order to prevent the escalation of conduct problems in young children who are showing high levels of aggression?

and promote positive social information-processing skills, as well as work with parents to foster effective behaviour-management strategies and good home–school partnerships. The approach has been shown to have significant impacts on young people at highest risk of developing externalising problems (Bierman *et al.*, 2007). Other school-based programmes with a cognitive focus have also been found to be effective in the prevention of anxiety and depression disorders (e.g. Barrett *et al.*, 2006; Gillham *et al.*, 1995).

The success of these kinds of approaches for addressing a range of behavioural and emotional difficulties has encouraged the development of universal programmes to promote social and emotional learning in schools. The Social and Emotional Aspects of Learning programme in England, for example, is designed to help primary and secondary school students develop a wide range of skills relating to self-awareness, empathy, academic motivation and goal setting, behavioural and emotional self-regulation, and social problem-solving (DCSF, 2005, 2007). Thus, psychological insights into individual differences in students' behavioural, emotional and social adjustment have heavily influenced the kinds of intervention and prevention strategies introduced to support students at school.

20.4.3 Summary

An examination of behavioural, emotional and social difficulties provides a valuable opportunity to see how, in the course of children's development, various biological, social, cognitive and emotional processes interact with each other to produce individual differences in sociobehavioural and emotional adjustment at school. Therefore, most researchers are of the opinion that a multifaceted approach to intervention and prevention – taking into account social experiences in and out of school as well as patterns of cognition and information processing – is critical for preventing and intervening in the development of problem behaviour and emotional distress.

20.5   CHAPTER SUMMARY

This chapter has reviewed a range of developmental, motivational and social processes that play a role in pupils' learning, achievement and behaviour in school settings. Researchers have taken various approaches to the question of how children's cognition changes as they get older, and we have seen how these approaches can complement each other in helping us understand different aspects of pupils' learning in the classroom. But in order to gain a full understanding of pupils' school adjustment, we need to consider not just their cognitive development, but also their motivation with regard to learning and achievement at school. Pupils' motivation in turn is heavily influenced by social agents such as parents, peers and teachers. Studying the case of young people with behavioural, emotional and social difficulties encourages us to put all of these factors together in a coherent model, so that we can devise effective strategies for preventing the escalation of problem behaviour and emotional distress in children and young people at school.

SELF-TEST QUESTIONS

- What is the difference between assimilation and accommodation in Piaget's theory of cognitive development?
- What are the main features associated with Piaget's stages of cognitive development?
- How does the concept of scaffolding relate to Vygotsky's sociocultural theory of cognitive development?
- What is the zone of proximal development?
- What is the microgenetic method?
- Explain the overlapping waves metaphor for strategy change.
- What are the three fundamental needs emphasised in self-determination theory?
- What are some of the differences between mastery and performance goal orientations?
- How is the idea of a self-fulfilling prophecy related to the impact of teacher expectations?
- What are the differences between authoritative, authoritarian and permissive parenting styles?
- How is social comparison relevant to pupils at school?
- What is the biopsychosocial model of conduct problems?
- Why might cognitive-behavioural therapy be helpful for pupils with anxiety problems at school?

ESSAY QUESTIONS

- Critically evaluate the educational implications of Piagetian and/or Vygostskyan theories of cognitive development.
- How have information-processing approaches influenced our understanding of children's cognitive development?
- How does research on achievement goal orientation help us understand pupils' learning and behaviour in the classroom?
- What role do parents and/or peers have in shaping the achievement motivation of pupils at school?
- Critically evaluate the role of social information processing in the development of behavioural, emotional and social difficulties of pupils at school.

TEXTS FOR FURTHER READING

Donaldson, M. (1978) *Children's Minds*, London: Fontana.

Grusec, J.E. & Hastings, P.D. (eds) (2008) *Handbook of Socialisation: Theory and Research*, New York: Guilford Press.

Siegler, R.S. & Alibali, M.W. (2005) *Children's Thinking*, 4th edn, Upper Saddle River, NJ: Prentice-Hall.

Wigfield, A. & Eccles, J.S. (eds) (2002) *Development of Achievement Motivation*, San Diego, CA: Academic Press.

Wood, D. (1998) *How Children Think and Learn*, 2nd edn, Oxford: Blackwell.

RELEVANT JOURNAL ARTICLES

Assor, A., Kaplan, H. & Roth, G. (2002) Choice is good, but relevance is excellent: Autonomy-enhancing and suppressing teacher behaviours predicting students' engagement in schoolwork, *British Journal of Educational Psychology* 72(2): 261–78.

Bleeker, M.M. & Jacobs, J.E. (2004) Achievement in math and science: Do mothers' beliefs matter 12 years later? *Journal of Educational Psychology* 96(1): 97–109, doi:10.1037/0022-0663.96.1.97.

Dodge, K.A. (1993) Social-cognitive mechanisms in the development of conduct disorder and depression, *Annual Review of Psychology* 44: 559–84, doi:10.1146/annurev.ps.44.020193.003015

Doise, W., Mugny, G. & Perret-Clermont, A. (1975) Social interaction and the development of cognitive operations, *European Journal of Social Psychology* 5(3): 367–83, doi:10.1002/ejsp.2420050309.

Elliott, E.S. & Dweck, C.S. (1988) Goals: An approach to motivation and achievement, *Journal of Personality and Social Psychology* 54(1): 5–12, doi:10.1037/0022-3514.54.1.5.

King, A., Staffieri, A. & Adelgais, A. (1998) Mutual peer tutoring: Effects of structuring tutorial interaction to scaffold peer learning, *Journal of Educational Psychology* 90(1): 134–52, doi:10.1037/0022-0663.90.1.134.

Ladd, G.W., Herald-Brown, S.L. & Reiser, M. (2008) Does chronic classroom peer rejection predict the development of children's classroom participation during the grade school years? *Child Development* 79(4): 1001–15, doi:10.1111/j.1467-8624.2008.01172.x.

Lepper, M.R., Corpus, J.H. & Iyengar, S.S. (2005) Intrinsic and extrinsic motivational orientations in the classroom: Age differences and academic correlates, *Journal of Educational Psychology* 97(2): 184–96, doi:10.1037/0022-0663.97.2.184.

Parsons, J.E., Adler, T.F. & Kaczala, C.M. (1982) Socialization of achievement attitudes and beliefs: Parental influences, *Child Development* 53(2): 310–21, doi:10.2307/1128973.

Radziszewska, B. & Rogoff, B. (1991) Children's guided participation in planning imaginary errands with skilled adult or peer partners, *Developmental Psychology* 27(3): 381–9, doi:10.1037/0012-1649.27.3.381.

Ryan, R.M. & Deci, E.L. (2000) Self-determination theory and the facilitation of intrinsic motivation, social development, and well-being, *American Psychologist* 55(1): 68–78, doi:10.1037/0003-066X.55.1.68.

Siegler, R.S. (1987) The perils of averaging data over strategies: An example from children's addition, *Journal of Experimental Psychology: General* 116: 250–64.

Stipek, D.J. & Gralinski, J.H. (1991) Gender differences in children's achievement-related beliefs and emotional responses to success and failure in mathematics, *Journal of Educational Psychology* 83(3): 361–71, doi:10.1037/0022-0663.83.3.361.

Wentzel, K.R., Barry, C.M. & Caldwell, K.A. (2004) Friendships in middle school: Influences on motivation and school adjustment, *Journal of Educational Psychology* 96(2): 195–203, doi:10.1037/0022-0663.96.2.195.

Wood, D., Wood, H. & Middleton, D. (1978) An experimental evaluation of four face-to-face teaching strategies, *International Journal of Behavioral Development* 1(2): 131–47.

RELEVANT WEB LINKS

Collaborative for Academic, Social, and Emotional Learning (CASEL), http://www.casel.org

Department for Children, Schools and Families, website on behaviour, attendance and SEAL (social and emotional aspects of learning), http://nationalstrategies.standards.dcsf.gov.uk/inclusion/behaviourattendanceandseal

Jean Piaget Society: Society for the study of knowledge and development, http://www.piaget.org

University of Rochester website on self-determination theory, http://www.psych.rochester.edu/SDT

REFERENCES

Assor, A., Kaplan, H. & Roth, G. (2002) Choice is good, but relevance is excellent: Autonomy-enhancing and suppressing teacher behaviours predicting students' engagement in schoolwork, *British Journal of Educational Psychology* 72(2): 261–78, doi:10.1348/000709902158883.

Baillargeon, R. & DeVos, J. (1991) Object permanence in young infants: Further evidence, *Child Development* 62(6): 1227–46, doi:10.2307/1130803.

Bandura, A. (1977) Self-efficacy: Toward a unifying theory of behavioral change, *Psychological Review* 84(2): 191–215, doi:10.1037/0033-295X.84.2.191.

Bandura, A. & National Inst of Mental Health (1986) *Social Foundations of Thought and Action: A Social Cognitive Theory*, Englewood Cliffs, NJ: Prentice-Hall.

Banerjee, R. (2002) Audience effects on self-presentation in childhood, *Social Development* 11(4): 487–507, doi:10.1111/1467-9507.00212.

Banerjee, R. (2008) Social cognition and anxiety in children, in C. Sharp, P. Fonagy & I. Goodyer (eds) *Social Cognition and Developmental Psychopathology*, pp. 239–69, New York: Oxford University Press.

Barrett, P.M., Dadds, M.R. & Rapee, R.M. (1996) Family treatment of childhood anxiety: A controlled trial, *Journal of Consulting and Clinical Psychology* 64(2): 333–42, doi:10.1037/0022-006X.64.2.333.

Barrett, P.M., Farrell, L.J., Ollendick, T.H. & Dadds, M. (2006) Long-term outcomes of an Australian universal prevention trial of anxiety and depression symptoms in children and youth: An evaluation of the Friends program, *Journal of Clinical Child and Adolescent Psychology* 35(3): 403–11, doi:10.1207/s15374424jccp3503_5.

Baumrind, D. (1967) Child care practices anteceding three patterns of preschool behavior, *Genetic Psychology Monographs* 75: 43–88.

Bierman, K.L., Coie, J.D., Dodge, K.A. *et al.* (2007) Fast track randomized controlled trial to prevent externalizing psychiatric disorders: Findings from grades 3 to 9, *Journal of the American Academy of Child & Adolescent Psychiatry* 46(10): 1250–62, doi:10.1097/chi.0b013e31813e5d39.

Bleeker, M.M. & Jacobs, J.E. (2004) Achievement in math and science: Do mothers' beliefs matter 12 years later? *Journal of Educational Psychology* 96(1): 97–109, doi:10.1037/0022-0663.96.1.97.

Borke, H. (1975) Piaget's mountains revisited: Changes in the egocentric landscape, *Developmental Psychology* 11(2): 240–43, doi:10.1037/h0076459.

Bruner, J. (1960) *The Process of Education*, Cambridge, MA: Harvard University Press.

Butler, A.C., Chapman, J.E., Forman, E.M. & Beck, A.T. (2006) The empirical status of cognitive-behavioral therapy: A review of meta-analyses, *Clinical Psychology Review* 26(1): 17–31, doi:10.1016/j.cpr.2005.07.003.

Case, R. (1985) *Intellectual Development: A Systematic Reinterpretation*, New York: Academic Press.

Chen, C. & Stevenson, H.W. (1995) Motivation and mathematics achievement: A comparative study of Asian-American, Caucasian-American, and East Asian high school students, *Child Development* 66(4): 1215–34, doi:10.2307/1131808.

Chi, M.T.H. (1978) Knowledge structures and memory development, in R.S. Siegler (ed.) *Children's Thinking: What develops?*, pp. 73–96, Hillsdale, NJ: Lawrence Erlbaum Associates.

Cobham, V.E., Dadds, M.R. & Spence, S.H. (1998) The role of parental anxiety in the treatment of childhood anxiety, *Journal of Consulting and Clinical Psychology* 66(6): 893–905, doi:10.1037/0022-006X.66.6.893.

Deci, E.L., Koestner, R. & Ryan, R.M. (1999) A meta-analytic review of experiments examining the effects of extrinsic rewards on intrinsic motivation, *Psychological Bulletin* 125(6): 627–68, doi:10.1037/0033-2909.125.6.627.

Department for Children, Schools and Families (2005) *Primary National Strategy, Social and Emotional Aspects of Learning: Guidance*, Nottingham: DfES Publications.

Department for Children, Schools and Families (2007) *Secondary National Strategy, Social and Emotional Aspects of Learning for Secondary Schools: Guidance Booklet*, Nottingham: DfES Publications.

Diener, C.I. & Dweck, C.S. (1978) An analysis of learned helplessness: Continuous changes in performance, strategy, and achievement cognitions following failure, *Journal of Personality and Social Psychology* 36(5): 451–62, doi:10.1037/0022-3514.36.5.451.

Dodge, K.A. (1993) Social-cognitive mechanisms in the development of conduct disorder and depression, *Annual Review of Psychology* 44: 559–84, doi:10.1146/annurev.ps.44.020193.003015.

Dodge, K.A. & Pettit, G.S. (2003) A biopsychosocial model of the development of chronic conduct problems in adolescence, *Developmental Psychology. Special Issue: Violent Children* 39(2): 349–71, doi:10.1037/0012-1649.39.2.349.

Doise, W., Mugny, G. & Perret-Clermont, A. (1975) Social interaction and the development of cognitive operations, *European Journal of Social Psychology* 5(3): 367–83, doi:10.1002/ejsp.2420050309.

Donaldson, M. (1978) *Children's Minds*, London: Fontana.

Eccles, J.S. & Wigfield, A. (2002) Motivational beliefs, values, and goals, *Annual Review of Psychology* 53: 109–32.

Eccles. J.S. & Roeser, R.W. (2005) School and community influences on human development, in M.H. Bornstein & M.E. Lamb (eds) *Developmental Psychology: An Advanced Textbook*, 5th edn, pp. 513–56, Hillsdale, NJ: Lawrence Erlbaum Associates.

Eccles-Parsons, J., Adler, T.F., Futterman, R. *et al.* (1983) Expectancies, values, and academic behaviors, in J.T. Spence (ed.) *Achievement and Achievement Motivation*, pp. 75–146, San Francisco, CA: Freeman.

Elliot, A.J. & Church, M.A. (1997) A hierarchical model of approach and avoidance achievement motivation, *Journal of Personality and Social Psychology* 72: 218–32.

Elliott, E.S. & Dweck, C.S. (1988) Goals: An approach to motivation and achievement, *Journal of Personality and Social Psychology* 54(1): 5–12, doi:10.1037/0022-3514.54.1.5.

Festinger, L. (1954) A theory of social comparison processes, *Human Relations* 7: 117–40.

Gauvain, M. (2001) *The Social Context of Cognitive Development*, New York: Guilford Press.

Gelman, R. & Baillargeon, R. (1983) A review of some Piagetian concepts, in J. Flavell, E.M. Markman & P.H. Mussen (eds) *Handbook of Child Psychology: Vol. 3. Cognitive Development*, pp. 167–230, New York: John Wiley & Sons, Inc.

Gillham, J.E., Reivich, K.J., Jaycox, L.H. & Seligman, M.E.P. (1995) Prevention of depressive symptoms in schoolchildren: Two-year follow-up, *Psychological Science* 6(6): 343–51, doi:10.1111/j.1467-9280.1995.tb00524.x.

Grolnick, W.S. & Ryan, R.M. (1989) Parent styles associated with children's self-regulation and competence in school, *Journal of Educational Psychology* 81(2): 143–54, doi:10.1037/0022-0663.81.2.143.

Harris, M.J. & Rosenthal, R. (1985) Mediation of interpersonal expectancy effects: 31 meta-analyses, *Psychological Bulletin* 97(3): 363–86, doi:10.1037/0033-2909.97.3.363.

Harter, S. (1981) A new self-report scale of intrinsic versus extrinsic orientation in the classroom: Motivational and informational components, *Developmental Psychology* 17(3): 300–12, doi:10.1037/0012-1649.17.3.300.

Juvonen, J. & Murdock, T.B. (1995) Grade-level differences in the social value of effort: Implications for self-presentation tactics of early adolescents, *Child Development* 66(6): 1694–705, doi:10.2307/1131904.

Kaplan, A., Gheen, M. & Midgley, C. (2002) Classroom goal structure and student disruptive behaviour, *British Journal of Educational Psychology* 72(2): 191–212, doi:10.1348/000709902158847.

Kendall, P.C. (1993) Cognitive-behavioral therapies with youth: Guiding theory, current status, and emerging developments, *Journal of Consulting and Clinical Psychology* 61(2): 235–47, doi:10.1037/0022-006X.61.2.235.

King, A., Staffieri, A. & Adelgais, A. (1998) Mutual peer tutoring: Effects of structuring tutorial interaction to scaffold peer learning, *Journal of Educational Psychology* 90(1): 134–52, doi:10.1037/0022-0663.90.1.134.

Klahr, D. (1992) Information-processing approaches to cognitive development, in M.H. Bornstein & M.E. Lamb (eds) *Developmental Psychology: An Advanced Textbook*, 4th edn, pp. 273–336, Hillsdale, NJ: Lawrence Erlbaum Associates.

Ladd, G.W., Herald-Brown, S.L. & Reiser, M. (2008) Does chronic classroom peer rejection predict the development of children's classroom participation during the grade school years? *Child Development* 79(4): 1001–15, doi:10.1111/j.1467-8624.2008.01172.x.

Lepper, M.R., Corpus, J.H. & Iyengar, S.S. (2005) Intrinsic and extrinsic motivational orientations in the classroom: Age differences and academic correlates, *Journal of Educational Psychology* 97(2): 184–96, doi:10.1037/0022-0663.97.2.184.

Lepper, M.R., Greene, D. & Nisbett, R.E. (1973) Undermining children's intrinsic interest with extrinsic reward: A test of the 'overjustification' hypothesis, *Journal of Personality and Social Psychology* 28(1): 129–37, doi:10.1037/h0035519.

Love, J.M., Kisker, E.E., Ross, C. *et al.* (2005) The effectiveness of early head start for 3-year-old children and their parents: Lessons for policy and programs, *Developmental Psychology* 41(6): 885–901, doi:10.1037/0012-1649.41.6.885.

Luria, A.R. (1979) *The making of mind: A personal account of Soviet psychology*. Cambridge, MA: Harvard University Press.

Marsh, H.W. & Hau, K. (2003) Big-Fish-Little-Pond Effect on academic self-concept: A cross-cultural (26-country) test of the negative effects of academically selsective schools, *American Psychologist* 58(5): 364–76.

McKown, C. & Weinstein, R.S. (2008) Teacher expectations, classroom context, and the achievement gap, *Journal of School Psychology* 46(3): 235–61, doi:10.1016/j.jsp.2007.05.001.

Melhuish, E., Belsky, J., Leyland, A. & Barnes, J. (2008) Effects of fully-established Sure Start local programmes on 3-year-old children and their families living in England: A quasi-experimental observational study, *The Lancet* 372(9650): 1641–7, doi:10.1016/S0140-6736(08)61687-6.

Mueller, C.M. & Dweck, C.S. (1998) Praise for intelligence can undermine children's motivation and performance, *Journal of Personality and Social Psychology* 75(1): 33–52, doi:10.1037/0022-3514.75.1.33.

Naylor, P. & Cowie, H. (1999) The effectiveness of peer support systems in challenging school bullying: The perspectives and experiences of teachers and pupils, *Journal of Adolescence* 22(4): 467–79, doi:10.1006/jado.1999.0241.

Parsons, J.E., Adler, T.F. & Kaczala, C.M. (1982) Socialization of achievement attitudes and beliefs: Parental influences, *Child Development* 53(2): 310–21, doi:10.2307/1128973.

Patrick, E. & Abravanel, E. (2000) The self-regulatory nature of preschool children's private speech in a naturalistic setting, *Applied Psycholinguistics* 21(1): 45–61, doi:10.1017/S014271640000103X.

Piaget, J. (1950) *The Psychology of Intelligence*, London: Routledge & Kegan Paul.

Piaget, J. (1970) Piaget's theory, in P. Mussen (ed.) *Carmichael's Manual of Child Psychology*, pp. 703–32, New York: John Wiley & Sons, Inc.

Plowden Report (1967) *Children and Their Primary Schools: A Report of the Central Advisory Council for Education (England)*, London: Her Majesty's Stationery Office.

Radziszewska, B. & Rogoff, B. (1991) Children's guided participation in planning imaginary errands with skilled adult or peer partners, *Developmental Psychology* 27(3): 381–9, doi:10.1037/0012-1649.27.3.381.

Reuman, D.A. (1989) How social comparison mediates the relation between ability-grouping practices and students' achievement expectancies in mathematics, *Journal of Educational Psychology* 81(2): 178–89, doi:10.1037/0022-0663.81.2.178.

Rosenthal, R. & Jacobson, L. (1966) Teachers' expectancies: Determinants of pupils' IQ gains, *Psychological Reports* 19(1): 115–18.

Rothbaum, F. & Trommsdorff, G. (2007) Do roots and wings complement or oppose one another? The socialization of relatedness and autonomy in cultural context, in J.E. Grusec & P.D. Hastings (eds) *Handbook of Socialization: Theory and Research*, pp. 461–89, New York: Guilford Press.

Rubie-Davies, C.M. (2007) Classroom interactions: Exploring the practices of high- and low-expectation teachers, *British Journal of Educational Psychology* 77(2): 289–306, doi:10.1348/000709906X101601.

Ruble, D.N., Boggiano, A.K., Feldman, N.S. & Loebl, J.H. (1980) Developmental analysis of the role of social comparison in self-evaluation, *Developmental Psychology* 16(2): 105–15, doi:10.1037/0012-1649.16.2.105.

Ryan, A.M. (2001) The peer group as a context for the development of young adolescent motivation and achievement, *Child Development* 72(4): 1135–50, doi:10.1111/1467-8624.00338.

Ryan, R.M. & Deci, E.L. (2000) Self-determination theory and the facilitation of intrinsic motivation, social development, and well-being, *American Psychologist* 55(1): 68–78, doi:10.1037/0003-066X.55.1.68.

Siegler, R.S. (1987) The perils of averaging data over strategies: An example from children's addition, *Journal of Experimental Psychology: General* 116: 250–64.

Siegler, R.S. (2005) Children's learning, *American Psychologist* 60(8): 769–78, doi:10.1037/0003-066X.60.8.769.

Siegler, R.S. & Alibali, M.W. (2005) *Children's Thinking*, 4th edn, Upper Saddle River, NJ: Prentice-Hall.

Siegler, R.S. & Crowley, K. (1991) The microgenetic method: A direct means for studying cognitive development, *American Psychologist* 46(6): 606–20, doi:10.1037/0003-066X.46.6.606.

Skinner, E.A. & Belmont, M.J. (1993) Motivation in the classroom: Reciprocal effects of teacher behavior and student engagement across the school year, *Journal of Educational Psychology* 85(4): 571–81, doi:10.1037/0022-0663.85.4.571.

Smith, P.K. & Watson, D. (2004) *An Evaluation of the ChildLine in Partnership with Schools (CHIPS) Programme. Department for Education and Skills Research Report RR570*, Nottingham: DfES Publications.

Stipek, D.J. & Gralinski, J.H. (1991) Gender differences in children's achievement-related beliefs and emotional responses to success and failure in mathematics, *Journal of Educational Psychology* 83(3): 361–71, doi:10.1037/0022-0663.83.3.361.

Storch, E.A. & Ledley, D.R. (2005) Peer victimization and psychosocial adjustment in children: Current knowledge and future directions, *Clinical Pediatrics* 44(1): 29–38, doi:10.1177/000992280504400103.

Urdan, T.C. & Maehr, M.L. (1995) Beyond a two-goal theory of motivation and achievement: A case for social goals, *Review of Educational Research* 65(3): 213–43, doi:10.2307/1170683.

Vallerand, R.J., Fortier, M.S. & Guay, F. (1997) Self-determination and persistence in a real-life setting: Toward a motivational model of high school dropout, *Journal of Personality and Social Psychology* 72(5): 1161–76, doi:10.1037/0022-3514.72.5.1161.

Vygotsky, L.S. (1978) *Mind in Society: The Development of Higher Mental Processes*, Cambridge, MA: Harvard University Press.

Weiner, B. (1985) An attributional theory of achievement motivation and emotion, *Psychological Review* 92(4): 548–73.

Wentzel, K.R. (1996) Social goals and social relationships as motivators of school adjustment, in J. Juvonen & K.R. Wentzel (eds) *Social Motivation: Understanding Children's School Adjustment*, pp. 226–47, New York: Cambridge University Press.

Wentzel, K.R., Barry, C.M. & Caldwell, K.A. (2004) Friendships in middle school: Influences on motivation and school adjustment, *Journal of Educational Psychology* 96(2): 195–203, doi:10.1037/0022-0663.96.2.195.

Wigfield, A. & Eccles, J.S. (2002) The development of competence beliefs, expectancies for success, and achievement values from childhood through adolescence, in A. Wigfield & J. S. Eccles (eds) *Development of Achievement Motivation*, pp. 91–120, San Diego, CA: Academic Press.

Wigfield, A., Eccles, J.S., Schiefele, U. Roeser, R.W. & Davis-Kean, P. (2006) Development of achievement motivation, in N. Eisenberg, W. Damon & R.M. Lerner (eds) *Handbook of Child Psychology: Vol. 3. Social, Emotional, and Personality Development*, 6th edn, pp. 933–1002, Hoboken, NJ: John Wiley & Sons, Inc.

Wood, D., Wood, H. & Middleton, D. (1978) An experimental evaluation of four face-to-face teaching strategies, *International Journal of Behavioral Development* 1(2): 131–47.

21 Educational Psychology: Professional Issues

JIM BOYLE

LEARNING OUTCOMES

WHEN YOU HAVE COMPLETED THIS CHAPTER, YOU SHOULD BE ABLE TO:

1. Describe the roles and remits of educational psychologists (EPs) and the structure of EP services in the United Kingdom.
2. Contrast the traditional 'medical model' approach to problems with ecological and social constructionist approaches.
3. Understand the importance of multi-agency working.
4. Describe the structure of EP training in the United Kingdom.
5. Demonstrate awareness of future challenges for the practice of educational psychology in the United Kingdom.

KEY WORDS

Applied Problem-Analysis Frameworks ● Common Assessment Framework (CAF) ● Ecological Approaches ● Every Child Matters ● Multi-Agency Working ● Organisational Change ● Reconstruction ● Social Constructivism ● Systems Theory ● Within-Child Deficits

CHAPTER OUTLINE

FOCUS POINT 21.2   EDUCATIONAL PSYCHOLOGY IN THE NEWS

THE WEST DUNBARTONSHIRE LITERACY INITIATIVE

The West Dunbartonshire Literacy Initiative was a 10-year authority-wide programme aimed at raising the literacy attainments of all children in the authority. The initiative achieved some remarkable outcomes, reducing the levels of marked reading difficulties from 20% to 3% in the authority as a whole over the 10-year period, which attracted considerable media interest, for example:

- http://www.guardian.co.uk/education/2007/jul/10/schools.primaryeducation
- http://www.dyslexia-teacher.com/t152.html
- http://www.independent.co.uk/student/career-planning/getting-job/one-mans-quest-to-eradicate-illiteracy-439238.html

Dr Tommy Mackay, the educational psychologist who directed the initiative, appeared on television programmes and was the subject of a chapter in a book by former Prime Minister Gordon Brown (*Britain's Everyday Heroes*, London: Mainstream Books, 2007). He was also awarded the British Psychological Society's Award for Distinguished Contributions to Professional Psychology in 2007. The text of his award lecture describes the literacy initiative and also the possibilities of educational psychology and psychology more generally: see http://www.thepsychologist.org.uk/archive/archive_home.cfm/volumeID_21-editionID_166-ArticleID_1427-getfile_getPDF/thepsychologist/1108mack.pdf.

FOCUS POINT 21.3   THE KEY FEATURES OF EP PRACTICE

There have been recent attempts to capture the key features of EP practice and to examine how these might differ from the contributions of clinical psychologists and other applied psychologists on the one hand, and from specialist teachers and social workers with additional training in psychology on the other (Cameron, 2006; Gersch, 2004).

Dr Brahm Norwich, Professor of Educational Psychology and Special Educational Needs at the University of Exeter,

argues that EPs may not have distinctive skills *per se*, and that much of their work could be carried out by suitably trained advisory and support teachers (Norwich, 2005). However, he points out that EPs can make important, even if not unique, professional contributions through links with academic psychologists and educational researchers, which inform the application of psychological theory and research, and also links with professional groups and policy makers.

psychologists should capitalise on their complementary skills and effective joint working practices.

The ECM agenda – with its shift away from traditional statutory assessments linked to SEN to the promotion of mental health and quality of life and the facilitation of learning and achievement – brings with it opportunities for educational psychology to have an impact on all pupils, not just those with SEN/additional support needs, in a way that was not possible in the past. Further, the reduction in time spent on statutory assessments may yield more time for research and training, which are

highly valued by schools (Boyle & MacKay, 2007), and also more time for community-based work with parents and carers.

The future of educational psychology in the United Kingdom may thus hinge on the quality of the evidence base for EPs' service delivery, the strength of collaborations with other professionals and parents, and the quality of training and staff development for EPs. But in addition, new legislation will shape the scope and formal requirements of future EP practice and it is thus important that EPs should have a voice in legislative change.

SELF-TEST QUESTIONS

- What social factors make an important contribution to an understanding of learning difficulties and behaviour problems?
- Why are theories of organisational change important for EPs?
- Describe examples of applied problem-analysis frameworks used by EPs.
- Describe the five outcomes of the Every Child Matters legislation.
- Why is good communication with other professionals an important part of multi-agency working?
- What core modules are central to the training of EPs in the UK?
- How important is work with parents?

ESSAY QUESTIONS

- Critically evaluate the impact of Every Child Matters legislation (or its policy counterparts) on the delivery of educational psychology services.
- How might EPs demonstrate a distinctive, 'psychological' contribution to multi-agency working?
- To what extent might the practice of EPs be held to be 'value free'?
- How important is it for EPs to have a strong evidence-base for their professional practice?

TEXTS FOR FURTHER READING

Edwards, A., Daniels, H., Gallagher, T., Leadbetter, J. & Warmington, P. (2009) *Improving Inter-Professional Collaborations: Multi-Agency Working for Children's Wellbeing*, London: Routledge.
Kelly, B., Woolfson, L. & Boyle, J. (2008) *Frameworks for Practice in Educational Psychology*. London: Jessica Kingsley.

RELEVANT JOURNAL ARTICLES

Cameron, R.J. (2006) Educational psychology: The distinctive contribution, *Educational Psychology in Practice* 22(4): 289–304.
Mackay, T. (2008) Can psychology change the world? *The Psychologist* 21(11): 928–31.
Norwich, B. (2005) Future directions for professional school psychology, *School Psychology International* 26(4): 387–97.

RELEVANT WEB LINKS

Association of Commonwealth Universities, www.acu.ac.uk
LGJobs.com, www.lgjobs.com
British Psychological Society Code of Ethics and Conduct, http://www.bps.org.uk/document-download-area/document-download$ .cfm?restart=true&file_uuid=E6917759-9799-434A-F313-9C35698E1864
Children's Workforce Development Council, http://www.cwdcouncil.co.uk/educational-psychology

Educational Psychology (Scotland), http://www.bps.org.uk/careers/society_qual/educational-psychology-scotland.cfm

Health Professions Council Standards of Conduct, Performance and Ethics, http://www.hpc-uk.org/aboutregistration/standards/standardsofconductperformanceandethics

REFERENCES

APA Presidential Task Force on Evidence-Based Practice (2006) Evidence-based practice in psychology, *American Psychologist* May–June: 271–85.

Association of Educational Psychologists (2008) *Educational Psychologists in Multi-Disciplinary Settings: Investigations into the work of Educational Psychologists in Children's Services Authorities*, Durham: Association of Educational Psychologists.

Bowen, S. & Zwi, A.B. (2005) Pathways to 'evidence-informed' policy and practice: A framework for action, *PLoS Medicine* 2(7), e166. doi:10.1371/journal.pmed.0020166.

Boyle, J. & Mackay, T. (2007) Evidence for the efficacy of systemic models of practice from a cross-sectional survey of schools' satisfaction with their educational psychologists, *Educational Psychology in Practice* 23(1): 19–31.

Boyle, J., Mackay, T. & Lauchlan, F. (2008) The legislative context and shared practice models, in B. Kelly, L. Woolfson & J. Boyle (eds) *Frameworks for Practice in Educational Psychology*, pp. 33–51, London: Jessica Kingsley.

British Psychological Society (2009) *Code of Conduct and Ethics*, Leicester: British Psychological Society.

Cameron, R.J. (2006) Educational psychology: The distinctive contribution, *Educational Psychology in Practice* 22(4): 289–304.

Children's Workforce Development Council (2008) *Postgraduate Courses in Educational Psychology, Handbook 2008*, Leeds: CWDC.

Department for Education and Employment (2000) *Educational Psychology Services (England): Current Role, Good Practice and Future Directions. Report of the Working Group*, London: HMSO.

Department for Education and Skills (2004) *Every Child Matters: Change for Children*, London: HMSO.

Edwards, A., Daniels, H., Gallagher, T., Leadbetter, J. & Warmington, P. (2009) *Improving Inter-Professional Collaborations: Multi-Agency Working for Children's Wellbeing*, London: Routledge.

Farrell, P., Woods, K., Lewis, S., Rooney, S., Squires, G. & O'Connor, M. (2006) *A Review of the Functions and Contributions of Educational Psychologists in England and Wales in Light of 'Every Child Matters: Change for Children'*, London: DfES Publications.

Gameson, J. & Rhydderch, G. (2008) The Constructionist Model of Informed and Reasoned Action (COMOIRA), in B. Kelly, L. Woolfson & J. Boyle (eds) *Frameworks for Practice in Educational Psychology*, pp. 94–120, London: Jessica Kingsley.

Gersch, I. (2004) Educational psychology in an age of uncertainty, *The Psychologist*, 17(3): 142–5.

Gillam, B. (1978) *Reconstructing Educational Psychology*. London: Croom Helm.

Health Professions Council (2008) *Standards of Conduct, Performance and Ethics*, London: HPC.

Health Professions Council (2009) *Standards of Proficiency for Practitioner Psychologists*, London: HPC, http://www.hpc-uk.org/assets/documents/10002963SOP_Practitioner_psychologists.pdf, accessed November 2010.

Her Majesty's Inspectors of Education (2007) *Quality Management in Local Authority Educational Psychology Services: Self-Evaluation for Quality Improvement*, Livingston: HMIE.

Kelly, B., Woolfson, L. & Boyle, J. (2008) *Frameworks for Practice in Educational Psychology*, London: Jessica Kingsley.

Lindsay, G. (2008) Ethics and value systems, in B. Kelly, L. Woolfson & J. Boyle (eds) *Frameworks for Practice in Educational Psychology*, pp. 52–66, London: Jessica Kingsley.

Monsen, J. & Frederickson, N. (2008) The Monsen *et al.* problem-solving model ten years on, in B. Kelly, L. Woolfson & J. Boyle (eds) *Frameworks for Practice in Educational Psychology*, pp. 69–93, London: Jessica Kingsley.

Norwich, B. (2005) Future directions for professional school psychology, *School Psychology International* 26(4): 387–97.

Rees, I. (2008) A systemic solution-oriented model, in B. Kelly, L. Woolfson & J. Boyle (eds) *Frameworks for Practice in Educational Psychology*, pp. 162–82, London: Jessica Kingsley.

Scottish Executive (2001) *For Scotland's Children: Better Integrated Children's Services*, Edinburgh: HMSO.

Scottish Executive (2002) *Review of Provision of Educational Psychology Services in Scotland* (The Currie Report), Edinburgh: HMSO.

Scottish Government (2008) *The Guide to 'Getting it Right for Every Child'*, Edinburgh: Scottish Government.

Wagner, P. (2008) Consultation as a framework for practice, in B. Kelly, L. Woolfson & J. Boyle (eds) *Frameworks for Practice in Educational Psychology*, pp. 139–61, London: Jessica Kingsley.

Woolfson, L. (2008) The Woolfson *et al.* Integrated Framework: An executive framework for service-wide delivery, in B. Kelly, L. Woolfson & J. Boyle (eds) *Frameworks for Practice in Educational Psychology*, pp. 121–36, London: Jessica Kingsley.

Part V
Occupational Psychology

22 Occupational Psychology in Practice – The Individual

ALMUTH McDOWALL, ADRIAN BANKS & LYNNE MILLWARD

LEARNING OUTCOMES

WHEN YOU HAVE COMPLETED THIS CHAPTER YOU SHOULD BE ABLE TO:

1. Understand employed life as an employment life cycle.
2. Describe and evaluate different paradigms on selection and relevant research.
3. Describe the basic principles of managing performance.
4. Describe what training is in the context of work.
5. Describe feedback-based activities such as coaching and counselling.
6. Describe and evaluate critical stages in the employment life cycle such as retirement or stress-related absence.
7. Describe and evaluate contemporary concepts such as work–life balance.

KEY WORDS

Coaching • Constructivist Perspective • Counselling • Employee Life Cycle • Employment • Feedback • Performance Appraisal • Predictivist Perspective • Recruitment • Redundancy • Retirement • Selection • Training • Unemployment

CHAPTER OUTLINE

ROUTE MAP OF THE CHAPTER

This chapter will introduce you to applied psychology in the workplace from the individual's perspective. First, we will outline some of the key issues and challenges in the contemporary world of work. Then, we will use the image of the employee life cycle to show how individuals go through different stages when working with a particular employer. This allows us to address key issues, such as what happens when an individual joins an organisation, in the light of practical issues as well as some underpinning psychological theory. We will cover established tools and techniques, such as psychometrics and meta-analytic evidence, and also contemporary issues and concepts such as work–life balance.

Rather confusingly, psychology as applied to the world of work has many different names, depending on what country you work in and what the focus of your work is. In the United Kingdom, the term *occupational psychology* is used and is the official title that is now protected by law. However, the term 'organisational psychology' is also used, in particular where this field is taught within a business school rather than a psychology department. In other countries in Europe, people use the term *work psychology*, whereas in the United States our profession is called *industrial and organisational psychology*, or *I/O psychology* for short.

So what do occupational psychologists actually do? In short, we apply the science and theory of the mind to the world of work. By and large we tend to think of work as paid **employment**. Recently researchers and practitioners have increasingly broadened their interested to the interface between work and nonwork, as work may also be undertaken in the home, and of course we need adequate recovery and respite from our day-to-day demands. Occupational psychologists may specialise in different areas, such as assessment and **selection** or coaching. Underpinning our practice are the eight knowledge areas (such as **training** or employee relations and motivation), which we describe in Chapter 26 and which underpin the whole of Part Five. We describe many applied examples of occupational psychology in the following chapters, such as using validated assessments to help employers select the right people, train and develop employees and understand how leadership behaviours have an impact on others. Our first two chapters focus on occupational psychology in practice, outlining underpinning theories at appropriate points.

employment work, occupation (usually paid).

selection a systematic process of choosing employees, usually in the context of hiring, but also for promotion for instance.

training in organisational settings, increasing one's learning and developing one's skills, usually in a formal, relatively structured manner.

22.1 INTRODUCTION

While work is commonly understood as an activity to generate income (Oxford English Dictionary, 2009), all of us work in some way or another, whether this is paid or unpaid, inside the home or outside the home. There is also no doubt that being in work is good for us. A now classic study by Marie Jahoda and colleagues (recently republished as Jahoda, Lazarsfeld & Zeisel, 2002) showed the effects of **unemployment** on a small community in Austria. The findings led the researchers to conclude that work is central to our identity and sense of worth and thus vital in modern-day industrial societies. Jahoda went on to develop the deprivation theory of unemployment (1981), identifying five different categories important for wellbeing, such as structure, time and social contact. She argued that the unemployed are deprived of these, which she claimed accounts for reported impaired physical and mental health in unemployed people. Work is evidently central to our lives, as one of the first questions that we are typically asked when meeting new people is 'So what do you do?'

unemployment being out of paid work.

That notwithstanding, we need to examine whether it is always true that work is good for us, as work has fundamentally changed over the last few decades. We are beginning to understand some of these changes, such as the influx of women into the workplace (Davidson & Cooper, 1993) and striving for equal opportunities. The content of work has also changed, moving away from manual tasks and structured roles and responsibilities to a service- and customer-oriented focus in many things we do (Patterson, 2001). We are also more likely to work in teams, and work on specific projects for a specified period. The physical place where we work may not be a static one either, as many organisations use hot desking to encourage fluid and flexible working styles (Millward, Haslam & Postmes, 2007). Workers may also communicate and/or work remotely, made possible through the advent of mobile technology, where it would be quite possible to see a project through to completion without ever having met other team members in person. In addition, it has long been argued that a solid 'job for life' is no more, as stability has been replaced by flexibility, self-reliance and adaptability (Hiltrop, 1995). Organisations are also undergoing transformations: following trends such as diversifying and downsizing, many organisations are now merging into larger corporations. Plus, the world is now a global marketplace where economic interdependence is one of the hallmarks of our time, manifest at the time of writing in the current global recession, a phenomenon never seen before at such a scale.

Therefore, individuals and organisations are now part of a world of work where the only constant is change. This chapter and Chapter 23 will outline on a practical level how we can understand the world of work first from the individual's and then from the organisation's perspective. Chapters 24 and 25 will build on these two contrasting accounts by outlining the theoretical perspective, whereas Chapter 25 will outline the professional issues associated with doing research and practice in organisational contexts.

22.2   THE EMPLOYEE LIFE CYCLE

As we have already discussed, change and uncertainty are now part of life in most organisations and it has become a human resource challenge to try to help individuals and organisations adapt to this (Hiltrop, 1995; Wright & Snell, 1998). There are some aspects where existing research can offer clear guidance, for instance when we think about the best tools for selecting an individual, but there are other aspects of work where research evidence lags behind. For example, we know that during the recent recession men were more likely to become unemployed than women in the United Kingdom (Eurostat, 2009) and workers were asked to take 'time out' from their paid jobs rather than losing them altogether, or to work reduced hours. While we observed these developments in practice, little is known about the psychological processes and outcomes involved.

One way of getting a handle on the complexities of employed life is by taking a cyclical timespan perspective depicting the employment life cycle. This is a popular model that is frequently used as an analogy in HR research and practice (e.g. CIPD, 2009) by mapping out different stages in employment onto a life cycle, as shown in Figure 22.1.

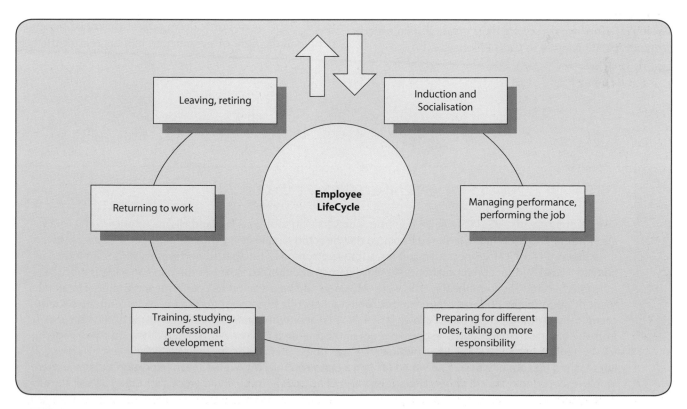

FIGURE 22.1 *The employee life cycle.*

The cycle shows how any one individual might progress through a job. First, the individual enters the job, being attracted and then selected into a particular role. There are of course logistic issues to go with this, such as learning about how things work in this particular organisation – induction – and getting used to the people you are working with – socialisation. From the day the job has started, there is a need to manage performance, as the organisation needs to know to what extent the employee can fulfil the given tasks to the required standards, and take appropriate action if this is not the case. Employees might move into a different role after a while, for instance take on more management responsibility, and might need to be prepared for such transitions. Professional study and development are also important, as there are few roles where workers and organisations can afford not to update skills. The **employee life cycle** might be interrupted at certain stages, for instance when workers become sick and/or are absent due to maternity or paternity leave. It is important to manage the return to work very carefully to ensure that people can integrate back into the organisation in a successful way. Finally, there will be the day when any job ends, whether this is out of choice or not.

employee life cycle a concept showing how individuals go through different stages when working with a particular employer

The following section will take you through the employment life cycle stage by stage by connecting it to key areas of research and practice in occupational psychology. Before we do so, we have given you an excerpt from a typical life cycle in Case History 22.1.

22.3 ENTERING THE LIFE CYCLE AND INDUCTION

Way before an employee enters an organisation, a whole host of processes has already taken place. First, the employee will have made decisions about why to apply for this job. For many job entrants, some of these thought processes will have been around career choices, deciding what they want to do and in what context. Other decision factors might be more mundane and to do with lifestyle choices, as there are times when any of us might have to take on a job that we don't particularly enjoy or want because we need the money. Considerable emphasis in practice and research has been on selecting and recruiting the right people. Consider Case History 22.2.

Francesca's experience mirrors that of many people in the current workplace. There is often a decision to be made between finding something that really interests you and something that pays well. It also shows that performance appraisal is not easy, as setting hard targets might be motivating but can have an impact on wellbeing. Finally, she has just experienced what seems to be a rather unstructured way of screening new employees, which is also a prevalent issue. It is to **recruitment** and selection that we now turn.

recruitment hiring people for work.

The first stage of the life cycle is absolutely crucial to get right, as not only do organisations need to screen people in the light of evidence to help us recruit the best

OKE – AN EXAMPLE OF AN EMPLOYEE LIFE CYCLE

Oke graduated with a BSc in Media Studies from a university in southeast England. His main concern after graduation was to find a job that was based locally so that he could remain living with his girlfriend. He saw an advert for a job as a technical support manager for a software company. He applied and was called for an interview, and did a weekly induction programme where he learned about his company [induction and socialisation]. Very quickly, it became apparent that his skills were very good, and based on his last performance appraisal [management of performance] he was offered and accepted a new role in account management, looking after a large client [moved into different role]. Following that, his management capability was recognised and with support from the organisation through a leadership programme [training], he is now managing others. Two years ago, he took extended paternity leave when his first child was born [interruption to the cycle]. Last week, his company approached him about whether he would take on a European role. This would mean relocation to Spain, where employment conditions are rather different (see also Chapter 26), so you could argue that the cycle will start all over again!

FRANCESA

Having completed a degree in fine arts, Francesca worked as a recruitment consultant in the City of London for several years to earn enough money to pay off her student debts. While she outwardly succeeded in doing so by being paid well and getting large bonus payments, she has recently confided in friends at work that her work targets are increasingly hard to meet. Her manager, who is pleased with her performance and wants to push her further, keeps setting her harder sales targets in order to 'really motivate her'. However, Francesca finds that to meet these she has to work evenings regularly, and also during weekends. This has led her to take stock and re-evaluate what she wants to do. She has now applied for a job with a local charity that supports arts schemes in local schools. Having gone for an interview, she liked what she heard about the job, but is contemplating whether she could afford to take a big pay cut. Francesca is also concerned that the manager who interviewed her just asked 'tell me about yourself', which, given her recruitment experience, did not seem a very structured way of going about the selection process.

people for the job, we also need to understand candidates' reactions and their perspective. We offer two different perspectives.

22.3.1 Finding and Fitting

There are two different perspectives that can be applied to understanding assessment and selection – predictivist or constructivist (Anderson & Cunningham-Snell, 2001).

22.3.1.1 The predictivist perspective

predictivist perspective in occupational psychology research and practice a paradigm concerned with predicting the extent to which results from particular selection tools are linked to positive performance outcomes in the workplace.

The **predictivist perspective** is all about matching the right people to particular jobs. This perspective rests on the notion that any job can be explained, made explicit and quantified in some way, so is a somewhat stable entity, and that organisations can find scientific and quantifiable processes for selecting and matching individuals to that job. Research and practice in this paradigm are therefore concerned with predicting to which extent results from particular selection tools, such as interviews or psychometric tests, are linked to positive performance outcomes in the workplace.

22.3.1.1.1 Psychometric principles

Psychometric principles are of paramount importance in this context (Coaley, 2009). First, any selection technique needs to be reliable, in other words generate replicable and stable results across people and situations. For instance, while unstructured employment interviews are very popular in industry, this popularity is at odds with continued criticisms of their *unreliability* (Anderson & Cunningham-Snell, 2001). Linked to the principle of reliability is *validity*, which refers to the extent to which a

particular measure is measuring what it says it measures. In order to establish validity, reliability is a necessary precondition, as if results come out differently every time, one cannot be sure what is being measured at all. There are different forms of validity. *Construct validity* is very important here, whether the overall concept is right and sound, as is predictive validity, which in the context of work would be measured through the correlation between any selection measure scores and a measure of job performance (Rust & Golombok, 2008). Finally, any process has to be standardised, as a meaningful and evidence-based point of comparison is needed when you obtain someone's test or assessment scores. Without this, it is not possible to make informed decisions. The first way of doing this is a *normative approach*, where you compare different people's scores, mapping them on to the normal distribution, to find out who the best-scoring individuals are. The second way of doing this is a *criterion-based approach*, where you specify in advance what an acceptable standard of performance is, and then ensure that everyone who is selected reaches this standard (Rust & Golombok, 2008). *Standardisation* also refers in a broader sense to how a testing process is administered. For instance, you would want to ensure that each candidate sits a test under similar conditions and that everyone is given the same chance to prepare. Taken together, the psychometric principles should ensure that a selection process is as evidence based and objective as possible. Key terms that relate to psychometrics and to a predictivist stance to assessment and recruitment are summarised in Table 22.1.

22.3.1.1.2 Meta-analytic evidence in selection

One of the biggest advances in occupational psychology over the last few decades has been the advent and subsequent refinement of meta-analytic techniques, which were particularly successfully applied to research on different

TABLE 22.1 *Key Terms in Psychometrics and Assessment Validation.*

Ability test	Psychological test that measures a person's mental capacity. Examples of these tests include verbal reasoning, numerical reasoning and spatial awareness.
Big five	Common abbreviation for the five factor model of personality. This takes a *psychometric* or *trait* approach to measuring personality, where behaviours that define human behaviour are summarised statistically into five factors. This model underlies popular psychometric instruments such as the Hogan or 16PF.®
Competency	Set of observable work behaviours that can be described with a label, an example of which is 'communication skills'.
Criterion-referenced testing	Someone's score is compared to an established measure of acceptable performance. A driving test is an example – no matter how you drive in comparison to others, you have to meet basic skills to pass the test.
Freedom from bias	The fourth of the *psychometric principles*, which refers to whether a measurement produces the same results for all people.
Meta-analysis	A systematic quantitative analysis of results from different studies that allows you to make certain generalisations; in the context of occupational psychology an example would be 'the extent to which someone's ability test scores predict how well they will do in a job'.
Normative or norm-referenced testing	Comparing someone's score to those of other people who have also taken that test; in other words, you try to establish whether someone is average, below or above compared to others.
Personality questionnaire	A questionnaire that measures people's underlying stable characteristics or preferences in an explicit, observable way.
Personality	An enduring (long-lasting) set of traits, usually measured as behaviours, that describes a person's characteristics.
Predictive validity	The association between a predictor measure (for instance personality questionnaire scores) and a subsequent measure of performance or behaviour (for instance manager ratings).
Psychometric model (of personality)	This holds that a model of personality can be derived statistically by summarising information (such as typical human behaviours or attributes).
Psychometric principles	These are *reliability, validity, standardisation* and *freedom from bias.*
Reliability	The first of the *psychometric principles*, which refers to whether a measurement is consistent in itself, across time and across people.
Standardisation	The third *psychometric principle*, which refers to whether a measurement has been set up in an objective and consistent manner.
Trait instrument	A *personality questionnaire*, which measures to what degree people behave on different scales, such as 'extraversion' (how outgoing someone is).
Validity	The second of the *psychometric principles*, which refers to whether something measures what it says it does. An example is criterion-related validity, which in the context of occupational psychology refers to the relationship between a set of predictor measures, for instance psychometric test scores, and an outcome measure, usually a measure of work performance.

PHOTO 22.1 *Professor Frank L. Schmidt, who holds the Gary C. Fethke Chair in Leadership at the University of Iowa, a very influential figure in industrial and organisational psychology research.*

selection methods. The advantages of meta-analyses are that they:

- Control variation between studies.
- Include moderators to explain variation.
- Test overall effect sizes.
- Allow generalisation to the population of studies included.

Typical steps are to review the literature, then formulate inclusion criteria for the studies to be analysed, select studies based on these criteria and decide which variables will be considered in the analysis.

Frank L. Schmidt, who is said to be one of the most published industrial and organisational psychology researchers, and John E. Hunter were particular pioneers in the development and advancement of validity-refining statistical methods to allow us to generalise from a set of studies. Before then, much research was heavily context dependent, so for instance one could not be sure whether findings that demonstrated the *predictive validity* of certain assessment techniques – how confident we can be from someone's test or assessment scores that they will do well on the job – would also hold elsewhere. In occupational psychology, their influence has been deep rooted and long lasting. Schmidt and Hunter's seminal review of different selection methods (1998) was rigorous and is widely cited to the present day. The authors reviewed the predictive power of General Mental Ability (GMA) tests and 18 other techniques. Findings showed that we can predict the largest variance in employee performance when we use a GMA combined with a work sample such as a so-called intray, where candidates are asked to deal with demands that mirror real-life scenarios. A GMA combined with an integrity test or a structured interview also has high validity. The findings underline that it is both rigorous and cost effective to combine selection techniques rather than rely on the results of one technique alone.

22.3.1.1.3 Ability and personality in the workplace
Research on ability and personality in the workplace needs to be discussed here. With regard to the former, measures of cognitive ability fall into two broad categories. The first category is ability and aptitude, which measure individuals' capacity to think and process information mentally. Silvester and Dykes (2007) conducted a study where potential political candidates for a major UK party were assessed through an assessment centre, which uses a mix of different exercises that in this instance included a measure of critical thinking. Results showed clearly that, among other factors, this ability to reason critically, for instance by deducing from facts and making logical inferences, predicts political performance.

While the academic and practitioner communities have embraced the use of ability tests and attainment measures in selection, opinions are more diverse and controversial regarding the use of personality measures. Guion and Gottier (1965) published a much-cited review that came to the conclusion that personality tests were too seriously flawed to be used in the workplace. In 1991, however, Barrick and Mount produced a very influential meta-analysis that reviewed the five factor model of personality (FFM). This piece of research cannot be under-estimated in its influence, as it integrated different ways of measuring personality into a common language, summarising five core traits with the OCEAN acronym. This stands for *Openness to Experience, Conscientiousness, Agreeableness, Extraversion* and *Neuroticism*. Its findings showed that personality does predict both workplace and training performance, and that in particular conscientiousness is a powerful predictor. Since then, other meta-analytic reviews have shown support for the criterion-related validity of personality questionnaires (e.g. Salgado, 1997). However, a strong opposition remains that considers the validities of these questionnaires questionable and inflated due to methodological flaws (Morgeson *et al.*, 2007).

Thus, this is one area in occupational psychology where research does not send a clear message to the practitioner community. In addition, there are various ways of measuring personality, all based on different models. So for those who accept personality as a useful concept and measurement framework in the workplace, guidance is needed as to which instruments to use when, which we outline in Focus Point 22.1. We will pick up on this gulf between research and practice in Chapter 26.

22.3.1.2   *Constructivist perspective*

constructivist perspective in occupational psychology research and practice, a paradigm that acknowledges that any selection process is a social one with the focus on matching people to organisations and teams.

A second paradigm in selection, the **constructivist perspective**, openly acknowledges that such purported objectivity is not always possible. Rather than concentrating on matching people to jobs, as with the predictivist perspective, this acknowledges that any selection process is a social one, in which different parties and stakeholders are involved (Herriot, 2002). Therefore the focus is on matching people to organisations and teams, so shifting the emphasis to context and 'fit'. Such a person–organisation fit is very important. Anyone who has ever had a job that isn't the right fit, say where the team atmosphere is not constructive, knows just how dispiriting an experience this can be. In the constructivist perspective the emphasis is on employers and employees using a selection process to find out facts about one another, so that each party can make a decision about whether the job is right, and trying to understand expectations and reactions.

It is a common misconception that people tend to think of selection as a very simple process, with one 'yes/no decision' at the end. The reality is that many stages are involved, with one or even several decisions at each stage (Anderson & Cunningham-Snell, 2001). Indeed, in each selection process the applicant has the last decision, as they can always turn the job down. Applicant reactions and face validity are therefore important considerations to ensure that a candidate takes up a job offer, as if the procedure is cumbersome, or seems not relevant to the job, this may put candidates off.

22.4   MANAGING PERFORMANCE AND PERFORMING THE JOB

Managing and understanding performance are key issues in occupational psychology (Arvey & Murphy, 1998). There is little to be gained from selecting people who then under-perform in their job, so the objectives of performance management should be very broadly to identify and nurture those who are performing well, but also to identify those who are under-performing and either manage their outputs to a more satisfactory level or determine appropriate mechanisms for terminating their employment contracts (Fletcher, 2004). It is of course a prerequisite to such decisions that each organisation has an understanding of and a framework for the measurement of effective performance. This is easier said than done!

22.4.1 *Measurement of Performance*

As we highlighted earlier, organisational contexts are now fast moving and performance is rarely a simple construct. There are many aspects to successful performance, which has come to be understood as a multi-layered phenomenon (Arvey & Murphey, 1998). In reality, many organisations use *competencies* as a framework for measuring performance, explicit behaviours that tap into certain knowledge, skills and abilities that make an employee good at a particular job. We return to the concept of competencies when we discuss stress, wellbeing and work–life balance.

So one way of measuring performance would be to use ratings on instruments or measurements that employ these competencies as a framework (see Focus Point 22.2),

FOCUS POINT 22.2   PERFORMANCE MEASUREMENT USING 360-DEGREE FEEDBACK

Excerpt from Performance 360 Report

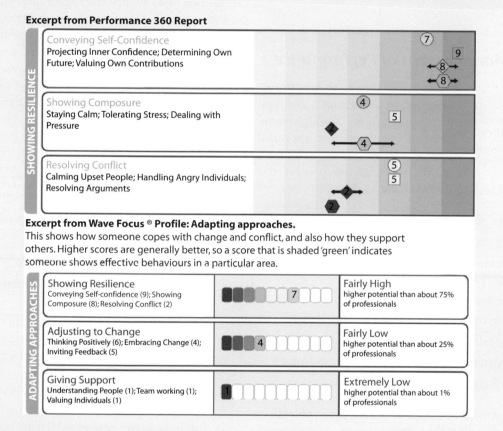

Excerpt from Wave Focus ® Profile: Adapting approaches.
This shows how someone copes with change and conflict, and also how they support others. Higher scores are generally better, so a score that is shaded 'green' indicates someone shows effective behaviours in a particular area.

Consider the illustration above. This shows you the 360-degree feedback for Jo Wilson, meaning that Jo has rated herself (shown as a square), has been rated by her boss (the circle) and her peers (the remaining symbols) on performance dimensions (think of these as questionnaire items) that were agreed and established beforehand. It shows that Jo and all other people rate her as very confident, and that she rates herself higher than others for showing composure and resolving conflict.

What are the performance issues here? First, Jo rates herself consistently higher than other people, suggesting that she may be somewhat blind to her weaknesses. Second, being so confident is not necessarily a good thing when working with others, as Jo may not be sensitive to others' needs and may also impose her view on others when conflicts arise. Of course, it is useful to know what the performance issues are, but also where they come from.

Consider the brief complementary excerpt from a personality profile, the Wave Focus (R), which was constructed by drawing on the OCEAN framework and other models. This shows that Jo is outwardly very confident, but actually feels uncomfortable when others are upset and has a general tendency to ignore others. Imagine what Jo might be like to work with – the chances are that she will come over as brusque and overpowering, even potentially bordering on bullying behaviour. Of course, as with all psychological measures, there is a degree of error in these reports, so it would be important to investigate these issues personally with Jo in a feedback interview.

which would usually be collated from the opinions of managers, sometimes also peers and occasionally even customers. Note that such measures are always based on individuals' somewhat subjective ratings.

Another way of measuring performance is to utilise objective performance data, such as sales figures, or a different output measure such as the number of successfully handled calls per day in a call centre. This is not perfect either, as there are many factors that can influence such outputs that are not under the individual's control. For instance, the recent global recession meant that many organisations struggled to make their targets, no matter how hard individual employees worked.

22.4.2 *Management of Performance*

performance appraisal the process of reviewing past work performance, usually combined with setting targets for the future.

Still, the reality is that performance has to be managed, and typically this is done through some form of **performance appraisal** system. From an organisation's point of view, the process has many objectives (see Fletcher, 2004):

- Reward employees for good performance.
- Improve on current performance.
- Identification, and where appropriate remedy, of under-performance.
- Provide the basis for formal disciplinary action.
- Motivate staff and setting objectives.
- Identify talent and succession planning.
- Link to training and development programmes.
- Promote communication and two-way processes.

The above list indicates that some of these objectives are opposed to each other. For instance, a disciplinary process is likely to bring friction and discontent with it, and is as such unlikely to be instrumental in fostering good employee relations. It is thus perhaps not surprising that appraisal systems are one of the biggest sources of discontent in organisations. In the United Kingdom, a recent survey of 2900 workers by Investors in People showed that 29% of those asked felt that the experience of formal appraisals was a waste of time and 44% believed the appraiser had been dishonest, while 41% felt that the process overall was useful (BBC, 2007). Organisations therefore need to strike a fine balance between making a performance appraisal system rigorous enough to fulfil its management functions on the one hand, and keeping it flexible and 'human' enough to ensure that managers and employees 'buy in' to it on the other hand.

22.5 TRAINING, FEEDBACK, PREPARING FOR DIFFERENT ROLES

One outcome of the appraisal process is to identify areas in which employees could develop their skills. Formal training is one of the mechanisms through which organisations can achieve this. Training is fundamentally about employees' learning, but learning for its own sake is not always sufficient to improve performance. Training is more than the acquisition of *ad hoc* tips and suggestions, but should relate to a process called the training cycle: training needs analysis is followed by instructional design, which is followed by evaluation, which informs future training needs analyses. Finally, it is important to maximise the transfer of training back to the workplace. It is all too easy for trainees to learn skills in the training environment and then be unable to apply these to make a difference in their jobs. Without this final step, the training will not have the desired impact. It is also important to evaluate outcomes in a systematic way, as otherwise much time and energy might be spent on an activity that does not reap benefits; however, in practice this is often overlooked.

The most common framework for evaluating training is Kirkpatrick's (Kirkpatrick, 2006), which uses four levels:

- The reaction level assesses what the trainees' response to the training was – did they find it interesting, useful or difficult?
- The *learning* level assesses whether trainees have acquired the knowledge, skills and attitudes that were identified in the learning objective through specific tests.
- The third level is *behaviour*: does the trainee change their behaviour back in the workplace and implement the new skills? This is often assessed by manager ratings.
- The final, and most difficult, is the *results* level. What is the impact of the training on organisational effectiveness? Often this is the ultimate goal of training, but establishing the impact of training on performance is very difficult.

Despite the difficulty of applying all four of Kirkpatrick's levels, some form of evaluation is very beneficial in ensuring that the formal training develops employees in useful ways, and ensures ongoing improvements to the training itself.

While formal training is very important for both employee and employer and to ensure a skilled workforce (Salas & Cannon-Bowers, 2001), there are many other ways of facilitating learning in employees. To start with, it is important to understand how development and learning differ from training. Linked with concepts such as the new or boundaryless career (Arthur & Rousseau, 1996), development refers to an ongoing process of personal and professional growth that goes way beyond the current job. The onus here very much rests with the employee, to ensure that a broad and updated portfolio of skills makes them attractive to current and future employers. Thus, development activities are broader than training and vary in how planned and formal they are (McDowall & Mabey, 2008).

coaching in business, one-to-one facilitation by a trained individual to improve specific performance issues and the effectiveness of the person being coached.

One of the biggest trends in organisations over the last decade has been the rising popularity of **coaching** in the realm of work (Passmore, 2006). In coaching, a trained individual, who can, but does not necessarily have to, be someone with an occupational psychology background, works one on one with an employee for an agreed timeframe. Often the remit is to address specific performance issues and make individuals more effective through techniques such as setting goals and then working towards these. There are several reasons for the growth of coaching. First, it is often much harder for senior managers, who have progressed through the employee life cycle, to

feedback response or reaction providing useful information or guidelines for further action or development.

improve their skills and also gain objective **feedback** on their performance from the internal workforce. Thus, executive coaches are contracted by organisations to work on specific aspects relating to work performance with an employee, referred to as the 'coachee'. Coaching is a two-way and personal process, where the focus and objectives for sessions are agreed up front, and where the coach may use a number of techniques and exercises, such as feedback and goal setting, to facilitate changes in behaviour and thought (McDowall & Millward, 2009). Research evidence is to date relatively sparse, however, so this is an area where practice is ahead of research. This is not uncommon when applying psychology to the world of work (see Chapter 26), but the onus is on researchers and practitioners alike to build an evidence base.

One of the central mechanisms of coaching is feedback, where the coach for instance comments on the coachees' progress, or uses objective feedback information such as psychometric profiles to structure sessions and facilitate (McDowall & Millward, 2009). The underlying assumption then is that feedback will have an impact on behaviour. Coaching may also help individuals to prepare for different roles, either in the stages of the employee life cycle, where individuals for instance take on more responsibility, or moving into a role that requires a different skill set.

22.6   INTERRUPTIONS TO THE EMPLOYMENT CYCLE – STRESS, WORK–LIFE BALANCE AND MATERNITY

22.6.1   Stress

There are many ways in which the employment cycle above could be interrupted, one of them being through illness or sickness-related absence. Such absence has a direct impact on any organisation, and comes at a vast cost to a national economy; for instance in the UK this is an estimated £12 billion every year (HSE, 2005). Absence is often attributed to stress, which has become an omnipresent buzzword. Recent estimates suggest that over half a million people are affected by work-related stress, costing UK industry an estimated £9.6 billion per year (HSE, 2005). Research concerned with stress is a prolific research area in occupational psychology, which generates thousands of publications. From an occupational psychological point of view, there are two main reasons for such prominence on the research agenda. First, we need to find ways of measuring stress levels and determining when pressure becomes excessive. Second, we need to find ways in which stress can be managed and prevented.

Given such a wide and important agenda, do we actually understand what stress is? Definitions are varied and rather confusing. Early work in the twentieth century saw stress as a largely physical response (e.g. Selye, 1956), whereas later, more detailed frameworks, such as Lazarus and Folkman's (1984) work over several decades, stressed the importance of people's strategies of dealing with stress, such as adapting behaviour or thinking about things differently (see also Chapter 9). These frameworks are also covered in Part Two on health psychology, as there is a pronounced link between stress and health outcomes. As we saw above, there is a vast cost to the economy, so recent initiatives have shifted to understanding how stress can be managed effectively. An example of current UK research is shown in Focus Point 22.3.

22.6.2   Work–Life Balance

Closely connected to the topic of stress but even wider in remit is work–life balance. Broadly speaking this refers to how demands from the home and work domain can be reconciled, and how different spheres in life can be successfully integrated (Frone, 2003). This topic has become of increasing importance and continues to move in different directions. Early research from the 1960s onwards

FOCUS POINT 22.3   MANAGING STRESS – THE ROLE OF THE LINE MANAGER

Over the last few years, the UK Health and Safety Executive (HSE) and the Chartered Institute for Personnel and Development (CIPD) have co-sponsored a research programme to investigate how stress in the workplace can be managed. This had three phases:

1. The elicitation of competencies needed by managers to manage stress effectively in employees, such as 'Managing Workload' and 'Resources and Empowerment'.
2. Validation of these competencies. This phase was concerned with refining the initial framework, resulting in 4 competencies, an example being 'Respectful and Responsible', with 12 sub-competencies and the construction of a 66-item stress-management competency-indicator tool.
3. Running and testing an intervention to develop these competencies in line managers. This phase involved specific training and targeted feedback.

The key messages from the research for line managers are that managing stress management should be part of normal general management activities; and that there is no single behaviour needed for effective stress management.

Therefore managers need to think about using and adapting a whole set of relevant behaviours. For instance, they need to take a participative approach rather than imposing on others what they think is best. They can do this through, for instance, providing an opportunity for employees to air their views, listening and consulting others on decisions.

Overall, the findings highlight the crucial role of the manager in managing stress, and that intervention has the greatest effects for managers who are ineffective at the beginning of the intervention. If you are interested in finding out more, the research reports relating to this project, which are open access, are well worth reading. Full references and web links are provided below. Not only do they provide a thorough review of extant literature, they also demonstrate the links between different areas of research and practice; for instance, feedback was found to be very important here as a developmental activity for fostering positive manager behaviour. Web links for the full reports are:

Phase 3: http://www.cipd.co.uk/subjects/health/stress/_preventing_stress

Phase 2: http://www.hse.gov.uk/research/rrhtm/rr633.htm

Phase 1: http://www.hse.gov.uk/research/rrhtm/rr553.htm

---

focused on the influx of women into the workplace and work–family conflict. In the 1990s the term 'work–life balance' became more widely used to indicate a broader agenda (Lewis, Gambles & Rapoport, 2007).

Showing some similarity to stress research, many earlier studies focused on potentially detrimental outcomes, and initially neutral terms such as *spillover*, where experiences in one domain in life mirror another (Edwards & Rothbard, 2000), came to be understood in a negative way. While there is no doubt that a negative work–life balance can have detrimental physical and mental outcomes, it is also important to understand how the interface of work and life can be managed positively and proactively. Recent frameworks such as *enrichment* (Rothbard, 2001) and *facilitation* are built around the premise that having different roles is not in itself necessarily a stressful or bad thing, but can be enriching. Different researchers use these terms, slightly confusingly, in different ways, but regardless of the exact wording they all entail the idea that having different areas and responsibilities in our lives can be a good thing. For instance, for an employee this means that being a mother, worker and partner, as well as engaging in hobbies and leisure time, makes for a richer life. For employers it means that acknowledging

that our lives don't stop when we go home at the end of the day is vital and necessary.

Research has shown that facilitation and conflict are orthogonal constructs, suggesting that their origins or antecendents might be different (Grywacz & Marks, 2000). *Border theory* (Clark, 2000) provides a contemporary conceptual framework illustrating how individuals might juggle different demands by negotiating and crossing borders between different domains in their lives. This theory acknowledges that some of us might prefer a more integrated approach, with similarity between the domains of work and family, whereas others prefer to keep different domains clearly separated. Another relatively new strand in this domain of psychology builds on Bronfenbrenner's (1979) ecological model, framing work and family as micro and meso systems (Voydanoff, 2001).

Now consider Case History 22.3 in the light of these notions.

Groundbreaking research by Virginia Schein (Schein *et al.*, 1998) has shown consistently that women are judged differently to men in the workplace around the globe, with sex-role stereotypes prevailing, arguing that 'think manager think male' is a global phenomenon. But are women at fault? Consider Focus Point 22.4.

CASE HISTORY 22.3

AN EXAMPLE OF WORK–LIFE BALANCE ISSUES

I just don't have a support network any more. My mum is getting on quite a bit and my dad is losing his memory. They both used to help with Milly [daughter] a lot, but now we have to beg and borrow favours from all sorts of people to get us through the week. We both work full time, but we have such a big mortgage that we can't afford to pay for help. Besides, I don't want Milly to spend too much time in school clubs etc., as I like having her around the house. Still, I feel guilty all the time that I don't spend enough time with her, as I often have to do my marking when we get home, or with my partner as he seems to have to take second place at the moment. In between things, I try and help out my parents as much as I can but I can never do enough. Sometimes I wish there was more help from the government for people like us. My career is important to me, so I had my daughter later in life, but sometimes I wish I had not left it so late, as it's hard without much help from the family. (Harriet, female head teacher, London)

This example illustrates how a relationship perspective can be helpful for considering work–life balance. Think about the following issues:

- What kind of things might affect the relationships within this family?
- What is the relationship between family and work for Harriet?
- What is the role of the community in the above scenario?

Having provoked you to give this some thought, the example has hopefully demonstrated to you that work–life balance is a wide issue that affects entire systems, rather than one individual at a time. You can imagine that, as a head teacher, it might be difficult for Harriet to draw very clear lines between her professional and private life. For instance, she may need to attend governors' meetings in the evenings. The example also shows how important others are for juggling the interface of work and life. Harriet used to call on her parents, but now has to rely on friends. She is also both caring for a child and for elderly, and in this case ill, parents. This scenario is typical of the present generation of parents, which is also referred to as the 'sandwich generation'.

FOCUS POINT 22.4   CAN WOMEN HAVE IT ALL?

In November 2009, the editor of UK *Vogue*, Alexandra Shulman, wrote a provocative article in the *Daily Mail*. She argued that no government can legislate over the difficult tightrope walk between career and motherhood, and that in fact recent legislation in the United Kingdom has lost sight of the needs of employers. She puts forward the idea that women should not expect to come back to exactly the same job as they had before childbirth. Shulman herself returned to work full time shortly after having her son, and has continued to work full time in a high-profile job ever since, giving as one reason that she wants to be able to provide a good life and education for her son.

WHAT IS YOUR OPINION ON THIS?

Lynne Millward's research (2006) showed that women feel 'invisible' as employees when returning to work after maternity leave, with their identity as functioning workers threatened. To what extent is this a justified experience? Can women really have it all? Are they damaging their own cause when they are asking for alternative or flexible working arrangements?

Source: Shutterstock.

22.7   LEAVING, RETIRING AND REDUNDANCY

The termination of employment, whether this is voluntary or involuntary, is a huge life change for employees. As alluded to before, this can have dramatic impact, as work is important for our psychological and physical wellbeing and our concept of self. One activity that is useful here is **counselling**, where specially trained individuals use techniques centred on listening, questioning and goal setting to help people to help themselves (see Egan, 1996). Lopez (1983; in Kidd, 1996) identifies several ways in which a counsellor can help an employee who has been dislocated from the workplace through **redundancy**:

counselling a purposeful relationship in which a specially trained person (trained in, e.g., listening skills and psychology) helps another to help him or herself.

redundancy process where one or more employees' work is terminated.

- Clarifying with employees their marketable, transferable and work skills and helping them to develop short-term plans by which skills might be realistically applied in other situations.
- Creating opportunities for employees who have been made redundant to vent their feelings about vocational and also personal concerns connected with this.
- Helping employees to identify and assess their sources of financial, marital/familial and other types of support.
- Helping employees to obtain and use timely information on referral services, employment outlook and available placement services.
- Reinforcing with employees that they are skilled and mature and that the job loss they have experienced is not due to personal incompetence.

Retirement is also a fundamental change. Retirement can be construed in terms of 'bereavement' or 'loss' in this case of one's job, identity and self-worth, in the sense that this is more often than not (at least for men) rooted in the employment world. Counselling may be required to prepare for, and help an employee deal with, this major life transition from work to nonwork, particularly in an employment climate where early retirement is seen as one way in which organisations are currently being streamlined. Transitions are most stressful when they are unpredictable and involuntary. No matter how undesirable the transition, there is always the opportunity for personal growth and development contained within it. It is the role of the counsellor to harness this potential.

retirement a major life-transition from working to not working.

Counselling is one of the areas of occupational psychology practice where practitioners have to be mindful not to act outside their competence and expertise. For instance, individuals nearing retirement may be in need of financial advice about pensions, benefits and so on. Clearly, such advice is outside the competence of someone who is psychologically trained, and should only be given by appropriately trained and registered financial advisers.

22.8   SUMMARY AND INTEGRATION

This chapter has depicted issues pertaining to individuals at work as a 'life cycle'. The various stages can all affect one another and it is important to recognise these links. For instance, someone who was made redundant may enter the life cycle all over again in a different organisation, but the chances are that they will not leave their prior experiences behind them completely.

In reality, occupational psychologists are likely to specialise in issues to do with one or more stages of this cycle, such as assessment and selection. Nevertheless, we argue that it is important to maintain a holistic perspective, and not to lose sight of other areas of research and practice.

SELF-TEST QUESTIONS

- What are the different stages in the employee life cycle?
- How do the predictivist and constructivist perspectives differ with respect to selection?
- How can you describe training at work?
- What are the reasons for managing performance at work?
- Why is it important to manage stress?
- What is counselling and how can it help us when faced with redundancy or retirement?

ESSAY QUESTIONS

- Describe the employee life cycle, illustrating this with psychological evidence for the different stages.
- Compare and contrast predictivist and constructivist perspectives in selection.
- What does psychological research say about the use of psychometric tests in selection?
- How can we measure performance at work?
- What is 'work–life balance'?

TEXT FOR FURTHER READING

Chmiel, N. (ed.) (2008) *Introduction to Work and Organizational Psychology: A European Perspective*, Oxford: Blackwell.

RELEVANT JOURNAL ARTICLES

Clark, S. (2000) Work/family border theory: A new theory of work/family balance, *Human Relations* 539: 747–70.
McDowall, A. & Mabey, C. (2008) Developing a framework for assessing effective development activities, *Personnel Review* 37(6): 629–46.
Millward, L.J. (2006) The transition to motherhood in an organizational context, *Journal of Occupational and Organizational Psychology*, Special Issue on Epistemology, *79(3)*: 315–33.
Morgeson, J.P., Campion, M.A., Dipboye, R.L., Hollenbeck, J.R., Murphy, K. & Schmitt, N. (2007) Reconsidering the use of personality tests in personnel selection contexts, *Personnel Psychology* 60: 683–729

RELEVANT WEB LINKS

Health and Safety Executive, for download of the stress management report and other useful info on health and safety more generally, www.hse.gov.uk
Project Epsom, http://www.savilleconsulting.com/campaigns/howvalidisyourquestionnaire/thanks.aspx
Psychological Testing Centre, run by BPS, www.psychtesting.org.uk

REFERENCES

Allen, N.J. & Meyer, J.P. (1996) Affective, continuance, and normative commitment to the organization: An examination of construct validity, *Journal of Vocational Behavior* 49(3, Dec.): 252–76.
Anderson, N. & Cunningham-Snell, N. (2001) Personnel selection, in N. Chmiel (ed.) *Introduction to Work and Organizational Psychology: A European Perspective*, London: John Wiley & Sons, Ltd.
Arthur, B.A. & Rousseau, D.M. (1996) *The Boundaryless Career: A New Employment Principle for a New Organizational Era*, Oxford: Oxford University Press.
Arvey, R.D. & Murphy, K.R (1998) Performance evaluation in work settings, *Annual Review of Psychology* 49: 141–68.
Barrick, M.R. & Mount, M.K. (1991) The big five personality dimensions and job performance: a meta-analysis, *Personnel Psychology* 44(1): 1–26.
BBC (2007) Staff appraisals waste of time, http://news.bbc.co.uk/1/hi/7126971.stm, accessed 25 January 2010.
Berridge, J.R. & Cooper, C.L. (1994) The employee assistance programme: Its role in organizational coping and excellence, *Personnel Review* 23(7): 4–20.

Bertua, C., Anderson, N. & Salgado, J. (2005) The predictive validity of cognitive ability tests: A UK meta analysis, *Journal of Occupational and Organisational Psychology* 78(3): 387–409.

Bronfenbrenner, U. (1979) *The Ecology of Human Development. Experiments by Nature and Design*, Boston: Harvard University Press.

Cheung, F.M., Leung, K., Fan, R.M., Song, W.Z., Zhang, J.X. & Zhang, J.P. (1996) Development of the Chinese personality assessment inventory, *Journal of Cross-Cultural Psychology* 27: 143–64.

CIPD (2009) Employee benefits: An overview, http://www.cipd.co.uk/subjects/pay/empbnfts/empbens.htm?IsSrchRes=1, accessed 25 January 2010.

Clark, S. (2000) Work/family border theory: A new theory of work/family balance, *Human Relations* 539: 747–70.

Coaley, K. (2009) *An Introduction to Psychological Assessment and Psychometrics*, London: Sage.

Colantonio, A. (1989) Assessing the effects of employee assistance programmes: A review of employee assistance program evaluations, *Yale Journal of Biology and Medicine* 62: 12–22.

Costa, P.T., Jr. & McCrae., R. R. (1992) *The Revised NEO Personality Inventory and NEO Five Factor Inventory: Professional Manual*, Odessa, FL: Psychological Assessment Resources.

Davidson, M.J. & Cooper, C.L. (1993) An overview, in M.J. Davidson & C.L. Cooper (eds) *European Women in Business and Management*, pp. 1–15, London: Paul Chapman.

Edwards, N. & Rothbard, N.P. (2000) Mechanisms linking work and family: Clarifying the relationship between work and family constructs, *Academy of Management Review* 25(1): 178–99.

Egan, G. (1996) *The Skilled Helper*, 6th edn, London: Brooks/Cole.

Eurostat (2009) Unemployment statistics. Retrieved from http://epp.eurostat.ec.europa.eu/statistics_explained/index.php/Unemployment_statistics#A_detailed_look_at_2009 (accessed January 2011).

Fletcher, C. (2004) *Appraisal and Feedback: Making Performance Review Work*, 3rd edn, London: Chartered Institute of Personnel and Development.

Frone, M.R. (2003) Work–family balance, in J.C. Quick & L.E. Tetrick (eds) *Handbook of Occupational Health Psychology*, Washington, DC: American Psychological Association.

Grywacz, J.G. & Marks, N.F. (2000) Reconceptualising the work–family interface: An ecological perspective on the correlates of positive and negatige spillover between work and family, *Journal of Occupational Health Psychology* 5: 111–26.

Guion, R.M. & Gottier, R.F. (1965) Validity of personality measures in personnel selection, *Personnel Psychology* 18: 135–64.

Health and Safety Executive (2005) *2005/6 Survey of Self Reported Work Related Illness*, (SW105/0), London: HMSO.

Heckley, G. (2005) Offshoring and the labour market: The IT and call centre occupations considered, *Labour Market Trends* 113(9): 373–85.

Herriot, P. (2002) Selection and self: Selection as a social process, *European Journal of Work and Organizational Psychology* 11(4): 385–402.

Hiltrop, J.M. (1995) The changing psychological contract: The human resource challenge of the 1990s, *European Management Journal* 13(3): 286–94.

HSE (2006) Absence costs UK economy £12 billion every year, HSE press release E009:06, http://www.hse.gov.uk/press/2006/e06009.htm, accessed 25 January 2010.

Jahoda, M. (1981) Work, employment, and unemployment: Values, theories, and approaches in social research, *American Psychologist* 36(2, Feb.): 184–91.

Jahoda, M., Lazarsfeld, P.F. & Zeisel, H. (2002) *Marienthal: The Sociography of an Unemployed Community*, Piscataway, NJ: Transaction Publishers.

Kidd, J.M. (1996) Career planning within work organizations, in A.G. Watts, B. Law, J. Killeen, J.M. Kidd & R. Hawthorn (eds) *Rethinking Careers Guidance and Education*, pp. 142–55, London: Routledge, Taylor & Francis.

Kirkpatrick, D.L. (2006) *Evaluating Training Programs: The Four Levels*, San Fransisco, CA: Berrett-Koehler.

Krause, N., Dasiner, L.K. & Neuhauser, F. (1998) Modifed work and return to work: A review of the literature, *Journal of Occupational Rehabilitation* 8(2): 1573–3688.

Lazarus, R.S. & Folkman, S. (1984) *Stress, Appraisal and Coping*, New York: Springer.

Lewis, Gambles & Rappoport (2006) *The Myth of Work-Life Balance. The challenge of our time for men, women and societies*, New York: John Wiley & Sons.

McDowall, A. & Mabey, C. (2008) Developing a framework for assessing effective development activities, *Personnel Review* 37(6): 629–46.

McDowall, A. & Millward, L. (2009) Feeding back, feeding forward and setting goals, in S. Palmer & A. McDowall (eds) *The Coaching Relationship: Putting People First*, London: Routledge.

McDowall, A. & Smewing, C. (2009) What assessments do coaches use in their practice and why? *The Coaching Psychologist*, December.

Millward, L.J. (2006) The transition to motherhood in an organizational context, *Journal of Occupational and Organizational Psychology*, Special Issue on Epistemology 79(3): 315–33.

Millward, L, Haslam, A. & Postmes, T. (2007) Putting employees in their place: the impact of hot desking on organizational and team identification, *Organization Science* 18(4): 547–59.

Morgeson, J.P., Campion, M.A, Dipboye, R.L., Hollenbeck, J.R., Murphy, K. & Schmitt, N. (2007) Reconsidering the use of personality tests in personnel selection contexts, *Personnel Psychology* 60: 683–729.

Office for National Statistics (2009) Migration Statistics Quarterly Report Statistical Bulletin, November, London: ONS.

Oxford English Dictionary (2009) Work, http://www.askoxford.com/concise_oed/work?view=uk, accessed 25 January 2010.

Passmore, J. (2006) Coaching: The emerging future, in J. Passmore (ed.) *Excellence in Coaching*, London: Kogan Page.

Patterson, F. (2001) Developments in work psychology: Emerging issues and future trends, *Journal of Occupational and Organizational Psychology* 74(4): 381–90.

Riketta, M. (2002) Attitudinal organizational commitment and job performance: A meta-analysis, *Journal of Organizational Behavior* 23(3): 257–66.

Rothbard, N.J. (2001) Enriching or depleting? The dynamics of engagement in work and family, *Administrative Science Quarterly* 46: 655–84.

Rust, J. & Golombok, S. (2008) *Modern Psychometrics*, London: Routledge.

Salas, E. & Cannon-Bowers, J.A. (2001) The science of training: A decade of progress, *Annual Review of Psychology* 52: 471–99.

Salgado, J.F. (1997) The five factor model of personality and job performance in the European community, *Journal of Applied Psychology* 82: 30–43.

Saville, P., MacIver, R., Kurz, R. & Hopton, T. (2008) *Project Epsom: How Valid is Your Questionnaire? Phase 1: A New Comparative Study of the Major Personality Questionnaires in Predicting Job Performance*, Esher: Saville Consulting.

Schein, V., Mueller, R., Lituchy, T. & Jiang, L. (1998) Think manage – think male: a global phenomenon? *Journal of Organizational Behaviour* 17(1): 33–41.

Schmidt, F.L. & Hunter, J.E. (1998) The validity and utility of selection methods in personnel psychology: Practical and theoretical implications of 85 years of research findings, *Psychological Bulletin* 124(2): 262–74.

Selye, H. (1956) *The Stress of Life*, New York: McGraw-Hill.

Shulman, A. (2009) Year-long maternity leave, flexi hours, four day weeks... why would *any* boss hire a women? *Mail Online*, 11 November, http://www.dailymail.co.uk/debate/article-1226157/Vogue-editor-Alexandra-Shulman-asks-boss-hire-woman.html, accesed 1 February 2010.

Silvester, J. & Dykes, C. (2007) Selecting political candidates. A longitudinal study of assessment centre performance and political success in the 2005 UK general election. 80(1), 11–25.

Voydanoff, P. (2001) Incorporating community into work and family research: A review of basic relationships, *Human Relations* 54(12): 1609–37.

Wright, P.M. & Snell, S.A. (1998) Toward a unifying framework for exploring fit and flexibility in strategic human resource management, *Academy of Management Review* 23(4): 756–72.

23 Occupational Psychology in Practice – The Organisation

Almuth McDowall, Lynne Millward & Adrian Banks

LEARNING OUTCOMES

WHEN YOU HAVE COMPLETED THIS CHAPTER YOU SHOULD BE ABLE TO:

1. Describe what is meant by 'organisational behavior' and why this is of interest to psychologists.

2. Explain why work motivation is important to managing performance.

3. Describe the role of the group and team in motivating performance.

4. Describe how the leader might motivate performance.

5. Explain what is meant by 'organisational development'.

6. Describe Lewin's approach to managing organisational change.

7. Describe the problems that can arise with human–machine interactions.

8. Describe the key factors that can be changed to improve job design.

KEY WORDS

Ergonomics • Group Processes • Human–Machine Interaction • Human Relations Approach • Job Characteristics Model • Organisational Culture • Organisational Culture Change • Organisational Development • Scientific Management • Sociotechnical Systems • Team Development • Work Motivation

CHAPTER OUTLINE

This chapter introduces you to psychology in the workplace through the lens of the organisation. We begin by considering how individuals are motivated by considering three core theoretical approaches. We then move on to teams and group influences, followed by an extended section on leadership. Finally, we consider the influence and importance of the working environment by outlining how errors occur in the workplace, human–machine interaction and the basic principles of job design.

23.1   INTRODUCTION

In this chapter we look at the organisation as the focus of applied psychology. It is only recently that psychologists have embraced the concept of the organisation not just as a context in which to understand individual behaviour, but as a focus in its own right. Of particular interest to psychologists is how individuals behave in organisational contexts, the impact of organisational contexts on this behaviour and how organisational behaviour can be most effectively managed and, if necessary, changed.

How to balance the needs of the employer with those of the employee is the primary concern of organisational psychology. Employers want to optimise performance, while employees want to ensure that their efforts are duly rewarded and that they have a positive work experience. This is a difficult balance to strike, but is the crux of what organisational psychology is about.

scientific management a carrot and stick approach to managing workers who were considered to be a commodity that had to be managed and controlled.

human relations approach an approach to managing employees that focuses attention on employee work needs and motivations, and recognises the importance and motivating power of workplace relationships.

work motivations motivation in a work environment.

In the early 1900s, psychology was concerned with 'efficiency engineering' (Moorrees, 1933). This was a production era, where efficiency and output were prioritised using the principles of **scientific management** (Taylor, 1911; Focus Point 23.1).

In the meantime, psychologists became concerned about the 'welfare spirit' of workers, sowing the seeds of the **human relations approach** (Roethlisberger & Dickson, 1939). This approach focused attention on employee work needs and **work motivations**, and recognised the importance and motivating power of workplace relationships.

Both scientific management and human relations approaches to managing performance ignored the role played by wider economic and social factors. It is clear, however, that performance is *contingent* on many different internal and external factors (Trist & Bamforth, 1951). Alongside this, psychologists have also increasingly become interested in looking closely at how employees experience and make sense of organisational life (Symon & Cassell, 1998); in other words they are interested in processes and qualitative approaches rather than merely considering outcomes, such as productivity.

23.2   ORGANISATIONAL BEHAVIOUR

Behaviour in organisational contexts is known as *organisational behaviour*. If psychology can help in the prediction and understanding of organisational behaviour, it can inform on how to increase desirable behaviours and eliminate and/or reduce the likelihood of undesirable behaviours. Desirable behaviours align with organisational interests, while undesirable behaviours are not (e.g. motivated absenteeism, high staff turnover, sabotage), which we illustrate in Table 23.1.

23.2.1   Motivation in the Workplace

An employee is recruited because they 'can do' a job and ideally also have the right type of personal qualities as well as being suitably motivated. Motivation is probably the most important aspect of performance, without which personal qualities (such as ability or personality traits) have no focus or application. How best to motivate employees is hence one of the most crucial issues to consider in the workplace. McGhee and Thayer (1961) defined the 'motivated person' as someone who 'is striving towards some goal'. In organisational contexts, it is

FOCUS POINT BOX 23.1 ASSUMPTIONS OF SCIENTIFIC MANAGEMENT

In the initial study, a detailed task analysis (where you break down what workers do into very fine elements) was used to decide how these tasks should be performed and by whom. For example, the 'science of shovelling' came from observing load per shovel and also the shovelling technique of 'first class shovellers' (Taylor, 1947, p. 64). Workers' knowledge, skill and ability were *precisely* matched to task requirements and their behaviour was tightly 'managed' using financial incentives and the threat of dismissal if they did not reach targets. Workers' welfare, satisfaction and voice were not relevant.

Unfortunately this carrot-and-stick approach to managing workers generated mass dissatisfaction and restriction of output. Considering the tactics in retrospect, the principles of scientific management saw workers as a commodity that had to be managed and controlled, rather than treating them as human beings who brought their own qualities and contributions to the workplace. Many organisations think differently today and we should not forget that these principles were deeply influential by highlighting the importance of efficiency and productivity.

TABLE 23.1 *Surrogate Performance Indicators and Indicators of Conflict or Dissatisfaction.*

Organisational commitment (OC) – Mathieu and Zajac (1990) found that OC predicts intention to search for another job, intention to quit and actual turnover. The stronger the OC, the more likely it is that the employee will go the extra mile in the way they do their job (see Chapter 22).	Classic examples of individual activity indicative of 'conflict' with the organisation include
Organisational identity (OI) – according to social identity theory (SIT; Haslam, 2005; see Chapter 25), organisational identity is a particular form of social identity and predicts a wide range of motivated organisational behaviour (e.g. increased cooperation, going the extra mile on behalf of the organisation).	<ul><li>Factory workers hiding key materials somewhere unexpected and hard to find</li><li>Conveyor belts being jammed with sticks</li><li>Weak fuses being put into electrical goods, slowing up processes at quality assurance</li><li>Textile workers 'knifing' through carpets</li><li>Petty pilfering</li><li>Viruses being unleased into vulnerable computer systems and critical files being deleted by disgruntled employees</li><li>Office workers spending hours playing computer games</li></ul>
Contextual performance – Borman (1991) uses the term 'organisational citizenship behaviour' to refer to spontaneous daily behaviours that assist others to perform effectively as well as complying with organisational rules and procedures.	
Relational psychological contracts (Conway & Briner, 2005; see Chapter 22) and employee *work engagement* (Little & Little, 2006) both predict desirable organisational outcomes.	Mars (1982) studied pilfering and cheating at work and argued that workplace crimes are not the exception. Fiddling (using company goods for personal gain, as an example) was found to be widespread and an integral part of all organisations. Strikes are the most visible but least common means of organisational conflict.

the alignment of personal and organisational goals that is crucial to performance (see Chapter 25).

Motivation theories can broadly be divided up into two different categories. Content theories are concerned with the content, in other words what motivates people's behaviour. Process theories focus on what the name implies, which are processes such as cost–benefit calculations and decisions that people make. In the following we outline an example of a need theory, an example of a process theory and also organisational justice, which takes a sociocognitive perspective.

23.2.1.1 Understanding employee needs

This approach assumes that individuals have innate needs that must be fulfilled in order to sustain their motivation. In other words, need theories propose that

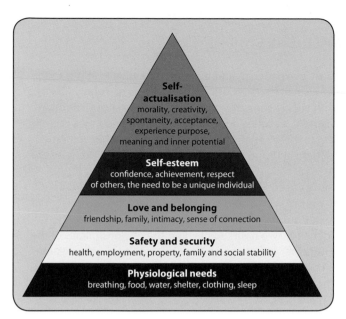

FIGURE 23.1 *Maslow's hierarchy of needs.*

our motivations are innate, such as needs to be secure, loved and fulfil one's potential. Only when these needs are met can we perform at our best. Managers can provide environments that harmonise with the salient needs of an individual employee, but they must first understand what they are. Maslow's hierarchy of needs (1954) is probably the most commonly known model of employee needs. This well-known and often cited model depicts different needs as a hierarchy (see Figure 23.1). According to the model, basic needs such as safety and belonging have to be met first before we can realise our full potential.

Maslow's model maintains that the needs have to be fulfilled in this order. Once one need is satisfied, people direct their energy to the next one. If needs cannot be met, this is a source of discomfort. The model has been criticised for these assumptions. First, we can probably all think of situations when several needs become important and crucial at the same time. Think of someone losing their job: this is a stressful life event that is likely to have an impact on all needs. Another criticism is that 'self-actualisation' is hard to define, and therefore we don't really know when someone has reached this stage.

Motive approaches to motivation postulate universal psychological motives and aim to specify the conditions and the processes that translate motives into action. *Equity theories* pre-suppose that individuals seek equity in their relationships with others, in that there

has to be a balance between the effort put into any task and the likelihood of good or favourable outcomes, and you as an individual should not be disadvantaged or treated unfairly compared to other workers around you. Employee's 'organisational justice' perceptions are based on two fairness principles: the fairness of how valued outcomes are distributed and the fairness of how decisions are made. When people make fairness judgements, they do so by comparing themselves with others: how do my rewards compare with those of others relative to how much effort I put in (Thibaut & Walker, 1978) and how fair were the procedures used to make the decision *not* to promote me (Greenberg, 1987)? We illustrate organisational justice principles in Case History 23.1.

23.2.1.2 *Understanding employees' cost–benefit calculations*

Some of the process theories of motivation depict employees as rational beings who weigh up costs and benefits when deciding how to act. The best-known example is Valence–Instrumentality–Expectancy (VIE) Theory (Vroom, 1964), where 'V' stands for 'valence' beliefs, I for 'Instrumentality' beliefs and E for 'expectancy' beliefs. The idea here is that people will put in effort to the extent that it is perceived to pay dividends. In terms of managing motivation, this means that managers should discover what employees value (valence), for instance which kind of rewards, such as pay or simply being praised. Managers also need to know what resources employees need (expectancy) so that they have the right levels of confidence. Last, managers need to manage the fulfilment of promises of rewards (instrumentality) and that employees are aware of this. Employees will be disappointed if expected pay-offs don't occur. If pay-offs are unclear or the link between effort and outcome is muddy (e.g. 'Is it worth the effort?'), there will not be much motivation to work hard. For instance, imagine an employee in a large public-sector organisation who has been working really hard and putting in extra hours as they want to advance in their career. However, they feel out of their depth as they have had little training, no one seems to notice their efforts and other colleagues are getting promoted, but not them. The chances are that this employee will reduce their efforts and start 'working to rule'.

The above discussion has focused on individuals and how they can be motivated. However, the reality of modern-day environments is that we work in groups or teams, which also provide an important motivational context (Haslam, 2005) that we now discuss.

ORGANISATIONAL JUSTICE – JIM'S EXPERIENCE

Jim is a 35-year-old IT manager, with many years of industry experience and postgraduate qualifications in the field. Having been made redundant by his old company, a small to medium-sized enterprise, he is now looking for a new job. Jim has recently applied for a position with a local company that provides specialist IT solutions. His initial application was via one of the national recruitment websites and Jim was pre-screened by a recruitment consultant, who having read his CV put him forward to the company. His qualifications suit the recruitment criteria exactly: he has 10 years' relevant experience, a degree in IT and up-to-date qualifications in the software platform that this organisation uses.

Jim was telephone interviewed by the company's outsourced HR department and was put forward as 'the ideal candidate for the vacancy'. The questions centred around 'why would you like to work for us, what kind of environment would you feel comfortable working in?' and questions about his personal background. The following week, two senior IT managers interviewed Jim for nearly two hours, explaining the responsibilities of the position, their current salary structure and all company benefits. Jim was given the opportunity to ask questions about the work set-up and was told he would hear directly from them by the beginning of the following week. The next Friday, Jim was rung late in the afternoon by the recruitment consultant, who told him that 'he was the bringer of bad news'. Jim was not offered the job, as the managers felt he was 'too wishy-washy for the job'.

We will now analyse this case study using some of Leventhal's rules of organisational justice. First, organisations should treat people consistently. This is unlikely to have been the case here, as Jim was passed from person to person and had what seems to have been a rather unstructured interview. Jim also had little voice – he was not given the opportunity to explain himself properly and outline why his skills were suited to the job; there was also no room for any decisions to be corrected or reviewed in the light of new evidence. You might be able to imagine the consequences the experience is likely to have for Jim. The chances are that this has eaten away at his self-confidence, and he might be less motivated to apply for subsequent jobs.

23.3 THE GROUP AS A SOURCE OF WORK MOTIVATION

Likert (1951, 1967) argued that supportive work groups are critical to employee satisfaction and motivation. As such, they are a potentially crucial unit in determining the success or failure of the organisation as a whole. Researchers have also begun to appreciate the importance of work groups and teams to social identity (e.g. Haslam, 2005). Groups are a way of structuring roles and activities to achieve organisational goals. A group does not always operate as a team. A team is an interdependent way of working (i.e. it has a particular group dynamic) to achieve a common goal. In a multidisciplinary context, team work requires the complementary expertise and skill of many different types of service professionals within time, budgetary and other resource constraints (Tannenbaum, Beard & Salas, 1992, p. 118). In other words, in teams there is some form of task dependency, some mandate for member coordination, and some structure within which this coordination is possible.

Central to the description and explanation of groups as a source of motivated behaviour is an understanding of how and in what ways group memberships can influence individual attitudes and behavior via a social identification process (Haslam, 2005; see Chapter 25). Schein's (1980) conceptualisation of group formation assumes that groups satisfy five sets of psychological needs:

- The need for affiliation – the need to be with others.

- The need for a sense of self-identity and self-esteem. Who we are, and our personal value and standing, are determined by our membership of various groups.

- The need to test out and establish social reality – groups develop beliefs about the way things are and how things work, possibly developing norms and behaviours (and ultimately, an **organisational culture**) of their own.

> **organisational culture**
> a system of shared beliefs and values that guides behaviour.

- The need for a feeling of security and mutual support to manage anxiety and reduce uncertainty.

- The group may also act as a problem solver for its members.

TABLE 23.2 *Elements of Intra-group Process that can Produce Both Gains and Losses in Group Performance.*

Process gains	Process losses
Social facilitation The energising effect derived from the presence of other group members.	**Social inhibition and social loafing** The presence of other group members leading to anxiety in relation to complex tasks. Group members exert less effort when their individual products are not identifiable.
Increased knowledge, ability and effort The availability of increased knowledge and skills such that 'many hands make light work'.	**Failure to use knowledge, ability and effort** Groups may assign weights to individual contributions to the group based on *perceived* rather than *actual* expertise.
Conformity Group pressure to conform can be a powerful force in implementing solutions, moving a group from just mulling over ideas to producing action.	**Group think** Groups can pressure their members into unthinking conformity or group think. In particular, cohesiveness can turn into group think that leads to blind decision making and action, with sometimes fatal consequences (e.g. plane crashes and shuttle disasters; Janis, 1972).
Diversity of views A diversity of opinions can serve as a valuable resource for innovation and creativity.	**Diversity of views can lead to conflict** Groups can fall into win–lose competition in which members fight to win arguments rather than to achieve group goals.
Alignment of team or group task with social identity Behaviour of members is premised on a shared social identity and that the norms and values on which this identity is premised are aligned with organisational interests (Haslam, 2005).	**Personal goals and interests more important to identity** Behaviour of members is premised on *personal interests* rather than with reference to any shared sense of social identity (Haslam, 2005).

Any one person can be a member of several groups, which will vary in relative importance for an individual and therefore in how much influence they have on personal attitudes and behaviour.

In practice, however, groups do not always perform to their potential. Steiner (1972) argued that many of the 'process gains' possible within groups do not happen; instead, commonly there is 'process loss', which can seriously detract from overall performance. *Process gains* come from the process of working as a group rather than as a collection of random individuals, whereas *process losses* arise from dysfunctional intra-group dynamics (see also Chapter 25), as we set out in Table 23.2.

team development a forum for team members to reflect on their performance and to overcome process difficulties.

group processes a general term referring to stages groups usually go through in forming and functioning.

Team development is a forum for team members to reflect on their performance and to overcome process difficulties. A typical intervention involves building trust, clarifying process problems (e.g. communication difficulty, conflict), generating internal responsibility for problem solving, and increasing awareness of the impact that **group**

processes can have on performance. Most would advocate a mixed approach tailored to the specific requirements of the team (see Table 23.3). Hackman (2005) argued that for team work to become effective, there must be a genuine need to work interdependently to achieve a goal, realistic expectations of what team development can achieve, long-term commitment to effecting lasting improvement, active and explicit support of senior management, and team members who believe in the team development effort.

23.4 LEADERSHIP AS MOTIVATION

The term 'leader' has popular currency. Most would agree with Stogdill's (1948, p. 3) definition that leadership is 'the process (act) of influencing the activities of an organized group in its efforts towards goal setting and goal achievement' (quoted in Bryman, 1996). In the early stages of leadership research, the *ability to influence* was said to be innate to personality. A landmark review by Stogdill (1948)

TABLE 23.3 *Approaches to Team Development.*

Goal setting: clarifying the shared goal and mobilising the team to this end, akin to goal setting at the individual level.
Interpersonal: changing team climate (increased trust, cooperation, cohesiveness) and process (e.g. conflict-resolution strategies, communication) by improving the way members feel about and interact with each other.
Role approach: clarifying role expectations and obligations (what is expected of each other on a task and a team level). A common technique for this particular approach is Belbin's (1981) Team Role Inventory.
Managerial grid: an approach designed to create a pattern of management emphasising concern for both production (task) and people (through engaging participation).

showed that leaders tend to be slightly more intelligent, self-confident and achievement oriented than nonleaders, but that these traits did not explain much of their behaviour. Researchers started to look at different types or *styles of leadership influence*.

23.4.1 Leadership Style

There are many different leadership terms and models, but common to all is that behaviour can be described in two main ways: *task oriented* and *relationship oriented* (Bass, 1990). The *task-oriented style* is about managing task accomplishment, while the *relationship-oriented style* is about managing interpersonal relations. The Ohio State University 'Leader Behaviour Description Questionnaire' or LBDQ was specifically designed to measure these two styles of leadership (Fleishman, 1953). Bales (1950) said that the task specialist is a different person to the socioemotional specialist. However, most now agree that any leader could in practice use both task and relationship styles simultaneously. The Managerial Grid, for example, assumes that leaders can be high on both people and task concern; low on both people and task concern; high on people concern but low on task concern; high on task concern but low on people concern; and midway on both scales (Blake & Mouton, 1964).

In contrast, Bass (1990) argues that *all* leadership practices range from purely autocratic to purely democratic. Autocratic describes leaders who seek sole possession of authority, power and control, while democratic describes leaders who tend to share authority, power and control with their followers. It is generally agreed that autocratic/democratic styles refer more to the *origin* of power and influence (leader versus group) rather than the *focus* of this power and influence (task versus people). Eagly and Johnson (1990) showed how it is possible for a leader to be directive in both a task-based (i.e. instructing subordinates) and people-oriented (i.e. structuring the interaction among group members) way. Conversely, a leader can act in a participative way yet still be task as well as people oriented. Consider Focus Point 23.2.

23.4.2 Leadership Effectiveness

Bass (1990) reviewed evidence on leadership style from a wide range of studies, and concluded that the effectiveness of different styles varied depending on the task, follower and organisational context. For instance, the importance of being task focused is greater when the task is ambiguous (i.e. lack of role clarity, task complexity and ambiguity), so long as the leader is *not coercive*. Followers are generally much more satisfied when their leader is also highly people focused. Bass (1990) complains of how difficult it is to integrate findings across studies because of the many and varied ways in which leadership style and also leadership effectiveness are measured by researchers.

Fiedler (1965) argued that different situations demand varied degrees of leadership influence. He identified three sets of factors that have an impact on how much leadership control is acceptable: how acceptable the leader is to team members, how clear the task is, and whether the leader has legitimate authority to deliver punishment and rewards. Task-oriented influence is most successful when the leader is already accepted by the group (i.e. has a good relationship with members), where the task is structured and unambiguous and the leader holds a legitimate position of authority. For a good relationship to build up between leader and followers, the leader must also be appropriately people oriented.

There is now much evidence suggesting that an effective leader can adapt their style to address the demands of the situation. Shiflett (1979), for instance, argues that the most important skill for a leader is 'resource recognition' (e.g. identifying, harnessing and building the competence of group members, and also garnering organisational support). He says that when selecting or training leaders, the question is whether the leader is able to recognise and implement the resources available rather than trying to describe their leadership style. For instance, the work in many organisations is now project based, where people come together on different projects, disband when the project is over and then

FOCUS POINT 23.2 OBSERVING MOTIVATION AND LEADERSHIP – GENE SIMMONS' *ROCK SCHOOL*

A good way to understand the concepts of leadership and motivation is to observe people around you and their effect on others. When we teach trainee occupational psychologists, one of the tasks we give to them is to observe a film or television programme of their choice, and observe and critically analyse motivational and leadership behaviours. One example to illustrate this in class is Gene Simmons, the lead guitarist with the rock band Kiss and not so long ago the key character in a reality programme called *Rock School*. Gene is fascinating to observe as he interacts with school children in order to put together a band. While he shows some signs of autocratic behaviour (because he seems to know exactly what he wants and does not tolerate slacking), he is also distinctly people oriented. He is also sensitive enough to adapt his behaviour to getting the best out of different individuals and

treats the school children with respect and encouragement to help them become confident musicians in very little time.

Source: Photo courtesy of Mark Johnson.

---

work on different projects with different people again. A good leader in this context would know intuitively which team member is particularly suited to lead a particular project and what resources they need to make this a success.

Gastil (1994) looked at the relative effectiveness of autocratic/democratic styles averaged across 23 different studies. Neither the democratic nor the autocratic leadership style was found to be especially effective at achieving group goals. However, Gastil (1994) did find that the democratic style was more strongly tied to effectiveness in naturally occurring field contexts rather than in experimentally induced contexts, especially when working on complex tasks. Gastil (1994, p. 402) argues that 'investigations should consider the influence of task complexity and recognise the importance of study design and setting'; that is, field versus laboratory based, naturally occurring versus experimentally induced leadership styles. However, Paul and Ebadi (1989) say that the power of 'participation' (requiring a democratic style of leadership) in group contexts is not clear cut, maybe because there are many different types and degrees of participation and many ways of measuring its effectiveness.

Paul and Ebadi (1989) argue that forms of employee participation can be functional when:

- The leader has the authority to make a decision.
- The decision can be made without stringent time limitations.

- Subordinates have the relevant knowledge, skills and abilities to discuss and implement the decision made.
- Subordinates' characteristics (values, needs, attitudes etc.) are congruent with the decision to participate.
- The leader is skilled in the use of participative techniques.

In the words of Gastil (1994, p. 403), the democratic style entails 'giving group members responsibility, improving the general abilities and leadership skills of other group members, and assisting the group in its *decision-making process*'. In short, while all group members can perform leadership functions (through increased participation), someone must be there to facilitate, coordinate and monitor the effectiveness of the 'empowerment' process.

On the issue of empowerment, recent research has focused on identifying the ingredients of leaders who are able to engage group members in transformational ways (Bass & Avolio, 1994). The concept of transformational leadership emphasises in particular the power of the leader to 'change' (i.e. literally transform) the way things are done. Bass (1990) argued that while transactional leadership motivates subordinates to perform expected goals, the transformational leader will inspire people to go further than originally expected. This type of leadership pre-supposes a strong identification of group members with the leader joining in a shared vision of the future (i.e. describing a commitment-based influence approach – see Chapter 25).

23.4.3 *The Role of the Leader in the Change Process*

organisational development a systematic effort applying behavioural science knowledge to the planned creation and reinforcement of organisational strategies, structures and processes for improving an organisation's effectiveness.

A review of the **organisational development** literature identifies leadership as one of the most important factors in the successful facilitation of change (Smirchich, 1983). The actions of leaders are generally found to be more powerful in delivering the message of change than are written statements and company policy. The appointment of a new leader is often used as a catalyst to a change, carefully selected to represent the organisation's new vision and values, express novel viewpoints and practices, and be more able to question the status quo (simply because they are not an integral part of it). An example of this kind would be Lord King as Chief Executive of British Airways, or think of the high hopes pinned on Barack Obama when he took office as US President. We have shown above that there are very different ways in which leaders can influence others, and that it is important that they can adapt their behaviour.

23.5 ORGANISATIONAL DEVELOPMENT AND CHANGE

The effective management of organisational change is upheld as key to corporate success in the contemporary business world. The need for change in response to contemporary economic turbulence has created an imperative for revolutionary change in all aspects of organisational structure, process and functioning.

23.5.1 *Organisational Development*

The concept of organisational development (OD) is premised on the assumption of 'planned' transformational change.

OD has been defined as:

> A systematic effort applying behavioural science knowledge to the planned creation and reinforcement of organizational strategies, structures and processes

for improving an organization's effectiveness. (Huse & Cummings, 1985)

In OD, the aim is to achieve widespread organisational commitment to change. An OD intervention pertains to a range of planned programmatic activities pursued by both clients and consultants. French, Bell and Zawacki (1994) differentiate between interventions directed at individuals (e.g. coaching and counselling), dyads (e.g. arbitration), teams (e.g. survey feedback, role analysis), inter-group configurations (e.g. survey feedback, group-level arbitration) and organisations as a whole (e.g. total quality management programmes, business process re-engineering). As we move from one level of focus to the next, the number of dimensions to consider is increased, which adds to the complexity of the intervention process. All interventions nonetheless rely heavily on some form of organisational diagnosis (see Table 23.4).

Most diagnosis begins with an assumption that something is wrong and in need of repair. However, there are many instances where organisations can benefit from taking preventative action. *Appreciative inquiry* is an OD model that focuses not on what is but what *might be*; what *should be* and what *will be* (Cooperrider & Srivastva, 1987). Appreciative inquiry seeks out ways of igniting the imagination of what might be and helps in carrying out that vision. The method involves an identification and analysis of so-called 'peak experiences' as the building block for envisioning how things could be better.

23.5.2 *Organisational Change*

Organisational change can be a major source of stress for employees, generating fear and inducing resistance. Organisational restructuring in particular can create uncertainty about future prospects. Change agents (whether internal or external) are commonly mistrusted by employees. Some common sources of resistance to change are:

- A need to hold on to the status quo.
- Disruption of relationships (e.g. through lay-offs, restructuring, reassignment or relocation).
- Perceived threats to identity and status.
- Fear of a loss of status and authority on the part of managers because of decentralisation and empowerment policies (i.e. vested interest in old systems).
- Economic factors (e.g. fear of loss of jobs and/or loss of future security or prospects).
- Problems with the consultant (e.g. mistrust, lack of rapport).
- Lack of resources for coping.

TABLE 23.4 *'Diagnostic' Methods in Organisational Development.*

Questionnaires	Sensing
Use of questionnaires (e.g. the managerial grid) is economical and produces data that can be numerically analysed. The anonymity afforded may reveal otherwise hidden thoughts and feelings among employees. However, this method is not conducive to creating personal involvement and discussion, which are otherwise integral to the process of 'changing hearts and minds'.	Sensing involves unstructured group interviews designed to explore group issues, concerns, needs and resource requirements. The 'group' is usually a sub-sector of an organisation (e.g. professional employees, nonsupervisory technical and office staff, supervisory staff). Sampling members from different parts of an organisation can afford the OD researchers with a feel for the organisation as a whole as well as what the organisation means to its members. Successful group interviews assume some level of trust, otherwise people will not disclose their real concerns. The group interviews are for listening, not for communicating rhetoric or commands from the top, and are best conducted by a third party.
Interviews	**Polling**
Interviews can also be used to invite discussion on a wide range of subjects including personal concerns that are rarely aired, but the interviewer must be skilled in doing this. Interviews are commonly used to explore team dynamics. Interviews can, however, take up to two hours per person and analysis is labour intensive and complex.	A group is 'polled' by questionnaire or structured 'round-Robin' exercises on issues or agendas that will otherwise remain buried and unspoken (and thus cause distress or anxiety, e.g. interpersonal conflict, the future of the group and its place in the organisation). The whole group takes part in the process and thus commitment to the results is obtained. It is important that the results are discussed and followed up rather than left 'open' and not properly addressed. The group facilitator should ensure full and balanced involvement of all members.
Collages/drawings	**Physical representation of organisations**
Individuals or groups are asked to prepare collages (with glue, material, paint etc.) on a theme (e.g. my feelings about the team or the organisation). If a single collage is produced by a group it can elicit deep but burning issues and as such can become the focal point of discussion. This is fun, but may not be taken seriously at first.	Group members 'sculpt' themselves physically according to some group characteristic or issue that is of worry to them (e.g. cliques, inappropriate influence, competition, communication channel). The method can yield dramatic results and create strong motivation for improvement. The exercise is run by a skilled third party. Some groups find this embarrassing so it must be carefully managed.

Probably the most popular model of organisational change is Lewin's (1951) three-step process called unfreezing, moving and freezing, applicable at individual, group and organisational levels of analysis. Unfreezing refers to opening the system up to change by breaking down or minimising resistance. Employees are confronted with the need for change by making them more aware of their behaviour. Once changes have been made, freezing will stabilise them. Stabilising change may also require an intervention, such as the introduction of a new reward system. Unfreezing may involve analysing the 'force-field' (Lewin, 1951) operating either to 'drive' or to 'restrain' the implementation of change. The management task is to pave the way for effective implementation by removing underlying 'restraints' (e.g. reducing the probability that change will be 'resisted' by the individuals affected by it).

Although many other, more complex models of **organisational culture change** have been proposed, most assume that the organisation is a force-field, in other words a bit like a protective barrier that wants to retain the atmosphere inside. For example, Weiss (1996) advocated the following 'unfreezing' strategies:

> **organisational culture change** usually top-down change to an organisation's culture that involves: clear strategic vision, management commitment, symbolic leadership and changes in membership.

- Education and communication
- Participation and involvement
- Facilitation and support
- Negotiation and agreement
- Manipulation and co-optation
- Explicit and implicit coercion

To effect culture change, Cummings and Huse (1989) suggest implementation and careful management of the following stages:

- *Clear strategic vision.* Often this will be embodied in the organisation's mission statement, which should be a clear and precise statement of *operationalisable* and *achievable* goals.
- *Management commitment.* Top management must be committed and *seen to be* committed to change. Only top management has the power to make changes in the values and deeper structures of the organisation.
- *Symbolic leadership.* Senior managers must behave in ways that are consistent with the new culture, e.g. management by walking about.

- *Supporting organisational changes.* Changes to organisational structure, reporting procedures, management styles, organisational processes and so on are likely to be required.
- *Changing organisational membership.* Bringing in new organisational members who subscribe to the required new organisational values and practices is likely to consolidate and 'freeze' the change. Existing organisational members can be encouraged to buy into the change through consultation, training and development, ensuring visible senior management commitment.

The last two sets of strategies are potentially very risky. In the case of manipulation, people may come to actually 'feel' manipulated and thus lose faith and trust in the intervention. In the case of coercion, people may simply not comply. You can probably think of examples of when people have tried to force you to do something, the result being that you really did not want to cooperate. Various transformational change models have evolved as frameworks for the process of engineering radical change. An example of transformation is provided by the case of British Airways, which 'transformed' from a bureaucratic to a customer service organisation. Transformational change involves culture change and is usually initiated from the top down, in response to strategic requirements (see Focus Point 23.3).

Furnham (1997) argues that although leadership may direct and support change, this is unlikely to be successful unless the organisation is also structurally redesigned. Structure and culture create leadership styles and leaders are part of the process of change. However, the decision of which model of change to use is a matter of personal choice and experience. In practice, the key task is to help employees engage constructively with the change. For example, Robinson, Kraatz and Rousseau (1994) note that people's response to change depends on whether it involves some gain or loss in value for the individual (i.e. what is in it for me?) and whether their personal values/attitudes and needs have been taken into account. Last, organisational change is often at a critical point in mergers or acquisitions, when two organisations are required to blend into one another. We illustrate this in Focus Point 23.4.

23.6   THE WORK ENVIRONMENT

Psychologists tend to focus on the people in an organisation (e.g. selecting the best person for a job and training them up), but in doing so we may overlook other important factors that can influence how the organisation works. There are not many workplaces that consist solely of people. Most are complex **sociotechnical systems** (Trist & Bamforth, 1951). That is, they comprise people and all manner of technology, ranging from calculators and desktop computers through to sophisticated nuclear power plants. The interaction between all of these elements is what determines the performance of the organisation. The individual elements may be good, but if they do not interact efficiently within the system then overall performance will be hindered. This sociotechnical systems perspective emphasises a particular way of thinking about how an organisation works. If a job is especially demanding, one solution is to select a talented individual to fulfil it, or to provide excellent training so that the job can be completed effectively. But another alternative is to change the job itself so that it is no longer as demanding. The approach of redesigning the system to better fit the people within it, rather than changing the people to fit the system, is the basis of the ergonomic approach to work design. This approach can provide an

> **sociotechnical systems** a term for organisations that are comprised of people as well as technology.

FOCUS BOX 23.4   THE REALITIES OF MERGERS

In their study of an organisational merger scenario, Buono, Bowditch and Lewis (1985) observed that it was the *style and visibility of the leader* that made a difference to how employees perceived the success of the merger. The CEO of each bank was perceived to have a different leadership style. In Bank A the style was described as 'participative and egalitarian', whereas in Bank B it was described as 'authoritarian and bureaucratic'. Management style and 'tone' were reported by employees in Bank A to be 'planned' and decisions made based on wide consultation. On the other hand, Bank B was perceived to be in a permanent state of 'crisis management'. Post-merger questionnaires showed that despite better pay and conditions in the merged organisation, employees from former Bank A were more satisfied with and committed to the new organisation than their colleagues from former Bank B.

Another real-life example is a small creative agency during the 'dot-com boom' that prided itself on its unconventional style. The focus of the office was a hammock that everyone could use, and the management had a very informal style. It then merged with another company, which meant that the senior management team changed. Suddenly, the employees were all told to 'dress appropriately', the hammock went and they had to account for each hour spent on every project. Many employees left, as they felt that the new leadership style was not suited to their style of working.

effective complement to other techniques within occupational psychology.

The sociotechnical systems approach is becoming more relevant as the workplace has changed to incorporate more technology. This has changed the nature of many jobs and raised new issues. Jobs that used to require manual labour, for example coal mining, increasingly involve the control of complex machines. So increased technology has led to a shift towards more cognitive over physical work. Much white-collar work has been transformed too. For example, the ease of communication through wireless networks, smartphones and so forth has enabled teleworking to become a common occurrence, with employees either based at home or otherwise geographically distributed. This has generated new implications for organisations. On the one hand performance can rise because of increased satisfaction and improved efficiencies such as cutting out commuting time and working while commuting (e.g. Hill, Ferris & Märtinson, 2003). On the other hand, new problems occur such as role conflicts and work–life balance issues when trying to work at home, and the problems of ensuring an ergonomically acceptable work station (Montreuil & Lippel, 2003). Clearly, technology is becoming an increasingly important part of the work environment, and while it solves many problems it can also generate some new ones if not used effectively to support the people who use it.

23.6.1   Human–Machine Interaction

One of the key elements of ensuring that technology is a help rather than a hindrance in the workplace is to optimise the interactions between the human and the machine. The goal of designing machines so that they fit humans rather than trying to fit humans to machines is the basis of studies of **human–machine interaction**. This field is called **ergonomics** (or human factors, the terms are used interchangeably). Before improving the interactions, however, it is necessary to decide which functions will be completed by the human and which by the machine. One way to think about the best allocation of functions is to consider which would be performed best by the machine and which would be performed best by the human (Fitts, 1954). Humans are particularly good at perceiving patterns in complex information, creativity, common sense, finding the meaning of actions and tolerating errors. Humans are much less good at remembering details accurately, monitoring unchanging states and making rapid calculations. In contrast, machines are excellent at storing detailed information in databases, making calculations with great precision and monitoring a system (e.g. a thermostat). They are poor at common-sense tasks.

> **human–machine interaction** in organisational settings the study of the interaction between the human workforce and the technology at work and the allocation of functions appropriate to each.
>
> **ergonomics** the science of designing the task to fit the person.

This seems like an ideal fit – machines can complete the functions where they work well and humans can complete the functions that suit our abilities. But how is the interaction designed? It is often designed to suit the technology rather than the human. Seemingly simple tasks such as programming a video recorder or switching on a washing machine involve remembering precise sequences of operations without which the machine will not operate. As a result, we frequently record the wrong programme or limit ourselves to two settings on the washing machine, the others remaining a mystery that only reading the instruction manual would solve. (And why would we bother doing that?) Machines have certainly transformed all aspects of our work and non-work lives; however, our interactions with them are not automatically straightforward. Good human–machine interaction must be carefully designed.

23.6.2 Designs and Controls

There are essentially two components through which humans interact with machines – displays and controls. The study of each of these has been subject to detailed research and different types of displays and controls are beneficial in different circumstances (cf. Kroemer & Grandjean, 1997). For example, digital displays are often better for monitoring small, slow-moving changes because the exact figure is given. In contrast, analogue displays are often better for making predictions about how quickly something is changing, such as altitude, because the speed with which the pointer moves in the dial indicates this change. Similar guidelines exist for controls. For example, when switching between different states (e.g. on or off), a discrete click into the alternatives ensures that the correct state is more likely to be chosen, whereas a continuous state such as volume is best controlled with variable settings. More resistance allows more precise control of variable settings (cf. Oborne, 1998).

In order to design the system to support the people using it – that is, to fit the task to the human – it is helpful to know people's strengths and weaknesses in processing information. Applying cognitive psychology provides an indication of typical information-processing capacities. For example, we have limited working memory capacity, which means that we can remember very little novel information in the short term and retain it only for a short period without rehearsal (Baddeley & Hitch, 1974). Therefore any information that is essential to the ongoing task should ideally be present in the display. We have limited attentional resources and if we attempt to divide our attention between too many tasks there may be insufficient resource to attend adequately to everything (Pashler, 1998). As a result, we may fail to notice information that could be critical.

23.6.3 Human Error

Despite the best efforts to design displays and controls well, these limitations mean that people will inevitably make mistakes. For example, despite using computers every day, we have all on occasion deleted a file that we intended to keep. Forgetfulness, inattention and fatigue – or many other factors – can all play a part in leading us to make these mistakes. Sometimes the consequences are more serious, however. In 1999 a train driver failed to stop at a red signal near London Paddington station and collided with an oncoming train, leading to 31 deaths and many more injuries. How could these accidents be prevented? Given that they have been caused by human failures of attention, training and so forth, techniques to improve employee motivation and skills seem like the best solution.

There is some evidence for the effectiveness of these techniques. For example, training employees in safe working practices and involving them in decisions about safety can help (Vredenburgh, 2002). Developing shared positive attitudes to safety – a safety culture – also improves safety (Zacharatos, Barling & Iverson, 2005). There are many effective interventions that reduce unsafe acts and so reduce accidents at work.

Often accidents such as the one above are attributed to human error alone. While this is a factor, an approach to preventing organisational accidents that focuses solely on the person that made the mistake has some limitations. First, it encourages a 'blame culture'. That is, a person responsible for the accident is identified and punished with the intention that this will prevent future accidents. However, this does not lead to constructive attempts to improve safety; it is more likely to lead to attempts to avoid blame, including covering up unsafe situations. Secondly, detailed analyses of organisational accidents reveal a much more complex picture than that suggested by a human simply making an error. In fact, many of the errors made by employees do not have serious consequences. The occasional slip can be recovered and the occasional mistake can be corrected by a colleague, or an automated safety system can override an unsafe act.

This more complex analysis follows naturally from the realisation that people in organisations work within complex sociotechnical systems, as described above. While a person may make a mistake, the system as a whole is designed to prevent that mistake turning into a serious accident by correcting the problem in some way. These defences can take many forms, for example a co-pilot can correct a pilot or an automated system can intervene, such as anti-lock brakes taking control of braking if a car begins to skid. Reason (1997) suggested that a system can have several defensive layers. None of these layers is perfect and all may have holes in them.

FOCUS POINT 23.5   THE SWISS CHEESE MODEL

The idea of multiple defensive layers, known as the 'Swiss cheese model' because each layer looks like a slice of holey cheese, highlights a distinction between two sorts of error. On the one hand, an active error is an unsafe act that leads directly to an accident. In the case of the Paddington Station rail crash mentioned on p. 478, failing to stop at a red signal was the active error that led to the collision. However, this wasn't the only problem. There were a number of other mistakes that had occurred in the past and caused weaknesses in the defences that had remained undetected. These are the latent conditions for accidents. As a result of these weaknesses the active error caused a crash, because if they had not been there then the train would have stopped safely.

Lawton and Ward (2005) identify the range of latent conditions that existed that day. Driver training was quite limited. Despite a general agreement that this signal was hard to see, the driver had not been specifically trained on it. Also previous incidents when the signal had been passed without leading to accident had been attributed to human error, meaning that no changes were made to the system. And finally the auditory warning, which must be acknowledged by the driver, is the same for yellow and red signals, but only a red signal requires a train to stop. So train drivers became accustomed to acknowledging the signal without stopping, perhaps undermining the benefit of this signal. As a result of these and other holes in the defences it became possible for the train driver to pass

the red signal onto the same track as an oncoming train. Eliminating these latent conditions could have prevented the active error leading to the accident. Or, more generally, seeking ways of supporting the human within the more complex sociotechnical system rather than expecting the person to adapt to difficult conditions could have prevented this incident and ensured smooth running of the task.

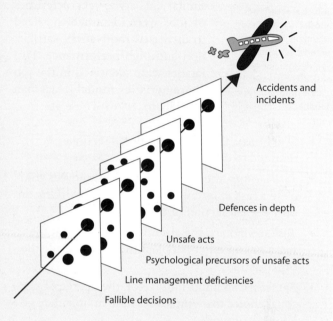

Accidents and incidents

Defences in depth

Unsafe acts

Psychological precursors of unsafe acts

Line management deficiencies

Fallible decisions

That is, circumstances may arise in which that defensive layer is penetrated. However, if this happens, the next defensive layer could well intercept the error. Only in the unlikely situation that the holes in all of the defensive layers are aligned will an error pass through all the defences and lead to an accident. This 'Swiss cheese model' is illustrated in Focus Point 23.5.

23.6.4   Design of Work

The previous section has looked at how machines can be designed to fit people and the benefits this has for their performance. The same is true for designing work – if you would like employees to be interested in their jobs, it helps to give them interesting jobs to do. The first systematic attempts to design work using scientific management certainly did not apply this principle.

While the process of rationalising how tasks are performed does lead to more efficient work (as exemplified by Henry Ford's assembly lines, which enabled him to make cheaper cars), this efficiency does come at a cost. Simplified jobs are repetitive and boring, meaning that employees' motivation can suffer. Designing jobs to improve satisfaction and motivation requires a quite different approach.

In 1966, Herzberg proposed a theory claiming that the factors that satisfied people in their work ('motivator factors') were different to those that dissatisfied them ('hygiene factors'). The *motivator factors* that are intrinsic to the job are achievement, recognition of achievement, the work itself, responsibility and growth or advancement. The *hygiene factors* that are extrinsic to the job include company policy and administration, supervision, interpersonal relationships, working conditions, salary, status and security. While tackling the hygiene factors will remove some sources of discontent, these will never cause employees to be really satisfied. To do that, you need to work on the motivator factors (which are akin to addressing an employee's needs). Herzberg claimed that developing these enriches the job and leads to a motivated workforce. Unfortunately, despite the enormous popularity of this model, the distinction between hygiene and motivator factors has not always been supported; it has been hard to identify separate effects of motivator and hygiene factors (Parker & Wall, 1998). Nonetheless, the idea of job enrichment through increasing the challenge and responsibility in a job remains an important aspect of job design.

The second major development in job design was similar in style: characteristics of jobs were identified that lead to increased motivation, satisfaction and high performance. Five factors were identified in the **job characteristics model** (Hackman & Oldham, 1976). These are:

job characteristics model a model that identifies five core characteristics important in job design: skill variety, task identity, task significance, autonomy and job feedback.

- *Skill variety*, the range of different actions required to do the job.
- *Task identity*, the extent to which employees complete a task in its entirety, rather than working on only a small section of the big picture.
- *Task significance*, the amount of impact that the work has on other people, inside and outside the organisation.
- *Autonomy*, an important factor, the degree of personal choice that employees have in how they go about their work.
- Finally, *feedback* from the job, the amount of information about job performance that comes from the job itself (rather than from other people).

These five characteristics of the job lead to three critical psychological states. Together, skill variety, task identity and task significance combine to influence how meaningful the work is. Autonomy influences how responsible employees feel about their work. After all, why would you feel responsible for something over which you have no control? Feedback directly informs employees' knowledge of their work outcomes. These psychological states in turn directly affect the work outcomes, such as motivation and satisfaction. As with Herzberg's model, although not all aspects of the theory have been supported (e.g. Fried & Ferris, 1987), it certainly leads to some practical and effective recommendations, such as the importance of giving workers a variety of tasks and empowering workers to have greater control of their working patterns.

PHOTO 23.1 *Call centre.*
Source: Shutterstock.

More recently, models of work design have been extended to tackle important changes in work that have subsequently arisen (e.g. Parker, Wall & Cordery, 2001). In addition to the increased use of technology at work, the increase in customer service roles has also emphasised the importance of managing emotions at work.

For example, call-centre workers dealing with complaints frequently talk to irate customers and must stay positive. This emotional labour can be demanding. Nonwork roles, such as family life, can conflict with work roles and balancing these elements can be difficult. Projects are increasingly tackled by teams rather than individuals too, so facilitating effective team work has become important. As customers demand services 24 hours a day, there must be people employed to deliver them. This means that shift work has increased across a range of jobs.

The physical design of the workplace can also make a difference. Early studies highlighted the difficulties of linking changes in the physical workplace to performance. A famous study investigated changes in illumination on employees' productivity at the Hawthorne Works. Oddly, decreasing the light to quite low levels seemed to increase performance. It transpired that the workers believed that they were being given better working conditions and worked harder as a result, even though the conditions were actually worse. This is known as the Hawthorne effect and illustrates a wider point about the effects of the physical work environment on workers. There is not a direct link between the environment and performance and so increasing one will not simply increase the other; it is mediated by the workers themselves. A major factor is the workers' perceptions of the link between the environment and performance. If they perceive that there are benefits, those benefits are much more likely to arise.

The humans in this system make these relationships more complex. For example, a popular notion is that painting walls a certain colour will affect performance. Striking findings include the fact that more proofreading errors are made in white rooms than blue rooms (Kwallek *et al.*, 1996). However, these findings are hard to replicate (Kwallek, Soon & Lewis, 2007). The physical environment of offices can make a difference, though. Open-plan offices can increase communication, but can also lower job satisfaction (Danielsson & Bodin, 2008). There are also important regulations on physical factors such as heat, noise and so on because of their implications for health and safety (e.g. Dul & Weerdmeester, 2001).

Overall, how jobs are designed has a clear effect on a number of outcomes. Unfortunately, though, it is hard to achieve everything, and changes to improve one factor can hinder another one. Increasing efficiency will reduce errors and idle time, but will also increase problems such as ill health. Conversely, increasing motivational factors by applying ideas from the job characteristics model will improve job satisfaction, but often this does not translate into an increase in efficiency. Improving the physical work environment will reduce discomfort and ill health, but can reduce the efficiency of work. Good job design is not simply applying all these principles at once, because they conflict. Instead, by careful redesign it is possible to find innovative ways to balance these factors in the best way and design the optimal fit of the job to the person (e.g. Morgeson & Campion, 2002).

In summary, we must not neglect the human element when considering the design of jobs and equipment. How we process information should have a bearing on equipment design to ensure safety and avoid accidents. Good job design, on the other hand, is more complex, as you often have to consider a trade-off between making the physical environment better and losing efficiency.

23.7 SUMMARY AND CONCLUSIONS

This chapter has considered work from the perspective of the organisation. We did this by first outlining how individuals can be motivated, by considering needs, organisational justice and how people calculate benefits. This led us to discuss the impact of teams and the crucial influence of leadership. While all of these aspects were concerned with the human element in organisations, it is also very important to consider the environment. Jobs have to be designed in ways that maximise efficiency while protecting health and wellbeing, and both job and equipment design should minimise the likelihood of errors and accidents occurring.

SELF-TEST QUESTIONS

- Compare and contrast a motivational theory that considers content and one that considers process.
- What are the key principles of organisational justice?
- What is the Swiss cheese model?
- What are the different elements of the job characteristics model?
- What can psychologists contribute to understanding performance management?
- What is the difference between a group and a team?
- Describe two different approaches to understanding leadership.
- What factors affect people during organisational change?

RELEVANT ESSAY QUESTIONS

- What is an organisation? Why is the answer to this question important to understanding organisational behavior?
- What can psychologists contribute to understanding performance management?
- How can an understanding of group processes be used to leverage better teamwork?
- How can leaders most effectively manage their staff?
- What can psychologists contribute to organisational development and change?
- What methods might a psychologist use to diagnose organisational needs with a view to designing interventions, and why?

TEXTS FOR FURTHER READING

Cannon, J.A. & McGee, R. (2008) *Organizational Development and Change*, London: CIPD.

Latham, G.P. (2007) *Work Motivation: History, Theory, Research and Practice*, London: Sage.

Mohrman, S.A., Cohen, S.G. & Mohrman, A.M. (1995) *Designing Team-Based Organizations: New Forms for Knowledge Work*, San Francisco, CA: Jossey Bass.

Norman, D.A. (2002) *The Design of Everyday Things*, New York: Basic Books.

Parker, S. & Wall, T.R. (1998) *Job and Work Design*, London: Sage.

Parry, K.W. & Bryman, A. (2006) Leadership in organizations, in S. Clegg, C. Hardy, T. Lawrence & W. Nord (eds) *Sage Handbook of Organization Studies*, London: Sage.

RELEVANT JOURNAL ARTICLES

Buono, A.F., Bowditch, J.L. & Lewis, J.W. (1985) When cultures collide: The anatomy of a merger, *Human Relations* 38(5): 477–500.

Gastil, J. (1994) A meta-analytic review of the productivity and satisfaction of democratic and autocratic leadership, *Small Group Research* 26(3): 384–410.

Greenberg, J. (1987) Organizational justice: Yesterday, today, and tomorrow, *Journal of Management* 16: 399–432.

Parker, S.K., Wall, T.D. & Cordery, J.L. (2001) Future work design research and practice: Towards an elaborated model of work design, *Journal of Occupational and Organizational Psychology* 74: 413–40.

RELEVANT WEB LINKS

Biomedcentral for a study using the Swiss cheese model, http://www.biomedcentral.com/1472-6963/5/71

Corporate Leadership Council, https://clc.executiveboard.com/Public/Default.aspx

REFERENCES

Baddeley, A.D. & Hitch, G.J. (1974) Working memory, in G.H. Bower (ed.) *The Psychology of Learning and Motivation, Vol. 8*, London: Academic Press.

Bales, R.E. (1950) *Interaction Process Analysis: A Method for the Study of Small Groups*, Reading, MA: Addison-Wesley.

Bass, B.M. (1990) *Bass and Stogdill's Handbook of Leadership*, New York: Free Press.

Bass, B.M. & Avolio, B.J. (1994) *Improving Organizational Effectiveness through Transformational Leadership*, Thousand Oaks, CA: Sage.

Belbin, R.M. (1981) *Management Teams: Why They Succeed or Fail*, London: Heinemann.

Blake, R.R. & Mouton, J.S. (1964) *The Managerial Grid,* Houston, TX: Gulf.

Borman, W.C. (1991) Job behaviour, performance and effectiveness, in M.D. Dunnette & L. Hough (eds) *Handbook of Industrial and Organizational Behaviour, Vol. 2*, pp. 271–326, Palo Alto, CA: Consulting Psychologists Press.

Bryman, A. (1996) Leadership in organizations, in S.R. Clegg, C. Hardy & W.R. Nord (eds) *Handbook of Organizational Studies*, pp. 276–92, Thousand Oaks, CA: Sage.

Buono, A.F., Bowditch, J.L. & Lewis, J.W. (1985) When cultures collide: The anatomy of a merger, *Human Relations* 38(5): 477–500.

Conway, N. & Briner, R.B. (2005) *Understanding Psychological Contracts at Work: A Critical Evaluation of Theory and Research*, London: Sage.

Cooperrider, D.L. & Srivastva, S. (1987) Appreciative inquiry in organizational life, in R.W. Woodman & W.A. Passmore (eds) *Research in Organizational Change and Development, Vol. 1*, pp. 129–69, Stamford, CT: JAI Press.

Cummings, T.G. & Huse, E.F. (1989) Organization development and change, in L.L. Cummings & B.M. Staw (eds) *Research in Organizational Behaviour*, Stamford, CT: JAI Press.

Danielsson, C.B. & Bodin, L. (2008) Office type in relation to health, well-being and job satisfaction among employees, *Environment and Behavior* 40: 636–68.

Dul, J. & Weerdmeester, B. (2001) *Ergonomics for Beginners*, London: Taylor & Francis.

Eagly, A.H. & Johnson, B.T. (1990) Gender and leadership style: A meta-analysis, *Psychological Bulletin* 108: 233–56.

Fiedler, F.E. (1965) *A Theory of Leader Effectiveness*, New York: McGraw-Hill.

Fitts, P.M. (1954) The information capacity of the human motor system in controlling the amplitude of movement, *Journal of Experimental Psychology: General* 112: 309–46.

Fleishman, E.A. (1953) The measurement of leadership attitudes in industry, *Journal of Applied Psychology* 37: 153–8.

French, W., Bell, C. & Zawacki, R. (eds) (1994) *Organizational Development and Transformation: Managing Effective Change*, Burr Ridge, IL: Irwin McGraw-Hill.

Fried, Y. & Ferris, G.R. (1987) The validity of the job characteristics model: A review and meta-analysis, *Personnel Psychology* 40: 287–322.

Furnham, A. (1997) *The Psychology of Behavior at Work*, Hove: Psychology Press.

Gastil, J. (1994) A meta-analytic review of the productivity and satisfaction of democratic and autocratic leadership, *Small Group Research* 26(3): 384–410.

Greenberg, J. (1987) Organizational justice: Yesterday, today, and tomorrow, *Journal of Management* 16: 399–432.

Hackman, J.R. (2005) Rethinking team leadership or Team leaders are not music directors, in D.M. Messick & R.M. Kramer (eds) *New directions in the psychology of leadership*, pp. 115–42, Mahwah, NJ: Lawrence Erlbaum Associates.

Hackman, J.R. & Oldham, G. (1976) Motivation through the design of work: Test of a theory, *Organizational Behavior and Human Performance* 16: 250–79.

Haslam, S.A. (2005) *Psychology in Organizations*, London: Sage.

Herzberg, F. (1966) *Work and the Nature of Man*, Cleveland OH: World.

Herzberg, F. (1968) One more time: How do you motivate employees? *Harvard Business Review* 46(1): 53–62. Reprinted in *Harvard Business Review* (1987) 65: 109–20.

Hill, E.J., Ferris, M. & Märtinson, V. (2003) Does it matter where you work? A comparison of how three work venues (traditional office, virtual office, and home office) influence aspects of work and personal/family life, *Journal of Vocational Behavior* 63: 220–41.

Huse, E. & Cummings, T. (1985) *Organizational Development and Change*, St Paul, MN: West.

Janis, I.L. (1972) *Victims of Group Think: A psychological study of foreign-policy decisions and fiascos.* Boston: Houghton Mifflin.

Kroemer, K.H.E. & Grandjean, E. (1997) *Fitting the Task to the Human: A Textbook of Occupational Ergonomics*, London: Taylor & Francis.

Kwallek, N., Soon, K. & Lewis, C.M. (2007) Work week, productivity, visual complexity, and individual environmental sensitivity in three offices of different color interiors, *Color Research & Application* 32: 130–43.

Kwallek, N., Lewis, C.M., Lin-Hsiao, J.W.D. & Woodson, H. (1996) Effects of nine monochromatic office interior colors on clerical tasks and worker mood, *Color Research & Application* 21: 448–58.

Lawton, R. & Ward, N.J. (2005) A systems analysis of the Ladbroke Grove rail crash, *Accident Analysis & Prevention* 37: 235–44.

Lewin, K. (1951) *Field Theory in Social Science*, London: Tavistock.

Likert, R. (1967) *The Human Organization*, New York: McGraw-Hill.

Little, B. & Little, P. (2006) Employee engagement: Conceptual issues, *Journal of Organizational Culture, Communications, and Conflict* 10: 1–11.

Mars, G. (1982) *Cheats at Work*, Hemel Hempstead: Allen and Unwin.

Maslow, A. (1954) *Motivation and Personality.* New York: Harper & Row.

Mathieu, J.E. & Zajac, D. (1990) A review and meta-analysis of the antecedents, correlates, and consequences of organizational commitment, *Psychological Bulletin* 108: 171–94.

McGhee, W. & Thayer, P.W. (1961) *Training in Business and Industry*, New York: John Wiley & Sons, Inc.

Montreuil, S. & Lippel, K. (2003) Telework and occupational health: A Quebec empirical study and regulatory implications, *Safety Science* 41: 339–58.

Moorrees, V. (1933) Industrial psychology at Rowntree's Cocoa Works. I. The work of the psychological department, *Human Factor* 7: 159–66.

Morgeson, F.P. & Campion, M.A. (2002) Minimizing tradeoffs when redesigning work: Evidence from a longitudinal quasi-experiment, *Personnel Psychology* 55: 589–612.

Oborne, D.J. (1998) *Ergonomics at Work: Human Factors in Design and Development*, Chichester: John Wiley & Sons, Ltd.

Parker, S. & Wall. T.R. (1998) *Job and Work Design*, London: Sage.

Parker, S.K., Wall, T.D. & Cordery, J.L. (2001) Future work design research and practice: Towards an elaborated model of work design, *Journal of Occupational and Organizational Psychology* 74: 413–40.

Pashler, H. (1998) *The Psychology of Attention*, Cambridge, MA: MIT Press.

Paul, R.J. & Ebadi, Y.M. (1989) Leadership decision making in a service organization: A field test of the Vroom Yetton model, *Journal of Organizational Psychology* 62: 201–11.

Reason, J. (1997) *Managing the Risks of Organizational Accidents*, Aldershot: Ashgate.

Robinson, S.L., Kraatz, M.S. & Rousseau, D.M. (1994) Changing obligations and the psychological contract: A longitudinal study, *Academy of Management Journal* 31(1): 137–52.

Roethlisberger, F.J. & Dickson, W.J. (1939) *Management and the Worker*, Cambridge, MA: Harvard University Press.

Schein, E.H. (1980) *Career Anchors: Discovering Your Real Values*, San Diego, CA: Pfeiffer.

Shiflett, S. (1979) Toward a general model of leadership effectiveness, *Journal of Leadership & Organizational Studies* 1(2): 3–26.

Smircich, L. (1983) Concepts of culture and organizational analysis, *Administrative Science Quarterly* 28: 339–58.

Steiner, I.D. (1972) *Group Process and Productivity*, New York: Academic Press.

Stogdill, R.M. (1948) Personal factors associated with leadership: A survey of the literature, *Journal of Psychology* 25: 35–71.

Symon, G. & Cassell, C. (1998) Reflections on the use of qualitative methods, in G.Symon & C.Cassell (eds) *Qualitative Methods and Analysis in Organizational Research: A Practical Guide*, pp. 1–9, London: Sage.

Tannenbaum, S.I., Beard, R. & Salas, E. (1992) Team building and its influence on team effectiveness: An examination of conceptual and empirical development, in K. Kelley (ed.) *Issues Theory, and Research in Industrial and Occupational Psychology: Advances in Psychology*, pp. 117–53, San Francisco: Jossey-Bass.

Taylor, F.W. (1911) *The Principles of Scientific Management*, New York: Harper.

Taylor, F. (1947) *Scientific Management*, London: Harper & Row.

Thibaut, J.W. & Walker, L. (1978) *Procedural Justice: A Psychological Analysis*, Hillsdale, NY: Erlbaum.

Trist, E.L. & Bamforth, K.W. (1951) Some social and psychological consequences of the long-wall method of coal getting, *Human Relations* 4: 3–38.

Vredenburgh, A.G. (2002) Organizational safety: Which management practices are most effective in reducing employee injury rates? *Journal of Safety Research* 32: 259–76.

Vroom, V.H. (1964) *Work and Motivation*, San Fancisco, CA: Jossey Bass.

Weiss, H.M. & Adler, S. (1984) Personality and organizational behavior, in B.M. Staw & L.L. Cummings (eds) *Research in Organizational Behavior*, Vol. 6, pp. 1–50, Greenwich, CT: JAI Press.

Weiss, J. (1996) *Organizational Behaviour and Change: Managing Diversity, Cross-Cultural Dynamics and Ethics*, St. Paul, MN: West.

Zacharatos, A., Barling, J. & Iverson, R.D. (2005) High-performance work systems and occupational safety, *Journal of Applied Psychology* 90: 77–93.

24 Cognition in the Workplace

ADRIAN BANKS, ALMUTH McDOWALL & LYNNE MILLWARD

LEARNING OUTCOMES

WHEN YOU HAVE COMPLETED THIS CHAPTER, YOU SHOULD BE ABLE TO:

1. Describe how people learn knowledge, skills and attitudes.
2. Describe the major approaches to decision making and their relevance in organisations.
3. Explain how people's cognitive capacity limitations contribute to errors.
4. Explain how sharing knowledge affects team performance.

KEY WORDS

Attitude • Automatic Processes • Biases • Bounded Rationality • Controlled Processes • Declarative Knowledge • Expected Utility Theory • Heuristics • Lapse • Mental Model • Mistake • Procedural Knowledge • Prospect Theory • Recognition-Primed Decision Making • Situation Awareness • Slip

CHAPTER OUTLINE

FOCUS POINT 24.1 PROVIDING GOOD FEEDBACK IN TRAINING

Providing good feedback to trainees is an essential component of skill acquisition. An obvious point, perhaps, is that skills are not learned without feedback (Fabiani *et al.*, 1989). Simply practising a skill without any sense of whether you are doing it correctly affords no benefits, and yet asking trainees to practise a skill without providing adequate feedback occurs more often than you would think. This places the onus on the trainer to ensure that adequate feedback is given, even though it can be difficult when there are a number of trainees and time is limited. The question is how to schedule this practice and feedback in order to speed up the process of skill acquisition and to make best use of time with the trainer.

Some tasks have intrinsic feedback: it is clear from the task itself if you are doing the right thing. One example is learning a new computer system. If it works, then you have operated it correctly. If the computer crashes, then you know that you did something wrong. But other skills do not have much intrinsic feedback and it is not always obvious if you are performing as you should be. An example of this is conducting an interview. You may be trying to ask questions in the correct manner and so on, but an external observer is often better placed to comment on

how you come across. In these situations it is helpful to have accurate and timely information about your performance in order to maximise learning. However, it is not necessary to receive this feedback after every attempt. In one study, receiving feedback only one third of the time was just as effective as receiving information after every attempt (Winstein & Schmidt, 1990).

The guidance hypothesis suggests that receiving too much feedback can actually be counter-productive. Over time, trainees come to rely on the feedback in order to guide them instead of evaluating their performance for themselves. This can lead to problems when the feedback is eventually removed. Therefore the best approach is often to begin with plenty of feedback (although not so much as to overload the trainee in the very early stages when they are trying to understand the task) and then tapering it by slowly reducing the frequency with which feedback is provided, to encourage trainees to reflect on their own performance and learn from the intrinsic feedback they are receiving from the task itself. In this way they are initially supported, but subsequently learn to develop their skills without always relying on the trainer.

FIGURE 24.1 *An emotive poster by The Hazards Campaign emphasising the importance of safety at work.*

sub@hazards.org.

consequences, for example strategic decisions taken by an organisation can result in its success or failure. The accumulation of poor decisions concerning loans by financial institutions seems to have been a major factor in a global recession. On a smaller scale, decisions are made daily on topics such as selection, negotiation and appraisal that combine to determine the effectiveness of employees and the organisations for which they work. Making good judgement calls is an important element of many jobs, especially managerial roles.

24.3.1 *Expected Utility Theory*

What exactly is meant by a decision? A decision refers to the process of selecting between two or more options. Within **expected utility theory** (e.g. Kahneman & Tversky, 1979) each of these options will lead to different outcomes, and the outcomes have two attributes (although decision makers may not explicitly think of their decisions in these terms). These attributes are (i) the value of each possible outcome – that is,

> **expected utility theory**
> a theory of decision making concerned with reviewing the value and risk of each potential outcome.

how beneficial or not it would be – and (ii) how likely that outcome is to arise – that is, how risky it is. The benefits of each outcome are weighted by how likely that outcome is, and the best option is the one that has the best weighted outcomes on average. If decision makers always evaluated their options in this way then they would maximise their chance of receiving the greatest benefit.

For example, which of the following two options would you prefer? Would you prefer to receive £5 right now, or let me toss a coin and if it lands on heads I will give you £11 but if it lands on tails I will give you nothing? Many people will settle for the £5, but this doesn't maximise your expected return. You don't know if the coin toss will be heads or tails, but you could expect it to be heads half of the time (giving you £11) and tails half of the time (giving you £0). So on average you would receive £5.50 with the risky option, making it a better bet. Of course you may be unlucky on this one occasion, but in the long run maximising your expected utility like this will pay dividends.

24.3.2 *Behavioural Decision Theory*

Unfortunately, it is common for people to take the non-optimal choice, documented by many studies in the field of behavioural decision theory. Their decisions are not solely influenced by random error, though;

there are systematic **biases** in the evaluations that are made. Many biases have been identified and they can all be seen to influence organisational and managerial decision making (e.g. Bazerman, 2005). There are biases influencing the evaluation of the outcomes, such as the *'sunk cost effect'*. This refers to the act of throwing good money after bad: a previous commitment to a course of action increases the desire to commit further. This can lead to large sums of money being spent to prop up failing schemes when a wiser course of action would have been to let them go. There are also biases influencing the evaluation of how likely events are to occur. For example, people tend to think that very unlikely events are more common than they really are (I might win the National Lottery!) and that very likely events are less certain than they actually are (well, you never know what might happen. . .). Many of these biases can be explained with **prospect theory**, an account of how people's judgements of outcomes and likelihoods deviate from the mathematically optimal (Kahneman & Tversky, 1979). As a result, making complex decisions is a challenging task and the best option is not always taken. Take a look at Focus Point 24.2.

biases systematic errors in judgement.

prospect theory a theory accounting for how peoples' judgements of outcomes and likelihoods deviate from the mathematically optimal.

FOCUS POINT 24.2 SUNK COSTS IN THE FINANCIAL WORLD

Nick Leeson was a trader at Barings Bank, trading derivatives in Singapore. In 1995 he bankrupted Barings by running up losses of £709 million. How did he generate such large losses? Leeson traded futures contracts, complex financial products that amount to gambles on the future direction of the stock exchange. After initial success he made a loss, which he hid from Barings and used more Barings money to try to recoup the loss. He lost this money too, and so used more money to try to recover the growing losses. This spiral grew until the debts were so great that he bust the bank. This is a good illustration of the sunk cost effect: the initial loss was small in comparison to the eventual loss, but Leeson dealt in greater and greater sums of money to try to recover it. A better course of action would have been to accept the initial loss, which would have had much less severe consequences in the long run.

It is easy to be wise after the event, however. The British government responded to the global recession in 2009 in part by quantitative easing or 'printing money' – injecting money directly into the economy. By 2010 a total of £200

billion – a huge sum – had been spent. Is this a sunk cost in which larger amounts of money were spent in order to prop up an unsuccessful policy? Or has it saved the economy? Opinion is divided, and we will never know what the consequences of a different route would have been.

Source: Getty Images.

Endsley, M.R. (1995) Toward a theory of situation awareness in dynamic systems, *Human Factors* 37: 32–64.

Endsley, M.R. & Jones, W.M. (2001) A model of inter- and intrateam situational awareness: Implications for design, training and measurement, in M. McNeese, E. Salas & M.R. Endsley (eds) *New Trends In Cooperative Activities: Understanding System Dynamics in Complex Environments*, pp. 46–67, Santa Monica, CA: Human Factors and Ergonomics Society.

Fabiani, M., Buckley, J., Gratton, G., Coles, M.G.H., Donchin, E. & Logie, R. (1989) The training of complex task performance, *Acta Psychologica* 71: 259–99.

Furnham, A. (1997) *The Psychology of Behaviour at Work: The Individual in the Organization*, Hove: Psychology Press.

Gigerenzer, G. & Goldstein, D.G. (1996) Reasoning the fast and frugal way: Models of bounded rationality, *Psychological Review* 103: 650–69.

Gore, J., Banks, A., Millward, L.J. & Kyriakidou, O. (2006) Naturalistic decision making and organisations: Reviewing pragmatic science, *Organization Studies* 27: 925–42.

Hollingshead, A.B. (1998) Communication, learning and retrieval in transactive memory systems, *Journal of Experimental Social Psychology* 34: 423–42.

Kahneman, D. & Tversky, A. (1979) Prospect theory: An analysis of decision under risk, *Econometrica* 47: 263–92.

Keppel, G. (1964) Facilitation in short and long term retention of paired associates following distributed practice in learning, *Journal of Verbal Learning and Verbal Behaviour* 3: 91–111.

Klein, G. (1998) *Sources of Power: How People Make Decisions*, Boston, MA: MIT.

Lee, T.D. & Magill, R.A. (1983) The locus of contextual interference in motor-skill acquisition, *Journal of Experimental Psychology: Learning, Memory and Cognition* 9: 730–46.

Loftus, G.R., Dark, V.J. & Williams, D. (1979) Short-term memory factors in ground controller/pilot communications, *Human Factors* 21: 169–81.

Luiten, J., Ames, W. & Ackerson, G. (1980) A meta-analysis of the effects of advance organisers on learning and retention, *American Educational Research Journal* 17: 211–18.

Mathieu, J.E., Goodwin, G.F., Heffner, T.S., Salas, E. & Cannon-Bowers, J.A. (2000) The influence of shared mental models on team process and performance, *Journal of Applied Psychology* 85: 273–83.

Mayer, R.E., Dyck, J.L. & Cook, L.K. (1984) Techniques that help readers build mental models from scientific text: Definitions, pretraining, and signalling, *Journal of Educational Psychology* 76: 1089–105.

Miller, G.A. (1956) The magical number seven, plus or minus two: Some limits on our capacity for processing information, *Psychological Review* 63: 81–97.

Orsburn, J.D. & Moran, L. (2000) *The New Self-Directed Work Teams: Mastering the Challenge*, New York: McGraw-Hill.

Pashler, H. (1998) *The Psychology of Attention*, Cambridge, MA: MIT Press.

Pearce, C.L., Gallagher, C.A. & Ensley, M.D. (2002) Confidence at the group level of analysis: A longitudinal investigation of the relationship between potency and team effectiveness, *Journal of Occupational and Organizational Psychology* 75: 115–19.

Petty, R.E. & Cacioppo, J.T. (1986) The elaboration likelihood model of persuasion, in L. Berkowitz (ed.) *Advances in Experimental Social Psychology, Vol. 19*, pp. 123–205, San Diego: Academic Press.

Reason, J. (1990) *Human Error*, Cambridge: Cambridge University Press.

Rouse, W.B. & Morris, N.M. (1986) On looking into the black box: Prospects and limits in the search for mental models, *Psychological Bulletin* 100: 359–63.

Seabrook, R., Brown, G.D.A. & Solity, J.E. (2005) Distributed and massed practice: From laboratory to classroom, *Applied Cognitive Psychology* 19: 107–22.

Shiffrin, R.M. & Schneider, W. (1977) Controlled and automatic human processing: II. Preceptual learning, automatic attending, and a general theory, *Psychological Review* 84: 127–90.

Simon, H.A. (1955) A behavioral model of rational choice, *Quarterly Journal of Economics* 69: 99–118.

Stanovich, K.E. (2009) *The Psychology of Rational Thought: What Intelligence Tests Miss*, New Haven, CT: Yale University Press.

Stanton, N.A., Stewart, R., Harris, D. *et al.* (2006) Distributed situational awareness in dynamic systems: Theoretical development and application of an ergonomics methodology, *Ergonomics* 49: 1288–311.

Taatgen, N.A. & Lee, F.J. (2003) Production compilation: A simple mechanism to model complex skill acquisition, *Human Factors* 45: 61–76.

Tversky, A. & Kahneman, D. (1974) Judgement under uncertainty: Heuristics and biases, *Science* 185: 1124–31.

Venturino, M. (1997) Interface and information organization in keeping track of continually changing information, *Human Factors* 39: 532–9.

Wickens, C.D. (1984) Processing resources in attention, in R. Parasuraman & D.R. Davies (eds) *Varieties of Attention*, London: Academic Press.

Winstein, C.J. & Schmidt, R.A. (1990) Reduced frequency of knowledge of results enhances motor skill learning, *Journal of Experimental Psychology: Learning, Memory and Cognition* 16: 677–91.

Zaccaro, S.J. (1991) Nonequivalent associations between forms of cohesiveness and group-related outcomes: Evidence for multidimensionality, *Journal of Social Psychology* 131: 387–99.

25 Social and Development Psychology in Work and Organisations

Lynne Millward, Almuth McDowall & Adrian Banks

LEARNING OUTCOMES

WHEN YOU HAVE COMPLETED THIS CHAPTER, YOU SHOULD BE ABLE TO:

1. Explain how employee attitudes and behaviour come to be socially regulated by and committed to the organisation.

2. Identify and describe mechanisms of social influence with reference to relevant theories of identity.

3. Describe various group and intergroup phenomena that can be either an impediment to or a facilitator of employee performance.

4. Explain how the psychology of careers requires an understanding of how personal development needs can be reconciled with organisational needs.

KEY WORDS

Career Anchors ● Commitment ● Compliance ● Group Think ● Informational Influence ● Membership Prototypes ● Normative Influence ● Personal Identity ● Role Theory ● Self-Categorisation Theory ● Social Identity ● Social Identity Theory ● Social Influence ● Social Loafing ● Social-Cognitive Career Theory (SCCT)

CHAPTER OUTLINE

26 Professional Issues in Occupational Psychology

Almuth McDowall, Lynne Millward & Adrian Banks

LEARNING OUTCOMES

WHEN YOU HAVE COMPLETED THIS CHAPTER, YOU SHOULD BE ABLE TO:

1. Describe and evaluate pathways into occupational psychology.
2. Describe the eight areas of knowledge underpinning practice and research.
3. Understand how the consultancy cycle can be applied.
4. Be able to describe core principles of ethical practice in organisations.
5. Describe the concepts of diversity, culture and inclusion.

KEY WORDS

Chartership • Consultancy Cycle • Discrimination • Diversity • Ethics • Inclusive Organisations • Knowledge Areas • Supervision

CHAPTER OUTLINE

TABLE 26.2 (*Continued*)

Will my training make me an attractive proposition for other careers? If so, which careers?	See above: the skills are highly transferable to other fields such as HR or business research.
What are the hours of work?	This depends on your job! In some consultancy jobs you work relatively long hours and do a lot of travelling, but this is not necessarily the case.
What are the working conditions like?	Again, this depends on where you work. But do remember that occupational psychology in some way or other has a commercial element, meaning that you have to deliver what the client asked for to specification and on time.
Will I have a job for life?	Many people come to occupational psychology as a second career. This is often valuable, as a mature outlook, paired with business experience, is a prerequisite for being a good occupational psychologist. While what we do continues to evolve, the reality is that people will always work and there will therefore always be a role for occupational psychology.
Where can I go for further information?	Check out the BPS website in the first instance: see relevant web links.

SELF-TEST QUESTIONS

- What are the eight areas of knowledge underpinning training in occupational psychology?
- How should you go about training to become a registered occupational psychologist?
- What are the core elements of common ethical frameworks?
- What is diversity?

ESSAY TITLES

- What, in your view, are the key issues that may face an occupational psychologist in practice?
- How can occupational psychologists ensure that their work adheres to ethical standards?

TEXT FOR FURTHER READING

Block, J. (2000) *Flawless Consulting: A Guide to Getting Your Expertise Used*, San Francisco, CA: Jossey Bass.

RELEVANT JOURNAL ARTICLES

Anderson, N., Herriot, P. & Hodgkinson, G.P. (2001) The practitioner–researcher divide in Industrial, Work and Organizational (IWO) psychology: Where are we now, and where do we go from here? *Journal of Occupational and Organizational Psychology* 74(4): 391–411.

Cheung, F.M., Leung, K., Zhang, J.X. *et al.* (2001) Indigenous Chinese personality constructs, *Journal of Cross-Cultural Psychology* 32(4): 407–33.

REFERENCES

American Psychological Association, Ethical Principles of Psychologists and Code of Conduct, http://www.apa.org/ethics/code/index.aspx#, accessed 1 February 2010.

Anderson, N., Herriot, P. & Hodgkinson, G.P. (2001) The practitioner–researcher divide in Industrial, Work and Organizational (IWO) psychology: Where are we now, and where do we go from here? *Journal of Occupational and Organizational Psychology* 74(4): 391–411.

Association for Coaching, Code of ethics and good practice, http://www.associationforcoaching.com/about/about02.htm, accessed 15 November 2009.

Australian Psychological Society (2007) APS Code of Ethics, http://www.psychology.org.au/Assets/Files/Code_Ethics_2007.pdf, accessed 1 February 2010.

BBC (2005) Offshoring has not hit UK jobs. BBC online, retrieved from http://news.bbc.co.uk/1/hi/business/4225604.stm, 17 January 2011.

Cheung, F.M., Leung, K., Zhang, J.X. *et al.* (2001) Indigenous Chinese personality constructs, *Journal of Cross-Cultural Psychology* 32(4): 407–33.

Costa, P.T., Jr. & McCrae, R.R. (1992) *The Revised NEO Personality Inventory and NEO Five Factor Inventory: Professional Manual*, Odessa, FL: Psychological Assessment Resources.

Fletcher, C. (2008) Performance appraisal, in N. Chmiel (ed.) *An Introduction to Work and Organizational Psychology*, London: Blackwell.

Kandola, B. (2008) Creating inclusive organizations, in N. Chmiel (ed) *An Introduction to Work and Organizational Psychology*, London: Blackwell.

Kandola, B. & Fullerton, J. (1998) *Diversity in Action: Managing the Mosaic*, London: Institute of Personnel and Development.

Kluger, A. & DeNisi, A. (1996) Effects of feedback intervention on performance: A historical review, a meta-analysis, and a preliminary feedback intervention theory, *Psychological Bulletin* 119(2): 254–84.

Mail Online (2009) Student with prosthetic arm awarded £9,000 after Abercrombie & Fitch 'banished her to stockroom', MailOnline, 13 August 2009, http://www.dailymail.co.uk/news/article-1206332/Disabled-student-wins-Abercombie-Fitch-case-store-banished-stockroom.html, accessed November 2009.

New Zealand Psychological Society (2008) Code of Ethics, http://www.psychology.org.nz/cms_display.php?sn=64&pg=2379&st=1, accessed 1 February 2010.

Office for National Statistics (2009) Labour Force Historical Quarterly Supplement. Economic Activity by ethnic group. Accessed at http://www.statistics.gov.uk/downloads/theme_labour/LFSHQS/2010/2010_LFS_HQS_CQ.pdf, 17 January 2011.

Practitioner Psychologists, Standards of proficiency (2009) Health Professions Council, http://www.hpc-uk.org/assets/documents/10002963SOP_Practitioner_psychologists.pdf, accessed 1 February 2010.

Qualification in Occupational Psychology, Candidate Handbook, 2007–08, British Psychological Society Qualifications Office, http://www.bps.org.uk/document-download-area/document-download$.cfm?restart=true&file_uuid=46A3F5BC-1143-DFD0-7E33-F849C52DE3EA, accessed 1 February 2010.

RELEVANT WEB LINKS

British Psychological Society, information on occupational psychology research and training, http://www.bps.org.uk/careers/what-do-psychologists-do/areas/areas_home.cfm#occupational

Part VI
Sports and Exercise Psychology

27 The Nature of Sport and Exercise Psychology

ANDY LANE & TRACEY DEVONPORT

LEARNING OUTCOMES

WHEN YOU HAVE COMPLETED THIS CHAPTER, YOU SHOULD BE ABLE TO:

1. Demonstrate how personal values and beliefs might influence how a sport and exercise psychologist works.
2. Explore some of the roles of a sport and exercise psychologist and what are the key related issues.
3. Examine validity and reliability issues related to conducting a needs analysis.

KEY WORDS

Behaviourist • Beliefs • Emotion • Goals • Humanist Philosophy • Performance Profile • Psychological Skills • Trait Theory • Values

CHAPTER OUTLINE

ROUTE MAP OF THE CHAPTER

The chapter begins by discussing the clients and key roles of a sport and exercise psychologist. Importantly, we propose that a sport psychologist and an exercise psychologist have markedly different clients. We also explore why someone might either become a sport or exercise psychologist, encouraging people to reflect on their own *beliefs* and *values*. We follow this by looking at some of the key issues involved in service delivery. We discuss the issue of performance enhancement versus the wellbeing of the client, a concern that is particularly relevant for sport psychology. Following this, we look at guiding philosophical issues as these influence how practitioners work with clients, including how to conduct a needs analysis. We finish by considering measurement issues related to applied psychology, and in doing so conclude an important point related to the performance versus wellbeing debate.

To get the most out of this chapter, we suggest that you read the case histories and complete all the activities, as these are designed to highlight key issues concerning your approach to consultancy. Start with Activity Box 27.1, which refers to Case History 27.1. Before getting engrossed in the literature, it is important to bear in mind that a psychologist is a person who comes with a set of **beliefs**, **values** and opinions. These personal characteristics can influence how they work in ways that are so subtle that the psychologist may not realise it is happening (Andersen, Knowles & Gilbourne, 2004).

beliefs opinions or judgements held by an individual.

values those aspects of behaviour that are significant for an individual within a culture, these may be shared by other/most members of that culture.

Therefore, from the outset we encourage you to reflect on your core beliefs and values and how this might affect how you think and what you do. By completing this task, it is hoped that this will prompt answers to the questions: Why do I want to be a psychologist? What is in it for me?

27.1 WHO ARE THE CLIENTS?

From the outset, it is important to clarify that professionals typically specialise in sport or exercise psychology, rather than both. Distinctions between a sport

SPORT AND EXERCISE PSYCHOLOGY – WHAT'S IT ALL ABOUT?

ACTIVITY BOX 27.1

There are two aims to this task. The first is to raise your awareness of any experiences/issues you bring to the table that may influence the way in which you process information and make decisions. The second is to begin identifying key issues faced by practising sport and exercise psychologists, and how one might go about providing appropriate support.

Read the stories of Alan and Brenda in Case History 27.1. Each case provides a snippet of information about the client. Psychologists often work in less than perfect conditions, where there is scant information provided on which to start making decisions.

What Key Issues are Presented by Each Case?

Try to put yourself in either Alan or Brenda's shoes – how would you feel? What would you be thinking? What

might you do to help yourself? If you have actually experienced a similar situation to that presented in either or both cases, then use your experiences to help answer the questions.

What are the key issues that need to be addressed? Is it to ensure that Alan's performance improves? Or is it Alan's wellbeing that needs addressing? Is it to get Brenda using the gym, or to address her perceptions of exercise and self-esteem? Consider your immediate reaction to the question. If you thought that the key issues are all about performance or exercise behaviours, then think about why this is the case. Alternatively, if you think that the mental health or self-esteem of the client is the key issue, then reflect on why you think that is the case.

SPORT PSYCHOLOGY – ALAN

Alan is a 22-year-old cyclist who is determined to get into the GB team for the next Olympic Games. He trains for around 20 hours per week while having a full-time job in a bank. He rides mornings and evenings, and races most weekends. For a while he felt he was improving, his times in training were good and he was doing well in races. Then he tried to raise his performance to a higher level and increased his training. He also lowered his food intake to reduce his weight. This left him feeling drained and tired and he struggled to concentrate at work. His confidence in training and performance in races dipped, and he would try to psych himself up by telling himself to try harder, but this seemed to make matters worse. He said he was tired, irritable and deep down lacking confidence, even if outwardly he gave the impression that everything was under control. At an emotional low point, he was considering giving up.

Eventually, he called a sport psychologist to see if they could help. He wanted to know how to improve his sports performance. The sport psychologist looked at what he was doing in training and races and what he said to himself during these events. During these meetings, Alan learned to identify and challenge the effectiveness of berating himself in an attempt to psych himself up in preparation for performance. The sport psychologist referred him to a sport nutritionist and sport physiologist, who offered advice on diet and training. The sport psychologist also helped him set goals around diet and training, and shortly after, he started performing well in training and races again. There are times when Alan catches himself resuming old habits. At this point, he goes through some of the strategies recommended by the sport psychologist.

EXERCISE PSYCHOLOGY – BRENDA

Brenda is clinically obese and has never really enjoyed or engaged in regular exercise. She often snacks on biscuits during the day to cheer herself up, although she cannot identify why she is feeling down or why these feelings started in the first place. She reports feeling tired frequently. She has spent literally thousands of pounds on diet products and gym memberships. On joining a gym, she exercises frequently at the start, following her good intentions, but after a few weeks thinks that she is not making enough progress and stops going. She also says that she finds it difficult to make time for exercise. On stopping exercise for a couple weeks, she reports feeling a failure and begins snacking more frequently to cheer herself up. When she contemplates going back to exercise, she thinks she does not fit in, and memories of miserable experiences of playing sport at school fill her mind.

At an emotional low point, which she felt was much worse than usual, she called an exercise psychologist to see if they could help. The exercise psychologist explored the emotions and thoughts she attached to exercising, considering how perceptions of previous experiences contributed to this cycle of failure and unhappiness. The exercise psychologist also looked at her personality characteristics, particularly her low self-esteem. During sessions with an exercise psychologist, Brenda learned strategies to raise her self-esteem and become less critical in evaluating her performance. The exercise psychologist worked on her inner dialogue, encouraging her to challenge negative ways of thinking. Through setting more realistic goals and learning to enjoy the experience of engaging in exercise itself, she began to take a more positive view of going to the gym. After a while, when presented with an option of eating a biscuit or exercising as a strategy to cheer herself up, she chose the gym and, on occasions where she chose a biscuit, she no longer criticised herself for doing so. There are times when Brenda catches herself resuming old habits. At this point, she goes through some of the strategies recommended by the exercise psychologist.

psychologist and an exercise psychologist largely derive from the type of client and the focus of their work. Sport psychologists typically work with individuals or teams wishing to enhance psychological aspects that influence performance. Exercise psychologists tend to work with individuals who have a health focus. At times, the distinction between a sport psychologist and an exercise psychologist is such that it could be possible to argue that each

represents a chapter in itself. At other times, however, the distinction between the two is blurry. We are minded by the differences, and cognisant that the roles of a sport and an exercise psychologist can vary hugely. For example, a sport psychologist can work with athletes experiencing performance issues in competition or in training, with recently injured athletes or with those returning to training from injury. In addition to working with athletes, sport psychologists also work with other sport scientists (e.g. physiologist, biomechanist, nutritionist), coaches and officials (Thelwell, 2008). Consequently, the list of potential clients and issues is substantial. Exercise psychologists have an equally diverse range of potential clients. They can range from people who struggle to maintain an exercise programme to those who are retiring from elite sport. Client characteristics are diverse and cover the full spectrum of age, social class and culture. If we then consider all the different sports, from aesthetically judged individual sports such as gymnastics to contact team sports such as rugby, and combine diverse clients with diverse sports and exercises, we start to hint at the intellectual dexterity required to be a sport and/or exercise psychologist.

Given the range of issues and clients a practitioner may face, it is unrealistic for one person to believe that they can be a master of all areas. A review of the services offered by an Applied Sport and Exercise Psychologist (ASEP) shows that they tend to specialise within the headings of a sport or an exercise psychologist. For example, some psychologists claim to specialise in certain sports, team sports or individual sports, whereas other sport psychologists might work with different groups (adolescent, elderly, elite, recreational etc). After gaining accreditation to become a sport or exercise psychologist, the British Association of Sport and Exercise Sciences (BASES) require

you to indicate your areas of specialism. For example, Lane (2006, 2009) indicates that his enthusiasm to work as a consultant in boxing was based on his experiences as an athlete. He argued that this helped glean an in-depth understanding of the demands of the sport, which in turn helped provide appropriate support (Lane, 2006). Trainee sport and exercise psychologists should gather a detailed knowledge of the demands of sports in which they might offer support services, but typically do so by observation. Equally, practitioners should also develop their understanding of specialist populations with which they wish to work (e.g. children, athletes with a disability, elderly population, athletes from different cultures). It should be noted that the usage, acceptance and perceived value of sport and exercise psychology can vary by sport or activity, and are also different between sport and exercise. We touch on all of these points within this chapter. Take a look at Activity Box 27.2.

Sport and exercise psychology is growing as a profession. It was not so long ago that the notion of an athlete working with a sport psychologist would be seen as unusual, and the athlete seeking support be seen as a 'nut case'. Nowadays, there are sport psychologists working with professional sports teams and Olympic sports. However, as Thelwell (2008) describes, athletes do not readily accept the information provided by sport psychologists. Sport and exercise psychologists face the challenge of

---

PROFILING CLIENTS AND ISSUES ADDRESSED BY SPORT AND EXERCISE PSYCHOLOGISTS

ACTIVITY BOX 27.2

Go to the home page of the Division of Sport and Exercise Psychology (http://www.bps.org.uk/spex/about-s&e-psych/about-s&e-psych_home.cfm). Look at what a sport and exercise psychologist claims to do and the type of issues involved. Write down this information in the boxes below. From this list, ask yourself: What are the recurring issues? And who are the recurring clients?

Sport psychologist Types of client	Issues involved	Exercise psychologist Types of client	Issues involved

selling their services to athletes, coaches and exercise participants alike. By the term selling, we mean provide a convincing case for why people might wish to use this service. This task is becoming easier, since scepticism surrounding sport and exercise psychology has steadily declined and there are many reports of effective support. In the last 10 years or so, sport and exercise psychology as a profession has thus gained acceptance. Most coaches and exercise instructors have been exposed to the work of a sport and exercise psychologist in their training, especially at a theoretical level. Many recently qualified coaches and exercise instructors are graduates of sport degree programmes that included sport and exercise psychology modules. Thus, the notion that an athlete or exerciser choosing to recruit the services of a sport and exercise psychologist is 'sick' has largely been dispelled.

While the profession has grown, career pathways (see Chapter 31) for sport and exercise psychologists and referral processes for clients remain unclear. An elite athlete might have access to a sport psychologist through their club or national governing body. For example, UK providers of sport science support such as the English Institute of Sport (EIS) employ sport psychologists to work with those training in sports at Olympic level. By contrast, a club athlete wishing to work with a sport psychologist

psychological skills in sport and exercise psychology, the systematic and consistent practice of thoughts or actions designed to enhance performance, increase enjoyment, or achieve greater satisfaction.

may have less understanding of how to contact a credible professional. To confound matters, it is common to see adverts placed by unqualified individuals claiming to enhance **psychological skills** for athletes and exercisers. Sport and exercise psychology seems to attract charlatans, possibly more than other disciplines of psychology (Andersen, 2009).

To make the task of finding a qualified practitioner easier, organisations such as the British Association of Sport and Exercise Sciences (BASES) and the British Psychological Society (BPS) have sought to clarify what a sport and exercise psychologist does, and appropriate training routes. They have developed accreditation schemes to qualify people so that clients seeking consultation are offered some quality assurance guarantees. Clients wishing to use a sport and exercise psychologist are not likely to know about BASES or the BPS and therefore can be hoodwinked by attractive claims from unqualified people. Fortunately, national organisations such as UK Sport insist that all sport psychologists employed to provide services are suitably qualified. At present, a sport and exercise psychologist can be either Chartered by the BPS or accredited by BASES, although, as will be seen in Chapter 31, changes are afoot within the profession. Some of these practical challenges are addressed in Activity Box 27.3.

Once a sport and exercise psychologist has secured work, the next key challenge is to gain acceptance among the group with whom they are working. If athletes or exercise participants do not trust the psychologist, they will act differently around them, complete self-report scales inaccurately and be unhelpful in their support of their work. Both Lane (2006) and Schinke (2004) describe the process of gaining acceptance by athletes and the importance of building relationships in the early stages of consultancy. Both authors go into some detail to explain how they worked carefully, particularly in the early stages, to gain acceptance and how acceptance can

---

EXPLORING PRACTICAL CHALLENGES   ACTIVITY BOX 27.3

The aim of this activity is to explore your views concerning what you feel a sport and exercise psychologist should do. This activity also encourages you to explore some of the practical issues that can make the work of a sport and exercise psychologist challenging. Your answer will be subjective, in that there will not be an answer that is easily marked as yes or no, but rather the best answer shows that you have reflected on the issues and can provide a convincing argument.

Key questions are: What does a sport psychologist or an exercise psychologist do? What are the limits to the support they can offer? How should these be communicated to the client from the outset?

Posters or websites advertising sport and exercise psychology services often refer to improved performance or other outcomes. Such a claim seems feasible; but if you think again, wouldn't a coach or exercise instructor make a similar claim? If so, is the sport and exercise psychologist another type of coach/instructor?

Consider your views on this matter. Briefly identify the roles of a coach/exercise instructor and the roles of a psychologist. Can you think of any similarities between a coach/exercise instructor and a psychologist, and if so, how do you think this could affect the working relationship?

HOW WILL MY PREVIOUS EXPERIENCE INFLUENCE MY WORK AS A PRACTITIONER?

A key question that a trainee sport or exercise psychologist should ask themselves is the extent to which their sport and exercise experience will influence their work. Most sport and exercise psychologists have played sport and/or taken part in exercise, and therefore their personal experiences could influence how they work as a practitioner. The key question to ask yourself is: How do such experiences influence what you think and do?

In our work with athletes from different sports, we ask athletes to develop a performance profile to identify the qualities needed to deliver successful performance. During such discussions, many athletes engage in a debate about which is the most demanding sport. These athletes typically contend that the most difficult sport is their own. This is not a surprising answer. Athletes invest a great deal of time in their sport and therefore have an in-depth knowledge of the intricacies and difficulties that must be overcome to ensure successful performance. By contrast, they have limited knowledge of other sports. If they watch a sport on television, the actor–observer phenomenon

(Bandura, 1997) influences their perception. Experts tend to make tasks look easy to do. If the observer sees certain similarities with themselves, this raises the belief: 'If they can do it, then so can I.' If one elite athlete looks at another performer, they could first say, 'I am an elite athlete also, and thus am similar in many ways to the person I am watching.' However, this athlete does not have access to the same knowledge, neither have they experienced the difficulties that the person being observed underwent in order to become an elite athlete. As such, it is possible that they will under-estimate the demands of the task in the sport they are observing.

What do You Believe to be the Most Challenging Sports?

- List three qualities that make these sports demanding.
- What are the least challenging sports?
- List three reasons why you think this is the case.
- Compare and contrast the two lists.

---

lead to effectiveness. For example, in soccer, the banter of players in the dressing room needs to be observed and understood before the psychologist judges its meaning. Players could be acting the role expected of them rather than expressing their true feelings. Lane (2006) describes scenarios in his work with boxers where he listened to advice from coaches to boxers such as following extreme diets in order to lose weight. He argues that if he challenged such views before gaining acceptance from key people in the sport, he would have ostracised himself, and therefore minimised his chances of being effective. What is clear from these guidelines is that sport and exercise psychologists need to learn the values and beliefs of the group with which they are working in order to be effective (Gilbourne & Richardson, 2005; Schinke, 2004; Thelwell, 2008). Take a look at Activity Box 27.4.

27.2 KEY ISSUES IN SERVICE DELIVERY

Offering a simple description of the role of sport and exercise psychologists allows the reader to begin to understand the nature of the job. If it can be described

simply, then the following sentence probably encompasses many of the roles involved. We propose that sport and exercise psychologists are interested in helping people to perform better, leading to the achievement of sport, exercise or health-related goals. A key aspect is the notion that psychologists seek to help people do things better in order to achieve their goals. We acknowledge that sport psychologists and exercise psychologists operate in different domains, but argue that they share a common goal of seeking to enhance the wellbeing of their clients.

goals targets, aims, or ends a person wishes to achieve.

While the reasons cited by athletes for engaging with sport psychologists can vary, performance issues are one of the most prevalent. Athletes tend to take performance in competition seriously and invest time preparing physically, tactically and psychologically. The balance of these factors will vary from sport to sport and from athlete to athlete. Evidence indicates that individuals devote time and invest effort in psychological preparation for competition (Thomas, Murphy & Hardy, 1999) and we know that people seem to develop strategies to manage performance states (Lane, 2007). It is typical for sport or exercise psychologists to be consulted as a 'fire-fighting' strategy when a team or athlete is experiencing a slump in performance, or a gym manager has exhausted all other avenues of trying to maintain exercise adherence. This is opposed to a sport or exercise psychologist being an integrated member of a support team (Lane, 2009). When the sport and exercise psychologist is a fully integrated member of the team, the work of a psychologist can be more proactive (Devonport & Lane, 2009) and support the building of skills and attributes needed to deal with task demands and challenges. Clearly, sport and exercise presents unexpected challenges and so some fire-fighting might be needed, but this is akin to having a bucket ready to put out a couple of burning sticks rather than a towering inferno!

A sport psychologist offered an attractive opportunity to work with a professional team on the basis that they can solve their psychological issues and bring about enhanced performance should consider such an offer carefully. The psychologist should question whether (i) it is a realistic goal to bring about such a change in the time available; and (ii) even if psychological factors improve, whether this will bring about improved performance. Remember the fire-fighting analogy: a sport or exercise psychologist does not want to be brought down in flames by entering a fire they stand no chance of putting out. Considering such issues should make people think about why they wish to become a sport and exercise psychologist. Someone who seeks to work with successful athletes or exercise franchises with a view to attaining reflected glory rather than helping the psychology of the participant would be encouraged to reconsider their motives. Activity Box 27.5 considers the demands of the sport and exercise psychologist's job.

WHAT ARE THE DEMANDS OF THE JOB?   ACTIVITY BOX 27.5

In relation to a sport or exercise in which you are currently participating, identify the key attributes or skills that help you to perform in that activity. What are the physical, technical, attitudinal, mental and tactical skills that enable you to perform well?

It may help to reflect on a recent best performance. What skills/qualities helped you to perform to a high standard during that performance? Alternatively, reflect on an elite athlete or successful exerciser in your sport/exercise activity. What skills/qualities/attributes do they possess that enable them to perform consistently at the highest level?

Write down these qualities in the boxes below:

One thing that strikes many individuals completing this task is how difficult it is to identify the skills that enable them to perform well, perhaps because they are rarely asked to consider what it takes to be good in their sport or exercise activity. Second, the list of qualities that you have identified in this first attempt is rarely a definitive list. Invariably you will need to reflect over time and add to the list before you can be sure that it closely resembles those required for elite/successful performance in your sport or exercise. This process of self-reflection and self-awareness is at the heart of the performance-profiling technique.

PERFORMANCE QUALITIES				
Physical e.g. Strength	**Technical** Passing	**Mental/Attitudinal** Concentration	**Tactical** Game awareness	**Other** Hydration

27.3 PERFORMANCE ENHANCEMENT VERSUS THE HEALTH OF THE ATHLETE DEBATE

A contentious argument is whether the sport and exercise psychologist should be responsible for the performance of their client. A series of articles offers a compelling argument that achieving sport or exercise success can be a collaborative goal with the client, but that the primary goal of the sport and exercise psychologist should be the client's welfare. Andersen (2009) proposed:

> Performance in real competition is multi-multi-determined and having some mental skills under one's belt is no assurance that things will go to plan. Sport psychologists claiming their interventions will enhance performance smacks of professional hubris. A softer kind of claim would be that sport psychologists may help some athletes learn some mental strategies that might be useful for athletes when it comes to the acid test of real competition. On the day of competition, however, as every coach knows, all bets are off. (Andersen, 2009, p. 13)

However, sport and exercise psychologists can become embroiled in the notion that the aim of their work is performance enhancement. A recent debate on anxiety issues in applied sport psychology by Mellalieu and Lane (2009) can be used to cast some light on this issue. Anxiety can help athletes perform; anxiety could also be part of a much deeper underlying issue related to a fragile sense of self-esteem. Students should read the debate by Mellalieu and Lane as the authors are highly critical of each other. The debate was followed up by Andersen (2009). Andersen (2009) guides the reader to consider how a sport or exercise psychologist might judge their contribution to success or failure, and we recommend a detailed reading of this article.

Andersen makes an insightful point concerning the nature of assessment in psychology. Assessment in psychology differs to other sciences, particularly other sports science disciplines where the claim to enhance performance can be evidenced by demonstrating improvement in the area intended. Andersen provides an example of a strength and conditioning professional who claims that their programme increases strength or fitness. They have the numbers to prove it (e.g. lifting more weights, jumping higher, longer time to exhaustion), but the claims stop there. The strength and conditioning professional can say to the coach: 'You asked me to help the athlete become stronger and fitter, and here are the numbers to show I did my job.' The strength and conditioning coach has delimited their role and can concentrate on those variables within their professional expertise. If a psychologist were asked to improve a client's mental strengths on the day of competition or in preparing to enter a gym class for the first time, what evidence can be used to support the psychologist as evidence to say they did their job? Andersen proposes that the psychologist might say, 'You asked me to improve an athlete's mental skills, and here are the numbers to prove it.' This refers to psychologists who use self-report as the means to assess psychological qualities. It is also common for a psychologist to use scores on a psychometric scale to assess clients. For example, asking how nervous you are, with the response rated on a 1–5 scale. Such numbers are arbitrary and rely on the honesty of the respondent (an issue we return to later in the chapter). What if an individual is genuinely uncertain of their feelings, what score do they put down? They might consult their feelings and report a value as close to their feelings as possible, but such a score would only represent an estimate and as such should not be used to judge the effectiveness of the consultant.

27.4 GAINING EVIDENCE TO SUPPORT PERFORMANCE ENHANCEMENT

The key difference between psychological data and data from other sciences is its subjective nature. An individual cannot measure their anxiety in the same way that a physiologist might measure body weight. Even psychologists who use physiological or neurological measures to infer *emotions* tend to validate these with self-report (Beedie, 2007; Beedie, Terry & Lane, 2005). We understand body weight through the relationship of the gravitational pull in the mass of two objects. With psychological concepts, we infer that something exists from multiple sources; people report feelings, thoughts and behaviours and from these, we assume that the concept exists. However, we cannot see psychological concepts in the same way as body weight. The abstract nature of a psychological construct makes it difficult to measure.

For example, if we ask an athlete how confident they feel shortly before competing on a scale from 1–10, where 1 is not confident and 10 is completely confident, and we receive a score of 10, we might assume that the athlete is confident. However, in order to do that we have to assume that the score is an accurate measure of confidence. By reporting a score of 10, the athlete might be reporting how they would like to feel, as opposed to how they are actually feeling. The scale might assess an ideal psychological state rather than the actual psychological state. It is possible that the athlete is low in confidence, but the process of asking them to rate their confidence initiated awareness of these feelings, and in doing so initiated regulatory actions. By telling someone you are confident you are also trying to tell yourself the same message, and by doing so, trying to raise your confidence. It is also possible that the person does not know how they are feeling and that they guess. When the person guesses, the answer might represent how confident they feel they ought to be or they might be genuinely unsure, but when presented with the question they feel they ought to provide an answer and so offer a number abstractly. When seen together, the threats to accuracy of self-report scores are considerable.

Although psychologists go to great lengths to develop valid and reliable self-report scales, the abstract nature of the process means that in the end, such scales can only provide an estimate. We infer that anxiety exists because a person reports negative thoughts, increases in physiological arousal and possibly certain behaviours. However, two states might show similarities and such similarities make it difficult to identify what they are and how they differ. For example, both anxiety and excitement show a similar physiological response and both have been shown to be associated with enhanced

performance (Jones & Uphill, 2004). Thus, it might not be surprising that researchers could confuse the two constructs, or find it difficult to distinguish between them. With this in mind, psychologists will struggle to claim that they have accurate measures to substantiate claims of improvement with any degree of confidence.

Differences between winners and losers in elite sport are often determined by the finest of margins. The nature of psychological constructs precludes practitioners and researchers alike from being able to demonstrate objectively fine assessment in parity with other sport scientists. As Andersen (2009) indicates, psychologists should seek to make softer claims. By such a statement, he is suggesting that sport and exercise psychologists should reflect on the subjective nature of their area. It is worth bearing this point in mind when evaluating the work of a psychologist. Read Focus Point 27.1, which considers what the goal of a sport psychologist should be.

In summary, the tools available for psychologists to assess the traits and states of their clients are fraught with subjectivity. A psychologist often relies on the person accurately reporting how they feel or think and this process is subjective. Sport scientists involved in performance enhancement are often asked to show improvements in performance and to do this they have to demonstrate changes in the variables related to their expertise. As

FOCUS POINT 27.1 PROFESSIONAL PRACTICE – WHAT IS THE GOAL OF A SPORT PSYCHOLOGIST?

As a practising sport psychologist, we are intrigued about how our professional colleagues advertise their worth to clients and reports of the benefits of their work. Websites for professional organisations such as the British Association of Sport and Exercise Sciences (BASES) and the British Psychological Society (BPS) offer an insight into how this is done.

'A performance enhancement guaranteed' was the slogan appearing on one sport psychologist's web page. Intrigued by this comment, I delved further into its origin. Contained on the website were numerous testimonials on the benefits of working with the sport psychologist from clients, typically high-profile clients, by which the sport psychologist was inferring that their sporting success and achievements were in part attributable to the work of the sport psychologist. Initially it is easy to be seduced by the impressiveness of such claims and to believe that if a high-profile athlete endorses the work, by implication it is good work. However, it is worth asking the question of what exactly the sport and exercise psychologist did in order to improve the athlete's psychological approach to

competition and mental state during competition. A physiologist can demonstrate that athlete X has improved their strength using relatively accurate means of assessment. If strength is a key factor related to sports performance, then improving strength has clearly been beneficial. For the sport psychologist such claims are more difficult to substantiate. Can the psychologist make the same claims based on self-report? I am less convinced. Is an athlete who is performing better and reporting feeling more confident suggesting that confidence predicts performance? Or is improved confidence simply a by-product of improved performance? Furthermore, if the performance in question is reliant on strength, could the physiologist also lay claim to helping improve confidence?

In a recent article, Andersen (2009) argued that the primary role of a sport psychologist was the welfare of the client. The psychologist might share the collaborative goal of seeking performance enhancement, but do so while recognising the influence of goal achievement on the wellbeing of the client. What is your view?

indicated above, this process seems more difficult for psychologists due to the subjective nature of the variables under consideration.

Several keys issues have emerged from this discussion that warrant further discussion. The first relates to philosophical issues related to consultancy and the second concerns the way in which psychologists assess their clients. Both issues will be tackled in the next sections.

27.5 GUIDING PHILOSOPHICAL ISSUES

Poczwardowksi, Shermanm and Ravizza (2004, p. 446) state:

> it is the professional philosophy of a consultant that drives the helping process and determines the points of both departure and arrival regarding the client's behaviour changes and guides consultants in virtually every aspect of their applied work.

Hence a philosophy provides the background to how someone works, it guides their thoughts and actions, and does so in a consistent way. How people operate as sport and exercise psychologists is in part a function of their training, an assessment of situational characteristics and, importantly, their philosophical views on the nature of human functioning. If the majority of my training focused on **behaviourist** conditioning (see Chapter 28), then my approach to assessing one of my client's needs would tend to focus on the effects of conditioned responses. By contrast, if my training was driven by a **humanist philosophy**, then I would look at how the individual ascribes personal meaning to situations. The key difference would be that the behaviourist would focus on the effects of environmental stimuli and conditions, the humanist on personal meaning. Extending this approach, if I was influenced staunchly by **trait theory**, I might be looking to identify the underlying traits responsible for behaviour. Further, if I followed a social-cognitive approach (see Chapter 28), I might look to see how efficacy expectations have been developed by looking at the four sources identified in self-efficacy theory (Bandura, 1997). This argument could continue by adding different approaches designed to explain human functioning.

behaviourist an adherent of *behaviourism.*

humanist philosophy any system that asserts human dignity and man's capacity for finding meaning and fulfillment through reason and scientific method.

trait theory a theory of personality that assumes that people possess enduring characteristics (traits) that determine their behaviour across different situations and across time.

An intriguing aspect of psychology is that there is evidence to defend the use of each theory. The textbook by Hill (2001) provides an in-depth examination of the way in which four traditional theoretical psychological frameworks (i.e. psychodynamic, behavioural, cognitive and humanistic; see Chapter 28) shape various aspects of the consulting process. It is an individual's innermost beliefs and values regarding the world and human behaviour that form the foundations of their professional philosophy. A key question that each person should ask is: 'What are my personal, core beliefs and values?' Activity 27.3 encouraged you to address such questions. When we work with students beginning their consultancy career, we get a range of different answers to these scenarios. Activity 27.4 asked you to explore the extent to which your own personal experiences with sport and exercise might influence your expectations concerning issues that may be encountered. Underlying these activities is the importance of a reflective process (see Chapter 28). Having completed the activities, we encourage you to compare your responses with others where possible. Engage in discussions to facilitate personal reflection regarding the origins and implications of your beliefs.

It is important for sport and exercise psychology consultants to reflect on these and similar questions to enhance their self-knowledge and self-awareness. For example, a homophobic consultant might find it difficult to address some personal issues with gay, lesbian or bisexual athletes. Exploring self-knowledge should be an ongoing process of self-reflection that should start during initial education and training.

In conclusion, it is important for sport and exercise psychologists to be introspective about their personal philosophy. When you are ready to start formal training, you will have been exposed to a number of psychological theories and these theories will tend to inform your approach. As Level 1 students, you are potentially beginning this process, and so if pursuing a career in this area is a possibility, you should start thinking of which approach you agree with. Application to Theory Box 27.1 is one example of an innovative approach.

27.6 MEASUREMENT ISSUES RELEVANT TO CONDUCTING A NEEDS ANALYSIS

Sport and exercise psychologists have a range of methods available with which to conduct a needs analysis. One approach is to use self-report measures, of which there are a vast number available. This results from the

---

BOX 27.1   APPLICATION TO THEORY

Listening to Music

By simply looking at how track and field athletes prepare for competition, by attending exercise classes and by being part of a vociferous crowd supporting a team, it is possible to see the extent to which listening to music is an integral part of sport and exercise. Unfortunately, there is not one type of music. Why do athletes listen to music and what type of music do they listen to? What is the best type of music to listen to when exercising and how can crowd singing inspire performance?

Attempts to answer this type of question have been driven by the pioneering work of Dr Costas Karageorghis (Karageorghis, 2008) at Brunel University. He has conducted numerous studies on the topic and has developed a theoretical framework for researchers to follow. As theory testing relies on the availability of valid and reliable methods, his team has developed and validated a scale for such a purpose. Not happy with the original scale, he developed a revised scale to advance research. From an observation of athletes and reflection on his own experiences, he developed a theory and methodology to facilitate scientific analysis.

---

contention by sport and exercise psychologists that there is a need to develop context-specific scales; that is, scales that are developed and validated for specific sports or exercises. For example, a measure of anxiety developed for hockey might be different to an anxiety measure for running, which in turn is different to rugby. Each scale would assess the parts of the situation that trigger anxiety and in doing so, hopefully produce a scale that is valid. To address this issue, several situational specific measures have been developed for constructs such as anxiety (Martens *et al.*, 1990), motivation (Duda & Nicholls, 1992) and cohesion (Carron, Brawley & Widmeyer, 1985). In fact, almost all psychological constructs have a sport- and exercise-specific equivalent. The concepts involved are addressed in Research Methods Box 27.1.

A key question is whether such scales are needed. Do the development and validation of a sport- or exercise-specific scale help understand the nature of the construct? Or should there be a sport anxiety scale as opposed to a scale to assess anxiety in a number of situations? The argument in favour of such research is based on the notion that measures developed among the general population might not be suitable. This is an argument we have used in numerous studies; for example, we developed and validated a version of the Profile of Mood States (POMS; McNair, Lorr & Droppleman, 1971) for use with adolescents and adults (Fazackerley, Lane & Mahoney, 2003; Terry, Lane & Fogarty, 2003; Terry *et al.*, 1999). We have even argued that validity does not generalise from one sport to another and sought to develop sport-specific measures. A principle underpinning this work has been the idea that theory testing depends on the availability of valid and reliable measures. Validity in this context means that the scale assesses what it is designed to measure, and reliability that it gets the same score each time. A set of scales is arguably a valid measure of weight. If the scales are not accurate, they can still be reliable. A person might weigh 60 kg and the scales indicate 63 kg. If the person weighs 63 kg each time, then the scales are reliable. However, as they overestimate by 3 kg, the measure is not valid. If measures cannot be trusted as valid and reliable, then it is not possible to infer meaning from them.

In some of the work above, findings have supported the value of such research. Using research to develop and validate a measure of **emotion** provides a good example of this approach. The original POMS has been widely used in research and, as such, its use facilitates comparisons between studies. If study A found that exercise improves mood whereas study B found no relationship, and the same validated measure is used, this suggests that exercise might not actually improve mood. If study A used one scale and study B used a different scale, we might not be able to draw the same conclusion as it may be influenced by the way in which mood was assessed. It is possible to argue that one scale was valid and one was not. Validity is considered in more depth in Research Methods Box 27.2.

The concept of emotion is a good one to use to illustrate measurement issues. Recent research developed and validated a Sport Emotion Questionnaire (Jones *et al.*, 2005) with the intention of producing contextually valid measure. Jones *et al.* found that emotions in sport are characterised by five emotions: excitement, happiness,

> **emotion** from the Latin meaning 'to stir up', emotion may perhaps be described as agitation of the mind combined with physical sensations which produce a variety of experiences that can be recognised generally as, e.g. happiness, anger, anxiety, sadness.

RESEARCH METHODS BOX 27.1

Where are the Psychological Concepts – I Want to See One, Feel One, Touch One ... How do I Know they Exist?

Psychologists typically examine the relationships between variables in order to try to understand their relationship. A difficulty in this process is that many of the variables that psychologists wish to study are not directly observable; we cannot observe anxiety in the same way that we can see muscle strength. Anxiety is often observed through biting nails, sweaty palms, increased perspiration, goose pimples and frequent visits to the toilet.

Let us consider these behaviours and explore whether they are reliable indicators of anxiety. Think back to a time when you were very nervous and then go through each indicator using the headings in the boxes below.

Anxiety indicator	Could this behaviour be attributed to something other than anxiety?	How easy would it be to spot that someone was anxious from this indicator?
Biting nails	Yes. The person might have long nails and so looking at how short the nails are is important. But they may habitually bite their nails irrespective of their mood.	Difficult. The person could hide their anxiety easily if they wished. Someone would have to know the person well in order to have a chance at saying that they were anxious.
Sweaty palms		
Increased perspiration		
Goose pimples		
Frequent visits to the toilet		

anger, anxiety and dejection. When they examined the relationship between the Sport Emotion Questionnaire and the mood measure developed by Terry et al. (1999, 2003) called the Brunel Mood Scale (BRUMS), they found that scores on the two scales were similar that is, the two scales correlated strongly. The BRUMS is a nonsport-specific measure of mood/emotion. What Jones et al. show is that the sport-specific scale produces very similar results to the nonsport-specific scale. If athletes conceptualise emotions differently to the general population, it might be feasible to expect that the relationship between the specific (Jones et al.) and general (Terry et al.) scales would be weaker. Thus the argument that athletes conceptualise emotions differently to individuals from other populations is not supported in terms of the structure of emotions. While Jones et al. set out to develop a scale that was domain specific, the resulting scale was similar to the BRUMS, which is used across different domains.

The above argument raises an important issue: was the research worth doing? Researchers argue strongly that athletes conceptualise emotions differently to people in the general population (Hanin, 2000). If this proposal is correct, then Jones et al. would have found that athletes produce different emotions. A counter-argument to developing sport- or exercise-specific scales is that such measures preclude comparison with the same construct assessed in other domains. Motivation, for example, while relevant to sport, is equally applicable to a host of other domains (Duda, 1998). Furthermore, if each domain developed a specific inventory this would make comparisons difficult. Any differences between samples could be a product of using a different measure and thus meaningful comparisons are problematic. Following this logic suggests that sport and exercise psychologists should use measures developed on the general population and then cross validated for the specific sub-group. Such an argument seems logical: concepts such as emotion, cohesion and motivation are proposed to be universal and exist across culture, age, gender and so on. Therefore, if a concept exists across domains and that the scale shows evidence of validity and reliability. It makes sense to use a commonly agreed scale as this facilitates accurate comparisons between different sub-groups. If a scale accurately assesses anxiety, then we could use that scale to see if running is associated with higher anxiety than circuit training. If we wish to see whether rugby players are heavier than soccer players, we would insist on using the same scales.

We will expand on the issue of selecting a measure that is appropriate for the research question through an

RESEARCH METHODS BOX 27.2

A Look at Validity

Let us consider the issue of validity. Terry *et al.* (1999) looked at the validity of the POMS for use among British athletes, particularly adolescent athletes. The POMS uses single adjectives (happy, sad, depressed etc.) to assess mood, against which participants indicate a response on a 0–4 scale, from 0 = not at all, to 4 = very much so. Terry *et al.* argued that the original POMS lacked cultural sensitivity, in that many items were biased towards a North American culture. In the United Kingdom, people rarely use the term 'blue' when feeling downhearted, for example. Terry *et al.* further suggested that the item 'ready to fight' intended for the anger scale could be interpreted as ready to compete in combat sports. It should be noted that mood has shown to be highly predictive of combat sport when using the POMS (Terry & Slade, 1995). In their study, which had several stages, Terry *et al.* (1999) demonstrated that items such as 'Grovely' and 'Bushed' were not suitable for participants in the United Kingdom. Further, that there was an age-related interpretation of the item 'sad'. Adolescents interpreted sad as 'pathetic' or 'uncool' rather than as an indicator of depressed mood.

PHOTO 27.2 *Awarding medals and giving prizes to winners provides positive reinforcement.*

Source: Photo courtesy of Andy Lane.

example. If researchers were interested in differences in emotion between athletes before competition, students before an exam or money-market traders before entering a transaction, the method used could be to administer the Positive and Negative Affect Schedule (Watson, Clark & Tellegen, 1988). The PANAS assesses two broad factors: positive affect and negative affect. Through a series of comprehensive studies, Watson *et al.* demonstrated that the scales were valid and reliable. Few would argue that the scale is widely used in the literature and therefore researchers and practitioners alike could ask the question: 'If the scale has been found to be valid and used in a number of studies, is there evidence to support continued further usage?' Evidence for usage of the PANAS is based on an argument suggesting that the scale will correctly assess the concept in the domain under investigation. The influence of sport and/or exercise on emotions necessitates the use of a specific measure.

The concept of emotion has been studied extensively in the sport and exercise as well as general psychology literature. An emotion such as anxiety is typically defined as something that feels unpleasant (Lane & Terry, 2000) and theoretically is proposed to lead to poor performance (Martens *et al.*, 1990). However, several sport psychologists have argued that unpleasant emotions such as anxiety can in fact lead to improved performance (Hanin, 2000; Lane & Terry, 2000); further, that athletes can develop meta-beliefs concerning this emotion, believing that anxiety can help performance (Hanin, 2003). When such athletes experience anxiety, they seek to sustain it rather than down-regulate it. Anxiety can be helpful for performance through acting as a warning signal that action is needed, for example, when a meaningful goal is under threat. However, when anxiety appears to

PHOTO 27.1 *The motivation for individuals to take part in sport and exercise varies. For some people it is about winning medals, for others taking part is about improvements in health and fitness. The photo above shows a Santa race, an event typically organised before Christmas. Enjoyment is likely to be a major motivator for these runners.*

Source: Photo courtesy of Andy Lane.

be helpful it is important to assess the entire emotional state (Baumeister *et al.*, 2007). An emotional state that includes anxiety, excitement and feeling vigorous is often perceived to be helpful for performance (Hanin, 2000; Lane & Terry, 2000). Athletes report that anxiety direction is closely related to feeling excited (Jones & Uphill, 2004). Therefore, as the PANAS merges unpleasant emotions into a single scale, this precludes examining interactions. We suggest that investigating interactions among emotions would be a more fruitful line of research and offer greater utility for applied practitioners. If the above argument is correct in that sport and exercise represent a domain where specific emotions should be assessed, then a global scale will be inadequate.

The key point emanating from the issues discussed above is that measurement tools need to be fit for purpose. We encourage student practitioners to consider what the assessment tool is needed for, and what measures fulfil those requirements. Researchers and practitioners alike should consider whether a scale designed to assess a construct in one population will adequately meet assessment needs when used in a different population.

In summary, as psychological variables such as anxiety are more difficult to identify than variables such as body weight or height, researchers are suggesting that they might be different in nature. The relative subjectivity of psychology as a science means that scales designed to assess any given construct should always be treated cautiously. To complicate matters, psychologists disagree on how to approach measuring constructs. Some psychologists argue that scales should be sport or exercise specific, while others propose that such an approach would make it difficult to compare anxiety levels, for example between soccer players and rugby players.

27.6.1 Methodological Factors Influencing a Needs Analysis

A construct routinely investigated in sport and exercise psychology is the use of psychological skills. Assessment of psychological skills is often recognised as an integral part of the work of an applied sport psychologist (see Thomas, Murphy & Hardy, 1999). Psychological skills refer to a systematic and consistent practice of thoughts or actions designed to enhance performance, increase enjoyment or achieve greater satisfaction of sport or exercise. One method of measuring the mental skills of athletes is by using psychological questionnaires or inventories, but the utility of such instruments depends fundamentally on their psychometric properties. Several researchers have recommended the use of the Test of

Performance Strategies (TOPS; Thomas, Murphy & Hardy, 1999) as the psychometric instrument of choice for assessing psychological skills usage. The TOPS is a 64-item measure, designed to assess the 'psychological processes thought to underlie successful athletic performance as delineated by contemporary theory' (Thomas, Murphy & Hardy, 1999, p. 699).

Thomas and his colleagues presented a dual rationale for developing the TOPS. First, they pointed out that the validity of previous measures of psychological skills usage had not been established beyond doubt. For example, the factor structure of the Psychological Skills Inventory for Sport (Mahoney, Gabriel & Perkins, 1987) was not fully supported by a subsequent validation study (Chartrand, Jowdy & Danish, 1992). Second, they emphasised the importance of distinguishing strategies used in competition from those used during practice; a context in which many athletes spend the vast majority of their time. Thomas and associates hypothesised that eight dimensions of psychological skills – activation, attentional control, automaticity, emotional control, goal-setting, imagery, relaxation and self-talk – would be common to both competition and practice contexts. Exploratory factor analyses supported this structure for the practice items, but identified a slightly different solution for the competition items, with negative thinking replacing attentional control as a competition-specific factor. Recent research has supported usage of the TOPS through findings showing scores relating to emotional intelligence, in which athletes reporting to use psychological skills frequently also reported higher emotional intelligence (Lane *et al.*, 2009).

The use of self-report to assess psychological skills usage or any other construct is not without limitations. For self-report measures to be valid, the respondent must provide an honest and accurate response. This seems an obvious statement, but when unpacked it reveals several levels of complexity. First, the athlete must provide an honest answer and to do that, must actually know what the answer is (again, this sounds obvious). When asked the question 'How confident do you feel you can win this contest?' the athlete might reply giving a high score, thereby suggesting high confidence. However, is the athlete providing an answer that reflects how they feel, or an answer on how they should be feeling? Most people recognise that confidence varies and low confidence is associated with poor performance (Bandura, 1997). Therefore, when asked how confident they feel, the athlete might provide an answer that reflects how confident they would like to feel. They might be giving a response that is desirable to them. It is also possible that the athlete is genuinely unaware of their score and a deep level of introspection is required. It is known that people vary in their self-awareness regarding their own thoughts and feelings (Baumeister *et al.*, 2007). When placed in the situation of being requested to provide a score, the athlete with low self-awareness guesses a likely response.

Andersen (2009) is highly critical of the use of such measures. He correctly points out that they cannot be relied on as valid or reliable. The issues mentioned above are consistent with this view. However, given the tradition of self-report in sport and exercise psychology, it raises the question of what valuable information is being gleaned through such an approach. The answer is partly based on how sport and exercise psychologists use self-report measures in their work. Many psychologists look to corroborate self-report data with individual data, behavioural data or data from a significant other (coach or parent). Terry (1995) suggests that mood profiling acts as the starting point for a discussion on the mood states of athletes. The athlete provides scores on the scale and these are used to prompt discussion in a one-to-one interview. Psychologists also use behavioural data. A great deal of research has investigated the effect of coach behaviour on athletes. Behaviourist principles propose that successful reinforcement strengthens the response, increasing the likelihood of repeat in the future.

Psychologists also adopt a humanist approach to assessing the athlete. The **performance profile** method (Butler & Hardy, 1992; Weston, 2008) involves identifying the ideal self and the current self, and reducing the difference between the current and ideal as the basis for the intervention. Performance profiling is a well-used method of assessment, particularly among UK-based sport and exercise psychologists, who have conducted most of the research on the effectiveness of performance profiling. Activity Box 27.5 provided an example (Weston, 2008). However, self-awareness is at the heart of the performance profile method and thus it is subject to many of the limitations described previously.

> **performance profile** a method of assessment used in the UK by sport and exercise psychologists, it involves identifying the ideal self and the current self, and reducing the difference between the current and ideal as the basis for intervening.

27.7 CONCLUSIONS

The aim of this chapter was to introduce some of the key issues related to applied sport and exercise psychology. We have asked you to look at the type of tasks a sport and exercise psychologist does and reflect on how you might work under such circumstances.

SELF-TEST QUESTIONS

- Write down two factors that distinguish a sport psychologist from an exercise psychologist.
- How might a potential client find a suitably qualified sport and exercise psychologist?
- Identify a common goal for a sport and exercise psychologist.
- Describe what Andersen (2009) said about the debate over performance enhancement versus the wellbeing of the athlete.
- The physiologist is asked to improve the strength of the athlete; he decides that strength can be assessed via 1 repetition maximum (1 rep max) bench press performance. He explains this approach to the coach, who agrees to this strategy. After 4 weeks' training, the physiologist shows the coach differences in 1 rep max performance. Consider issues and difficulties with following a similar procedure if a psychologist was asked to improve the confidence of an athlete.
- An athlete reports a score of 10 out of 10 for a self-confidence item. State reasons why the athlete might be misrepresenting their data.
- Describe what Poczwardowksi, Shermanm and Ravizza (2004) mean by the term 'professional philosophy'.
- Describe in layperson's terms what is meant by validity and reliability.
- The items below are selected from the Test of Performance Strategies (TOPS). Look at each item carefully and then provide an honest rating. After that, consider how you might complete the scale if it formed part of a training weekend in a sport of your choice and you wished to be invited to attend further weekends. Consider how and why scores might change and try to identify items that seem easier to present false information for than others.

Each of the following items describes a specific situation that you may encounter in your training and competition. Please rate how frequently these situations apply to you on the following scale:	Never	Rarely	Sometimes	Often	Always
1. I set realistic but challenging goals for practice	1	2	3	4	5
2. I say things to myself to help my practice performance	1	2	3	4	5
3. During practice I visualise successful past performances	1	2	3	4	5
4. My attention wanders while I am training	1	2	3	4	5
5. I practise using relaxation techniques at workouts	1	2	3	4	5
6. I practise a way to relax	1	2	3	4	5

ESSAY QUESTIONS

- An athlete reports feeling high anxiety and says that this is due to wanting to win 'so badly'. Consider how a sport psychologist might go about working with this athlete.

- 'How confident are you of winning the contest?' the coach asks the athlete before the contest. '100% confident,' replies the athlete. With reference to validity issues, consider how a sport and exercise psychologist might interpret the athlete's self-efficacy score.

- 'Performance in real competition is multi-multi-determined and having some mental skills under one's belt is no assurance that things will go to plan. Sport psychologists claiming their interventions will enhance performance smacks of professional hubris.' With reference to Andersen (2009), discuss ways in which a sport and exercise psychologist should evaluate the effectiveness of their work.

- Sport and exercise psychologists should develop specific inventories. Consider the above statement with reference to measures of emotion.

TEXTS FOR FURTHER READING

Lane, A.M. (2007a) *Mood and Human Performance: Conceptual, Measurement, and Applied Issues*, Hauppauge, NY: Nova Science.

Lane, A.M. (2007b) Developing and validating psychometric tests for use in high performance settings, in L. Boyar (ed.) *Psychological Tests and Testing Research*, pp. 203–13, Hauppage, NY: Nova.

Lane, A.M. (2008) *Sport and Exercise Psychology: Topics in Applied Psychology*, London: Hodder Arnold.

Lane, A.M. (2009) Consultancy in the ring: Psychological support to a world champion professional boxer, in B. Hemmings & T. Holder (eds) *Applied Sport Psychology*, pp. 51–63, Chichester: John Wiley & Sons, Ltd.

RELEVANT JOURNAL ARTICLES

Lane, A.M. (2006) Reflections of professional boxing consultancy, *Athletic Insight* 3(8), http://www.athleticinsight.com/Vol8Iss3/Reflections.htm.

Lane, A.M. & Whyte, G. (2006) From education to application: The role of sport sciences courses in the preparation of Applied Sport Scientists, *Journal of Hospitality, Leisure, Sport and Tourism Education* 5: 88–93.

Lane, A.M., Thelwell, R. & Devonport, T. (2009) Emotional intelligence, mood states and performance, *E-journal of Applied Psychology* 5: 67–73, http://ojs.lib.swin.edu.au/index.php/ejap/issue/current, accessed November 2010.

Lane, A.M., Meyer, B.B., Devonport, T.J. *et al.* (2009) Validity of the Emotional Intelligence Scale for use in Sport, *Journal of Sports Science and Medicine* 8: 289–95, http://www.jssm.org/vol8/n2/19/v8n2-19text.php, accessed November 2010.

Mahoney, A., Devonport, T. & Lane, A. M. (2008) Interval feedback and self-efficacy of netball umpires, *Journal of Sports Sciences and Medicine* 7: 39-46, http://www.jssm.org/content.php, accessed November 2010.

RELEVANT WEB LINKS

E-academy – What is a Sport Psychologist and What Do They Do? http://www.ecademy.com/node.php?id=94982
How to Do Performance Profiling in Sport Psychology
Part 1 http://www.5min.com/Video/How-to-do-Performance-Profiling-in-Sport-Psychology-Part-1-34094979
Part 2 http://www.5min.com/Video/How-to-do-Performance-Profiling-in-Sport-Psychology-Part-2-34094990
Part 3 http://www.5min.com/Video/How-to-do-Performance-Profiling-in-Sport-Psychology-Part-3-34094995
Peak Performance – Performance Profiling, http://www.pponline.co.uk/encyc/performance-profiling-strengths-and-weaknesses-athletes-27
Radio 4 – The Science of Sport: Programme 1 Psychology, http://www.bbc.co.uk/radio4/science/thescienceofsport.shtml
BASES Accreditation in Sport and Exercise Psychology, http://www.bases.org.uk/Individual-Accreditations
BPS Chartered Status in Sport and Exercise Psychology, http://www.bps.org.uk/careers/society_qual/spex/spex_home.cfm
HPC regulation of sport and exercise psychologists, http://www.hpc-uk.org/mediaandevents/news/index.asp?id=256

REFERENCES

Andersen, M.B. (2006) It's all about sport performance... and something else, in J. Dosil (ed.) *The Sport Psychologist's Handbook: A Guide for Sport-Specific Performance Enhancement*, pp. 687–98, Chichester: John Wiley & Sons, Ltd.

Andersen, M.B. (2009) Performance enhancement as a bad start and a dead end: A parenthetical comment on Mellalieu and Lane, *Sport & Exercise Scientist* 20: 12–13.

Anderson, A.G., Knowles, Z. & Gilbourne, D. (2004) Reflective practice for sport psychologists: Concepts, models, practical implications, and thoughts on dissemination, *Sport Psychologist* 18: 188–203.

Bandura, A. (1997) *Self-Efficacy: The Exercise of Control*, New York: W.H. Freeman.

Baumeister, R.F., Vohs, K.D., DeWall, D.C. & Zhang, L. (2007) How emotion shapes behavior: Feedback, anticipation and reflection, rather than direct causation, *Personality and Social Psychology Review* 11: 167–203.

Beedie, C.J. (2007) Towards empirical distinctions between emotion and mood: A subjective contextual model, in A.M. Lane (ed.) *Mood and Human Performance: Conceptual, Measurement, and Applied Issues*, pp. 63–88, Hauppauge, NY: Nova Science.

Beedie, C.J., Terry, P.C. & Lane, A.M. (2005) Distinguishing mood from emotion, *Cognition and Emotion* 19: 847–78.

Butler, R.J. & Hardy, L. (1992) The performance profile: Theory and application, *Sport Psychologist* 6(3): 253–64.

Carron, A.V., Brawley, L.R. & Widmeyer, W.N. (1985) The development of an instrument to measure cohesion in sport teams: The Group Environment Questionnaire, *Journal of Sport Psychology* 7: 244–66.

Chartrand, J.M., Jowdy, D.P. & Danish, S.J. (1992) The Psychological Skills Inventory for Sports: Psychometric characteristics and applied implications, *Journal of Sport and Exercise Psychology* 14: 405–13.

Devonport, T.J. & Lane, A.M. (2009) Utilizing mentors to facilitate the delivery of a longitudinal coping intervention amongst national junior netball players, *International Journal of Evidence Based Coaching & Mentoring* 7: 50–63.

Duda, J.L. (1998) *Advances in Sport and Exercise Psychology Measurement*, Morgantown, WV: Fitness Information Technology.

Duda, J.L. & Nicholls, J.G. (1992) Dimensions of goal achievement motivation in schoolwork and sport, *Journal of Educational Psychology* 84: 290–99.

Fazackerley, R., Lane, A.M. & Mahoney, C. (2003) Confirmatory factor analysis of the Brunel Mood Scale for use with water-skiing competition, *Perceptual & Motor Skills* 2: 657–61.

Gilbourne, D. & Richardson, D. (2005) A practitioner focused approach to the provision of psychological support in soccer: Adopting action research themes and processes, *Journal of Sports Sciences* 23(6): 651–8.

Hanin, Y.L. (2000) Individual zones of optimal functioning (IZOF) model: Emotion–performance relationships in sports, in Y.L. Hanin (ed.) *Emotions in Sport*, pp. 65–89, Champaign, IL: Human Kinetics.

Hanin, Y.L. (2003) Performance related emotional states in sport: A qualitative analysis, *Qualitative Social Research* 4, http://www.qualitative-research.net/fqs-texte/1-03/1-03hanin-e.htm, accessed November 2010.

Hill, K.L. (2001) *Frameworks for Sport Psychologists: Enhancing Sport Performance*, New York: Human Kinetics.

Jones, M.V. & Uphill, M. (2004) Responses to the Competitive State Anxiety Inventory-2(d) by athletes in anxious and excited scenarios, *Psychology of Sport and Exercise* 5: 201–12.

Jones, M.V., Lane, A.M., Bray, S.R., Uphill, M. & Catlin, J. (2005) Development and validation of the Sport Emotion Questionnaire, *Journal of Sport & Exercise Psychology* 27(4): 407.

Karageorghis, C.I. (2008) The scientific application of music in sport and exercise, in A.M. Lane (ed.) *Sport and Exercise Psychology: Topics in Applied Psychology*, pp. 109–38, London: Hodder.

Lane, A.M. (2006) Reflections of professional boxing consultancy: A response to Schinke (2004), *Athletic Insight* 8(3): 1–7.

Lane, A.M. (2007) *Mood and Human Performance: Conceptual, Measurement, and Applied Issues*, Hauppauge, NY: Nova Science.

Lane, A.M. (2009) Consultancy in the ring: Psychological support to a world champion professional boxer, in B. Hemmings & T. Holder (eds) *Applied Sport Psychology*, pp. 51–63, Chichester: John Wiley & Sons, Ltd.

Lane, A.M. & Terry, P.C. (2000) The nature of mood: Development of a conceptual model with a focus on depression, *Journal of Applied Sport Psychology* 12(1): 16–33.

Lane, A.M., Thelwell, R.C., Lowther, J.P. & Devonport, T. (2009) Relationships between emotional intelligence and psychological skills among athletes, *Social Behaviour and Personality* 37: 195–202.

Mahoney, M.J., Gabriel, T.J. & Perkins, T.S. (1987) Psychological skills and exceptional athletic performance, *Sport Psychologist* 1: 181–99.

Martens, R., Vealey, R.S., Burton, D., Bump, L. & Smith, D.E. (1990) Development and validation of the Competitive Sports Anxiety Inventory-2, in R. Martens, R.S. Vealey & D. Burton (eds) *Competitive Anxiety in Sport*, pp. 117–78, Champaign, IL: Human Kinetics.

McNair, D.M., Lorr, M. & Droppleman, L.F. (1971) *Manual for the Profile of Mood States*, San Diego, CA: Educational and Industrial Testing Services.

Mellalieu, S. & Lane, A. (2009) Debate: Is studying anxiety interpretations useful for sport and exercise psychologists? *Sport & Exercise Scientist* 19: 28–31.

Poczwardowski, A., Sherman, C.P. & Ravizza, K. (2004) Professional philosophy in the sport psychology service delivery: Building on theory and practice, *Sport Psychologist* 18: 445–6.

Schinke, R.J. (2004) The contextual side of professional boxing: One consultant's experience, *Athletic Insight*, http://www.athleticinsight.com/Vol6Iss2/Professionalboxing.htm, accessed November 2010.

Terry, P.C. (1995) The efficacy of mood state profiling among elite competitors: A review and synthesis, *Sport Psychologist* 9: 309–24.

Terry, P.C., Lane, A.M. & Fogarty, G.J. (2003) Construct validity of the Profile of Mood States – Adolescents for use with adults, *Psychology of Sport & Exercise* 4(2): 125–39.

Terry, P.C. & Slade, A. (1995) Discriminant effectiveness of psychological state measures in predicting performance outcome in karate competition, *Perceptual & Motor Skills* 81(1): 275–86.

Terry, P.C., Lane, A.M., Lane, H.J. & Keohane, L. (1999) Development and validation of a mood measure for adolescents, *Journal of Sports Sciences* 17(11): 861–72.

Thelwell, R.C. (2008) Applied sport psychology: Enhancing performance using psychological skills training, in A.M. Lane (ed.) *Sport and Exercise Psychology: Topics in Applied Psychology*, pp. 1–16, London: Hodder & Stoughton.

Thomas, P.R., Murphy, S. & Hardy, L. (1999) Test of Performance Strategies: Development and preliminary validation of a comprehensive measure of athletes' psychological skills, *Journal of Sports Sciences* 17: 697–711.

Watson, D., Clark, L.A. & Tellegen, A. (1988) Development and validation of brief measures of positive and negative affect: The PANAS scales, *Journal of Personality and Social Psychology* 54: 1063–70.

Weston, N. (2008) Performance profiling, in A.M. Lane (ed.) *Sport and Exercise Psychology: Topics in Applied Psychology*, pp. 91–108, London: Hodder & Stoughton.

28 Psychological Skills Interventions in Sport and Exercise Psychology

TRACEY DEVONPORT & ANDY LANE

LEARNING OUTCOMES

WHEN YOU HAVE COMPLETED THIS CHAPTER, YOU SHOULD BE ABLE TO:

1. Be aware of the influence of consultancy perspectives (e.g. behaviourist) on client assessment and the subsequent selection and application of psychological skills interventions.
2. Be aware of the stages of trainee ASEP supervision and the implications of each stage for the experiences of a trainee practitioner.
3. Understand the need for a code of conduct and adherence to ethical principles among practitioners.
4. Understand the principles of reflective practice and models that guide its use.

KEY WORDS

Cognitive Distortions • Cognitive Restructuring • Confidentiality • Humanistic Approach • Informed Consent • Psychological Skills Interventions (PSI) • Reinforcement • Schema • Self-Actualisation • Sociocultural Conditioning

CHAPTER OUTLINE

28.1 PSYCHOLOGICAL SKILLS INTERVENTIONS

Applied Sport and Exercise Psychology (ASEP) practitioners around the world appear to address many of the same issues, using similar intervention techniques (Taylor, 1995). To appropriately select and increase the efficacy of **psychological skills interventions (PSI)**, it is necessary to understand the client and the goal for the work. The ASEP practitioner should seek to establish client characteristics, including their existing skills and abilities, personal dispositions (e.g. beliefs, motives, emotional responses) and those demands within the situations they typically face that trigger key behaviours (Gardner & Moore, 2006). In a further attempt to ensure that interventions utilised by ASEP appropriately match client needs, they must also be grounded within a scientific evidence base. Theory and research underpin the work of an applied psychologist, and this approach often differentiates appropriately qualified practitioners from charlatans.

> **psychological skills interventions (PSI)** in sport and exercise psychology, the focus of a PSI is to change thinking processes and patterns to increase productivity, desirable outcomes and, by extension, happiness.

Psychological skills have been defined as a

> systematic and consistent practice of mental or psychological skills for the purpose of enhancing performance, increasing enjoyment, or achieving greater sport and physical activity self-satisfaction. (Weinberg & Gould, 2007, p. 250)

Psychological skills include imagery training, goal setting, relaxation training, attentional control training, activation training and self-talk (Thomas, Murphy & Hardy, 1999). Studies have found that higher achievers employ psychological skills more effectively, and on a more regular basis, both in training and competition. These skills facilitate higher levels of confidence that enable individuals to perform to their potential (Gould *et al.*, 1999; Greenleaf, Gould & Dieffenbach, 2001). The results from three meta-analytic studies point to the value of using PSI in terms of benefit to the performer, with 85% of studies included demonstrating positive effects (Greenspan & Feltz, 1989; Vealey, 1994; Weinberg & Comar, 1994).

The following sections will examine three approaches used in assessing client needs and delivering interventions. By reviewing the major assumptions of the three perspectives, it is possible to demonstrate implications for the consultants' role, intervention goals and subsequent intervention techniques.

28.1.1 *Behaviourist Approach*

Behaviourist approaches incorporate various sub-theories, including classical, operant and **sociocultural conditioning**. In respect of classical conditioning, does the name Pavlov ring any bells? Pavlov is a famous psychologist whose name is used in everyday language. He was testing the amount of saliva dogs produce while eating when he observed dogs salivating before the presentation of food. This occurred in response to the stimulus of hearing their food bowls being prepared. Pavlov then showed that he could produce this salivatory response with other stimuli when paired simultaneously with food. He conditioned dogs to salivate to the sound of a ringing bell because the dogs learned to associate this sound with food.

> **sociocultural conditioning** a theory that contends that behaviour is learnt by individuals observing others receiving rewards or punishment dependent on their behaviour.

Watson and Rayner (1920) are often credited as exemplifying classical conditioning in humans. However, as reported in a special edition of *The Psychologist* entitled 'Unravelling psychology's myths', these studies were poorly controlled (Jarrett, 2008). It is commonly reported that little Albert, a young male participant, was allowed to play with a white rat, and that in doing so he exhibited a response of curiosity. The researchers then presented a loud noise that made Albert cry at the same time as presenting the white rat. This conditioning meant that Albert began to fear and avoid the white rat (see Figure 28.1).

It is often suggested that this fear generalised to all things white and fluffy, including things never actually tested, such as a cat, a man's beard and a teddy bear. In reality Albert did show a fearful response to the rat, a rabbit, a dog (which also scared the experimenters) and a sealskin coat. He also exhibited a negative response to a Santa Claus mask and Watson's hair, and a mild response to cotton. What contaminated these results is that Albert would happily play with the hair of assistants. Also on subsequent re-tests Albert barely reacted when presented with the rabbit and dog in a different room; he even initiated contact with the rabbit in one re-test. As such, the evidence supporting classical conditioning with humans is not as strong as is commonly reported in contemporary literature. You may now want to take a look at Activity Box 28.1.

In summary, for classical conditioning to be effective the neutral and unconditioned stimulus must be paired consistently and almost simultaneously. Classically conditioned behaviours can be removed by repeatedly exposing the learner to the conditioned stimulus without the unconditioned stimulus.

Skinner extended behavioural approaches by suggesting that learners would exhibit behaviours if they thought that it would result in a reward. In operant conditioning, the learner associates behaviours with consequences. Using **reinforcement**, punishment and appropriate shaping, a learner could be conditioned to behave voluntarily in a particular way. This is because behaviour is determined by its consequences: it is strengthened when rewarded and weakened when punished. People learn to engage in behaviours that have positive effects, or positive reinforcement. During positive

> **reinforcement** the use, by applied sport and exercise psychologists influenced by behaviourism, of positive and negative reinforcers to increase desired behaviours and punishments to decrease undesired behaviour.

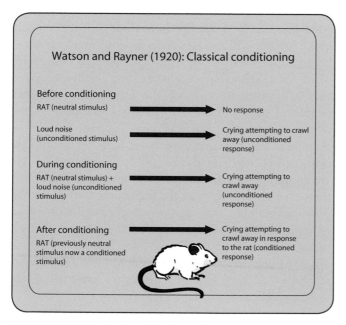

Watson and Rayner (1920): Classical conditioning

Before conditioning
RAT (neutral stimulus) → No response

Loud noise (unconditioned stimulus) → Crying attempting to crawl away (unconditioned response)

During conditioning
RAT (neutral stimulus) + loud noise (unconditioned stimulus) → Crying attempting to crawl away (unconditioned response)

After conditioning
RAT (previously neutral stimulus now a conditioned stimulus) → Crying attempting to crawl away in response to the rat (conditioned response)

FIGURE 28.1 *Classical conditioning in humans.*

FOUNDATIONS OF SAND

Read the article 'Foundations of sand' at http://www.thepsychologist.org.uk/archive/archive_home.cfm?volumeID=21&editionID=164&ArticleID=1394. This article explores academic myths and their influence in psychology. Focus on the classical conditioning experiment with Little Albert.

Having read the article, consider the following questions:

- What do you believe is the impact of consistently misrepresenting classic experiments in psychology?

- What are the implications of this for reading primary (original article) and secondary source (cited in) information?
- What are the implications for sport and exercise psychologists in reporting research methodologies and findings?
- Having read a full account of their work, how can Watson and Rayner's (1920) work exploring classical conditioning be tested among sport and exercise participants?

reinforcement learner behaviours are rewarded with a desired consequence, for example being selected to play for the first team. They also learn to perform acts because they permit them to avoid undesirable consequences, or negative reinforcement. Negative reinforcement involves the removal of an unpleasant event that is also satisfying, for example not having to face a cold shower because you didn't finish a cross-country run in last place. Punishment involves presenting an undesired behaviour beside an unwanted behaviour. Whereas negative reinforcement removes an aversive stimuli, punishment applies the aversive stimuli, thereby decreasing the strength of the response that led to its presentation. Punishment represents a negative or unsatisfying consequence of behaviour, for example being sent off during a game (see Table 28.1).

There are factors that influence the application and outcomes of classical and operant conditioning:

- If the learner feels that they are being manipulated, they can refuse to be conditioned.

- Alternatively, if reinforcement is predominantly external, the learner may not enjoy the experience itself, only maintaining involvement for external rewards.

- Those learners being punished may associate negative emotions with the activity and drop out,

TABLE 28.1 *Behaviourist Principles of Reinforcement Schedules.*

Procedure	In sport and exercise	Behavioural effect
Positive reinforcement	Coach or personal trainer compliments an individual after working hard during training/exercise	Increases desired behaviour
Negative reinforcement	Coach indicates that unless a player increases their effort they will be substituted Personal trainer indicates that unless their client works harder they will not lose weight	Increases desired behaviour
Punishment	Coach/personal trainer increases training load when the person is perceived as not trying hard enough	Decreases undesired behaviour

or be preoccupied with what not to do as opposed to desired behaviours.

- Alternatively, they may only exhibit undesired behaviour at times they believe they will not be caught, or in some cases the learner may feel that any attention is good, therefore reinforcing the behaviour associated with punishment.

A more recent behavioural approach is sociocultural conditioning (Bandura, 1986). This theory contends that individuals could learn the appropriate behaviours simply by observing others receiving rewards or punishment. Where a person is observed receiving positive consequences for a specific behaviour, it is more likely that a learner will model that behaviour at a later time. Conversely, where an individual is observed being punished for a behaviour, a learner may resolve to avoid that behaviour. Because of the importance of other people in sociocultural conditioning, Bandura (1986) referred to this as social learning. The anticipated consequences and attitudes associated with behaviours are proposed to mediate the extent to which behaviours are conditioned. For example, if a learner believes that the potential punishment for behaviour outweighs the potential benefits, they may not replicate the observed behaviour. The characteristics of the person (model) being observed also influence the extent to which observed behaviours are modelled. Models with similar attributes, or those held in high regard, are more likely to be modelled.

There are clear implications in using a behaviourist approach for an applied sport and exercise psychologist. These include:

- Behaviour is conditioned (learned) in response to the external environment. A sport and exercise psychologist can use observational analysis to identify how an individual's environment and reinforcement schedules help shape their behaviour.

- Behaviour can be modified by a variety of techniques (e.g. positive and negative reinforcement, punishment, shaping). A sport and exercise psychologist should be aware of existing reinforcement schedules that are taking place.

- Behaviours can be learned and unlearned and, as such, the focus of interventions is on learned experiences as reflected in present behaviours and learning processes.

A behaviourist intervention commonly used by ASEP when working with coaches and instructors is the use of feedback. Bandura (1997) contends that the attainment of response information is a central aspect of learning. Response patterns learned observationally are further refined using informative performance feedback (Bandura, 1997). This highlights the importance of feedback within sport and exercise in terms of evaluating and refining performance. Feedback provides information known to provide self-evaluations about performance, ability and understanding (Bandura, 1986). When learning a new skill or refining existing skills, feedback can be used to reinforce, discourage, shape or punish behaviours. The meta-analysis of Kluger and DeNisi (1996) suggests that two-thirds of studies investigating the effects of feedback found that it positively affected performance. Several studies have indicated that feedback has a positive effect on self-efficacy, performance and decision making (Escarti & Guzmán, 1999; Fitzsimmons *et al.*, 1991; Mahoney, Devonport & Lane, 2008; Sinclair & Vealey, 1989).

Feedback can be intrinsic or extrinsic. Intrinsic feedback is gained via the individual's own sensory and muscular systems. That is, when an exerciser uses a gym ball they can use the gym mirrors to ensure they are using correct technique, which is reinforced by the way the activity feels. They should feel the activity working the core muscle groups. Extrinsic feedback is obtained via an external source such as a coach, instructor or stopwatch (Williams, 2001). Verbal instruction is the most commonly used method of extrinsic feedback intended to develop knowledge of performance in sport and exercise (Mononen *et al.*, 2003). External feedback from others that may reinforce behaviour includes verbal praise, facial expressions and pats on the back. Phrases such as 'well done' and 'that's much better' can be referred to as positive feedback. Not only can this form of feedback reinforce desirable behaviours, it may also increase confidence.

Negative feedback can also be used and often takes the form of criticism or corrective statements, with phrases such as 'you failed to…' or 'you were in the wrong position'. Bandura (1992) suggests that negative feedback could be used to increase an individual's motivation for future learning effort. For example, feedback indicating how a sub-standard performance could be improved might be motivational if the person believes that a change in behaviour will bring about improved performance. Further, Kanfer (1990) argues that the use of negative feedback can serve to indicate that an individual is not performing to an acceptable standard, and therefore increases the amount of effort invested as a consequence. In contrast, research by Lindsley, Brass and Thomas (1995) suggests that negative feedback can lead to individuals questioning their ability, or believing that their best efforts are not good enough. As such, the content, timing and frequency of all forms of feedback must be carefully considered if desirable outcomes are to be achieved.

There are guidelines that may enhance the efficacy of verbal feedback in increasing desired behaviours. These guidelines suggest that by managing the relationship between behaviours and verbal feedback, teachers, coaches and instructors can increase desired behaviours. It is important to identify desired behaviours and the feedback given for particular behaviours. These behaviours must be measurable and objective and the learner must know what they have to do to receive feedback. The learner must also know what feedback they will receive for which behaviours.

Regarding the timing of feedback, it appears that immediate feedback provides a better opportunity to improve or correct performance when compared with delayed feedback (Mononen *et al.*, 2003; Sinclair & Vealey, 1989). It has also been suggested that immediate feedback could have a positive effect on the self-efficacy of performers, including those performers who are lacking in confidence (Sinclair & Vealey, 1989; Stewart & Corbin, 1988). Detailed feedback, if used appropriately, will enhance motivation. For example, feedback that focuses on self-improvement rather than comparisons with other players should be emphasised. Intrinsically motivated athletes can use skill enhancement, learning and mastery as a source of motivation. They typically enjoy competition, focus on having fun and want to make the most of their ability. Extrinsically motivated individuals participate to gain recognition or some other external reward, for instance financial rewards or praise from a parent (Ryan & Deci, 2000).

In conclusion, applied sport and exercise psychologists using a behaviourist approach should strive to identify existing reinforcement schedules experienced by an individual. Thereafter, these can be manipulated as appropriate to optimise behaviour change via the use of techniques including shaping, negative reinforcement and rewards. Now take a look at Activity Box 28.2.

28.1.2 Cognitive Approach

Cognitive practitioners argue that an individual's interpretation of external stimuli is more influential in determining behaviours than the external stimuli itself. Cognitive processes such as appraisal and attitudes (see Focus Point 28.1) are neglected by behaviourists. For example, people can plan and make decisions on the basis of information stored in memory, selectively choosing among stimuli that require attention. While cognitive theory began in response to the limitations of behavioural approaches, in practice the two theories are compatible and are often employed together in developing

CHANGING BEHAVIOUR

ACTIVITY BOX 28.2

Consider and makes notes on the following questions:

- What behaviours do you currently exhibit in your sport or exercise activity(ies) that you would like to remove? E.g. in aerobics you are often half a step behind the rest of the class and feel uncoordinated as a result.
- What behaviours would you like to replace these with? E.g. the warm-up routine is always the same

using the same music. You would like to time your movements accurately to the music.
- What strategies will you utilise to change your behaviours? E.g. reinforcement, punishment, shaping. Explain how you would apply these strategies.
- If you succeed in substituting these old behaviours for new ones, what is likely to be the outcome? E.g. you will feel more coordinated and less self-conscious.

FOCUS POINT 28.1   KEY TERMS DEFINED

COGNITIVE APPRAISAL

Cognitive appraisal can be defined as the cognitive process by which a person evaluates a stimulus in accordance with their memories, beliefs and expectations before responding. It helps a person evaluate whether a particular encounter with the environment is relevant to their wellbeing and, if so, in what ways (Folkman *et al.*, 1986, p. 992). This appraisal process accounts for the wide variation in responses to the same stimulus.

ATTITUDE

An attitude can be defined as the tendency to think, feel or act positively or negatively towards an object, person or concept (Eagly & Chaiken, 1993; Petty, 1995). Attitudes comprise three components: the cognitive, the affective and the behavioural (Reid, 2006). The cognitive component is a set of beliefs about the attributes of the object, person or concept. The affective component includes feelings about the object, person or concept. Finally, the behavioural component pertains to the way people act towards the object, person or concept (Eagly & Chaiken, 1993). When the cognitive and affective elements are highly correlated, there is a stronger relationship between attitude and behaviour (Bagozzi & Burnkrant, 1979). In practical terms, the stronger the attitude, the greater the degree of activity performed. It can therefore be seen that some evaluation of attitudes is essential for understanding behaviours and the choices made by individuals.

SCHEMATA

A schema (plural schemata) refers to a unit of knowledge (or representations) that guides memory, aids in the interpretation of events and influences how we retrieve stored memories (Flannery & Walles, 2003). Piaget (1985) considered schemata to be the basic building blocks of thinking. Accumulated experiences gradually increase the number (things known and therefore represented) and the complexity of these schemata, allowing an individual to adapt more effectively to the environment (Taylor, 2005). The process of assimilation organises existing schemata to better understand events in the external world, whereas accommodation involves changing pre-existing schemata to adapt to a new situation. Cognitive development is evidenced through changes in behaviour as adaptation takes place.

METACOGNITION

Being able to reflect on the nature of thought is known as metacognition (Taylor, 2005). As such, metacognition is often simply defined as thinking about thinking. It refers to higher-order thinking, which involves active control over the cognitive processes engaged in learning. Activities such as planning how to approach a given learning task, monitoring comprehension and evaluating progress towards the completion of a task are metacognitive in nature. Because metacognition plays a critical role in successful learning, it is important to study metacognitive activity and development to determine how students can be taught to better apply their cognitive resources through metacognitive control (Flavell, 1987).

interventions. Many practitioners using a behaviourist approach accept revised conceptualisations of the causes of human behaviour, accepting a cognitive orientation. Similarly, behaviourist principles have had a significant influence on cognitive practitioners. The cognitive-behavioural approach to behaviour change emerged as a result of a merger of these two approaches, and is one of the most widely used among ASEP (Brewer *et al.*, 1998; Hill, 2001).

Cognitive psychology focuses on specific behaviours, as behaviourism does, but these are interpreted in terms of underlying mental processes. Cognition refers to the mental processes of perception, memory and information processing by which the individual acquires knowledge, solves problems and makes plans for the future. There are implications of a cognitive approach for the consultant's role, intervention goals and subsequent intervention techniques. Since the cognitive approach contends that cognitive processes determine behaviour, practitioners adopting this approach seek to develop and empower individuals to be in control of their thought processes. The focus of interventions is to change thinking processes and patterns to increase productivity, desirable outcomes and by extension happiness. By inspecting **schemas**, cognitive practitioners strive to help individuals think in more productive and satisfying ways.

schema an individual's organised knowledge about self, events and beliefs.

Meta-cognitive processes are used to recognise areas where thought processes can be enhanced along with resultant emotions and behaviour.

There are many techniques used to help an individual change their thought processes, including imagery, attribution and self-talk. A commonly used intervention that will be explored in more detail is **cognitive restructuring**. Anderson (1977) developed schema theory, describing the mechanism by which perceptions and interpretations of experiences allow people to build schemas, organise abstract principles that help us make sense of our world and categorise new experiences in terms of previous experience. Each schema is embedded in another and itself contains sub-schema. For example, if I were to say 'athlete' do you know what I am referring to? You probably have a generalised idea of a sports person that trains regularly and participates competitively (a schema of what it is like to be an athlete). However, you would need more information to know exactly what I am referring to. It is generally agreed that we arrange schemas hierarchically. For example, you have a schema for 'athlete' and you probably also have a sub-schema for 'gymnast' and one for

cognitive restructuring methods used to challenge the biases that a client might hold about how frequently bad events might happen and to generate thoughts that are more accurate.

'rugby player' (gymnast and rugby would represent two separate sub-schemas), and so these can exist at different levels.

Schema change by the acquisition of new information, and an individual can be helped to create new schema through new experiences. **Cognitive distortions** can take place due to errors in schemas, or the biased selection and assimilation of information into them (Ellis, 1993). Distortions include focusing on one thing above all others, attributing inappropriate significance to events, personalising events inappropriately or being too narrow in inferences made. Ellis (1982) identified the following list of distorted thoughts in athletes:

cognitive distortions inaccurate ways of thinking, e.g., personalising and catastrophising, that reinforce negative thinking and feeling and may lead to inappropriate behaviour.

- Holding perfectionist beliefs.
- Catastrophising about the future.
- Believing that self-worth depends on achievement.
- Personalisation, meaning that everything is centred around you.
- A fallacy of fairness, or unfairness, particularly regarding officials.
- Blaming and polarised thinking.

Such errors in thinking can lead people to behave inappropriately (Ellis, 1993).

Cognitive restructuring is a technique with origins in cognitive-behavioural therapy. Changes in thinking are achieved through a process of identifying maladaptive cognitions, automatic thoughts, distortions in information processing and dysfunctional schemata (Meichenbaum, 1986). These thoughts are replaced with more appropriate thinking, positive affirmations and self-encouragement. Seligman (1991) argued that pessimistic thinkers could be coached into optimistic viewpoints, changing outcomes in all aspects of daily life for the better. For example, I (Tracey Devonport) was working with a junior tennis player who expressed pessimistic thinking and generalisations when noting that she 'always played badly on court number three' at her home tennis venue. This is clearly an example of maladaptive thinking. In order to address this, the player, coach and myself endeavoured to complete training on court three. The focus was to integrate positive affirmations into training with the objective of transferring them into competitive play. To reinforce positive self-talk, the tennis player was asked to visualise herself playing well against opponents on court three. Over time, the pessimistic thinking, which had become habitual, was replaced by more appropriate thinking.

As demonstrated in this example, when implementing cognitive restructuring, it is essential that the restructuring task remains the primary focus, not the skill being learned (Boggianno *et al.*, 1992). Graham and Golan (1991) observed that a focus on performance can interfere with remembering the primary objective of positive changes in thinking.

By applying techniques such as reframing, thought stopping, modelling and scaffolding, individuals can assume control in changing their thinking and maintaining change, therefore decreasing the risk of relapse (Brownell, 1982). Individuals should be assisted in identifying effective and ineffective thought patterns as a means to modify them (Williams & Leffingwell, 1996).

Techniques that can then be used to enhance thinking include thought stopping (saying 'stop' to a negative thought that comes to mind); changing negative to positive thoughts; countering (creating an internal debate to rationalise perception); and reframing (changing thinking patterns from pessimistic to optimistic, e.g. 'I lost the last game but I learned new skills'). Individuals should be encouraged to develop a repertoire of constructive statements to incorporate into thought patterns (Hill, 2001). The skills learned are transferable from one aspect of life to another, so learning to restructure thinking in a sport or exercise environment may be transferable to a work or educational environment. Now complete Activity Box 28.3.

COGNITIVE RESTRUCTURING

ACTIVITY BOX 28.3

Using a sport or exercise activity of your choice, identify in the table below maladaptive or erroneous thinking. Then identify an alternative way of thinking that is more adaptive and functional. Finally, identify those strategies you would utilise to implement and maintain cognitive restructuring. In order to support your completion of this task, refer back to the information provided on cognitive restructuring techniques (contained under the sub-heading of cognitive approaches).

Maladaptive thinking	Adaptive thinking	Strategies
I can never exercise in a morning (generalising thought)	*If I sort out my gym bag the night before, and have an early breakfast, mornings would be a good time to exercise*	*Countering, Reframing*

28.1.3   *Humanistic Approach*

humanistic approach
an approach that values each individual as having a unique perception of the world, freedom of choice and the ability to set goals driven by a motivational tendency towards growth and self-actualisation.

self-actualisation a term that has two meanings: in motivational terms it is the motive or drive to realise one's full potential; according to the personality theory of Abraham Maslow, it is the final level of personal development.

The underlying assumption of the **humanistic approach** is that every person has a unique perception of the world. Individuals are free to make choices and set goals, driven by a motivational tendency towards growth and **self-actualisation**. Self-actualisation is the basic need to develop potential to its fullest, progressing beyond existing competencies and overcoming environmental and social barriers (Hill, 2001). The object is to help people become self-actualised, capable of achieving their best in every possible way. This is achieved by seeking changes in thoughts and feelings that result in positive changes in behaviour. By examining an individual's perceptions, humanistic interventions aim to promote responsibility, personal growth and self-actualisation.

At the forefront of the humanistic movement was Carl Rogers. Rogers (1961) claimed that he could see the need for self-actualisation in small children when they were learning to walk. Rogers contended that children are continually changing because they consistently strive towards self-actualisation, a goal that will carry on throughout our lives. According to humanists, it is an individual's concept of self that most influences behaviour. This concept of the self develops as an individual interacts with the environment and struggles to maintain what has been achieved while also striving

to achieve more. Happiness is the result of how closely the ideal self corresponds to the behaving self (Ibrahim & Morrison, 1976). It also appears that individuals are happier when their locus of evaluation is internal rather than external. Clear personal standards of performance allow an individual to know exactly what needs to be done in order to feel fulfilled. As long as the individual sets goals realistically and invests appropriate effort to accomplish them, they can find satisfaction with themselves. Where an individual attempts to find satisfaction through social comparisons, they are more likely to end up unhappy and dissatisfied because these external motives are much more inconsistent.

The aim of humanist interventions is to explore personal goals and create new meanings in life, as opposed to focusing on behaviours. This approach is nondirective and client centred. ASEP adopting this approach tend to reject the belief that behaviour is controlled by external stimuli (behaviourism), or by the simple processing of information in perception and memory (cognitive psychology). Many psychologists believe that behaviour can only be understood objectively, but humanists argue that this suggests that an individual is incapable of understanding their own behaviour, a view that they see as both paradoxical and threatening to wellbeing. Humanists argue that the meaning of behaviour is essentially personal and subjective because each person has a background of unique experiences, which causes them to view a situation in a unique way. Their perceptions determine their individual reactions, and therefore psychologists should attempt to see the world through the individual's eyes.

There are many interventions based on humanist principles that are applied in teaching, coaching or instructing contexts. Where behaviourists perceive these roles as developing core skills, behaviours and competencies, humanists undertake these roles as a facilitator of the sport and exercise experience. They would strive to increase an individual's self-concept to facilitate, assist and be flexible, not to manipulate and coerce behaviour. The intention is to help athletes find out what *they* want to be, and not mould them to what *you* want them to be.

An example of a commonly used intervention derived from a humanist approach is performance profiling. Devised and developed by Butler (1989), performance profiling is a natural application of Kelly's (1955) personal construct theory in sport and exercise psychology. Personal construct theory contends that individuals strive to make sense of the world and themselves by constructing personal theories. These theories are validated or revised on the basis of how well they enable the individual to see into the immediate and long-term future (Bannister & Fransella, 1986). Each individual is unique in the way they perceive and interpret situations. Issues that are considered important to some people are irrelevant

PHOTO 28.1 *Establishing motives for exercising is an important part of the humanistic approach. Health benefits may be of no value to the individual, exercise may simply be a means to access nature.*

Source: Photo copyright Tracey Devonport.

to others. As such, it is necessary to explore each individual's self-perception of the ideal self to achieve success in that particular sport or exercise (Butler & Hardy, 1992). Ravenette (1977) argues that construct systems are built up and maintained at a low level of awareness. Exploring the performer's perspective thus enhances their awareness and enables the coach, instructor and sport or exercise psychologist to discern something of the performer's perspective.

The repertory grid proposed by Kelly (1955) prevails as the principal method of facilitating a person's construct system (Beail, 1985), although this has not been used in sport and exercise psychology. Butler (1989) adapted the repertory grid for the sport and exercise context by mapping an individual's personal construct system on to a performance profile. This provides a visual display of those areas perceived by the athlete to be important in achieving a top performance, and their assessment of current self is also mapped (Butler & Hardy, 1992). Constructs that the performer perceives as constituting the fundamental qualities of elite or good performance are elicited by asking: 'What in your opinion are the qualities or characteristics of an elite athlete in your sport?' The individual then assesses themselves using these constructs and the scores are presented on a visual profile. When constructing performance profiles, it is important to retain the labels generated by the performer (Bannister & Fransella, 1986), since the profile then accurately reflects what the athlete perceives as important in terms of performance. This perception may or may not be at odds with what the coach and sport psychologist consider important. Qualities selected can be clustered in categories such as physical, technical, attitudinal, team and psychological characteristics and profiled accordingly (Butler & Hardy, 1992; Lane, 2009). In the example provided in Focus Point 28.2, the focus is on psychological characteristics. The exemplar performance profile is presented as both a repertory grid and a visual display.

Typically a scale of zero ('couldn't be any worse') to ten ('couldn't be any better') is used to rate qualities and is displayed on a visual profile (Jones, 1993; Lane, 2009). Including an ideal self-assessment on each quality enables the production of a discrepancy or priority rating, where the current rating is subtracted from the ideal or top performance score (Jones, 1993). Areas of desired change are identified by a large discrepancy between 'now' and 'ideal'.

The rapid spread of performance profiling across a number of sports has arisen because coaches have recognised potential uses of performance profiles (Butler & Hardy, 1992). These include enhancing understanding of an individual; identifying areas of perceived strength and areas for improvement; establishing an individual's perception of what constitutes good performance; monitoring progress; and establishing discrepancies in an individual's and coach/teacher's view of performance, and what is considered important in producing a good performance. Such benefits help realise Kelly's (1955) concept of sociality corollary, which suggests that effective coaching is based on an understanding of each other's construction process. The performance profile allows the performer's self-perceptions to be understood by the coach, and also allows the athlete to establish how the coach construes the performer.

It should be noted that the way in which practitioners portray a performance profile can differ. Weston (2008) outlines the different approaches used, concluding that although the assessments can look different, the theoretical principles underpinning them remain. Student practitioners should therefore avoid making inferences based on differences in a profile's appearance.

Having explored three approaches to consultancy, the next section will investigate key issues that aspiring ASEP must consider if they wish to pursue a career in this domain. These include supervision, ethical issues and the value of reflective practice.

28.2 SUPERVISION

Supervision has been described as a process that allows trainees to improve the quality of services they provide through practice and feedback with a trained professional in the field (Andersen, Van Raalte & Brewer, 2000). When exploring the developmental path from student to master practitioner, there appear to be various key stages that trainees undergo. Gardner and Moore (2006) categorised these under cognitive, associative and autonomous stages of learning (Ericsson, 2003; Fitts & Posner, 1967). The cognitive stage is dominated by cognitive activity, self-consciousness and an emphasis on structure. Trainees are dependent on the explicit guidance of their supervisors because they lack sufficient knowledge about service delivery. The application of this knowledge is very structured and requires considerable concentration. As a result, Gardner and Moore contend that trainees respond poorly to the words and actions of clients, as they miss critical cues and comments (environmental and situational cues). In autobiographical accounts, trainee ASEP have described the anxieties they experienced with clients and the help they received from supervisors (Tammen, 2000). It is suggested that during this

FOCUS POINT 28.2   PERFORMANCE PROFILING

The aim of performance profiling is to identify factors that an individual believes determine successful performance and then conduct a self-assessment against these factors. This leads to the identification of gaps between current and ideal self, which are used to inform the objective of subsequent intervention work. Performance profiling is a humanist approach and assumes that each person has a unique set of beliefs regarding what constitutes successful performance.

The process of conducting a performance profile begins by each person looking to identify factors influencing performance. Following this, key strengths and areas for improvement are identified. Individual plans for using strengths more effectively, prioritising and developing weaknesses can then be agreed, implemented and monitored. Each element can be changed as agreed between athlete and coach to make the profile as individual as possible.

HOW TO COMPLETE A PROFILE

Athlete and coach complete the profiles independently. All elements of the profile must be scored. The results are then discussed and development needs identified.

Each element of the profile should be given a score from 1–10 (10 = could not be any better/best the player can possibly be; 1 = could not be any worse/the player has little or no conscious understanding of the element and has not yet learned to apply or facilitate it).

Below is an example of a performance profile undertaken with a swimmer and the resulting map.

Area for development	Athlete	Coach
Confidence in ability to perform	8	8
Maintaining concentration	5	5
Controlling self-talk	5	4
Controlling emotions	3	3
Self-motivation	6	5
Effective goal setting	8	8
Ability to shut out distractions	5	5
Using imagery	2	3

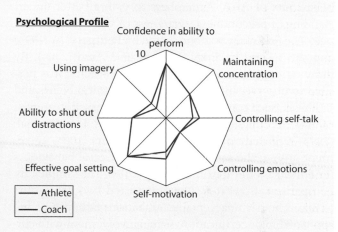

Psychological Profile

stage, supervisors help trainees identify and respond to situational and environmental cues and move away from structured, rule-governed behaviours.

During the associative stage, trainees begin to identify and appropriately respond to environmental and situational cues, making a shift from structured, rule-governed behaviours. As such, trainees exhibit greater flexibility in the choice and implementation of interventions, and develop a more effective connection with clients. Trainees become less self-conscious and are able to engage more task-focused attention. During this stage, supervisors should help trainees reflect on and in action to enhance their use of contingency-based and flexible practice.

In the autonomous stage, the trainee has evolved to a trainee expert who exhibits automated and rapid responses, perceiving clients' actions and responses and attending to their needs. The identification and implementation of interventions requires less attentional processing, allowing the practitioner to focus on contextual features and cues. Trainee experts draw on internalised models developed from their extensive histories with clients; they are flexible in using intervention techniques and adjust them to suit their clients. At this stage, supervisors encourage trainees to maintain continued professional development and motivation to improve further.

In conclusion, developing an understanding of the developmental path from student to master practitioner can help establish the expectations of trainee and supervisor. It is suggested this information can be used to inform the development and evaluation of a learning programme established to meet the needs of individual trainees.

28.3   ETHICS OF PRACTICE

In an attempt to ensure that ASEP practitioners will do no harm, and protect the dignity and welfare of clients, professional organisations (such as the British Psychological Society [BPS] or the Association for the Advancement of Applied Sport Psychology [AAASP]) have developed ethical guidelines that regulate their members' professional conduct. In recent decades, a growing number of articles and book chapters concerning ethics have appeared in the sport and exercise psychology literature (Andersen, 2005; Andersen, Van Raalte & Brewer, 2000; Etzel, Watson & Zizzi, 2004; Heyman, 1990; Petitpas *et al.*, 1994). In 2008, the online journal *Athletic Insight* devoted a special edition to the ethics of ASEP. Despite the growing body of literature exploring the ethics of applied practice, Etzel and Watson (2009) suggest that many contemporary publications still do not sufficiently emphasise the importance of ethics.

Two studies sought to explore the ethical beliefs and behaviours of AAASP members to gain a better understanding of practitioners' awareness of the ethics of practice. The first study was conducted by Petitpas *et al.* (1994) and the second by Etzel, Watson and Zizzi (2004). By drawing comparisons across these two studies, it is possible to observe shifts in practitioners' ethical beliefs and practices. Such comparisons reveal an increased awareness of AAASP ethics, principles and standards. Petitpas *et al.* (1994) reported no unanimous behaviours (100% agreement among the sample) or nearly universal behaviours (endorsed as ethical by more than 90% of the sample). By comparison, Etzel *et al.* (2004) reported two behaviours as unanimously unacceptable (affiliations falsely implying sponsorship or certification; sexual involvement with current clients) and one (maintaining professional competencies) as nearly universal. Etzel *et al.* identified five items as rare behaviours in the 2004 survey (gaining less than 5% endorsement), of which three replicated behaviours identified by Petitpas *et al.* (1994). These behaviours included:

- Betting on a team one is working with.
- Developing a sexual relationship after discontinuation of a professional relationship.
- Entering into a business relationship with a recent client.

Participants in the 2004 survey identified 11 controversial behaviours compared to 24 identified in Petitpas *et al.* As such, there appears to be less controversy almost a decade later. Etzel *et al.* (2004) argued that these outcomes demonstrate greater clarity among AAASP members concerning ethics. They suggest that this is due to more frequent inclusion of ethics in education and training. This contention was supported by their finding that nearly twice the percentage of the respondents than in the 1994 survey reported undertaking one or more courses in which ethics were covered. These two studies highlight a growing awareness of, and adherence to, ethical practice among applied practitioners. In recent years, more practitioners are undertaking training and education regarding the ethics of practice, and there is more consistency in practitioners' ethical beliefs and practices.

Aspiring and practising ASEP practitioners should thoroughly read, discuss and remain aware of nationally relevant codes of ethics. This section will explore those ethical considerations that commonly appear in the ethics codes of national professional bodies. These include the following: the use of **informed consent**, **confidentiality**, practising within areas of professional competence and maintaining professional relations (Andersen, Van Raalte & Brewer, 2001; Brown & Cogan, 2006; Moore, 2003).

> **informed consent** agreement or permission by a client for the use of a professional intervention based on the client having all the information necessary and the personal ability to make an educated, informed decision about the likely benefits and risks of the specific intervention.

> **confidentiality** an ethical requirement of many professions in which the client has the right to expect that information gathered about or from the client will not be made public without the client's consent and if limitations are placed on the terms of confidentiality these are generally discussed and agreed before the start of any professional relationship.

28.3.1   Informed Consent

The term 'informed consent' reflects

> all information necessary for clients to make an educated, informed decision about the likely benefits and risks of the specific intervention to be used in the development of a professional working relationship with a therapist/consultant. (Moore, 2003, p. 603)

Practising sport and exercise psychologists should develop and utilise a clear and thorough method of informed consent for the client to comply with ethical principles (Gardner & Moore, 2006). The informed consent given by the ASEP should describe the services offered, parameters of the services, the service methods, fees, practitioner availability and limitations of confidentiality (Braaten & Handelsman, 1997). From the legal standpoint, if a client is injured or harmed as a result of a failure on the part of the practitioner to disclose information about their methods, the client can collect compensation from the psychologist for causing the damage (Faden, Beauchamp & King, 1986). Where the client is not of a legal age to be able to give consent (over 16 years), then it is necessary to gain the permission of a guardian or parent prior to conducting any work (Canter *et al.*, 1994). The need to obtain the consent of a parent or guardian also applies when consulting with clients of

PHOTO 28.2 *It is an ethical requirement that confidentiality and limits of confidentiality are discussed from the outset.*
Source: Photo copyright Andy Lane.

diminished responsibility, such as athletes with a cognitive disability.

28.3.2 Confidentiality

Confidentiality refers to a general standard of professional conduct that obliges a professional not to discuss information about a client with anyone (Koocher & Keith-Spiegel, 1998). When cited as an ethical principle, confidentiality implies an explicit contract or promise not to reveal anything about a client except under certain

circumstances agreed to by both parties. Confidentiality may appear relatively straightforward, but it is not. ASEP work in a variety of ways: with an individual; with an individual and their coach; with an individual but contracted by their parent(s); and with a team and coaches, contracted by a national sport or exercise organisation. These multiple relationships can be problematic from the perspective of confidentiality. It is important to clarify who the client is, and what are the contractual obligations of employment. It is not unusual for a coach or other member of the sport organisation to request access to information gained about an individual without their prior consent.

The ethical guidelines offered by a range of professional bodies (e.g. APA, BPS) suggest that ASEP disclose and discuss relevant limits of confidentiality from the outset, also discussing the foreseeable use of information generated through consultancy. ASEP should inform clients of the full range of potential issues concerning confidentiality before services are initiated (Gardner & Moore, 2006). In many countries, psychologists are required by law, and by their ethical codes, to waive confidentiality in certain circumstances. Evidence of child or elder abuse and threat of harm to self or others (and an accompanying duty to warn) are examples of instances where breaks in confidentiality are deemed acceptable (Andersen, 2005), but in such cases the psychologist's decision to break confidentiality is endorsed by a legal body rather than taken on their own. Where clients request that information is shared, the ASEP should first have the client sign a release of information form. This form should outline the information that is to be shared, with whom and when. The ASEP should not provide information beyond that agreed. Consider Focus Point 28.3.

FOCUS POINT 28.3   ADDRESSING CONFIDENTIALITY

Andersen (2005, p. 10) provides an exemplar of the dialogue that could take place to initiate the discussion and clarification of confidentiality:

Coach, for many of your athletes, they are going to want some help with things like staying focussed, relaxing, running their events over in their heads, and so forth. For them, the services will be mainly about performance enhancement strategies. For some of your other athletes, their performances may be deeply tied to feelings of worth, parental pressures, big anxieties about what you think of them, and other problems outside of sport. For all the athletes I work with, I encourage them to let you know what we are working on, but I also

need to let them all know that what passes between me and them is confidential and doesn't go outside our sessions unless they want it to. Some athletes may need to talk about stuff that they would be embarrassed or anxious about if you knew. By keeping things confidential, it frees the athletes to say whatever is on their minds, and helps the athletes and me get to the source of their worries. It's all part of the ethical code of my profession, and it's there to ensure the privacy of the athletes, and the development of a trusting open relationship. That trust and confidence is what will help me help the athletes get the most out of their sports and maybe help in other aspects of their lives too.

28.3.3 Practising within Areas of Professional Competence

An ASEP may only intervene with a client in those areas where they possess the relevant training and expertise. Take the scenario of an ASEP exploring performance-related issues. During early discussions, the client discloses that they have an eating disorder. It would be unethical for the ASEP to issue advice on or intervene in an attempt to resolve the eating disorder, however well intentioned, if they do not possess the relevant training or knowledge. This would be classed as negligence on the part of the practitioner as they breach their limits of professional competence. For this reason, many professional organisations are striving to develop a comprehensive referral network of individuals where their area of expertise is clarified (Van Raalte & Andersen, 2002). A licensed ASEP who has experience dealing with personal or interpersonal issues may be considered for one referral, but an ASEP qualified to work with athletes suffering from anxiety and depression may be required for another referral (Heyman & Andersen, 1998).

Van Raalte and Andersen (2002) suggest that ASEP practitioners should prepare clients for the possible need for referral from the outset, explaining why this is intended to be of benefit to the client. They also suggest that where it becomes apparent that the client's requirements are beyond the professional competency of the ASEP practitioner, the consultant should explain why a referral is being made, to whom the referral is being made and what services are usually offered by the alternative professional. It may be that in some instances a refer-in approach is most suitable, where the ASEP continues to work with and alongside alternative professionals. This can be advantageous, as the trust and rapport already established with the ASEP may help the client to develop relations with the professional to whom they are being referred (Heyman & Andersen, 1998; Van Raalte & Andersen, 2002). Importantly, the client may be more comfortable with this arrangement (Van Raalte & Andersen, 2002). Whether an alternative professional is referred in or not, it is important that ASEP continue their work with their client while the referred professional deals with issues that exceed the ASEP's limits of competency, to ensure that the client does not feel abandoned (Heyman & Andersen, 1998). A team approach such as this may provide a more complete service for the client, offering the greater protection of their general welfare.

28.3.4 Maintaining Professional Relations

An ASEP may be required to perform activities that do not replicate those of many psychologists in order to meet demands of third parties such as sports organisations (Knapp & Slattery, 2004). For example, ASEP may be required to conduct late-evening meetings or consultation sessions in public and private spaces, or attend tours with clients (Haberl & Peterson, 2006). Dilemmas faced by ASEP may include where to meet with an athlete, whether to take up an invite for drinks with the coaches or attend a team social engagement, or whether to offer consultation in the home of the client. These scenarios may challenge the psychologist–client relationship in ways that would not ordinarily occur in office-based services. Supervisees or inexperienced ASEP may be unprepared for the boundary challenges that could occur (Knapp & Slattery, 2004). For example, regarding the issue of where to meet a client, it is usually possible to find a space to sit and meet away from the earshot of others. This could be a corner of the cafeteria in the training centre, on a bench away from the team living area, or at the far end of the warm-up track (Haberl & Peterson, 2006). When invited to attend a social event, the ASEP may feel obligated to attend and perceive that failing to do so may be viewed negatively by clients. In such circumstances, the practitioner must represent themselves professionally, restrict conversations to a superficial level of engagement and avoid issues dealt with during work (Canter *et al.*, 1994; Gardner & Moore, 2006).

In conclusion, when reviewing the ethics of ASEP, irrespective of the level of experience possessed practitioners must become familiar with and adhere to the codes of ethics for their country of practice. For a useful ethical self-awareness checklist, see Gardner and Moore (2006, pp. 218–20). Contained in Activity Box 28.4 is an exercise that we complete with undergraduate students to introduce the ethics of practice. We recommend that readers engage with this activity and consider how they would practice ethically with the full spectrum of personalities.

28.4 ENGAGING IN REFLECTIVE PRACTICE

Reflective practice is becoming more commonplace in ASEP, with associations such as the British Association of Sport and Exercise Sciences (BASES) including it within the accreditation process. In professions such as ASEP, while it is difficult for external parties to assess proficiency due to the confidential and individual nature of practitioner–client relationships (Anderson *et al.*, 2002), it has been argued that practitioners must have their performance evaluated if they are to improve (Devonport & Lane, 2009). Self-assessment through reflection has been offered as an acceptable method for professionals

CONSIDERING ETHICS   ACTIVITY BOX 28.4

- Identify three or four people you have felt very close to or liked. Identify the physical qualities and personal characteristics (good or bad) that may be similar between these individuals.
- Identify three or four people you have disliked. Identify the physical qualities and personal characteristics (good or bad) that may be similar between these individuals.
- The characteristics that you have identified for those individuals you like and dislike are risk factors. Can

you identify how you would respond to people with these characteristics?
- Feeling disdain towards people is not in itself problematic. It is acknowledging and dealing with those feelings that can be. You must be aware of a client's characteristics and your feelings towards them. You must ensure that the services you offer are not influenced by your feelings toward a client.

FOCUS POINT 28.4   REFLECTION EXEMPLIFIED

When reviewing their experiences there were many stories recited by mentors and mentees that I could relate to, which at times mirrored my own experiences. For example, one mentor expressed disappointment as she tried different strategies to encourage her mentee in becoming more talkative, each of which she perceived as failing. I was privy to the views of her mentee, in her eyes, her mentor was a source of encouragement, a 'sounding board', someone on 'her side'. Where the mentor perceived failure the mentee saw success. Incidents such as this highlighted the need to clarify and monitor expectations. In the example provided, the mentee did not perceive a need to talk more, she desired an additional source of social support. Such experiences, either my own or vicarious, have taught me valuable lessons, such as avoiding assumptions, striving for honest two-way com-

munication, engaging in ongoing critical reflection and accepting that which is uncontrollable and non-harmful. In my applied work, I establish client expectations from the outset, seeking to explore motives, attainability, perceived barriers, and agree roles and responsibilities. I reinforce the importance of honest critical reflection as a contributor to an effective working relationship. I consciously endeavour not to make assumptions and feel in doing so this facilitates open and exploratory communication. As suggested by Andersen (2005, p. 295) 'sport psychologists in practice often trip over their own blind spots'. These blind spots are often caused by assumptions such as those exemplified above.

Source: Devonport & Lane (2009, p. 171)

---

such as ASEP to manage their own practice, increase understanding of their practice and enhance continuing professional development (Anderson, Knowles & Gilbourne, 2004; Knowles *et al.*, 2007).

Reflective practice is the process of thinking about thinking (Knowles *et al.*, 2001). Practitioners use reflective practice to give meaning to past experiences and use the insights and understanding gained from examining past performance to improve future practice (Devonport & Lane, 2009; Johns, 1994). There has been criticism that graduates are unable to link theory with practice when they begin work in applied settings (Grey & Fitzgibbon, 2003; Schön, 1987). Reflection has been found to be an effective method of linking research and applied practice

(Grey & Fitzgibbon, 2003; Knowles *et al.*, 2001; Lane & Whyte, 2006). Furthermore, reflection allows practitioners to think about the whole experience of consultancy rather than the theoretical framework alone. Reflection can improve a sport psychologist's performance and increase accountability to self, client and profession (Anderson *et al.*, 2002). Traditionally in ASEP, the emphasis has been placed on performance rather than athlete-centred issues (Anderson *et al.*, 2002). However, there has been a shift towards a more holistic attitude regarding client care in health professionals (Johns, 1994). Some ASEP practitioners advise that it is unethical for practitioners to focus on improving performance without considering client welfare (Anderson *et al.*, 2002). See Focus Point 28.4.

There are different types of reflective practice and many ways to reflect. Knowles *et al.* (2001) found that successful coaches use reflection in and on practical experience. Anderson, Knowles and Gilbourne (2004) call this dual-staged reflection. Reflection-in-action pertains to thinking about a situation while it is occurring in order to clarify thoughts; this then influences decisions made and allows more desirable procedures to be implemented (Knowles *et al.*, 2001). Consultants reflect mid-action and must therefore be flexible to change, and conscious of their own thoughts and feelings. Reflecting on past practice is known as knowledge-on-action (Schön, 1987). Encouraging practitioners to review experiences identifying factors that made them successful or not facilitates the development of action plans intended to enhance future practice (Grey & Fitzgibbon, 2003). Knowledge-on-action is integral to effective practice as it is proposed to incorporate values, prejudices, experiences, knowledge and social norms (Knowles *et al.*, 2007).

Formal models of reflection can be used to guide reflection, although it is recommended that these are adapted to suit individual practices (Anderson *et al.*, 2002; Johns, 1994). Models of reflection commonly used in sport psychology are Gibbs' (1988) six-staged cyclic model, and Johns' (1994) model of structured reflection. See Table 28.2.

There are several different ways to reflect, which may include professional conversations, spontaneous thoughts, written reflection, meetings and using a mentor. One of the most common methods of reflection is keeping a portfolio or journal. Grey and Fitzgibbon (2003) found logs and reflective essays successful aids for reflection in their study. Johns (2004) suggests that keeping a journal has therapeutic benefits and allows us to connect with ourselves and others if we share it. However, journal writing is limited by the individual's own knowledge and understanding, and also it can be 'forced' if individuals feel obliged to log their thoughts at regular intervals (Anderson *et al.*, 2004; Knowles *et al.*, 2007). However, Irwin, Hanton and Kerwin (2004) recommend reflective writing for promoting craft knowledge in elite coaching; and keeping journals or portfolios has been found to be an effective means of providing evidence of competency for evaluation purposes (Anderson *et al.*, 2002). Practitioners can be limited by their own understanding of a situation. Knowles *et al.* (2007) suggest that sharing experiences with other consultants increases and widens practitioner knowledge. Supervisors or mentors may assist neophyte ASEP practitioners in learning the process of reflection. Schön (1987, p. 17) states that mentors should assist the practitioner in self-discovery and not try to teach them; a mentor should 'help him [practitioner] see what he needs to see'. Dialogue is an important part of reflection and may be experienced during meetings with a supervisor or mentor (Anderson *et al.*, 2004; Johns, 2002).

In conclusion, this section has demonstrated the utility of reflective practice. Not only is it a requirement of many professional bodies for certification (see Chapter 31), it is also valued as a central part of continued professional development.

TABLE 28.2 *Contrasting Models of Reflection.*

Model of reflection	Key features	Suited to
Gibbs (1988)	Iterative, dynamic cycles: Repeat the same loop of actions over and over again. Practitioners to describe an incident, evaluate what was good and bad about the experience, followed by an analysis. Using academic sources they reflect on how they would react in similar future situations, developing an action plan. This is then implemented and the cycle starts again.	Experienced reflective practitioners
Johns (1994)	Structured model: Steps with prompts, questions and activities to aid reflection. Questions are concerned with describing the experience and its key issues, to reflect on what was trying to be achieved, why the practitioner acted in a certain way, what were the consequences of the action to self and to the client, what feelings were evoked by the action and what academic sources of knowledge should have influenced any decisions made. Finally, the model questions how the situation could have been dealt with differently and what would be done in future.	Novice reflective practitioners (offers more guidance)

28.5 CONCLUSION

This chapter has demonstrated that there is no exact way in which psychological skills should be delivered, and although there are more 'desirable' approaches, practitioners are encouraged to gauge the situation while also being aware of the appropriate underpinning research evidence. This chapter also demonstrates the role of practitioner issues in mediating consultancy efficacy, irrespective of the approach to consultancy adopted. For example, the ability of trainee ASEP to be reflexive to the needs of a client may vary in accordance with their stage of learning. Alternatively, a client must be confident that the ASEP practitioner will behave responsibly and ethically in order for them to share potentially sensitive personal information. It is hoped that this chapter and the tasks contained within have facilitated an enhanced understanding of ASEP with reference to psychological skills and practitioner issues.

SELF-TEST QUESTIONS

- Identify the key features of a behaviourist, cognitive and humanist approach to consultancy.
- With reference to Gardner and Moore's (2006) stages of learning, identify the challenges you would expect to face at each stage of development.
- Identify two ethical issues that may be encountered by an ASEP.
- Identify the ways in which you feel reflective practice may assist your ongoing professional development as a trainee sport and exercise psychologist.
- Identify the key points for your own professional development that you have gained from this chapter. How will you act on these?

ESSAY QUESTIONS

- Select an intervention of your choice (e.g. imagery, self-talk, relaxation, attentional control) and describe the way in which a behaviourist, cognitive or humanist practitioner may differ in their use and application of this intervention.
- Identify the approach (behaviourist, cognitive or humanist) that you believe best complements your personal philosophy of consultancy. Provide a rationale for this decision and explain how it would guide your practice.
- Describe the three stages of learning associated with ASEP supervision identified by Gardner and Moore (2006). Identify the implications for your own development, anticipated experiences and use of supervisory support.
- Identify and explore the ethical requirements of ASEP. What benefits does adherence to ethical guidelines offer a practitioner?
- Explore guidelines for the effective use of reflective practice. To what extent does your use of reflective practice comply with these guidelines? Identify the areas where you could improve your own use of reflective practice and the anticipated benefits of change.

TEXTS FOR FURTHER READING

Andersen, M.B., Van Raalte, J.L. & Harris, G. (2000) Supervision II: A case study, in M.B. Andersen (ed.) *Doing Sport Psychology*, pp. 167–79, Champaign, IL: Human Kinetics.

Gardner, F. & Moore, Z. (2006) Ethics in clinical sport psychology, in F. Gardner & Z. Moore (eds) *Clinical Sport Psychology*, pp. 199–220, Champaign, IL: Human Kinetics.

Gardner, F. & Moore, Z. (2006) Professional development and supervision in sport psychology, in F. Gardner & Z. Moore (eds) *Clinical Sport Psychology*, pp. 221–37, Champaign, IL: Human Kinetics.

Hill, K.L. (2001) *Frameworks for Sport Psychologists: Enhancing Sports Performance*, Champaign, IL: Human Kinetics.

Johns, C. (2002) *Guided Reflection: Advancing Practice*, Oxford: Blackwell Science.

Moran, A. (2004) Introducing sport and exercise psychology: Discipline and profession, in A. Moran (ed.) *Sport and Exercise Psychology: A Critical Introduction*, pp. 3–33, London: Routledge.

Van Raalte, J.L. & Andersen, M.B. (2000) Supervision I: From models to doing, in M.B. Andersen (ed.) *Doing Sport Psychology*, pp. 153–65, Champaign, IL: Human Kinetics.

Weinberg, R.S. & Williams, J.M. (2001) Integrating and implementing a psychological skills training program, in J.M. Williams (ed.) *Applied Sport Psychology: Personal Growth to Peak Performance*, 4th edn, pp. 347–77, Mountain View, CA: Mayfield.

Williams, J.M. & Leffingwell, T.R. (1996) Cognitive strategies in sport and exercise psychology, in J.L. Van Raalte & B.W. Brener (eds) *Exploring Sport and Exercise Psychology*, pp. 51–73, Washington, DC: American Psychological Association.

RELEVANT JOURNAL ARTICLES

Andersen, M.B. (2005) 'Yeah, I work with Beckham': Issues of confidentiality, privacy and privilege in sport psychology service delivery, *Sport and Exercise Psychology Review* 1(2), http://www.bps.org.uk/downloadfile.cfm?file_uuid=8DEE01EC-1143-DFD0-7E98-A2F921B5066C&ext=pdf, accessed 21 September 2009.

Anderson, A.G., Knowles, Z. & Gilbourne, D. (2004) Reflective practice for sport psychologists: Concepts, models, practical implications, and thoughts on dissemination, *Sport Psychologist* 18: 188–203.

Butler, R.J. & Hardy, L. (1992) The Performance Profile: Theory & application, *Sport Psychologist* 6: 253–64.

Etzel, E.F., Watson, J.C., II & Zizzi, S. (2004) A web-based survey of AAASP members' ethical beliefs and behaviors in the new millennium, *Journal of Applied Sport Psychology* 16: 236–50.

Ibrahim, H. & Morrison, N. (1976) Self-actualization and self-concept among athletes, *Research Quarterly* 47: 68–79.

Jarrett, C. (2008) Foundations of sand, *The Psychologist* 21: 756–9, http://www.thepsychologist.org.uk/archive/archive_home.cfm?volumeID=21&editionID=164&ArticleID=1394, accessed 19 November 2009.

Jones, G. (1993) The role of performance profiling in cognitive behavioural interventions in sport, *Sport Psychologist* 7: 160–72.

Petitpas, A., Brewer, B., Rivera, P. & Van Raalte, J. (1994) Ethical beliefs and behaviors in applied sport psychology: The AAASP ethics survey, *Journal of Applied Sport Psychology* 6: 135–51.

Taylor, J. (1995) A conceptual model for integrating athletes' needs and sport demands in the development of competitive mental preparation strategies, *Sport Psychologist* 9: 339–57.

RELEVANT WEB LINKS

Association of Applied Sport Psychology professional resources (including tips for undergraduate students interested in a career in sport and exercise psychology and ethics), http://appliedsportpsych.org/Resource-Center/professionals

Athletic Insight for sport and exercise psychology links, http://www.athleticinsight.com/Links.htm

British Association of Sport and Exercise Sciences, www.bases.org.uk

International Association of Applied Psychology newsletters, http://www.iaapsy.org/index.php?page=Newsletter

REFERENCES

Andersen, M.B. (2005) 'Yeah, I work with Beckham': Issues of confidentiality, privacy and privilege in sport psychology service delivery, *Sport and Exercise Psychology Review* 1(2), http://www.bps.org.uk/downloadfile.cfm?file_uuid=8DEE01EC-1143-DFD0-7E98-A2F921B5066C&ext=pdf, accessed 21 September 2009.

Andersen, M.B., Van Raalte, J.L. & Brewer, B.W. (2000) When applied sport psychology graduate students are impaired: Ethical and legal issues in supervision, *Journal of Applied Sport Psychology* 12: 134–49.

Andersen, M.B., Van Raalte, J.L. & Brewer, B.W. (2001) Sport psychology service delivery: Staying ethical while keeping loose, *Professional Psychology: Research and Practice* 32: 12–18.

Anderson, A.G., Knowles, Z. & Gilbourne, D. (2004) Reflective practice for sport psychologists: Concepts, models, practical implications, and thoughts on dissemination, *Sport Psychologist* 18: 188–203.

Anderson, A.G., Miles, A., Mahoney, C. & Robinson, P. (2002) Evaluating the effectiveness of applied sport psychology practice: Making the case for a case study approach, *Sport Psychologist* 16: 433–54.

Anderson, R. (1977) The notion of schemata and the educational enterprise: General discussion of the conference, in R. Anderson, R. Spiro & W. Montague (eds) *Schooling and the Acquisition of Knowledge*, Hillsdale, NJ: Lawrence Erlbaum Associates.

Bagozzi, R.P. & Burnkrant, R.E. (1979) Attitude organization and the attitude–behavior relationship, *Journal of Personality and Social Psychology* 37: 913–29.

Bandura, A. (1986) *Social Foundations of Thought and Action: A Social Cognitive Theory*, Englewood Cliffs, NJ: Prentice Hall.

Bandura, A. (1992) Exercise of personal agency through the self-efficacy mechanism, in R. Schwarzer (ed.) *Self-Efficacy: Thought Control of Action*, pp. 3–38, Washington, DC: Hemisphere.

Bandura, A. (1997) *Self-Efficacy: The Exercise of Control*, New York: W.H. Freeman.

Bannister, D. & Fransella, F. (1986) *Inquiring Man: The Theory of Personal Constructs*, London: Croom Helm.

Beail, N. (ed.) (1985) *Repertory Grid Technique and Personal Constructs*, London: Croom Helm.

Berliner, D.C. (1994) Expertise: The wonder of exemplary performances, in J.M. Mangier & C.C. Block (eds) *Creating Powerful Thinking in Teachers and Students: Diverse Perspectives*, pp. 161–86, Fort Worth, TX: Holt, Rinehart & Winston.

Boggianno, A.K., Shield, A., Barrett, M. *et al.* (1992) Helplessness deficits in students: The role of motivational orientation, *Motivation and Emotion* 16: 271–96.

Braaten, E.B. & Handelsman, M.M. (1997) Client preferences for informed consent information, *Ethics & Behavior* 7: 311–28.

Brewer, B.W., Van Raalte, J.L., Petipas, A.J., Bachman, A.D. & Weinhold, R.A. (1998) Newspaper portrayals of sport psychology in the United States, 1985–1993, *Sport Psychologist* 12: 89–94.

Brown, J.L. & Cogan, K.D. (2006) Ethical clinical practice and sport psychology: When two worlds collide, *Ethics & Behavior* 16: 15–23.

Brownell, K.D. (1982) Obesity: Understanding and treating a serious, prevalent, and refractory disorder, *Journal of Consulting and Clinical Psychology* 50: 820–40.

Butler, R.J. (1989) Psychological preparation of Olympic boxers, in J. Kremer & W. Crawford (eds) *The Psychology of Sport: Theory & Practice,* pp. 74–84, Leicester: British Psychological Society.

Butler, R.J. & Hardy, L (1992) The Performance Profile: Theory & application, *Sport Psychologist* 6: 253–64.

Canter, M.B., Bennett, B.E., Jones, S.E. & Nagy, T.F. (1994) *Ethics for Psychologists: A Commentary on the APA Ethics Code*, Washington, DC: American Psychological Association.

Devonport, T.J. & Lane, A.M. (2009) Reflecting on the delivery of a longitudinal coping intervention amongst junior national netball players, *Journal of Sports Science and Medicine* 8: 169–78.

Eagly, A.H. & Chaiken, S. (1993) *The Psychology of Attitudes*, Fort Worth, TX: Harcourt Brace Jovanovich.

Ellis, A. (1982) Self-direction in sport and life, *Rational Living* 17: 27–33.

Ellis, A. (1993) Reflections on rational-emotive therapy, *Journal of Consulting and Clinical Psychology* 61: 199–201.

Ericsson, K.A. (2003) Development of elite performance and deliberate practice: An update from the perspective of the expert performance approach, in J.L. Starkes & K.A. Ericsson (eds) *Expert Performance in Sports: Advances in Research on Sport Expertise*, pp. 49–84, Champaign, IL: Human Kinetics.

Escarti, A. & Guzmán, J.F. (1999) Effects of feedback on self-efficacy, performance, and choice in an athletic task, *Journal of Applied Sport Psychology* 11: 83–96.

Etzel, E. & Watson, J. (2009) Ethics and legal issues in sport psychology today, in T. Morris & P. Terry (eds) *Sport and Exercise Psychology: To the Cutting Edge*, Morgantown, WV: Fitness Information Technology.

Etzel, E.F., Watson, J.C., & Zizzi, S. (2004) A web-based survey of AAASP members' ethical beliefs and behaviors in the new millennium, *Journal of Applied Sport Psychology* 16: 236–50.

Faden, R.R. Beauchamp, T.L. & King, N.N. (1986) *A History and Theory of Informed Consent*, Oxford: Oxford University Press.

Fitts, P. & Posner, M.I. (1967) *Human Performance*, Belmont, CA: Brooks/Cole.

Fitzsimmons, P.A., Landers, D.M., Thomas, J.R. & van der Mars, H. (1991) Does self-efficacy predict performance in experienced weightlifters? *Research Quarterly for Exercise and Sport* 62: 424–31.

Flannery, K.A. & Walles, R. (2003) How does schema theory apply to real versus virtual memories? *Cyberspychology and Behavior* 6: 151–9.

Flavell, J.H. (1987) Speculations about the nature and development of metacognition, in F.E. Weinert & R.H. Kluwe (eds) *Metacognition, Motivation and Understanding*, pp. 21–9, Hillside, NJ: Lawrence Erlbaum Associates.

Folkman, S., Lazarus, R.S., Dunkel-Schetter, C., De Longis, A. & Gruen, R.J. (1986) The dynamics of a stressful encounter: Cognitive appraisal, coping, and encounter outcomes, *Journal of Personality and Social Psychology* 50, 992–1003.

Gardner, F. & Moore, Z. (2006) *Clinical Sport Psychology*, Champaign, IL: Human Kinetics.

Ghaye, T. & Lillyman, S. (1997) *Learning Journals and Critical Incidents: Reflective Practice for Health Care Professionals*, Salisbury: Mark Allen.

Gibbs, G. (1988) *Learning by Doing: A Guide to Teaching and Learning Methods*, Oxford: Oxford Brookes University, Further Education Unit.

Gould, D., Guinan, D., Greenleaf, C., Medbery, R. & Peterson, K. (1999) Factors affecting Olympic performance: Perceptions of athletes and coaches from more and less successful teams, *Sport Psychologist* 13: 371–95.

Graham, S. & Golan, S. (1991) Motivational influences on cognition: Task involvement, ego involvement and depth of information processing, *Journal of Educational Psychology* 83: 187–94.

Greenleaf, C., Gould, D. & Dieffenbach, K. (2001) Factors influencing Olympic performance: Interviews with Atlanta and Nagano U.S. Olympians, *Journal of Applied Sport Psychology* 13: 154–84.

Greenspan, M.J. & Feltz, D.L. (1989) Psychological interventions with athletes in competitive situations: A review, *Sport Psychologist* 3: 219–36.

Grey, A. & Fitzgibbon, K. (2003) Reflection-in-action and business undergraduates: What learning curve? *Journal of Reflective Practice* 4: 11–18.

Haberl, P. & Peterson, K. (2006) Olympic-size ethical dilemmas: Issues and challenges for sport psychology consultants on the road and at the Olympic Games, *Ethics & Behavior* 16: 25–40.

Heyman, S.R. (1990) Ethical issues in performance enhancement approaches with amateur boxers, *Sport Psychologist* 4: 48–55.

Heyman, S.R. & Andersen, M.B. (1998) When to refer athletes for counselling or psychotherapy, in J.M. Williams (ed.) *Applied Sport Psychology: Personal Growth to Peak Performance*, 3rd edn, pp. 359–71, Mountain View, CA: Mayfield.

Hill, K.L. (2001) *Frameworks for Sport Psychologists: Enhancing Sports Performance*, Champaign, IL: Human Kinetics.

Ibrahim, H. & Morrison, N. (1976) Self-actualization and self-concept among athletes, *Research Quarterly* 47: 68–79.

Irwin, G., Hanton, S. & Kerwin, D. (2004) Reflective practice and the origins of elite coaching knowledge, *Reflective Practice* 5: 425–42.

Jarrett, C. (2008) Foundations of sand, *The Psychologist* 21: 756–9, http://www.thepsychologist.org.uk/archive/archive_home.cfm?volumeID=21&editionID=164&ArticleID=1394, accessed 19 November 2009.

Johns, C. (1994) Guided reflection, in A. Palmer, S. Burns & C. Bulman (eds) *Reflective Practice in Nursing*, pp. 110–30, Oxford: Blackwell Science.

Johns, C. (2002) *Guided Reflection: Advancing Practice*, Oxford: Blackwell Science.

Johns, C. (2004) Becoming a transformational leader through reflective practice, *Reflections on Nursing Leadership* 30: 24–6.

Jones, G. (1993) The role of performance profiling in cognitive behavioural interventions in sport, *Sport Psychologist* 7: 160–72.

Kanfer, R. (1990) Motivation and individual differences in learning: An integration of developmental, differential, and cognitive perspectives, *Learning and Individual Differences* 2: 221–39.

Kelly, G.A. (1955) *The Psychology of Personal Constructs, Vols. I & II*, New York: Norton.

Kluger, A.N. & DeNisi, A. (1996) The effects of feedback interventions on performance: A historical review, a meta-analysis, and a preliminary feedback intervention theory, *Psychological Bulletin* 119: 254–84.

Knapp, S. & Slattery, J.M. (2004) Professional boundaries in non-traditional settings, *Professional Psychology: Research and Practice* 35: 553–8.

Knowles, Z., Gilbourne, D., Borrie, A. & Nevill, A. (2001) Developing the reflective sports coach: A study exploring the processes of reflective practice within a higher education coaching program, *Reflective Practice* 1: 924–35.

Knowles, Z., Gilbourne, D., Tomlinson, V. & Anderson, A.G. (2007) Reflections on the application of reflective practice for supervision in applied sport psychology, *Sport Psychologist* 21: 109–22.

Kolb, D.A. (1984) *Experiential Learning: Experience as the Source of Learning and Development*, Upper Saddle River, NJ: Prentice Hall.

Koocher, G.P. & Keith-Spiegel, P. (1998) *Ethics in Psychology: Professional Standards and Cases*, 2nd edn, New York: Oxford University Press.

Lane, A.M. (2009) Consultancy in the ring: Psychological support to a world champion professional boxer, in B. Hemmings & T. Holder (eds) *Applied Sport Psychology*, pp. 51–63, Chichester: John Wiley & Sons, Ltd.

Lane, A.M. & Whyte, G. (2006) From Education to application: The role of Sport Sciences courses in the preparation of Applied Sport Scientists, *Journal of Hospitality, Leisure, Sport and Tourism Education* 5: 88–93, see http://www.hlst.heacademy.ac.uk/johlste/vol5no2/contents.html

Lindsley, D.H., Brass, D.J. & Thomas, J.B. (1995) Efficacy-performance spirals: A multilevel perspective, *Academy of Management Review* 20: 645–78.

Mahoney, A., Devonport, T. & Lane, A.M. (2008) Interval feedback and self-efficacy of netball umpires, *Journal of Sports Sciences and Medicine* 7: 39–46, http://www.jssm.org/content.php, accessed November 2010.

Meichenbaum, D. (1986) Cognitive behaviour modification, in F.H. Kanfer & A. P. Goldstein (eds) *Helping People Change: A Textbook of Methods*, pp. 346–80, New York: Pergamon Press.

Mononen, K., Viitasalo, J.T., Konttinen, N. & Era, P. (2003) The effects of augmented kinematic feedback on motor skill learning in rifle shooting, *Journal of Sports Sciences* 21: 867–76.

Moore, Z.E. (2003) Ethical dilemmas in sport psychology: Discussion and recommendations for practice, *Professional Psychology: Research and Practice* 34: 601–10.

Petitpas, A., Brewer, B., Rivera, P. & Van Raalte, J. (1994) Ethical beliefs and behaviors in applied sport psychology: The AAASP ethics survey, *Journal of Applied Sport Psychology* 6: 135–51.

Petty, R. (1995) Attitude change, in A. Tesser (ed.) *Advanced Social Psychology*, pp. 195–255, New York: McGraw-Hill.

Piaget, J. (1985) *Equilibration of Cognitive Structures*, Chicago, IL: University of Chicago Press.

Ravenette, A.T. (1977) PCT: An approach to the psychological investigation of children and young people, in D. Bannister (ed.) *New Perspectives in Personal Construct Theory*, pp. 251–80, London: Academic Press.

Reid, N. (2006) Thoughts on attitude measurement, *Research in Science & Technological Education* 24: 3–27.

Rogers, C. (1961) *On Becoming a Person*, Boston, MA: Houghton Mifflin.

Ryan, R.M. & Deci, E.L. (2000) Self-determination theory and the facilitation of intrinsic motivation, social development, and well-being, *American Psychologist* 55: 68–78.

Schön, D. (1987) *Educating the Reflective Practitioner*, San Francisco, CA: Jossey Bass.

Seligman, M.E.P. (1991) *Learned Optimism: How to Change Your Mind and Your Life*, New York: Pocket Books.

Sinclair, D.A. & Vealey, R.S. (1989) Effects of coaches' expectations and feedback on the self-perceptions of athletes, *Journal of Sport Behavior* 12: 77–91.

Stewart, M.J. & Corbin, C.B. (1988) Feedback dependence among low confidence preadolescent boys and girls, *Research Quarterly for Exercise and Sport* 59: 160–64.

Stoltenberg, C. (1981) Approaching supervision from a developmental perspective: The Counsellor-Complexity Model, *Journal of Counselling Psychology* 28: 59–65.

Tammen, V.V. (2000) First internship experiences, or what I did on holiday, in M. Andersen (ed.) *Doing Sport Psychology*, pp. 181–92, Champaign, IL: Human Kinetics.

Taylor, J. (1995) A conceptual model of the integration of athletic needs and sport demands in the development of competitive mental preparation strategies, *Sport Psychologist* 9: 339–57.

Taylor, L.M. (2005) *Introducing Cognitive Development*, Hove: Psychology Press.

Thomas, P.R., Murphy, S. & Hardy, L. (1999) Test of Performance Strategies: Development and preliminary validation of a comprehensive measure of athletes' psychological skills, *Journal of Sports Sciences* 17: 697–711.

Van Raalte, J.L. & Andersen, M.B. (2000) Supervision I: From models to doing, in M.B. Andersen (ed.) *Doing Sport Psychology*, pp. 153–65, Champaign, IL: Human Kinetics.

Van Raalte, J.L. & Andersen, M.B. (2002) Referral processes in sport psychology, in J.L. Van Raalte & B.W. Brewer (eds) *Exploring Sport and Exercise Psychology*, 3rd edn, Washington, DC: APA.

Vealey, R.S. (1994) Current status and prominent issues in sport psychology interventions, *Medicine and Science in Sports and Exercise* 26: 495–502.

Watson, J.B. & Rayner, R. (1920) Conditioned emotional reactions, *Journal of Experimental Psychology* 3: 1–14.

Weinberg, R.S. & Comar, W. (1994) The effectiveness of psychological interventions in competitive sport, *Sports Medicine* 18: 406–18.

Weinberg, R. & Gould, D. (2007) *Foundations of Sport Psychology*, 4th edn, Champaign, IL: Human Kinetics.

Weston, N. (2008) Performance profiling, in A.M. Lane (ed.) *Sport and Exercise Psychology: Topics in Applied Psychology*, pp. 91–108, London: Hodder & Stoughton.

Williams, J.M. (ed.) (2001) *Applied Sport Psychology: Personal Growth to Peak Performance*, 4th edn, Mountain View, CA: Mayfield.

Williams, J.M. & Leffingwell, T.R. (1996) Cognitive strategies in sport and exercise psychology, in J.L. Van Raalte & B.W. Brener (eds) *Exploring Sport and Exercise Psychology*, pp. 51–73, Washington, DC: American Psychological Association.

29 Sport and Exercise Psychology – Understanding Cognitive and Biological Factors

ANDY LANE & TRACEY DEVONPORT

LEARNING OUTCOMES

WHEN YOU HAVE COMPLETED THIS CHAPTER, YOU SHOULD BE ABLE TO:

1. Identify and describe the relationship between cognitive factors such as self-efficacy and self-esteem, self-efficacy and memory.
2. Identify relationships between cognitive states associated with performance.
3. Identify relationships between psychological and physiological factors.

KEY WORDS

Acute Mountain Sickness • Binge Eating • Body Image • Concentration • Coping • Dehydration • Glycogen Depletion • High Altitude Cerebral Edema (HACE) • High Altitude Pulmonary Edema (HAPE) • Hypobaric Hypoxia • Meta-beliefs • Mood-Incongruent Effect • Oxidative Stress • Performance Accomplishments • Self-Belief • Self-Esteem • Ventilation • Verbal Persuasion • Vicarious Experiences

CHAPTER OUTLINE

ROUTE MAP OF THE CHAPTER

The chapter utilises examples to discuss cognitive and biological factors relevant for sport and exercise psychologists. The first section describes self-referent issues focusing on *self-efficacy* and *self-esteem*. We then look at memory, particularly memories of psychological states associated with variations in performance. We continue by exploring concentration and decision making, concepts that lead into a discussion on *stress* and *emotion*. In the second half of the chapter, we focus on biological factors. We explore factors such as diet, extreme environments and physical fitness to look at relationships between physiological and psychological states. We conclude the chapter by acknowledging clinical issues, with a focus on eating disorders.

29.1 COGNITIVE FACTORS

Finlay's story in Case History 29.1 is a common experience in sport and exercise psychology. He is experiencing low self-efficacy in his ability to exercise as often as he would like, and given the importance he places on doing this to maintain his sense of **self-esteem**, it is influencing other aspects of his life. His self-efficacy in relation to exercise is diminishing, as are his efficacy expectations across a spectrum of activities in his daily life. Finlay's story is a case of the self-efficacy and performance relationship affecting each other in line with theoretical predictions (Bandura, 1997); and from the reduction in self-efficacy, his self-esteem also suffers.

self-esteem the value that one places on one's self.

29.1.1 Self-Efficacy and Self-Esteem

Self-efficacy is defined as the levels of confidence individuals have in their ability to execute courses of action or attain specific performance outcomes (Bandura, 1997). It is a situationally specific form of self-confidence that can vary from task to task, or even moment to moment. For example, a soccer player might have high self-efficacy in relation to how he or she will play in terms of tackling, but have low self-efficacy if required to take a penalty. Equally, a player might start a game with high self-efficacy to take a penalty, but after missing a few clear shots on goal may experience reduced self-efficacy. In terms of exercise, a person might be confident about their ability to perform a weight-training session and be less confident about performing in a yoga class. Someone might begin an aerobics session full of confidence but, after experiencing difficulties keeping up with the instructor, find

---

CASE HISTORY 29.1

FINLAY'S STORY

Finlay is 17 and a highly successful junior tennis player. As he starts playing on the senior tour, he finds he is losing more points during matches, and not surprisingly, so begins to lose matches. He notices that the quality of his performance changes during games. During parts of the game, he finds winning points effortless and can concentrate on what he is doing. At other parts of his game, he loses self-belief in his ability. He starts making errors on his first serve, and begins to question his ability to perform at this level. During such runs in performance he tries very hard: he concentrates on his technique, thinking through each part of the shot in his mind; he tries to talk to himself, coaching himself on what to do, and he says to himself he will put his utmost effort into winning each point. Tennis is the main thing in his life and after losing a few matches, his self-esteem is very low.

He consults a sport psychologist who looks at how he thinks during matches and how his self-perception is affected by success and failure at tennis. Specifically, the sport psychologist looks at how his confidence sways during matches, his concentration style during games, and the value he places on success in tennis in terms of his self-esteem.

that their self-confidence starts diminishing rapidly, even to the point of wishing to leave early.

In contrast, self-esteem is more global, more stable and therefore resistant to change. Self-esteem has been found to be closely related to a number of stable personality traits (Baumeister, 1993). Self-esteem is a term used to reflect a person's overall evaluation or appraisal of their own worth (Baumeister, 1993). Importantly, self-esteem is often seen to be one of the most important indicators of psychological wellbeing. A person's self-esteem is more general and is an amalgam of estimates of confidence and self-evaluations over all aspects of life. Estimates of confidence can range hugely and can include being good at sport, being able to maintain successful relationships, being good at a job or being a good academic. The number of aspects of a person's life that influence self-esteem can vary. Some people can compartmentalise their self-esteem based on relatively few aspects of life (e.g. being a good athlete), whereas others base their self-esteem on a whole host of different activities or factors (being kind to people, providing support to a friend, trying hard at work etc).

As we discuss in this chapter, self-efficacy and self-esteem are separate concepts. However, it is also worth noting that if your self-esteem is tied into success in one area of your life (e.g. being an athlete, or being an exerciser), then the two concepts can be closely related. Self-efficacy relates to successful performance in numerous areas, and being successful is closely related to some people's sense of self-esteem. In sport, plenty of athletes are high in both self-efficacy and self-esteem when they are succeeding. Equally, people with naturally low self-esteem seem to struggle to acquire confidence to succeed. However, there can be a downside to having a close relationship between self-efficacy and self-esteem. Many young athletes base their self-esteem on success in a few compartments and can struggle to cope with slumps in performance (Devonport et al., 2005). Exercisers returning to physical activity can have fragile self-efficacy expectations towards exercise and, because being good at exercise is not a key part of their self-esteem, will stop exercising if efficacy expectations diminish from perceptions of poor performance (Duncan, 2008). Self-esteem is very much a key variable to the health and performance of the individual, and thus also to the sport and exercise psychologist.

Terry (1989) described self-efficacy as the guardian angel of successful performance. Evidence for a positive relationship between self-efficacy and performance has been found in meta-analytic studies in sport (Moritz et al., 2000) and work (Stajkovic & Luthans, 1998). Self-efficacy is also a strong predictor of exercise adoption and adherence (Willis & Campbell, 1992). Personal efficacy expectations are proposed to influence initiating

PHOTO 29.1 *High self-confidence, controlling emotions and focusing on key factors are important in sports such as cycling. Mat Wilson, rider in the 2008 Ride Across America, demonstrates high-speed descending.*

Source: Photo courtesy of Mat Wilson.

behaviour and how much effort will be applied to attain a successful outcome in the face of difficulties and setbacks (Bandura, 1997, 1999). Bandura suggests that self-efficacy judgements derive from the cognitive processing of information from four principal sources:

- **Performance accomplishments**: success raises and failure lowers self-efficacy, creating the belief that 'I succeeded last time, I can succeed again' (Feltz & Lirgg, 2001; Lane & Terry, 1996).

  performance accomplishments see mastery experience.

- **Vicarious experiences**: watching success creates a symbolic view, potentially creating the belief that 'if he/she can do it, so can I' (Chase, Feltz & Lirgg, 2003; George, Feltz & Chase, 1992).

  vicarious experiences a term generally used to indicate experience that has not been direct but rather observation of another's experience.

- **Verbal persuasion**: being told you can do something, creating the belief that 'if he/she thinks I can do it, then maybe I can' (Chase, Feltz & Lirgg, 2003).

  verbal persuasion influencing someone by what is said, often enhanced by maximising the trustworthiness and expertise of the speaker.

negative moods recall positive experiences to prevent their mood from worsening or to enhance it (Terry, Stevens & Lane, 2005). Individuals engage in conscious efforts to improve their emotional states, thus if they are feeling nervous, they try to recall times when they were successful as a strategy to reduce unpleasant feelings, or interpret unpleasant feelings as meaning that they are 'ready to perform' (Lane & Terry, 2000). Thus when individuals make efficacy judgements, they do so in less than perfect conditions. Their emotional state can influence what information can be retrieved; if a person is in a negative mood, accessibility to negative experiences seems easier. However, it is possible that individuals feeling negative emotions consciously seek to up-regulate emotions by thinking about positive experiences (Parkinson *et al.*, 1996).

meta-beliefs beliefs about beliefs.

Hanin (2003) proposed that individuals develop **meta-beliefs** about how emotions influence performance. The process that unfolds is that an individual experiences intense emotions before and during a competition or exercise session. They link these feelings with performance outcome; for example, a positive outcome fosters a belief that the accompanying emotions experienced are in some way responsible for that successful performance (Baumeister *et al.*, 2007). Baumeister *et al.* (2007) recently argued that emotions promote the learning of rules concerning how emotions influence performance. When an individual experiences a similar situation, this evokes memories of emotions experienced, which the individual consults to determine the extent to which they believe these emotions will be helpful or harmful for performance. This line of research demonstrates that memories of emotion have a powerful influence on future behaviours. Practitioners may need to consider how they might go about changing meta-beliefs on emotions.

In conclusion, at first glance, memory represents a simple concept: people recall factual information from experience. We selected emotion as an example of a factor that can influence the accuracy of memory. In simple terms, it seems that being in a positive mood helps recall times when you felt positive emotions and vice versa for negative emotions. However, people can deliberately try to counter this process. If a person identifies that they are feeling unpleasant emotions, then they might consciously try to change that feeling by recalling positive thoughts or thinking about positive experiences. As indicated by Hanin (2003), people might be content with feeling unpleasant emotions if they believe that such feelings help generate motivational states. When seen collectively, memory is a complex process, of which emotional states represent one of the many influencing variables.

29.1.3 *Attention and Decision Making*

One cognitive variable that is particularly relevant to applied sport and exercise psychologists is attention. The terms 'attention' and '**concentration**' are often used synonymously. Moran (2004) suggests that this is acceptable

concentration to direct attention to internal or external events.

because researchers usually define attention as the concentration of mental effort on internal or external events. There are two crucial features of attention: (i) the selectivity of attention, and (ii) the 'mental effort' required to maintain alertness for prolonged periods. It is widely acknowledged that in sport, the ability to pay attention to the task without being distracted by irrelevant cues is necessary for effective performance (Singer *et al.*, 1991). The ability of individuals to selectively perceive and process information underpins effective decision making. Research exploring the accuracy of decision making among officials exemplifies the importance of decision making in sport (Balmer, Nevill & Lane, 2005; Balmer *et al.*, 2007; Lane *et al.*, 2006).

We begin by discussing the importance of decision making by considering the following example. Imagine a scenario of 50 000 supporters watching a soccer game. The home-team defender lunges into the path of an attacking forward; the forward falls down, the ball wobbles away and the crowd roar 'dive'. Does the referee blow the whistle and give a penalty to the away team? This looks like it should be the accurate decision. Does the referee wave play on, arguing that he was not 100% sure that it was a foul? If he gives the penalty, it is a decision that will receive vociferous protest from the crowd, and given the likelihood of worldwide television coverage, be subject to post-match analysis and potential criticism. If he waives play on, the response from the home crowd will be supportive, and although away fans will heckle, these will be fewer in number. If the situation is reversed, would the referee give the same decision if the home team forward fell and the crowd called for a penalty?

A wealth of anecdotal evidence suggests that referees tend to give decisions in favour of the home team. Statistical examination of game records indicates that home teams win more often than away teams; home teams are awarded more penalties and receive fewer bookings (Nevill, Newell & Gale, 1996). A great deal of research has investigated the home advantage phenomenon in sport, with studies being conducted in soccer, boxing and the Olympic games (Balmer, Nevill & Williams, 2003; Holder & Nevill, 1997; Nevill *et al.*, 1997). A summary of the findings from these studies indicates that the home advantage phenomenon occurs in sports where a referee's decision(s) can influence the result, such as soccer and boxing. For example, in a study of the number of penalties awarded to home teams in the English and Scottish soccer leagues, results showed clear evidence that home teams with large crowds receive more penalties, and away teams are penalised with more players being sent off, for example (Nevill, Newell & Gale, 1996). In short, evidence suggests that the relative supportiveness of the crowd influences how referees make decisions, and therefore that designing an intervention to teach attentional control training for referees is desirable.

In a quest to identify factors associated with crowd noise, Nevill, Balmer and Williams (2002) conducted experimental research in which participants were asked to give decisions in two crowd noise conditions. In one condition, participants gave decisions in silence; but in the other condition, they gave decisions when listening to the sounds of a vociferous crowd. It should be explained that the referees acting as participants did not actually interact with a crowd, but were asked to give decisions about incidents on a videotaped game. Nevill, Balmer and Williams (2002) used 40 qualified referees who viewed an edited videotaped game between Liverpool v Leicester City, played at Liverpool in the season 1999–2000. Immediately after one of 47 challenges, the video was stopped for six seconds. In this time, each referee was asked to say whether the challenge was a foul or not, and if it was a foul, to which team the decision should be awarded. Half the referees watched the videotape with crowd noise audible and the other half watched in silence. Results showed that the referees who watched the game with audible crowd noise gave significantly fewer decisions against the home team, hence supporting the notion that referees consistently give decisions in favour of the home team (Nevill & Holder, 1999).

This research team conducted a follow-up study using qualitative methods to explore the factors that influence experienced referees when making decisions (Lane *et al.*, 2006). Five experienced referees volunteered to participate in semi-structured interviews of 30–40 minutes' duration. Examples of questions/probes included 'Are there times when it is difficult to make a decision on whether there was a foul or not? When? Why?' and 'Do you worry about making the wrong/unpopular decision? What effect does this have on you?' Qualitative analysis found themes such as 'ideal decision making' and 'concentration', 'experience' and 'personality'. They found that referees with a resilient **self-belief** who had experience of dealing with hostile crowds made fewer wrong decisions. Lane *et al.* (2006) argued that at an applied level, practitioners should develop strategies that accelerate the process of learning to concentrate on the appropriate cues and exclude performance-related stressors such as the crowd noise at

self-belief confidence in one's own abilities and judgements.

the point of making a decision on whether to blow the whistle and award a free kick.

However, as indicated above and demonstrated elsewhere, improving attentional control skills is not simply a case of trying harder to concentrate. It is a case of knowing what to concentrate on and focusing attention on these factors. Concentration is defined as 'the process by which all thoughts and senses are focused totally upon a selected object or activity to the exclusion of everything else' (Terry, 1989). It is worth emphasising at this point that concentration is a process that changes over time and that maintaining the intensity and focus will require some effort. Recognising this factor is important, because it means that concentration can vary in both intensity and focus. We can be focusing on the key parts of performance at one moment, but be distracted the next. It also suggests that expressing concentration in terms of a percentage is a helpful way of examining the concept. The percentage of effort given to focusing on relevant cues is important. Figure 29.2 graphically illustrates the concentration profile of two soccer referees.

In the example, both referees are concentrating equally hard, but one referee is focusing predominantly on relevant cues and the other on irrelevant performance cues. The key skill is to be able to identify the relevant performance cues at each moment of competition. It is likely that referee A will perform better than referee B.

Anecdotal reports from athletes conducted postcompetition reveal phrases such as 'I needed to concentrate more' following poor performance. Conceptualising

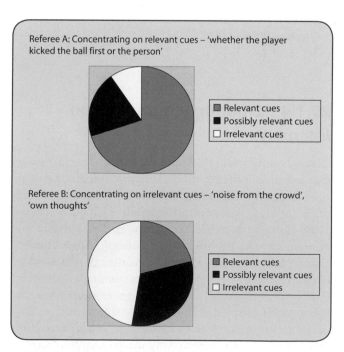

FIGURE 29.2 *Concentration profiles of two referees during a game.*

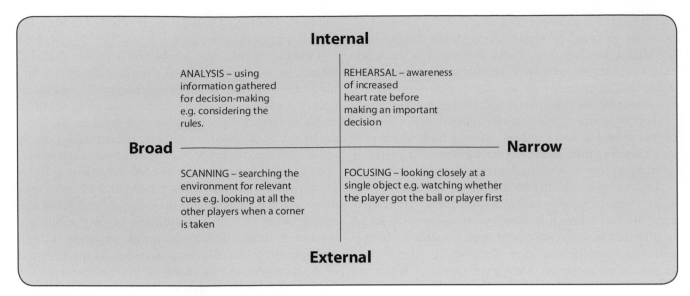

FIGURE 29.3 *Characteristics of different concentration (attentional) types applied to refereeing.*

concentration as a singular concept is not helpful; it does not identify what information needed to be looked at. As a starting point, we can break concentration down into two broad dimensions: a 'broad–narrow dimension' and an 'external–internal dimension'. Characteristics of each concentration type are described in Figure 29.3.

It is important to highlight that all four attentional styles are useful at times, and that athletes need to be able to switch attentional styles appropriately. Clearly, most athletes will need to be able to switch attention: a broad–external style is useful for planning and decision making, and a narrow–external style is required to deal with the 'here and now'. You may now want to complete Activity Box 29.1.

29.1.4 Emotion–Concentration Interplay

Given the importance of concentration for performance, it is worth identifying the factors that influence it. One such variable is emotions. Evidence shows that as emotions intensify, concentration tends to narrow (Terry, 1989). Initially, increased emotions such as anxiety and excitement can be helpful for concentration. Anxiety, characterised by feelings of nervousness and tension, is coupled with negative thoughts about performance. Excitement, characterised by feelings of adrenaline and liveliness, is coupled with optimistic thoughts regarding performance success. Both excitement and anxiety affect concentration in a similar way. As arousal and anxiety begin to intensify, what follows is that attention narrows and this makes it easier to ignore irrelevant cues,

with performance improving accordingly. However, as emotional states intensify, both relevant and irrelevant cues are ignored, with the consequence that performance begins to deteriorate (Nideffer, 1986).

Individuals need to be able to control their emotions to reduce the risk of poor decision making. To illustrate this phenomenon, let us use an example of a racing driver overtaken because of lapses in concentration, who subsequently becomes angry and then increases efforts to re-overtake. However, individuals tend to take poorly calculated risks when over-aroused as their attentional control becomes clouded. In such cases, the athlete needs to be in control of their attention. Recognising situations where emotions can hamper performance is particularly important. Sport psychologists need to explore emotional states, patterns of concentration and variations in performance in their work with athletes. It is important to identify meta-beliefs (Hanin, 2003) on the impact of emotions on performance, and explore whether such beliefs are associated with effective concentration. For example, an individual might believe that getting angry is helpful for performance based on experiences when they became angry and this led to success. Such a belief might not be erroneous. Anger might reduce attentional control and the individual might increase effort, thereby attaining successful performance outcomes.

You may now want to take a look at Activity Box 29.2.

29.1.5 Risk Taking

Athletes often need to take some risks to succeed in competition (Robazza & Bortoli, 2005). Risk reflects the probability that a difficult situation will turn into a success or a disaster. Risk is the balance between attaining

CONCENTRATION ERRORS IN MOTORSPORT   ACTIVITY BOX 29.1

Provide examples from a sport of your choice.

Concentration category	Examples of errors in concentration			Your turn. Think back to when you lost concentration. Classify errors into the four categories. In doing so you might find that you are prone to one type of concentration error.
	Example 1	**Example 2**	**Example 3**	
External focus too narrow	Failure to notice an opponent	Failure to notice course conditions	Missing important performance-related details	
External focus too broad	Failure to focus on the racer in front of you	Making simple errors, gear-change errors, going over bumps, racers slowing down in front	Attending to unimportant details	
Inappropriate narrow internal focus	Saying negative things to yourself	Becoming fixed on a particular thought or feeling and missing important things going on around you	Worrying about a recent mistake	
Inappropriate broad internal focus	Over-analysing situations	Not racing in the here and now, i.e. going over the past in your mind or anticipating the future	Daydreaming	

sporting goals against undesirable outcomes such as incurring possible personal injury, losing possession or making errors, and not achieving your personal goal.

How much risk will an athlete or exerciser take? The answer is not so straightforward, but the decision will be influenced by how much the person wants to achieve their performance goals. While examining risk in sport seems more apparent, especially in sports such as boxing and motor racing, people take risks during exercise sessions. For example, an individual might push themselves very hard at the start of an exercise class and risk having to stop early from exhaustion. A safer strategy might be to pace yourself at the start, but following this strategy might mean that fitness does not improve that fast.

The ability to maintain concentration and make accurate decisions during exercise or competition requires knowledge of the likely consequences of making a poor

decision. Experienced athletes tend to be able to identify the relevant environmental cues that can influence their performance much earlier than a novice. Research shows that emotions influence risk-taking behaviour (Robazza & Bortoli, 2005). Intense emotional states such as anger and tension can lead to individuals assessing risk inappropriately, resulting in reduced chances of success (Tenenbuam & Elran, 2003). If an individual becomes angry because of an incident during competition or during their exercise session, that reduces the likelihood of goal attainment, and the athlete's goal becomes to reduce anger by improving performance. This response is commonplace for motivated people. However, it is important to assess course conditions, the capability of the equipment and the physiological state when deciding when to overtake. If goal-directed behaviour is focused on reducing anger by trying to achieve a highly difficult

DEALING WITH EXTERNAL DISTRACTIONS THAT NEGATIVELY INFLUENCE CONCENTRATION IN A SPORT OF YOUR CHOICE

ACTIVITY BOX 29.2

By looking through the list of possible external distractions indicated below and simply placing a tick beside some of the distractions listed, you can identify what distracts you. Once you have identified these distractions, you can start developing strategies to cope with them.

- Noise in the crowd
- Poor weather conditions
- Clicking of a camera
- People observing your gym class through the window
- Movement seen in peripheral vision
- Verbal attempts to intimidate by opponents
- Seeing coach get up and leave
- Gym instructor correcting your technique
- **What distracts you?**

_____

_____

_____

Dealing with Internal Distractions

Even in the absence of external distractions, your mind can present a range of internal distractions. This may result in an inability to identify the relevant cues, which in turn can lead to anxiety. We know that becoming anxious leads to an increase in physiological arousal, which in turn makes it more difficult for us to control concentration. Listed below are some of the internal distractions that athletes and exercisers typically report:

- Worrying about the importance of the next event
- Thinking about a previous error
- Comparing your performance against other people
- Anger at an official's poor decision
- Feeling self-conscious in a gym environment
- Concern about whether a previously injured knee will influence performance
- Getting too analytical about the contest
- **How do you distract yourself?**

_____

_____

_____

_____

---

goal, it is possible that poor performance will result, due to over-arousal. Over-arousal is associated with missing key performance cues. An awareness of the tendency to become highly emotional and its impact on concentration emphasises the value of learning strategies to manage concentration (see Activity Box 29.3).

29.1.6 Conclusion

This section has alluded to some of the cognitive factors relevant to the work of a sport and exercise psychologist. As indicated, cognitive variables interact and one variable can be influenced by a second variable, or have a knock-on effect on that variable. Cognitive processes can be used to illustrate why some people can acquire confidence more quickly than others, particularly through its relationship with self-esteem. The effects of emotion on cognitive factors were also explored. Emotion influences not only memory processes but also attention, concentration and the appetite for risk.

29.2 BIOLOGICAL FACTORS

The range of biological factors related to psychological states is vast. In this section we focus on exploring a selection of topics, including:

- Physiological states and factors associated with sport and exercise.
- Impact of extreme environments on physiology and psychological variables.
- Relationships between diet, nutrition and psychological states.

LEARNING TO RECOGNISE YOUR EMOTIONAL PROFILE ASSOCIATED WITH SUCCESS

ACTIVITY BOX 29.3

We have all experienced intense emotions before important events. Some athletes can channel these feelings to enhance performance; some athletes can regulate these feelings and reduce anxiety; while other athletes become debilitated by these feelings, increasing anxiety.

Identify Your Positive and Negative Emotions

Go over the list of *positive (pleasant)* emotions below and select from the list *up to five words* that describe the emotions you felt *before* competitions or exercise activities in the past where you were successful.

Each line on the list consists of several synonyms. You may select only one word on the same line. Circle the words that you select. If you don't find a word describing an emotion that is important to you, you may add your own word at the end of the list.

Repeat this process for *negative emotions*.

For each emotion selected, identify whether you perceived the emotion to contribute positively or negatively towards your performance. If you thought it had a positive contribution indicate this with a +, if negative a –.

Positive emotions:

active	dynamic	energetic	vigorous
relaxed	comfortable	easy	
calm	peaceful	unhurried	quiet
cheerful	merry	happy	
confident	certain	sure	
delighted	overjoyed	exhilarated	
determined	set	settled	resolute
excited	thrilled		
brave	bold	daring	dashing
glad	pleased	satisfied	contented
inspired	motivated	stimulated	
lighthearted	carefree		
nice	pleasant	agreeable	
quick	rapid	fast	alert

Your own emotion _____

Negative emotions:

afraid	fearful	scared	panicky	
angry	aggressive	furious	violent	
annoyed	irritated	distressed		
anxious	apprehensive	worried		
concerned	alarmed	disturbed	dissatisfied	
discouraged	dispirited	depressed		
doubtful	uncertain	indecisive	irresolute	
helpless	unsafe	insecure		
inactive	sluggish	lazy		
intense	fierce			
jittery	nervous	uneasy	restless	
sorry	unhappy	regretful	sad	
tense	strained	tight	rigid	cheerless
tired	weary	exhausted	worn out	

Your own emotion _____

29.2.1 Physiological States and Factors Associated with Sport and Exercise

A great deal of research has focused on the relationship between physiological factors and psychological states (Acevedo & Ekkekakis, 2001). Evidence suggests that how hard you exercise associates with how you feel, although there is some debate as to whether this is always the case. For example, research shows that participating in intense exercise can lead to experiencing negative emotions. By contrast, participating in low- to moderate-intensity exercise tends to lead to feeling pleasant emotions (Berger & Motl, 2000). Continuing the use of changes in emotion as an example, results show that people report feeling more vigorous and less angry, confused, depressed, fatigued and tense following exercise (see Figure 29.4). One explanation for improved mood during exercise is the endorphin hypothesis. It has been suggested that endorphins released during exercise trigger enhanced emotion (Hamer & Karageorghis, 2007). However, if the endorphin hypothesis were correct, people would show similar mood improvements in relation to endorphin release.

Although a plethora of studies report the mood-enhancing effects of exercise (Berger & Motl, 2000), such studies tend to be conducted with people who are already regular exercisers. A research design might be to investigate changes in emotions among people at an aerobic session rather than recruiting people for a laboratory study. What you have with this sample is people who have made the decision to go and exercise rather than thinking about exercising or not exercising at all. The assumption is that people who are already exercising believe that there are some benefits, and one of these benefits could be that they experience pleasant emotions. The story might be different if studies used a sample of people who were not currently exercising. A key point is that the previous experience and beliefs of the exercisers might be an important factor in whether people experience positive emotions following exercise.

PHOTO 29.2 *Exercise and Positive Emotions*

Some people can recognise the potential for the mood-enhancing effects of running, whereas to others, running will always be a turn-off. These running enjoy a scenic run in front of Lichfield Cathedral.

Source: Photo courtesy of Andy Lane.

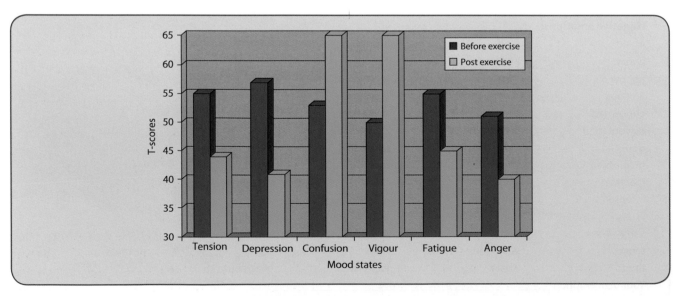

FIGURE 29.4 *Typical mood-enhancing effect of exercise.*

One comprehensive study showed that approximately 50% of people use exercise to enhance their mood (Thayer, Newman, & McClain, 1994); this is an impressive finding at first hand, but it also means that 50% of people do not like exercising. The challenge for the exercise psychologist is to develop beliefs that exercise can be enjoyable, particularly with the known health-related benefits deriving from it. The annual round of New Year's resolutions of 'getting fit' or 'losing weight' and the upsurge of physical activity evidenced through increased gym membership are testimony to the need for exercise psychology interventions. Results show that beliefs about the exercise are also important (Lane, Jackson & Terry, 2005). Lane, Jackson and Terry found that mood enhancement was related to beliefs about whether the exercise was enjoyable rather than the intensity of the exercise. In this study, the key factor that determined mood enhancement was a belief that exercise would lead to pleasant emotions following exercise. Lane, Jackson and Terry (2005) found that people who enjoyed running, for example, gained the most mood-enhancing benefits from running, but if someone who liked running did weight training, the emotions might not be so pleasant. The same story was found for people who liked weight training. When people switched to a less enjoyable activity, mood enhancement reduced. It should be noted that Lane, Jackson and Terry did not adequately control for exercise intensity and so these findings should be viewed with caution.

On the issue of how methodological factors can influence results, few studies use a rigorous research design that controls for all factors that could affect the findings (exercise intensity, beliefs on whether participating in the exercise will be enjoyable etc.). A great deal of research has been conducted in ecologically valid settings in which the researcher attempts to capture emotions as they are experienced in real life. While such research is praiseworthy on one level, a limitation is that it is not possible to determine causative relationships. Therefore, although there is clearly a relationship between physiological and psychological factors, methodological issues complicate the study of this topic. Take a look at Research Methods Box 29.1 and Focus Point 29.1.

As indicated previously, exercising at a high intensity is associated with unpleasant emotions. When this issue is considered more closely, it shows that exercising above the lactate threshold increases unpleasant emotions (Lane, 2009b; Lane *et al.*, 2003, 2005, 2007). It is argued that when people exercise at intense levels, physiological cues predominate (Rejeski & Ribisl, 1980). However, although this is often the case, many elite or well-trained athletes learn to cope with fatigue (Baron *et al.*, 2008). Lane *et al.* (2007) report data from the London Marathon showing that most runners reported extreme fatigue,

---

RESEARCH METHODS BOX 29.1

T-Scores

T-scores can also be called standard scores. Psychologists encourage use of T-scores because raw scores on their own carry little meaning.

A standard T-score is calculated as follows:

Observed – average score (often taken from tables of norms) / standard deviation, multiplied by 10 + 50

Raw scores are subjected to T-score transformations using the following formula:

$$T = 50 + 10 \frac{(n - m)}{s}$$

where n = raw score; m = mean; s = standard deviation. This transformation converts raw scores to scores on a standard scale with a mean of 50 and a standard deviation of 10.

Psychologists use standard T-scores to interpret data. If the mean is 50 and the standard deviation (SD) 10, then scores of 60 and 40 are within 1 SD of the average. A score of 60 is 1 SD above the average, and a score of 40 is 1 SD below the average. As data conforms to normal distribution theory, 68% of data will be within $+/-1$ SD; 34% of data will be within $+/-2$ SD, and almost all data will be within $+/-3$ SD. It is argued that converting data to standard scores helps practitioners interpret the meaning of data.

---

and that while some of these runners reported a concurrent increase in anger, tension and depression, others reported no changes in these unpleasant emotions (see Figure 29.5). Lane *et al.* (2007) proposed that some athletes accept that they will perceive sensations of intense fatigue and attribute this to a sense of goal achievement.

29.2.2 Impact of Extreme Environments on Physiology and Psychological Variables

Extreme environments place physiological and psychological **stress** on an individual (Lane *et al.*, 2004b). We will delimit discussion of the effects of extreme environments by focusing on altitude, although as Lane *et al.* (2004b) describe in their review article, exercising in adverse

FOCUS POINT 29.1   LACTATE THRESHOLD

As people exercise they use energy, and the waste product for this energy can be carbon dioxide when exercising at a low intensity. As the intensity of exercise increases, the aerobic system fails to cope and the by-product is lactic acid. When people exercise at a high intensity, they produce lactic acid. If aerobic exercise is characterised by a noticeable increase in the depth and breadth of breathing rates, anaerobic exercise is characterised by a sensation of burning in the muscles; lactic acid is partly responsible for this burning feeling. The lactate threshold is a point during exhaustive, all-out exercise at which lactic acid builds up in the bloodstream faster than the body can remove it.

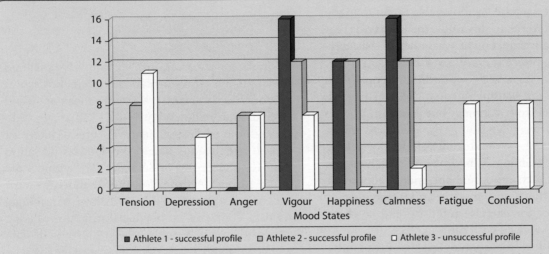

- **Athlete 1** is an emotional profile typified by feeling vigorous, lively and alert, and in control. This athlete has regulated negative and unpleasant emotions.
- **Athlete 2** shows a different emotional profile associated with success. In contrast to athlete 1, athlete 2 has a profile depicted by feeling vigorous, tense and angry. They will use feelings of tension and anger to aid motivation. For athlete 2, feeling tense can be like a warning signal – 'I am about to try to achieve an important goal, and unless I work really hard, I will not achieve my goal.'
- **Athlete 3** is a different story. This athlete feels anxious, angry and depressed. These emotions are likely to interfere with performance. Feeling tense might make you want to try harder, but when it is combined with feeling depressed it can make you feel like giving up. Our research has found that feeling depressed is possibly the most damaging emotion to experience before and during competition (Lane & Terry, 2000). When athletes feel depressed, angry and fatigued at the same time, they tend to turn anger inwards to self-blame and implode; poor performance is then likely.

FIGURE 29.5 *Mood profiles of runners.*

environments tends to be associated with unpleasant psychological states. Evidence shows that living and exercising at altitude have pronounced psychological and physiological effects (Bolmont, 2007; Lane *et al.*, 2004b). With less oxygen available for use, these effects are not surprising. Responses occurring at altitudes over 1500 metres above sea level include increased heart rate, **ventilation**, **oxidative stress**, **dehydration** and **glycogen depletion**, and decreased exercise capacity and immune function. In the initial stages, exercise simply feels harder than that performed at the same pace at sea level due to the increased physiological demands. If athletes consider that these increased demands outweigh their perceived ability to cope, then

ventilation the bodily process of breathing in and out.

dehydration excessive loss of water from the body's tissues.

oxidative stress a condition of increased oxidant production in human cells, characterised by the release of free radicals, the physical and medical consequences of which are unclear but may play a role in fostering an adaptive response to altitude exposure.

glycogen depletion the process whereby stores of glycogen (from carbohydrates) in the muscles and liver are reduced and blood glucose levels begin to fall causing athletes to experience, e.g., fatigue and lack of coordination.

hypobaric hypoxia a deficiency of oxygen reaching the tissues of the body related to conditions of low air pressure and low oxygen as can be found at high altitudes.

acute mountain sickness a set of maladaptive physiological and psychological disorders, caused by rapid ascent to heights of more than 3000m.

high altitude pulmonary edema (HAPE) a life-threatening form of fluid accumulation in the lungs of otherwise healthy mountain climbers that occurs typically at high altitudes.

high altitude cerebral edema (HACE) a severe (frequently fatal) form of altitude sickness.

exercising at altitude represents a stressful task (Bolmont, 2007).

Rapid ascents to heights of more than 3000 metres cause further physiological responses triggered by **hypobaric hypoxia**, associated with a reduction in barometric pressure leading to a reduced partial pressure of oxygen (Whyte, 2006). Arterial oxyhaemoglobin saturation decreases and may produce a set of maladaptive physiological and psychological disorders known as **acute mountain sickness** (AMS; Whyte, 2006). AMS involves experiencing breathlessness, headache, insomnia, dizziness and abnormal tiredness, and mood disturbances (Lane & Whyte, 2008). Other effects are visual disturbances, adverse changes in cognitive functions such as having difficulties concentrating, remembering key information, postural stability, sensory motor coordination, eye–hand coordination and neuromuscular control. AMS includes two major life-threatening conditions: **high altitude pulmonary edema (HAPE)** and **high altitude cerebral edema (HACE)** (Lane & Whyte, 2008). Treatment for these conditions must be immediate to avoid long-term injury and fatality (Whyte, 2006). The primary treatment for HAPE and HACE is evacuation to a lower altitude/sea level as rapidly as possible (Lane & Whyte, 2008). Other associated health issues with moderate altitude (up to 3000 metres) and in particular high altitude range from nonfreezing cold injury and frostbite to hypothermia.

For a given altitude, AMS symptoms usually show maximal effects during the first or second day of exposure and then recede rapidly in those who adapt (responders). AMS symptoms can reappear if the person's ascent continues too rapidly. It should be noted that some people do not adapt to altitude (labelled nonresponders). The number of symptoms, the severity and rapidity of the onset and the duration of high-altitude symptoms vary between individuals. Pronounced changes that occur include alterations in mood states such as irritability, hostility, depression and anxiety. Figure 29.6 shows changes in mood states reported in previous research. The message is clear: the higher the altitude, the more pronounced the effects on emotional and cognitive processes.

Of the plethora of factors found to influence how people adapt to altitude, possibly the most convincing are the effects of experience (Lane & Whyte, 2008). While this might seem an obvious statement, the precise mechanisms through which experience assists with **coping** efforts are not clear. It is possible that repeated exposure to altitude leads to physiological changes that make adaptation to altitude much easier; however, evidence indicates that the physiological acclimatisation to altitude is relatively transient. The benefits from one trip to altitude have depreciated by the time the person goes on the next trip.

coping constantly changing effort in the form of thoughts and behaviours to manage demands that are appraised as challenging or beyond the resources of the individual.

Nevertheless, it could be that individuals expect to experience the acute physiological responses and change their behaviour accordingly. This explanation would suggest that people exercise less intensely or gauge the exercise–rest ratio more effectively. Figure 29.7 shows improvements in mood states from a group of elite athletes who attended two training camps at an altitude of 2000 metres (Lane *et al.*, 2003). In the second camp, some four months after the first camp, athletes reported feeling more vigorous and less fatigued.

The issue of whether successful adaptation is driven by physiological or experiential mechanisms is a question best answered in academic circles. Practically, athletes should look to maximise the benefits of experience of altitude. Each trip to altitude represents a learning

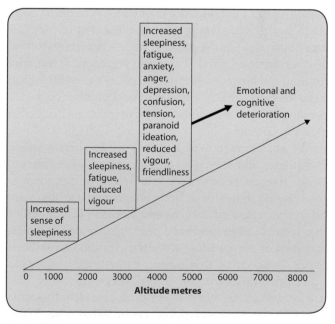

FIGURE 29.6 *Emotional and cognitive changes to living and exercising at altitude.*

Source: Bolmont (2007), figure from Lane (2007).

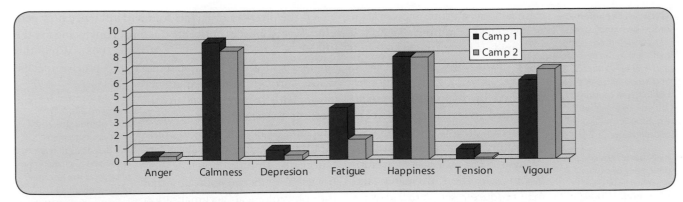

FIGURE 29.7 *Improvements in mood states as athletes gain experience of managing the effects of altitude.*

opportunity. The perceptual nature of stress is an important issue to consider here. It seems that it helps if people hold a positive perception of their ability to manage the physiological effects.

In conclusion, given the nature of physical activity and subsequent physiological responses, the relationship with psychological states represents a worthwhile line of future research.

29.2.3 Food and Unhealthy Eating

The biological basis of diet at first glance appears to be common sense: people consume food and drink for energy requirements. People regulate their consumption around perceived energy requirements in the same way that animals in the wild do. If one looks at animal body shape in the wild, it is readily apparent that obesity is a rare condition. This is the case even when animals have an abundance of food. The same argument is not true for humans, however. Although there is a clear biological basis for eating, there appears to be a number of social, personality and environmental factors that contribute to eating behaviours.

Weight management and diet are important issues for athletes and exercisers alike (Hausenblas & Carron, 1999). Exercisers tend to be interested in diet for reasons realted to health or body image, while athletes are often motivated to lose weight because of the belief that it can lead to improved performance or is a necessary part of preparation in weight-classified sports. It is generally accepted that having a low body weight can be helpful for health and/or sports performance, but it is important to avoid developing obsessive thoughts about food and/or unhealthy eating behaviours. Thus, there are clear social drivers pushing athletes and exercisers to try to regulate their diet. This section describes unhealthy eating behaviours in more detail and

attempts to explore how individuals may develop eating disorders. By using a case study, strategies intended to prevent food obsessions and increase self-control around food are explained.

Some individuals, including athletes and exercisers, have very unhealthy eating behaviours and become obsessed with their diet. It is of course possible that people who already hold extreme beliefs about diet are drawn to sport and exercise as these are settings where they find like-minded people. Unhealthy eating patterns and weight-management behaviours can include regularly dieting, fasting or exercising excessively to lose weight. Alternatively, unhealthy eating patterns can include over-eating uncontrollably and then vomiting to prevent weight gain. These are all symptoms of an eating disorder. Although researchers do not know fully how eating disorders develop, they know that there are many factors that cause unhealthy eating and suspect that unhealthy eating and eating disorders are related.

Therefore, if sport and exercise are associated with unhealthy eating patterns, with which sports and activities does this phenomenon seem to occur? Evidence suggests that aesthetic activities such as gymnastics and ice skating, where body image is important, and sports where power to weight ratio is important, such as distance running, tend to show a higher proportion of athletes reporting eating disorders. Athletes that are commonly linked to eating disorders tend to be from weight-making sports such as weightlifting, wrestling and boxing (Hausenblas & Carron, 1999). It is common in such sports to use excessive weight-loss techniques, including rapid dehydration by fasting, fluid restriction, diuretics, laxatives and purging (Hall & Lane, 2001). Although making the weight can clearly be detrimental, leading to dehydration, reduced energy levels and poor performance (Hall & Lane, 2001), many athletes believe that they will gain a number of benefits from the process. For example, some athletes believe that making the weight will develop mental toughness and improve performance. Sports like boxing and wrestling can positively reinforce extreme dieting, because two boxers who are both equally starved can compete and one boxer will win. This means that the winning boxer positively reinforces the use of extreme weight-making strategies.

For example, Hall and Lane (2001) conducted a study in which boxers competed in a simulated contest at their competition weight and their normal weight. Their normal weight describes their condition shortly before competition. Boxers reported engaging in strategies to get down to competition weight, and normally did so one or two days before competition. The difference between the competition weight and the normal weight was around 10% of body weight. Hall and Lane found that boxers used a range of potentially dysfunctional strategies to lose weight, including dehydrating strategies such as using a sweat suit, reducing food and liquid intake, and in some cases vomiting. Boxers recognised that this would produce a weakened state, but believed that energy levels could be restored after the weigh-in and before the contest. For example, a boxer may go on an 'lemon-only' diet as they believe that this will increase weight loss. If they make the weight, this belief is reinforced. They will experience positive emotions when they feel they can make the weight and they utilise these emotions to help endure unpleasant feelings to achieve this goal (Lane, 2009a). Unfortunately, if these methods are repeated they can form a habit, and once the habit is formed, it is hard to break. As Figure 29.8 shows, athletes develop a belief that they could perform better at the reduced weight and this runs counter to actual performance.

Take a look also at Activity Box 29.4.

29.2.4   How Do Eating Behaviours Develop?

Diet and patterns of eating behaviour derive from a number of individual and environmental factors. Amid a number of possible factors, cognitive aspects and particularly thought processes about food and eating behaviours are particularly important. We should remember that for most of us, what we eat, how much we eat and when we eat are choices we freely make; we are not force fed. Most people have the opportunity to walk by a sweet shop or walk in and buy some sweets. While acknowledging this point, individuals make choices around food along with a number of issues. The desire to eat is a biological urge and trying to deny this urge can be very difficult. You will start feeling hungry, your sleep will be affected, you will starting thinking about food,

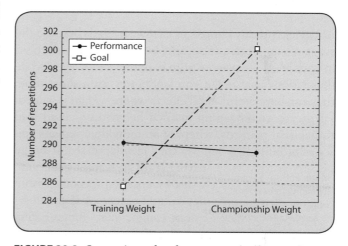

FIGURE 29.8 *Comparison of performance and self-set goals at training weight and championship weight.*
Source: Hall & Lane (2001).

ATTITUDES TO EATING

ACTIVITY BOX 29.4

Complete the questionnaire at http://www.mnsu.edu/shs/bodyimage/eatingattitude.html. As you complete this measure we would like you to think about the pros and cons of using it.

This questionnaire can be a useful tool in recognising someone who may be at risk. However, it should be used with extreme caution. First, using this questionnaire does not qualify you to diagnose an eating disorder; only a

professional in the field can do this. Second, it requires some form of support mechanism. Ethically, if you identify someone with possible symptoms of disordered eating, you should direct them towards appropriate support.

If you are concerned about your results on the EAT-26 or those of another person, you should visit the 'Help and Support' section of the beat website (http://www.b-eat.co.uk/HelpandSupport).

and this information will be telling you the message 'eat'. When faced with a decision on which food to eat, if you have deprived yourself the message will be loud and clear: 'Eat the food with the most calories and eat lots of it'.

People who experience obsessive thoughts and unhealthy eating behaviour such as binging and extreme dieting tend also to experience negative emotions. For example, an individual who reports feeling stressed, frustrated or depressed might binge eat on unhealthy foods as a strategy to enhance their emotions (Lane, 2007; Lane & Lane, 2008). Data from a recent study illustrates this point (Lane, 2007). An exerciser named Abbey who was asked if she ate when feeling emotional indicated:

> When I'm depressed I eat. I eat lots of really unhealthy foods like biscuits, chocolates and crisps – the sweeter and fattier the better and I keep eating even though I am full – what is that saying? I know by eating it won't make me happier, but I keep trying all the same. (Lane, 2007)

Abbey may partly choose to eat sweet foods because the surge of sugar can temporarily boost levels of endorphin in your brain, associated with happiness. However, while these foods may make you feel better for a short time, they can have detrimental effects where weight is gained. Furthermore, engaging in such behaviours could lead to habitual patterns, whereby an individual repeats episodes of binging whenever they feel depressed. If **binge eating** leads to weight gain, individuals can then become more depressed because of their subsequent weight gain. Binge eating as a response to stress and depression can in turn become the cause of subsequent feelings of stress and depression, and a negative cycle of unpleasant emotions and binge eating emerges (Lane, 2007).

binge eating a self-defeating behaviour in which an individual eats to excess (as defined by the individual) in order to regulate emotion and/or self-soothe.

Dysfunctional eating behaviours, and particularly the moment a person decides to eat unhealthily, might be related to their emotional state. The key to controlling eating behaviours is to explore the extent to which the individual is aware of the emotions that accompany food, and what causes these emotions in the first place. Individuals who have difficulty controlling their weight are often unaware of the cause of these feelings. One factor that may influence future eating behaviour is eating behaviour in childhood (Brown & Ogden, 2004). For example, adults may choose to eat more sweet foods when they are upset partly because they were given sweet foods to cheer them up when they were children. Research also shows strong support for the link between poor dietary control and stress (Laitinen, Ek & Sovio, 2002). An inability to control diet and an inability to cope with the stresses of everyday life are closely related.

29.2.5 Developing Strategies to Control Eating Behaviours

We will look at the results from recent applied work (Lane & Lane, 2008). Lane and Lane provide details of a 39-year-old male who previously competed at national level, but more recently exercised for health and fitness-related reasons. At the start of the intervention, Lane and Lane screened the athlete for possible indicators of eating disorders using the Eating Attitude Test (Garner *et al.*, 1982). They used a dual approach to interpreting scores on the EAT. First, they checked to see if the overall score was above 20. A score of 20 or more is a potential indicator of a clinical issue, and if this score was identified, the next step should be to refer the individual for clinical assessment. They also interpreted data using norms from an exercise population of 598 exercisers (Lane, Lane & Matheson, 2004). As Figure 29.9 shows, it is normal for exercisers to engage in dieting behaviours, but very few exercisers are preoccupied by food or show bulimic tendencies. In this case study, the participant reported scores that closely resembled normative data other than that he engaged in a greater number of dieting behaviours.

Lane and Lane (2008) asked their athlete to complete the TEES. As Figure 29.10 indicates, he engaged in weight-making activities, experienced unpleasant emotions after eating, and tended to eat when experiencing unpleasant emotions such as depression and anxiety. He also had a poor **body image**, believing himself to be overweight. Following assessment, the authors concluded that there were no symptoms of an underlying clinical condition.

body image the cognitions, emotions and behaviours related to how one perceives one's body.

The authors followed an intervention to unravel and change the diet–emotion link. Part of the process was for him to start recording his daily intake and emotional states through the use of a daily diary. He was asked to keep a diary of when he was eating, what he was eating and what emotions were being experienced. The process of recording a diary is important, as it not only provides

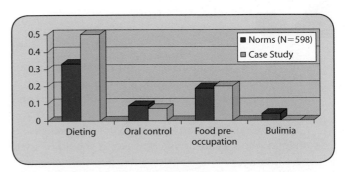

FIGURE 29.9 *Eating Attitude Test scores: A case study from applied work (see Lane & Lane, 2008).*

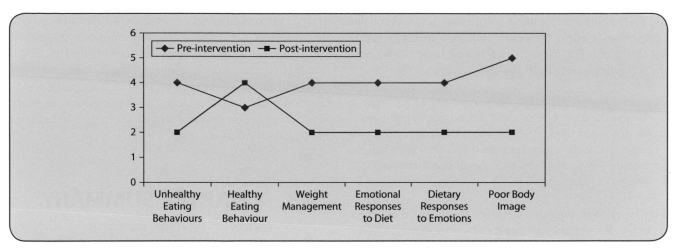

FIGURE 29.10 *Changes in attitudes to diet following an intervention: A case study from applied work (see Lane & Lane, 2008).*

RESEARCH METHODS BOX 29.2

The Exerciser's Eating Scale

Recent research has explored the emotions that link diet and eating. A measure called The Exerciser's Eating Scale (Lane, 2007), or *TEES* for short, has been developed to examine eating behaviour (i.e. what we eat), weight-management techniques, dietary responses to emotions, emotional responses to diet and body image. Examples of items for each factor are contained below. By using TEES, emotions related to diet, eating behaviour and body image can be assessed and an intervention package can be developed to improve healthy eating behaviours and weight control. The TEES can be used to monitor progress, with reassessment being done at regular intervals.

The Exerciser's Eating Scale (TEES)

	Strongly disagree					Strongly agree
Unhealthy eating behaviours						
1. I eat lots of fatty foods	1	2	3	4	5	6
2. I eat lots of sweets and sugary foods	1	2	3	4	5	6
Healthy eating behaviours						
3. Most days I eat more than three portions of fruit and/or vegetables	1	2	3	4	5	6
4. I eat a variety of fruit and/or vegetables	1	2	3	4	5	6
Weight management						
5. I control my weight by limiting my calorie intake	1	2	3	4	5	6
6. I omit some foods from my diet to lose weight	1	2	3	4	5	6
Emotional responses to diet						
7. I feel guilty when I eat high-calorie foods	1	2	3	4	5	6
8. I worry when I eat certain foods because I may gain weight	1	2	3	4	5	6
9. I feel disgusted with myself if I over-eat	1	2	3	4	5	6
10. I feel disappointed with myself when I over-eat	1	2	3	4	5	6
Dietary responses to emotions						
11. I eat more unhealthy foods when I am under stress	1	2	3	4	5	6
12. I eat more when I'm nervous	1	2	3	4	5	6
13. I eat unhealthy foods when I am depressed	1	2	3	4	5	6
14. When I'm angry, I often eat more	1	2	3	4	5	6
15. When I'm tense I eat more	1	2	3	4	5	6
Body image						
16. My stomach is too fat	1	2	3	4	5	6
17. I think I am overweight	1	2	3	4	5	6

the consultant with valuable information, but also helps raise self-awareness of factors that lead to binge eating for the client. For example, Lane and Lane (2008) note the following exerts from the daily diary:

> I came home from work after a bad day today, went to the gym and ate a huge meal when I got home. Later, I sat down and thought about why I binged. Partly it was because I felt I could because I had exercised, but the exercise just masked the real reason that I was unhappy over an incident at work.

The work was intended to offer the client a different strategy for regulating unpleasant emotions (Thayer, Newman & McClain, 1994). In this case, he engaged in regular exercise to enhance emotions. Information in the diary helped develop self-talk scripts to assist the client when facing similar situations in the future. It is important for clients to realise that they are active in the decision-making process on whether to binge eat, and self-talk should be targeted to enhance self-confidence towards the use of a different strategy. We asked our client to think back to the situations in which he made a decision to eat chocolate and to explore what he said to himself. He then replayed the scenario and sought to remove the link between eating chocolate and improved mood, choosing a different strategy.

A second key aspect of the use of a diary is to recognise the process through which an individual can be confident enough to take control of decisions around food changes during the intervention. It is important that success is positively reinforced and individuals should seek to reward themselves when they have made a good decision around food. However, this reward should not be linked with food. It is important for the consultant to closely monitor the food diary in the initial stages of the intervention, and to encourage individuals to congratulate themselves on their achievements. As individuals become more confident in their ability to make appropriate decisions around food, they also think less about weight-management issues and engaging in dieting behaviours. Furthermore, once food is no longer seen as a primary strategy for emotional regulation, individuals tend to eat a healthier diet. This trend is evidenced in our case study, as depicted in Figure 29.10.

29.2.6 Summary

Diet and exercise are inextricably linked: diet provides the fuel for engaging in exercise, and exercise provides a strategy for maintaining body shape. Both diet and exercise are strategies for enhancing our emotions. However, exercise can serve as a strategy for masking dysfunctional eating patterns, and experiencing unpleasant emotions following binge eating can be part of a negative food–emotion cycle. In this section we reported a case study of an intervention that challenged exercisers' beliefs and attitudes around food.

29.3 CHAPTER SUMMARY

In this chapter we have looked at some cognitive and biological factors and how they might influence an applied sport and exercise psychologist. We began by describing two self-referential issues. We focused on self-efficacy because previous research shows that measures of self-efficacy are predictive of performance. We looked at how Bandura's (1997) theoretical framework might be used to guide practice. We considered how self-esteem might influence this process. Participating in sport and exercise often involves trying to win contests or races, achieving personally important goals such as completing a marathon, or using exercise to achieve a goal (such as losing weight). People high in self-esteem appear to be able to cope with failure better than people with low self-esteem. We extended this discussion by looking at the influence of memory on psychological states. We focused on how emotion can colour memory and the notion that if a person feels positive this can lead to recalling positive information. We concluded the section on cognitive factors by looking at concentration and decision making and factors such as emotions, which appear to influence our ability to focus on relevant information.

In the second half of the chapter, we focused on biological factors. We looked at how psychological states respond to exercise and, in particular, the notion that exercise can enhance mood. We looked at how changes in physiological states as a response to being in extreme environments alter psychological states. In both cases, the key message is that variations in physiological states can influence psychological states. We continued this theme by considering diet. In sports where weight making is seen as a way to improve performance, athletes can engage in extreme dietary behaviour. We looked at research and applied work where this was a factor, offering suggestions on how practitioners might challenge athletes' beliefs on diet and thereby manage psychological wellbeing.

SELF-TEST QUESTIONS

- Can you describe the four sources of self-efficacy as proposed by Bandura (2007)?

- Which source of self-efficacy is suggested to be the most dependable?

- Research has found that individuals low in self-esteem tend to respond to experiences in a balanced way; positive events lead to positive psychological states and negative events lead to negative ones. Describe how people high in self-esteem might respond to failure.

- 'Memories are more accessible when mood is similar to when the memories were originally encoded.' What factors are proposed to influence this process?

- Describe how Hanin (2003) proposes that meta-beliefs influence people's memories of emotional states.

- According to home advantage research, referees tend to favour the home team in which type of sports or activities?

- Describe how Nevill, Balmer and Williams (2002) conducted their experiment on home advantage.

- Describe the concentration styles of broad internal, broad external, narrow internal and arrow external.

- According to Thayer, Newman and McClain (1994), what proportion of people use exercise as a self-regulating strategy?

- Describe the symptoms of acute mountain sickness.

- List sports reported to be associated with poor eating attitudes.

ESSAY QUESTIONS

- Compare and contrast similarities and differences between self-efficacy and self-esteem.

- Given the predictive effectiveness of self-efficacy on subsequent performance, sport and exercise psychologists focus their work on enhancing self-efficacy. Discuss this statement with reference to attentional control.

- Outline the effects of exercising at altitude on physiological and psychological variables.

- 'I have exercised and therefore I can eat loads.' Evaluate this statement with reference to biological and social theory of diet.

TEXTS FOR FURTHER READING

Bandura, A. (1997) *Self-Efficacy: The Exercise of Control*, New York: W.H. Freeman.

Lane, A.M. (2007) *Mood and Human Performance: Conceptual, Measurement, and Applied Issues*. Hauppauge, NY: Nova Science.

Lane, A.M. (2009) Consultancy in the ring: Psychological support to a world champion professional boxer, in B. Hemmings & T. Holder (eds) *Applied Sport Psychology*, pp. 51–63, Chichester: John Wiley & Sons, Ltd.

Whyte, G. (2006) *The Physiology of Training*, Oxford: Elsevier Health Sciences.

RELEVANT JOURNAL ARTICLES

Baron, B., Noakes, T.D., Dekerle, J. *et al.* (2008) Why does exercise terminate at the maximal lactate steady state intensity? *British Journal of Sports Medicine* 42(10): 528–33.

Baumeister, R.F., Vohs, K.D., DeWall, C.N. & Zhang, L. (2007) How emotion shapes behavior: Feedback, anticipation, and reflection, rather than direct causation, *Personality and Social Psychology Review* 11(2): 167–203.

Berger, B.G. & Motl, R.W. (2000) Exercise and mood: A selective review and synthesis of research employing the Profile of Mood States, *Journal of Applied Sport Psychology* 12(1): 69–92.

Dodgson, P.G. & Wood, J.V. (1998) Self-esteem and the cognitive accessibility of strengths and weaknesses after failure, *Journal of Personality and Social Psychology* 75: 178–97.

Hall, C.J. & Lane, A.M. (2001) Effects of rapid weight loss on mood and performance among amateur boxers, *British Journal of Sports Medicine* 35(6): 390–95.

Hausenblas, H.A. & Carron, A.V. (1999) Eating disorder indices and athletes: An integration, *Journal of Sport & Exercise Psychology* 21(3): 230.

Hausenblas, H.A., Cook, B.J. & Chittester, N.I. (2008) Can exercise treat eating disorders? *Exercise & Sport Sciences Reviews* 36(1): 43–7.

Lane, A.M., Jones, L. & Stevens, M.J. (2002) Coping with failure: The effects of self-esteem and coping on changes in self-efficacy, *Journal of Sport Behavior* 25(4): 331–45.

Lane, H. J. (2007) Emotions and eating behaviours in exercisers, in A.M. Lane (ed.) *Mood and Human Performance: Conceptual, Measurement, and Applied Issues*, pp. 189–202, Hauppauge, NY: Nova Science.

Moritz, S.E., Feltz, D.L., Fahrbach, K.R. & Mack, D.E. (2000) The relation of self-efficacy measures to sport performance: A meta-analytic review, *Research Quarterly for Exercise and Sport* 71: 280–94.

Nevill, A.M. & Holder, R.L. (1999) Home advantage in sport: An overview of studies on the advantage of playing at home, *Sports Medicine* 28(4): 221–36.

REFERENCES

Acevedo, E. & Ekkekakis, P. (2001) The transactional psychobiological nature of cognitive appraisal during exercise in environmentally stressful conditions, *Psychology of Sport & Exercise* 2(1): 47–67.

Balmer, N.J., Nevill, A.M. & Lane, A.M. (2005) Do judges enhance home advantage in European championship boxing? *Journal of Sports Sciences* 23(4): 409–16.

Balmer, N.J., Nevill, A.M. & Williams, A.M. (2003) Modelling home advantage in the Summer Olympic Games, *Journal of Sports Sciences* 21(6): 469–78.

Balmer, N.J., Nevill, A.M., Lane, A.M., Ward, P., Williams, A.M. & Fairclough, S.H. (2007) Influence of crowd noise on soccer refereeing consistency in soccer, *Journal of Sport Behavior* 30(2): 130–45.

Bandura, A. (1997) *Self-Efficacy: The Exercise of Control*, New York: W.H. Freeman.

Bandura, A. (1999) *Self-Efficacy: Toward a Unifying Theory of Behavioral Change*, Hove: Psychology Press.

Baron, B., Noakes, T.D., Dekerle, J. *et al.* (2008) Why does exercise terminate at the maximal lactate steady state intensity? *British Journal of Sports Medicine* 42(10): 528–33.

Baumeister, R.F. (1993) *Self-Esteem: The Puzzle of Low Self-Regard*, New York: Plenum.

Baumeister, R.F. & Scher, S.J. (1988) Self-defeating behavior patterns among normal individuals: Review and analysis of common self-destructive tendencies, *Psychological Bulletin* 104(1): 3–22.

Baumeister, R.F., Vohs, K.D., DeWall, C.N. & Zhang, L. (2007) How emotion shapes behavior: Feedback, anticipation, and reflection, rather than direct causation, *Personality and Social Psychology Review* 11(2): 167–203.

Berger, B.G. & Motl, R.W. (2000) Exercise and mood: A selective review and synthesis of research employing the Profile of Mood States, *Journal of Applied Sport Psychology* 12(1): 69–92.

Blaney, P.H. (1986) Affect and memory: A review, *Psychological Bulletin* 99: 229–46.

Bolmont, B. (2007) Relationships between mood states and motor performances: What can you learn from high altitude, in A.M. Lane (ed.) *Mood and Human Performance: Conceptual, Measurement, and Applied Issues*, Hauppauge, NY: Nova Science.

Bower, G.H. (1981) Mood and memory, *American Psychologist* 36: 129–48.

Brown, J.D. & Dutton, K.A. (1995) The thrill of victory, the complexity of defeat: Self-esteem and people's emotional reactions to success and failure, *Journal of Personality and Social Psychology* 28: 712–22.

Brown, J.D. & Mankowski, T.A. (1993) Self-esteem, mood, and self-evaluation: Changes in mood and the way you see you, *Journal of Personality and Social Psychology* 64: 421–30.

Brown, R. & Ogden, J. (2004) Children's eating attitudes and behaviour: A study of the modelling and control theories of parental influence, *Health Education Research* 19: 26.

Campbell, J.D. (1990) Self-esteem and clarity of the self-concept, *Journal of Personality and Social Psychology* 59: 528–49.

Chase, M.A., Feltz, D.L. & Lirgg, C.D. (2003) Sources of collective and individual efficacy of collegiate athletes, *International Journal of Sport and Exercise Psychology* 1: 180–91.

Devonport, T.J. (2008) Stress and coping among competitive athletes in sport, in A.M. Lane (ed.) *Sport and Exercise Psychology: Topics in Applied Psychology*, pp. 73–90, London: Hodder & Stoughton.

Devonport, T.J., Biscomb, K., Lane, A.M., Mahoney, C.A. & Cassidy, T. (2005) Stress and coping in elite junior netball, *Journal of Sports Sciences* 22: 162–3.

Dodgson, P.G. & Wood, J.V. (1998) Self-esteem and the cognitive accessibility of strengths and weaknesses after failure, *Journal of Personality and Social Psychology* 75: 178–97.

Duncan, M.J. (2008) Physical activity and self-esteem, in A.M. Lane (ed.) *Sport and Exercise Psychology: Topics in Applied Psychology*, pp. 173–88, London: Hodder & Stoughton.

Feltz, D.L. & Lirgg, C.D. (2001) Self-efficacy beliefs of athletes, teams and coaches, in R.N. Singer, H.A. Hausenblas & C.M. Janelle (eds) *Handbook of Sport Psychology*, pp. 340–61, New York: John Wiley & Sons, Inc.

Garner, D.M., Olmsted, M.P., Bophr, Y. & Garfinkel, P.E. (1982) The Eating Attitudes Test: Psychometric features and clinical correlates, *Psychological Medicine* 12: 871–8.

George, T.R., Feltz, D.L. & Chase, M.A. (1992) Effects of model similarity on self-efficacy and muscular endurance: A second look, *Journal of Sport & Exercise Psychology* 14: 237–48.

Hall, C.J. & Lane, A.M. (2001) Effects of rapid weight loss on mood and performance among amateur boxers, *British Journal of Sports Medicine* 35(6): 390–95.

Hamer, M. & Karageorghis, C.I. (2007) Psychobiological mechanisms of exercise dependence, *Sports Medicine* 37(6): 477–85.

Hanin, Y.L. (2003) Performance related emotional states in sport: A qualitative analysis, *Forum: Qualitative Social Research* 4(Feb.), http://www.qualitative-research.net/fqs-texte/1-03/1-03hanin-e.htm, accessed November 2010.

Hausenblas, H.A. & Carron, A.V. (1999) Eating disorder indices and athletes: An integration, *Journal of Sport & Exercise Psychology* 21(3): 230.

Hausenblas, H.A., Cook, B.J. & Chittester, N.I. (2008) Can exercise treat eating disorders? *Exercise & Sport Sciences Reviews* 36(1): 43–7.

Hausenblas, H.A. & Symons Downs, D. (2002) Exercise dependence: A systematic review, *Psychology of Sport & Exercise* 3(2): 89–123.

Holder, R.L. & Nevill, A.M. (1997) Modelling performance at international tennis and golf tournaments: Is there a home advantage? *Statistician* 46(4): 551–9.

Laitinen, J., Ek, E. & Sovio, U. (2002) Stress-related eating and drinking behavior and body mass index and predictors of this behavior, *Preventive Medicine* 34: 29–33.

Lane, A.M. (2009a) Consultancy in the ring: Psychological support to a world champion professional boxer, in B. Hemmings & T. Holder (eds) *Applied Sport Psychology*, pp. 51–63, Chichester: John Wiley & Sons, Ltd.

Lane, A.M. (2009b) Physiological correlates of emotion Self-Regulation during prolonged cycling performance, paper presented at the International Society for Research on Emotion, Leuven, Belgium, August.

Lane, A.M., Jackson, A. & Terry, P.C. (2005) Self-regulatory mechanisms to explain mood changes following exercise, *Journal of Sports Science and Medicine* 4: 195–200.

Lane, A.M., Jones, L. & Stevens, M.J. (2002) Coping with failure: The effects of self-esteem and coping on changes in self-efficacy, *Journal of Sport Behavior* 25(4): 331–45.

Lane, A.M. & Lane, H.J. (2008) Psychology of eating and food control: A case study, *International Journal of Psychology* 43: 148.

Lane, A.M. & Terry, P.C. (1996) Predictors of self-efficacy in amateur boxing, *Journal of Sports Sciences* 14: 93–4.

Lane, A.M. & Terry, P.C. (2000) The nature of mood: Development of a conceptual model with a focus on depression, *Journal of Applied Sport Psychology* 12: 16–33.

Lane, A. & Whyte, G. (2008) Head in the clouds – altitude climbing psychology, *Peak Performance* 260: 1–4.

Lane, A.M., Nevill, A.M., Ahmad, N.S. & Balmer, N. (2006) Soccer referee decision-making: 'Shall I blow the whistle?' *Journal of Sports Science and Medicine* 5: 243–53.

Lane, A.M., Terry, P.C., Beedie, C.J. & Stevens, M. (2004a) Mood and concentration grid performance: Effects of depressed mood, *International Journal of Sport & Exercise Psychology* 2(2): 133–45.

Lane, A.M., Terry, P.C., Stevens, M.J., Barney, S. & Dinsdale, S.L. (2004b) Mood responses to athletic performance in extreme environments, *Journal of Sports Sciences* 22(10): 886–97.

Lane, A.M., Whyte, G.P., George, K., Shave, R., Stevens, M.J. & Barney, S. (2007) Marathon: A fun run? Mood state changes among runners at the London Marathon, in A.M. Lane (ed.) *Mood and Human Performance: Conceptual, Measurement, and Applied Issues*, pp. 265–74, Hauppauge, NY: Nova Science.

Lane, A.M., Whyte, G.P., Godfrey, R. & Pedlar, C. (2003) Adaptations of psychological state variables to altitude among the Great Britain biathlon team preparing for the 2002 Olympic Games, *Journal of Sports Sciences* 21(4): 281–2.

Lane, A.M., Whyte, G.P., Shave, R., Barney, S., Stevens, M.J. & Wilson, M. (2005) Mood disturbance during cycling performance at extreme conditions, *Journal of Sports Science and Medicine* 4: 52–7.

Lane, A.M., Whyte, G.P., Shave, R. & Wilson, M. (2003) Mood state responses during intense cycling, *Journal of Sports Sciences* 21(4): 352–3.

Lane, H.J. (2007) Emotions and eating behaviours in exercisers, in A.M. Lane (ed.) *Mood and Human Performance: Conceptual, Measurement, and Applied Issues*, pp. 189–202, Hauppauge, NY: Nova Science.

Lane, H.J., Lane, A.M. & Matheson, H. (2004) Validity of the eating attitude test among exercisers, *Journal of Sports Science and Medicine* 3: 244–53, http://www.jssm.org/vol3/n4/7/v3n4-7.htm, accessed November 2010.

Michela, M. & Parisolla, M. (2001) The contemporary construction of perfect body image: Bodybuilding, exercise addiction and eating disorders, *Quest* 53: 216–30.

Moran, A.P. (2004) *Sport and Exercise Psychology: A Critical Introduction*, London: Routledge.

Moritz, S.E., Feltz, D.L., Fahrbach, K.R. & Mack, D.E. (2000) The relation of self-efficacy measures to sport performance: A meta-analytic review, *Research Quarterly for Exercise and Sport* 71: 280–94.

Nevill, A.M., Balmer, N.J. & Williams, A.M. (2002) The influence of crowd noise and experience upon refereeing decisions in football, *Psychology of Sport & Exercise* 3(4): 261–72.

Nevill, A.M. & Holder, R.L. (1999) Home advantage in sport: An overview of studies on the advantage of playing at home, *Sports Medicine* 28(4): 221–36.

Nevill, A.M., Holder, R.L., Bardsley, A., Calvert, H. & Jones, S. (1997) Identifying home advantage in international tennis and golf tournaments, *Journal of Sports Sciences* 15(4): 437–43.

Nevill, A.M., Newell, S.M. & Gale, S. (1996) Factors associated with home advantage in English and Scottish soccer matches, *Journal of Sports Sciences* 14(2): 181–6.

Nideffer, R.M. (1986) Concentration and attention control training, in J.M. Williams (ed.) *Applied Sport Psychology: Personal Growth to Peak Performance*, pp. 257–69, Palo Alto, CA: Mayfield.

Parkinson, B., Totterdell, P., Briner, R.B. & Reynolds, S. (1996) *Changing Moods: The Psychology of Mood and Mood Regulation*, London: Longman.

Petrie, T.A. (1996) Differences between male and female college lean sport athletics, non-lean sport athletics and non-athletics on behavioural and psychological indices of eating disorders, *Journal of Applied Sports Psychology* 8: 218–30.

Rejeski, W.J. & Ribisl, P.M. (1980) Expected task duration and perceived effort: An attributional analysis, *Journal of Sport Psychology* 2(3): 227–36.

Robazza, C. & Bortoli, L. (2005) Changing students' attitudes towards risky motor tasks: An application of the IZOF model, *Journal of Sports Sciences* 23(10): 1075–88.

Singer, R.N., Cauraugh, J.H., Tennant, L.K., Murphey, M., Chen, D. & Lidor, R. (1991) Attention and distractors: Considerations for enhancing sport performance, *International Journal of Sport Psychology* 22: 95–114.

Stajkovic, A.D. & Luthans, F. (1998) Self-efficacy and work-related performance: A meta-analysis, *Psychological Bulletin* 124: 240–61.

Tenenbaum, G. & Elran, E. (2003) Congruence between actual and retrospective reports of emotions for pre and post-competition states, *Journal of Sport & Exercise Psychology* 25(3): 323–40.

Terry, P.C. (1989) *The Winning Mind*, Wellingborough: Thorsons.

Terry, P.C., Stevens, M.J. & Lane, A.M. (2005) Influence of response time frame on mood assessment, *Anxiety, Stress & Coping* 18(3): 279–85.

Thayer, R.E., Newman, R. & McClain, T.M. (1994) Self-regulation of mood: Strategies for changing a bad mood, raising energy, and reducing tension, *Journal of Personality and Social Psychology* 67: 910–25.

Whyte, G. (2006) *The Physiology of Training*, London: Elsevier Health Sciences.

Willis, J.D. & Campbell, L.F. (1992) *Exercise Psychology*, Champaign, IL: Human Kinetics.

30 Sport and Exercise Psychology – Understanding Social, Developmental and Personality Factors

Tracey Devonport & Andy Lane

LEARNING OUTCOMES

WHEN YOU HAVE COMPLETED THIS CHAPTER, YOU SHOULD BE ABLE TO:

1. Be aware of the influence of social psychological factors on engagement with and outcomes of sport and exercise participation.

2. Be aware of the role of developmental factors on engagement with and outcomes of sports and exercise participation.

3. Be aware of the influence that personality may have on engagement with and outcomes of sport and exercise participation.

4. Appreciate the influence that social, developmental and personality variables may have on the services offered by ASEP.

KEY WORDS

Cultural Models ● Culture ● Group Dynamics ● Group Environment Questionnaire ● Multicultural Training Models ● Personality ● Scaffolding ● Social Cohesion ● Task Cohesion ● Trait Anxiety ● Trait Emotional Intelligence ● Trait Theory

CHAPTER OUTLINE

DEVELOPING SOCIOGRAMS

A sociogram is a graphic representation of the social links that a person has. It is a sociometric chart that plots the structure of interpersonal relations in a group situation. Those individuals on a sociogram who have many attraction lines are called Stars. Those with few or no choices are called Isolates. Individuals who choose each other are known to have made a Mutual Choice. One-Way Choice refers to individuals who choose someone but the choice is not reciprocated. Cliques are groups of three or more people within a larger group who all choose each other (Mutual Choice).

Constructing sociograms can help identify individuals at risk of exclusion and/or dropping out of the group. An example of a sociogram is provided below. We can see that Finlay is the star and Dave is the isolate. Once social patterns are established, interventions can then be utilised to identify the reasons behind the social dynamic and ways of better integrating isolates.

To construct a sociogram ask a group/team questions such as:

- Name those individuals who you prefer to exercise/train/compete with (i.e. not just one person).
- Name those individuals whom you definitely would not want to exercise/train/compete with (i.e. assessing

rejection – be careful about generating negative feelings).
- Name the person whom you talk to the most/the least.
- Name the person whom you know the best/least.

Using a sports team, exercise group or alternative group (e.g. art or music club) construct a sociogram. Identify the stars and isolates (present information sensitively). What would you do to enhance the social group dynamic?

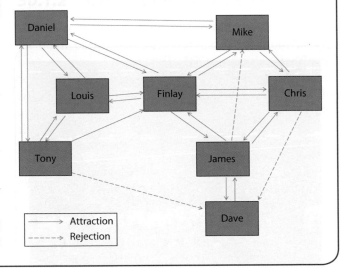

- Task type – tasks that require interaction, communication, interdependence and coordination increase cohesion over tasks requiring a minimal presence of these factors.

Personal factors include:

- Team member cognitions – cohesion is associated with more team-enhancing attributions (Widmeyer, Brawley & Carron, 1990).
- Affect – greater cohesion has been shown to be related to lower pre-competition anxiety as well as to greater athlete satisfaction (Lowther & Lane, 2002).
- Behaviours – cohesion is positively associated with adherence behaviour, personal effort and conformity behaviour.

Leadership factors include:

- Training and instruction behaviours. For example, social support, democratic and positive feedback behaviours have been associated with greater perceptions of cohesiveness (Shields et al., 1997).

- A more democratic approach to decision making has been linked to greater cohesiveness. Team members invest more effort, persist and engage for longer where they have had an opportunity to participate in decision making (Carron et al., 1998).

Team factors include:

- Team success, collective efficacy and group communication. As team cohesiveness increases, the team is more successful, collective efficacy is greater and communication is improved.
- Team roles also influence cohesion. A role is a set of behaviours expected of an individual occupying a specific position within a group (Mabry & Barnes, 1980). Teams whose members have role clarity, accept and understand the scope of their responsibility, know the behaviours necessary to fulfil these roles and how they are evaluated. They also know the consequences should they fail to fulfil their responsibilities and tend to be more cohesive (Eys & Carron, 2001).

- Team norms are standards of behaviours expected for group members that are also associated with increased group cohesion where they are agreed and adhered to (Gammage, Carron & Estabrooks, 2001). These may include norms for productivity during competition, practice and off-season (Munroe et al., 1999).

The growing body of cohesion literature in ASEP offers a sound empirical basis on which to base interventions intended to enhance the functioning of a sport or exercise group. Interventions typically focus on one or more of the categories of situational factors, personal factors, leadership factors and team factors. They commonly address role relationships, interpersonal relationships, goal setting or leadership (Martin, Carron & Burke, 2009). Continued research in this area will inform the evolution and enhancement of interventions intended to enhance group cohesion.

30.2 DEVELOPMENTAL FACTORS

Before you begin this section, consider Activity Box 30.3.

When exploring sport and exercise behaviours among individuals, it is important to acknowledge the influence of developmental factors. This section describes the main considerations of each key developmental stage, including children, adults and elderly populations.

30.2.1 Children

There is substantial evidence to suggest that active play, sport and exercise are central to a child's physical, mental and social wellbeing (Pellegrini, 2008; Tomkinson et al., 2003). A greater understanding of developmental psychology may inform opportunities to promote children's physical activity and development. Furthermore, few studies have explored the impact of cognitive development on children's ability to engage with and utilise sport psychology interventions. In exploring the cognitive development of children, the work of two influential theorists will be presented here, Piaget and Vygotsky.

30.2.1.1 Piaget's (1952) theory of cognitive development

Piaget's (1952) theory of cognitive development is the most widely used theory in the study of human development, but is not without its critics (Beilin, 1992). The central tenants of Piaget's theory are as follows. Children

---

PIAGET'S STAGES OF COGNITIVE DEVELOPMENT   **ACTIVITY BOX 30.3**

View a short video of Piaget's stages of cognitive development at http://www.youtube.com/watch?v=9yhXjJVFA14. You may need to watch and consider this video on a number of occasions before answering the following question:

What are the implications of the information presented in the video for a child's development in the sport and exercise domain? Address this question for each of the four stages of cognitive development.

Stage	Implications
Sensorimotor stage	
Pre-operational stage	
Concrete operational stage	
Formal operational stage	

construct their own reality as they manipulate and explore the world around them by developing schemata. A schema is an interrelated set of actions, memories, thoughts or strategies used to predict and make sense of the environment. As children grow, they develop and refine their schemata through a process of organisation, assimilation and accommodation. Assimilation and accommodation enable adaptation: during assimilation existing schemata are used to interpret new knowledge; by contrast, accommodation occurs where old schemata are adapted to better fit environmental demands (Piaget, 1952). Piaget proposed that the organisation of cognitive structures occurs in four stages, that these stages progress in a fixed order and that no stage is missed.

30.2.1.1.1 Sensorimotor stage

The sensorimotor stage is the first stage occurring during the first two years of an infant's life. In this period (which has six sub-stages) children progress from a simplistic reflexive response to the environment, gradually developing the ability to think about the environment, learn motor meaning, begin the development of symbolic representation (also known as language) and utilise symbolic abilities (mental representation/memory). The main achievement of this stage is the development of object permanence, whereby children learn that objects continue to exist independently of our ability to perceive them. The acquisition of object permanence (at about 7 months of age) marks the beginning of the ability to think using representations (memory) rather than via actions. This means that the developing child can think things through before they act.

30.2.1.1.2 Pre-operational stage

The second stage is the pre-operational stage, which occurs from 2 to 7 years of age. The rapid growth of representational abilities, including language, numbers, pictures and spatial representation, is considered to be a key achievement of this stage (which has two sub-stages). Egocentric thinking predominates, in that the child has a tendency to think from their own perspective and fails to consider alternative viewpoints.

30.2.1.1.3 Concrete operational stage

The third stage is the concrete operational stage that occurs from 7 to 11 years of age. In this stage, operational thinking develops and egocentric thought diminishes. Children develop their ability to apply the logical and systematic manipulation of symbols related to concrete objects. For example, children understand that the physical characteristics of an object or substance remain the same (e.g. volume of water) even if their appearance changes (e.g. water is transferred from a short to a tall glass).

30.2.1.1.4 Formal operational stage

The fourth stage, which occurs from 11 years and above, is the formal operational stage. In this stage, children can reason in logical, propositional, abstract and hypothetical ways. Children may apply hypothetico-deductive reasoning, whereby they start with a general theory of all possible factors that might affect an outcome and deduce from it specific hypotheses (or predictions) about what might happen. They then test these hypotheses in order to test and if necessary revise their theory. A second key element of this stage is that children can utilise propositional thinking, in that they can reason based on the logical properties of a set of statements rather than requiring concrete examples. There appears to be variation in the attainment of formal operational reasoning and so it cannot be assumed that this will be attained by all. It has been suggested that this finding may partially be as a result of schooling practices in literate societies emphasising logical thinking and problem solving (Moshman, 1998). For more information regarding the sub-components and criticisms of Piaget's theory, see Keenan and Evans (2009, pp. 159–70).

30.2.1.2 Utility of the theory

In terms of the potential utility of Piaget's theory for ASEP in the promotion and development of children's physical activity, the developmental stage of a child affects their ability to understand and apply motor/psychological skills and informs the social support required for the individual. Practitioners must integrate each child's cognitive, emotional and physical development into an intervention, while recognising the socio environmental (e.g. teacher, coach, parents, peers) and task constraints (e.g. readiness for competition) imposed on them.

For example, for children in the pre-operational stage (aged 2 to 7), thinking is largely restricted to thoughts about the physical world, including where an activity takes place and what it involves. During this stage, children may struggle to categorise, classify and serialise information. As such, they may be incapable of determining the necessary order of information and establishing mutually exclusive categories, or of appreciating that the features of an object remain the same when it is transformed (the water in a glass example). An intervention such as performance profiling (Butler, 1989) requires an individual to identify key factors related to performance and rate themselves against these factors on a scale (for more information on performance profiling see Chapter 28). This type of format used by older children and adults would be inappropriate for pre-operational children (Foster & Weigand, 2008). A developmentally beneficial task would be to explore what the child thinks about the world, and what they believe they need to do in order to succeed in sport and exercise. While the child will not rate these factors, engaging them in conversations about what they do and why this is useful is relevant.

During the concrete operational stage, children (aged 7 to 11) reason logically, yet their ability to solve problems and think in abstract terms is under-developed compared with children aged 12 and older (formal operational stage). Studies show that the inability to think hypothetically and use abstract reasoning influences what children do to cope with stress, in that they predominantly use external and behaviourally orientated coping strategies (Garnefski *et al.*, 2002). By contrast, children utilise cognitive coping skills to a greater extent as they progress to the formal operational stage and have mastered more advanced cognitive skills (Aldwin, 1994).

To exemplify this, take the example of a junior national athlete (aged 15) who is asked to compete for their school team, club, county and country. These combined demands may mean that they are competing three or four times in a single week and training on the remaining evenings. This is clearly an excessive demand if they are also to accommodate school, family and social commitments. The effective management of these demands requires more advanced cognitive skills such as solution generation, hypothesis testing, abstract thinking (recalling solutions in previous contexts and considering their utility) and effective planning. However, research indicates that junior national athletes may struggle to apply these cognitive skills (Devonport, 2008). Recall the finding that there is variation in the attainment of formal operational reasoning. As such, it is quite feasible that this individual may not yet have mastered advanced cognitive skills. This predisposes them to utilise behaviourally focused coping strategies such as venting, crying or avoiding the situation. In such instances, helping young athletes to consider alternative solutions may be an effective way to help them make better decisions and apply cognitive coping skills (Fischhoff, Crowell & Kipke, 1999).

Although research has supported the existence of Piaget's sub-stages, methodological developments have enabled researchers to demonstrate that children may have more advanced cognitive abilities than is suggested by Piaget (Baillargeon & DeVos, 1991). It appears that the stages a child progresses through in developing cognitive abilities may be heavily dependent on cultural and social factors (Rogoff, 1998). Vygotsky recognised the influence of social and cultural processes in his sociocultural theory of cognitive development (Vygotsky, 1981), which we consider next.

30.2.1.3 Vygotsky's (1981) sociocultural theory of cognitive development

Vygotsky disagreed with Piaget's assumption that development could not be impeded or accelerated through instruction, asserting that development is complex and is influenced by social and cultural contexts. While Piaget suggested that concepts should not be taught until children are in the appropriate developmental stage,

Vygotsky's zone of proximal development (ZPD), which forms a substantive part of the sociocultural theory, runs counter to this suggestion.

30.2.1.3.1 Zone of proximal development ZPD is argued to be one of the sociocultural theory's most important contributions to developmental psychology. The ZPD is described as the difference between a child's actual development (determined by independent problem solving) and their potential development (determined through problem solving under adult guidance or in collaboration with more capable peers; Vygotsky, 1978). Capable others can assist a child's development by working with them at a level that fractionally exceeds their current capabilities. Vygotsky believed that the established techniques of testing cognitive abilities only determine the actual level of development and not the potential ability of the child. He contends that it is a child's potential capability that should be the focus of assessment. He did not offer guidance on the way in which capable others can help a child progress from one level to the next, but while researching sociocultural theory the concept of **scaffolding** was proposed by others (Bruner, 1983).

> **scaffolding** the way in which a child's efforts to master a new or challenging task can be supported in a flexible and contingent way by adults or more competent partners

30.2.1.3.2 Scaffolding Scaffolding refers to an interactive process whereby adults adjust the type and amount of support offered to a child to assist with the mastery of a skill being taught. Where a child does not operate to the limit of their capability, an adult will tend to utilise specific behaviours to direct the learner and vary the type of instruction. As a child experiences success, an adult will tend to reduce the amount of instruction being given and encourage the child to move on (removing the scaffold of directive instructions). According to Donato (1994), scaffolding can occur during social interactions where a knowledgeable other creates supportive conditions in which the learner can extend current skills and knowledge to a higher level of competence. In an educational context, scaffolding occurs when the instructor models the desired learning strategy or task, then gradually shifts responsibility to the learner. McKenzie (1999) suggests that scaffolding provides a number of advantages, including providing clear directions for learning; clarifying the purpose of the task; keeping the child on task; and reducing uncertainty, surprise and disappointment.

Vygotsky's theory has not received the same level of critical analysis as the work of Piaget. However, his almost exclusive focus on the influence of culture on cognitive development has been criticised. It has also been suggested that sociocultural theory does not explain how basic processes such as attention and memory contribute to cognitive development (Wertsch & Tulviste, 1992). Finally, the way in which the interactive processes between learner and knowledgeable other determine the goals of collaboration has not been explained, along with the interactive processes of larger **group dynamics**. Despite these limitations, the theory is still perceived as offering a valid contribution to the understanding of cognitive developmental psychology.

> **group dynamics** the forces operating in groups that affect group performance and member satisfaction.

30.2.1.4 Utility of the theory

In terms of the potential utility of the sociocultural theory for encouraging children's participation and mastery in sport and their use of mental skills, it acknowledges the dynamic nature of interactions between knowledgeable others, learners and tasks, and provides a view of learning as arising from interactions with others. According to Ellis (2000), sociocultural theory assumes that learning arises not *through* interaction but *in* interaction. Learners first succeed in performing a new task with the help of another person and then internalise this task so that they can perform it on their own. In this way, social interaction is advocated to mediate learning.

Mediation is central to sociocultural theory and refers to the role of knowledgeable others in enhancing learning by selecting and shaping the learning experiences presented to children. Vygotsky (1978) claims that effective mediation leads to effective learning and that scaffolding contributes to successful mediation (Ellis, 2000). An example in ASEP is where a practitioner helps a child identify the self-talk statements they are currently using when playing sports or exercising. When scaffolding, the practitioner may provide hints or partial answers to help identify the self-talk statements that may be most appropriate for use in those situations commonly faced by the child. As the child internalises this new knowledge and can engage in the self-talk statements independently, the practitioner reduces the frequency of instructions offered regarding self-talk use. In this way the child is challenged, but still supported in developing and enhancing their use of self-talk.

30.2.2 Adults

Recent guidelines (Haskell *et al.*, 2007) advocate that adults up to the age of 65 should pursue at least 30 minutes of moderate- to high-intensity activity five days a week. These recommendations are based on the physical, psychological and social benefits associated with regular physical activity, including a reduced incidence of coronary heart disease (Paffenbarger *et al.*, 1993), improved self-concept (Raglin, 1990) and social wellbeing (Hassmén, Koivula & Uutela, 2000). Currently many members of the adult population fail to meet these recommendations, which is undesirable considering the potential implications for health.

30.2.2.1 Participation trends

Stamatakis and Chaudhury (2008) explored temporal trends and patterns of adult sports participation in England during 1997–2006. They found that overall participation exhibited a small increase (<0.5% for men and <3% for women), but that this increase did not occur equally across socioeconomic, demographic and ethnic groups. The upward trend was apparent only among middle-aged and older adults. Young men (<30 years), particularly men in late adolescence, showed marked decreases in participation. This is of practical significance given the finding that physical activity habits acquired in adolescence not only continue into later adult life, but may also have consequences for adult health (Hallal *et al.*, 2006). A further cause of concern was the finding that the gap between men from lower and higher socioeconomic groups, and white and nonwhite ethnic backgrounds, appears to be widening (Stamatakis, 2006). Encouraging are findings indicating that the gap in participation between men and women has narrowed, with considerable increases in participation among most female population groups. It is also encouraging that participation increased by approximately 4–5% among respondents aged 45 years and above. Gym and fitness club-based activities showed the most consistent and noticeable increase. The authors suggest that this may be due to increased time pressures, which force individuals to pursue activities that are flexible and individual in nature, such as gym workouts, aerobics and calisthenics.

30.2.2.2 Encouraging adult participation

30.2.2.2.1 Role models Research suggests that the role models used to promote physical activity should be realistic for the target age group and ethnicity, as this has been found to be effective in encouraging participation (Crone-Grant & Smith, 2001). The lack of realistic role models has been found to be a problem for members of the South Asian and black communities (Rai & Finch, 1997). Failing to provide realistic role models might explain why some athletes become anxious or lack confidence about entering unfamiliar settings such as gyms. Take the example of an Asian woman in her 50s with a body mass index indicating that she is overweight. On considering entering a gym environment, she may perceive this to be predominantly habituated by fit, Caucasian, male youths. This may engender concerns that can act as a barrier to participation, such as not knowing other people, poor body image and not fitting in with the gym culture (Crone-Grant & Smith, 1999). Generally women display more social anxiety about appearance than men (Davis & Cowles, 1991). Exercise scientists/professionals need to be aware of such concerns when planning exercise programmes. Providing a suitable role model who inducts new gym members, or acts as a gym instructor, may help alleviate some of the concerns that individuals may have.

30.2.2.2.2 Exploring motives

Personal enjoyment and the social networks offered by sport and physical activities are important participation motivators for many adults from different cultural and ethnic backgrounds. Those individuals who are intrinsically motivated are inclined to adhere to self-monitored exercise programmes for longer than those who are not highly self-motivated (Crone-Grant & Smith, 1999). However, it is important to recognise that the specific motives can differ subtly between individuals within a single group. For example, Smith (1998) interviewed members of a running club and found a distinction between 'runners' and 'joggers'. Runners were elite members of the club and were motivated by intense competition and winning. Conversely, joggers did not consider themselves competitive in races, but aimed to better their own previous best time. Joggers were more motivated by the health benefits of running and the increased status afforded to them by nonexercisers, who saw them as fit and healthy. Equally, Lane, Jackson and Terry (2005) found that exercise preference played a significant role in determining whether individuals enjoyed exercise. Exercise preference was more significant in determining enjoyment than the exercise itself. As such, practitioners should ensure that they establish the participation motives in individuals as opposed to groups.

30.2.2.2.3 Exploring childhood experiences

Research suggests that exercise habits in adulthood are often established in childhood (Aarts, Paulussen & Schaalma, 1997). It is during these formative years that attitudes towards physical activity in general, interest in a specific activity and self-confidence in the ability to maintain an activity programme are established. These are all important to long-term involvement. Adults do not typically initiate or attempt to continue exercise programmes without the benefit of having acquired the necessary skills in childhood. According to Seefeldt (1986), students who participate in quality physical education programmes of sufficient length can increase levels of fitness and acquire the necessary knowledge and enjoyment levels essential to have an impact on future patterns of adherence to exercise programmes.

This explains the importance of establishing and exploring an individual's childhood experiences with sport and exercise. For example, nonexercisers may recall negative school experiences as reasons for not participating into middle age (Porter, 2002). The practitioner may explore these childhood experiences by looking to establish what it was that generated negative perceptions. This can then act as a starting point for establishing a preferred sport or exercise experience.

30.2.2.2.4 Making time for exercise

Finding sufficient time to train is a concern raised by many adult athletes and exercisers alike, as they often have to contend with high work demands. There are benefits to be gained from spreading goals across domains such as work and sport. Evidence suggests that investing self-worth in a single domain can have a negative impact on self-esteem where the individual fails to achieve their goals (Park, Crocker & Kiefer, 2007). Individuals whose self-esteem is accrued by achieving success in a range of domains tend to show greater resilience in the face of setbacks (Park, Crocker & Kiefer, 2007). As such, it is desirable to pursue goals across domains, as opposed to exclusively prioritising goals in any one domain.

Time management, according to Lakein (1973), involves determining needs, setting goals to achieve needs, prioritising the tasks required and matching tasks to time and resources through planning, scheduling and making lists. By managing time effectively, an individual may more efficiently accommodate personal goals across domains. Efficient time management can be achieved by effectively planning time and keeping to schedule (Francis-Smythe & Robertson, 1999).

This section has identified participation trends and factors that may have an impact on sport and exercise engagement in adult populations, including the use of role models, motives for exercise, previous experiences and time management. Developing an understanding of those factors that influence adult participation is necessary to inform the content and delivery of interventions intended to increase participation in sport and exercise.

30.2.3 The Elderly Population

By the year 2030, it is speculated that 22% of the population of the United States will be older than 65 years, approximately 70 million people (Laurie, 2000). Recent guidelines (Haskell *et al.*, 2007) advocate that individuals aged 65 and older should pursue at least 30 minutes of moderate-intensity activity, five days a week. The recommendations for those 65 and older do differ from those for younger adults, in that it is recommended that older individuals exercise at a moderate intensity level rather than a high intensity level. Stretching exercises that promote flexibility are also recommended, as are activities that promote balance for those individuals at risk of falls. Modest increases in life expectancy result from exercise even where individuals did not initiate regular exercise until the age of 75, and also when compared with those who were active during their younger years and subsequently stopped exercising (Paffenbarger *et al.*, 1986). As such, it is never too late for individuals to benefit from exercise and physical activity.

30.2.3.1 *Encouraging exercise amongst elderly populations*

30.2.3.1.1 Motives for exercise The motives for exercise and physical activity among older adults may vary from those of younger adults. Older adults are more likely to identify the health benefits of physical activity as motives in terms of reducing the effects of ageing and being fit and able to play with grandchildren (Finch, 1997). The consequences of ageing that such individuals seek to manage include progressively impaired static balance (Gustafson *et al.*, 2000), chronic diseases (Wild *et al.*, 1997), drop in cognitive performance (Pirani *et al.*, 1984) and increased memory loss (Fabre, Masse-Biron & Chamari, 1999).

While older adults may be motivated to exercise to improve physical/cognitive attributes, they may be unsure about the most effective way to engage in physical activity (Finch, 1997). Most older adults can safely begin a moderate aerobic and resistance training programme if they start slowly and gradually increase their level of activity. For those individuals who plan to begin exercising at a vigorous intensity, or for those where there are potential contra-indications to exercise, the American College of Sports Medicine recommends that exercise stress testing is first completed (Franklin, Whaley & Howley, 2000).

30.2.3.1.2 Facilitating adherence While perceived health benefits and/or GP referrals may encourage the uptake of exercise in older adults, adherence is maintained through enjoyment and strong social networks (Stathi, McKenna & Fox, 2003). Applied practitioners can help motivate older adults by exploring individual goals, concerns, physical limitations and barriers to exercise. Subsequent exercise recommendations should be simple, enjoyable and meet an individual's health needs, beliefs and goals (Neid & Franklin, 2002). Structuring exercise and physical activity around existing activities can help make it easier to remember, especially in very old and cognitively impaired persons. The individual must be confident that they can carry out the planned exercise or physical activity behaviours, as self-efficacy is a strong predictor of exercise participation, especially in women (Biddle, Goudas & Page, 1994).

30.2.3.1.3 Role models Finally, as discussed with adult populations, the lack of realistic role models available to older adults within the community is perceived as a deterrent. Exercise classes and activities are commonly perceived as targeting young people and not relevant to older groups. Because of the perceived lack of realistic role models, the exercise beliefs of family and close friends become especially important influences. Consequently, the education of significant others regarding the safety and benefit of exercise in older adults is advisable (Shephard, 1994).

This section has demonstrated the need to consider the impact of ageing on the motives for and ability to exercise among elderly populations. The consequences of ageing must be established and accommodated when seeking to develop interventions intended to increase exercise participation.

30.3 PERSONALITY FACTORS

References to **personality** attributes are commonly made by the layperson, and as such are prevalent in daily interpersonal interactions. For example, we may say 'Andy always makes jokes' or 'Tracey is always on time'. Here we allude to stable properties of the individual in question. Within this section we will explore personality in sport and exercise with the intention of identifying its relevance to ASEP service delivery.

> **personality** the overall profile or combination of traits that characterise the unique nature of a person.

Lazarus and Monat (1979, p. 1) define personality as

> the underlying, relatively stable psychological structure and processes that organise human experience and shape a person's activities and reactions to the environment.

The stable psychological structure and processes refer to the core components of personality by which we know ourselves and are known by others. They are relatively hardy to life's trials and do not change much once established. Allport (1937, p. 48) defined personality as 'the dynamic organisation within the individual of those psycho-physical systems that determine his unique adjustments to his environment'. Allport suggested that in addition to a psychological core, behaviour is also determined by peripheral states, which are aspects of personality that are variable. Allport proposes that it is the dynamic interactions between core (trait) and peripheral (state) elements that comprise personality.

TABLE 30.1 *Personality Theories.*

Name	Author	Summary
Constitutional theory	Sheldon (1940, 1942)	Suggests that basic body types predict personality. Ectomorphs (lean build) have a high level of activity, tension and introversion. Mesomorphs (muscular and athletic) can respond to environmental stimuli with aggression, they take risks and are leaders. Endomorphs have a rounder physique and are jovial, generous, affectionate and sociable.
Psychodynamic theory	*Freud (1873–1923)*	Personality has a tripartite structure consisting of the id, the ego and the superego. The id represents the unconscious instinctual aspect of the personality and is essentially biologically driven. The ego represents the rational and conscious psychological aspect of personality. The ego ensures that the impulses of the id can be expressed in a manner acceptable in the real world. The superego is the aspect of personality that holds all of our internalised moral standards and ideals that we acquire from both parents and society, our sense of right and wrong. The superego provides guidelines for making judgements.
Humanistic models		These models contend that human nature is basically good and based on free choice rather than dominated by instincts. Two such models are:
	Maslow – hierarchy of needs (1943)	Maslow's hierarchy of needs suggests that if basic human needs are fulfilled, people will strive to actualise to their highest potential. Self-actualisation is the final psychological need and cannot be attained until basic physical and psychological needs are met.
	Rogers – person-centred perspective (1951)	Rogers' person-centred perspective also refers to the human tendency for someone to fulfil their human potential. Self-actualisation is a central theme. Fulfilled individuals will tend to see congruence between their sense of who they are (self) and who they feel they should be (ideal self).
Social learning theory	*Bandura (1977)*	Social learning theory emphasises the importance of the social environment in shaping personality. Personality attributs are not necessarily a genetic predisposition, rather they are learned through modelling (learning through observation) or social reinforcement (e.g. having a behaviour rewarded in some way, and therefore making it more likely to be repeated).

trait theory a theory of personality that assumes that people possess enduring characteristics (traits) that determine their behaviour across different situations and across time.

There are many theories of personality and, while a sample of these are presented in Table 30.1, this section will focus on **trait theory**.

Trait theorists, including Allport (1937), Cattell (1965) and Eysenck (1952, 1992), maintain that individuals can be described by trait names such as 'sociable' or 'aggressive', which refer to enduring, stable and consistent characteristics. Personality traits comprise general dimensions of individual differences in tendencies to show consistent patterns of thoughts, feelings and actions (McCrae & Costa, 1990). The combination and interaction of various traits combine to form a personality that is unique to each individual. To exemplify traits, Cattell's 16 personality factors are presented in Table 30.2.

A great deal of sport and exercise research has utilised the trait approach in seeking to better understand and predict behaviour (LeUnes & Nation, 2002). This is because trait theorists contend that personality comprises relatively enduring traits or predispositions to respond in similar ways across a variety of situations. As such, the suggestion is that individuals respond in predictable and measurable ways. Two concepts will be presented and discussed to further exemplify the trait approach to understanding and predicting human behaviour in a sport and exercise context: emotional intelligence and self-confidence.

30.3.1 Trait Emotional Intelligence

Emotional intelligence (EI) is defined as 'the ability to perceive, monitor, employ, and manage emotions within oneself and in others' (Salovey & Mayer, 1990, p. 189). Trait EI is defined as 'a constellation of emotion-related self-perceptions and dispositions located at the lower levels of personality hierarchies' (Furnham & Petrides, 2003, p. 816). Trait approaches assess these self-perceptions, which are based on experiences and determine emotional behavioural dispositions (Meyer & Zizzi, 2007). As trait EI relates to behavioural tendencies and self-perceived abilities, it has been argued that it should be studied as part of the personality framework (Petrides & Furnham, 2001).

TABLE 30.2 *Cattel's (1965) 16 Personality Factors.*

Reserved	←→	Outgoing	Unintelligent	←→	Intelligent
Stable	←→	Unstable	Humble	←→	Assertive
Sober	←→	Happy-go-lucky	Expedient	←→	Conscientious
Shy	←→	Adventurous	Tough-minded	←→	Tender-minded
Trusting	←→	Suspicious	Practical	←→	Imaginative
Forthright	←→	Shrewd	Placid	←→	Apprehensive
Conservative	←→	Experimenting	Group-dependent	←→	Self-sufficient
Undisciplined	←→	Controlled	Relaxed	←→	Tense

Trait EI is measured through self-report, which Tett and Fox (2006) contend is the most effective way to measure emotional intelligence. Examples of self-report measures of **trait emotional intelligence** include the Emotional Intelligence Scale (EIS; Schutte *et al.*, 1998); Trait Emotional Intelligence Questionnaire (TEIque; Petrides & Furnham, 2003); and Trait Emotional Intelligence Questionnaire Short-Form (TEIque-SF; Petrides & Furnham, 2006). Trait measures offer opportunities for assessing participants' emotional intelligence and to identify areas that may be in need of enrichment. Researchers contend that because trait EI relates to self-perception, it is more likely to allow change (Petrides *et al.*, 2006).

> **trait emotional intelligence** a constellation of emotion-related self-perceptions and dispositions located at the lower levels of personality hierarchies.

Recent research in sport psychology has tested the validity of the Emotional Intelligence Scale (Lane *et al.*, 2009). Lane *et al.* (2009) reported that a revised version of the scale was suitable for use in sport. In light of such findings, EI is subject to growing interest in sport and exercise psychology (Devonport, 2007; Thelwell *et al.*, 2008).

Individuals high in trait EI believe that they are in touch with their own emotions, and that in regulating these emotions wellbeing is promoted (Furnham & Petrides, 2003). Research demonstrates that efficacious emotion regulation can lead not only to pleasant emotional states before and during performance, but also optimal performance states (Totterdell & Leach, 2001). Recent research has found that emotional intelligence is associated with frequent use of psychological skills (Lane *et al.*, 2009) and anger regulation (Lane *et al.*, 2007). Evidence pointing to emotional intelligence being associated with the ability to regulate emotions to optimal levels in different domains appears to make it a potentially useful construct to target interventions. Lane, Thelwell and Devonport (2009) found that athletes high in emotional intelligence could identify emotional states that help sport performance and academic performance.

The value of assessing EI is supported by research demonstrating that high scores on the EIS correlated significantly with psychological skills usage (Lane *et al.*, 2009). It is possible that emotionally intelligent athletes see the value in psychological skills and utilise these as part of a self-regulatory process. If this contention is accepted, athletes lower in self-reported EI are less likely to adopt psychological skills as part of their preparation for sports and exercise participation or performance. This has implications for ASEP practitioners, in that the support offered for athletes demonstrating low EI could focus on establishing and developing confidence in the use of psychological skills. The psychological skills addressed could serve the dual purpose of enhancing EI, for example by exploring emotions experienced before, during and after competition with a view to developing strategies to alter unwanted emotions (e.g. feeling downhearted when you would like to feel excited).

A number of interventions intended to influence emotions exist, along with supporting evidence for their efficacy (Thelwell & Greenlees, 2003; Thomas, Murphy & Hardy, 1999). Strategies to control emotions have been found to be used by athletes both during training and while competing (Thomas, Murphy & Hardy, 1999), including strategies such as imagery, self-talk and goal setting (Thelwell & Greenlees, 2003). As such, it is important to explore and develop their use in both training and competition contexts.

30.3.2 Trait Anxiety

The relationship between anxiety and sport and exercise performance has attracted a great deal of research attention. Within the study of anxiety, distinguishing between state and **trait anxiety** is commonplace (Spielberger, 1972, 1983). State anxiety is defined as an unpleasant emotional arousal in the face of threatening demands or dangers. A cognitive appraisal of threat is a prerequisite for the

> **trait anxiety** a person's disposition to experience anxiety, whereby some individuals are more anxious than others.

experience of this emotion (Lazarus, 1991). Trait anxiety is described as a personality disposition to experience anxiety whereby some individuals are more anxious than others. Such people also become anxious more easily when anticipating threatening situations (Spielberger, 1966). The anxiety-prone individual is predisposed to perceive threat and experiences state anxiety in a wide variety of situations, many of which would be perceived as innocuous by those with lower trait anxiety (Martens, Vealey & Burton, 1990). In a sport and exercise context, trait anxiety may predispose an individual to view competition and social evaluation as more or less threatening.

As would be expected given the definition of trait anxiety (a predisposition to be more or less anxious), the focus of questions for trait measures is different to that for state measures. Rather than rating feelings 'at this moment', individuals are asked to rate how they 'typically feel'. Measures of trait anxiety include the Sport Competition Anxiety Test (SCAT; Martens, 1977); the Spielberger State-Trait Anxiety Inventory (STAI; Spielberger, 1983); and the Sport Anxiety Scale (SAS; Smith, Smoll & Schutz, 1990).

Trait anxiety has been used to predict outcomes such as burnout and sports injury. For example, Vealey, Udry, Zimmerman and Soliday (1992) examined the relationship between trait anxiety and coaching burnout among high school and college coaches. Results revealed that trait anxiety was the strongest predictor of burnout. It also indicates that trait anxiety may be a psychological risk factor contributing to an increased risk of sports injury (Petrie, 1993). Kerr and Fowler (1988) found that athletes with a high level of trait anxiety more frequently reported an inappropriately narrow focus of concentration and attention. If high trait anxiety leads to peripheral narrowing, then the athlete may face an increased risk of injuries as they fail to assess ongoing contextual risks accurately.

If an ASEP practitioner establishes that an individual exhibits high trait anxiety, they then need to identify and facilitate the ongoing implementation and review of anxiety-reduction techniques. Each individual will have specific needs and find different techniques more effective, therefore an ASEP would devise an intervention programme with individual differences in mind. Techniques used to lower arousal levels can be loosely divided into somatic, cognitive and behavioural techniques, examples of which are presented in Focus Point 30.2.

FOCUS POINT 30.2   SOMATIC TECHNIQUES

Somatic techniques deal with identifying the physical symptoms of anxiety, such as muscle tension, and then focusing on reducing the symptoms. A popular technique for reducing somatic symptoms of anxiety is progressive muscular relaxation (PMR), which is based on the work of Jacobson (1938). Jacobson believed that it is impossible to be anxious or have tension anywhere in the body if all skeletal muscles are in a complete state of relaxation, and that an anxious mind cannot exist in a relaxed body (Cox, 1998).

PMR involves an individual lying down and tensing a muscle before relaxing it, as this helps the individual to identify the difference between tension and relaxation; so muscle groups are systematically tensed and relaxed in a specified order to gain total relaxation or lack of muscular tension. The process takes around 20 minutes and the relaxation of the body results in relaxation of the mind as well. This is often referred to as muscle-to-mind relaxation and needs to be practised regularly over a period of months, so that the individual can start to relax more quickly and use the technique when they are in a situation where they need to relax quickly.

COGNITIVE TECHNIQUES

Cognitive techniques focus on relaxing the mind to transmit feelings of relaxation to the rest of the body and are beneficial for reducing the symptoms of anxiety. Imagery, which is the use of developing images in the mind, is a popular cognitive method of anxiety control (Martin, Moritz & Hall, 1999). It can involve the individual imagining themselves in a place they find relaxing, such as somewhere they have been on holiday. Alternatively, they can imagine themselves performing confidently and successfully incorporating the emotions associated with a successful performance (Holmes & Collins, 2001). Because these techniques transfer relaxation to the body, they are often known as mind-to-muscle techniques.

BEHAVIOURAL TECHNIQUES

These techniques involve identifying situations that produce feelings of anxiety and developing strategies to avoid or deal with them. For example, a simple technique for reducing anxiety that is created by overload is learning to say 'no' and mean 'no'. Assertiveness and time-management skills are useful behavioural techniques.

30.4   CONCLUSION

This chapter has explored social, developmental and personality factors that may influence sport and exercise performance and satisfaction. In doing so, the implications for ASEP have been identified and reinforced using activity boxes and focus points. It is important that students of sport and exercise psychology are cognisant of such variables and the way in which they may be influential. For example, by identifying personality traits that may influence engagement with and performance in sport and exercise activities, it is possible for ASEP to develop and implement individualised interventions intended to accrue desirable outcomes. These may include a personal best time, technical improvements, greater performance satisfaction or enhanced wellbeing. It is hoped that the examples presented will encourage you to consider alternative variables that may have an impact on performance and satisfaction.

SELF-TEST QUESTIONS

- Identify reasons why multicultural training would facilitate the roles of ASEP.
- List situational, personal, leadership and team factors that may mediate performance–cohesion relationships.
- Identify the utility of Piaget's stages of cognitive development in the promotion and development of children's physical activity.
- How might the principle of scaffolding be used by a sports coach or exercise instructor?
- What are the stages of cognitive development outlined by Piaget?
- What are the main principles of Vygotsky's sociocultural theory?
- What factors predict exercise behaviours among adult populations?
- What are the exercise guidelines for older adults?
- How is personality defined?
- What do you understand by the term 'trait anxiety'?
- How might high trait anxiety influence performance outcomes?
- What is trait emotional intelligence?

ESSAY QUESTIONS

- Describe the influence that the belief systems of different cultures may potentially have on client–practitioner interactions.
- Describe the utility of group cohesion literature in the development of interventions intended to increase adherence to exercise programmes.
- Compare Piaget's cognitive development theory and Vygotsky's sociocultural theory, identifying the strengths and limitations of each.
- Identify factors that have an impact on the ability of children, adults and older adults (65 plus) to engage with and maintain regular exercise.
- How may trait personality theory be used to help achieve desirable outcomes for sport and exercise participants?

TEXTS FOR FURTHER READING

Carron, A.V. & Hausenblas, H. (1998) *Group Dynamics in Sport*, 2nd edn, Morgantown, WV: Fitness Information Technology.

Ewen, R.B. (1998) *Personality: A Topical Approach,* Mahweh, NJ: Lawrence Erlbaum Associates.

Lutz, D.J. & Sternberg, R.J. (1999) Cognitive development, in M.H. Bornstein & M.E. Lamb (eds) *Developmental Psychology: An Advanced Textbook*, 4th edn, pp. 275–311, Mahwah, NJ: Lawrence Erlbaum Associates.

Meyer, B.B. & Zizzi, S. (2007) Emotional intelligence in sport: Conceptual, methodological, and applied issues, in A.M. Lane (ed.) *Mood and Human Performance: Conceptual, Measurement, and Applied Issues*, pp. 131–54, Hauppauge, NY: Nova Science.

Parham, W.D. (2005) Raising the bar: Developing an understanding of athletes from racially, culturally and ethnically diverse backgrounds, in M.B. Andersen (Ed.) *Sport Psychology in Practice*, pp. 201–16, Champaign IL: Human Kinetics.

Shephard, R.J. (1994) Determinants of exercise in people aged 65 years and older, in R.K. Dishman (ed.) *Advances in Exercise Adherence*, pp. 343–59, Champaign, IL: Human Kinetics.

RELEVANT JOURNAL ARTICLES

Carron, A.V., Colman, M.M., Wheeler, J. & Stevens, D. (2002) Cohesion and performance in sport: A meta analysis, *Journal of Sport and Exercise Psychology* 24: 68–188.

Devonport, T.J. & Lane, A.M. (2009) Reflecting on the delivery of a longitudinal coping intervention amongst junior national netball players, *Journal of Sports Science and Medicine* 8: 169–78.

Fabre, C., Masse-Biron, J. & Chamari, K. (1999) Evaluation of quality of life in elderly healthy subjects after aerobic and/or mental training, *Archives of Gerontology & Geriatrics* 28: 9–22.

Fisher, L.A., Butryn, T. & Roper, E.A. (2003) Diversifying (and politicizing) sport psychology through cultural studies: A promising perspective, *Sport Psychologist* 17: 391–405.

Foster, D.J. & Weigand, D.A. (2008) The role of cognitive and metacognitive development in mental skills training, *Sport and Exercise Psychology Review* 4: 21–9.

Hallal, P., Cesar, V., Azevedo, M. & Wells, J. (2006) Adolescent physical activity and health: A systematic review, *Sports Medicine* 12: 1019–30.

Lane, A.M., Meyer, B.B., Devonport, T.J. *et al.* (2009) Validity of the Emotional Intelligence Scale for use in sport, *Journal of Sports Science and Medicine* 8: 289–95, http://www.jssm.org/vol8/n2/19/v8n2-19text.php, accessed November 2010.

Lane, A.M., Thelwell, R. & Devonport, T. (2009) Emotional intelligence, mood states and performance, *E-journal of Applied Psychology* 5: 67–73, http://ojs.lib.swin.edu.au/index.php/ejap/issue/current, accessed November 2010.

McCrae, R.R. & Costa, P.T. (1997) Personality trait structure as a human universal, *American Psychologist* 52: 509–16.

Smith, R.E., Smoll, F.L. & Schutz, R.W. (1990) Measurement correlates of sport-specific cognitive and somatic trait anxiety: The Sport Anxiety Scale, *Anxiety Research* 22: 263–80.

RELEVANT WEB LINKS

Association of Applied Sport Psychology professional resources, http://appliedsportpsych.org/Resource-Center/professionals

Athletic Insight, an online journal of Sport Psychology, www.athleticinsight.com

Emotional intelligence forum, http://eqi.org/eitoc.htm

Journal of Sport Science and Medicine, www.jssm.org

REFERENCES

Aarts, H., Paulussen, T. & Schaalma, H. (1997) Physical exercise habit: On the conceptualization and formation of habitual health behaviours, *Health Education Research* 12: 363–74.

Aldwin, C.M. (1994) *Stress, Coping, and Development: An Integrative Perspective*, New York: Guildford.

Allport, G.W. (1937) *Personality: A Psychological Interpretation*, New York, Holt.

Baillargeon, R. & DeVos, J. (1991) Object permanence in young infants: Further evidence, *Child Development* 62: 1227–46.

Bandura, A. (1977) *Social Learning Theory*, New York: General Learning Press.

Beilin, H. (1992) Piaget's contribution to developmental psychology, *Developmental Psychology* 28: 191–204.

Biddle, S., Goudas, M. & Page, A. (1994) Social-psychological predictors of self-reported actual and intended physical activity in a university workforce sample, *British Journal of Sports Medicine* 28: 160–63.

Bruner, J. (1983) Education as social invention, *Journal of Social Issues* 39: 129–41.

Butler, R.J. (1989) Psychological preparation of Olympic boxers, in J. Kremer & W. Crawford (eds) *The Psychology of Sport: Theory & practice*, pp. 74–84, Leicester: British Psychological Society.

Carron, A.V. (1982) Cohesiveness in sport groups: Interpretations and considerations, *Journal of Sport Psychology* 4: 123–38.

Carron, A.V. & Ball, J.R. (1977) Cause – effect characteristics of cohesiveness and participation motivation in intercollegiate hockey, *International Review of Sport Sociology* 12: 49–60.

Carron, A.V., Brawley, L.R. & Widmeyer, W.N. (1998) The measurement of cohesiveness in sport groups, in J.L. Duda (ed.) *Advances in Sport and Exercise Psychology Measurement*, pp. 213–26, Morgantown, WV: Fitness Information Technology.

Carron, A.V., Colman, M.M., Wheeler, J. &Stevens, D. (2002) Cohesion and performance in sport: A meta analysis, *Journal of Sport and Exercise Psychology* 24: 68–188.

Carron, A.V. & Hausenblas, H. (1998) *Group Dynamics in Sport*, 2nd edn, Morgantown, WV: Fitness Information Technology.

Carron, A.V., Widmeyer, W.N. & Brawley, L.R. (1985) The development of an instrument to assess cohesion in sport team: The group environment questionnaire, *Journal of Sport Psychology* 7: 244–66.

Cattell, R.B. (1965) *The Scientific Analysis of Personality*, Baltimore, MD: Penguin Books.

Chakravarty, K. & Webley, M. (1993) Shoulder joint movement and its relationship to disability in the elderly, *Journal of Rheumatology* 20: 1359–61.

Cox, R.C. (1998) *Sport Psychology: Concepts and Applications*, 4th edn, Boston, MA: WCB McGraw Hill.

Crone-Grant, D.M. & Smith, R.A. (1999) Broadening horizons: A qualitative inquiry on the experience of patients on an exercise prescription scheme, *Journal of Sports Sciences* 17: 12.

Crone-Grant, D.M. & Smith, R.A. (2001) Exercise referral schemes in public and private leisure: A qualitative investigation, *Journal of Sports Sciences* 19: 19.

Daleiden, S. (1990) Weight shifting as a treatment for balance deficits: A literature review, *Physiotherapy Canada* 42: 81–6.

Davis, C. & Cowles, M. (1991)Body image and exercise: A study of relationships andcomparisons between physically active men and women, *Sex Roles* 25: 33–44.

Devonport, T.J. (2007) Emotional intelligence and the coping process amongst adolescent populations: A case study of student athletes, in A.M. Lane (ed.) *Mood and Human Performance: Conceptual, Measurement, and Applied Issues*, pp. 167–18, Hauppauge, NY: Nova Science.

Devonport, T.J. (2008) Stress and coping among competitive athletes in sport, in A.M. Lane, *Sport and Exercise Psychology: Topics in Applied Psychology*, pp. 73–90, London: Hodder & Stoughton.

Donato, R. (1994) Collective scaffolding, in J.P. Lantolf & G. Appel (eds) *Vygotskian Approaches to Second Language Research*, pp. 33–56, Norwood, NJ: Ablex Publishers.

Dustman, R.E., Ruhling, R.O., Russell, E.M.*et al.* (1984) Aerobic exercise training and improved neuropsychological function of older individuals, *Neurobiology of Aging* 5: 35–42.

Ellis, R. (2000) Task-based research and language pedagogy, *Language Teaching Research* 4: 193–220.

Evans, C.R. & Dion, K.L. (1991) Group cohesion and performance: A meta analysis, *Small Group Research* 22: 175–86.

Evans, W. & Rosenberg, I.H. (1991) *Biomarkers: The 10 Determinants of Aging You Can Control*, New York: Simon & Schuster.

Eys, M.A. & Carron, A.V. (2001) Role ambiguity, task cohesion, and task self-efficacy, *Small Group Research* 32: 356–72.

Eys, M.A, Burke, S.M., Carron, A.V. & Dennis, P.W. (2006) The sport team as an effective group, in J.M. Williams (ed.) *Applied Sport Psychology: Personal Growth to Peak Performance*, 5th edn, pp. 157–73, Boston, MA: McGraw-Hill.

Eysenck, H.J. (1952) *The Scientific Study of Personality*, London: Routledge & Kegan Paul.

Eysenck, H.J. (1992) Four ways five factors are not basic, *Personality and Individual Differences* 13: 667–73.

Fabre, C., Masse-Biron, J. & Chamari, K. (1999) Evaluation of quality of life in elderly healthy subjects after aerobic and/or mental training, *Archives of Gerontology & Geriatrics* 28: 9–22.

Finch, H. (1997) *Physical Activity 'At our Age': Qualitative Research among People over the Age of 50*,London: Health Education Authority.

Fischhoff, B., Crowell, N.A. & Kipke, M. (eds) (1999) *Adolescent Decision Making: Implications for Prevention Programmes*,Washington, DC: National Academy Press.

Fisher, L.A., Butryn, T. & Roper, E.A. (2003) Diversifying (and politicizing) sport psychology through cultural studies: A promising perspective, *Sport Psychologist* 17: 391–405.

Foster, D.J. & Weigand, D.A. (2008) The role of cognitive and metacognitive development in mental skills training, *Sport and Exercise Psychology Review* 4: 21–9.

Francis-Smythe, J.A. & Robertson, I.T. (1999) On the relationship between time management and time estimation, *British Journal of Psychology* 90: 333–47.

Franklin, B.A., Whaley, M.H. & Howley, E.T. (eds) (2000) *ACSM's Guidelines for Exercise Testing and Prescription*, 6th edn, Baltimore, MD: Lippincott, Williams & Wilkins.

Freud, S. (1923) *The Ego and the Id*, New York: W.W. Norton.

Frydenberg, E. & Lewis, R. (1993) Boys play sport and girls turn to others: Age gender and ethnicity as determinants of coping, *Journal of Adolescence* 16: 252–66.

Furnham, A. & Petrides, K.V. (2003) Trait emotional intelligence and happiness, *Social Behavior and Personality* 31: 815–24.

Galloway, M.T. & Jokl, P.M.D. (2000) Aging successfully: The importance of physical activity in maintaining health and function, *American Academy of Orthopaedic Surgeons* 8: 37–44.

Gammage, K.L., Carron, A.V. & Estabrooks, P.A. (2001) Team cohesion and individual productivity: The influence of the norm for productivity and personal identifiability, *Small Group Research* 32: 3–18.

Garnefski, N., Legerstee, J., Kraaij, V., Van Den Kommer, T. & Teerds, J. (2002) Cognitive coping strategies and symptoms of depression and anxiety: A comparison between adolescents and adults, *Journal of Adolescence* 25: 603–11.

Gridley, H. (2005) Commentary on Chapter 11, in M.B. Andersen (ed.) *Sport Psychology in Practice*, pp. 217–22, Champaign IL: Human Kinetics.

Gully, S.M., Devine, D.J. & Whitney, D.J. (1995) A meta-analysis of cohesiveness and performance: Effects of level of analysis and task interdependence, *Small Group Research* 26: 497–520.

Gustafson, A.S., Noaksson, L., Kronhed, A.C., Moller, M. & Moller, C. (2000) Changes in balance performance in physically active elderly people aged 73–80, *Scandinavian Journal of Rehabilitation Medicine* 32: 168–72.

Hallal, P., Cesar, V., Azevedo, M. & Wells, J. (2006) Adolescent physical activity and health: A systematic review, *Sports Medicine* 12: 1019–30.

Hardcastle, S. & Taylor, A. (2001) Looking for more than weight loss and fitness gain: Psychosocial dimensions among older women in a primary-care exercise-referral program, *Journal of Aging and Physical Activity* 9: 313–28.

Haskell, W.L., Lee, I.M., Pate, R.R. *et al.* (2007) Physical activity and public health: Updated recommendation for adults from the American College of Sports Medicine and the American Heart Association, *Medicine and Science in Sport and Exercise* 39: 1423–34.

Hassmén, P., Koivula, N. & Uutela, A. (2000) Physical exercise and psychological well-being: A population study in Finland, *Preventative Medicine* 30: 17–25.

Hill, T.L. (1993) Sport psychology and the collegiate athlete: One size does not fit all, *Counseling Psychologist* 21: 436–40.

Holmes, P.S. & Collins, D.J. (2001) The PETTLEP approach to motor imagery: A functional equivalence model for sport psychologists, *Journal of Applied Sport Psychology* 13: 60–83.

Jacobson, E. (1938) *Progressive Relaxation*, Chicago, IL: University of Chicago Press. (Original work published 1929.)

Keenan, T. & Evans, S. (2009) *An Introduction to Child Development,* 2nd edn, London: Sage.

Kerr, G. & Fowler, B. (1988) The relationship between psychological factors and sports injuries, *Sports Medicine* 6: 127–34.

Kolt, G.S., Kirkby, R.J., Bar-Eli, M.*et al.* (1999) A cross-cultural investigation of reasons for participation in gymnastics, *International Journal of Sport Psychology* 30: 381–98.

Kontos, A.P. & Arguello, E. (2005) Sport psychology consulting with Latin American athletes, *Athletic Insight*, http://www.athleticinsight.com/Vol7Iss3/LatinAmerican.htm, accessed April 21, 2007.

Lade, L., Frydenberg, E. & Poole, C. (1998) Daughters don't merely imitate their mothers' coping styles: A comparison of the coping strategies used by mothers and their daughters, *Australian Educational Psychologist* 15: 62–9.

Lakein, A. (1973) *How to Get Control of Your Time and Your Life*, New York: David McKay.

Lane, A.M. (2006) Reflections of professional boxing consultancy, *Athletic Insight* 3(8), http://www.athleticinsight.com/Vol8Iss3/Reflections.htm, accessed November 2010.

Lane, A.M., Devonport, T.J., Davies, K., Lane, H.J., Gill, G. & Diehl, C. (2007) Anger, emotional intelligence, performance and interventions, pp. 235–56, in E.I. Clausen, *Psychology of Anger*, Hauppage, NY: Nova.

Lane, A.M., Jackson, A. &. Terry, P.C. (2005) Self-regulatory mechanisms to explain mood changes following exercise, *Journal of Sports Science and Medicine* 4: 195–200.

Lane, A.M., Thelwell, R. & Devonport, T. (2009) Emotional intelligence, mood states and performance, *E-journal of Applied Psychology* 5: 67–73, http://ojs.lib.swin.edu.au/index.php/ejap/issue/current, accessed November 2010.

Lane, A.M., Meyer, B.B., Devonport, T.J. *et al.* (2009) Validity of the Emotional Intelligence Scale for use in sport, *Journal of Sports Science and Medicine* 8: 289–95, http://www.jssm.org/vol8/n2/19/v8n2-19text.php, accessed November 2010.

Lane, A.M., Thelwell, R., Lowther, J.P. & Devonport, T. (2009) Relationships between emotional intelligence and psychological skills among athletes, *Social Behaviour and Personality* 37: 195–202.

Langfred, C.W. (1998) Is cohesiveness a double edged sword? *Small Group Research* 29: 124–39.

Laurie, N. (2000) Healthy People 2010: Setting the nation's public health agenda, *Academic Medicine* 75: 12–13.

Lazarus, R.S. (1991) *Emotion and Adaptation*, London: Oxford University Press.

Lazarus, R.S. (1999) *Stress and Emotion: A New Synthesis*, New York: Springer.

Lazarus, R.S. & Monat, A. (1979) *Personality*, 3rd edn, Englewood Cliffs, NJ: Prentice Hall.

LeUnes, A. & Nation, J.R. (2002) *Sport Psychology*, 3rd. edn, Pacific Grove, CA.: Wadsworth.

Lowther, J. & Lane, A.M. (2002) Relationships between mood, cohesion and performance among soccer players, *Athletic Insight* 4, http://www.athleticinsight.com/Vol4Iss3/MoodandPerformance.htm, accessed November 2010.

Lutz, D.J. & Sternberg, R.J. (1999) Cognitive development, in M.H. Bornstein & M.E. Lamb (eds) *Developmental Psychology: An Advanced Textbook*, 4th edn, pp. 275–311, Mahwah, NJ: Lawrence Erlbaum Associates.

Mabry, E.A. & Barnes, R.E. (1980) *The Dynamics of Small Group Communication*, Englewood Cliffs, NJ: Prentice-Hall.

Martens, R. (1977) *Sport Competition Anxiety Test*, Champaign, IL: Human Kinetics.

Martens, M.P., Mobley, M. & Zizzi, S.J. (2000) Multicultural training in applied sport psychology, *Sport Psychologist* 14: 81–97.

Martens, R., Vealey, R.S. & Burton, D. (1990) *Competitive Anxiety in Sport*, Champaign, IL: Human Kinetics.

Martin, K.A., Moritz, S.E. & Hall, C.R. (1999) Imagery use in sport: A literature review and applied model, *Sport Psychologist* 13: 245–68.

Martin, L.J., Carron, A.V. & Burke, S.M. (2009) Team building interventions in sport: A meta-analysis, *Sport and Exercise Psychology Review* 5: 3–18.

Maslow, A. (1943) A theory of human motivation, *Psychological Review* 50: 370–96.

McCrae, R.R., & Costa, P.T., Jr. (1990) *Personality in Adulthood*, New York: Guilford.

McKenzie, J. (1999) Scaffolding for success. From now on, *Educational Technology Journal* 9(4), http://fno.org/dec99/scaffold.html, accessed 13 October 2009.

Meredith, C.N., Frontera, W.R., O'Reilly, K.P. & Evans, W.J. (1992) Body composition in elderly men: Effect of dietary modification during strength training, *Journal of American Geriatrics Society* 40: 155–62.

Mesquita, B. & Albert, D. (2007) The cultural regulation of emotions, in J.J. Gross (ed.) *Handbook of Emotion Regulation*, New York: Guilford.

Mesquita, B. & Ellsworth, P.C. (2001) The role of culture in appraisal, in K.R. Sherer & S.A. Schorr (eds) *Appraisal Processes in Emotion: Theory, Methods, Research*, pp. 233–48, New York: Oxford University Press.

Mesquita, B. & Haire, A. (2004) Emotion and culture, in C.D. Spielberger (eds) *Encyclopedia of Applied Psychology*, pp. 731–7, New York: Elsevier.

Meyer, B.B. & Zizzi, S. (2007) Emotional intelligence in sport: Conceptual, methodological, and applied issues, in A.M. Lane (ed.) *Mood and Human Performance: Conceptual, Measurement, and Applied Issues*, pp. 131–54, Hauppauge, NY: Nova Science.

Moshman, D. (1998) Cognitive development beyond childhood, in D. Kuhn & R. Siegler (eds) *Handbook of Child Psychology: Vol. II. Cognition, Perception, and Language*, 5th edn, pp. 947–78, New York: John Wiley & Sons, Inc.

Mudrack, P.E. (1989) Group cohesiveness and productivity: A closer look, *Human Relations* 42: 771–85.

Munroe, K., Estabrooks, P., Dennis, P. & Carron, A.V. (1999) A phenomenological analysis of group norms in sport teams, *Sport Psychologist* 13: 171–82.

Neid, R.J. & Franklin, B. (2002) Promoting and prescribing exercise for the elderly, *American Family Physician* 65: 419–27.

Nelis, D., Quoidbach, J., Mikolajczak, M. & Hansenne, M. (2009) Increasing emotional intelligence: (How) is it possible? *Personality and Individual Differences* 47: 36–41.

Paffenbarger, R.S. Jr., Hyde, R.T., Wing, A.L. & Hsieh, C.C. (1986) Physical activity, all-cause mortality, and longevity of college alumni, *New England Journal of Medicine* 314: 605–13.

Paffenbarger, R.S., Jr., Hyde, R.T., Wing, A.L., Lee, I.M., Jung, O.L. & Kampert, J.B. (1993) The association of changes in physical-activity level and other lifestyle characteristics with mortality among men, *New England Journal of Medicine* 326: 538–45.

Parham, W.D. (2005) Raising the bar: Developing an understanding of athletes from racially, culturally and ethnically diverse backgrounds, in M.B. Andersen (ed.) *Sport Psychology in Practice*, pp. 201–16, Champaign IL: Human Kinetics.

Park, L.E., Crocker, J. & Kiefer, A.K. (2007) Contingencies of self-worth, academic failure, and goal pursuit, *Personality and Social Psychology Bulletin* 33: 1503–17.

Pellegrini, A. (2008) The recess debate: A disjunction between educational policy and scientific research, *American Journal of Play* 1: 181–91.

Peters, H.J. & Williams, J.M. (2009) Rationale for developing a cultural sport psychology, in R.J. Schinke & S.J. Hanrahan (eds) *Cultural Sport Psychology*, Champaign, IL: Human Kinetics.

Petrides, K.V. & Furnham, A. (2000) On dimensional structure of emotional intelligence, *Personality and Individual Differences* 29: 313–20.

Petrides, K.V. & Furnham, A. (2001) Trait emotional intelligence: Psychometric investigation with reference to established trait taxonomies, *European Journal of Personality* 15: 425–48.

Petrides, K.V. & Furnham, A. (2003) Trait emotional intelligence: Behavioural validation in two studies of emotion recognition and reactivity to mood induction, *European Journal of Personality* 17: 39–57.

Petrides, K.V. & Furnham, A. (2006) The role of trait emotional intelligence in a gender-specific model of organizational variables, *Journal of Applied Social Psychology* 36: 552–69.

Petrides, K.V., Sangareau, Y., Furnham, A. & Frederickson, N. (2006) Trait emotional intelligence and children's peer relations at school, *Social Development* 15: 537–47.

Petrie, T.A. (1993) Coping skills, competitive trait anxiety and playing status: Moderation effects on the life stress-injury relationship, *Journal of Sport and Exercise Psychology* 5: 1–16.

Piaget, J. (1952) *The Origins of Intelligence in the Child*,New York: Norton.

Pirani, A., Neri, M., Belloi, L., Dinelli, M. & Vecchi, G.P. (1984) Do mental and physical performances have different patterns in elderly? *Journal of Sports Medicine and Physical Fitness* 24: 303–6.

Pollock, M.L., Mengelkoch, L.J., Graves, J.E.*et al.* (1997) Twenty-year follow-up of aerobic power and body composition of older track athletes, *Journal of Applied Physiology* 82: 1508–16.

Porter, S. (2002) *Physical Activity: An Exploration of the Issues and Attitudes of Men in Mid Years*, London: Scott Porter Research and Marketing.

Prepavessis, H. & Carron, A.V. (1996) The effect of group cohesion on competitive state anxiety, *Journal of Sport and Exercise Psychology* 27: 269–85.

Raglin, J.S. (1990) Exercise and mental health: Beneficial and detrimental effects, *Sports Medicine* 9: 323–9.

Rai, D. & Finch, H. (1997) *Physical Activity 'From Our Point of View'*, London: Health Education Authority.

Rees, C.R., Brettschneider, W.D. & Brandl-Bredenbeck, H. (1998) Globalization of sports activities and sport perceptions among adolescents from Berlin and suburban New York, *Sociology of Sport Journal* 15: 216–30.

Rogers, C.R. (1951) *Client-Centered Therapy*, Boston, MA: Houghton Mifflin.

Rogoff, B. (1998) Cognition as a collaborative process, in D. Kuhn & R.S. Siegler (eds) *Cognition, Perception and Language. Vol. 2, Handbook of Child Psychology*, 5th edn, pp. 679–744, New York: John Wiley& Sons, Inc.

Ryba, T.V. & Wright, H.K. (2005) From mental game to cultural praxis: A cultural studies model's implications for the future of sport psychology, *Quest* 57: 192–212.

Salovey, P. & Mayer, J.D. (1990) Emotional intelligence, *Imagination, Cognition, and Personality* 9: 185–211.

Schinke, R.J. (2004) The contextual side of professional boxing: One consultant's experience, *Athletic Insight,* http://www.athleticinsight.com/Vol6Iss2/Professionalboxing.htm, accessed October 2010.

Schinke, R.J., Hanrahan, S.J. & Catina, P. (2009) Introduction to cultural sport psychology, in R.J. Schinke & S.J. Hanrahan (ed.) *Cultural Sport Psychology*, Champaign, IL: Human Kinetics.

Schutte, N.S., Malouff, J.M., Hall, L. E.*et al.* (1998) Development and validation of a measure of emotional intelligence, *Personality and Individual Differences* 25: 167–77.

Seefeldt, V. (ed.) (1986) *Physical Activity and Well-Being*, Reston, VA: National Association for Sport and Physical Education.

Sheldon, W. (1940a) *The Varieties of Human Physique: An Introduction to Constitutional Psychology*, New York: Harper.

Sheldon, W. (1940b) *The Varieties of Human Temperament: A Psychology of Constitutional Differences*, New York: Harper.

Shephard, R.J. (1994) Determinants of exercise in people aged 65 years and older,in R.K. Dishman (ed.) *Advances in Exercise Adherence*, pp. 343–59, Champaign, IL: Human Kinetics.

Shields, D.L., Gardner, D.E., Bredemeier, B.J. & Bostrom, A. (1997) The relationship between leadership behaviors and group cohesion in team sports, *Journal of Psychology: Interdisciplinary & Applied* 131: 196–210.

Siegler, R.S. (1998) *Childrens Thinking*, 3rd edn, Upper Saddle River, NJ: PrenticeHall.

Singh, M.A., Ding, W., Manfredi, T. J. *et al.* (1997) Why are GP exercise schemes so successful (for those who attend)? Results from a pilot study, *Journal of Management in Medicine* 11: 233–7.

Smith, R.E., Smoll, F.L. & Schutz, R.W. (1990) Measurement correlates of sport-specific cognitive and somatic trait anxiety: The Sport Anxiety Scale, *Anxiety Research* 22: 263–80.

Smith, S.L. (1998) Athletes, runners, and joggers: Participant-group dynamics in a sport of 'individuals', *Sociology of Sport Journal* 15: 174–92.

Spielberger, C.D. (1966) Theory and research on anxiety, in C.D. Spielberger (ed.) *Anxiety and Behavior*, pp. 3–20, New York: Academic Press.

Spielberger, C.D. (1972) *Anxiety: Current Trends in Theory and Research, Vol. I*, New York: Academic Press.

Spielberger, C.D. (1983) *Manual for the State-Trait Anxiety Inventory (STAI)*, PaloAlto, CA: Consulting Psychologists Press.

Stamatakis, E. (2006) Physical activity,in R. Craig & J. Mindell (eds) *The Health Survey for England 2004. The Health of Minority Ethnic Groups*, London: The Stationery Office.

Stamatakis, E. & Chaudhury, M. (2008) Temporal trends in adults' sports participation patterns in England between 1997 and 2006: The Health Survey for England, *British Journal of Sports Medicine* 42: 901–8.

Stathi, A., McKenna, J. & Fox, K. (2003) The experiences of older people participating in exercise referral schemes, *Journal of the Royal Society for the Promotion of Health* 124: 18–23.

Terry, P.C. (2009) Strategies for reflective cultural sport psychology practice, in R.J. Schinke & S.J. Hanrahan (eds) *Cultural Sport Psychology*, Champaign, IL: Human Kinetics.

Tett, R.P. & Fox, K.E. (2006) Confirmatory factor structure of trait emotional intelligence in student and worker samples, *Personality and Individual Differences* 41: 1155–68.

Thelwell, R.C. & Greenlees, I.A. (2003) Developing competitive endurance performance using mental skills training, *Sport Psychologist* 17: 318–37.

Thelwell, R.C., Lane, A.M., Weston, N.J.V. & Greenlees, I.A. (2008) Examining relationships between emotional intelligence and coaching efficacy, *International Journal of Sport and Exercise Psychology* 6: 224–35.

Thomas, P.R., Murphy, S. & Hardy, L. (1999) Test of Performance Strategies: Development and preliminary validation of a comprehensive measure of athletes' psychological skills, *Journal of Sports Sciences* 17: 697–711.

Tomkinson, G., Leger, A., Olds, T. & Cazorla, G. (2003) Secular trends in the performance of children and adolescents (1980–2000): An analysis of 55 studies of the 20m shuttle run test in 11 countries, *Sports Medicine* 33: 285–300.

Totterdell, P. & Leach, D. (2001) Negative mood regulation expectancies and sports performance: An investigation involving professional cricketers, *Psychology of Sport and Exercise* 2: 249–65.

Triandis, H.C. (1991) Cross-cultural differences in assertiveness/competition vs group loyalty/co-operation, in R.A. Hinde & J. Groebels (eds) *Co-operation in Social Behaviour*, Cambridge: Cambridge University Press.

Triandis, H.C. (1994) *Culture and Social Behavior*, New York: McGraw-Hill.

Vealey, R.S., Udry, E.M., Zimmerman, V. & Soliday, J. (1992) Intrapersonal and situational predictors of coaching burnout, *Journal of Sport & Exercise Psychology* 14: 40–58.

Vygotsky, L.S. (1962) *Thought and Language*, Cambridge, MA: MIT Press.

Vygotsky, L.S. (1978) *Mind in Society: The Development of Higher Psychological Processes*, Cambridge, MA: Harvard University Press.

Vygotsky, L.S. (1981) The genesis of higher mental functions, in J.V. Wertsch (ed.) *The Concept of Activity in Soviet Psychology*, pp. 144–88, Armonk, NY: M.E. Sharpe.

Wertsch, J.V. & Tulviste, P. (1992) LS Vygotsky and contemporary developmental psychology, *Developmental Psychology* 28: 548–57.

Widmeyer, W.N., Brawley, L.R. & Carron, A.V. (1990) The effects of group size in sport, *Journal of Sport and Exercise Psychology* 12: 177–90.

Wiggins, M.S. (2001) Direction and intensity of trait anxiety: A comparison of high school male and female athletes' competitive anxiety, *International Sports Journal* 5: 153–9.

Wild, G.M., Peeters, M.P.D., Hoefnagels, W.H.L., Oeseburg, B. & Binkhorst, R.A. (1997) Relative exercise intensity of long-distance marching (120 km in 4 days) in 153 subjects aged 69-87 years, *European Journal of Applied Physiology and Occupational Physiology* 76: 510–16.

Zaman, H. (1997) Islam, well-being and physical activity: Perceptions of Muslim young women, in G. Clarke & B. Humberstone (eds) *Researching Women and Sport*, pp. 50–67, London: Macmillan Press.

31 Sport and Exercise Psychology – Professional Structure and Applied Case Study

TRACEY DEVONPORT & ANDY LANE

LEARNING OUTCOMES

WHEN YOU HAVE COMPLETED THIS CHAPTER, YOU SHOULD BE ABLE TO:

1. Be aware of existing training structures currently available for becoming an applied sport and exercise psychologist (UK, Europe, US & Australian).
2. Be cognisant of the need to establish training needs early in undergraduate studies to maximise continued professional development.
3. Be aware of the importance of using theory to underpin and evaluate applied interventions.

KEY WORDS

Applied Sport and Exercise Psychology (ASEP) ● Association for the Advancement of Applied Sport Psychology (AAASP) ● Australian Psychological Society (APS) ● British Association of Sport and Exercise Sciences (BASES) ● College of Sport Psychologists (CoSP) ● Division of Sport and Exercise Psychology (DSEP) ● Dutch Society for Sport Psychology (VSPN: Vereniging voor SportPsychologie in Nederland) ● European Credit Transfer and Accumulation System (ECTS) ● European Federation of Sport and Exercise Psychology (FEPSAC) ● European Masters' Programme consortium in Sport and Exercise Psychology (EMPSEP) ● European Network of Young Specialists in Sport Psychology (ENYSSP) ● German Association for Psychologists (Berufsverband Deutscher Psychologinnen und Psychologen) ● International Society of Sport Psychology (ISSP) ● United States Olympic Committee (USOC)

CHAPTER OUTLINE

31.1 TRAINING STRUCTURE OF APPLIED SPORT AND EXERCISE PSYCHOLOGY (ASEP)

Since its inception in the 1970s the number of applied practitioners in the field of sport and exercise psychology has increased (Roper, 2002), with the profession established or currently being established in many nations around the world. As the discipline continues to evolve, so too do the challenges posed. Anderson and Lavallee (2005) suggest that **applied sport and exercise psychology (ASEP)** currently faces three key challenges:

> **applied sport and exercise psychology (ASEP)** the application of proven psychological techniques to sports performance, concerning itself with how the mind influences and is influenced by participation in physical competition and exercise generally.

- Clearly defining itself and its practitioners (see Chapter 27).
- Clarifying and quality assuring the pathways that prepare individuals for applied practice.
- Enhancing the ongoing professional development of applied professionals with a view to ensure and maintain competence in applied work.

While it is not the intention of this chapter to champion one approach or offer any form of quality assurance, a selection of training structures currently available will be outlined.

The **International Society of Sport Psychology (ISSP)** has highlighted a need to examine the development of sport and exercise psychology around the world and to state its position with regard to the way sport psychologists are trained and selected to offer services (Morris *et al.*, 2003). Since the 1970s various registration and certification schemes have been created around the globe. For example, Australia, Belgium, the United Kingdom and the United States have developed schemes to ensure that individuals practising ASEP have minimum standards of training and experience. However, there is a lack of consistency throughout the world regarding the education and experience necessary for practice (Morris *et al.*, 2003).

The training, registration and practice standards of ASEP have generated considerable controversy, partially resulting from confusion surrounding the terms associated with affiliation. Terms used vary and include certification, licensure, registration and accreditation (Zizzi, Zaichkowsky & Perna, 2002). It is suggested that sharing worldwide practices will help develop an understanding of different cultural, political, economic and social structures factors influencing practice (Morris *et al.*, 2003).

> **International Society of Sport Psychology (ISSP)** the only worldwide organisation of scholars explicitly concerned with sport psychology, it exists to encourage and promote the study of human behaviour within sport, physical activity and health settings; facilitate the sharing of knowledge through a newsletter, meetings and a quadrennial congress; improve the quality of research and professional practice in sport psychology.

31.1.1 Training in Sport and Exercise Psychology: United Kingdom

There are a number of postgraduate programmes in ASEP offered by UK-based educational institutions. However, recent developments by the health professions council (HPC) have had an impact on the extent to which many postgraduate programmes contribute to the training of aspiring ASEP. Before a review of the HPC route, introduced in July 2009, is undertaken, the previous routes to practitioner status will be presented. While these routes still exist,

British Association of Sport and Exercise Sciences (BASES) a professional body promoting excellence in sport and exercise sciences through evidence-based practice.

they do not enable the individual to use the title 'Sport and Exercise Psychologist'. The **British Association of Sport and Exercise Sciences (BASES)** and the british psychological society (BPS) both provide supervised experience programmes that result in, respectively, Accreditation or Chartered Status in sport and exercise psychology. The BPS route (see Table 31.1) has been adopted unchanged as the pathway towards HPC registration as a Sport and Exercise Psychologist, but does not in itself permit an individual to use that title. BASES accreditation, before it was revised in September 2009, provided recognition of a member's ability to provide scientific support services and/or complete quality research in the areas of psychology, physiology, biomechanics or interdisciplinarily.

A three-year period of supervised experience was normally the recommended route towards attaining the standards required for accreditation. To initiate supervised experience, individuals rated themselves against the competencies required for accreditation (guided by written criteria that underpin a certain rating). The trainee then set appropriate yearly goals and self-directed consulting and training activities (aided by a privately organised supervisor) to progress themselves through the rating scale. As the trainee progressed, a yearly report and portfolio of work were submitted to BASES. Two BASES accredited psychologists provided feedback and agreed or disagreed with the estimates of goal attainment submitted by the candidate. When their final supervised experience report was passed, the candidate could then apply for full accreditation with a report including a detailed case study and reflective summary of their applied experiences and competency development.

To gain accreditation, the individual was required to meet a range of criteria. They must be a full member of BASES, holding a first degree at honours level and also a higher degree (both in Sport and Exercise Science or a related discipline). They must have followed an appropriate programme of continuing professional development, including attending workshops and conferences approved by BASES. They must provide evidence via a portfolio submission (including a case study of working with a client) of the application and dissemination of knowledge to client groups or the lay public. The support work provided must demonstrate intellectual rigour and clear scientific underpinnings, as well as the ability to translate scientific knowledge into effective practice. Applicants must demonstrate reflective practice that

considers, among other things, the aforementioned criteria for accreditation. Finally, applicants must give evidence of collaboration with recognised sports organisations or exercise and health client groups.

Accreditation was awarded for up to a maximum of five years in the first instance and could be renewed at five-yearly intervals thereafter. Individuals accredited through the association could use the title 'Accredited Sport and Exercise Scientist'. The section through which their application for accreditation was processed was recognised on the certificate of accreditation to indicate the area of professional competence along with the type of accreditation, for example Sport and Exercise Scientist (Psychology – Scientific Support). BASES accreditation was recognised by bodies such as the Sports Council, British Olympic Association, British Psychological Society, and home-country sport science providers such as the English Institute of Sport, National Sports Medicine Institute and the National Coaching Foundation.

Following HPC developments, BASES reviewed the accreditation process in order to increase compatibility with HPC requirements and made a number of changes (see Table 31.1). At the time of writing the updated requirements of applicants for accreditation include having the required level of underpinning scientific knowledge, fully understanding the delivery context, being able to apply knowledge to make a positive difference relative to the delivery context, and having the personal skills required to bring about the action or change required.

PHOTO 31.1 *Many training pathways incorporate workshops endorsed by relevant professional bodies.*
Source: Photo copyright Andy Lane.

Regarding the training and application process, the following changes were made. Trainees maintain online records of their professional development over a two-year supervised experience process. There is one application for the domain of expertise and, as before, accreditation is assessed against meeting core competencies (see Table 31.1). There is a greater focus on application as opposed to knowledge when compared to the previous accreditation process. Additional differences are that supervised experience is directly linked to accreditation, there are mandatory BASES workshops (four core, two elective) that form part of the training programme, and there are also 500 mandatory supervised/reflective practice hours. The process recognises BASES-endorsed undergraduate and postgraduate courses as part of training, and the individual is accredited as a 'Sport and Exercise Scientist'. Further information on BASES supervised experience and accreditation can be obtained at http://www.bases.org.uk/Supervised-Experience.

BASES was established in 1984 and offered the first training route for sport and exercise psychologists in the United Kingdom. By contrast, the BPS **Division of Sport and Exercise Psychology (DSEP)** is relatively young, having been formed in 2004, although the parent association is considerably older. It was established in response to the growing academic status and public recognition of sport and exercise psychology. The DSEP's aims are to promote the interests, development and standards of professionals working in sport and exercise settings. The BPS model of postgraduate supervised experience launched in 2008 (termed the Stage Two Qualification) remains unchanged, as it was able to accommodate HPC regulations from the outset. In order to access Stage Two an individual must attain a psychology-accredited undergraduate degree or equivalent that provides graduate basis for chartered membership (GBC) with the BPS. They must then successfully complete a one-year MSc programme in Sport and Exercise Psychology (termed the Stage One Qualification).

The Stage One Qualification undertaken by examination is divided into two core syllabus areas (Paper 1: Research Methods; Paper 2: Professional Skills/Counselling) plus six optional areas, of which candidates must complete four (Paper 3: Performance – The Theoretical Basis; Paper 4: Psychological Skills and Approaches; Paper 5: Lifespan Issues; Paper 6: Social Processes; Paper 7: Exercise and Physical Activity; Paper 8: Individual Differences). Candidates also undertake a research portfolio in Sport and Exercise Psychology, which is a core requirement of the Stage One Qualification.

Division of Sport and Exercise Psychology (DSEP) a division of the BPS, its aims are to promote the interests, development and standards of professionals working in sport and exercise settings.

This requires candidates to be able to critique relevant areas of knowledge and also demonstrate an awareness of ethical practice and issues of diversity. Only when these criteria are met can an individual undertake Stage Two.

The Stage Two Qualification in Sports and Exercise Psychology provides an award whereby independent trainees can demonstrate their competence as Sport and Exercise Psychologists and thereby become eligible to be entered on the Register of Chartered Psychologists of the British Psychological Society. It also conveys eligibility for full membership of the Division of Sport and Exercise Psychology. More information on BPS Stage 1 and 2 qualifications can be obtained at http://www.bps.org.uk/careers/society_qual/spex/spex_home.cfm.

During Stage Two, there are some similarities between the BPS and BASES routes. The Stage Two Qualification is not a course of study; as with BASES, it is a competency-based framework of evidence requirements and assessments around which trainees create their own training programme. Individuals rate themselves against competencies required for Chartered status and a self-directed, supervisor-supported programme of work is designed to enhance relevant knowledge and practical competencies. There are, however, some clear differences between the BPS and BASES routes. Notably, the BPS route requires the trainee to become proficient in four key roles relating to national occupational standards in psychology. These roles are intended to enhance expertise in consulting, teaching/educational and research-related activities. The supervisee's plan of training is segmented into these four key roles, which are the development and practice of ethical principles; the application and delivery of psychological services; expertise in research and research methods; and the communication and dissemination of psychological knowledge. Trainees are also required to complete a research project as part of the qualification programme. The BPS model is based on two years full time or three to four years part time (460 days) to develop competencies in these four key roles. Assessments of the trainee psychologist are based on yearly reports, practice diaries, an ongoing portfolio and four different consulting case studies submitted by the trainee. Once the final documentation has been submitted, the trainee completes an oral examination as the final element of Stage Two assessment.

On attaining GBC, passing Stage One and Stage Two an individual becomes eligible to apply for registration as a Chartered Sport and Exercise Psychologist. On gaining Chartered status individuals are then eligible to enter the HPC register of Sport and Exercise Psychologists. Psychologists offering services to the public are required to be registered with the HPC to meet statutory regulations, which came into effect in July 2009. The terms 'Sport and Exercise Psychologist', 'Sport Psychologist' and 'Exercise Psychologist' are now protected titles and only HPC members are able to use them.

To conclude, the process and core competencies addressed by the BPS and BASES routes are presented in Table 31.1.

31.1.2 Training in Sport and Exercise Psychology: Europe

Throughout Europe, there are many postgraduate programmes in ASEP offered by educational institutions and national associations representing psychology professionals. These fall under three categories. The first are courses comprising the

European Masters' Programme Consortium in Sport and Exercise Psychology (EMPSEP) one of three categories of postgraduate programmes in ASEP offered by European educational institutions and national associations representing psychology professionals.

European Masters' Programme Consortium in Sport and Exercise Psychology (EMPSEP). Second are courses developed and offered by host education institutions. Third are advanced courses developed by national associations representing sport and exercise psychology professionals and hosted by educational institutes, or developed in collaboration between psychology associations and educational institutes. The following sections will offer an overview of the EMPSEP and also sample courses developed via educational institutions and psychology association collaborations.

European Federation of Sport and Exercise Psychology (FEPSAC) intended to promote and disseminate scientific, educational and professional work in sport and exercise psychology in Europe.

The EMPSEP was initiated and coordinated by the **European Federation of Sport and Exercise Psychology (FEPSAC;** Vanden Auweele, 2003). Launched in 1996–97, the European Master's Programme consortium comprises 12 European universities with acknowledged expertise, high research profiles and longstanding associations with the field of sport and exercise psychology. Universities comprising the consortium include University of Leuven, Belgium; Lund University, Sweden; Norwegian University of Sport and PE, Norway; University of Copenhagen, Denmark; University of Jyväskylä, Finland; University of Leipzig, Germany; University of Montpellier, France; and the University of Thessaly, Greece (for full list see http://www.fepsac.com/index.php/european_master_s_degree/network_coordinators.

The programme works around a **European Credit Transfer and Accumulation System (ECTS)**, intended to improve transparency and facilitate study across the European Union. The programme is open to students holding a degree in Sport Sciences, Physical Education or Psychology. The 60 ECTS European Master's Programme in Sport and Exercise Psychology involves a minimum of one year full time, comprising a period of study abroad of four to six months (at a recognised host university) and a series of jointly designed modules. These include a common introductory reading package (10 ECTS); a two-week international intensive course where students from all partner universities congregate and study together (10 ECTS); courses at home and foreign universities (17 ECTS); and a master's thesis (23 ECTS). In working towards a master's degree specialising in sport and exercise psychology, students engage in the scientific study of people and their behaviour in sport and exercise contexts. A key feature is the practical application of that knowledge for health, wellbeing and performance enhancement. On completion of an individualised study plan, students receive their master's degree and a certificate of European collaborative study. The programme purports to qualify graduates for practice both in the private and public sectors, for instance as performance enhancement consultants, health and fitness leaders, instructors or academic researchers (http://www.fepsac.com/index.php/european_master_s_degree).

A product of the EMPSEP is the **European Network of Young Specialists in Sport Psychology (ENYSSP)**. Students from the 1996–97 and 1997–98 cohorts were inspired to start up a network for the sharing of ideas and knowledge between young professionals in the field. The ENYSSP was officially formed in 2003 at the FEPSAC congress in Copenhagen). Some of the main objectives of ENYSSP are to coordinate European links between students, young researchers, educators and professional practitioners; to promote and facilitate cross-national cooperation for research, education and applied work in sport and exercise psychology (SEP); and to support the development and standardisation

European Credit Transfer and Accumulation System (ECTS) a credit system successfully tested and used across Europe to facilitate the recognition of periods of study abroad and thus enhance the quality and volume of student mobility in Europe, it has recently been developing into an accumulation system to be implemented at institutional, regional, national and European levels.

European Network of Young Specialists in Sport Psychology (ENYSSP) a network for the sharing of ideas and knowledge between young professionals in the field with some of its main objectives being: to coordinate European links between students, young researchers, educators and professional practitioners; to promote and facilitate cross-national cooperation for research, education and applied work in Sport and Exercise Psychology (SEP); to support the development and standardisation of official degrees in SEP within Europe.

TABLE 31.1 *Core Competencies Addressed by BASES and BPS Training.*

BPS: Stage 1 and 2 qualifications	BASES: Supervised experience (SE)
Stage 1 The Stage 1 Qualification is undertaken by examination. This is divided into two core syllabus areas plus six optional areas (of which candidates must undertake examination in four). *Core Papers (candidates must undertake all core papers)* Paper 1: Research Methods Paper 2: Professional Skills/Counselling Candidates must also submit a Research Portfolio, which is a core requirement of the Stage 1 Qualification. This requires candidates to be able to critique relevant areas of knowledge and also to demonstrate an awareness of ethical practice and issues of diversity. *Optional Papers (candidates must undertake four of the six optional papers)* Paper 3: Performance – The Theoretical Basis Paper 4: Psychological Skills and Approaches Paper 5: Lifespan Issues Paper 6: Social Processes Paper 7: Exercise and Physical Activity Paper 8: Individual Differences **Stage 2** The Stage 2 Qualification is not a course of study; it is a competency-based framework of evidence requirements and assessments around which trainees create their own training programme. Competencies include: • **Ethical Competence**, e.g. respond to unpredictable contexts and events professionally and ethically • **Consultancy Competence**, e.g. establish, develop and maintain working relationships with clients • **Research Competence**, e.g. conduct psychological research activities • **Communication Competence**, e.g. promote psychological principles, practices, services and benefits	It is possible to complete SE within two years. Supervisees must complete a postgraduate degree, or demonstrate a similar level of underpinning knowledge, along with 500 hours of logged supervised practice. They must also attend four compulsory workshops and two elective workshops. The compulsory workshops are: • Entry Workshop • Ethical Practice and Confidentiality • Reflection and Self-Evaluation • Understanding Your Client Market The two elective workshops can be selected from those offered by BASES, the BPS or other organisations. Supervisees must demonstrate that they have attained the required level for 10 competencies, including: • **Technical Skills**, e.g. be able to select, undertake and record a thorough, sensitive and detailed assessment, using appropriate techniques and equipment • **Scientific Knowledge**, e.g. understand and be able to apply the theoretical concepts underpinning sport and exercise science delivery within their domain of expertise • **Application of Knowledge and Skills**, e.g. know and be able to apply the key concepts that are relevant to safe and effective practice within their domain of expertise as a sport and exercise scientist • **Understanding and Use of Research**, e.g. to recognise the value of research to the critical evaluation of practice • **Self-Evaluation and Professional Development**, e.g. be able to adapt their practice as a result of new and emerging ideas and information within the area of sport and exercise science • **Communication**, e.g. recognise the need to use interpersonal skills to encourage active participation of service users • **Problem Solving and Impact**, e.g. be able to demonstrate a logical and systematic approach to problem solving • **Management of Self, Others and Practice**, e.g. understand the need to establish and maintain a safe practice environment • **Understanding of the Delivery Environment**, e.g. understand the need to agree the goals, priorities and methods of the proposed intervention in partnership with the service user • **Professional Relationships and Behaviours**, e.g. understand the importance of and be able to maintain confidentiality

of official degrees in SEP within Europe. The structure of ENYSSP includes three departments: Research, Applied and Education. Services offered by ENYSSP include a website (www.enyssp.org), forum, newsletters, annual workshops and ENYSSP e-mail flashes (e.g. job adverts).

In addition to the EMPSEP, across Europe there are programmes resulting from collaborations between educational institutes and sport psychology associations and/or national governing bodies. An example is the collaboration between Vrije Universiteit Amsterdam (VUA) and the **Dutch Society for Sport Psychology (VSPN: Vereniging voor SportPsychologie in Nederland)**. In 2007, they established a two-year part-time 80 ECTS credits post-academic programme for applied sport psychologists. Entrants must possess a master's or doctoral programme in psychology or in movement sciences and must also have acquired a minimum of 30 ECTS credits in sport psychology, as recognised by the VSPN. The programme provides courses (e.g. psychodiagnostic and interview skills, performance physiology, working with teams and individuals, intervention techniques) and supervised applied work with athletes, coaches and/or teams. As a result of successful course completion, students attain accreditation as an applied sport psychology practitioner with the VSPN as well as with the Dutch Olympic Committee (Nederlands Olympisch Comite).

An example of courses developed by National Governing Bodies (NGB) and hosted by educational institutions are those produced by the **German Association for Psychologists (Berufsverband Deutscher Psychologinnen und Psychologen)**. It developed two postgraduate supervised training programmes. The first course, 'Sport Psychology in Prevention and Rehabilitation' (Sportpsychologie in Pravention und Rehabilitation), is hosted by the University of Freiburg. The second, 'Sport Psychology in Competitive Sports' (Sportpsychologie im Leistungssport), is organised by Munich Technical University. In Germany, only people who have graduated in psychology as their main subject are entitled to call themselves 'Diplom-Psychologe' or even 'Psychologists'. It is a legal requirement that clients may not be misled about professional skills or about the use of the professional title of 'Psychologist'. The illegitimate use of this professional title is a violation of the German Unfair Competition Act (http://kindergesundheit.org/psychologie/faq_recognition.html#01). In Germany, if

Dutch Society for Sport Psychology (VSPN: Vereniging voor SportPsychologie in Nederland) aims to enhance the professionalisation of sport psychology in the Netherlands creating an accreditation system in 2004.

German Association for Psychologists (Berufsverband Deutscher Psychologinnen und Psychologen) the recognised professional association of German psychologists representing the professional interests of psychologists from all fields of activity.

TABLE 31.2 *European Training Routes.*

1. Courses comprising the European Master's Programme consortium in Sport and Exercise Psychology (EMPSEP). Comprises 12 European universities and works around a European Credit Transfer and Accumulation System (ECTS). The 60 ECTS European Master's Programme in Sport and Exercise includes a common introductory reading package (10 ECTS); a two-week intensive course (10 ECTS); courses at home and foreign universities (17 ECTS) and a master's thesis (23 ECTS).

2. Courses developed and offered by host education institutions. These operate in much the same way as in the United Kingdom, in that the course content is guided by the requirements of key national governing bodies. For example, Dutch courses incorporate curriculum recommendations from the Dutch Society for Sport Psychology.

3. Advanced courses developed by national associations representing sport and exercise psychology professionals and hosted by educational institutes, or developed in collaboration between psychology associations and educational institutes. For example, there are postgraduate supervised training programmes developed by the professional association of German psychologists and hosted by the University of Freiburg and Munich Technical University.

people call themselves 'Sport or Exercise Psychologists' without having graduated in psychology as a main subject, they risk legal action. This position is desired by the British Psychological Society, since in the United Kingdom it is common to see unqualified people claim to be sport or exercise psychologists. While efforts are now being undertaken to implement this, enforcement is evidently a long way from being commonly accepted.

The three categories of European training routes are summarised in Table 31.2.

United States Olympic Committee (USOC) a non-profit organisation that serves as the National Olympic Committee (NOC) for the United States. As part of its services USOC maintains a registry of sport psychology consultants from around the US and Canada from which to make an appropriate referral for service. These sport psychology consultants are required to meet standards for educational training and supervised practice in order to achieve Registry membership.

31.1.3 Structure of Sport and Exercise Psychology: USA

A sport psychology registry was established by the **United States Olympic Committee (USOC)** in 1983. This identified three categories in which ASEP practitioners could be registered: clinical counselling, educational and research. Andersen (2004, p. 453) was critical of this system, contending that the boundaries between teaching, counselling and research are unclear. To exemplify this he observed that researchers investigating interventions often teach athletes therapeutic techniques to enhance performance, and thus blur the boundaries between research and education. However, despite such criticisms this tripartite division remains.

The **Association for the Advancement of Applied Sport Psychology (AAASP)**, founded in 1985, established another form of nonstatutory credentialing via its certification of sport and exercise psychologists. In 1995, a partnership was established between the USOC and AAASP, enabling all consultants certified by AAASP who were also members of the American Psychological Association to be accepted on the USOC registry. AAASP certification is recognised by USOC as the only measure of training competence in the field.

> **Association for the Advancement of Applied Sport Psychology (AAASP)** an international, multidisciplinary, professional organisation that offers certification to qualified professionals who practice sport, exercise and health psychology, it promotes the ethical practice, science and advocacy of sport and exercise psychology.

In order to become a certified consultant with AAASP, applicants must have current AAASP membership status; have a doctoral degree from an accredited institution of higher education, in an area clearly related to sport science or psychology; and successfully complete the necessary coursework. Coursework requirements include three sport and exercise psychology courses (two at graduate level). Applicants must have completed courses in key areas, including professional ethics and standards; biomechanical and/or physiological bases of sport; historical, philosophical, social or motor behaviour bases; psychopathology and its assessment; counselling skills (a graduate course); research design, statistics or psychological assessment; biological bases of behaviour; cognitive-affective bases of behaviour; and individual behaviour. The AAASP website lists online courses that address each of these key areas (http://appliedsportpsych.org/consultants/online-courses). In addition to these academic requirements, applicants must complete 400 hours of supervised experience in ASEP, of which 100 hours must be direct contact hours with clients. They must receive 40 hours of supervision by an AAASP-approved supervisor, and all 400 hours must be verified by their supervisor.

The criteria to become AAASP certified establish clear guidelines concerning the minimum training requirements to be addressed by graduate courses in ASEP. However, despite the clarity of these guidelines, Van Raalte *et al.* (2000) concluded from an analysis of 79 graduate programmes in ASEP that there was no consensus among programmes on the content offered. All the academic content areas required for AAASP certification were provided by just 27% of institutions included in the survey.

31.1.4 Structure of Sport and Exercise Psychology: Australia

In 1991 the **Australian Psychological Society (APS)** supported a proposal for the establishment of a **College of Sport Psychologists (CoSP)**. This is the national body representing ASEP professionals. It has developed a training route meeting APS guidelines and possessing equivalence to training routes in the other specialties. Four years of undergraduate psychology accredited by the APS are followed by a two-year master's programme. APS-accredited qualifications include the completion of supervised service delivery experience (1000 hours), a research thesis or dissertation, and coursework. The supervised practical experience includes both ASEP and general psychology placements. Students complete subjects in ASEP, psychological practice, research methods and sport and exercise science. In order to register as psychologists with the Australian State Registration Boards, applicants must be members of the APS and have completed APS-accredited master's and doctoral degrees. While there is no formal certification process, full members of CoSP are recognised as qualified to practise sport psychology. CoSP has informal agreements with organisations such as the Australian Olympic Committee regarding the exclusive selection of CoSP full members as service providers.

> **Australian Psychological Society (APS)** the largest professional association for psychologists in Australia.

> **College of Sport Psychologists (CoSP)** the national body representing ASEP professionals in Australia.

Alternatively, separate from the processes established by APS, in most Australian states individuals may apply for registration as ASEP using specialist titles. The criteria for specialist registration mirror those for membership of CoSP. Applicants must complete four years of training before undertaking supervised experience. They then complete two years of supervised work experience rather than APS-accredited postgraduate qualifications. These training pathways were developed because the Australian federal government required states to enact legislation to make registration of psychologists compulsory in order for them to be able to practise. In some Australian states there are specialist titles, including 'Sport Psychologist', whereas in others all psychologists, including those who specialise in sport, are designated by the general title 'Psychologist'. The legal registration of psychologists is entirely independent of their membership of professional associations such as the Australian Psychological Society. For further discussions surrounding training issues in Australia and the US, see Anderson and Lavallee (2005).

In conclusion, when reviewing the training, registration and identity of ASEP worldwide there is clearly a lack of consistency. Encouraging transparency and continued debate will enable training pathways to be updated and the discipline to evolve. Given the diversity and debate surrounding training, registration and identity, it is unsurprising that students can find training and registration topics unsettling. Students wishing to embark on a career in sport and exercise psychology should invest time during their undergraduate training to identify and become familiar with the current training requirements for the country in which they wish to practise.

Now you have read information pertaining to different training routes worldwide, read the information presented in Activity Box 31.1. You are encouraged to consider the extent to which athlete wellbeing is highlighted or addressed in the training routes that have been outlined. You are then encouraged to consider whether you feel athlete wellbeing should be addressed by applied practitioners, providing a rationale for your decision.

31.2 CASE STUDY: SPORT PSYCHOLOGY IN PRACTICE

In concluding the five chapters that explore sport and exercise psychology, the following case study is presented to exemplify the work of an ASEP practitioner. This is intended to offer evidence of issues addressed throughout the chapters, including needs analysis, ethics, reflective practice and the use of theory to inform interventions. While reading this case study the reader is encouraged to consider ethical issues, the benefits of reflective practice and the utility of theory in informing interventions.

The following offers a sample of the support work completed by Tracey Devonport with a junior female tennis player. Throughout this case study the reader will be signposted back to key materials in the previous four chapters addressing applied sport and exercise psychology. The purpose of this is to reinforce the utility of theory in practice.

HEALTH AND WELLBEING IN SPORT AND EXERCISE PSYCHOLOGY

ACTIVITY BOX 31.1

The excerpt below is taken from Wylleman *et al.* (2009, p. 436). Read it and then consider these questions:

- To what extent are health and wellbeing overtly described in the training pathways described?
- To what extent do you feel that wellbeing contributes to performance-related outcomes in sport and exercise?
- Should athlete wellbeing be addressed as part of the services offered by applied practitioners?

Another step forward in outlining the aim of Applied Sport Psychology (ASP) was taken in the wake of sport psychologists using a more holistic perspective on the development of athletes (e.g., Wylleman & Lavallee, 2004). For example, Anderson *et al.* (2002) elaborated that the aim of ASP should include athletes' development when describing it as 'principally concerned with the application of theories, principles, and techniques from psychology to induce psycho-behavioural change in athletes to enhance performance, the quality of the sport experience, and the personal growth of the athlete'

(p. 434). Thus, beyond psychological skills training and use of mental skills (McCann, 2005), ASP also focused on lifestyle development, and use of life skills amongst athletes. FEPSAC (2008) supported this perspective recently in its position statement on the quality of ASP services by referring not only to athletes' personal growth, but also to their relational and vocational development, and by including a reference to athletes' well-being. FEPSAC stated that while in ASP 'a central focus is usually on optimising performance, other psychological themes such as well-being, work-life-balance or interpersonal issues may also come across'. In fact, by stating in this position paper that its services should not be geared solely towards athletes, but also to provide 'efficient psychological support for coaches, sport clubs, organisations and significant others', FEPSAC added a new element and took another step in elaborating on the aim of ASP.

In order to answer the questions, re-read the information on training routes provided within this chapter. You are encouraged to follow the web links provided to complete further research.

Age 17, Kirsty (a pseudonym) had a top ten under-18 national ranking, and was also national champion in the girls' under-18 doubles. She was in full-time education and her aspirations were to become a professional tennis player. To provide context to this case study, we will focus on the initial contact and assessment, a sample of psychological strategies utilised in responding to the needs of the client and, finally, an evaluation and reflections concerning the intervention process. Throughout this case study, we will utilise direct quotes recorded from Kirsty when reflecting on the interventions used. Further information on this intervention work can be found in Lane *et al.* (2007).

31.2.1 Initial Contact and Assessment

The ASEP was approached by the head club coach and the client shortly after Kirsty arrived as a new club member. She had transferred from another regional club after experiencing decreasing self-efficacy, which she attributed to the coaching climate. In addition to her self-efficacy, an issue Kirsty wished to address from the outset was the impact that her emotions, in particular anger, were having on her tennis performance.

Kirsty was able to describe vividly the relationship between her emotions, self-efficacy and performance prior to the completion of any intervention work (see Chapter 29 for more information on self-efficacy). The following excerpts taken from reflective interviews with Kirsty identify the emotions she experienced, their manifestation in terms of body language and self-efficacy, and the situations in which these emotions arise.

> I used to go mad and bang my racquet, I used to get really p****d off, every time I lost a point literally, whether it was a good point I just played I wouldn't see that it was a good point, I'd just see I lost a point, it wasn't good enough. I used to be really negative on myself and that always got me down even more. I always used to have a lot of pressure on me; I put a lot of pressure on myself.

In the description provided by Kirsty, she indicated that she assessed her performance with the use of outcome goals. In addition to the need to win points, she explained how she was also heavily influenced by other outcome measures.

> I used to focus on ratings and rankings, so if I was playing a girl who was lower ranking than me, I used to put pressure on myself thinking, I shouldn't lose to this girl, she's not the same rating.

Research indicates that failure to attain personally important goals may foster negative feelings such as depression, and also detract from self-efficacy (Klein *et al.*, 1999). Kirsty wanted to win points, win matches and improve her ranking, and clearly makes reference to negative self-statements associated with depressed mood, and a reduced sense of self-efficacy when her objective was not achieved. She demonstrates an ego orientation when setting goals, and emotional and behaviourally focused coping strategies when these are threatened. Research suggests that task-orientated goals are more controllable, and as such task orientation is associated with less negative thinking in sport (Hatzigeorgiadis & Biddle, 1999). Task orientation is linked to problem-focused coping strategies and, consequently, is more likely to lead to the mastery of adverse situations and self-efficacy gains. The efficacy of such a goal orientation has been evidenced in tennis (Harwood & Swain, 1998, 2001).

When Kirsty was asked if she was aware of the impact her emotions were having on her performance, she replied, 'I was aware of it but I didn't know how to control it.' When then asked which emotion had the most noticeable effect on her performance, she replied 'anger'. In trying to manage her anger, she sometimes tried to use behaviourally based coping strategies, but found that these had limited impact.

> I used to throw my racquet all the time, stamp my feet like a spoilt child, walk round like a loser basically with my shoulders down, dragging my feet. I used to scream so bad, scream everything like 'oh this is not good enough', sometimes I used to scream at my Dad as well, tell him to go away. I think because all of it was bottled up inside I needed to get rid of it, but it was after every point so it was tiring.

When exploring how effective these strategies were in managing anger, Kirsty explained:

> It got rid of the anger for then, but sometimes it would get even worse my anger did. I would get heated even more because I've just tried to get myself out of the situation by whacking the ball into the back fence, but when I whacked the ball I was still aroused in that anger area, so I was like aaaargh.

The intervention that followed this preliminary assessment facilitated ongoing profiling by systematically assessing pre-competition emotions, cognitions and self-efficacy longitudinally.

31.2.2 Psychological Strategies Utilised in Responding to the Needs of the Client

Prior to embarking on any intervention work, limits of confidentiality were discussed (see Chapter 28 for more information on confidentiality). The athlete expressed a desire to share information and ideas with her coach, whom she wished to involve. The ASEP was happy to utilise an equal-expertise model with the athlete, coach and ASEP triad (Hardy & Parfitt, 1994) to stimulate discussion and reflection. However, consent for information sharing was always sought before this occurred. Having agreed procedures regarding confidentiality, an overview of the ways in which the ASEP would assess psychological states, the types of psychological skills that could be used, behavioural changes that could be made and how effectiveness of work completed would be assessed were then discussed. The client agreed that a preferred starting point would be to develop her ability to recognise different emotions, those factors that elicited them and their symptomology. One of the first steps in acquiring psychological skills is to develop self-awareness, which is central to gaining control of any pressure situation (Ravizza, 2001). In tennis this may involve physical aspects of the game such as becoming more aware of appropriate focal points on which to lock concentration (Ravizza, 2001), or mental aspects such as being more aware of negative thoughts, emotions, comments or acts prior to or during matches (Mamassis & Doganis, 2004). Such activities will help ensure that the athlete is focused on the task at hand (or processes) rather than the outcome (Ravizza, 2001).

In order to develop her self-awareness, Kirsty kept a diary of emotional episodes for three months. This was adapted from the work of Hanin (2000). It has previously been utilised successfully by sport psychologists in applied practice (Devonport, Lane & Hanin, 2005; Robazza & Bortoli, 2003). This ideographic approach allows athletes to select their own terminology to describe emotional experiences, allowing them to offer a narrative description of pre-competition and post-competition thoughts and feelings. Kirsty also provided insightful comments in a tennis diary. While this could be seen as over-using self-report measures as a means to gather data, this process should be seen against the process through which the support programme was explained to and agreed by the athlete (see Chapter 27 for further information regarding measurement issues relevant to conducting a needs analysis).

Subsequent meetings were arranged to provide feedback to Kirsty regarding the data collected. Mood profiles associated with successful and unsuccessful performance were discussed, along with the associated cognitions and relationship with self-efficacy (see Chapter 29 for more information on emotions and their consequences). What emerged from these discussions were profiles of emotions associated with success. This is an important process, as the athlete begins to recognise those emotional states that tend to be associated with successful performance, and that strategies that seek to maintain these psychological states are worth pursuing.

Increasing Kirsty's awareness of her emotions and their impact on performance directly addressed, and sought to enhance, her emotional intelligence, specifically awareness of her own emotions (see Chapter 30 for more information on emotional intelligence). The influence that emotional intelligence can have on sports performance is starting to be acknowledged in sports domains (Lane et al., 2005a, 2005b) and was reinforced by Kirsty's personal experiences. Once Kirsty was better able to identify emotions, the next stage was to address her ability to manage these emotions. Self-regulatory techniques are essential in that they enable an athlete to control and direct emotions, thoughts and attention (Singer, 2002). The ability to regulate one's own emotions forms a second component of emotional intelligence, and enhancing this aspect offers a number of benefits for Kirsty's tennis performance. When exploring mood states and performance, emotionally intelligent athletes appear more capable of attaining desirable emotional states before competition (Lane et al., 2005a). In such challenging situations, emotional intelligence competencies influence the selection and control of coping strategies directed towards the immediate situation (Matthews & Zeidner, 2000; Mayer, Salovey & Caruso, 2000). Furthermore, significant relationships have also emerged between emotional intelligence and psychological skills usage, including imagery, goal setting and positive self-talk (Lane & Lowther, 2005; Lane et al., 2009). Theoretically, developing Kirsty's emotional intelligence would enhance her ability to apply interventions intended to help manage her emotions and self-efficacy.

A review of her self-set goals showed they all related to outcomes such as winning and Lawn Tennis Association (LTA) rankings. Kirsty agreed that establishing performance goals would result in goals that were more controllable. Goal setting is a popular technique used by tennis players to enhance motivation and self-efficacy (Harwood & Swain, 1998, 2001; Mamassis & Doganis, 2004) and the use of appropriate goals can help engender self-belief (Jones, Hanton & Connaughton, 2002). Bull et al. (2005) proposed that self-belief is related to robust self-confidence, which leads to the ability to overcome self-doubts and maintain self-focus. As Kirsty set outcome goals, modifying these to performance goals could exert a positive impact on her motivation and self-efficacy. A further advantage is that performance goals make available problem-focused coping strategies and reduce negative thinking (Hatzigeorgiadis & Biddle, 1999; Ntoumanis, Biddle & Haddock, 1999). Goals were established according to present priorities and included technical, physical, tactical and psychological goals. As part of the goal-setting process, enhancing her ability to manage her emotional state was identified as a key goal. As such, a number of interventions intended to manage her emotional states were introduced. These included pre-serve and return of serve routines, breathing techniques, imagery, positive self-talk, attentional control, use of music and developing social support.

Kirsty makes reference to a number of these interventions when describing those actions that she perceived to be of value in managing emotions and developing her self-efficacy. First, when describing routines she explains how she believed her breathing and attentional control strategies to be of value:

> Try and relax by taking time in between points and using deep belly breathing which really helps. It helps 'cause you're thinking about breathing and relaxing, and then when you let the breath out, you just let everything go and everything just feels so relaxed. Plus you're taking time to recover as well and not thinking about 'I just played a point and lost it'. For example, after a serve I'd think 'okay forget about it', breathe, then everything's gone, and then walk up to the service line and think about the next point in a positive way, forget about the last one. It takes your mind off things.

In terms of those actions she would take in order to attain her 'peak state', as she described it, she found a number of strategies introduced by the ASEP to be effective:

> When I used to go to tournaments I used to hate being on certain courts, so I used to imagine being on those courts in bad situations, and I used to imagine playing my shots like Federer or Justine Henin, and you'd be like wow, and go out and try it and it was a really good feeling actually. It relaxed me more, now I've been to more or less every place in country so I can imagine myself on every court. I get myself into a state where I can imagine myself playing on any court I know I might be playing on. It makes me happy and its inspirational imagining myself playing tennis. It's a good thing but in a way it's really bad because I'll be in school and my teacher is talking about something and I'll be seeing myself playing tennis, I can multi-task [laughs].

Imagery can be used as a self-modelling technique to image successful performance. To reinforce good play or correct an error, the tennis player can preview a performance feeling energised and powerful. These benefits are clearly described by Kirsty. Callow, Hardy and Hall (2001) used a successful motivational general mastery imagery (Hall et al., 1998) intervention to increase feelings of self-confidence with badminton players. Two objectives in utilising imagery with Kirsty were to enhance her self-efficacy expectations to cope with competition and to maintain a positive emotional profile. She was encouraged to use imagery to strengthen strategies utilised during training. For example, she was encouraged to imagine herself coping successfully with tough rallies or periods of poor play. She was encouraged to try to anticipate a difficult situation and see herself coping with it successfully.

An important part of this process is to imagine successfully tackling a number of the factors that make the task difficult, never under-estimating the difficulty of the task as this can create a false sense of self-confidence. For example, she imagined herself coping successfully when feelings of anger and depression started to build up in situations where she was unable to attain the standard of performance set as a goal. During imagery sessions, she rehearsed the psyching up strategies that would be used to raise her vigour, confidence, motivation and determination. This developed effective coping strategies for successfully dealing with unpleasant emotions experienced during competition. In addition to imagery, music and singing (internally) formed a strategy that Kirsty used as part of a consistent pre-match routine. Three folders of music were set up on her iPod: (i) her chillout tracks, (ii) her psych-up tracks and (iii) her random play list. A great deal of time was invested exploring the where, when and why of iPod use.

> I sing to myself, that song search for a hero inside yourself, I sing that when I'm on court now, or something inside so strong, that one, and I always listen to my iPod. I have a relaxing play list which I have on, on the way to a tournament in the car, then half an hour before I play I have my pump up play list which has got all my upbeat songs, and then after my match I go back to my relaxing play list again. If I'm just walking around at a tournament I have a random play list on to get myself in a good mood.

Previous research has indicated that music may be an effective regulator of negative mood as it can have a stimulating or sedative effect (Karageorghis, 2008). Given that the influence of music appears to be dependent on individual factors (such as age and musical preferences), allowing Kirsty to select her own music is a strategy endorsed by previous research (Karageorghis, Terry & Lane, 1999). Kirsty was able to select music to manipulate her mood according to the stage of her pre-match routine. In the car she was looking to relax and chose music accordingly; between games she wanted to be in a good mood, and chose music accordingly. Having a selection of music available on her iPod enabled her to select music easily.

When reviewing the efficacy of her pre-match routine, Kirsty utilised a number of different interventions, including music, self-talk, controlled breathing, performance goals and imagery. Consistent with previous research, this multimodal intervention was effective in identifying and manipulating debilitating perceptions of pre-competitive emotions to more facilitative ones (Hanton & Jones, 1999). During competition her pre-serve, pre-return or serve routines facilitated decision making, positive thinking, attentional control and physical preparation (Hanton & Jones, 1999).

The final example of a strategy utilised by Kirsty to manage her emotions and self-efficacy was the use of social support. In the following description Kirsty outlines developments in her interpersonal skills. She explains how she is better able to identify and utilise social support, and also appreciates the importance of giving something back. This is evidenced when she describes her improved relationship with other players.

> I used to keep things inside, I never used to talk about things, but when I was on court what I learned was when you keep things inside it just makes you even more mad. Like I use 'Team Kirsty' [refers to social support network]. I don't know what I'd do without my friends, 'cause I speak to them a lot, and like my coach, if I'm having an off day I tell him and he understands. We have a really good relationship and that's really important. I get on well with the other players as well. I'm better than the other girls and I used to hate going on court with them, when they missed I used to get really p****d off and angry, I used to want to hit with somebody better, but now, it's not about who's better or not, it's what you get out of the session, and I've realised now that I can hit against a brick wall and get out of it what I want.

When describing her use of social support in managing mood and self-efficacy, Kirsty describes good interpersonal skills. This component of emotional intelligence was described by Bar-On (2002, p. 16) as being 'able to establish cooperative, constructive, and satisfying inter-

personal relationships'. Having initially been frustrated with the technical competencies of her training partners, she reappraised the situation, in order to establish satisfying, confidence-building relationships. This ultimately enhances her ability to manage her moods and confidence via the use of social support. The ASEP spent a great deal of time identifying and discussing the role of 'Team Kirsty' members, in particular ways of nurturing these relationships by returning support, or giving thanks for support. This enhanced the satisfaction of all members of Team Kirsty and enhanced communication among its members.

In summary, having identified a need to equip Kirsty with strategies to better manage her moods and enhance her self-efficacy, consideration was given to emotional intelligence as a factor mediating the success of interventions. A longitudinal intervention programme sought to enhance her ability to recognise emotions and their impact, and to develop strategies to manipulate her mood. It also sought to enhance her ability to communicate emotions and utilise social support. This intervention ultimately conditioned a different mindset, helping Kirsty manage emotions and self-efficacy via enhanced emotional intelligence.

31.2.3 Evaluation and Reflections Concerning the Intervention Process

When assessing an athlete, introducing, developing and refining interventions, the ASEP continually engages in self-reflection and encourages the client to engage in the same reflective process (see Chapter 28 for more information on reflective practice). It is for this reason that a wealth of qualitative data are available from the client, enabling their perceptions regarding the intervention and consultancy process to be explored. This enables the early identification of interventions that are not functioning optimally, and their refinement as necessary. The ASEP in this case study introduced herself to the client as a facilitator of mental skills development, explaining that the client has the primary responsibility for change. Kirsty demonstrates the efficacy of this approach, by engaging with the process of behavioural change and clearly understanding the rationale for it. Kirsty demonstrates an increased awareness of intrapersonal and interpersonal skills, and enhanced competencies in utilising these appropriately.

Now complete Activity Box 31.2.

USE OF THEORY IN DEVELOPING AND REVIEWING INTERVENTIONS ACTIVITY BOX 31.2

Identify the theories used to underpin and evaluate the applied interventions presented in the case study example provided. Specifically, identify the key implications of the theory for intervention development and application.

Identify the theory	Identify key aspects of the theory	Identify how the theory informed interventions

31.3 CONCLUSION

This chapter has reviewed the international training routes available for becoming a professional ASEP. Comparing and contrasting these training pathways has highlighted inconsistencies in training practice worldwide. We then presented a case study to exemplify many of the issues discussed throughout the five chapters addressing sport and exercise psychology. It is hoped that this chapter will encourage you to consider your own professional development irrespective of the domain of psychology in which you practise. It is important that aspiring practitioners clearly identify their training needs and engage with professional bodies that may facilitate their development.

Table 31.3 provides answers to some frequently asked questions about sport and exercise psychology.

TABLE 31.3 *Frequently Asked Questions about Sport and Exercise Psychology.*

What income can I expect while I am training?	Few people earn an income while training. It is possible to charge clients as a trainee sport and/or exercise psychologist, and BASES offer some tentative guidelines. However, it would be misleading to suggest that people could earn a living during training, as most supervisors charge trainees.
What salary can I expect when I am fully trained?	A recently qualified sport psychologist employed by the English Institute of Sport could expect to earn a salary of around £25 000 per year (current to 2010). There is not a clearly defined career structure or salary and therefore many sport and exercise psychologists operate as independent consultants and charge varying fees.

Many sport and exercise psychologists combine consultancy with lecturing, therefore the usual salary for lecturers would be applicable. Salaries for lecturers at FE and HE institutions range from:

Lecturer: £17 000–£25 500
Senior Lecturer: £24 000–£31 500
Principal Lecturer: £30 000–£37 000

University lecturers' salaries range from:
Lecturer: £23 500–£29 500
Senior lecturer: £27 000–£36 500
Principal lecturer: £34 000–£43 000
Professorial from £43 500

For up-to-date information visit the Universities and Colleges Union website (http://www.ucu.org.uk).

What job opportunities are there?	UK jobs are advertised on the BASES website, www.bases.org.uk. Most positions are based in universities as lecturers in sport and exercise psychology and therefore can also be found on www.jobs.ac.uk.
What unique skills will I learn?	Some of these have been described within this chapter
What qualifications and experience should I have prior to training?	In order to use the title Sport and Exercise Psychologist, you will need to be registered with the Health Professionals Council (HPC). At present this is achieved via the British Psychological Society (BPS) training route. For this you will need the following qualifications before undertaking Stage 2 training: 1. Graduate Basis for Chartered Membership (GBC, previously known as GBR). This is achieved by completing a Society-accredited degree or conversion course. 2. A Society-accredited Master's in Sport and Exercise Psychology or Stage 1 of the Society's Qualification in Sport and Exercise Psychology. For accreditation with BASES to use the title Sport Scientist, you will require an undergraduate and postgraduate degree in sport and exercise sciences. You can then embark on the BASES-supervised experience programme. See Chapter 31 or the BPS and BASES websites for further information.
What further training and development can I do once I have qualified?	BASES and BPS both run workshops to ensure continuing professional development. For a list of these workshops please visit the respective websites: www.bases.org.uk www.bps.org.uk
What particular qualities will employers look for?	• The ability to demonstrate good interpersonal skills • Evidence of appropriate training (BPS or BASES) • Evidence of successful applied work • Evidence of ongoing professional development
What career progression opportunities are there?	Sport and exercise psychologists working in academia can follow the well-established career progression route. Sport psychologists working as consultants develop careers based on previous successes and recommendations. Sport psychologists working with the EIS can progress to Regional lead for psychology and the National lead.
Will my training make me an attractive proposition for other careers? If so, which careers?	Sport psychologists tend to work in business psychology, as both involve addressing psychological states associated with performance. Exercise psychologists can work with the national health or other health-focused organisations.

(Continued)

TABLE 31.3 *(Continued)*

What are the hours of work?	Working with professional sport often involves working flexible hours and being available for consultation on demand. Sport psychologists working in organisations such as the EIS are contracted to a number of hours per week, but a caveat to this contract is to work hours as required.
What are the working conditions like?	Sport and exercise psychology can be very rewarding. However, a practitioner must be prepared to travel and immerse themselves in the culture of the sport or exercise.
Will I have a job for life?	Possibly, but sport and exercise psychologists typically operate in performance-enhancement climates (including outcomes such as performance, adherence, wellbeing and so on). If performance deteriorates, their position is questioned. The decision to use a sport or exercise psychologist can depend on a number of factors that are beyond the control of either the practitioner or the client (in the case of a practitioner working in an Olympic sport, for example).
Where can I go for further information?	www.bases.org.uk www.bps.org.uk http://www.bps.org.uk/careers/what-do-psychologists-do/areas/sport.cfm

SELF-TEST QUESTIONS

- What are the main differences in the training routes offered by the BPS and BASES?
- According to Anderson and Lavallee (2005), what are the three key challenges faced by the profession of Applied Sport and Exercise Psychology (ASEP)?
- What are the ten competencies addressed during BASES supervised experience?
- What are the competencies addressed during stage 2 of the BPS training pathway?
- What are the three categories of European training routes?
- What are the three categories in which ASEP practitioners could be registered in the United States of America?

ESSAY QUESTIONS

- Describe existing quality assurance pathways that prepare individuals for applied practice.
- It is suggested that there is a lack of consistency in the training, registration and identity of ASEP worldwide. What are the grounds for this contention?
- Why is the use of theory in informing ASEP interventions strongly advocated and incorporated in training pathways?
- Describe the key roles of ASEP practitioners and outline the way in which existing training pathways facilitate these roles.

TEXTS FOR FURTHER READING

Andersen, M.B., Van Raalte, J.L. & Harris, G. (2000) Supervision II: A case study, in M.B. Andersen (ed.) *Doing Sport Psychology*, pp. 167–79, Champaign, IL: Human Kinetics.

Gardner, F. & Moore, Z. (2006) Professional development and supervision in sport psychology, in F. Gardner & Z. Moore (eds.) *Clinical Sport Psychology*, pp. 221–37, Champaign, IL: Human Kinetics.

Lavallee, D., Kremer, J., Williams, M. & Moran, A. (2004) Introduction, history and development, in D. Lavallee, J. Kremer, M. Williams & A. Moran (eds) *Sport Psychology: Contemporary Themes*, pp. 1–17, London: Palgrave.

Moran, A. (2004) Introducing sport and exercise psychology: Discipline and profession, in A. Moran (ed.) *Sport and Exercise Psychology: A Critical Introduction*, pp. 3–33, London: Routledge.

RELEVANT JOURNAL ARTICLES

Anderson, A.G. & Lavallee, D. (2005) Professional development issues in Britain: Lessons from Australia and the USA, *Sport and Exercise Psychology Review* 1: 12–16, http://www.bps.org.uk/downloadfile.cfm?file_uuid=E946D6CE-1143-DFD0-7E44-ABF3BFC9E0B4&ext=pdf, accessed 21 September 2009.

Rubin, N.J., Bebeau, M., Leigh, I.W. *et al.* (2007) The competency movement within psychology: An historical perspective, *Professional Psychology: Research and Practice* 38: 452–62.

Sanchez, X., Godin, P. & De Zanet, F. (2005) Who delivers sport psychology services? Examining the field reality in Europe, *Sport Psychologist* 19: 81–92.

Tod, D. (2007) The long and winding road: Professional development in sport psychology, *Sport Psychologist* 21: 94–108.

Van Raalte, J.L., Brown, T.D., Brewer, B.W., Avondoglio, J.B. & Hartmann, W.M. (2000) An on-line survey of graduate course offerings satisfying AAASP certification criteria, *Sport Psychologist* 14: 98–104.

Weiss, M.R. (1998) 'Passionate collaboration': Reflections on the directions of applied sport psychology in the coming millennium, *Journal of Applied Sport Psychology* 10: 11–24.

Williams, J.M. & Scherzer, C.B. (2003) Tracking the training and careers of graduates of advanced degree programs in sport psychology, 1994 to 1999, *Journal of Applied Sport Psychology* 15: 335–53.

Wylleman, P., Harwood, C.G., Elbe, A.M., Reints, A. & de Caluwe, D. (2009) A perspective on education and professional development in applied sport psychology, *Psychology of Sport and Exercise* 10: 435–46.

RELEVANT WEB LINKS

Association for Applied Sport Psychology, http://appliedsportpsych.org/home

Australian Psychological Society College of Sport Psychologists, http://www.groups.psychology.org.au/csep

British Association of Sport and Exercise Sciences, www.bases.org.uk

Division of Sport and Exercise Psychology (within the British Psychological Society), http://www.bps.org.uk/spex/spex_home.cfm

European Federation of Sport Psychology, www.fepsac.com

Full list of the 12 European master's degree network members, http://www.fepsac.com/index.php/european_master_s_degree/network_coordinators

REFERENCES

Andersen, M.B. (2004) The evolution of training and supervision in sport psychology, in T. Morris & J.J. Summers (eds) *Sport Psychology: Theory, Applications and Issues*, 2nd edn, pp. 452–69, Brisbane: John Wiley & Sons, Ltd.

Anderson, A.G. & Lavallee, D. (2005) Professional development issues in Britain: Lessons from Australia and the USA, *Sport and Exercise Psychology Review* 1: 12–16, http://www.bps.org.uk/downloadfile.cfm?file_uuid=E946D6CE-1143-DFD0-7E44-ABF3BFC9E0B4&ext=pdf, accessed 21 September 2009.

Anderson, A., Miles, A., Mahoney, C. & Robinson, P. (2002) Evaluating the effectiveness of applied sport psychology practice: Making the case for a case study approach, *Sport Psychologist* 16: 432–53.

Bar-On, R. (2002) *Bar-On Emotional Quotient Inventory: Short (EQ-I: S): Technical manual*, Toronto: Multi-Health Systems.

Bull, S.J., Shambrook, C.J., James, W. & Brooks, J.E. (2005) Towards an understanding of mental toughness in elite English cricketers, *Journal of Applied Sports Psychology* 17: 209–27.

Callow, N., Hardy, L. & Hall, C. (2001) The effect of a motivational-mastery imagery intervention on the confidence of high-level badminton players, *Research Quarterly for Exercise and Sport* 72: 389–400.

Devonport, T.J., Lane, A.M. & Hanin, Y. (2005) Affective state profiles of athletes prior to best, worst and performance-induced injury outcomes, *Journal of Sports Science and Medicine* 4: 382–94.

FEPSAC (2008) European master's programme in sport and exercise psychology, http://www.fepsac.com/index.php?cID=79, accessed 2 December 2010.

Hall, C., Mack, D., Paivio, A. & Hausenblas, H. (1998) Imagery use by athletes: Development of the Sport Imagery Questionnaire, *International Journal of Sport Psychology* 29: 73–89.

Hanin, Y.L. (2000) Successful and poor performance and emotions, in Y. Hanin (ed.) *Emotions in Sport*, pp. 157–88, Champaign, IL: Human Kinetics.

Hanton, S. & Jones, G. (1999) The acquisition and development of cognitive skills and strategies. I: Making the butterflies fly in formation, *Sport Psychologist* 113: 1–21.

Hardy, L. & Parfitt, G. (1994) The development of a model for the provision of psychological support to a national squad, *Sport Psychologist* 8: 126–42.

Harwood, C. & Swain, A.B.J. (1998) Antecedents of pre-competition achievement goals in elite junior tennis players, *Journal of Sports Sciences* 16: 357–71.

Harwood, C. & Swain, A.B.J. (2001) The development and activation of achievement goals in tennis: I. Understanding the underlying factors, *Sport Psychologist* 15: 319–41.

Hatzigeorgiadis, A. & Biddle, S. (1999) The effects of goal orientation and perceived competence on cognitive interference during tennis and snooker performance, *Journal of Sport Behavior* 22: 479–501.

Jones, G., Hanton, S. & Connaughton, D. (2002) What is this thing called mental toughness? An investigation of elite sport performers, *Journal of Applied Sport Psychology* 14: 205–18.

Karageorghis, C.I. (2008) The scientific application of music in sport and exercise, in A. Lane (ed.) *Sport and Exercise Psychology*, pp. 109–38, London: Hodder Education.

Karageorghis, C.I., Terry, P.C. & Lane, A.M. (1999) Development and initial validation of an instrument to assess the motivational qualities of music in exercise and sport: The Brunel Music Rating Inventory, *Journal of Sports Sciences* 17: 713–24.

Klein, H.J., Wesson, M.J., Hollenbeck, J.R. & Alge, B.J. (1999) Goal commitment and the goal setting process: Conceptual clarification and empirical synthesis, *Journal of Applied Psychology* 84: 885–96.

Lane, A.M. & Lowther, J.P. (2005) Relationships between emotional intelligence and psychological skills among athletes, *Journal of Sports Sciences* 23: 1253–4.

Lane, A.M., Devonport, T.J., Davies, K., Lane, H.J., Gill, G. & Diehl, C. (2007) Anger, emotional intelligence, performance and interventions, in E.I. Clausen (ed.) *Psychology of Anger*, Hauppage, NY: Nova.

Lane, A.M., Soos, I., Leibinger, E., Karsai, I. & Hamar, P. (2005a) Emotional intelligence, mood states and successful and unsuccessful performance, *Journal of Sports Sciences* 23: 1254.

Lane, A.M., Thelwell, R., Lowther, J. & Devonport, T.J. (2009) Emotional intelligence and psychological skills use among athletes, *Social Behaviour and Personality* 37: 195–202.

Lane, A.M., Thelwell, R., Weston, N. & Devonport, T. (2005b) Emotional intelligence, mood states and performance, *Journal of Sports Sciences* 23: 1254–5.

Mamassis, G. & Doganis G. (2004) The effects of a mental training program on junior's pre-competitive anxiety, self-confidence, and tennis performance, *Journal of Applied Sport Psychology* 16: 118–37.

Matthews, G. & Zeidner, M. (2000) Emotional intelligence, adaptation to stressful encounters, and health outcomes, in R. Bar-On & J.D.A. Parker (eds) *The Handbook of Emotional Intelligence: Theory, Development and Application at Home, School, and in the Workplace*, pp. 459–89, San Francisco, CA: Jossey-Bass.

Mayer, J., Salovey, P. & Caruso, D. (2000) Competing models of emotional intelligence, in R.J. Sternberg (ed.) *Handbook of Human Intelligence*, 2nd edn, New York: Cambridge University Press.

McCann, S. (2005) Roles: The sport psychologist, in S. Murphy (ed.) *The Sport Psych Handbook*, pp. 279–92, Champaign, IL: Human Kinetics.

Morris, T., Alfermann, D., Lintunen, T. & Hall, H. (2003) Training and selection of sport psychologists: An international review, *International Journal of Sport and Exercise Psychology* 1: 139–54.

Ntoumanis, N., Biddle, S.J.H. & Haddock, G. (1999) The mediating role of coping strategies on the relationship between achievement motivation and affect in sport, *Anxiety, Stress, and Coping* 12: 299–327.

Ravizza, K. (2001) Increasing awareness for sport performance, in J.M. Williams (ed.) *Applied Sport Psychology: Personal Growth to Peak Performance*, pp. 179–89, Mountain View, CA: Mayfield Publishing Company.

Robazza, C. & Bortoli, L. (2003) Intensity, idiosyncratic content and functional impact of performance-related emotions in athletes, *Journal of Sports Sciences* 21: 171–89.

Roper, E.A. (2002) Women working in the applied domain: Examining the gender bias in applied sport psychology, *Journal of Applied Sport Psychology* 14: 53–66.

Singer, R.N. (2002) Pre-performance state, routines, and automaticity: What does it take to realize expertise in self-paced events? *Journal of Sport & Exercise Psychology* 24: 359–75.

Vanden Auweele, Y. (2003) Sport psychology and education. The European masters in exercise and sport psychology, in E. Apitzsch & G. Schilling (eds) *Sport Psychology in Europe. FEPSAC – An Organisational Platform and a Scientific Meeting Point*, pp. 39–50, Biel: FEPSAC.

Van Raalte, J.L., Brown, T.D., Brewer, B.W., Avondoglio, J.B., Hartmann, W.M. & Scherzer, C.B. (2000) An on-line survey of graduate course offerings satisfying AAASP certification criteria, *Sport Psychologist* 14: 98–104.

Wylleman, P. & Lavallee, D. (2004) A developmental perspective on transitions faced by athletes, in M. Weiss (ed.) *Developmental Sport and Exercise Psychology: A Lifespan Perspective*, pp. 507–27, Morgantown, WV: Fitness Information Technology.

Wylleman P., Harwood, C.G., Elbe, A.M., Reints, A. & de Caluwe, D. (2009) A perspective on education and professional development in applied sport psychology, *Psychology of Sport and Exercise* 10: 435–46.

Zizzi, S.J., Zaichkowsky, L. & Perna, F.M. (2002) Certification in sport and exercise psychology, in J. Van Raalte & B. Brewer (eds) *Exploring Sport and Exercise Psychology*, 2nd edn, pp. 459–77, Washington, DC: American Psychological Association.

Glossary

4-what assessment a simplified SORC functional assessment of four questions beginning with 'what' that a client asks when considering his or her negative emotional reaction.

ABC A functional psychological model involving: Antecedents, Behaviour and Consequences.

ability grouping pupils are grouped with other pupils at school on the basis of their ability in a given subject or task

abnormal attributional processes biases or faults in the normal attribution process which may lead to errors in the interpretation of one's own and others' behaviour.

abnormal psychology an alternative definition of psychopathology albeit with negative connotations in regard to being 'not normal'.

accommodation in Piagetian theory, a type of adaptation in which a child creates or makes changes to existing schemas.

achievement goal orientations in education research, a theory of goals in which those who hold a performance goal orientation are focused on the visible end product of learning, while those who hold a mastery goal orientation are focused on the process of learning itself and progress in mastering the task at hand.

actuarial risk assessment a means of predicting aggression by putting risk factors into a statistical formula.

acute mountain sickness a set of maladaptive physiological and psychological disorders, caused by rapid ascent to heights of more than 3000m.

acute stress an urgent and usually distressing bodily response to 'fight or flight' situations to prepare the body to respond appropriately to help ensure survival.

adherence following advice provided by health care professionals.

adoption studies research conducted on children who are biologically similar but have been reared apart.

adrenal glands two glands within one located on the top of each kidney, secreting hormones and steroids.

aetiology a term widely used in psychopathology to describe the causes or origins of psychological symptoms.

aftermath later consequences of a particular incident or occurrence.

aggression function motivation for aggression.

agreeableness one of the dimensions of personality as suggested by the Big Five personality model.

allostasis the ways in which the HPA axis, the ANS, and the cardiovascular and immune systems together help the body to adapt to stress.

American Psychiatric Association (APA) a scientific and professional organisation that represents psychiatry in the United States.

amphetamine psychosis a syndrome in which high doses of amphetamines taken for a long time produce behavioural symptoms that closely resemble symptoms of psychosis.

anorexia nervosa (AN) an eating disorder featuring a refusal to maintain a minimal body weight, a pathological fear of gaining weight and a distorted body image.

antecedents things that go before, namely triggers.

antibody-mediated immunity an immune response produced by B cells which attack and destroy infectious agents by stimulating the release of antibodies.

antisocial personality disorder a personality disorder, the main features of which are an enduring disregard for, and violation of, the rights of others.

anxiety disorder excessive or aroused states characterised by feelings of apprehension, uncertainty and fear.

anxiety sensitivity fears of anxiety symptoms based on the belief that such symptoms have harmful consequences.

applied behaviour analysis (ABA) applying the principles of behaviourism and operant conditioning to the assessment of treatment of those exhibiting behavioural difficulties.

applied problem-analysis frameworks tools used by educational psychologists to clarify concerns, structure hypothesis-testing and information gathering, involve clients and stakeholders, devise, implement and evaluate intervention plans to achieve change.

applied sport and exercise psychology (ASEP) the application of proven psychological techniques to sports performance, concerning itself with how the mind influences and is influenced by participation in physical competition and exercise generally.

appraisal a thought (usually automatic and often negative) in response to a stressor which itself will affect how a person responds to the original stressor.

apprentices individuals who learn a craft or trade through the guidance of a more skilled or competent person.

Asperger's syndrome severe and sustained impairment in social interaction and the development of restricted, repetitive patterns of behaviour, interests and activities.

assess understand and explain the determinants of an individual's health or wellbeing problems.

assessment a process of gathering information about the client's or clients' difficulties and goals.

assimilation in Piagetian theory, a means of extending existing schemas by incorporating a new experience.

Association for the Advancement of Applied Sport Psychology (AAASP) an international, multidisciplinary, professional organisation that offers certification to qualified professionals who practice sport, exercise, and health psychology, it promotes the ethical practice, science, and advocacy of sport and exercise psychology.

associations in research methodology, links between variables.

atherosclerosis the build-up of fatty plaques in the lining of the blood vessels which leads to narrowing of the arteries, partly caused by repeated activation of the stress response systems.

attention part of the information-processing system of the human brain related to taking notice and observing.

attention deficit hyperactivity disorder (ADHD) a persistent pattern of inattention and/or hyperactivity-impulsivity that is at a significantly higher rate than would be expected for a child at their developmental stage.

attention problems disorders involving difficulties in concentration, such as attention deficit/hyperactivity disorder (ADHD).

attitude construct describing a person's like or dislike of something.

attitude change a shift in a person's hypothetical construct in one or more of its three components: cognition, affect and behaviour.

attitudes a hypothetical construct with three components: cognition, affect and behaviour.

attribution theory an explanation of the ways in which people assess the causes of their own or the behaviour of others.

attributional theories of depression the argument that people learn to become helpless and hopeless because they explain their behaviour and events by attributing them to causes that generate pessimistic thinking.

attributions assessments about our own or the behaviour of others.

Australian Psychological Society (APS) the largest professional association for psychologists in Australia.

autistic spectrum disorder (ASD) an umbrella term referring to all disorders that display autistic-style symptoms across a wide range of severity and disability.

automatic processes in humans, processes that require no attentional resources, or very little.

autonomic nervous system a sub-division of the peripheral nervous system concerned with regulating internal body processes that require no conscious awareness.

aversion therapy a treatment based on classical conditioning which attempts to condition an aversion to a stimulus or event to which the individual is inappropriately attracted.

Axis I disorders commonly diagnosed disorders such as anxiety disorder, depression and schizophrenia.

Axis II disorders chronic, long-term psychopathologies and disorders such as personality disorder.

battered woman syndrome the view that a pattern of repeated partner abuse leads battered women to believe that they are powerless to change their situation.

Beck's cognitive therapy a form of therapy that considers depression is maintained by 'negative schema' leading depressed individuals to hold negative views about themselves, their future and the world.

behaviour analysis an approach to psychopathology based on the principles of operant conditioning (also known as behaviour modification).

behaviour modification an approach to psychopathology based on the principles of operant conditioning (also known as behaviour analysis).

behaviour therapy a form of treatment that aims to change behaviour using principles based on conditioning theory.

behavioural data in educational psychology research, data relating to students' observable behaviour or task performance.

behavioural determinants underlying causes of behaviour including beliefs, attitudes and intentions.

behavioural model an influential psychological model of psychopathology based on explaining behaviour.

behavioural pathways the ways in which psychological factors can influence health indirectly by changing health behaviours.

behaviourism an approach to the study of psychology which focuses entirely on observable events and the behaviours associated with them, without referring to the mind and emotions.

behaviourist an adherent of behaviourism.

beliefs opinions or judgements held by an individual.

benefit finding the ability by those who have experienced major stressors to find the benefits and advantages in the experience.

biases systematic errors in judgement.

big fish–little pond effect the effect whereby students' academic self-perception depends on comparison with the ability of peers in their school.

Big Five personality model a model of personality sometimes known as the OCEAN model derived through taking the initial letter of each of the five key dimensions.

binge eating a self-defeating behaviour in which an individual eats to excess (as defined by the individual) in order to regulate emotion and/or self-soothe.

binge-eating disorder an eating disorder characterised by recurrent episodes of binge eating.

biofeedback in pain management, a technique taught to patients to help them manage stress by exerting control over autonomic and voluntary bodily processes.

biological challenge test research in which panic attacks are induced by administering carbon dioxide-enriched air or by encouraging hyperventilation.

biopsychosocial model an integrated model of health psychology drawing on many other disciplines, including biology, medicine, social psychology, developmental psychology and economics in order to provide a comprehensive picture of the causes and processes underpinning health and illness.

bipolar mood disorder a psychological disorder characterised by periods of mania that alternate with periods of depression.

body dysmorphic disorder a preoccupation with assumed defects in physical appearance.

body image the cognitions, emotions and behaviours related to how one perceives one's body.

borderline personality disorder a personality disorder, featuring inability in personal relationships, a lack of well-defined and stable self-image, mood changes and impulsive behaviour.

bounded rationality the idea that one's thought is limited by cognitive limitations yet within those limits one is rational.

brain the central part of the nervous system which helps control our behaviour.

British Association of Sport and Exercise Sciences (BASES) a professional body promoting excellence in sport and exercise sciences through evidence-based practice.

British Psychological Society (BPS) the representative body for psychology and psychologists in the UK.

broken leg problem the term given to the failure of actuarial approaches to risk to account for unexpected change.

B-SAFER the acronym for Brief Spousal Assault Form for the Evaluation of Risk.

bulimia nervosa (BN) an eating disorder featuring recurrent episodes of binge eating followed by periods of purging or fasting.

bullying aggressive acts by individuals or groups that are directed, repeatedly and over time, towards victims in order to hurt them emotionally or physically.

cardiovascular system the circulatory system comprising the heart and blood vessels.

career anchors five career drivers, with one being primary: autonomy, creativity, technical or functional competence, security, and power.

caricatured composite a composite image with the facial distinctiveness changed, for the purpose of improving recognition.

case formulation a clinical psychologist's attempts to provide a theoretical rationale for how an individual's problems have developed and how they might best be treated.

catastrophic misinterpretation of bodily sensations an influential model of panic disorder which hypothesises that panic attacks are precipitated by the individual catastrophically misinterpreting their bodily sensations as threatening.

catastrophising an example of magnification, in which the individual takes a single fact to its extreme.

causal attribution an explanation by an individual of the cause of a particular behaviour.

cause-and-effect relations in experimentation, the relations between the independent variable that is manipulated (hypothesised as the cause) and the dependent variable or resultant change in behaviour (the effect).

cell-mediated immunity an immune reaction produced by T cells which attack and destroy infectious agents by triggering release of killer cells.

central executive the key part of the working memory system which directs the manipulation and transformation of information.

central nervous system the brain and the spinal cord protected by bone.

central route the term for high (effortful) processing of messages according to the elaboration likelihood model of Petty and Cacioppo.

cerebrum the largest part of the human brain consisting of a mass of intricate tissue divided into two halves, the left and right cerebral hemispheres.

chartership the title of Chartered Psychologist is the benchmark of professional recognition for psychologists and the pathway towards it involves undertaking a recognised degree in psychology, a postgraduate qualification, working under supervision and demonstrating competence in the knowledge, research and practice.

child-centred education approach to education which focuses on the needs, abilities, and other attributes of the child.

child sexual abuse abuse of a child by an adult or older adolescent for sexual stimulation.

chronic stress a long-term, ongoing bodily response to 'fight or flight' situations to prepare the body to respond appropriately to help ensure survival.

classical conditioning the learning of an association between two stimuli, the first of which (the conditioned stimulus) predicts the occurrence of the second (the unconditioned stimulus).

classroom goal structures orientations within classrooms that can parallel personal goal orientation as being either performance or mastery focused.

classroom management the approaches and strategies used by teachers to create a positive learning environment.

client-centred therapy an approach to psychopathology assuming that if individuals are unrestricted by fears and conflicts, they will develop into well-adjusted, happy individuals.

clinical psychology the branch of psychology responsible for understanding and treating mental health problems.

clinical risk assessment a 'hypo-deductive' means of assessing the risk a person presents with.

coaching in business, one-to-one facilitation by a trained individual to improve specific performance issues and the effectiveness of the person being coached.

cognitive behaviour therapy (CBT) an umbrella term for many different therapies that share the common aim of changing both cognitions and behaviour.

cognitive-behavioural a psychotherapeutic approach that focuses on the interrelationships between thoughts, behaviours and feelings.

cognitive development in neuroscience and psychology the study of a child's development in terms of information processing, conceptual resources, perceptual skill, language learning, and other aspects of brain development.

cognitive dissonance an unpleasant feeling arising in an individual when two or more cognitions are inconsistent or when the person's behaviour is inconsistent with their underlying attitudes.

cognitive distortions inaccurate ways of thinking, e.g., personalising and catastrophising, that reinforce negative thinking and feeling and may lead to inappropriate behaviour.

cognitive interview (CI) an interview used to help a person recall information about a face to locate subsets of features within a composite system for presentation to eyewitnesses.

cognitive model an influential psychological model of psychopathology.

cognitive restructuring methods used to challenge the biases that a client might hold about how frequently bad events might happen and to generate thoughts that are more accurate.

cognitive script based on previous experience and learning, mental 'guides' which a client has which will tell him or her how to respond in certain situations.

cognitive techniques in pain management, interventions taught to individuals to identify and change cognitions and emotions which increase pain.

cognitive therapy a form of psychotherapy based on the belief that psychological problems are the products of faulty ways of thinking about the world.

College of Sport Psychologists (CoSP) the national body representing ASEP professionals in Australia.

commitment a social influence outcome fulfilling a motivational goal.

Common Assessment Framework (CAF) an approach shared by educational psychologists and social services for assessment and planning to meet children's additional support needs.

common cold a viral illness affecting the respiratory system.

communication deviance a general term used to describe communication that is difficult for ordinary listeners to follow and leaves them puzzled and unable to share a focus of attention with the speaker.

community-level intervention a health initiative using media and resources at the level of the community, such as local radio and voluntary organisations.

community psychology the branch of psychology dealing with relationships between the individual and community and their wider society.

comorbidity the co-occurrence of two or more distinct disorders.

competencies skills that are essential to perform certain functions and roles, acquired during a professional's training.

compliance externally-motivated behaviour based and dependent on the presence of rewards and punishments.

compulsions repetitive or ritualised behaviour patterns that an individual feels driven to perform in order to prevent some negative outcome happening.

computerised CBT an alternative to therapist-delivered cognitive behaviour therapy whereby an individual interacts with sophisticated software delivered via a variety of media.

concentration to direct attention to internal or external events.

concordance studies research designed to investigate the probability with which family members or relatives will develop a psychological disorder depending on how much genetic material they have in common.

conduct disorder a pattern of childhood behaviour exhibited by a child including fighting, lying and running away from home.

conduct research for example, developing theoretical understandings, collecting data and interpreting the meaning of findings for theory and intervention.

confidentiality an ethical requirement of many professions in which the client has the right to expect that information gathered about or from the client will not be made public without the client's consent and if limitations are placed on the terms of confidentiality these are generally discussed and agreed before the start of any professional relationship.

conflict a conflict situation is one in which an individual has orchestrated a hostile situation of some kind with a clear plan and focus in mind.

conscientiousness one of the dimensions of personality as suggested by the Big Five personality model.

constructivist an approach in cognitive-development theory focusing on how children construct their knowledge and understanding based on their experiences.

constructivist perspective in occupational psychology research and practice, a paradigm that acknowledges that any selection process is a social one with the focus on matching people to organisations and teams.

consult to negotiate the nature of a piece of work requested by a client and then undertake this competently, delivering what has been agreed to a good standard and on time.

consultancy cycle the process through which work is structured when applying occupational psychology in a project or piece of work, the stages are: establishing agreements with customer/client, identifying needs and problems, analysing needs and problems, formulating solutions, implementing and reviewing solutions, evaluating outcomes and reporting and reflecting on outcomes.

consultant clinical psychologist a senior clinical psychologist whose role includes managerial responsibilities and functions.

consumer psychology the study of human responses to product and service-related information and experiences.

context a visual scene which can influence the decision processes of eyewitnesses.

continuing professional development (CPD) training and development undertaken post-qualification to retain and develop one's professional competencies.

control group in an experiment, the group in which an intervention is not applied, making it possible to assess how far any change that occurs in the experimental group is attributable to the intervention itself, rather than something that would have happened anyway over that period of time.

controlled conditions in experimental survey research, the circumstances surrounding data collection are kept as comparable as possible across participants.

controlled processes in humans, processes that require attentional resources.

conversational management (CM) a tool applicable in any investigative interviewing context.

conversion disorder the presence of symptoms or deficits affecting voluntary motor or sensory function.

coping constantly changing effort in the form of thoughts and behaviours to manage demands that are appraised as challenging or beyond the resources of the individual.

coping strategies ways of coping that are problem-focused or emotion-focused.

cortisol commonly known as the 'stress hormone', it is secreted when a person encounters a stressful situation in order to help the body respond appropriately.

counselling a purposeful relationship in which a specially trained person (trained in, e.g., listening skills and psychology) helps another to help him or herself.

counselling psychology the application of psychological knowledge generally to therapeutic practice.

counterconditioning a behaviour therapy using conditioning techniques to establish a response that is antagonistic to the psychopathology.

counterfactual thinking an attributional process commonly used by victims to make sense of their victimisation, it is characterised by the phrase, "If only …".

crisis a crisis situation is one in which the individual concerned has no clear goals and his or her emotional distress is high.

cross-sectional design a research design where the same task or questionnaire is completed at the same point in time by individuals within different groups.

cued recall memories called to mind in response to specific prompting from an interviewer.

cultural models the way in which the underlying values and beliefs inherent in the culture influence perceptions of self and perceptions of others

cultural tools products of human culture that are passed on to children in order to promote and extend their cognitive development.

culturally mediated according to Vygotsky, a child's mental functions emerge within the context of social interactions, particularly with others who are more competent in the use of cultural tools.

culture a set of human-made objective and subjective elements that in the past have increased the probability of survival and resulted in satisfaction of the participants in an ecological niche, and thus became shared among those who could communicate with each other because they had a common language and lived in the same time and place.

cycle of abuse a term with a variety of meanings including multiple victimisation whereby an individual is victimised again and again throughout his or her life.

cytokines chemicals in the body that play a crucial role in the functioning of the body's immunity.

daily diaries an approach to research whereby an individual records data every day, either using rating scales or open-ended responses (for example, ratings of moods or descriptions of stressors).

daily hassles daily happenings causing the repeated activation of the stress response system.

declarative knowledge knowledge that can be declared or stated (often verbally).

deduction the process of drawing conclusions from premises assumed to be true.

defensive attribution hypothesis a motivational theory of victim blame in which the role of relevance is emphasised.

dehydration excessive loss of water from the body's tissues.

demonology the belief that those exhibiting symptoms of psychopathology are possessed by bad spirits.

dependent variable in an experiment, the variable that is measured to demonstrate whether its value was affected by the independent variable.

depersonalisation disorder a disorder characterised by feelings of detachment or estrangement from the self.

depression a mood disorder involving emotional, motivational, behavioural, physical and cognitive symptoms.

description-identification relationship the relationship that appears to exist between the quality and quantity of a person's description of a face and his or her accuracy in distinguishing the guilty from the innocent in a line-up.

developmental coordination disorder (DCD) a specific learning difficulty involving problems with movement and motor coordination, characterised by difficulties in object recognition and planning of movement.

developmental dyslexia specific learning difficulty involving problems in reading accuracy and spelling, related to a number of cognitive and neurobiological processes.

developmental psychology the branch of psychology concerned with change and development over the lifespan, focused on development during childhood and adolescence.

diagnostic assessment a forensic psychologist who has some professional mental health experience and training can diagnose mental health problems and personality disorders in individuals.

Diagnostic & Statistical Manual (DSM) an APA handbook for mental health professionals listing different categories of mental disorders and criteria for diagnosing them.

dialogic using talk between partners to enhance learning.

diathesis-stress perspective a view that psychopathology is caused by a combination of a genetically inherited biological predisposition to schizophrenia and environmental stress.

didactic designed to instruct.

diencephalon a sub-division of the forebrain which comprises the thalamus and hypothalamus.

differential exposure hypothesis a theory that proposes that the higher prevalence of health problems in low socioeconomic status groups is associated with a greater exposure to psychological stressors.

differential vulnerability hypothesis a theory that suggests that low socioeconomic status individuals are less well equipped to cope with stressors because they have fewer material and social resources.

diploma in forensic psychology the formal qualification (regulated by the BPS and approved by the HPC) to become a forensic psychologist in the UK.

direct aggression overt aggression.

discovery learning an enquiry-based form of learning in which the student explores and finds answers rather than merely receives instruction.

discrimination treating an individual or group differently (for or against) as a result of feelings or prejudices about their difference.

disequilibrium a state experienced by a child when encountering new experiences that do not map onto his or her existing schemes.

disputation techniques methods in which a client can learn to argue, debate or negotiate with their own thoughts.

dissociative amnesia an inability to recall important personal information that is usually of a stressful or traumatic nature.

dissociative experiences a disorder in which the mind separates or compartmentalises certain mental contents from normal consciousness.

dissociative fugue the instance of an individual suddenly and unexpectedly travelling away from home or work and being unable to recall some or all of his or her past history.

dissociative identity disorder (DID) a dissociative disorder characterised by the individual displaying two or more distinct identities or personality states that take turns to control behaviour.

distraction techniques methods for disturbing one's thoughts using attention-shifting or physical distraction.

diversity the state of being different, visibly or invisibly.

Division of Sport and Exercise Psychology (DSEP) a division of the BPS, its aims are to promote the interests, development and standards of professionals working in sport and exercise settings.

domain-specific applicable to a specialised area of knowledge or activity.

dopamine a compound that exists in the body as a neurotransmitter and as a precursor of other substances including adrenalin.

dopamine hypothesis a theory which argues that the symptoms of schizophrenia are related to excess activity of the neurotransmitter dopamine.

downward drift a phenomenon in which individuals exhibiting psychotic symptoms fall to the bottom of the social ladder or even become homeless due to impairment.

dream analysis the analysis of dream content as a means of accessing unconscious beliefs and conflicts.

DSM-IV-TR the most recent version of the *Diagnostic and Statistical Manual*.

DSM-IV-TR Axes of Disorder the five dimensions (axes) of classification in DSM-IV-TR.

Dutch Society for Sport Psychology (VSPN: Vereniging voor SportPsychologie in Nederland) aims to enhance the professionalisation of sport psychology in the Netherlands creating an accreditation system in 2004.

dynamic risk factors influencing an offender that may be open to change through therapy.

dyscalculia a term used to describe specific difficulties in recognising and working with numbers.

eating disorders serious disruptions of the eating habits or the appetite.

ecological approaches in the practice of educational psychology, they emphasise the influences of the different contexts of a young person's experience (such as family, school, community) upon problems and in turn inform assessment and intervention.

ecologically valid when research accurately describes psychological functioning in the 'real world'.

educational psychology psychology as applied to educational practice and related research.

effect–danger-ratio theory a theory indicating that when a perpetrator chooses an aggressive strategy he or she will adopt one that carries the least cost for the perpetrator but still has an impact on the victim.

effort–reward imbalance a model which suggests that negative health outcomes will result if there is an imbalance between the efforts the employee puts in at work and the rewards they receive.

E-FIT-V a facial composite system.

ego in psychoanalysis, a rational part of the psyche that attempts to control the impulses of the id.

ego defence mechanisms means by which the ego attempts to control unacceptable id impulses and reduce the anxiety these may arouse.

elaboration likelihood model a model by Petty and Cacioppo that considers the amount of systematic processing devoted to a message, known as 'cognitive elaboration'.

electro-encephalography (EEG) a means of gathering information about brain activation in terms of changes over time.

elementary mental functions according to Vygotsky, mental capacities that are independent of any cultural learning, such as attention, perception, and memory.

elicitation research seeks to elicit or diagnose the deficits or problems which explain why people are not taking actions that are in their own interests.

emotion from the Latin meaning 'to stir up', emotion may perhaps be described as agitation of the mind combined with physical sensations which produce a variety of experiences that can be recognised generally as, e.g. happiness, anger, anxiety, sadness.

emotion-focused coping coping strategies focused on regulating the individual's emotions rather than changing the stressful situation.

emotional acceptance accepting rather than inhibiting or suppressing emotion and the cognitions underpinning the emotion.

emotional intelligence (EQ) intelligence relating to the perception, understanding, and management of emotions.

emotional reactivity the extent to which an individual reacts to a negative or positive event.

emotional regulation the strategies an individual employs, consciously or subconsciously, to manage his or her emotion.

empathising-systematising theory particularly relevant to autism spectrum disorder, this theory seeks to classify people on the basis of their skills in two factors – empathising and systemising.

empathy an ability to understand and experience a client's own feelings and personal meanings and convey this understanding to the client.

employee life cycle a concept showing how individuals go through different stages when working with a particular employer.

employment work, occupation (usually paid).

encode the term for the cognitive systems an individual uses to remember a face.

endocrine system an integrated system of small glands that work closely with the ANS.

enhanced cognitive interview (ECI) an enhanced interviewing system based on sound psychological principles, developed in the US by Fisher *et al.* (1987)

environmental psychology the study of the interrelationships between the physical environment and human behaviour.

epidemiological transition a wealth threshold which, when crossed by a country, means that increased national wealth has little effect on the overall health of the population.

ergonomics the science of designing the task to fit the person.

ethics a consideration of what is acceptable behaviour in the pursuit of a particular personal or professional goal, often formalised in professional codes.

ethology the study of animal behaviour, particularly its function and evolution.

European Credit Transfer and Accumulation System (ECTS) a credit system successfully tested and used across Europe to facilitate the recognition of periods of study abroad and thus enhance the quality and volume of student mobility in Europe, it has recently been developing into an accumulation system to be implemented at institutional, regional, national and European levels.

European Federation of Professional Psychologists Associations the representative body for 32 European national psychological associations, including all European Union Member States.

European Federation of Sport and Exercise Psychology (FEPSAC) intended to promote and disseminate scientific, educational and professional work in sport and exercise psychology in Europe.

European Masters' Programme consortium in Sport and Exercise Psychology (EMPSEP) one of three categories of post-graduate programmes in ASEP offered by European educational institutions and national associations representing psychology professionals.

European Network of Young Specialists in Sport Psychology (ENYSSP) a network for the sharing of ideas and knowledge between young professionals in the field with some of its main objectives being: to coordinate European links between students, young researchers, educators and professional practitioners; to promote and facilitate cross-national cooperation for research, education and applied work in Sport and Exercise Psychology (SEP); to support the development and standardisation of official degrees in SEP within Europe.

evaluation an appraisal of the impact and success of any intervention once it is complete and during its use.

Every Child Matters a UK government programme introduced in England and Wales in 2003 providing a detailed framework for services for children, young people and families based upon integrated multi-agency partnership working. Getting it Right for Every Child (GIRFEC) is the equivalent national initiative in Scotland.

evidence-based practice practice whose efficacy has been proven through research using the scientific method.

evoFIT a commercial 'holistic' facial composite system.

executive dysfunction impairment of the cognitive skills involved in problem-solving, planning and engaging in goal-directed behaviour.

executive functioning processes that are involved in planning and attentional control.

exemplar example of work (eight are required) which, together with a practice dairy, evidences a trainee's competence to gain a diploma in forensic psychology in order to practise at the level of chartered psychologist.

existential therapies humanistic therapies orientating themselves around a shared concern relating to human lived experience, its 'givens' and meanings.

expectancy-value account a theory whereby an individual's engagement in a given academic task will depend on both estimated probability of success as well as the subjective value attached to the task.

expected utility theory a theory of decision making concerned with reviewing the value and risk of each potential outcome.

experiential learning theory a model of the learning process. It differs from other models of learning in that it suggests experience is central to adult learning (as opposed to cognitive theories which emphasise the role of cognition over emotion).

experimental conditions the various groups used in an experiment, to which participants are assigned.

experimental group in an experiment, the group exposed to a particular value of the independent variable, which has been manipulated by the experimenter.

experimental methods methods of research using tightly controlled studies to identify cause-and-effect relations.

explicit tests self-report tests administered by psychologists that measure tendencies overtly so that their purpose is clear to participants.

exposure therapies treatments in which sufferers are helped by the therapist to confront and experience events and stimuli relevant to their trauma and their symptoms.

expressed emotion a qualitative measure of the 'amount' of emotion displayed, typically in the family setting.

expressive aggression aggressive behaviour used by an individual to manage a negative emotion provoked in reaction to an event, also known as reactive aggression.

external facial features non-central parts of the face including the hair, face shape and ears.

externalising disorders outward-directed behaviour problems such as aggressiveness, hyperactivity, non-compliance or impulsiveness.

extraversion one of the dimensions of personality as suggested by the Big Five personality model.

extrinsic motivation doing something because of incentives and pressures applied to the individual from outside.

eyewitness an individual (who may be a witness or victim) who sees something happening or being done.

facial composite a visual likeness of an offender's face.

facial configuration the relative positioning of elements of the face.

factorial designs a form of experimental design that manipulates two or more independent variables at the same time, by combining or crossing the levels of each.

false memory a memory that is not real or may be inaccurate due to having been affected or created by the way in which a question is asked, for example during investigative interviewing.

false positives in risk assessment, seeing risk as elevated when in reality the risk should not necessarily be viewed as elevated.

familiar face recognition the ability to correctly identify a familiar face.

family therapy a form of intervention involving family members designed to treat mental health problems arising from the relationship dynamics within the family.

feature composite systems methods of building a face involving selection of individual facial features – eyes, nose, hair, mouth etc.

feedback response or reaction providing useful information or guidelines for further action or development.

feminist an advocate for women's social, economic and legal equality with men.

flooding a form of desensitisation for the treatment of phobias and related disorders in which the patient is repeatedly exposed to highly distressing stimuli.

forebrain one of the three major anatomic components of the brain, situated towards the front.

forensic psychologist in training the term used to refer to individuals enrolled on the diploma to qualify as a forensic psychologist.

forensic psychology the application of psychological knowledge within the criminal justice system.

formulation an account of the causes and maintenance of a client's difficulties that draws on both information from the assessment and psychological theory.

free association a technique used in psychoanalysis where the client is encouraged to verbalise all thoughts, feelings and images that come to mind.

free recall memories called to mind unprompted by direct questions beyond the request that the individual reports everything he or she can remember.

functional analysis the use of operant conditioning principles to try to understand what rewarding or reinforcing factors might be maintaining behaviour.

functional assessment a way of assessing motivation based on learning theory.

functional magnetic resonance imaging (fMRI) a means of visually monitoring the flow of blood to different areas of the brain showing which regions are active.

gate-control theory the idea that a neural gate in the spinal cord can open and close thus modulating incoming pain signals

gender dysphoria a gender identity disorder in which an individual has a sense of gender that is opposite to his or her biological sex.

gender identity disorder (GID) a sexual disorder where an individual is dissatisfied with his or her biological sex and has a strong desire to be a member of the opposite sex.

general aggression model a social information processing model which places emphasis on aggression as a product of multiple interacting factors, including: social cognition, emotional aggression, predisposition and factors based on learning and developmental history.

generalised anxiety disorder (GAD) a pervasive condition in which the sufferer experiences continual apprehension and anxiety about future events which leads to chronic and pathological worrying about those events.

generalising in information-processing theory, taking a strategy applicable to one specific domain and applying it to other domains.

generic professional competencies everyday skills that all psychologists need, e.g., the ability to talk to clients and keep accurate records in a confidential manner.

generic standards standards of conduct, performance and ethics applicable to any practitioner working in the health professions generally.

German Association for Psychologists (Berufsverband Deutscher Psychologinnen und Psychologen) the recognised professional association of German psychologists representing the professional interests of psychologists from all fields of activity.

Gestalt therapy a humanistic therapy that takes into account all aspects of a person's life and experience to bring about a sense of the whole person, characterised by a sense of self-awareness and integration.

glycogen depletion the process whereby stores of glycogen (from carbohydrates) in the muscles and liver are reduced and blood glucose levels begin to fall causing athletes to experience, e.g., fatigue and lack of coordination.

goals targets, aims, or ends a person wishes to achieve.

graded tasks manageable tasks that are only increased in difficulty as confidence and skill in task performance grow.

graduate basis for charted membership (GBC) eligibility to become a chartered member of the British Psychological Society and to train as a clinical psychologist requires that applicants have completed qualifications specifically accredited by the Society.

group dynamics the forces operating in groups that affect group performance and member satisfaction.

group environment questionnaire a means of assessing team cohesion.

group identification an identification procedure whereby police may escort an eyewitness to a public place to see if he or she can identify the offender.

group processes a general term referring to stages groups usually go through in forming and functioning.

group think false consensus within a group generated by conformity pressures.

group work a way of organising students into groups to actively engage them in study.

habitual aggression frequently or continually occurring behaviour that results in harm.

hair one of the most important external features for unfamiliar face perception.

hallucinogenic drugs psychoactive drugs which affect the user's perceptions, either sharpening the individual's sensory abilities or creating sensory illusions or hallucinations.

HCR-20 a structured clinical risk assessment for violence.

health behaviours behaviours that affect one's health protectively (through prevention, detection and avoidance of health-harming behaviours) and positively (e.g. exercise participation and healthy eating).

health belief model a model that considers that health behaviours are mainly determined by two aspects of an individual's cognitions about a health behaviour: perceptions of illness threat and evaluation of behaviours to reduce this threat.

health-enhancing behaviour patterns behaviours that have an immediate or long-term positive affect on an individual's health and are at least partially within the individual's control.

health inequalities differences between the health and life expectancy of individuals affected by social and economic factors, amongst others.

Health Professions Council (HPC) the regulator of Practioner Psychologists in the UK. The HPC aims primarily to protect the public and maintains a register of health professionals (e.g. Practioner Psychologists) who meet set standards for their training, professional skills, behaviour and health.

health psychology the professional application of psychological knowledge to the solution of problems associated with human health behaviour.

health trainers lay people recruited from the community and given brief training on facilitating health behaviour change in others in the community.

hearing impairment loss of hearing of various degrees including total deafness.

heuristics simple rules for making a judgement.

high altitude cerebral edema (HACE) a severe (frequently fatal) form of altitude sickness.

high altitude pulmonary edema (HAPE) a life threatening form of fluid accumulation in the lungs of otherwise healthy mountain climbers that occurs typically at high altitudes.

higher mental functions mental capacities developed through the use of 'cultural tools' enabling a child to control his or her attention, build a conceptual understanding of the world, and engage in logical problem solving.

hindbrain part of the brain involved in coordinating the body's movements, sleep, arousal and regulation of the cardiovascular system and respiration.

hindsight bias an attributional phenomenon related to self-blame that is used to make sense of events.

holistic cognitive interview a cognitive interview including additional procedures (such as personality attribution) used to improve the quality of an individual composite.

homophobia fear and/or a strong dislike of homosexual men.

hopelessness a cluster of symptoms in an individual connected to his or her expectation that negative not positive outcomes will occur and that the individual has no responses available that will change this.

hostile attribution bias a tendency that an individual has to see hostility where it may not exist.

hostility a negative attitude towards others, consisting, e.g., of enmity and unfriendliness.

human–machine interaction in organisational settings the study of the interaction between the human workforce and the technology at work and the allocation of functions appropriate to each.

human relations approach an approach to managing employees that focuses attention on employee work needs and motivations, and recognises the importance and motivating power of workplace relationships.

humanist philosophy any system that asserts human dignity and man's capacity for finding meaning and fulfillment through reason and scientific method.

humanist-existentialist approach an approach that aims to resolve psychological problems through insight, personal development and self-actualisation.

humanistic approach an approach that values each individual as having a unique perception of the world, freedom of choice and the ability to set goals driven by a motivational tendency towards growth and self-actualisation.

humanistic therapies psychotherapies that attempt to consider the 'whole' person and not just the symptoms of psychopatholgy.

hybrid disorders an illness containing elements of a number of different disorders.

hyperventilation a rapid form of breathing that is a common feature of panic attacks.

hypobaric hypoxia a deficiency of oxygen reaching the tissues of the body related to conditions of low air pressure and low oxygen as can be found at high altitudes.

hypochondriasis unfounded preoccupation with fears of having or contracting a serious disease or illness based on misinterpreting bodily symptoms.

hypothalamic-pituitary-adrenal (HPA) axis response system a physiological response to stress leading to the release of the stress hormone cortisol.

hypothalamus part of the forebrain, it regulates many of the body's systems, including controlling how an individual responds to stress.

hypothetical scenario a tool used by social psychologists to investigate how people think and feel about something by presenting participants with a hypothetical story and asking them how they think and feel about the contents of the story.

id in psychoanalysis, the concept used to describe innate instinctual needs – especially sexual needs.

identification parade an identification procedure whereby police create a line-up of the suspect together with at least eight other individuals ('foils') from which the eyewitness is asked to pick out the offender, if present.

imitation the direct copying of another organism's behaviour.

immune system a network of organs and cells that protects the body from invading bacteria, viruses and other foreign substances.

implicit association test a test designed to measure in a non-transparent way underlying aggressive attitudes.

implicit cognition thoughts an individual may not be consciously aware of.

implicit tests assessments of an individual's tendencies towards being aggressive without the individual knowing what the tests are designed to assess.

impression management an attempt by an individual to present himself favourably to others.

imprinting an instinctive process of learning the features of other members of the same species that occurs shortly after hatching or birth, usually focused on the mother.

inclusion a process focused on fulfilling each child's entitlement to high quality education.

inclusive education a policy to provide access to mainstream education for those with disabilities unless good reason can be shown that this is counterproductive.

inclusive organisations organisations that manage diversity with an emphasis on communality rather than differences.

increased access to psychological therapies (IAPT) a programme in the UK having the principle aim of supporting Primary Care Trusts in improving access to psychological therapies for people suffering from depression and anxiety disorders.

independent variable in an experiment, the variable that is manipulated by the experimenter as a means of determining cause-and-effect relations.

indirect aggression subtle aggression in which the victim is harmed but the perpetrator is protected from social or official retribution by virtue of the subtle nature of the aggression.

individual education plan in the UK, an individualised plan for a child in education that identifies the child's needs, profiles his or her strengths and weaknesses, sets targets for the child, plans specific intervention to achieve those targets, and reviews the child's progress towards those targets.

individual facial features any part of the face such as the nose.

induction observation of repeated associations which is often the first step in theory building.

inflated responsibility the belief that one has power to bring about or prevent subjectively crucial negative outcomes either actually or in a moral sense.

information–motivation–behavioural skills model provides a useful guide to identifying key behavioural determinants.

information processing a theory that suggests that cognition can be explicit or implicit.

information-processing accounts an array of theories that seek to describe cognitive development in terms of changes in the processing of information.

information-processing biases biases in interpreting, attending to, storing or recalling information that may give rise to dysfunctional thinking and behaving.

informational influence influence to accept information obtained from another as evidence of reality.

informed consent agreement or permission by a client for the use of a professional intervention based on the client having all the information necessary and the personal ability to make an educated, informed decision about the likely benefits and risks of the specific intervention.

instrumental aggression planned acts of aggression an individual chooses to engage in, also known as proactive aggression.

integrated a model of information processing outlined by Huesmann in 1998.

intellectual disabilities one of the two main Axis II categories, sometimes referred to as learning disabilities.

intelligence a complex concept which incorporates intellectual capability, reasoning and understanding.

intelligence quotient (IQ) tests means of comparing the mental age of a child with their chronological age, to determine the child's current intellectual capacity.

interaction effects any effects independent variables have in combination with each other.

internal facial features the central part of the face containing eyes, brows, nose and mouth.

internalising disorders inward-looking and withdrawn behaviours, which in children may represent the experience of depression, anxiety and active attempts to socially withdraw.

International List of Causes of Death (ICD) the international standard diagnostic classification developed by the World Health Organisation.

International Personality Item Pool a scientific collaboratory for the development of advanced measures of personality and other individual differences.

International Society of Sport Psychology (ISSP) the only worldwide organisation of scholars explicitly concerned with sport psychology, it exists to encourage and promote the study of human behaviour within sport, physical activity, and health settings; facilitate the sharing of knowledge through a newsletter, meetings and a quadrennial congress; improve the quality of research and professional practice in sport psychology.

interpretation in psychoanalysis, helping the client to identify important underlying conflicts.

intervene designing, implementing and evaluating any programme or materials to promote psychological or behavioural change.

intervention a psychological 'treatment' implemented on the basis of the formulation.

intervention mapping a step-by-step method for planning, developing and evaluating behaviour change interventions.

interview schedule the sequence of questions in an interview.

interviews a non-experimental method of research using a prepared set of questions delivered via conversation between respondent and researcher.

intolerance of uncertainty an inability to tolerate uncertainty which gives rise to anxiety and worrying.

intrinsic motivation doing something because of one's own internal drives and the interest and enjoyment that it brings.

intrusive thoughts disturbing thoughts over which an individual feels he or she has little or no control.

item selection The method of choosing the items included in a survey, determined by going through one or more cycles of design, testing and weeding out.

job characteristics model a model that identifies five core characteristics important in job design: skill variety, task identity, task significance, autonomy and job feedback.

job decision latitude also known as job control, this refers to the extent to which an employee has a say in decisions about their job and is able to develop their abilities.

job demand-control model a well-known approach to work stress that focuses on the two core aspects of job demands and job control.

job design the planned arrangement (or rearrangement) of the characteristics of a job (such as the level of job control) usually to improve motivation, satisfaction and performance and/or reduce stress.

job insecurity lack of security concerning one's job which adds to work stress and impacts on one's health.

job strain the extent to which a job is stressful depending on the combination of demand and control, i.e. a job which is high in demand and low in control is likely to be stressful.

just world theory a belief that individuals are motivated to believe that the world is a fair and just place.

key roles professional psychologists are expected to be able to fulfil six key roles, four achieved with qualification, a further two with post-qualifying work experience.

knowledge areas in occupational psychology there are eight knowledge areas: human–machine interaction, design of work environments, personnel selection and assessment, performance appraisal and career development, counselling and personal development, training, organisational development and change.

lapse action when the intention is correct, but the one acting omits to carry out the action, resulting in an error or unintended action.

learned helplessness a theory of depression that argues that people become depressed following unavoidable negative life events because these events give rise to a way of thinking that makes them learn to become 'helpless'.

learning disability an umbrella term to cover specific learning disabilities, intellectual disabilities and pervasive developmental disorders.

learning theory the body of knowledge encompassing principles of classical and operant conditioning applied to explain and treat psychopathology.

life change unit (LCU) a numeric value assigned to individual life events to determine the social readjustment each event would require.

life events positive or negative events which represent a change in a person's circumstances. It should be possible to objectively check this life change.

limbic system evolutionarily old, this part of the brain interacts with the endocrine system, plays an important role in motivational and emotional aspects of behaviour and is involved in aspects of memory processes.

line-up the arrangement in a line of the suspect and at least eight other individuals for the purposes of the eyewitness identifyng the suspect.

longitudinal studies research which takes measures from the same participants at two or more different times in order to specify the time relationships between variables over time. This may extend over months or years or even over a participant's whole lifetime.

Mad Pride a UK organisation dedicated to changing the way society views people with mental health problems.

main effects the effects of each independent variable by itself.

major theorists model a model developed by Martin Fishbein and colleagues which suggests that behaviour is determined by intentions, environmental constraints and skills.

maladaptive behaviour behaviour which inhibits a person's ability to adjust to a particular situation.

mania an emotion characterised by boundless, frenzied energy and feelings of euphoria.

mastery experience past experience of successfully performing a behaviour thus giving a person confidence that he or she can tackle a new task providing a similar challenge.

mastery or learning goals in education, goals whereby an individual is motivated to master the task and/or increase his or her ability and knowledge

medical model an explanation of psychopathology in terms of underlying biological or medical causes.

membership prototypes those who typify or most represent the social category of the group and in so doing hold positions of influence and power.

memory a term used in many ways, including referring to the information that an individual remembers.

Mental Health Review Tribunal (MHRT) MHRT are independent judicial bodies that operate under the provisions of the Mental Health Act 1983 and the Mental Health Review Tribunal Rules 1983. A tribunal's main purpose is to review the case of a patient detained under the Mental Health Act and to direct the discharge of any patient for whom the statutory criteria for discharge have been satisfied.

mental model a cognitive representation of something, symbolising its key elements and the relationships between them.

mental retardation a DSM-IV-TR-defined disorder in which an individual has significantly below-average intellectual functioning characterised by an IQ of 70 or below.

meta-analysis a statistical technique which combines the statistical findings of a number of studies.

meta-analytic study a study which combines evidence from many other studies.

meta-beliefs beliefs about beliefs.

metacognition the awareness of one's own thought processes, enabling effective learning through correction.

microgenetic designs a specialised form of experimental study, the key characteristic of which is the use of a small sample and many more observations than would be employed in an ordinary repeated measures design with these being densely packed together.

microgenetic methodologies a research approach whereby measurements of a child's problem-solving are made repeatedly over the period of change being studied.

midbrain one of the three major anatomic components of the brain which includes the brain stem, it regulates critical bodily functions such as breathing.

miscarriages of justice convictions that are shown to be incorrect. Such cases are sometimes due to unreliable eyewitness evidence and, as a result, suspects are now not convicted on the basis of eyewitness evidence alone.

mistake action when the intention is correct but not appropriate and results in an error.

mixed-motive aggression aggression that can be considered to be reactive as well as proactive.

mock witness paradigm a procedure used to test the fairness of a line-up.

moderate learning difficulties (MLD) as defined by government guidance in the UK, difficulties by pupils in all or most areas of the curriculum, particularly literacy, numeracy and conceptual understanding, despite appropriate intervention.

monoamine oxidase (MAO) inhibitors a group of antidepressant drugs which have their effects by increasing levels of both serotonin and norepinephrine in the brain.

mood-incongruent effect the term for an individual recalling more positive memories while in a negative mood than in a neutral mood (possibly as a means of self-regulation).

morphed composite a facial 'portrait' made from combining or 'averaging' a number of individual composites.

motivation an internal force pushing behaviour in certain directions.

motor skills those involved in bodily movement and functioning.

multi-agency working the practice of different services, agencies, teams of professionals and other staff working together to provide services that meet the needs of children, young people, and their parents or carers.

multicultural training models models of training that take into account difference in the following with regard to trainees and future clients: socioeconomic status, gender, sexual orientation, race, cultural background and ability status.

multidisciplinary settings health psychologists work in a variety of settings in which a variety of professionals work together.

multidisciplinary teams (MDTs) teams of workers from a range of disciplines specialising in different aspects of health and social care so that clients may receive holistic care.

multiple intelligence a theory that distinguishes between various distinct intelligences, including logical-mathematical, spatial, musical, interpersonal, and kinaesthetic components.

multiple victimisation the term for the process in which an individual is victimised on more than one occasion by different perpetrators over a period of time.

myocardial infarction, destruction of heart tissue resulting from an interruption of blood supply to the area, possibly triggered by emotional upset.

narrative therapy variously a term referring specifically to the ideas and practices of Michael White and David Epston, as well as the general term for psychotherapy that used stories and 'storying' to make meaning.

National Institute for Health & Clinical Excellence (NICE) an independent UK organisation responsible for providing national guidance on promoting good health and preventing and treating ill health.

National Occupational Standards identified levels of knowledge, skill and performance expected after professional qualification, enabling professionals and employers to match acquired skills or competencies against job demands.

near infra-red spectroscopy (NIRS) a means of gathering similar data to that gained by a functional MRI, but with the participant wearing a cap-like arrangement and acting normally rather than being placed in a large scanner.

need for cognition a tendency to enjoy thinking.

needs assessment initial research to ascertain what, if anything, needs to change to enhance the health and wellbeing of a group.

negative affect affect is generally a loose term for emotion or mood, thus negative affect refers to negative or difficult emotion.

negative reinforcement in learning theory, something that is intended to strengthen behaviour by removing something an individual considers unpleasant.

negative schema a set of beliefs that tends individuals towards viewing the world and themselves in a negative way.

negative triad the three-part negative schema whereby depressed individuals hold negative views about themselves, their future and the world.

nerves bundles of fibres that transmit information in and out of the nervous system.

nervous system the brain, the spinal cord and the nerves (bundles of fibres that transmit information in and out of the nervous system).

neural networks a set of interconnected neurons producing complex patterns of inhibitory and excitatory activation.

neuropsychology the study of the structure and function of the brain related to psychological processes and behaviours.

neuroticism one of the dimensions of personality as suggested by the Big Five personality model.

nonexperimental methods methods of research using questionnaires, interviews or observations in order to provide descriptions of the 'real world' that are as far as possible complete, accurate, and ecologically valid.

norepinephrine an adrenal hormone which functions as a neurotransmitter and is associated with symptoms of both depression and mania.

normative influence influence to conform to the positive expectation of another.

observational learning learning through imitation.

observational methods in research, observation and recording of behaviour exhibited by a participant.

obsessive-compulsive disorder (OCD) an anxiety disorder characterised by uncontrollable obsessive thoughts and compulsive, ritualised behaviours.

obsessions intrusive and recurring thoughts that an individual finds disturbing and uncontrollable.

occupational health psychology the application of psychology to protecting and promoting the safety, health and wellbeing of workers.

occupational psychology the professional application of psychological knowledge to organisations to make them better places in which to work.

openness to experience one of the dimensions of personality as suggested by the Big Five personality model.

operant conditioning the learning of a specific behaviour or response because that behaviour has certain consequences.

operant techniques in pain management, the idea that pain behaviours are learned responses which become conditioned through reinforcement.

optimism an expectation that in the future good things will happen to you and bad things will not.

organisational change in organisational psychology, a cycle encompassing identifying what needs to be done, planning how to do it, carrying out the plan, evaluating the delivery of the plan and then going back to identify whether there are any additional needs to be addressed.

organisational culture a system of shared beliefs and values that guides behaviour.

organisational culture change usually top-down change to an organisation's culture that involves: clear strategic vision, management commitment, symbolic leadership and changes in membership.

organisational development a systematic effort applying behavioural science knowledge to the planned creation and reinforcement of organisational strategies, structures and processes for improving an organisation's effectiveness.

organism variables in functional assessment the 'O' of SORC which includes, e.g,. the previous experiences of the individual and his or her learning experience.

orienting response a physiological reaction consisting of changes in skin conductance, brain activity, heart rate and blood pressure.

overcommitment the motivational component of the effort–reward imbalance model.

over-controlled aggression a strategy whereby an individual tries, ultimately unsuccessfully, to inhibit and repress his or her negative emotions.

over-justification effect an effect whereby the existence of an extrinsic reward can lower intrinsic motivation to complete a task.

overlapping waves a theory of child development suggesting that as a child develops, different strategies that are available to the child rise and fall in frequency of use and become dominant at different ages but at any given age there are multiple strategies available to the child.

oxidative stress a condition of increased oxidant production in human cells, characterised by the release of free radicals, the physical and medical consequences of which are unclear but may play a role in fostering an adaptive response to altitude exposure.

P scales operating in England and Wales, a system for measuring performance falling below the basic levels of the National Curriculum.

pain management the treatment and management of pain using any combination of approaches – psychological, behavioural and medical.

panic attack an attack of sudden uncontrollable fear or anxiety lasting from several minutes to several hours.

panic disorder an anxiety disorder characterised by repeated panic or anxiety attacks.

parallel development models a model that understands proactive and reactive aggression as originating from different background factors and developing almost independently in parallel.

paraphilias problematic, high-frequency sexual behaviours or unusual sexual urges and activities that are often directed at inappropriate targets.

parasympathetic division a sub-division of the ANS, it restores the body's energy by reducing heart rate and respiration while increasing the rate of digestions.

parenting style according to Baumrind (1967) there are three major parenting styles: authoritarian, authoritative and permissive.

pathology model a view of psychopathology which sees symptoms as produced by underlying causes.

PEACE interview in the UK, a police interview the name of which is formed from the initial letter of each of its five stages.

pedagogy the art and science of teaching.

peer relationships relationships with friends, in peer group affiliations, and within the broader peer network.

perception a two-part process integrating physiological sensory input and processing within the brain by which information in the environment is 'translated' into a recognition of objects, sounds, etc.

perception of physiological reactions one's performance can be affected positively or negatively depending on how one perceives and interprets one's physical and emotional responses during performance.

perfectionism the setting of excessively high standards for performance accompanied by overly critical self-evaluation.

performance accomplishments See mastery experience.

performance appraisal the process of reviewing past work performance, usually combined with setting targets for the future.

performance-approach orientation a focus on performance goals leading to a desire to demonstrate competence in front of others.

performance-avoidance orientation a goal orientation leading to withdrawal from a task that is perceived to carry a risk of negative evaluation of performance.

performance or ego goals in education, goals whereby an individual is motivated to maintain a positive judgement of self by proving or demonstrating ability.

performance profile a method of assessment used in the UK by sport and exercise psychologists, it involves identifying the ideal self and the current self, and reducing the difference between the current and ideal as the basis for intervening.

peripheral nervous system a network of nerves that connects the brain and spinal cord to the rest of the body.

peripheral route the term for low (effortless) processing of messages according to the elaboration likelihood model of Petty and Cacioppo.

person descriptions general descriptions of a person used for public appeals and computer searches.

personal identity a self-description denoting specific attributes of the individual.

personality the overall profile or combination of traits that characterise the unique nature of a person.

personality disorders a group of disorders marked by persistent, inflexible, maladaptive patterns of thought and behaviour that develop in adolescence or early adulthood.

pervasive developmental disorders (PDD) a group of disorders characterised by serious abnormalities in the developmental process, usually associated with impairment in several areas of development.

pessimistic thinking a form of dysfunctional thinking where sufferers believe nothing can improve their lot.

phenothiazines a group of antipsychotic drugs that help to alleviate the symptoms of psychosis by reducing dopamine activity.

phobic beliefs beliefs about phobic stimuli that maintain the phobic's fear and avoidance of that stimulus or situation.

phonological awareness in learning to read, the ability (possibly innate) to identify sound values in speech, and to decompose spoken words into these.

photofit a UK system for face construction using individual reference features printed onto rigid card from which eyewitnesses select the best matching hair, eyes, nose, etc., with each part being slotted together as if assembling a jigsaw.

physical disabilities difficulties or impairments in normal physical functioning.

physical health the primary focus of health psychologists (as opposed to psychological problems or mental illness).

picture matching a term used to describe a perceptual strategy whereby pairs of images are matched not by identity but by properties of the image (picture). This happens when exactly the same photograph is used during the study and test phases of an experiment. (Cf. structural code.)

pituitary gland the 'master' gland regulating the endocrine gland secretions.

positive reappraisal cognitive restructuring so that one sees the stressful situation in a more positive light.

positive reinforcement in learning theory, something that is intended to strengthen behaviour by 'adding' something an individual perceives as a gain following their behaviour.

post-traumatic stress disorder (PTSD) a disorder diagnosed according to DSM IV when an individual presents with three behavioural clusters: re-experiencing a traumatic event; avoidance concerning the trauma; generalised increased arousal or anxiety.

practice diary an example of a learning journal, designed to guide reflective practice and document the tasks completed by the forensic psychologist in training. The diploma in forensic psychology requires trainees to maintain a practice diary throughout their period of supervised practice (Stage II). The trainee is required to reflect within this log upon new learning experiences.

predictive validity the extent to which a test or measure can predict a specified outcome.

predictivist perspective in occupational psychology research and practice a paradigm concerned with predicting the extent to which results from particular selection tools are linked to positive performance outcomes in the workplace.

primal therapy a form of psychotherapy created by Arthur Janov based on the theory that a client's buried birth or childhood distress can resurface as neurosis, the treatment of which occurs through the client's 'return' to the 'primal scene' to re-experience and resolve the old trauma.

primary appraisal the process of assessing the threat or challenge posed by a stressor.

primary prevention interventions to prevent illness.

private speech talking to oneself as a child which, according to Vygotsky, plays a critical role in enabling a child to develop from being regulated by others to self-regulation.

proactive aggression planned acts of aggression an individual chooses to engage in, also known as instrumental aggression.

problem-focused coping coping that involves making plans or taking actions to help change the situation or reduce its impact.

procedural knowledge knowledge of procedures, i.e. knowing how something can be done.

profession-specific standards HPC standards of proficiency representing minimum standards necessary for safe and effective practice by registered psychologists working in their individual applied psychology professions.

PRO-fit a UK software system containing a database of individual facial features.

profound and multiple learning difficulties (PMLD) a diagnostic term for those with IQ scores of below 25 who have severe and complex needs, evident from infancy, often accompanied by physical disabilities and sensory impairments.

progressive muscle relaxation in pain management, a technique taught to patients to help them tighten and relax different muscle groups.

prospect theory a theory accounting for how peoples' judgements of outcomes and likelihoods deviate from the mathematically optimal.

protected titles a specified set of titles that practitioners can use only if they are registered with the HPC.

protective factors factors which effectively buffer against risk and reduce risk.

prototype the name for the average face created in the mind when an individual is shown a series of faces.

psychiatry a scientific method of identifying the biological causes of mental health problems and treating them with medication or surgery.

psychoanalysis a term for the theory developed by Freud to explain normal and abnormal psychological functioning and for the psychotherapy derived from that theory.

psychobiological pathways the ways in which psychological factors directly impact on physiological disease-related processes.

psychodynamic a psychotherapeutic approach concerned with the impacts of past relationships on a person's present, and that of an active unconscious.

psychological skills in sport and exercise psychology, the systematic and consistent practice of thoughts or actions designed to enhance performance, increase enjoyment, or achieve greater satisfaction.

psychological skills interventions (PSI) in sport and exercise psychology, the focus of a PSI is to change thinking processes and patterns to increase productivity, desirable outcomes and, by extension, happiness.

psychological wellbeing includes feeling happy and contented, maintaining good social relationships and using one's time to achieve realistic goals.

psychology of education the application of psychological knowledge to the processes of learning.

psychometric measures a form of survey method employing fixed questions, and giving rise to quantitative scores of psychological or intellectual functioning.

psychoneuroimmunology an area of science that explores the interplay between psychological processes and the nervous and immune systems.

psychotic experiences experiences characterised by disturbances in thought and language, sensory perception, emotion regulation, and behaviour. Sufferers may experience hallucinations and develop thought irregularities leading to false beliefs or delusions about themselves and the world.

punishment in learning theory, something that, when it follows a response, has the effect of reducing the probability of that event occurring again in the future, i.e. it weakens behaviour.

quasi-experimental designs experiments that examine the effects of a variable that is not directly under the researcher's control (e.g., student age or gender) on outcomes such as achievement or performance level.

questionnaire a nonexperimental method of research using a prepared set of written questions for self-completion.

random assignment the allocation, according to chance not design, by experimenters of participants into the different experimental conditions so that there is no bias in the distribution of participant characteristics.

randomised control trial an experiment in which people are randomly allocated to an intervention group or a control group for comparison purposes.

randomised design the most basic form of experimental design, in which participants are randomly assigned to a number of experimental conditions.

rape foreful and unlawful sexual intercourse with another person without their consent.

rapport building one of the techniques used in the cognitive interview whereby the interviewing achieves connection with and cooperation from the interviewee as well as their confidence in the process and the interviewer.

reactive aggression aggressive behaviour used by an individual to manage a negative emotion provoked in reaction to an event, also known as expressive aggression.

recall rememberance of things learned or experienced.

recognition identifying something as known or experienced before.

recognition-primed decision making a theory stating that decision makers can recognise the best course of action and implement it directly without comparing it to alternatives.

reconstruction a movement in educational psychology in the 1970s and 1980s, based on dissatisfaction with traditional 'within-child' deficit explanations of problems and a recognition of the importance of ecological approaches and systems theory.

recruitment hiring people for work.

redundancy process where one or more employees' work is terminated.

reflective practice a process of reflection to enhance and improve professional practice by building on existing knowledge and learning from experience.

reflective-practitioner someone who has developed the competency of being able to reflect on their work.

reinforcement the use, by applied sport and exercise psychologists influenced by behaviourism, of positive and negative reinforcers to increase desired behaviours and punishments to decrease undesired behaviour.

reinforcers those responses that happen after a behaviour which strengthens the likelihood of the behaviour reoccurring in the future.

reinstating the context a technique whereby an eyewitness thinks about an event they have witnessed and attempts to recreate it in his or her mind.

relaxation a coping strategy based on the theory that reducing muscle tension also reduces autonomic activity and thereby lowers anxiety levels.

repeat victimisation the term for the process whereby a person is re-victimised by the same perpetrator.

repeated measures design a very common form of experimental study in education using tests before and after introducing an intervention.

repeated recall a technique to draw out previously unremembered components of an eyewitness account.

report everything an instruction to eyewitnesses.

research an umbrella term used for the studying of a problem through the collection and/or analysis of data, often using scientific methods.

resilience the ability to withstand and recover from harmful experiences.

respiratory infectious illness an illness caused by a virus that affects the respiratory system.

retirement a major life-transition from working to not working.

retrograde amnesia loss of memory of events that occurred before a traumatic event.

risk assessment an appraisal by a forensic psychologist who will consider the dangers posed to others by an offender, as well as attempt to understand the individual offender.

role theory theory regarding the pattern of behavioural rights and obligations that accompanies a particular position or office and which the person is expected to learn and perform.

routine activities theory (RAT) the theory that certain routine activities engaged in by people make them more vulnerable to becoming victims.

Sally-Anne false belief task a method used to test whether a child has developed a 'theory of mind'.

SAVRY an acronym for Structured Assessment for Violence Risk in Youth.

scaffolding the way in which a child's efforts to master a new or challenging task can be supported in a flexible and contingent way by adults or more competent partners.

schema an individual's organised knowledge about self, events and beliefs.

schemes in Piagetian theory, an organised structure of knowledge (of self, beliefs and events) or abilities that change with age or experience.

schizophrenia the main diagnostic category for psychotic symptoms.

School Action as laid down in the SEN Code of Practice guidelines for a graduated response to pupil difficulty, this is the first phase of response, which uses existing school resources.

School Action Plus the SEN Code of Practice second phase of response for pupils who display continued difficulties and inadequate progress, involving external support services including those of educational psychologists.

scientist-practitioner a psychologist who can apply a hypothesis-testing approach to their clinical work.

scientific management a carrot and stick approach to managing workers who were considered to be a commodity that had to be managed and controlled.

secondary appraisal the process of assessing the coping options and resources available with regard to a particular stressor.

secondary prevention interventions designed to change patients' responses to their illness and so prevent long-term damage.

sedatives central nervous system depressants which slow the activity of the body, reduce its responsiveness and reduce pain, tension and anxiety.

Seizisman a state of psychological paralysis found in the Haitian community.

selection a systematic process of choosing employees, usually in the context of hiring, but also for promotion for instance.

selective serotonin reuptake inhibitors (SSRIs) a group of antidepressant drugs that selectively affect the uptake of only one neurotransmitter – usually serotonin.

self-actualisation a term that has two meanings: in motivational terms it is the motive or drive to realise one's full potential; according to the personality theory of Abraham Maslow, it is the final level of personal development.

self-belief confidence in one's own abilities and judgements.

self-categorisation theory in leadership theory, one that attempts to explain the mechanisms of social influence involved in the leadership process.

self-determination theory a theory that conceptualises human motivation in terms of three needs: need for competence; need for relatedness; need for autonomy.

self-efficacy the belief that one can perform an action or series of actions successfully.

self-esteem the value that one places on one's self.

self-fulfilling prophecies a prediction that causes itself to become true because people respond to it in such a way that they bring about the prophecy.

self-presentation efforts to control the way one presents oneself, in order to convey desired images of the self to others.

self-regulated learning comprises the deliberate application of known strategies to tasks, planning their use in advance, monitoring them in action, evaluating their output, and modifying subsequent behaviour on the basis of performance.

self-regulation the ability of an individual to regulate his or her own behaviour and thinking.

self-regulatory skills skills used to control everyday action including, e.g., goal setting, planning and self-monitoring.

SEN Code of Practice a code of practice in England and Wales concerning the provision of education for those with special educational needs.

sensitive period a specific and usually short period of time in early development during which learning of a particular type is especially active.

sequential development model a developmental model that suggests that reactive aggression develops first and proactive aggression develops after this.

sequential line-up the presentation of suspect and foils one after the other rather than simultaneously.

serotonin an important brain neurotransmitter where low levels are associated with depression.

service user groups groups of individuals who are end users of mental health services provided, e.g., by the NHS.

setting change objectives identifying behavioural determinants and change mechanisms.

severe learning difficulties (SLD) a diagnostic term in the UK applied to those children who at best will progress academically to no more than early primary school levels, and may not be able to do more than master simple counting and sight-reading of a few words.

sex offenders individuals who have committed crimes of a sexual nature and who may be characterised by: sexual pre-occupation; deviant sexual interests; conflicts in intimate relationships and intimacy deficits; hostility; the use of sex as a coping strategy.

sexual assault an indecent attack, attempted rape or rape.

sexual dysfunctions disturbances in the processes that characterise the sexual response cycle or pain associated with intercourse.

simultaneous line-up the presentation to the eyewitness of suspect and foils at the same time.

situation awareness a cognitive representation of reality as it is perceived in the present moment.

sketch artist a person skilled in portraiture who would draw by hand the face described by an eyewitness.

slip action when the intention is correct, but the one acting accidentally does not carry it out as intended, resulting in an error or unintended action.

social-cognitive career theory (SCCT) a highly influential career theory incorporating developmental principles that shows how the following impact on career behaviour: self-efficacy, outcome expectations, goals, the environment, personal attributes and learning experiences.

social cohesion in a group, the desire to develop and maintain social bonds between members.

social comparison comparison made by individuals regarding their abilities and attributes relative to those of others.

social constructionist a person who believes that there can be no objective truths about reality, only subjective constructions of reality

social constructivism the proposition that all knowledge, including so-called 'scientific knowledge' is not a neutral body of data independent of cultural norms and values, but is actually socially constructed in support of particular values and understandings.

social ecological model of change a model emphasising the different levels at which intervention may be required to successfully change behaviour.

social identity social identifications and self-descriptions that derive from membership in social categories.

social identity theory theory concerned with the individual's categorisation of self and others into in- and out-groups.

social influence a concept typically understood as a change in attitudes of an individual as a consequence of exposure to the attitudes of another.

social information processing as used in models of psychological and interpersonal functioning, cognitive processes whereby events in the social world are encoded and interpreted, and possible responses are identified and evaluated.

social information processing models influenced by social cognition, there are a variety of models used by psychologists to try and explain aggressive responses.

social labelling the theory that the development and maintenance of psychotic symptoms are influenced by the diagnosis itself.

social-learning models of aggression models that define aggression as an acquired behaviour driven and reinforced by the actual or anticipated rewards of aggression that an individual receives or observes being received by those he or she respects or admires.

social loafing the tendency of people not to work as hard in groups as they would individually.

social psychology the study of how the thoughts, feelings and behaviours of individuals are influenced by the presence of others.

Social Readjustment Rating Scale a checklist of life events developed by Holmes and Rahe which includes events such as bereavements as well as those events which are normally regarded as positive such as marriage.

social referencing the acquisition by infants of emotional reactions through using as a guide the emotional reactions of others, notably their care giver.

social-selection theory the theory that individuals displaying psychotic symptoms will move into the lower socioeconomic classes as a result of their disorder.

social skills the ability to interact successfully with other people.

social support a coping strategy in which an individual uses social relationships as a resource.

society a term that is often used to mean the collective citizenry of the country in which a person lives.

sociocultural conditioning a theory that contends that behaviour is learnt by individuals observing others receiving rewards or punishment dependent on their behaviour.

sociocultural or cultural–historical theory of cognitive development a theory developed by Vygotsky that focuses on the way in which people, such as parents and teachers, play an active role in transmitting cultural knowledge to the child.

socioeconomic hierarchies different levels of financial status in society.

socioeconomic status a summary measure of a person's economic and social position (compared to others) based on income, education and/or occupation.

sociogenic hypothesis the theory that individuals in low socioeconomic classes experience significantly more life stressors than individuals in higher socioeconomic classes.

sociotechnical systems a term for organisations that are comprised of people as well as technology.

Socratic method learning through dialogue and asking questions.

somatic nervous system a sub-division of the peripheral nervous system concerned with coordinating the 'voluntary' body movements controlled by the skeletal muscles.

somatisation disorder a pattern of recurring, multiple, clinically significant somatic symptoms that require medical treatment and cause significant impairment in functioning.

somatoform disorders the experiencing of physical symptoms suggestive of a medical or neurological condition for which there is no diagnosable evidence.

somatogenic hypothesis the theory that causes or explanations of psychological problems can be found in physical or biological impairments.

specific language impairment (SLI) specific delays in language development which cannot be explained by other conditions such as hearing impairment, severe learning difficulties, cerebral palsy, Down's syndrome or autism.

specific learning difficulties impairment in one narrowly defined area of a pupil's learning, accompanied by normal or near-normal ability in other areas.

specific phobias excessive, unreasonable, persistent fears triggered by a specific object or situation.

spinal cord the main neural axis in humans and other vertebrates.

sport & exercise psychology a profession dealing with sport and physical performance requiring knowledge of factors that can facilitate and enhance sporting performance.

Stage 1 Qualification in Health Psychology having acquired Graduate Basis for Chartered Membership of the BPS students proceed to study for a one-year, accredited Master's course in Health Psychology or they may study independently and take a Stage 1 examination set and assessed by the BPS.

Stage 2 Qualification in Health Psychology the qualification gained after completing Stage 1 training, this may be taken as a stand-alone qualification or as part of a doctoral programme.

standard interview a police question-and-answer style interview.

standards of proficiency in applied psychology, a minimum set of standards, necessary for the safe and effective practice of the profession, which psychologists must meet before they can be registered.

static risk factors influencing an offender that are historical and cannot be changed.

statistical norm a statistical unit that is representative of the range of scores on a particular variable.

statutory assessment the third phase of response for pupils about whom there is continuing cause for concern, involving a comprehensive assessment of the pupil's history, characteristics, and needs and can potentially give rise to a Statement of Special Educational Need.

stereotypes fixed and often simplistic generalisations about particular groups or classes of people.

stigma a sense of shame felt by those as a result of having mental health problems.

stimulants substances that increase central nervous system activity and increase blood pressure and heart rate.

stimulus–response (SR) mechanisms the basic building blocks of behaviour in which an object (the stimulus) marked out as significant for survival triggers a specific effective response.

strategies in information processing accounts of cognitive development, particular ways of performing information-processing tasks, especially those related to memory and problem-solving.

stress in health psychology, a general term used to refer to a range of negative perceptions and reactions experienced when pressure becomes too much.

stress-diathesis model a model that states that some people are more genetically susceptible to stressors.

stress-management training the teaching of techniques by psychologists, counsellors and trainers to individuals and groups to help people improve their coping.

stress response a bodily response to 'fight or flight' situations to prepare the body to respond appropriately to help ensure survival.

stressors an event, factor or agent that causes or triggers stress.

Stroop test a classic implicit association test which uses words in different colours, designed to assess the participant's unconscious aggression.

structural code a method of processing a face based on person identity rather than non face-specific properties of an image. (Cf. Picture matching.)

structural MRI a means of gathering data on the organisation of cells in different areas of the brain.

structured clinical assessment an assessment using a structured clinical tool such as the HCR-20 by a researcher or clinician that focuses only on empirical (i.e. researched) risk factors.

subjective values the worth to an individual of doing a task, which can be categorised into intrinsic value, attainment value, utility value and perceived cost.

substance abuse a pattern of drug or substance use that occurs despite knowledge of the negative effects of the drug, but where use has not progressed to full-blown dependency.

substance dependence a maladaptive pattern of substance use, leading to clinically significant impairment or distress.

suffocation alarm theories theories suggesting that a sensitivity to increases in carbon dioxide are a risk factor for panic disorder.

superego in psychoanalysis, a development from both the id and ego which represents our attempts to integrate 'values' that we learn from our parents or society.

supervise and manage to monitor directly and develop the work of others.

supervision a form of supervision in occupational psychology whereby a supervisor 'signs-off' on relevant work experience recorded by and discussed with the practitioner.

survey methods research methods utilising questionnaires, reports on children's behaviour by parents or teachers, or systematic observations of behaviour by researchers.

suspect in criminology, a person suspected of committing a crime.

sympathetic adrenal medullary (SAM) system a physiological response to stress leading to the release of adrenalin and noradrenalin to put the body on alert.

sympathetic division a sub-division of the ANS, it mobilises the body by increasing heart rate and blood pressure for example.

syndrome a distinct set of symptoms.

systematic desensitisation an exposure therapy based on the need to expose clients to the events and situations that evoke their distress and anxiety in a graduated and progressive way.

systemic a psychotherapeutic approach concerned with the system(s) in which the client lives and how changes in relationships within the system may lead to improvement in the client's wellbeing.

systems theory emphasises the importance of viewing families and schools as complex social organisations and the cyclical, recursive nature of processes of change.

task cohesion in a group, the desire of members to complete a given task.

team development a forum for team members to reflect on their performance and to overcome process difficulties.

telencephalon a sub-division of the forebrain which is composed of the cerebrum and limbic system.

Terman life-cycle personality cohort study a study measuring conscientiousness, optimism, self-esteem, sociability, stability of mood and energy level in around 1000 children from the age of 11 years.

tertiary prevention interventions designed to promote coping with illness or minimise the effects of established illness, rather than prevent illness.

thalamus part of the forebrain, it plays an important role in regulating states of sleep, arousal and consciousness.

theory of mind the ability to understand one's own and other people's mental states.

theory of planned behaviour a theory that sets out the key factors that determine the decision to act by an individual, these being intention to engage in that behaviour and perceived behavioural control over that behaviour.

thought–action fusion a dysfunctional assumption held by OCD sufferers that having a thought about an action is like performing it.

thought suppression a defence mechanism used by individuals with obsessive thoughts to actively suppress them.

top-down processing direction of information processing by pre-existing neural and cognitive structures aimed at confirming the presence of expected features.

train and supervise facilitate the development of health psychology competencies in others.

training in organisational settings, increasing one's learning and developing one's skills, usually in a formal, relatively structured manner.

training needs analysis the formal process of identifying the training gap and its related training need.

trait anxiety a person's disposition to experience anxiety, whereby some individuals are more anxious than others.

trait emotional intelligence a constellation of emotion-related self-perceptions and dispositions located at the lower levels of personality hierarchies.

trait theory a theory of personality that assumes that people possess enduring characteristics (traits) that determine their behaviour across different situations and across time.

transactional approach a psychological approach to stress which is viewed as a transaction between the individual and the environment whereby the stress experienced by an individual is highly dependent on their appraisal of the stressor and the coping methods they use.

transference a technique used in psychoanalysis where the analyst is used as a target for emotional responses.

transpersonal therapy any form of therapy which places emphasis on spirituality, human potential or heightened consciousness.

trauma in psychology, the term used for a psychological injury caused by a physical or emotional shock or wound.

traumagenic model a model of sexual re-victimisation explaining how some child victims become further victimised in adulthood.

triarchic theory of intelligence a theory that distinguishes three components of intelligence: analytic, creative, and practical.

tricyclic drugs antidepressant drugs which have their effect by increasing the amount of norepinephrine and serotonin available for synaptic transmission.

triggers in learning theory, an antecedent, something that begins the behavioural sequence.

twin studies studies in which researchers compare the probability with which monozygotic and dizygotic twins both develop symptoms indicative of a psychopathology in order to assess genetic contributions to the psychopathology.

Type A behaviour pattern a pattern of behaviour characterised by a competitive drive, aggression, chronic impatience and a sense of time urgency.

unconditional positive regard valuing clients for who they are without judging them.

under-controlled aggression a strategy whereby an individual is unable to manage even minor emotional fluctuation and reacts strongly to their own negative emotions.

unemployment being out of paid work.

unfamiliar face recognition the ability to recognise a face that is not familiar to us.

unified model of social information processing a model devised by Huesmann (1998) that focuses on understanding the acquisition and maintenance of repeated aggressive behaviour.

unipolar depression a psychological disorder characterised by relatively extended periods of clinical depression that cause significant distress to the individual and impairment in functioning.

United States Olympic Committee (USOC) a non-profit organisation that serves as the National Olympic Committee (NOC) for the United States. As part of its services USOC maintains a registry of sport psychology consultants from around the US and Canada from which to make an appropriate referral for service. These sport psychology consultants are required to meet standards for educational training and supervised practice in order to achieve Registry membership.

values those aspects of behaviour that are significant for an individual within a culture, these may be shared by other/most members of that culture.

ventilation the bodily process of breathing in and out.

verbal persuasion influencing someone by what is said, often enhanced by maximising the trustworthiness and expertise of the speaker.

vicarious experience a term generally used to indicate experience that has not been direct but rather observation of another's experience.

vicarious learning learning how to behave by observing important models and imitating what they do.

victim in criminology, a person subject to a crime.

victim proneness a somewhat controverial term that suggests that some people are more prone than others to victimisation.

video identification a method enabling an eyewitness to view line-ups via video clips.

VIPER (Video Identification Parade Electronic Recording) a tool used in the UK to present to an eyewitness a sequence of video clips showing suspect and foils.

visual impairment loss of sight of various degrees including blindness.

V-RAG an actuarial risk assessment that has been developed for use with mentally disordered men.

vulnerability hypothesis a model of multiple victimisation.

waves of intervention model a three-tier model of intervention to support pupils' learning: universal provisions intended to benefit all pupils; additional support for some groups of pupils; intense individual support for pupils with severe difficulties.

weak central coherence an atypical way of processing information focusing on individual details rather than on the meaningful whole.

weapon focus attention drawn to a weapon and away from other objects which reduces information available for recall.

Western Collaborative Group study an examination of the risk factors for coronary heart disease (CHD) in a sample of over 3000 healthy middle-aged men.

within-child deficits traditionally, problems of children and young children were often pathologised by the use of labels which located the difficulties at the level of the child, ignoring additional factors at the level of the home, school or community that may contribute to difficulties (e.g. family relationships, the appropriateness of the curriculum and teaching etc.).

witness in criminology, someone who has witnessed a crime.

work–family conflict pressure arising from potentially conflicting work and family roles.

work–life balance a concept concerned with people balancing their working life with other responsibilities and roles such as caring for children or older adults or engaging in community activities or other interests.

work motivation motivation in a work environment.

working memory a short-term store for visual and verbal information which allows that information to be actively manipulated and transformed.

worry a cognitive activity in which the individual attempts to deal with problems and potential threats, and which may sometimes be accompanied by anxiety.

wound healing the healing of wounds.

zone of proximal development the distance between what a child can do unaided and what he or she can achieve with the guidance and support of a more competent other.

Index